D1242204

OLD RIOT, NEW RANGER

At his Alamo City office Captain Jack Dean, with his Colt .45 autoloader in the easily accessible cross-draw carry, deferentially displays an inscribed plaque and badges honoring Texas Rangers. Though difficult to read absent a magnifying glass, the wording sums up the outfit as being comprised of that "Special Breed of Men." Courtesy the SAN ANTONIO CURRENT.

Presented to

Kingwood Branch Library

In Memory of Jere Joiner

Harris County
    Public Library
your pathway to knowledge

WITHDRAWN

OLD RIOT, NEW RANGER

Captain Jack Dean, Texas Ranger and U.S. Marshal

BOB ALEXANDER

Number 17 in the Frances B. Vick Series

University of North Texas Press
Denton, Texas

Permissions:
University of North Texas Press
1155 Union Circle #311336
Denton, TX 76203-5017

The paper used in this book meets the minimum requirements of the American National Standard for Permanence of Paper for Printed Library Materials, z39.48.1984. Binding materials have been chosen for durability.

Library of Congress Cataloging-in-Publication Data

Names: Alexander, Bob, 1943- author.
Title: Old riot, new Ranger : Captain Jack Dean, Texas Ranger and U.S.
    Marshal / Bob Alexander.
Other titles: Frances B. Vick series ; no. 17.
Description: Denton, Texas : University of North Texas Press, [2018] |
    Series: Number 17 in the Frances B. Vick series | Includes bibliographical
    references and index.
Identifiers: LCCN 2018010438| ISBN 9781574417296 (cloth : alk. paper) | ISBN
    9781574417401 (ebook)
Subjects: LCSH: Dean, Jack, 1937- | Traffic police—Texas—Biography. | Peace
    officers--Texas--Biography. | United States marshals—Texas,
    West--Biography. | Texas Rangers—Biography. | Law
    enforcement—Texas—History.
Classification: LCC HV7911.D418 A44 2018 | DDC 363.28/2092 [B] --dc23
LC record available at https://lccn.loc.gov/2018010438

Old Riot, New Ranger: Captain Jack Dean, Texas Ranger and U.S. Marshal is Number 17 in the Frances B. Vick Series

The electronic edition of this book was made possible by the support of the Vick Family Foundation.

Cover and text design by Rose Design

Contents

Preface & Acknowledgments

J ack O. Dean warrants a biography, it's as simple as that. Perhaps all career lawmen do. However, from a publisher's perspective such would be unworkable and financially impractical. In turn, that logical tumbling domino of reality falls into the laps of researchers and writers. Therefore, actually winnowing the gargantuan field of potential protagonists is a true challenge. What demonstrable criterion qualifies the cut? Certainly within the demanding historical context recognizing exceptionality is commonplace, a prerequisite for building a biography. Jack Dean through his captivating life's story links to that benchmark.

Within today's policing subculture the clear-cut expression "cocked and locked" carries dual connotations, figurative and literal. For the biography in hand, Jack O. Dean's law-enforcing life story, the axiom is apt. In the first instance, metaphorically, the precise words translate to being prepared—ready at but a moment's notice to tackle any assignment regardless the uncertain eventualities; the hardships and hazards—or political repercussions. Career lawman Jack Dean, as will become abundantly clear, was creatively geared to do what needed to be done—however, whenever, and wherever. Such a maxim applied to Jack O. Dean was/is an exalted compliment, one made even more meaningful when spoken by his law-enforcing peers. Colleagues' comments are telling. There, too, is the literal interpretation. For the latter case, the wording is applicable to carrying a specific sidearm in a particular and practical mode. As Jack Dean's stirring story unfolds the underlying theme of his mental acuity and physical preparedness will be noticeable throughout. Secondarily, when chronologically appropriate for this nonfiction narrative, the literal meaning of "cocked and locked" will be clarified.

There is, always has been and—probably always will be—a ubiquitous fascination with the Lone Star State's iconic Texas Rangers. Organizationally, bona fide history of the Texas Rangers now dramatically touches three centuries: The historical record is unassailable. Their longevity is legitimate, despite earlier dogmatic efforts to wholly disband and destroy them institutionally. There truly is no shortage of literature, good and bad, documenting the personalities and doings of Texas Rangers. With such a lengthy history to draw from, not unexpectedly, journalistic treatments vary from venerating tales of unconquerable champions wearing pristine white hats, to altogether unprincipled partisan men twisted toward ensuring ethnic superiority—at any costs. In the first instance and, undeniably so, any discomforting truths interfering with maintenance of an unspoiled legend are mislaid—obvious by omission.[1] Likewise, for the latter case treatments of patently agenda-driven detractors and debunkers, the trickery, chicanery, and obfuscation are translucent—sometimes shamefully so, even while impotently masquerading as scholarship.[2] Blindly bending to political correctness is not correct.

For the volume in hand a salient fact is unambiguous. As this book goes to press (2018) only five men have served in the Officer's Corps of the Rangers and also as a Presidentially appointed United States Marshal. When factoring in the hard fact that thousands of individuals have served as Texas Rangers over that time-span the percentage, in reality, does seem small—infinitesimal.[3] A special note of straightforward clarification is not inappropriate and, in fact, is compulsory. Numerous are the Texas Rangers who have through cross-deputation banked law enforcing service as a Deputy U.S. Marshal, but holding down that politically powerful top job is not in their repertoires. Prior to this undertaking, of that top-tier handful, the other four have by now been subject material for full-scale biographies. This try sets right the historical deficit.

Chronologically serving at a level above enlisted and noncom ranks as a Texas Ranger and as a U.S. Marshal was Ben McCulloch, the biographical focus of Professor Thomas W. Cutrer's 1993 *Ben McCulloch and the Frontier Military Tradition*. From his base as

Professor of History and Division Chair at Wharton Junior College, Paul N. Spellman biographically profiled another Texas Ranger who held at different times both titles with his excellent *Captain John H. Rogers, Texas Ranger* released by the University of North Texas Press in 2003. A half-dozen years later again UNT Press followed through with publication of the outstanding research and writing labors of Professor Emeritus Harold J. Weiss, Jr. culminating in *Yours to Command: The Life and Legend of Texas Ranger Captain Bill McDonald*, a celebrated Ranger who parlayed his career into appointment as a U.S. Marshal. While in fact published before the above enumerated volumes, during 1980 the esteemed Professor and past Director of the Texas State Library and Archives, James Milton Day, presented the reading public with his pleasantly readable although somewhat sycophantic treatment *Captain Clint Peoples, Texas Ranger: Fifty Years a Lawman*. Interestingly, but two former Rangers have also served as a U.S. Marshal since birth of the Texas Department of Public Safety in 1935: Captains Peoples and Dean, and only one, Jack Dean, can claim law enforcing service moving into the twenty-first century.[4] And only one of that somewhat elite group banking envied dual titles is yet walking on the topside of daises and not pushing them up. Jack Dean's unstinting contribution to this project is incalculable.

Lest there be any unintended confusion, another former Texas Ranger of the Wild West epoch was a U.S. Marshal, but his highest level with the state law enforcing outfit was as a 2nd-Sergeant during the Frontier Battalion era. Richard Clayton "Dick" Ware was the Texas Ranger that killed Seaborn Barnes during the blistering shootout with Sam Bass and gang in 1878 at Round Rock, Williamson County. One of his Texas Ranger partners, the ever plucky George Herold, planted the rifle ball into Sam's back that ultimately ended his der-ring-do string of armed robberies and the yahoo's twenty-seventh year of life. Such favorable publicity for Dick Ware propelled him into office as the Sheriff of Mitchell County (county seat Colorado City), a job he held onto through numerous election cycles. Thereafter, he and Texas Ranger Captain Frank Jones vied for the position of U.S. Marshal for the Western District of Texas, but Jones didn't have the political firepower and President Grover Cleveland handed Dick Ware the trophy and the paycheck.[5]

Ironically, and it is certainly germane for the text in hand, a century later Jack Dean pinned on the federal badge as the newly installed U.S. Marshal for the Western District of Texas, a gigantic jurisdictional parcel of the Lone Star's real-estate.[6] As will become crystal clear, Texas Ranger Captain Jack Dean had the political horse-power to land the job—a statement not disputed now after-the-fact, nor then when the highly sought appointment was awarded. Captain Jack Dean's law enforcing credentials were unsullied, his long-standing tenure and favorable stature within DPS's ranks was secure.

More than half a century ago former Ranger and Adjutant General William Warren Sterling wrote *Trails and Trials of a Texas Ranger* wherein he made reference to and awarded a quartet of Texas Ranger commanders with a subjective standing that stuck: "Rogers, Brooks, Hughes and McDonald, by virtue of their long, outstanding, and unhampered service, aptly have been called the 'Four Great Captains.'"[7] No contrarian argument is proffered herein and as earlier mentioned, two of those four "Great Captains," John Rogers and Bill McDonald, did own terms of service as U.S. Marshals. Of course W.W. Sterling's assessment could only be based upon history up until the time he wrote those words, not having the luxury of a fortune-teller's forecast. Although these four enumerated Ranger captains have by now been subjects for biographers, such a lengthy passage of time—more than fifty years—should open the historic doorway for updating any register of top-quality Texas Ranger captains, especially one that also donned the prized title as a U.S. Marshal. Jack Dean has earned his spot on that illustrious roster.

Generally speaking, because books demand a closing chapter, published works about the Texas Rangers are understandably subdivided along chronologic timelines. One eminent and knowledgeable academician thoughtfully postulated: "In the mechanism of western law enforcement the Texas Rangers singly or in groups, played a memorable role. Through revolution, statehood, and the rise of an urban Texas, the operations of the Rangers can be divided into three different periods: 1823–1874, 1874–1935, and 1935 onward."[8] While a gentlemen's argument may not be apropos regarding those first two partitions, the time-period of "1935 onward" in this writer's mind and for Jack Dean's riveting biography bears and will withstand tweaking.

Jack Dean's place in Texas Ranger history corresponded almost exactly with the time the fêted institution was undergoing a philosophical revamping and restructuring, due in large part simply to changing times. Fortuitously Jack Dean walked onto the Texas Ranger stage when sociological transformation and enlightened thinking was literally swamping the conventional methodology and management style of Texas Rangers schooled during an earlier and somewhat romantic generational epoch. In a nutshell, what was acceptable shortly before Ranger Jack Dean pinned on his first star-and-wheel badge was no longer deemed suitable. Unquestionably, the transformation was hastened by America's Civil Rights Movement, landmark decisions handed down by the United States Supreme Court, zooming advances in forensic technology, focused efforts designed to diversify the workforce, as well as forward and progressive thinking regarding professionalizing the law enforcing family. Jack Dean saw the old giving way to the new. There were, now, even courses leading to official Criminal Justice diplomas at the end of the accumulated college-hour rainbow. An observable hallmark of the Rangers has—over that time touching three centuries—been an organizational ability to adapt; to restructure and outfit themselves to meet head-on the new challenges criminals and ever evolving technology throw at them. Institutional viability is guaranteed only by weathering the sociological storms; otherwise the only option is to wither and die. As the life story of Jack Dean unfolds, there will be no room for doubt that he was—through no predisposed effort on his part—literally standing at the cusp of institutional transformation. Texas Ranger Jack Dean measured up: The historical record is now marked and is indelible.

That said, it is likewise relevant to point out that Texas Ranger Captain/United States Marshal Jack Dean was/is no infallible superman, just a man, a member of the human race, sometimes successful, sometime not. Unadulterated perfection is not the qualifier for lawmen's biographies. A quick backwards looking reality check vis-à-vis W.W. Sterling's purported "Great Captains" is in this instance more than fitting. Among other things, commendable and censurable, Captain James Abijah Brooks could pocket a Presidential Pardon subsequent to a trial jury finding him courtroom guilty on a reduced charge of Manslaughter due to an arrest gone terribly bad in Indian Territory.[9] Unquestionably, a fact well known, Captain William Jesse McDonald owned a flair for the flamboyant, leading one writer to insinuate that: "In the history of the Texas Rangers no one had ever moved more swiftly to capture a horse thief or a headline than Captain McDonald."[10] Captain John Harris Rogers, though it pained him to make the obligatory acknowledgement, was dismayed and disarmed, then sent packing by a genuinely notorious badman after a disastrous gunplay confrontation in the Sand Dunes of West Texas.[11] Though it's been tendered that Captain John Reynolds Hughes was a "premier gunman of that violent-prone era," and then highlighted in the very same paragraph that another Ranger captain woefully suffered stinging embarrassment because he had to report a self-inflicted gunshot wound, a persnickety little detail was either unknown or inadvertently glossed over. Ruefully, it seems, Captain John Reynolds Hughes was forced by bleeding circumstances to update Texas Ranger headquarters that he would be out of service for awhile: He had accidently shot himself in the foot with a brand-new Smith & Wesson .38 caliber revolver.[12] These four "Great Captains," notwithstanding occasional blunders or personality flaws, rightfully—peeking at their lives in the round and on balance—merit thoroughgoing biographies. Jack Dean does too. His slip-ups—and, yes, there will be cases in point—will not be deferentially sugarcoated in an inane effort to delegitimize any irrefutable evidence: Jack Dean is committed to candor.[13] Additionally, it's but equitable to register that since the aforementioned precipice of time wherein society was in want—demanded—more and more of its law enforcers during the last quarter of the twentieth-century and into this one, independent biographies of the Texas Ranger managerial staff personnel are, indeed, noticed—by their absence! Publication of Jack Dean's story rectifies part of that historical deficit and, hopefully, makes a somewhat worthy contribution moving the Ranger narrative forward and into the twenty-first century.

What then can be gained by meticulously examining Jack Dean's life story? For scoring that query there could be—technically and truthfully—as much as a tenfold answer: Texas Ranger Captain/U.S. Marshal Jack Dean's biographical chronicle, besides highlighting a significant number of humanity's bizarre contradictions, will fundamentally stand on its own merit in that it also serves as a genial legacy component to Texas history; provides an emblematical chapter preserving facets of the Lone Star State's law enforcement history; appropriately documents Texas Ranger evolutionary transitions; substantively contrasts administrative doctrines vis-à-vis state/federal bureaucracies; adequately surveys the very real dichotomy between truth and fiction, myth and legend; frankly showcases the genuine challenges of suitably supervising and disciplining a gun-carrying workforce of unquestionably type-A personalities; makes use of a biographical platform to put human faces on Texas Rangers; makes use of that same biographical platform to spotlight the everyday work of Texas Rangers; appropriately honors the lifetime law enforcing commitment and accomplishments of Jack Dean; and provides an easy to read, yet forthright and factual book for a general audience, as well as students and/or scholars.

Aside from the more or less abstract justifications for penning Jack Dean's personal story the reader will not be shortchanged should he/she be hungry for a taste of down-in-the-trenches police doings. With such a wide-ranging law enforcing career to delve into, it should come as no surprise that Jack Dean's on-the-job experiences were plentiful: sometimes days of monotonous drudgery, sometimes days of electrifying but sickening samples of humanity gone haywire, but at all times but a heartbeat away from excitement and/or sheer terror, that inexplicable stimulant drawing men and women to selflessly pin badges over their hearts. On the topside, society is made up of kindhearted and honest everyday folks, those building—or trying to—bright futures for themselves and their children. There is, however, an underbelly. Lawman Jack Dean never lost sight of the good, but his job choice caused him to circulate in the duplicitous underworld of dishonesty and criminality where twisted self-interest overrode compliance with societal norms. Therefore this biography is jam-packed with true-crime calamities: double murders, single murders, negligent homicides, suicides, jailbreaks, manhunts, armed robberies and home invasions, kidnappings, public corruption, sexual assaults, illicit gambling, car-theft rings, dope smuggling, arms trafficking, untangling perjured testimony, as well as authentic accounts of counterfeiting, cow stealing, con-games and cockfights. Comprehensive biographies require fuel, and this one is hotly charged. Texas Ranger Captain/U.S. Marshal Jack Dean's life story—to some extent—is also intricately tied to the criminal history of a twentieth-century outlaw, a cunning and conspiratorial fellow callously triggering assassinations in trade for cash payments. And though there may be a smattering of hyperbole, it's not altogether outlandish and is provable that the clichéd saw "One Riot. . . . One Ranger," might very well apply to Ranger Jack Dean's participation during an instance of overt social unrest taking place in South Texas, just north of the Rio Grande/Río Bravo.[14] Jack Dean's biography, in all honesty, is rich with drama.

And just as importantly, Jack Dean's story typifies—as with most law enforcers—that there is a life outside workaday battles with bureaucracy, bad men, *mal hombres*, and lawless women. When appropriate for the timeline of Jack Dean's journey down life's highway, matters of family, pride and problems, joy and sadness, will be addressed.

◆ ◆ ◆

Nonfiction work requires helpmates. Although a simple reeling off names and institutional enumerations seems a somewhat anemic methodology, the reader with Jack Dean's biography in hand will readily note the end-product was the work of many. There is no way to do them justice or pay sufficient homage, but the exceptional talents and contributions of each was never undervalued and is—and will be—forevermore appreciated. Standing before them, hat in hand, is my privilege.

Certainly the Texas Rangers and Department of Safety (DPS) are deserving tribute. Several years ago at the administrative decision making level the historic merit in giving Jack Dean his personnel records, personal correspondence, executive decision making blueprints, and Texas Ranger investigative case files and photographs was ably and intelligently recognized. Safeguarding a significant story was fulfilled. Thankfully, now, those archived treasures are not hopelessly lost in the dustbin of indifference. The inherent forethought and wisdom of proffering that workplace gift is well-nigh incalculable with regards to preserving Jack Dean's rich story. The solicitous calculation was also a truly masterful step forward in conserving the spellbinding history of the Rangers and DPS. Too, by straightforward extrapolation it also chronicles the modern-era epoch, at least a snapshot in time, of institutional transitions affecting the Rangers.

Likewise, worthily earning praise was/is the stellar contribution of Christina Stopka, Deputy Director, and Head of the Armstrong Research Center at the Texas Ranger Hall of Fame and Museum (TRHF&M) at Waco, Texas. The aforementioned documents, to be of real historic value, would require a thoughtful review, meticulous cataloguing, all within the framework of professionally accepted museum and library protocols—as well as proper storage in a climate controlled atmosphere, one guaranteeing preservation. This undertaking proved a tremendous and time-consuming task. Christina Stopka is topnotch. Though the multi-month process was trying and tiring, Christina never lost sight of the ultimate goal—boxes of loose papers are almost meaningless—while appropriately organized and retrievable records are the gemstones protecting an institutional history. Squirreled away and/or undisclosed history is valueless. Enthusiastically Christina Stopka, a consummate professional, knew what to do—and did it!

Without doubt this biography could not—and would not—have culminated in an ambitious project absent the participation of Rick Miller. Aside from being a very dear personal friend, the multi-talented and well-versed Miller brings to the table an unconquerable résumé. First and, perhaps, foremost in one sense, Rick has banked service as an on-the-ground peace officer and later in his illustrious career as a Chief of Police in two Texas municipalities. He understands the realities of police work. After completion of law school and earning credentials to hang out his shingle, Rick Miller was later—through multiple voting cycles—the elected County Attorney for Bell County, a position from which he retired. Therefore, turning to Rick Miller for assistance regarding legal issues and appellate court decisions was a natural—his interpretative analysis being not only spot-on accurate, but handily decipherable, too—no legalese shrouded gibberish. One might presume—always dangerous—that was enough levelheaded know-how, the deep well having been plumbed. The ever industrious Rick Miller is also a painstaking researcher and award-winning writer. His constructive 2012 UNT Press treatment in *Texas Ranger John B. Jones and the Frontier Battalion, 1874–1881* not only settled a nonfiction debt long in arrears, but garnered the title Best Book of the Year from the Wild West History Association.

Rick Miller is, subsequent to his richly-deserved retirement from Bell County, dreadfully busy atop the alluring hillside at Harker Heights. But that clumsy generalization demands a no-nonsense caveat. Rick always—always—has time to help a friend, colleague, researcher, or neophyte wannabe writer—or genealogical descendants infatuated with climbing family-trees. Rick Miller will do to tie to! There is nothing pretentious or haughty coming from the kind words and guiding hand of Rick Miller. For this treatment, Jack Dean's biography, Rick Miller's touch was indispensable. Thank you, my friend.

There too, is a cadre of *amigos* ever standing ready, dependable fellows each. My co-author for *Texas Rangers: Lives, Legend, and Legacy*, Donaly E. Brice, now retired and living at Lockhart, is a fountainhead of wisdom with regards to navigating the paper-work maze archived inside the Texas State Library and Archives Commission at Austin. He knows how to find any and everything—and does it willingly. Lieutenant Doug Dukes, Austin PD, Ret., is not only a cherished friend but he is the go-to guy with regards to questions concerning Texas Ranger firearms, from the outfit's inception right through today. His expertise is extraordinary and is exceeded only by his amicability and commitment to fully share that knowledge with researchers and writers not having a clue about technical issues and six-shooter nomenclature. A telephone call or a quick trip to Doug's acreage at Liberty Hill nets meaningful results—again and again. From his base near Zionsville, Indiana, Old West nonfiction writer Dave Johnson can always be counted on to clarify historical issues, especially as they relate to touchy issues spilling forth from feud mentality. Particularly, too, Dave Johnson can be counted on with regards to locating arcane source material and forwarding it to Texas. No challenge is too steep; the depth of his friendship is unfathomable. In somewhat the same vein, fellow TRHF&M Board Member Steve Wharram, from his CPA office at Cleburne, Texas, is never so far caught up in his internal business affairs to lend a helping hand to a writer stuck behind the eight-ball of computer illiteracy and possessing an unexplained phobia to all things that might suffer erasure with an inadvertent touch of but one button on the keyboard. And along those lines, there seems no one with more technical expertise with regards to electronic gismos when they are working as designed and—when they are not—than Josh Lehew of Waxahachie, Texas. Josh has saved this writer's bacon more than once. And for that, thank you Josh—a heartfelt thank you!

Because it interplays into the biography at hand, Jack Dean's thrilling story, piercingly highlighting the madness and meanness of Oklahoma/Texas outlaw Gene Paul Norris is apropos. Though suggesting that when compared to Gene Paul Norris, John Wesley Hardin was a darling little Sunday School pupil—that hyperbole might prove rich. On the other hand, provably, by most contemporary accounts Gene Paul Norris may have had by the mid 1950s as many as forty kills on his notch-stick. Norris was bad to the bone. And who is good to the bone is writer and researcher Michael Koch, Coweta, Oklahoma. When asked to lend a helping hand with fleshing out part of the Gene Paul Norris narrative, Mike jumped to, passionately and promptly. Herein the mention is but fleeting, but his commitment to clarity will forevermore be appreciated—and never undervalued.

Simply spooling off names of other contributors and help-mates seems insufficient, but their positive donations to this tome must not pass unrecognized or unmentioned. Each admirably stepped to the plate and stood tall, altruistically helping when their counsel was sought: Richard K. Alford, TDCJ Region I Director, Institutional Division, Ret., Huntsville, TX; Robin Amy, TRHF&M, Waco, TX; Susan Blackwood, TRHF&M, Waco, TX; Raymond "Rusty" Bloxom, Research Librarian, TRHF&M, Waco, TX; Jason Bobo, Texas Ranger, Lampasas, TX; Vickie Bryant, Historian, Top O' Hill Terrace, Arlington, TX; Captain Barry K. Caver, Texas Rangers, Ret., Denton, TX; Matt Cawthon, Texas Rangers, Ret., Waco, TX; Shelly A. Crittendon, Collections Manager, TRHF&M, Waco, TX; Lisa Daniel, Retail Services Manager, TRHF&M, Waco, TX; Cody Dean, Seguin PD, Seguin, TX; Janie Dean, San Antonio, TX; Kyle Dean, Texas Rangers, Ret., Kerrville, TX; Lieutenant Jim Denman, Texas Rangers, Ret., Austin, TX; Kemp Dixon, Austin, TX; Captain Jamie Downs, Texas Rangers, Austin, TX; Casey Eichhorn, Education Programs Manager, THRF&M, Waco, TX; West Gilbreath, CID Captain, University of North Texas PD, Denton, TX; Charles H. Harris III, Las Cruces, NM; Jude Grochoske, Program Analyst and Fiscal Officer, TRHF&M, Waco, TX; Joe Haralson, Texas Ranger, Texas City, TX; Darren Ivey, Manhattan, KS; Mariena Knueppel, TRHF&M, Waco, TX; Mike Konczak, Baird, TX; Assistant Chief Frank Malinak, Texas Rangers, Ret., Austin, TX; Doug Mankin, Ranger, TX; Reuben T. Mankin, Texas Ranger, McKinney, TX; Nathan R. Mutz, Texas Ranger, Laredo, TX; Robert R. "Bobby" Mutz, former Sheriff of Karnes County, Falls City, TX; Bill O'Neal, former State Historian of Texas, Carthage, TX; Patrick Peña, Texas Ranger, Waco, TX; Lisa Powell, TRHF&M, Waco, TX;

Christine W. Rothenbush, Marketing, Promotions, & Development Coordinator, TRHF&M, Waco, TX; Ronna Roulhac, TRHF&M, Waco, TX; Louis R. Sadler, Las Cruces, NM; Robert W. Stephens, Dunwoody, GA; David S. Turk, Historian, U.S. Marshals Service, Washington, DC; Lieutenant George Turner, Texas Rangers, Ret., Cleburne, TX; Dominic Villa, TRHF&M, Waco, TX; Bryan Warren, Maintenance Coordinator, TRHF&M, Waco, TX; H.L. "Hank" Whitman, Jr., Chief of the Texas Rangers, Ret., Floresville, TX; Jim Willett, former TDCJ Walls Unit Warden and now Director of the Texas Prison Museum, Huntsville, TX; and Jeremy Youngs, Assistant Manager, Visitor and Retail Services, TRHF&M, Waco, TX.

Too, an especial citation should be extended Jan Devereaux. Not only is she a fine writer and public speaker in her own right, but as well she is an authoritatively named TRHF&M Laureate, an honorary distinction of no little significance. Admittedly our relationship is more personal than professional. On the other hand, Jan can always—patiently—be counted on to stand as a sounding board and bring rationality to the table when a cockamamie theory or backwards sentence is served. She is a treasure—my lady love—and my best friend!

And certainly it would be a shameful oversight if the University of North Texas Press was not mentioned. Director Ron Chrisman has and is carving an enviable reputation for acquiring and publishing first-rate Texas Ranger histories. His commitment to excellence within this context has earned UNT Press accolades—well deserved accolades. It may be now argued—with legitimacy—that UNT Press catalogues some of the most prominent Texas Ranger histories. And since the splendid Texas Ranger saga is an ongoing story—additional treatments are a guarantee. Texas History is in good hands at UNT Press. Moving the manuscript from aspiration to fruition is in the most capable hands of Karen J. DeVinney, Assistant Director/ Managing Editor. She is, as would be expected, steadily practiced and superiorly proficient. She, too, is personable—and that makes working with her an absolute delight and pleasure. And though not likely to receive acknowledgment outside the publishing house, certainly two persons are deserving recognition for their unstinting workplace contributions at UNT Press and maintaining institutional merit: April Eubanks, Administrative Coordinator, and Bess Whitby, Marketing Manager.

And, too, herein it's appropriate to mention another contributor: Byron Johnson, Executive Director, TRHF&M, Waco, TX. Tirelessly working to objectively preserve and promote Ranger history—which by extrapolation is Texas history—Byron Johnson has carved an enviable record of achievements within the genre and museum administrative circles. At the helm of TRHF&M for more than twenty years, Mr. Johnson and his most capable staff of credentialed professionals have diligently shaped a first-class facility: Truly a historic resource of consequence, one with international recognition and worldwide acclamation. The journey has been long. Not only does he appreciate the importance of safeguarding the institutional integrity of the Texas Rangers' nineteenth and twentieth century histories, but Bryon Johnson is attuned to the significance of ensuring that today's accomplishments are not offhandedly swept from memory. Contemporary Texas Rangers are making history—everyday! Due to his undying commitment and breadth of knowledge, Byron Johnson has been named as official steward for the Texas Ranger Bicentennial Publications Program. As such he has the somber responsibility and independent authority to judge the intrinsic value of nonfiction journalistic Texas Ranger treatments and whether or not they can be and should be formally recognized as Publications of Merit for the Texas Ranger Bicentennial. Understandably such acknowledgment is well-received by the writer and publisher, but such formalized trademark stamps of approval assures potential casual readers and/or serious students and scholars that the product in hand meets exacting standards and is a worthwhile publication.

Of course, another earnest acknowledgment is imperative: A quick thank-you to Jack Dean. This treatment is a full-scale biography not an autobiography, therefore this writer's researching methodology and writing style underpinned and influenced the end product. When broached with the idea of writing his biography

Jack Dean's response was understandably mixed. Thankfully, in the end, he graciously consented. Therein was but a single admonition; simply tell the truth. As readers will promptly discover the primary source materials were accessible and the first-hand interviews were enlightening. That said, it must also be remembered that there is always the prospect for and possibility of innocent miscommunication—even among well-intentioned folks. Rigorous was the effort expended at trying to get Jack Dean's life story right. Past experience would stubbornly suggest, however, that seldom is any book wholly error free. Though for this tome—whatever the inadvertent slipups or misinterpretations—Jack Dean gets a free pass and this writer regretfully earns the blame. So, should there be mistakes of fact or interpretative misunderstandings Jack Dean and readers or gift-giving purchasers are awarded the sincere and heartfelt apology. Blunders, though certainly unintentional, are the sole property of this writer. Hopefully they are minimal.

1

"That was kinda scary"

For an iniquitous phase of her past Fort Worth was—at least in part—decadently wicked and not secretly corrupt. Such an assertion, perhaps, would not be too surprising to folks reading of her wild and woolly Old West upbringing. Whatever the village's offhandedly awarded moniker, "Where the West Begins" or simply "Cowtown," the North Texas settlement along the banks of the Trinity River was tough ground to cover. Fort Worth was the county seat of Tarrant County, a sprawling piece of real-estate covering near 900 sq. miles and formally surveyed during 1849. The new county was officially organized the following year on 5 August 1850 and then, ten years later, the city captured shiretown honors, wresting them away from Birdville during a heated electoral contest.[1]

From the blood and thunder perspective Fort Worth and Tarrant County was especially rich. The second and fourth sheriff, John B. York, was mortally stabbed and shot during a dustup with lawyer Archibald Young "Arch" Fowler and his teenaged nephew Willie (?), on the twenty-fourth day of August 1861. During labor strife revolving around strikers and the Missouri Pacific Railroad, a special deputy for Tarrant County, Richard W. "Dick" Townsend, was fatally gunned down while his partners of that disastrous day, Charles Sneed and John J. Fulford, were lucky to be alive but wounded, the first in the face, the latter by bullets tearing into both legs. City policeman Christopher Columbus Fitzgerald was fatally shot while trying to restore sanity to the madness two fighting adversaries were inflicting on each other during that sweltering day in August 1877. And again in August, but a couple of years later, Deputy City Marshal George H. White was shotgunned to death by the family of George Alford as he was transporting his prisoner back to the city lockup subsequent to an arrest in Arlington, the budding suburban community just east of downtown Fort Worth. Before he went down in that hail-fire of buckshot, Officer White managed to kill one ambusher and wound another. But a two-year veteran of the Fort Worth PD, C. Lee Waller, was bushwhacked as he and his partner foot-patrolled in the vicinity of Twelfth and Rusk Streets in Fort Worth. Wearing a lawman's gleaming badge was, at best honorable, at worst affording a shiny target. And probably the best known of all—especially for aficionados of the so-called Wild West's gunfighter era—was the very real and somewhat questionable killing of Timothy Isaiah "Longhair Jim" Courtright (carrying a deputy's commission) by the well-known gambler and gunman Luke Short on the boardwalk in front of Fort Worth's notorious White Elephant Saloon.[2] Residents of Fort Worth and Tarrant County could, if they wanted to, legitimately boast of real tough nineteenth-century doings.

Lest there be any undue and untrue assertion that Fort Worth and Tarrant County garnered unto themselves the sole reputation for nineteenth-century North Texas badness, one only has to move east a few miles to burgeoning Dallas and Dallas County. Just for the 1890s Dallas area lawmen paid the ultimate price, as five brothers of the badge mortally succumbed to gunfire during the decade.[3] Provably so, Dallas County's legally mandated hangings and extra-legal lynching are fodder enough for a book-length labor.[4] But, for the bona fide high drama and for relevance to the story in hand, it would be twentieth-century malice and murders that pushes the story and sparks the burning interests of a young Texas man that would be facing vacillating career choices on the pages of life's timelessly turning calendar.

Tarrant County's immediate neighbor to the north is Denton County, founded and organized even four years earlier. Subject to the typically heated rivalries between fledgling communities, the township of Denton ultimately emerged as the county seat of local home-rule government.[5] As the crow flies it's not too far north of Denton to the tiny hamlet of Green Valley. And it was there that the Sarepta, Webster Parish, Louisiana-born William Hershel Dean, twenty-two, and his eighteen-year-old wife Juanita Lucille (Day) Dean, a native of McKinney, Collin County, Texas, made their home. Mr. Dean was an accomplished painter, specifically of airplanes and airplane parts, an in-demand skillfulness not commonly found in those hardworking fellows contracting to paint business houses and barns. Incredibly Mr. Dean was a dually accomplished specialist. He, too, would become an expert at proficiently sealing the fuel tanks of the nation's WWII aircraft, in due time repairing fissures from the inside out, particularly for the America's flight-line of B-24 and B-36 bombers. Mrs. Dean had proficiently developed secretarial skills in accord with her pre-pregnancy employment at an insurance agency. Everyday life was good in North Texas before WWII and the Deans were a happy couple.

Blissful as they were, 16 June 1937 would be a good day but a hard day. During the wee morning hours, before sunrise, Juanita Dean's labor pains commenced. The delivery would not be easy. Whether notified by a hastened party-line telephone call or responding to a hurried nighttime knock at their residence's door is—at this point not now known and is truly irrelevant. The medical practitioners, a father and son physician team, were onsite at the Dean household, tending to Juanita who was undergoing a most difficult delivery. One doctor wanted to write the childbirth off as a heartbreaking but impossible task, the other rebuffed giving up—thankfully! At eight o'clock in the morning, in that little rural home, a brown-eyed bouncing baby boy cried his way into the world: Jack O'Day Dean had arrived.[6]

Understandably, from the biographic standpoint, painstakingly following—or trying to—each and every footstep toddler Jack Dean made before he could run, hop, skip, and jump is not viable and, if it were otherwise doable, extraneous for advancing his story. Schoolboy Jack Dean learned well—or well enough—the early-day classroom lessons of literacy and reckoning with numbers, the necessary exercises of adding and subtracting; counting the black spots on firehouse Dalmatians and tallying how many sheep were yet in the farmer's pen if one slipped through the wire-fence. Though it would not register at the time, but would later beneficially impact his life, Jack's classmates were a hodgepodge, a culturally diverse lot. Like most carefree kiddos romping and stomping and playing tag or dodge ball or Red Rover, they were innocently colorblind to certain social issues plaguing grownups. Santa Claus came once a year. Jack Dean dressed properly for Easter Sunday—mama Dean made sure of that. Jack Dean's early boyhood, happily, was normal.

Though his memories are understandably somewhat hazy, eight-year-old Jack Dean did accompany his parents on an out-of-state trip. A private contractor had a job for his daddy at Allentown, on the eastern side of Pennsylvania. Thankfully and by design, the sojourn to the Keystone State was of short duration—June through August—and Jack Dean's third grade school year was not handi-capped. Back in the Lone Star State, the Dean family finally settled at Fort Worth, the spot Jack Dean would remember best and the place he would call home.

There really is little doubt that by the time Jack Dean was a Fort Worth student he was to some degree aware at least subliminally of the gangster goings-on vilely affecting the city. At mid-century, Fort Worth was Mecca for chaos. Cowtown was and had always been home to a conglomeration of double-crossing underworld characters. Bloodshed makes its own bed in history. Local histories, newspapers, and neighborhood gossip were rife with stories about gambling and corruption and prostitution, car-bomb murders, thoroughly dead bod-ies pulled from Lake Worth, after-hours drinking emporiums, and particular local lawmen looking the other way—for pay. Representing lawfulness—at least on the surface for public consumption—the Tarrant County Grand Jury was rather active for awhile during the 1940s-50s. And so were the hired killers. While Jack Dean had been but an innocent first-grade schoolboy, an ex-convict from Oklahoma, Ray Sellers, Clyde Barrow's former brother-in-law, was filled full of smoking hot lead and pitilessly dumped from a car, but he had slyly opted not to finger his assailant before giving up the ghost. Area police character James B. "Red" Cavanaugh disappeared—for keeps.[7]

While the young and innocent Jack Dean was yet a public school student, Lon Holley took two to the back of the head and died slumped over the steering-wheel of his late-model roadster, murdered before he could cut a plea-bargain deal and snitch others into Huntsville's electric chair for a West Texas murder or clear police books for the bank robbery below Waco at Rosebud, Falls County.[8] Que Robert Miller, ex-sheriff of Foard County at the southeastern edge of the Texas Panhandle and an ex-convict, bought the farm, so to speak, a .45 slug to the back of his head. Then there was that horrific explosion that set the towns of Fort Worth and Dallas agog, the one wherein Texas gangster Herbert "The Cat" Noble's wife was accidently blown to smithereens when she turned the ignition switch on her husband's car that twenty-ninth day of November 1949.[9] And before year's end, Hollis DeLois "Lois" Green, a big-time gangster and murderer, a "desperate and depraved thug" and "really bad actor" purportedly with more than twenty kills on his notch-stick, was put under by multiple shotgun blasts in the parking lot of a Dallas nightspot, the Sky Vu Club,— the buckshot bought sweet revenge and eternal silence. Schoolboy Jack Dean, though not particularly overly interested in such gangster goings on in North Texas at the time, was not immune to the widespread media reports and hearing grownups rattle about them.[10]

Less than a year later, as Jack Dean was yet embarking on that journey to adulthood, he hazily recalls Fort Worth's next headlining newspaper copy. Gangsterdom's earthquake had erupted. Nelson Harris and his pregnant wife, Juanita, had been sent henceforth to mark their place in the hereafter, thanks to the expertise of a "nitro man," a shadowy guy adept at rigging automobiles with lethal charges of nitroglycerin.[11] Headline copy carried the news. Radios and televisions blared the, by now, seemingly habitual Fort Worth/Dallas area story. But the wholesale killing was far from over. The failed attempts on gangster Herbert Noble's life were near habitual headlines, so much so that the May 14, 1951, issue of *Life Magazine*, with photos, ran their underworld feature: "Ex-Gambler Has More Lives Than a Cat."[12] Shortly, relatively speaking, Herbert Noble reached into to his mailbox, not knowing that underneath the surrounding ground, well, it had been "wired." Presumably he never heard the explosion as his body parts shredded into little and nearly unrecognizable pieces of meat, bone, and gristle. Not surprisingly Texas Rangers responded to the blood-spattered crime scene, a fact not lost on ravenous newsmen or naive kiddos always curious about such ghoulish goings-on. Jack Dean was, at the time, an inquisitive fourteen-year-old. And that very same volatile month, August 1951, Fort Worth resident James Clyde "Jim" Thomas, an ex-convict having Nebraska and Texas prison time everlastingly inked on his lengthy rap sheet, also possessed a somewhat charming and dashing, but deceiving demeanor: "Police, however, saw him as half of the team that killed Lon Holley and Que Miller, as well as a strong suspect in the Nelson Harris bombing." In due course the seemingly but deceptively mild-mannered Jim Thomas was mortally cut down at Durant, Oklahoma, by two shotgun blasts fired by one Hubert Deere, one to the lower stomach, the other below the beltline—to his groin.[13]

Though a direct tie to Jack Dean's story is not there, a mention of Tarrant County's posh dinning room, ornate gaming hall, and upscale whorehouse is not altogether cheap or tactless.[14] When contrasted with the seedy side of Fort Worth's underworld society and its rough-edged environs it will, indeed, play into Jack Dean's true-life narrative. Any voyeuristic peek at the Fort Worth area with respect to it being a wide-open paradise for high-rollers and hedonists must include mention of the Top O'Hill Terrace in nearby Arlington. Though the signature activity of Top O'Hill Terrace was an under-the-table business, the top side was lavishly fixed, at least one penman so declares:

> As the name implies, it was situated on the top of a hill, and it was known not only for its exclusiveness but also for the luxury of its appointments. The floors were covered with costly rugs and lighting was provided by elegant chandeliers. . . . Fred Browning, saw to it that dinner guests were provided with sterling silver flatware, that they ate off priceless china and drank from imported crystal.[15]

Fred Browning's entertainment venue was perhaps Fort Worth's most unguarded secret, though real guards stood as sentinels cautiously eyeing potential players and good-timing gals as they passed through five locked doorways.[16] Access was by invitation—no strangers, no Rangers. According to an adroit and academic chronicler, basing his assessment on the knowledge of someone in the know, it is explicitly proffered "that it was not unusual for half a million dollars to change hands at Top O'Hill Terrace on a single good weekend during the horse racing season" at nearby Arlington Downs.[17] By any man's or woman's standard Top O'Hill Terrace was, before Las Vegas grabbed the spotlight, the elite's playground. But a circumspect check of the guest list from a blend of sources reveals that such celebrated and high-profile personalities as Don Ameche, Gene Autry, Marlene Dietrich, Tommy Dorsey, W.C. Fields, Benny Goodman, Jean Harlow, Howard Hughes, H.L. Hunt, Buster Keaton, Heddy Lamarr, Dean Martin, Tom Mix, Sally Rand, Ginger Rogers, Frank Sinatra, Lana Turner, W.T. Waggoner, and Mae West, enjoyably sampled the fare at Fred Browning's luxurious nightspot and casino. And, of course, that's not counting the well-known Fort Worth/Dallas crowd of risk-taking underworld bettors and bribers, cardsharps and cheats, conmen and killers.[18]

Not surprisingly, with his thumb in so many lucratively illicit pies, area gambler, racketeer, and rounder Lester Ben "Benny" Binion had a major behind-the-scenes slice of the action. For awhile the glitter and glamour and greenbacks slyly blinded police notice—and engagement. After clearing security, guests could participate in games of chance like roulette, blackjack, craps, or voraciously feed one-arm bandits coins to their heart's content—or the money ran out. Naturally, the big moneyed players had a liberal line of credit.[19]

At least one Texas Ranger captain was purportedly dragging his feet and fiddling with excuses for not shutting down the Top O'Hill Terrace.[20] Ultimately, though, it would be the Texas Rangers shutting down the illicit gaming operation with a triumphant raid captained by the now somewhat legendary Manuel Terrazas "Lone Wolf" Gonzaullas on Sunday night, 10 August 1947. Sneaking up on the backside of the casino, Texas Rangers pre-positioned themselves, and were successful when bewildered patrons—flushed like a covey of quail from the front side—vainly tried to flee through the not so hush-hush escape tunnel, a landmark of trickery existing to this very day.[21] Though it necessitates that niggling backwards chronological peek, the notable gambling raid had been of no concern or curiosity for Jack Dean. He had been, at that time, yet a fun-lovin' schoolboy more interested in playing cowboys and Indians, cops and robbers, and owning his very own pocket knife before the upcoming academic year had kicked-off at the Denver Avenue Elementary School.[22]

Being handed ownership of a firearm was a rite of passage for a boy growing up in Texas. Such parental confidence moved them to big boy status, then onto the march leading to maturity. At about age ten or eleven Jack Dean's grandfather on his mothers' side, Charley Day, gave young Jack a shotgun and, as it turned out, his very first gun-toting job. The assignment was simple, the pay acceptable. At granddad's farm near Pilot Point northeast of Green Valley, his chest thumping with pride, Jack Dean was to be paid bounty money; $1.00 for every varmint he sent scampering to the hereafter and terminally out of the fruitful garden plot. Visits to the farm, now were more fun than ever before. The reality check is measurable, he was tramping toward manhood, the jingling coins in his blue denim pockets from dispatching pests, well, that total never really amount to too very much, but the grown-up type challenge was what, in the end, really mattered.[23]

Jack Dean finished what are now classified as middle school years at Cowtown's Washington Heights Junior High, while living with his caring parents at 2516 Leming Street. And although it was a city address and a municipal school, some of Jack's fondest memories revolve around outings with his daddy to the countryside—like granddad Charley's farm—where shooting and squirrel hunting was on the day's agenda.[24] Recreational target practice was, really, the cat's meow for adolescent Jack Dean. And it was during these formative years that firearms safety was relentlessly drilled into Jack's head. The jaunts were fun, as well as practically instructional. Thankfully, at least no doubt from older brother Jack Dean's perspective, little brother, Jerry Glenn, nine years his junior, was too small to make the trips, interfering with the fun and/or vying for attention and ammunition.[25]

Perhaps more attuned with this biography is a compulsory geo-graphical and chronological notation that Jack Dean came along too late in life to sample the sinfulness or shy away from the Top O'Hill Terrace, but along a disreputable strip of Fort Worth's Jacksboro Highway meanness and madness still flourished, twenty-four and seven. Not lovingly, Fort Worth police sometimes referred to the depraved locale as the "Jax Beer Highway." Other folks, primarily upstanding Tarrant County citizens knew it, at the time, to be "the toughest, wildest piece of real estate in Texas." According to one eyewitness remembrance, along the iniquitous Jacksboro Highway profitable success of the clubs was calculated by the number of ambulance calls on any given night: The more shootings and cut-tings and cracked craniums and bruised knuckles was the palpa-ble clear-headed signal that scads of money was actually changing hands. Fortunately long-time educator Ann Arnold, in her single vol-ume treatment, painstakingly captured the not so pretty essence of this part of North Fort Worth with her insightful and intriguing and chilling *Gamblers and Gangsters: Fort Worth's Jacksboro Highway in the 1940s and 1950s*. A little closer in, "crime and carousing" in bar-rooms throughout the Stockyards Section was generating a not envi-able reputation, at least among Fort Worth's tea sippin' socialites, according to academician J'Nell Pate in her neat tome *North of the River: A Brief History of North Fort Worth*.[26] This was the timeframe that Jack Dean and his parents and siblings (sister Hershelene was eleven years his junior) were happily contented Cowtown residents.[27]

Jack Dean, by his own recollection, sporadically let some of that gangland noise bleed into his psyche and, it must not be under-played, but if truth be told there were more pressing matters taking up his time and occupying his mind. He was attending Fort Worth's Diamond Hill-Jarvis High School, seemingly a little more interested in girls and football than conquering geometry and physics and algebra and "hunt and peck" typing on a manual typewriter. With regards to attaining some pie-in-the-sky scholastic status, though his IQ score was high, Jack Dean had opted out of too much study-hall bookwork and skirted around doing too much after-school homework. His dedicated high-school principal, Clyde Brown, noted that Jack "was an average student, but that he was very neat, dependable, easy-going, quiet natured, and mixed well with other students." To a certain extent, rather importantly it seems, Principal Brown also recalled that Jack was "a very good football player and the team depended on him a great deal."[28] In fact, during two of those high-school years Jack "lettered" in football and earned a V-shaped scar on the top of his left hand attesting to the neat little fact that when he played, he played hard, giving it his all. Though an active member of the Athletic Club, and with no little effort spent on the basketball court and participation in track and field events, neither sport held the lure or the "letter" for a lean and lanky Jack Dean.[29] Among other things, one of his classroom teachers, John Rumfield, openly noted that although bookwise Jack was but an average student, he was "cool headed, got along with others excellently and was a good mixer. . . ." Another more than encouraging high-school teacher, T.B. Hudgins, Jr., amplified his educational colleagues' assessment stating that Jack "got along with other students well, was a hard worker, not lazy, [and] appeared to be a good worker. . . ." According to a friend and classmate, Bobby J. Means, Jack Dean really came from "an excellent family," and went to church "fairly often."[30] From the best evidence at hand, it would seem that Jack Dean was an all-around pretty good boy.

He too was smitten. Janie Lee Hill was also a student at Diamond Hill-Jarvis High School. The very pretty and especially petite girl was stunning as well as smart. Originally from Denison, Grayson County, just below the Red River's Texas/Oklahoma borderline, Janie had moved to several towns within the Lone Star State prior to coming to Fort Worth. As a small child she had lived at such places as centrally situated Brady in McCulloch County, the geographical heart of the Lone Star State, and for awhile in West Texas at Lamesa in Dawson County as well as Plainview (Hale County). Janie's father, Gerald A. Hill, during WWII and had been stationed at these small town airfields as an accomplished Flight Instructor, teaching young American and English aviators how to safely take off, navigate, and land their assigned aircraft on concrete and/or grass runways. Janie's mother, Myrtie Jewel, a sometimes seamstress, tended the home front as the couple patriotically transferred from town to town as orders dictated. Eventually, subsequent to WWII, the Hill family had settled at Fort Worth where Janie was enrolled in the city's public school system.[31]

Budding romance, yes, there was one. The stories of childhood or high-school sweethearts are oft told, and in the case of Jack Dean and Janie Hill, Cupid's arrow flew true. What is also true to the core is that Jack Dean was all boy—all the time—and that pathway to maturity is sometimes rocky and strewn with temptation. It was certainly common knowledge that during the 1950s along the infamous Jacksboro Highway, if you were tall enough to lay your money on the bar, you were big enough to drink—no questions asked, no ID required. Jack was tall, six foot, one inch—and thirsty. He and a couple of friends cut class and bellied up to the bar, testing the veracity of what they had been told of the Jacksboro Highway's loosely enforced laws and titillating wickedness. Was it really true that you had to be but breathing and have a dollar or two to wet your whistle? Luckily, as it turned out that afternoon, during the daytime inside that dark and smoke-filled and foul-smelling barroom there was naught to mention—nothing worth telling. The high school boys' money spent just as well as the grey-headed fellow with long sideburns guzzling beer from long-neck brown bottles and suitably racking the next game of Eight-Ball. The corner juke-box at 5¢ a play blared and the 50s' melodies reverberated, drowning any soft spoken conversation. It was, for teenagers, really rather heady stuff, hanging out with grown men and buxom waitresses in a bona fide beer joint. One helluva hiding place for three otherwise good guys, but this day was geared for skipping school. On the other hand, the Jacksboro Highway was one tough zone. The trio of truants was aghast when they afterwards learned that at that very same taproom, sometime after their afternoon departure but that very evening, someone was fatally gunned down in the parking lot beneath the forever flashing and enticing neon sign. Jack Dean, to this day, humbly and unpretentiously remembers, "That that was kinda scary." Less memorable, however, was whether or not this was the time Jack Dean glumly suffered his disciplinary three-day suspension from Diamond Hill-Jarvis High School, but nevertheless the Assistant Principal's demand for a dose of punishment was genuine, as was Janie's displeasure with Jack's errant conduct.[32]

Mid-point of the decade, 1955, would be consequential for Forth Worth's gangland annals as well as for Jack Dean's unfolding narrative. On the sleazy side gambler and pimp Edell Evans disappeared for awhile—about six months—until his decomposing body was found in a shallow grave at the north end of Lake Worth.[33] The dead Lois Green's brother, Cecil, a career criminal and alleged hit-man, was himself ambushed and murdered while sitting in a parked vehicle outside the By-Way Drive-In on Fort Worth's Jacksboro Highway.[34] And, putting a cap on the Fort Worth madness for 1955 was the slaying of Leroy "Tincy" Eggleston. The remorseless gangster's crimson-soaked Oldsmobile, dripping blood from the doorjamb, was found abandoned in the asphalt parking lot of a supermarket near the Fort Worth Stockyards. Shortly, after lawmen pocketed an alleged anonymous phone tip, Tincy's remains were recovered from a well, not too terribly far from where Edell Evans's body at been unearthed near Lake Worth.[35]

Aside from the real headlines for 1955 there was entertainment news, and though the message was subconscious, Jack Dean bends to reality—acknowledging, like most television viewers and movie goers he was hooked. Although the black and white adventures of a masked-man atop a charging white stallion and shooting silver bullets was obviously hokey, even for Jack Dean, other fabrications were not. James Arness and Amanda Blake were making their unforgettable marks as Marshal Dillon and Miss Kitty in the *Gunsmoke* TV series, a fictionalized production billed as a Western drama for an adult audience. There was even then, at that point in time, the debut of Willard Parker assuming the role of Ranger Jace Pearson and actor Harry Lauter becoming Ranger Clay Morgan for *Tales of the Texas Rangers*, a feature that ran for fifty-two episodes and actually spawned a colorful comic book.[36] And through the gravely voice and gruff persona of

Hollywood's Broderick Crawford in *Highway Patrol* there was a drama not centered on Texas Rangers or U.S. Marshals, but those tales of uniformed state troopers and criminal investigators also held an inexplicit—and as of then certainly vicarious—allure for Jack Dean. Like many other young men, he was not blind or immune to all that entertainment hoopla. In fact, his Diamond Hill-Jarvis High School buddy, Bob Means, had pinned on the badge and buckled on the Sam Browne leather as a Smith & Wesson carrying Fort Worth policeman.

Not every bit of 1955 news was about bad men doing bad things or actors doing good things. Jack Dean, on the first day of June 1955, was a student no more. He had successfully earned enough credits to graduate from Diamond Hill-Jarvis High School and had earned matrimonial credit with Janie. During the Christmas Holiday vacation, Jack a recent graduate, and Janie halfway through her senior year, raced to Gainesville in Cooke County and civilly tied the knot on 20 December 1955. The couple's impromptu marriage was legal and poignant but, nevertheless, it was an elopement. Back at Fort Worth the news was received with mixed results. W.H. and Juanita Dean, though surprised, were really "not too upset." At first the same could not be said at the bride's household. Gerald Hill was not ready to see his beloved girl child shackled with the responsibilities of keeping house and caring for a husband—especially with another semester of high school on the books. Myrtie Hill for the short-term went ballistic. After securitizing the Marriage License, she threw it in Janie's face. Tempers cooled. The displeasure was short-lived, and Myrtie did have to admit Jack Dean was a good boy and a good catch—and he really was personable, one of her favorites. Soon, in the end, all was well.[37]

Aside from now having a wife, young Jack Dean had a real job. He had landed grown man's wages, $2.29 per hour as a tool and dye maker at the city of Fort Worth's leading employer Convair: That is when the huge payroll at Cowtown's booming meat packing plants, Swift and Armour, at the east end of Exchange Avenue in the fragrant Stockyards Section is discounted. On the west side of Fort Worth, the mammoth Convair facility (earlier Consolidated Vultee

Aircraft Cooperation and somewhat later General Dynamics), was a bomber building factory during and subsequent to WWII. Physically the plant was staked next to the United State's Air Force's Tarrant Field Airdrome, which would eventually become the recognized and strategic Carswell Air Force Base.[38] Employment at Convair for the Dean family, father and son, but scratched the service. Janie, after graduation from Diamond Hill-Jarvis, worked there too, in the office. Jack's father-in-law Gerald, after health reasons knocked him off the flight-line, was gainfully employed at Convair as an accredited Inspector. For a solid middle-class living, the Deans and Hills were doing just fine at Fort Worth—economically.

On the educational front, Jack Dean gave it a part-time try at Fort Worth's Texas Christian University, majoring in History. As with so very many young folks, the first college effort is sometimes thwarted for one reason or another and Jack Dean, in this instance, is no exception. Though this cycle of university level studies would not be his swansong with regards to earning college credits, as far as Cowtown's TCU was concerned, Jack's first semester would be his last. At this point in his young life, Jack Dean opted to put accumulating college hours on hold. Estimably he makes no whinny excuses. What it is, is what it was!

While Jack Dean was ecstatic with his personal life regarding the marriage to Janie and their real prospects of making a tolerable medium-wage income home at Fort Worth, on another front something was missing. The post-WWII economy was booming, perhaps in someway energized by threats of Cold War preparedness, but the everyday humdrum of assembly-line production at the Convair plant was repetitively mundane. Though realizing it at the time, somewhere rising from the depths of his soul was an aspiration—a yearning—for something more exciting and meaningful career-wise. Jack Dean was an action oriented guy and there was, unhappily, no exhilarating labor for him at the Convair facility.

Such could not be said about the Jacksboro Highway. Another homicidal try—an ingenious murder plot—captured headlines in bold print. Naturally unbeknownst to underworld character Charles

Frank Cates, one of the prime suspects in the killings of Lon Holley, Nelson Harris, and Que Miller, plans were underway for his demise. Beneath his house, at the exact spot below the floor where his telephone stand stood, sticks of dynamite were placed—the unnoticed wires "trailing 250 feet down the Jacksboro Highway."[39] With one fellow sitting in a 1956 Buick holding the tail ends of electrical wires and another in a nearby telephone booth, dropping a dime for a dial tone, there is little need to speculate as to what was sneakily planned to happen next. The phone rang and Frank Cates answered. The ensuing explosion was horrific, but somehow Frank Cates survived even though his modest house was utterly destroyed. His good luck was fleeting. After a three-week hospital stay, on the night of 8 October 1956, two shotgun blasts did what a bomb-maker had failed to do, provide money for the dead Frank Cates's undertaker to buy Halloween costumes for his kiddos.[40] All of Fort Worth took note.

Fortuitously, for the day-after-day grinding Jack Dean was putting in at Convair, it happened, another of those spellbinding Fort Worth headlines, a story that sparked interest and muddled thoughts about his real purpose in life, his future.

If there really was a bad mid-twentieth-century outlaw it was Gene Paul Norris.[41] He and his older brother Thomas Nathan "Pete" Norris had been registered on the FBI's and other law enforcing agencies' recurring lists of most sought after fugitives. By many Lone Star State folks' standard—even the underworld's police characters—the Norris brothers were the most dreaded hoodlums into or out of raucous Fort Worth. "Within inner circles of the Southwest's gangland world Gene Paul Norris, his shotgun for hire, was well-established and unanimously feared."[42] One steadfast nonfiction scribe frankly posited: "He seemed a very pleasant and polite young man. Looks, however, deceived, for Gene Paul Norris was a psychopathic, cold-blooded killer whose likes had not been seen in Texas since the days of John Wesley Hardin. . . . Police believed he murdered more than forty men. . . ."[43] Somewhat irrefutably for measuring the man, Gene Paul Norris owned a string of twenty-five arrests and had been into and out of prison a half-dozen times.[44]

Though it somewhat may kick sideways any romantic or vicarious fascination with genuine gangsters, Gene Paul Norris, among numerous other gangland slayings, was the prime suspect in mortally gunning down one of Fort Worth's most dangerous underworld creatures, the ever incorrigible Cecil Green. Shortly thereafter, killer Gene Paul Norris married Cecil Green's widow, Rita (Davis) Green, more or less keeping faith with the tenet that there is not a scrap of honor among underworld thieves—or degenerate hired guns. That Gene Paul Norris was a snake is sustainable. Provably, too, Gene Paul Norris had—at gunpoint—even helped his brother Pete break out of the Ferguson Prison Farm of the Texas Department of Corrections penitentiary system at Midway, Madison County, roughly the halfway point between Dallas and Houston.[45] And it would be a Houston homicide—a double murder—that would trigger a spine-tingling episode that would, though he knew not at the time, help shape the life and give purpose to needs burning inside Jack Dean.

Pete Norris had been sent to prison in large part due to the courtroom testimony of Houston gambler and bookmaking kingpin Johnny Brannan. Gene Paul Norris vowed revenge. Years later the state's star witness and his wheelchair-bound wife, Lillie, had been found dead in their home, bludgeoned to death, hands tied, blankets covering their heads, their skulls beaten to "pulp." Although it was described as one of the most brutal and bloodiest crime scenes that Houston detectives could recollect, there was no doubt in anyone's mind just who had been responsible: Gene Paul Norris, "The Smiling Killer" and his sometimes sidekick William Carl "Silent Bill" Humphrey.[46] The remorseless killer had—with help—finally fulfilled his spiteful promise to off Brannan and had momentarily sated his bloodlust.[47]

Not surprisingly Rangers were called on to add their expertise and breadth of knowledge to the murder investigation. Their network of informants was vast, their forensic training first-rate. Within Ranger ranks the task fell to the captain of Company A, John J. "Johnny" Klevenhagen, a well-seasoned forty-five-year-old lawman from New Braunfels, Comal County. Though in truth an authentic cowboy, two descriptions of the veteran Texas Ranger ring true, loud and clear:

Captain Klevenhagen was essentially "unstoppable." And, Johnny Klevenhagen's boss, the revered Colonel Homer Garrison, Jr., too, characterized the Company A Captain: "He combined the qualities of the frontier Ranger and his modern counterpart. The lean leathery lawman was a peerless horseman and deadly shot but he was also versed in ballistics, fingerprints, and other facets of advanced criminology." Besides family Johnny Klevenhagen's life revolved around but three things: coffee, cigarettes, and career. The captain was a hopelessly addicted workaholic! The Department of Public Safety (DPS) Director, Colonel Garrison, had also noted that Captain J.J. Klevenhagen was a credibly licensed pilot and frequently used an airplane in furtherance of his nonstop policing and investigative duties. Captain John Joseph Klevenhagen was, quite truthfully, at least in the American Southwest, a law enforcing legend in his own time.[48]

Although it seemed surreal, the draft of the next caper for Gene Paul Norris was on the mean villain's drawing board, and it was no joking matter. The blueprint would be drawn with blood. Gene Paul and Silent Bill, subsequent to conspiratorial planning with a couple of other dubious police characters, had slyly concocted a murderous plan to enrich themselves. At her home on Meandering Road the wholly unsuspecting Elizabeth Barles and her twelve-year-old son, John, according to plan, would quickly be taken hostage temporarily—then executed: No witnesses. No testimony.[49] Gene Paul Norris was, perhaps, at this point in the 1957 time zone known as "the most vicious gangster in the Southwest."[50]

The gist of the gangster's plan was plain. After killing the mother and son, Gene Paul and Silent Bill would take the home-owner's automobile, leaving their getaway car parked in the victim's driveway. What then? Mrs. Barles was employed at Fort Worth's First National Bank, the branch located behind Carswell Air Force Base boundaries. Glued to the windshield of her personal vehicle was that ever important decal, the one allowing for entry onto the military base. Early in the morning, prior to the bank opening, and once Gene Paul Norris and Silent Bill Humphrey were waved past the checkpoint, they would proceed to the bank and using the dead Mrs. Barles's office keys secret themselves inside, waiting to make prisoners—presumably dead prisoners—of First National employees arriving at the worksite. After rifling the cash drawers and making withdrawals from the vault, they would wait for the armored car, the one delivering $500,000 for the airmen's monthly payroll. Gene Paul and Silent Bill would allow the money-laden guards inside, greeting them with the business end of pistols. Gene Paul Norris abhorred witnesses and there would be none—not one. The body count would be high, but so too would be the tally of freshly minted cash.[51]

Further south at Houston, Captain Klevenhagen ceaselessly working on the Brannan murders was at length able to develop sufficient information to file an official Complaint setting forth Probable Cause. Enthusiastically it might be surmised, the magistrate handed Ranger Captain Klevenhagen arrests warrant for Gene Paul Norris and Silent Bill Humphrey. So, while twenty-year-old Jack Dean, nose to the grindstone at Convair in his dead-end job, was pondering the prospects for his future in light of the projected RIF (Reduction in Force), Company A's Captain Klevenhagen was figuratively hotfooting to Fort Worth, Colt .45 autoloader at his side, arrest papers in hand. The Ranger's arrival at Cowtown would prove meaningful to not just a few folks, including a discontented and restless Jack Dean.

Captain Klevenhagen's timing had been perfect—almost as if Fate had winked and beckoned him to Fort Worth. Unbeknownst to Norris, area lawmen were aware of the diagram for death. Aside from forensics, cracking difficult criminal cases often depends on confidential sources and the inside information they own. Though their reasoning may vary, snitches snitch. And at Cowtown, subsequent to a debriefing, the Rangers, Tarrant County Sheriff's Office, FBI, and the Fort Worth Police Department were attuned to the outlaws' plan.

Though the actual full-length story is a thriller, for the purpose at hand, a shortened version must suffice. Through covert physical surveillance and electronic monitoring of an adjoining motel room, lawmen knew that Gene Paul Norris and Silent Bill Humphrey would make a dry run, clandestinely casing Mrs. Barles's neighborhood and eyeing potential escape routes the day before the murders and bank robbery. "From the prosecutorial perspective that dry run—an overt act—would help move the conspiracy from talk to deed—the law demanded that; juries needed assurance before throwing away the jailhouse keys."[52] Cautiously but smartly, and with a pledge of absolute secrecy, Mrs. Barles was apprised of the situation and her residence placed under the watchful eye of police snipers. The trap had been carefully set. When Gene Paul Norris and Silent Bill Humphrey entered the Meandering Road neighborhood, the jaws would snap shut. That is if everything went right. It didn't!

According to plan, FBI agents would tail the suspects from the motel to the Meandering Road locality then—via radio transmission—hand off to the Texas Rangers for the take-down, they being the outfit actually holding murder warrants. On paper it was a great plan; in reality it went to hell-in-a-hand-basket in but a jiffy. Gene Paul and Silent Bill "knocked off" the surveillance and the madcap car chase was on, the desperadoes driving a souped-up 1957 Chevrolet. Occupying the first police chase car, a super-charged Dodge driven by Texas Ranger Captain E.J. Banks, were Ranger Captain Klevenhagen, Tarrant County Sheriff Harlon Wright, Fort Worth Police Chief Cato Hightower, and the city's Homicide Detective Captain, O.R. Brown. In the second unit were Rangers Arthur Hill and Jim Ray (a future Chief of DPS Criminal Law Enforcement), along with Fort Worth's Chief of Detectives, Andy Fournier. Texas Ranger Ernest Daniel and additional local officers followed at high-speed in a third unit. If the excessive speed—sometimes 120 mph—wasn't danger enough, the peril was ramped up when Gene Paul Norris leaned from the Chevrolet's passenger widow and opened fire on the pursuing officers. As one would expect, unshakable lawmen returned the compliment. While recklessly careening around corners on two wheels and zigzagging on highway straight-aways, it comes as no great shocker, as of yet neither side was inflicting serious damage with bullets. But, just as predictable, that would soon change.

The 29 April 1957 car chase ended that Monday afternoon when Silent Bill lost control of the getaway vehicle along the muddy banks of Walnut Creek, wrecking just south of Springtown,

Parker County, Tarrant County's western neighbor. Bailing out of their stock-still automobile the two gangsters—firing at lawmen as they ran—raced afoot toward the finish-line, a stand of thick timber shading Walnut Creek. The frantic race ended with heartless brigands Gene Paul Norris and Silent Bill Humphrey earning the red-ribbon premium. Unluckily for them, as a well-known U.S. Border Patrol shootist duly noted, in a bona fide gunfight there are no second place winners. Norris and Humphrey lay dead, lifelessly riddled with bullets fired by Texas Ranger Captains Klevenhagen and Banks—and other area lawmen.[53] Not dead was local newsmen's legit interest! It was, by any journalistic standard, a whopping good news story, and keeping with editors' widespread doctrine that that if it bleeds it leads, a Johnny-on-the-spot newspaperman and photographer for the *Fort Worth Star-Telegram* were quickly onsite—as was the sizeable crowd of rubber-necking spectators. There's hardly any doubt that most Fort Worth folks were, though shocked, attracted to the newsy story. Jack Dean was. After all, the robbing and killing had been set to take place nearby— almost adjoining his jobsite. And, besides that, what young man of the place and time would not be drawn in by those photos of boot-wearing and Stetson covered lawmen, star-in-wheel badges pinned over their hearts, stalwart guys with pistols in fancy scabbards supported by intricately tooled gunbelts at the hip, shotguns in hand. Assuredly those dashing fellows weren't bored to death, inexorably trapped in some humdrum job.[54]

Adding to Jack Dean's internal dilemma and sparking perplexing career choice questions was Hollywood's release of another popular product for TV viewers to devour, *Trackdown*, starring Robert Culp, purportedly true-life episodes actually drawn "from files of the Texas Rangers."[55] There was/is even an iconic photograph of Texas Ranger Hoby Gilman (Culp's character) posing with a half-dozen two-gun Texas Rangers and the renowned DPS Director, Homer Garrison, Jr., in front of the University of Texas Tower at Austin.[56] Real life drama and make believe, to a certain extent fused in many minds. Hitting the television market the same year, 1957, that Texas Rangers had interdicted the wickedly concocted plan of real-life gangsters Gene Paul Norris and Silent Bill Humphrey, *Trackdown* would instinctively stir the coals of unrest burning in many a young Texan's belly. Jack Dean was at a crossroads.

Janie Dean wasn't standing at any crossroad of indecision; her course had been set. Before 1958 was history, during their third year of marriage, she and Jack would become proud parents. Jack was absolutely elated. The only downside would be that Janie would have to give up her coveted office job at Convair. The couple would, at least for awhile, be solely dependant on Jack as the family's bread-winner. Big time responsibilities were, now, more than ever before, laid at young Jack Dean's doorstep. With what he deemed appropriate thought processes and Janie's solid blessing, Jack Dean, a strapping twenty-year-old, applied for an entry-level position as a Texas Highway Patrolman with DPS on 18 March 1958.[57]

Again, his timing seems fortuitous but relevant. Although having 1935 as an actual birth year as an institution, just the year before, in 1957, DPS had been handed the critical analysis of its operations and organizational structuring, an authoritative subcontracted examination conducted by the Texas Research League at the behest of the Public Safety Commission. So, as a practical matter, 1957 was the year DPS was undergoing a major revamping. The clear target was, among other stated objectives, professionalizing the workforce and administratively streamlining the appropriate implementation of its extensive traffic and criminal law enforcement responsibilities. Part of that restructuring called for Texas to be subdivided into six geographical regions, each under the command of a Regional Commander, who would oversee the day-to-day operations of the uniformed divisions within DPS and answer to the outfit's Director at Austin. Additionally, "pursuant to 1957 Legislative authority, a limited crime laboratory was developed in each regional headquarters." The Texas Rangers, one of the criminal enforcement arms of DPS, and in accordance with the committed lawmakers' fiat, "were not to be abolished." They, too, would be reshuffled, formalized into six companies. Each of those investigative components would be assigned the same geographical territory as the DPS regional commands, with a Ranger Captain in charge of their field operations and criminal enforcement duties. "Headquarters functions were consolidated into four major divisions responsible for the support of the regional commands, and for services to local law enforcement agencies. These were termed the Identification and Criminal Records Division, the Personnel and Staff Services Division, Driver and Vehicle Records Division and the Inspection and Planning Division."[58] For Jack Dean's narrative, he had chosen a career with DPS at the exact time constructive transitions were underway.

If accepted into the Highway Patrol, Jack would turn twenty-one by the time of graduation from the DPS Academy, the training school for new recruits. Hearing naught of his application, the following month, on 17 April 1958, aspirant Jack Dean punched out a type-written query to the Personnel and Training Division of DPS: "I am writing in regards to my application for employment with the Texas Department of Public Safety, which was submitted in March of this year."[59] Somewhat unbelievably it would now seem, within the normally tangled web of most governmental bureaucracies, the fidgeting Jack Dean received an official reply within the week. J.R. Arnold, in charge of managing the Personnel and Training Division, informed the hopeful Texas Highway Patrol candidate: "We have placed your application for the position of Patrolman in our files. . . . You will be notified of the time and location of the examination which will be given in Fort Worth, Texas, May 22, 1958."[60]

Not surprisingly, Jack Dean, Applicant No. 413, promptly appeared in Fort Worth as ordered and, among other hurdles, answered the craftily constructed bank of questions for The Minnesota Multiphasic Personality Inventory. Additionally, for an essay question Jack Dean was asked to elaborate in but a few words why he was personally interested in becoming a Highway Patrolman, rather than a Drivers License Examiner/Patrolman or a License and Weight Patrolman or a Motor Vehicle Inspection Patrolman. His reply was, maybe not eloquent, but straightforward: "I am interested in this field because it is to my way of thinking the highest law enforcement branch in Texas due to its many varied activities."[61]

Jack Dean would have to withstand a thoroughgoing physical examination, fingerprinting, and in-depth background investigation—which he predictably came through with flying colors. And though it's politically indelicate at this day and age, one of the type-written questions on the preprinted background survey shows how times have changed, but in the case of Jack and Janie Dean, is also illustrative of their life-long commitment. The question, "Family atmosphere: Who is the 'Boss' in the home?" The answer was clear-cut, "Appears to be mutual." And it is!

Subsequent to jumping through the administrative and personnel hoops, Jack Dean was offered his preferred position with DPS as a Texas Highway Patrolman. He was quick to reply. Via a Western Union telegram to the Personnel and Training Division at DPS Headquarters in Austin, Jack Dean responded: "Dear Sir: I greatly accept your offer to attend the safety department training school. Sincerely. Jack Dean."[62]

On 6 August 1958 at Austin, before Travis County Notary Public Martha Chudej, THP recruit Jack O'Day Dean raised his right hand and was solemnly sworn, then signed his formalized Oath of Office, acknowledging gravity of the commissioning document. At the same ceremony he also affixed his signature on DPS's Oath of Allegiance, vowing to uphold, support, and defend the Constitution of the United States and the Constitution of the State of Texas. And, he also swore to a legally binding Loyalty Oath, one declaring he was not a Communist and was not a party to any organization bent towards overthrowing "the Government or the United States, or of any State, by force, violence or any other unlawful means. . . ."[63] As of that day Jack Dean was officially a THP Recruit—scheduled for the DPS Basic Training School—at a salary of $300 per month until the post graduation raise to $350. Jack Dean was a lawman, albeit a rookie, but a Lone Star State lawman nonetheless.

2

"All these beautiful trees"

Highway Patrolman Jack Dean's tenure as a Texas lawman may or may not have qualified for the DPS record book, but this career journey was short-lived: not fully twenty-four hours. Subsequent to taking his Oath of Office, the very next day, 7 August 1958, Jack Dean resigned.[1] He was no longer a lawman. Janie's delivery date was near, the DPS Training Academy was lengthy, and students were required to live at the state police instructional facility, not as renters at Austin or its nearby suburbs. Family life and nights with the wife would have to be put hold. Sculpting everyday citizens into first-rate lawmen, then arming them with pistols and shotguns, assigning them high-speed patrol cars, and granting them the discretion to issue citations or make handcuffed custodial arrest was real serious business, and DPS's command staff took it real seriously. There was no room at DPS for slackers or whiners or indecisiveness. Jack Dean, now reflectively looking back, chalks this short phase of his law-enforcing career up to "immaturity," nothing less. No silly excuse making.[2]

Fortunately, Jack Dean's pleasantly disposed personality and workplace industriousness had stood him well; he hadn't burned his employment bridge at Convair. Though it certainly wasn't a personally fulfilling job, it paid the freight of life's everyday living expenses. Money was tight and crucial, especially now that the Dean household headcount had grown by a factor of one. Kyle Lynn Dean was born on the twenty-seventh day of September 1958, the month following Jack bidding *adios* to DPS. Janie and Jack were on cloud nine. Like any young married couple there were the good times and economic struggles, days of joy interlaced with days robbing Peter to pay Paul. Then a pervasive nightmare blanketed the governmentally contracted airplane-building business, and Jack Dean was laid off, joining the ranks of the unemployed. Times had passed for breadline poverty of the horrid Depression Era and, gratefully, Jack regained his financial footing rather quickly. Although it obliged a punctual relocation, Jack, Janie, and toddler Kyle Lynn left Tarrant County in the rearview mirror.[3]

Jack Dean had accepted a position with the S.H. Kress & Company as a Management Trainee at Temple, Bell County, Texas. Conceivably managing a retail chain store would be a pathway of upward mobility and financial stability for Jack Dean. Foregoing to have a telephone installed in their rent home at 1508 South 3rd Street, Jack and Janie made the best of what the tax-man left them from that $280 monthly salary. Temple was not a bad place to live and its Central Texas location not too far directly south of Fort Worth/Dallas, then south of Waco, created but minimal hardship for grandparents desirous of keeping up with Kyle's playtime activities. For sure the stork was not flying blind by the Deans' moving; Kelly Lenea made her debut on the thirteenth day of August 1960. Once again, Janie and Jack were ecstatic.

On the other hand, Jack was less than rapturous regarding his workaday endeavor, despite the fact that within six months he would be part-way up the teetering career ladder as a retail store's Assistant Manager. That was all but in the bag. And just as certainly, it was definite that wearing a coat and tie, fiddling with inventories, adjusting calling-in-sick sales-clerks' daily schedules, kissing up to corporate bigwigs, all the while soothing ruffled feathers of disenchanted customers was not inspiring—or appealing—even if such work guaranteed beans in pot. Wasn't there more to be had from living life than that? Maybe abandoning that DPS ship two years before had been premature—as well as immature. That Highway Patrolman job might yet be the right thing to try for and do. Jack Dean reapplied.[4]

Not wishing to hurt his chances with S.H. Kress & Co. should something, somehow, go awry, THP Sergeant L.M. Hancock, tasked with part of Jack Dean's background investigation, noted: "Certainly the Kress Co. has spent a good deal of money in training this man and they would not be impressed if they knew he was considering a move."[5] Sergeant Hancock, politely keeping Jack's secret, submitted a sterling and painstaking statement. THP Sergeant Edwin D. Pringle, assigned the Fort Worth area part of Jack Dean's thorough background investigation, was also more than favorably impressed with the reapplying job seeker: "This applicant was previously investigated, I believe in 1958, and was recommended for appointment to the Academy. I concur most heartedly with Sergeant Hancock's evaluation of this applicant and I too, would be most happy to have him in my Area."[6]

On 7 December 1960, after again going through the mandated administration of oaths and promises, Jack Dean was accepted as a "Student Patrolman."[7] He had upped his salary by $45 per month, and during training would now be paid $325. Janie and the two kiddos moved in with her parents and Jack embarked on a grueling sixteen-week adventure rivaling any outfit's boot-camp. Taking a boy (girls need not apply at the time) from the farm or off the assembly-line or from some other lackluster job station and molding them into independently operating law enforcers, Texas Highway Patrolmen, was a real man's challenge. It was a chore not taken lightly by the grizzled instructors, those no-nonsense veteran state peace officers displaying years of service by the string of hash-marks sewed onto long sleeves.

Between 6:00 a.m. and 10:00 p.m. the spanking-new THP recruit—for every second—handed his body and soul to instructors and/or class evaluators. There was no expensive gym equipment. Rookies' physical conditioning would be attained via the old-fashioned and time-proven method: a seemingly ruthless regimen of calisthenics and running and running and running some more until sweat poured, lungs heaved, and cramping muscles cried for amnesty. Students by their own volition had sought the job and drillmasters weren't fooling. Anyone could quit—anytime! No one was a prisoner.

The schedule of classroom work was seemingly just as intense and uncompromising. But a sample illustrates recruit Jack Dean was—or was supposed to be learning and would be tested for— behind-the-desk course work in Texas History, Texas Government, Motor Vehicle Law, Spelling, First Aid, Texas Geography, Social Psychology, Traffic Law Enforcement, Accident Investigation, Criminal Law, Reports and Report Writing, Scientific Investigative Aids, Case Preparation and Police Courtesy.[8]

Then, just as importantly, there was that exhaustive hands-on work—sometimes now referred to as Offensive/Defensive Tactics: How to safely search, handcuff, and transport prisoners. Sometimes arrestees resisted and/or became belligerent, so there was no little emphasis placed on physical restraints, boxing, and judo. Instructors' general hypothesis at the time was that every student should suffer an ass whippin'. To their way of thinking, every graduate must be infused with the notion that no matter how big and bad they were (or thought they were), the day might come when they would suddenly confront a terrible guy, one much taller and ten-times tougher. Caution and commonsense must be instilled as everyday watchwords. Life-threatening business was at hand. There weren't any indestructible Highway Patrolman. While alone and alongside the lonesome roadway, standing with a violator or violators, students had best remember: Complacency was dangerous, alertness was crucial.

Just as essential, should the horrible necessity arise, was a lawman's ability to properly handle and accurately discharge firearms. A fellow that couldn't shoot straight was useless and, in fact, posed a real danger to fellow peace officers and innocent bystanders. Qualifying scores on bulls-eye and silhouette targets were mandatory—exceptions zero. There was no little time spent familiarizing recruits with available weaponry, but it should be remembered this was prior to common usage of such nonlethal tools as pepper-spray, stun-guns, and Tasers. Lawmen did not then routinely wear protective vests or body armor. During this law enforcing day, with regards to when an astonishing situation turned "Western," it boiled down to exchanging blows or bullets. God and supervisors and trial courts could sort out the substantive rights and wrongs later. On the firing range, at all times under watchful eagle-eyed instructors, even neophytes were brought up to speed with regards to daily carrying and shooting revolvers and tearing gaping holes in situational designed targets with buckshot. Already a rather masterful shooter, time on the training academy's firing range was enjoyable for Jack Dean—a young man well accustomed to handling firearms.

During Jack Dean's days at the DPS Academy he bunked in a six-man room, sharing quarters with five other THP hopefuls—hopeful in the fact that triumphant completion of the course work, physical conditioning, firearms qualifications, and scoring a passing grade on the wide-ranging final exam guaranteed the corridor to graduation: the only passageway to victory. There were no safe-space shortcuts. Jack Dean particularly recalls one night while in training at recruit school. Subsequent to an extraordinarily exhaustive and perspiring day running and following an intensive brain-teasing written examination, he and his roommates were sound asleep within seconds of heads hitting the pillows—so thought Jack Dean. Unbelievably it now seems, but it was damn sure real, when the figurative bugle blew and the literal 6:00 a.m. lights came on, wiping sleep from eyes, Jack Dean bounded out of bed abruptly and shockingly noting he was alone—his five campmates had quietly departed during the night for parts unknown, presumably home but classmates at DPS no more[9]

Though it mentally seemed as if it would never end, long days giving way to short nights, Jack Dean hung tough. He was bound and determined to graduate. Not unexpectedly and, no surprise to DPS management, but 50 percent of Jack Dean's class opted to stay with the program and earn their symbolic badges—the other half overtly threw in the towel or faded away into the darkness when no one was looking.

Yet reviewable is Jack Dean's Grade Record, and it's reasonably impressive. In a nutshell Jack was ranking in the top 10 percent of his class, earning particularly high marks as to physical conditioning, achieving a 100 percent score for boxing and 92 percent for judo. His overall academic rating was an A, 92 percent and his revolver qualification scores were well—well—above the minimum standard. The objective grades were assuredly important, but so, too, were subjective comments. THP Patrolman, G.D. Winstead, assigned as a class evaluator for Jack's class, said: "With the proper instruction during the first 6 months in the field, I believe this man will develop into one of our better men."[10] For his more formal Student Evaluation Report, Sergeant J.A. Dumas, answering prearranged questions, said quite a lot, in part: "Gets along well with other students and instructors. Has shown good judgment in school. Works well without close supervision. Even-tempered. No display of emotions. Excellent condition; good coordination. Good abilities and skills and will not hesitate to use them when necessary. Good driver and will make a good driver in any service. A very good student and should work well on any assignment. Makes good use of his time." And, perhaps the most important question, an overall assessment? "Should make a very good employee without a great deal of supervision."[11]

Not at all surprisingly, Jack Dean graduated, meeting training standards set by the state for certifying its officially commissioned peace officers.[12] Decked out in his spiffy new uniform, "which was of a unique color called 'Texas Tan' accented with blue trim," and wearing his regulation western-style hat and black Sam Browne leather rig and revolver, Jack Dean cut a dashing pattern.[13] He, too, was most pleased that Janie and little Kyle, and Kelly yet a baby in arms, were in attendance to witness his new-found career status. As of 24 March 1961, Jack O'Day Dean was nearly, but not quite, a full-fledged career THP Patrolman, a probationary patrolman. His job performance for the next six months—and management's assessment of that job performance—would be key: He could cut it and would be a Highway Patrolman, or he couldn't and wouldn't be a Highway Patrolman. On city streets, rural roads, and state highways big boys and badmen played for keeps. The choices probationary patrolman Jack Dean made, and the judgment he brought into play, would determine whether or not the state's monetary investment and expenditure of DPS instructors' time would pay its dividend for the citizens of the Lone Star State.

For the general public, DPS graduations were newsy, a signal fact noted by the photograph appearing the *Fort Worth Star-Telegram*.[14] Jack Dean was now entitled to that raise in pay, $350 per month.

Quite naturally the big question in the life of Janie Dean was where would her husband be posted after graduation? Where would she raise her beloved son and daughter? Texas was and is an enormous state and THP Patrolman perambulated every inch of every highway and/or every inch of FM (Farm to Market) and RR (Ranch Road) byways. Going in, greenhorn student Highway Patrolmen had not a clue as to where their actual duty stations would be after graduation—just somewhere within the Lone Star. The upper-tier management philosophy was plain: they knew best about manpower deployment and staffing patterns, and new hires were expected to report for duty at new stations with a smile, honored to be part of an outfit brimming with *esprit de corps* and solidly grounded by tradition.

THP Patrolman Jack Dean was assigned to Pecos, Reeves County, a sizable geographical swathe of West Texas west of the Pecos River.[15] One of Reeves County's northeastern neighbors was Loving County—adjoining the New Mexico state line—and a county boasting the smallest population numbers in the state—then or now registering less than one hundred souls: men, women, and children, not counting yelping dogs, a backyard donkey, and two stray cats.[16] The city of Pecos was, of course, more metropolitan than the only town in Loving County, Mentone, but she rightfully tallied below the 10,000 citizen indicator.[17]

It was, indeed, a far cry from the burgeoning population numbers in Fort Worth or Temple, the cities that had been home to the Deans. Nevertheless, Jack and Janie, leaving the kiddos with Grandmother Hill while house hunting, traversed West Texas during the dead of night, finally arriving at their destination, checking into a rather nondescript motel. The next morning after good light, while Jack was shaving and making ready to report for duty, he gazed out the bathroom window. What prompted his foolishness he knows not, other than an uncalled-for spasm of insensitivity. Jack called out to Janie, "Come look at all these beautiful trees." Excitedly and enthusiastically

Janie joined Jack at the window, primed to ogle Reeves County's heavenly landscape, the place she would call home. Jack stepped aside and Janie peered outside. There was, according to Jack's now remorseful confession, not a tree in sight and not even a bush higher than a person's knee for seventy-five miles. The mist in Janie's eyes dampened Jack's futile try at levity. Janie was, though, the type of lady that could make a home out of haunt. She adapted as she knew she must. Janie was a stand-by-your man gal and a devoted mama.[18]

That morning at the Highway Patrol office Jack Dean met his immediate supervisor, the short and stocky and noticeably muscular Sergeant Randal W. Howie, an old-hand with years of DPS service behind him. And, according to Jack Dean, at the time, DPS Sergeants, as far as Highway Patrolmen were concerned, "made all the law." Sergeant Howie was no exception. What he said went—to put it mildly. Well-known throughout Reeves County for being meaner than the proverbial junkyard dog in a serious scrap, the ever plucky but always fair-minded Sergeant Howie was doggedly protective of his assigned Highway Patrolmen and, leading by example, perpetually earned their respect. As far as rookie lawman Jack Dean was concerned Sergeant Randal W. Howie, as a lawman, was legit![19]

THP Patrolman Jack Dean would also soon meet and develop a close personal working relationship with the Reeves County Sheriff, A.B. Nail, himself a former THP Patrolman and Inspector for the Texas Liquor Control Board.[20] Interagency cooperation and the strong bond of law enforcing camaraderie was/is an imperative dynamic, especially in such locales as far-flung West Texas where the number of peace officers were few, the territorial topography massive, and the violators buzzing and darting like transitory bees—always ready to sting. Slobbering drunks in barrooms and beer joints may feel ten feet tall and bullet proof, but THP Patrolmen and deputy sheriffs and city cops and U.S. Border Patrolmen knew that they themselves weren't—and had to depend on each other at any given moment—Come Hell or High Water!

Country west of the Pecos River, though cut by paved highways and graveled county roads was, it may be argued, still part of the Wild and Woolly West. There were big ranches and little ones in between. The native populace was, for the most part, fiercely independent and not just a few were roughhewn, cut from well-seasoned and sturdy genealogical stock. Jack Dean was paired with Highway Patrolman Charley Bolinger, most but not all days working in tandem. These were days long before there was anything as progressive as federal workplace tinkering like the Fair Labor Standards Act, and THP Patrolmen were scheduled to work six days a week. At Pecos the single day off was either a Wednesday or Thursday. Those half-dozen work days were equally divided into three day-shifts, three night-shifts, but the THP Patrolmen were always on call, twenty-four and seven.[21]

As previously noted these were days prior to uniformed lawmen been tightly wrapped in wide belts weighted with a seemingly ungodly mélange of policing paraphernalia. Highway Patrolman Jack Dean, at first, carried on his Sam Browne a state-issued Colt New Service .38 Special revolver, a cartridge slide with a dozen spare rounds, and handcuffs in a leather case. Inside the patrol car were his flashlight, a clipboard, and ticket-book. At the leading edge of the front seat, near the floorboard, was a horizontally positioned gun pouch, one home to the standard issued Winchester Model 94, .30-30. In the car's trunk were the first-aid kit, a rudimentary camera, extra flashlight batteries, tape-measure, chalk, rain gear, road flares, and the magazine loaded but not a round chambered, slide-action 12-gauge shotgun.

Governmental bureaucracies are continuously behind the financial eight-ball, sometimes slow with advantaging themselves of the latest technological advances. Just as the state of Texas was transitioning to the Smith & Wesson .357 Magnum revolvers for issue to its THP Patrolmen, Jack Dean caught the posting at Pecos. Taking pity on the newbie, the Reeves County Chief Deputy, Gary Ingram, "one helluva a guy," insisted that Jack Dean accept the loan of his Smith & Wesson Model 27 .357 Magnum revolver until the state's inventory reached the boys at the bottom end of the pecking-order in far—and seemingly sometimes forgotten—West Texas. THP Patrolman Jack Dean, eagerly and thankfully, accepted the gesture of good will, carrying the Chief's piece "for a year or so."[22]

After but one month in the field, the ever thoughtful but thoroughly salty Sergeant Howie noted that rookie Highway Patrolman Jack Dean had "shown that he has a fairly high potential in all of his endeavors," and with all probability would "develop rapidly."[23]

Though THP Patrolman Jack Dean would investigate many motor vehicle accidents while stationed at Pecos, one in particular is permanently etched in his memory. Called from home, working alone, Jack Dean responded to the horrific scene of a head-on collision on the highway between Pecos and Barstow, the latter town situated just east of the Reeves County line in Ward County. Before there were ambulances run by fire departments and private emergency service contractors, ambulances were generally operated by funeral homes and looked more like the traditional hearse or family station-wagon. At any rate, the critically injured were taken to town at high-speed, red lights flashing, sirens blaring. Wreckers were naturally soon onsite and Jack Dean was taking basic measurements and overseeing traffic issues and tending to the necessary accident investigation. Part of those tasks also involved efficiently clearing the roadway and kicking debris to the side, as well as thoughtfully recovering and protecting injured victims' scattered personal property, such as suitcases and/or electronic gismos and/or other bits and pieces of nostalgic or monetary value. Walking along the bar-ditch, Patrolman Dean noticed a quilt and bent to recover it when he felt something inside and peeled back a soft layer of cover. Lo and behold, the bulge was a big-eyed black baby, obviously bewildered and altogether terrified, unable to even whimper much less cry. The ambulances were by this time gone and Patrolman Jack Dean had—in his mind—but one choice. He carefully placed the apparently uninjured but obviously traumatized infant in his state police cruiser and at near breakneck but safe speed rushed to Pecos, where he transferred his package into the waiting hands of medical professionals.[24] At home Jack Dean had quite a story to tell Janie—and two small children to caress.

Though it seemed as if the day would never come, it finally did. Jack Dean had successfully completed his six-month probation period and Sergeant Howie was recommending that he be officially removed from provisional standing to that of permanent status, a fully commissioned THP Patrolman. Lending their signatures to the request and making it official were the DPS Region IV Commander, Wilson E. "Pat" Speir, and THP Captain Ray B. Butler.[25] With permanent status went the emoluments of office; now Jack Dean's end of the month cash tallied at a whopping $388.33.[26]

A full year later THP Patrolman Jack Dean was in good graces for his dedicated exertion. Sergeant Randal Howie particularly noting for a mandated Performance Development Summary: "This man continues to rate high in the amount of work that he does. He is fast and capable of doing a large quantity of work." Jack's lieutenant, Hugh Shaw, based at Midland, concurred and signed off on the most favorable personnel assessment.[27]

Though most of his off-duty time was spent with Janie and the children, Jack did find occasional relief from the day to day job stress and a modicum of relaxation by participating with a few other firearms and shooting enthusiasts—sometimes taking little Kyle with him—as they enjoyed a few downtime hours plinking at tin cans or bottle-caps or cardboard targets with a makeshift bulls-eye colored with a stumpy red Crayola. Not unexpectedly, though he was but a mere child, Kyle Dean has fond memories—snapshot memories— of pleasant times at Pecos, capturing horny-toads and marveling that tumbleweeds incessantly blew across the windswept and pancake flat landscape—but they were the tallest plant for miles and miles and miles. Fleetingly he remembers his very first deer-hunt, tramping around, not even waist high to his daddy. But he was a big boy, allowed to carry a .30 caliber M1 Carbine, not necessarily an optimum deer hunting tool, but a diminutive weapon well suited to little hands and big dreams. The hunt did not produce a hanging carcass, even if there had been a place to hang it, but such an outing began the molding process of making a little boy into a grown man. Although another scenario for that maturation course would now earn a THP Patrolman unpaid time-off or termination, the 1960s allowed for some of Kyle Dean's most memorable Reeves

County times. At night, if things were really quiet on the law and traffic enforcement front, Kyle could ride in the THP car for a sneaky sojourn to the outskirts of town, which really was a short trip. Then the nighttime spotlighting and shooting of jackrabbits was on tap—no worry, no neighbors—no complaints. It was fun![28]

On the other hand, and of a more serious nature, Jack Dean was a member in good standing with a small-bore rifle team, and when time permitted he and his fellow marksmen traveled a mini-circuit shooting in competitive matches. Such diversion was enjoyable, but in the world of reality, with shifting hours and a subject to callout status, THP Patrolmen were tethered on a short and stout leash—the job!

Enumerating every traffic citation Highway Patrolman Jack Dean issued, or reconstructing all the motor vehicle accidents he investigated, and inclusively profiling all those folks he hauled off to the jailhouse is, of course, not realistic and is not requisite for telling his full-of-life story. Various highlights will suffice.

Certainly one arrest scenario was a twofold catch. For the first instance, Patrolman Dean, near Monahans in adjoining Ward County, apprehended two fellows driving a brand-new 1962 Buick stolen at Atlanta, Georgia. The interstate nature of the automobile theft opened the legal doorway for charging the thieves with a violation of the federal Dyer Act. Subsequent to the defendants being successfully prosecuted and formally sentenced, Francis E. Crosby, Special Agent in Charge (SAC) FBI, El Paso, Texas, in a laudatory letter to Colonel Homer Garrison, Jr., the DPS Director, specifically commended Jack Dean.[29]

In another cooperative arrest a youthful offender was attempting to burglarize the farm and outbuildings of a local agriculturist. How the burglar managed the journey from the state of Kansas is not now knowable, but his heretofore good shiftless luck ran out in Reeves County. Collectively responding to the scene of action were THP Patrolman Jack Dean, and Deputy Boyd Terin—a genuine cowboy turned lawman—from Toyah, and Chief Deputy Gary Ingram from Pecos. The newsy arrest was not unnoticed by an editor for the *Pecos Enterprise*.[30] Another arrest was noticed—by spectators.

Toyah, west of Pecos, and the oldest townsite in Reeves County, was and always had been one tough spot. Early on, during 1883, Texas Ranger Captain George Wythe Baylor notified his Austin-based headquarters via telegraph: "Cow boys tried to take town of Toyah one killed three wounded & five prisoners none of rangers hurt am on my way down."[31] But a scant two years later, another instance of uncalled for nastiness caused Texas Ranger Captain James T. Gillespie to acknowledge one more whopping tragedy at Toyah. His telegram sadly spotlighted the potential for trouble when outrageously stirring firewater with the long barrel of a Colt's six-shooter.

> Morris, sheriff of Reeves Co. Came here drunk abusing rangers Sargent [sic] Cartwright with three men went to arrest him a fight ensued private Nigh and Sheriff Killed full particulars by mail.[32]

Though many years had past since these examples of Old West badness had taken place, Toyah was yet tough—as THP Patrolman Jack Dean discovered.

Just outside the tiny town, on the highway, Patrolman Jack Dean executed a traffic stop on what turned out to be a Known Offender, a mean fellow owing Texas more penitentiary time due to his outstanding felony warrant. The outlaw was wholly committed to sustaining his status running free and a return visit behind Huntsville's tall walls wasn't in his close by playbook. The fight was on! And it would be tooth and toenail. What started on the side of the highway had morphed into a tornadic tussle and surefire slugfest. Locking up, the two combatants—Jack Dean ever mindful of keeping control of his revolver—fell to the ground and rolled down a steep embankment. The scuffling and swinging and swearing were grinding into minutes—neither the good guy or the bad guy could gain the upper hand. Both gladiators were desperately gasping for breath and hoping someone would, somehow, hurriedly call a timeout. The thug wouldn't quit, and Jack Dean couldn't quit. Dean didn't want to shoot him, but as energy faded and limbs weakened alternatives were dwindling. Drawing from somewhere deep within—in a last-ditch effort—Jack Dean finally got astraddle the prostrate and exhausted fellow, managing through sheer grit to get him cuffed. While yet on the ground Jack Dean detected what was growing into a thunderous ovation. From the bottom of the embankment, looking up to the roadway, Jack Dean saw five or six parked cars—the occupants outside clapping and cheering for a job well done—but none had had balls big enough to sail down the hill and offer that helping hand or thump an abhorrent yahoo's head.[33]

Huffing and puffing Patrolman Dean, at last, had safely secured the prisoner in his patrol car and started the fifteen-mile trip to Pecos and the Reeves County Jail, near breathlessly notifying the dispatcher that he would be 10-95 one time (transporting a prisoner). Hearing the radio traffic and detecting the hollowness in Jack Dean's wobbly voice, Sergeant Howie transmitted his understandable query to Jack: "Are you okay?"[34] Yes, Jack was okay.

At the county jail Patrolman Jack Dean went through the routine of booking in his prisoner but before he could take him upstairs to the cellblock in the cramped three-person elevator, he was forcefully ordered to sit down, rest and catch his breath. Sergeant Howie barked that he would escort the badass upstairs. Whether or not the elevator actually stopped, Jack Dean does not know—but he can recall and testify to the loud noises and echoes emanating from that narrow elevator shaft, bumping and banging and dull thuds. Shortly, Sergeant Howie, alone, stepped out of the elevator, winked at Jack Dean and postulated: "Bet he don't ever hit any of my Highway Patrolmen again!"[35] No doubt, on the way up, the belligerent prisoner had spat at, swung at, or kicked at Sergeant Randal W. Howie—no doubt!

There plainly was no doubt about THP Patrolman Dean's one and only citizen's complaint while stationed at Pecos. A disgruntled motorist, who Dean had cited for blistering down the road at an excessive speed, was not happy, though most of his ire was directed at the local justice of the peace at Pyote who had assessed the fine and court cost. The angry Dallasite wrote the governor about his alleged mistreatment and, as would be expected, odorous stuff rolls downhill and landed in the lap of DPS Director Garrison, who kicked the stinky matter further down the chain-of-command mountain.

The resultant full-scale investigation by impartial DPS supervisors rather quickly determined that the complaining fellow was somewhat of a "Crack Pot" and "fancies himself a 'do-gooder'" and was thoroughly convinced that the justice of the peace was "running a crooked court." From outside the DPS, Ed Keys, the County Attorney of Ward County where the traffic ticket was issued, was more than quick to reply about the lower court judge and THP Patrolman Jack Dean, scorching off a letter to Pat Speir, now Assistant Director of DPS. After internalizing part of the complainer's letter, Ed Keys remarked that the local JP "is a fine, hard-working man and that the letter is ridiculous. . . . This Judge is one of the most respected men in our community. . . . He happens to be the Judge who handles the traffic cases on one of the toughest sections of highway in West Texas, to wit: from Wickett, Texas to a point just east of Barstow, Texas. . . . He sees too many mangled bodies on this highway resulting from too much speed and too much alcohol. . . . However, I would like to go farther and say that one of the finest highway patrolman I know, Mr. Jack Dean, made the arrest in this case. Without talking to him I know he did what was right and that the Defendant was making 90 miles an hour or more; otherwise, Mr. Dean would not have put 90 miles an hour on the ticket." Jack Dean's reputation was outstanding and his word was good, a fact duly noted by him being wholly absolved by DPS of any infraction—big or little, intentional or unintentional.[36]

While THP traffic enforcement on Interstate 20 at Peyote had generated disgruntlement for a whining driver with a heavy foot, the area also imprinted an indelible image in the psyche of a little boy. One mile from town was the WW II Peyote Army Air Base, a 2,745-acre installation, at one time the largest bomber base in the United States with its twin 8,400-ft runways. At its 1940s height, it was home to thousands of officers, enlisted men, and civilian employees, housed in its hundreds of buildings. By the time the Deans were West Texas residents the existing facility—no longer flight active—had been rationally relegated to the less than sensational function as an officially designated United States Military Storage Depot, accommodating at one time as many as 2,000 aircraft, one being the *Enola Gay*, the bomber dropping the Atomic Bomb on Japan. Additional surplus military hardware was also stored there. Two dynamics caulked the memory in a child's malleable mind. During the early 1940s construction phase, the unearthing of an ungodly number of Western Diamondback dens, spawned a vivid nickname for the facility: "The Rattlesnake Bomber Base," and signs were yet posted—"Danger: Rattlesnakes, Watch Where You Step, Watch Where You Reach!" What little boy could forget that? And there was that other thing. From time to time THP was tasked with monitoring and directing traffic in accord with humongous convoys of military vehicles—trucks and tanks and jeeps and such stuff. On those occasions where Jack Dean drew such an assignment and the convoys were scheduled to be massive, Kyle Dean accompanied his daddy, sitting in the squad car, while Jack directed traffic. It was one grand show—unforgettable.[37]

The FBI's Special Agent in Charge at El Paso had routinely changed, but Highway Patrolman Jack Dean's attentiveness to duty was fixed, once again catching notice. On 2 September 1963, while patrolling near Pecos, a 1950 Chevrolet caught Jack Dean's interest. Grinding daily experience and numerous violator contacts predictably fertilizes an uncanny sixth-sense in many an officer's mind. The sedan driver's demeanor—furtive—trying to shroud his behavior in a mist of anonymity, meekly blending in with other motorists traveling the highway, was hopeless. Jack Dean alerted. Falling in behind, in but short order via his radio request, the ever alert Highway Patrolman learned that the Chevrolet was in fact stolen three days earlier, illicitly taken at Alhambra, California. No traffic stop is routine and, this one was ordained to end with an arrest. Aptly Jack Dean approached with caution. For the driver, Rudolph Anthony Bernal, aka Rudy Bernal, aka Rudolph Gomez, as the colloquial saying goes, "the jig was up." Not only was the suspect driving a stolen automobile, but inside were a cache of "six fully prepared forged checks which he had transported from California to Texas." Once again Jack Dean's vigilance had paved a bumpy road to the federal

penitentiary, following the defendant's courtroom conviction for a
Dyer Act violation, submissively standing before the U.S. District
Court's Judge, Sarah T. Hughes. The head of the FBI's El Paso office,
Herbert E. Hoxie, made sure that DPS Director Garrison was well
aware of a West Texas Highway Patrolman's performance:

> Patrolman Dean not only did a fine job in discovering these vio-
> lations and assisting greatly in the preparation of this case but he
> also testified as a Federal Government witness against the defen-
> dant; he testified in an exemplary manner. I want to commend
> Patrolman Dean for his performance in this case. . . .[38]

Another traffic stop is worth mentioning—for THP Patrolman Jack
Dean it would be one like no other. Relaxing at home with Janie
and the kids, Jack winced when the telephone rang, never knowing
whether it was family, friends, or the dispatcher. This balmy day it
was the latter. Someone was erratically driving down the highway in
an Armored Personnel Carrier, perhaps a military surplus vehicle,
perhaps not. Nonetheless inquiry into the unpredictable operation
and/or ownership was called for. In a reasonably short time Jack
Dean had his quarry in sight, moving down an exceptionally lonely
stretch of West Texas highway populated by more jackrabbits and
rattlesnakes than people in Fords and Chevys. Closing the distance
Jack Dean flipped the toggle switch, turning on his vehicle's flashing red-lights, clear indication the person driving the APC should
immediately give way, pull to the right side of the road—and stop.
Such was not to be. The suspected violator and the vehicle continued, ignoring Patrolman Dean's implied command. Jack Dean was
in a tight spot. The driver, whoever he was, would be maintaining
the high ground—a tactical advantage—when and if he ever opted
for rolling to a stop. Standing on the roadway, THP Patrolman Jack
Dean would be looking up, a decidedly awkward and perilous positioning for an inquiring lawman. Compounding the dilemma facing
Jack Dean was prickly reality; the APC operator could simply be a
harmless nitwit or a depraved desperado, either way, right now and
on this stretch of highway, Jack Dean was totally on his own. [39]

Certainly unknown to THP Patrolman Dean at the time, the APC operator was a multi-convicted felon with a rather lengthy string of violent crimes in his prison portfolio. And, also yet to be discovered by Jack Dean was the cocked 1911 Colt .45 autoloader concealed under a shop-rag on the seat, next to the spoiling for a fight ex-convict refusing stop. And, of course, there was no mindreading capability for Dean, but the rolling outlaw had blueprinted his plan for a solitary THP Patrolman on a forsaken expanse of cacti-studded West Texas highway, one where there would be no witnesses. Then it happened. Whether or not it was Divine Intervention will, in fact, never be known—but THP Patrolman Jack Dean thought it might have been.[40]

THP Captain Ray B. Butler, returning from a training school or some other administrative duty at El Paso, had heard Jack Dean's radio transmissions and, providently, was in close-by proximity to the unfolding drama. Captain Butler let-the-hammer-down on his unmarked unit and soon had the under grill red-lights flashing. Captain Butler pulled in behind Jack Dean, the third vehicle in a slow speed chase. Sensing inevitability, the APC driver grudgingly pulled to the side of the roadway and stopped forward momentum—but did not put the brakes on his mouthing. Guns drawn, Captain Butler and Patrolman Dean made their cautious approach and arrested the wanted felon who, in fact, had stolen the APC. Though handcuffed, the prisoner defiantly looked Jack Dean square in the eye and coldly pronounced: "I'd shot you in the head if that old gray-headed son-of-a-bitch hadn't shown up!"[41] Though he surely knew better than to say it aloud, THP Patrolman Jack Dean was more than glad that old gray-headed S.O.B. had been nearby. There was a good chance Captain Butler had saved his bacon—so to speak!

What was in short supply at the Jack and Janie Dean household was bacon—and buttered biscuits—and baked beans—and barbequed brisket—and a burgeoning bank account or even a chocked-full piggy bank. Through action of the legislature Jack Dean had pocketed a raise in salary to $453.00 but such was not an extravagant wage.[42] By any reckoning the Deans were thrifty but lean times more often than not are a lawman's lot. Although it was figurative speech,

Jack Dean in speaking of everyday life at Pecos on a THP Patrolman's pay, glumly recalled: "We were starving to death."[43]

THP Patrolman Jack Dean was betwixt and between. Always scrimping pennies and doing without was a high price to pay for job satisfaction. Should Janie and the kids sacrifice solely for his internal gratification? Was it a crime to like your job? There definitely was not any hidden agenda at the DPS shop; there were no acute personality conflicts or scheming. Nobody was pushing Jack Dean out. In fact, throughout the entire region, the DPS Supervisory Staff thought extraordinarily well of him: "Patrolman Dean has always had high job interest. He is quick, active and can do far more work than the average Patrolman. He has done some very good work in case preparation. Usually uses good judgment. Always a good attitude and easy to counsel with. Will readily correct errors when brought to his attention."[44] Furthermore, according to Sergeant Howe:

> Patrolman Dean has a very good working knowledge of the laws of the State and Department policies. He has done a good job in putting the laws and policies into effect in his assigned area. He has worked well with his public officials and supervisors. This man has a rather pleasing personality and can do a good job of dealing with people of any level. Patrolman Dean usually uses good judgment in making decisions concerning the Department and I have never received what I consider a justified complaint on him. Patrolman Dean has used his skill and time very effectively since he has been with the Department. He has always had high job interest and takes personal pride in any job assigned to him.[45]

While making the choice was tormenting, Jack Dean had chosen, once again, to say goodbye to the THP.[46] The new job at bustling Fort Worth would reunite the extended family and the Montgomery Ward Department Store's offering to pay trustworthy Jack Dean $507 per month as Chief Investigator was appealing and accepted.[47]

3

"I have no right to ask"

Settling at 7940 Tumbleweed Trail in White Settlement, a Tarrant County suburb west of downtown Fort Worth, the Deans had happily left desolate Pecos as but a fond memory of genial acquaintances and motivating employment, but it had been a dollars and cents nightmare. They had not been poor, though at the end of the month hunting payday they felt as if they were. The new gig at Montgomery Ward held promise of extraction from the financial quagmire and, besides, it was akin to police work—wasn't it? Chief Investigator Dean had the easy answer. Commercial security drudgery was different.

Store executives were much more concerned with the bottom-line: cutting financial losses and maintaining a lily-white public relations image. In most instances true-blue lawmen grade loss prevention and catching shoplifters, even if having a highfaluting title, as less than compelling. Jack Dean all too soon became conscious of on-the-ground reality. Although his prescribed workplace designation as Chief Investigator sounded nice on paper he was, in fact, tasked with trying to snare sneak-thieves and put the brakes on pilfering employees.[1] His department store policing was uninspiring and tame stuff when contrasted with the independence of patrolling highways and reeling in small fry and big fish violators as spontaneous situations dictated. Sergeant Randal Howie wouldn't have surrendered to corporate games and greed and boredom. Real career lawmen policed and then retired to a cushy misdemeanor vocation, not vice versa. The business world—looking through greenback lenses—focused on things foreign to lawmen. In point of fact there was no little controversy and an exchange of bristly correspondence between Montgomery Ward administrative personnel and A.A. Archer, District Attorney, 143rd Judicial District of Texas, with regards to Jack Dean being subpoenaed as the investigating THP Patrolman for a horrific West Texas fatality accident in Reeves County, a wreck resulting in a felony criminal charge of Murder With a Motor Vehicle.[2] Chief Investigator Dean was not happy knowing the real action took place outside the confines of a big-box department store or up and down the narrow corridors connecting cubicles of pencil-pushers not having a clue about actual policing. Hardly had three months gone by when Jack Dean, on Christmas Eve Day 1964, submitted another Application for Employment with DPS.[3] With the formal application Jack enclosed a hat-in-hand personal letter, sheepishly but truthfully declaring: "I now find that I have made a mistake in leaving the department as I feel I am better suited to Patrol work than in my present employment. . . . I realize that due to my resignation I have caused the Department great inconvenience and will again do so with the reinstatement request. But I feel that I will be a better patrolman due to the realization that patrol work is exactly what I want to do."[4]

DPS Assistant Director Pat Speir dictated the letter notifying an admittedly antsy Jack Dean of his remarkable, but extremely good fortune:

> Your request to reinstate with the Texas Department of Public Safety Highway Patrol Service has been evaluated by this office. Your reinstatement has been approved effective March 15, 1965, contingent upon your successful passing of the physical examination to be administered by this Department. . . . You will be assigned to Region 1B and stationed at Tyler. . . .[5]

Ninety miles east of Dallas, Tyler people had bragging rights Pecos citizens did not have: Trees! The Smith County shiretown was a hub for commerce and education and medical facilities in the geographical region simply referred to as the Piney Woods of East Texas. Smith County, when numerically contrasted with Reeves County, was shamelessly ahead in the population count.[6] Unlike Pecos, vacationers vacationed at Tyler. There they took in such popular events as the annual Rose Festival or marveled while traveling and taking photographs along the Azalea Trail or were mesmerized when visiting the picturesque and sweet-scented Rose Garden. There was no lack of interest for visitors and/or residents to pass away spring and summertime days swimming and boating and water-skiing the numerous area reservoirs, such as Lake Palestine or Lake Tyler. Fishing for mouthwatering catfish in the Sabine and/or Neches Rivers and/or their spider-web tributaries netted ample fare for deep-fryers and the ravenous picnickers impatiently standing by with an ice-cold Budweiser in hand. East Texas—and Smith County in particular—was a great place to live and raise a family. Of course, there was that niggling little downside that would affect the newly arrived Dean family. Increased census number correlated to more motor vehicle traffic, more major and fender-bender accidents, and more criminality than what THP Patrolman Jack Dean had been used to in forlorn and less peopled West Texas.

Jack and Janie, along with the ever-growing kiddos, moved to Tyler taking up residence at 1718 South Mahon. Especially for Janie the new surroundings were more appealing than Jack's previous DPS assignment, and at Tyler she couldn't be temporarily hoodwinked by any silliness about trees or the lack thereof; they were everywhere. As a courteous welcoming gesture a nice biographical profile of the family appeared in the *Tyler Morning Telegraph*.[7] At Tyler on the windy morning of 15 March 1965 Jack Dean, having already undergone and passed the required physical exam and the issuance of equipment and uniforms at Austin, energetically reported to the THP Office. The seasoned law enforcing veteran in charge was Captain Glen B. Warner, but Jack Dean's immediate supervisor—the one he really had to please the most—was THP Sergeant Frank L. Fasel. The grandfatherly looking sergeant had already banked two decades of life and practical law enforcing experience ahead of any of the Highway Patrolman under his command. Such hard-earned seniority had tempered Sergeant Fasel's backbone into ramrod straight steel. Due to the break in service, THP Patrolman Jack Dean would once more have to prove his worth and survive six-months of probationary service.

THP Patrolman Jack Dean started his new job on the right foot and with a good attitude. For his three-month evaluation Sergeant Fasel noted the probationary patrolman, "Is very dependable and shows good judgment."[8] Two months later the assessment was yet registering favorably, "This patrolman is very dependable and generally uses good judgment."[9]

On the first day of October 1965, THP Patrolman Jack Dean pocketed the report of Sergeant Fasel—the one recommending his retention with permanent status. Sergeant Fasel, in removing him from probationary standing particularly noted: "Jack O'Day Dean has completed six months of field service as a Highway Patrolman. His performance as a patrolman, his conduct, both on and off duty, and his general character traits, has been highly satisfactory."[10]

Although through the words of a biographer it may register as somewhat hyperbolic, such is not the case in reality. THP Patrolman Dean was aggressively tackling each workday with vigor; making violator contacts (stopping vehicles) either issuing warning tickets or ones more pricey. In Texas there never was a shortage of sports sailing down the highway—swerving—beer on breaths and in bloodstreams, possessing an incapacity for straight thinking or straight driving. For everyone's wellbeing, inebriates were escorted to the pokey. Most went wobbling but easily, others however wanted to fight and for those mindless folks THP Patrolmen kindly obliged. Passenger car and big-rig truck traffic on Interstate 20 cutting through Smith County never stopped; day or night, good weather or bad and backing up local officers on "hot calls' was but routine. Rather quickly—in the Grand Scheme—Jack Dean was shaping and sharpening his law enforcing persona. The fact is substantiated by a DPS supervisor's dispassionate assessment: "This patrolman is one of the hardest workers in this area."[11]

At this point a modicum of journalistic mercy is sought in light of blending chronological data regarding THP Patrolman Jack Dean's off-duty life. The Deans were members in good standing at the Friendly Baptist Church, where Jack "taught a junior college age boys' Sunday School class." Additionally Jack Dean somehow found the time to productively participate with the coaching of both baseball and flag-football teams for youngsters. Sometimes, taking his dinner break, Jack Dean would park the THP unit, adjust the volume so he wouldn't miss any 10-33 radio traffic (emergency), remove his Sam Browne and uniform shirt, and in a T-shirt pitch a few practice balls for the kiddos—Kyle among them. And, it was at Tyler that Kyle marked the noticeable difference between Reeves County and Smith County: water. When not on the field in an organized practice or game, Kyle roamed the nearby creek, catching crawdads with bacon on a string, trying to and sometimes gigging a frog, and digging worms for his cane-pole fishing adventures— he was an outside boy.[12]

Were the enumerated off-duty activities for Jack Dean not enough, he also graciously served as a "committeeman" for the Cub Scouts. Adding to his already full schedule he took on added responsibility as the official "safety coordinator at Bell Elementary School." Meanwhile, following a stint as a part-time employee at Tyler's City Hall, Janie accepted a full-time position on the administrative side with General Electric's Smith County setup. And as with most moms, Janie captained the Dean's taxi service, hustling Kyle and Kelly to this or that game, this or that extracurricular activity, when Jack was busy patrolling the Interstate again and again searching for less well-intentioned drivers.[13]

And one of those traffic stops is more than revealing about THP Patrolman's Jack Dean's overall demeanor. He could, if one laudable letter is typical, issue a traffic citation and make the violator feel pleased to have been stopped and ticketed. ". . . Mr. Jack Dean, Badge No. 454, had occasion to issue me a citation for speeding. He was most courteous and very attentive to duty. . . ."[14] And this very motorist keyed on that ever present bugaboo haunting most lower level lawmen: skimpy paychecks. "Under the circumstances it was most gratifying to know that the department can still attract fine young men into its service even at what I still consider to be substandard salaries."[15] Though at this point in Jack Dean's story it should come as no shocker, once again he was having second thoughts—the prospects of riches were enticingly peeking over the East Texas pine trees, on the near financial horizon.

Jack's second-cousin on his mother's side had a proposition. Were Jack to forego police work and come to work for him, he would not have to relocate but could office at the Fair Petroleum Building in Tyler, earning a higher monthly salary—and one lucratively supplemented by hefty sales commissions. The tease was tempting and, once more, Jack Dean wavered between what he really liked to do and what he thought he really should do. The timeworn story is growing stale; THP Patrolman Jack Dean, on 28 May 1966, gave notice that as of the fifteenth day of April 1966 he would be a pistol-wearing state-paid peace officer no longer, "I am resigning to accept a position that will increase my income substantially and, therefore, better enable me to support my family."[16] Clearly Sergeant Fasel was sorry to lose such a valuable and respected patrolman: "his work has been completely satisfactory and I would consider him a good, well-rounded Highway Patrolman. He presents a good appearance, is energetic, a good investigator and gets along well with the public and the people with whom he works. I would recommend this man be considered for reinstatement if he should apply."[17] Somewhat conflicted, Jack Dean went to work for Robert G. Day, Investment Securities as a "Registered Representative."[18]

Like the fleeting sojourn with Montgomery Ward as the Chief Investigator, Jack Dean's tenure was short. Trying to talk fellows out of money with a percentage coming his way was less than fulfilling. Janie was thoroughly devoted, wanting only the best for her dearly loved Jack. Though he was well-liked in Tyler business circles, restless Jack Dean tossed and turned at night, dreaming of real-life highway thrills, two-way radio traffic figuratively buzzing between his ears. He knew it at the time, there was and would be but one sedative for salesman Jack O. Dean. Apologetically, with unadulterated contrition, the troubled ex-Highway Patrolman would give it another go—if they but would have him back. Jack Dean opined:

> I realize I have no right to ask this but hope you will realize my deep desire to return to the Patrol. I have discussed this with Major Smith and he advised me that he will recommend my reinstatement. As I explained to Major Smith, I have been and am now employed at a higher salary but I have been unable to replace the Patrol with this. I know now that I will be unhappy doing anything else. The only thing I have to offer the Department in return is my performance as a patrolman. . . .[19]

Needless to say, by this time the DPS hierarchy had expansive room for bona fide skepticism. DPS Assistant Director Speir asked DPS Major Guy Smith for judicious guidance, one way or the other.[20] After thoughtful consideration—and as Jack Dean alluded to—Major Smith penned his written remarks and recommendation: "I would highly recommend that Patrolman Dean be reinstated. He was one of our better Patrolmen. . . ."[21] Assistant Director Speir would okay the reinstatement, but in light of Jack Dean's past history with DPS, he had a strongly worded caveat: "Dean's employment record indicates that he has wavered considerably in making a final decision in what position he desires. Excessive and frequent breaks in service are not desirable for employees in this Department. . . . let it be noted in his personnel file that another reinstatement request will not be considered should he once again terminate his employment and later apply for reinstatement."[22] The die had been cast.

Although it unquestionably derailed DPS's standard operating procedures, when Jack Dean had been reinstated on 15 January 1967 he was allowed to remain posted at Tyler. Benevolently the DPS Command Staff had opted not to transfer the rehired Jack Dean to another DPS Region, which would have been customary, but allowed that he would not have to move. Six-year-old Kelly Dean was suffering an imperfectly functioning thyroid gland, and had even received specialized treatment at the eminent John Sealy

Hospital along Gulf Coast beaches at Galveston. The medical situation had somewhat stabilized under the care of a prominent Tyler physician, and staff at the Tyler School District was also considerately working with the Deans.[23]

DPS Sergeant Frank L. Fasel was pleased to have Jack Dean back in harness, flatly declaring: "This patrolman was a very dependable man when he was with us previously and his present attitude indicates that he will be so again."[24] After the passage of a year, almost to the day, there was no reason for Sergeant Fasel to regret his earlier measure of Highway Patrolman Jack Dean: "His violator contacts are among the top in this area. He is cooperative and dependable."[25]

During this timeframe (1968) THP Patrolman Jack Dean felt the heat of an internal spark that reasonably soon would consequentially alter his life. As previously noted, the earlier assignment to West Texas had surely been educational but geographical remoteness and the sheer population numbers—even passing-through motorists' numbers—were appreciably lower than those in bustling Smith County. Counties throughout East Texas may have measured smaller in square miles on the unfolded roadmap, but the cluster of small towns and emerging cities dwarfed those in faraway West Texas. Statistically there were many more traffic and criminal matters to worry DPS Headquarters and, therefore, the manpower deployment model was dissimilar. Though their physical areas of responsibility were a great deal smaller, DPS personnel were scattered all through East Texas as if salt had been thrown to the wind. Such was not haphazard but fastidiously planned. The carefully drawn staffing pattern applied not only to THP Patrolmen but to the Texas Rangers as well. And therein was the flicker that would ignite Jack Dean's career choice curiosity.

In West Texas, though he irregularly saw a Texas Ranger, there was a significant age gap: "I had known some Rangers, when I was at Pecos, but they were older gentlemen, I mean quite a bit older. . . . They were in their 60s and they didn't have a retirement then. I was 23–24 years old, so you know, so for them to speak to me was unusual."[26] That changed in East Texas. There were several—and younger—Texas Rangers stationed in towns within reasonable proximity to Tyler and THP Patrolman Jack Dean's sphere of activity. Personally meeting and occasionally monitoring radio traffic of Texas Rangers as they conducted felony investigations and ably assisted sheriff's office and police department personnel was not only fascinating but personally rewarding. There was, though THP Patrolman Dean couldn't necessarily put into words, a certain mystique about Texas Rangers. Generally wearing Western attire and carrying their personal handguns—typically—Colt Model 1911 .45 autoloaders, Texas Rangers projected their own unique image, establishing a certain aura of independence and invincibility as they strove to honor tradition of Texas Rangers whose figurative shoulders they were deferentially standing on. Of course they were but mere mortal men, but for anyone to suggest there was not an impression of supremacy would be mistaken—not in the eyes and minds of many Anglo native Texans and Jack Dean was an Anglo native Texan. As an active Highway Patrolman Jack Dean's contact with such respected Rangers as Glenn Elliott from Longview and Robert M. "Red" Arnold posted at Mount Pleasant was not infrequent. Both had seen prior service as THP Patrolmen, and each of these Texas Rangers was bootstrap tough, but fair-minded and never too busy to pass a moment with the hardworking Jack Dean.[27] However, a most profound introduction—though Jack Dean would not know it at the given time—was when he was introduced to Texas Ranger Robert K. "Bob" Mitchell, a THP veteran, assigned to Tyler.[28]

Usually known for his amicability, one night Dean's blood boiled over—figuratively—but his anger at another Highway Patrolman was literal and lasting. Riding with a less- experienced partner for the night, Jack Dean was working the Interstate north of Tyler—doing what good Highway Patrolmen were supposed to do—their job. Though no violator contact should ever be classed as routine, there was not reason to think stopping this vehicle for speeding would be problematic. The three black men, for whatever reason, had figured their odds, calculating that their steam-spewing Dodge couldn't be counted on to outdistance the state's superior squad car, and that two Highway Patrolmen couldn't catch three sprinters escaping in diverse directions. So, when red lights turned on for the THP car, the four-door Dodge pulled to the highway shoulder as expected, but most unexpectedly the three fellows inside immediately bailed out of the car and "broke for the brush" afoot.

Having not a clue as to why the helter-skelter yahoos were running—be they professional armed robbers or just having overdue parking tickets—Jack Dean radioed the mile-marker location so that DPS backup wouldn't be utterly unawares—and quickly launched his foot-chase, this being well before everyday Highway Patrolmen having anything as extravagant as a walkie-talkie. Smith & Wesson .357 Magnum in hand, Jack Dean directed his partner to head one way, he'd go another and, with good luck, they would head-off the runners and effect the arrests, sorting out who was wanted for what later. Jack Dean took off at a high-lope, scanning the tree line and brushy hillside, hunting for the absconders. It was thorny business to be sure, but legit lawmen were paid to do what others couldn't or wouldn't do. Hearing something behind him, Jack Dean turned, speedily and apprehensively supposing that he might have to shoot a harebrained outlaw stampeding on his back-trail. Jack Dean's amazement was epic, his disbelief near unfathomable. Right behind him was his Highway Patrol partner for the day, revolver un-holstered. Dutifully, but with dripping disdain, Jack Dean queried: "I thought you were going to head them off?" Forthcoming was an answer that shocked and shook Jack Dean to the very core. Catching his breath, Dean's partner had said: "I got shot at in Vietnam and I'm damn sure not going to get shot at doing this job!" Then and there Jack Dean made a decision, one he would civilly cut Sergeant Fasel in on before shift's end: He would never, ever, work with that fellow again—and he didn't.[29] What of the chase? It was soon learned that the car had been stolen and that had prompted the foot race. Later, further down the highway, an alert deputy sheriff latched onto three hitchhikers—three black fellows that couldn't keep their stories straight.[30]

Although his role would not necessarily be that of a pure investigative nature, a ferocious brouhaha in far northeast Texas redirected

THP Patrolman Jack Dean's everyday routine and amplified his awareness about what Texas Rangers did. At the Lone Star Steel works south of Dangerfield, Morris County, on 16 October 1968 the second labor strike at the plant skyrocketed into newspaper head-lines when 2000 plus union members walked off the job. Wages were not in dispute, working conditions were, and both management and labor were at loggerheads—neither keen on showing even a smid-gen of weakness.[31] Lone Star Steel executives flatly refused to cool the facilities' furnaces, while union bosses vowed to shut down pro-duction at all costs, spilling of blood to be the spit-in-you-face down payment! When management rolled up their shirtsleeves to take up the laborers' slack and non-union workers—"scabs"—crossed pick-et-lines it turned nasty. The Morris County Sheriff, Joe Starrett, with but a couple of deputies on the payroll was understandably power-less to protect anyone's life and/or property. Especially if required to work around the clock and try to face down overwhelming numbers of angry and armed agitators.[32] Petulantly and poisonously a few riled strikers "broke out their guns and used them freely."[33] Credibly the call for help was forthrightly answered by DPS. Texas Rangers were handed the investigative assignments and the THP redeployed manpower to Morris County. The horrific strike would last a tire-some seven months and consume policing services of from "six to twenty-six Rangers and forty-six highway patrolmen. . . ."[34] THP Patrolman Jack Dean

Though sometimes such madness results in more mouthing than meanness, such was not the case for this mess. Texas Ranger Glenn Elliott, who was there for the duration, summarized: "Shootings, bombings, Molotov Cocktails, threats, intimidation, beatings, killing of children's pets, families breaking up, murder—you name it, and we had it in the '68 strike."[35] Texas Ranger Bob Mitchell, who was also there, chimed in: "And we got up there and that little old strike lasted seven months and three days. And violence like you would not believe and ah. . . . bombings, killings, beatings, clubbing. . . ."[36] On one occasion trucks loaded with steel pipe were parked at the Holiday Inn while drivers grabbed a bite inside the restaurant before hitting the road for their long distance haul. "Both trucks were blown to bits, as well as the motel having all its windows blown out."[37] A bomb consisting of "several sticks of dynamite hooked up with a timing device and set to explode at the lunch hour," and concealed inside a coat was left inside the plant's dining room.[38] Thankfully, it was soon discovered and disarmed before detonation. Rangers investigated and arrested the perpetrators. Texas Ranger Bob Favor who was there for two separate stints, said of one seven-day schedule: "I walked the picket line keeping the strikers from attacking the *scabs*, for 128 hours. A week only has 168 hours anyway you figure it."[39]

Assuredly one event caught every lawman's attention: the shootout between Ranger Captain Robert Austin "Bob" Crowder, Commander of Company B, and Ranger Mitchell on the one side and three imprudent union members and sympathizers on the other. Subsequent to shooting and a car chase south into northern Upshur County, the pursuing Rangers "got 'em hemmed up on a dead end street. . . . I [Mitchell] was young, but I was with an experienced old man [Crowder] and he said 'Robert, don't kill 'em,' and it was as good advice as I ever had."[40] All players survived the Grim Reaper's touch that night, but the trio of mechanics from Lone Star Steel's maintenance department had bitten from a hard plug—more than they could chew. Jack Dean began incorporating all this news, especially the thrilling accounts Texas Rangers were experiencing into his ever ginning thought processes. THP Sergeant Fasel took note, too. Although he incontestably wasn't fussing, he did recognize reality about Patrolman Jack Dean's performance or lack thereof in Smith County: "Strike duty has affected his work to a major degree."[41]

Finally, after 210 days, the Lone Star Steel strike was dumped into annals of the past after labor union members voted to go back to work, "ending the longest and most violent strike in Texas history."[42] For THP Patrolman Jack Dean it had been an eye-opener. There had been lessons to be learned and Jack Dean was a good student. Following the Lone Star Steel strike, THP Patrolman Dean was back on duty in Smith County for awhile—a little while.

With but a gentle reminder its appropriate to remember that the 1960s and 1970s in America were active times of anti-Vietnam War protests, Civil Rights marches, Labor Union Organizers' hustling farms workers into the fold, and National Guard callouts. Too, aside from the more or less peaceful activists and demonstrations, the timeframe was also abhorrently and sometimes violently or murderously marked by militant underground movements, such as the Weathermen and/or the Symbionese Liberation Army and/or the Black Panthers, etc. Private and government buildings were being bombed and/or burglarized, as well as banks and armored cars being robbed to finance this or that extremist revolutionary faction. Unmistakably it was a period of the United States' history punctuated with social unrest and upheaval.[43] Thoroughly attuned to the potential for a breakdown down in social order and with an eye toward public safety issues, DPS had sensibly blueprinted a specialized training program, one generically dubbed "Riot Control." Highway Patrolman Jack Dean had been a graduate of two such continuing education schools. Such instruction would fit well with his professionalization as a well-rounded DPS lawman.[44] Whether the sociological or cultural cause is justifiable or unjustifiable, the sworn duties of peace officers were then, and are now, unambiguous: Keep the peace—idyllically—impartially. THP Patrolman Jack Dean was all too soon suddenly immersed in the societal flood washing across the country.

East of Tyler is Harrison County, adjacent to the western Louisiana state line, not far from the Pelican State's Shreveport/Bossier City multiplex. Serving as the county's seat of government is Marshall, an East Texas city with a rich and colorful history tracing its birthday to Republic of Texas days, several years before statehood.[45] An integral component of that vivid history centers on Wiley College, a noteworthy institution, the oldest black college west of the Mississippi River, founded by the Freedman's Aid Society of the Methodist Episcopal Church shortly after the Civil War during 1873.[46] Students at Wiley did not dodge the 1960s unrest: "The concept of nonviolent sit-ins that began in Greensboro, North Carolina, in 1960 soon spread across the South. Students at Wiley and Bishop Colleges in Texas staged demonstrations that year. . . . In 1962 Wiley and Bishop College students held sit-ins at the local Woolworth store—demonstrations that helped integrate public facilities in Marshall."[47] The demonstrations and protests and boycotting and picketing at Marshall by Wiley College students during those earliest years, of course, did not involve THP Patrolman Jack Dean. However, a 1969 installment at Wiley College did.

During April of that year, predominantly nonviolent demonstrations uncorked and spewed at Wiley College, pointedly with regards to "faculty hiring practices, primitive dormitory facilities, and cutbacks in the intercollegiate athletic program. . . ."[48] Emphatically, not all fiery speeches and acidic wrangles over real or perceived wrongs volcanically erupt into wanton bloodshed or malicious property destruction, but the undercurrent for a flashpoint ignition is there. Coolness is crucial. Though it's been written that the hubbub resulted in sending 100 Texas Rangers to Marshall, such is technically a rich overstatement; there were, at that time, not even 100 Rangers in the whole state of Texas. An assertion that Texas officialdom dispatched some Rangers and a healthy contingent of Highway Patrolmen would be more accurate, and Jack Dean was a member of that assemblage.

THP Patrolman Jack Dean's avowed obligation was not to question why he was being sent to Marshall, but to follow lawful orders. Their sole responsibility was to maintain order and should criminal behavior emit, make arrests. That said, it's always wise to hope for the best, but be prepared for the worst, an axiom not lost on frontline peace officers. For this recount of Jack Dean's personal story and for this particular response to Marshall, thankfully, there are surviving photographs of his unit. Noting that the Highway Patrolmen were ostensibly on riot duty, but not wearing protective body armor or bullet-proof vests is reflective of the times; the minimally protective headgear being all that was issued for such uncertain duty. The troupe's armament is also noteworthy—especially for firearms enthusiasts. Though well past the mid-century mark, the THP Patrolmen carrying state-issued carbines were armed with Winchester Model 1894 .30-30s, a throwback to the nineteenth-century. More up to date were those armed with state-owned shotguns, slide-actions, a decided improvement over the iconic sawed-off double barrels of Old West days. Not illogically is Jack Dean's armament for this potentially touchy assignment. Due to his uncanny marksmanship ability and time spent target shooting—sometimes competitively—Jack Dean cradled a telescopic sighted high-powered rifle, a sniper's tool, one capable of protecting his fellow officers should they draw fire from a distance. Fortunately the Highway Patrolmen did not have to pull a trigger. though, according to Dean, during one buildup of agitation and near conflagration, the mere clicking sounds of the unsmiling Highway Patrolmen chambering rounds quieted the crowd.[49]

In the end, at Wiley College, the 1969 unrest was resolved administratively by faculty and staff, not by hardcore police work thumping heads and filling the Harrison County jailhouse to capacity. Though he certainly had no way to know it at the time, the levelheaded and unruffled response at Wiley College would, relatively soon, well-serve peace officer Jack Dean.

On the twenty-first day of April 1969 THP Patrolman Jack Dean formally submitted his letter to Colonel Speir requesting that he be considered for a transfer into the Texas Rangers: "During this period [THP service] I have been involved in investigative work related to traffic on many occasions and in some criminal investigations. I enjoy this type work very much. I am 31 years of age and in good health. I feel that I have the qualifications to perform the duties of a Ranger and any consideration given this request will be appreciated by me."[50]

Before too much time had elapsed, THP Patrolman Dean had occasion to exhibit some of that investigative acumen. On the fourth day of November 1969 he responded to a 2:30 p.m. motor vehicle accident on humming Interstate 20, an overturned automobile. That in and of itself, for a reasonably well-seasoned trooper, was not too unusual. What Jack Dean found at the scene, however, was. During his investigation, THP Patrolman Dean discovered "a sawed off shotgun, .380 cal auto pistol and a large amount of change. . . ." The handgun had been tossed into a drainage ditch—and some of the money was stuffed into a paper sack near the upside down car. Additionally, as Jack Dean soon discovered the stunned occupants—all three of them—had pockets bulging with jingling coins. Something wasn't upright, to be sure? Through some quick and skilled field-interrogation THP Patrolman Dean was able to articulate enough Probable Cause to make arrests. Paul W. Fisher, now the THP Sergeant and now on the scene concurred. The three black fellows, surprisingly uninjured, were hauled off to the Smith County Jail, proper charges to be determined shortly. And ever so shortly it was learned that the unlucky and violent visitors to the Tyler area were prime suspects in an Armed Robbery at Houston, Harris County. Texas Rangers Bob Mitchell and Glenn Elliott conducted the final and formal phase of the criminal investigation, both noting that THP Patrolman Jack Dean was made of the right stuff—a solid peace officer with potential.[51]

Texas Highway Patrolman Jack Dean's admitted immaturity when he first pinned on the badge had given way to levelheadedness and personal introspection. Now, just short of a decade later, he was valiantly working toward self-betterment and the major career change within DPS. On the eighth day of September he enrolled in the Criminal Justice program at Tyler Junior College, registering for LE-113, Introduction to Law Enforcement and LE-113A, Police Administration. He would, from start to finish, maintain an A average.[52]

On the morning of 24 November 1969 THP Patrolman Jack Dean, though he wished he were there, was not on the busy Interstate Highway chasing a speeder or working a wreck or wrestling a DWI into the backseat of his black and white cruiser with the State of Texas gold decals on the sedan's front doors. He, along with several other DPS cohorts, were at the Smith County Courthouse on standby, waiting to testify in a criminal matter before the District Court. The news broke fast. The Southside State Bank at Tyler had been held-up at 10:30 and the robber was on the loose. Under explicit hurried orders from Sergeant Fisher, the Highway Patrolmen broke for their cars. Hunting for an armed highjacker took precedent over standing around or sitting on wooden benches in the courthouse hallway doing nothing. Jack Dean was working alone that crisp fall day, a one-man unit. The frightening criminal offense had not been a long and drawn out affair.[53]

At an outside drive-in window, the idiotic bank robber had threatened the teller, Vera Cooper: "I'm going to hold this place up—give me your money," shakily handing her a brown paper bag and further accenting his scowling demand, "put all your money in it, I've got a bomb. . . ." Getting visibly nervous the crook blurted to the thoroughly terrified bank employee as she was stuffing bills into the sack, "that's enough" and grabbing the loot sped away in a yellow sports car. Luckily there had been a witness, other than the caged bank teller, a nice young man attending Tyler Junior College. Cautiously but adeptly he trailed the robber to a department store parking lot, where carrying a suitcase the desperado traded his get-away car to a young female accomplice, driving away in a striking late model green Buick Riviera. The feminine misfit went the other direction in the yellow vehicle.[54]

Subsequent to the dispatcher's APB broadcast, the DPS Highway Patrolmen and other area lawmen were diligently crisscrossing the circuitous back roads north and south of Interstate 20, and east and west on the four-lane slab. Collectively but separately the lawmen eyeballed any and every green automobile, specifically hunting for that suspect Buick Riviera and its sneaky bomb-carrying occupant. West of Tyler at the Stuckey's Travel Center, DPS Highway Patrolman Jack Dean and a local FBI Special Agent, John Faulks, indeed struck pay dirt. With more than sufficient Probable Cause they detained twenty-four-year-old Barry Joe Kuykendall from Dallas. They were soon joined by DPS Highway Patrolman Ralph Byrd and his partner, THP trainee Mike Farrar. Jack Dean duly noted and pegged on the fact that the suspect's Buick was displaying a fictitious license plate, a "homemade" example of ineptness. Incidental to a cursory

and legal search for weapons, it was found that the alleged bank robber had a .380 autoloading pistol and a brown paper sack stuffed
full of cash on the Buick's front seat. Jack Dean, knowing it had
been reported that the man had a suitcase or suitcases, asked for a
Voluntary Consent to Search. Realizing the absolute futility of his
situation and the unmitigated mess he was already in, Kuykendall
willingly agreed to let lawmen carry on with their look-see absent
having to send someone back into downtown for a search warrant.
Bingo! Inside one of the valises was a "dummy bomb made of wood
sticks and a cheap clock." Shortly, via radio traffic from Tyler PD
units it was announced that they had just arrested a gal driving a
snazzy yellow sports car, a twenty-three-year-old from Garland, the
bustling municipal suburb east of Dallas. It was a job well done. One
and all involved received merited kudos from the Tyler Police Chief,
L.B. Odom. From the time of the robbery to the apprehension had
burned but fifty minutes; the interagency cooperation had been
exemplary.

The quest after bank robbers and having his daddy pictured
in newspapers highlighting the story was, truly, an eye-opener for
young Kyle Dean. Where were the boys that wouldn't be proud having a father decked out in a spiffy and professionally pressed uniform, carrying a revolver and handcuffs—driving a car equipped
with red lights and a siren? And catching bad guys to boot—what a
job! Then and there Kyle internalized the fact that his father really
was a "source of pride," and someone worthy of emulating.[55]

Though the FBI's fan-base within local law enforcing circles vacillates, having its ups and downs, THP Patrolman Jack Dean did
not deny that he appreciated the laudatory letter from none other
than the outfit's top man, J. Edgar Hoover. Writing to Colonel Speir
regarding the recent bank robbery and capture of crooks at Tyler,
Director Hoover singled out two DPS lawmen for complimentary
recognition:

> It is a pleasure to express my appreciation to the officers involved
> in swiftly bringing about the arrest of the individuals charged with

this crime. The highly effective work of Patrolman Jack Dean and Gorman Ralph Byrd was particularly noteworthy and my associates and I are indeed grateful.[56]

Although getting in on a major criminal case such as the Tyler bank robbery was assuredly not Highway Patrolman's Jack Dean's first felony investigation, it had refueled that burning desire for him to put traffic work and writing tickets on the backburner and concentrate his policing efforts on matters more intriguing. Would he ever hear from the DPS powerbrokers about that Texas Ranger business? He was, as far as his work was concerned, standing on solid ground. DPS Sergeant Paul Fisher's latest evaluation of Highway Patrolman Jack Dean was one that he could have shared with his mother:

> This officer presents a good appearance in uniform. He keeps his patrol unit in good repairs with a minimum of cost. He has a very high production with good quality, and a good variety of contacts. He has arrested more DWI's than any other man in the area. He was involved in the arrest of a bank robbery suspect and did a good job. He has also made several good arrests over the past six months.[57]

Shortly and favorably, in response to a verbal request from his supervisor to actively search for outstanding candidates, Texas Ranger Bob Mitchell would make known his thoughts regarding Jack Dean's application for a transfer, writing his Company B Commander, Captain W.D. "Bill" Wilson: "Jack's supervisors rate him very high as a Highway Patrolman and for his criminal work. His sergeant showed me, at my request, his evaluation report which reflects the good work Patrolman Dean does. Jack is very interested in criminal law enforcement and I feel that he would make an excellent Ranger and I recommend him highly to you."[58]

Appointment as a Texas Ranger no longer was accomplished simply in accord with political whim or patronage payoff—much more was now required of applicants, a hard fact reiterated by Pat Speir, now DPS's headman, in his personal letter to THP Patrolman Jack

Dean. He had not been forgotten, his paperwork kicked into a waste-basket of inaction: "Please be advised than an entrance examination for prospective Texas Rangers will be given at the Texas Department of Public Safety Regional office in Dallas. You are invited to report to this location on July 6, 1970, at 1:00 P.M., for the purpose of partici-pating in this examination. In addition to an examination for mental acuity and personality factors, you will be examined on your knowl-edge of Texas History, Texas Government, Texas Penal Code, Code of Criminal Procedure, Laws of Search and Seizure, Laws of Arrests, Laws of Evidence, and Techniques of Criminal Investigation."[59]

Before mid-month of July, the ever hopeful but fidgeting Jack Dean was notified he had successfully cleared the first hurdle in the Texas Ranger hiring Olympics. The next step was to make an appearance at Austin and take questions—a grilling—from the Oral Interview Board. During that phase, on the twentieth day of July 1970, he would be "closely evaluated."[60]

Though it seemed to Jack and Janie, who was also heavily and emotionally invested, that an answer to Jack's dream of wanting to be a Texas Ranger would never come to fruition, the DPS's bureau-cratic wheels were really turning rather rapidly. On the last day of July 1970, the letter came. Jack was notified that, as of 1 September 1970, he would be a Texas Ranger, assigned to Company D and sta-tioned in the tropical Lower Rio Grande Valley at McAllen, Hidalgo County. Furthermore, he would, after an official touching base at McAllen, then report to Austin headquarters for the swearing-in ceremony so that DPS Director Speir could "personally present" him with his new badge.[61]

Indicative of the fact that Jack Dean had now stepped into a realm thus far unfamiliar to him, was the personal letter bearing the official State Seal of Texas, conveying "the warmest personal congratulations and sincere best whishes" from Governor Preston Smith.[62]

Photo Gallery

1

A young Jack Dean. And, as with many boys, a Jack Dean sans shoes. *COURTESY JACK DEAN.*

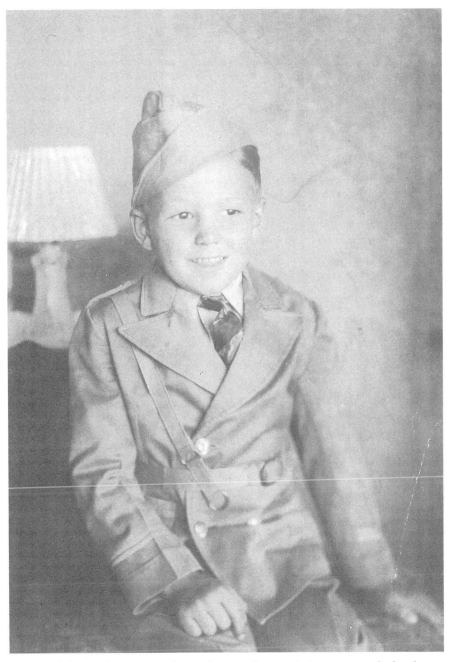

Jack Dean's boyhood years were during that era when patriotism was preached and practiced. COURTESY JACK DEAN.

A smiling Jack Dean accepted his very first badge-wearing assignment: A Safety Patrol Boy. *COURTESY JACK DEAN*.

Jack Dean was athletically inclined— a first-rate varsity football player. *COURTESY JACK DEAN*.

Jack Dean's high-school graduation photo. *COURTESY JACK DEAN.*

The ever vivacious Janie Lee Hill (Dean).
COURTESY JACK DEAN.

While working the assembly line (Jack Dean's back to camera) was good solid work—a dependable paycheck—there was something lacking for a young man bent toward adventure. COURTESY JACK DEAN.

Though the thrills were assuredly vicarious, as a young man Jack Dean, like most of the young fellows of his era, were fascinated with movies about outlaws and lawmen and Texas Rangers. COURTESY TEXAS RANGER HALL OF FAME & MUSEUM, WACO, TX.

At the time most households had televisions. On a weekly basis, actors Willard Parker [L] and Harry Lauter [R] rode into living rooms playing the parts of Texas Rangers Jace Pearson and Clay Morgan. The popular duo starring in *Tales of the Texas Rangers* captured imaginations of young and old throughout America—Jack Dean's included. *FROM THE TEXAS RANGER ANNUAL, VOL. IV, COURTESY TEXAS RANGER HALL OF FAME & MUSEUM, WACO, TX.*

While he lived, Texas Ranger Captain Johnny J. Klevenhagen was a legend in his own time, a superlative lawman—and one of the shooters that finally capped the career of Gene Paul Norris on the banks of Walnut Creek in nearby Parker County—a dramatic 1957 gunplay capturing the attention of an assembly-line working young man growing tired of monotony. *Courtesy Texas Ranger Hall of Fame & Museum, Waco, TX.*

Pictured here are two of the better known North Texas lawmen of the mid-twentieth century: Texas Ranger Captains R.A. "Bob" Crowder [L] and J.E. "Jay" Banks [R]. Ranger Banks was with Ranger Klevenhagen the day Gene Paul Norris and Silent Bill Humphries met their Maker and morticians. Note both are two-gun Texas Rangers. Additionally, Crowder is sporting a Thompson submachine gun, while Banks is armed with a rifle. FROM *THE TEXAS RANGER ANNUAL* IV, *COURTESY TEXAS RANGER HALL OF FAME & MUSEUM, WACO, TX.*

TEXAS DEPARTMENT OF PUBLIC SAFETY

RECRUIT TRAINING SCHOOL

December 7, 1960 – March 24, 1961

THP Patrolman Jack Dean's DPS Phase I graduating class. Jack Dean is first from left, second row. COURTESY JACK DEAN.

The day Jack Dean graduated from the DPS Academy, becoming a Texas Highway Patrolman. Janie is holding their son Kyle Lynn, while Jack has baby Kelly Lenea in arms. Indeed, it was a proud day at the Dean household. *COURTESY JACK DEAN.*

Jack Dean's official Texas Highway Patrolman photographic portrait. *COURTESY JACK DEAN*.

Texas Highway Patrolman Jack Dean's first day on the job at Pecos, Texas. COURTESY JACK DEAN.

Jack Dean would soon smartly learn that cooperation and collaboration with law enforcing colleagues, especially in the wilds of West Texas and, later, in the Lower Rio Grande Valley borderlands, was the key to success, as evinced by this period photograph of old-time lawmen. Advantaging themselves of latest technology—automobiles and submachine guns—these early twentieth-century Texas Rangers seem to be working hand-in-glove with U.S. Border Patrolmen. COURTESY TEXAS RANGER HALL OF FAME & MUSEUM, WACO, TX.

The windswept plains of West of the Pecos country are captured in this image of an accident being investigated by Highway Patrolman Jack Dean and partner. Not a beautiful tree in sight. COURTESY JACK DEAN.

Here, pictured at right, THP Patrolman Jack Dean interviews and investigates another motor-vehicle accident near Toyah in Reeves County. Violator and witness contacts sculpt good lawmen and hone investigative and interrogative skills. COURTESY JACK DEAN.

After a go in private industry, Jack Dean returned to service with the State of Texas, posted at Tyler. Turned out in a spiffy and pressed uniform and presenting his characteristic smile, there's little doubt THP Patrolman Jack Dean cast a favorable shadow for DPS throughout East Texas while stationed there. *COURTESY JACK DEAN.*

Wiley College at Marshall in Harrison County, is the oldest black college west of the Mississippi River. There were at times during the 1960s social unrest sweeping throughout America with regards to issues of overt racial discrimination and Civil Rights violations. Wiley College was not exempt. During 1969 DPS Troopers were deployed to provide a peace-keeping presence. THP Patrolman Jack Dean was one of those stalwart fellows, herein pictured standing at far left. *COURTESY JACK DEAN.*

Noting the DPS armament for the deployment to Wiley College is interesting. Even during 1969 the Troopers were issued lever action carbines, as well as the standard slide-action riot shotguns. Of particular note is Jack Dean's weapon, a scope-sighted sniper's rifle. Note none of the personnel are wearing protective vests. DPS Patrolman Jack Dean is seated in foreground on left. *COURTESY JACK DEAN.*

THP Patrolman Jack Dean, while posted in far West Texas, had but limited working contact with Texas Rangers. Such changed in the much more heavily populated East Texas region. Two of the better known Texas Rangers making a favorable impression on Jack Dean were Red Arnold [L] posted at Mount Pleasant and Glenn Elliott [R] stationed at Longview. They were amicable and never too busy to chat with or update uniformed DPS personnel. The career spark had ignited. COURTESY TEXAS RANGER HALL OF FAME & MUSEUM, WACO, TX.

Here Highway Patrolman Jack Dean and his Sergeant are investigating a major traffic accident on Interstate 20 in the Tyler, Texas, area, one that would eventually lead to the undoing of Armed Robbery perpetrators from Harris County. COURTESY JACK DEAN.

4

"Good image with good citizens"

Prior to his appointment becoming official, another message was driven home to Jack Dean. Not only did the governor wish him well, so did Lewis C. Rigler, a twenty-three-year Ranger veteran, one of the North Texas lawmen who had responded to the gruesome bomb blast blowing gambling gangster Herbert "The Cat" Noble to smithereens in 1951. Ranger Rigler was desirous of Jack Dean knowing he would now be part of a privileged investigative outfit and, furthermore, "If I may at any time be of help to you, please let me know."[1] Along the Rio Grande at McAllen, Ranger Jack Dean would be in a distant land, but only a phone call away from help. The Lone Star State was gargantuan. The cachet of carrying a Texas Ranger commission would give Jack Dean a statewide reach; he would not have to inordinately travel just to conduct an interview or see what vehicle was parked in a suspect's driveway. Safecrackers and hit-men were mobile creatures but a quick phone call could, sometimes, short-circuit their success. Aside from adaptability, Texas Rangers, especially those working in the field, prided themselves on a swift follow-through for investigative requests made by a brother badge-wearer stationed far away. Such reciprocal practice was a hallmark of many a criminals' downfall by the collaborative efforts of widely disbursed Rangers.[2]

And certainly in that territory then covered by Company D Texas Rangers, McAllen could be characterized as far away. Hidalgo County in and of itself was rather large on the topside, but disproportionally larger on the bottom end, with not just a few miles snaking along banks of the Rio Grande and its various U.S. Ports of Entry. Though the seat of local government would be Edinburg, on paper and in truth Texas Ranger Jack Dean would be stationed and living at McAllen, the county's most populous municipality. For Rangers the Texas/Mexico borderlands had always presented unparalleled challenges. Wanted hoodlums fleeing across the Rio Grande seeking safe sanctuary certainly was no twentieth-century phenomenon. Border jumping bandits and blue-eyed desperadoes had in the past and were then advantaging themselves of its proximity. Then, too, there were conflicting cultural issues. Disparate to Tyler where the Deans were part of the majority population, in temperate Hidalgo County, understandably, they would be in the minority—by overwhelming numbers, ranging well past ninety percentage points.[3] The fact that a tenderfoot Texas Ranger was not bilingual was of little concern to DPS's management team—their overall policing strategy was centered on a much larger and more complex dilemma. All too soon, Jack Dean would be privy to their pragmatism.

Immediacy forestalled Jack Dean pondering why he was being sent so far from interior Texas to the Lower Rio Grande Valley. The new Ranger and his family would need a home—they were not Bedouins proficient at nomadically unpacking and pitching tents beneath scanty shade at some South Texas oasis. Sergeant Paul W. Fisher gave his verbal blessing for Jack Dean to zip down to Hidalgo County via his state-owned THP squad car and find a suitable place to live for himself and brood. After all, it was the great State of Texas calling for THP Patrolman Dean's transfer into the Texas Rangers and relocation to the Texas/Mexico international line—a little state-paid gasoline would go a long way—and it was a long way to the borderlands, a long way. Though there would be the anticipated fits and starts, eventually the frazzled Jack Dean located a suitable place to live, taking up residence at 1204 Tamarack, McAllen, Texas—the

State of Texas picking up the commercial mover's tab of $387.85 for hauling household goods "from Tyler to McAllen, Texas, required by official DPS transfer."[4] Uprooting and relocating was never easy. Preceding permanent placement on the Texas Ranger's payroll there was that other obligation: a command appearance at Austin.

By prearrangement Jack Dean did not travel from McAllen to Austin by himself that Sunday. For the first leg of the 318-mile journey he was accompanied by Texas Ranger Jerome H. Preiss, at the time stationed at San Benito in Cameron County about halfway between Brownsville and Harlingen. The pair motored straight north out of the Lower Rio Grande Valley for about seventy miles to Falfurrias, Brooks County: the county named after the legendary Texas Ranger of the Frontier Battalion era, James Abijah Brooks. There they made contact with thirty-nine-year-old Billy J. Green, formerly a THP Patrolman, who like Jack Dean, had effectively tested for Ranger, withstanding the oral interview and background scrutiny. For the next 360 minutes Jack Dean and Billy Green keenly quizzed the well-seasoned Preiss about Ranger life: the dos and don'ts. They were somewhat surprised to learn that he was also one of the named defendants, along with Captain A.Y. Allee and Rangers Tolliver "Tol" Dawson and Jack Van Cleve, in a pending federal suit styled *Francisco Medrano et al. v. A.Y. Allee et al.* Candidly it seemed, there was some sort of complicated mess about a farm strike at Rio Grande City. As capable THP Patrolmen, Dean and Green knew DPS badges were not free passes to do harm. Preiss told them there were yet pretty irate folks demanding that real and/or perceived wrongs should be righted. At last, the trio pulled into Austin at 8:30 p.m. but Jack Dean and Billy Green weren't especially sleepy or extraordinarily tired. They were, putting it mildly, keyed up—the morrow would portend an exhilarating day.[5]

By next day's close of business Jack Dean was a THP Patrolman no longer. He was a Ranger, sworn into service by the DPS Director, Pat Speir, who really did take personal pride in pinning on brand-new Texas Ranger's badges, as had his late predecessor, Homer Garrison, Jr., the fellow who had commanded DPS for thirty years. Assistant Director Leo E. Gossett was there too. Also present was the

Senior Captain of Rangers, Clint Peoples, and Company A Captain Pete Rogers, Company B Captain Bill Wilson, and Company D Captain A.Y. Allee. Protocol and respect dictated their presence when new Rangers assigned to their companies were sworn. And for Texas Rangers, as an institution of historic merit, deference to and maintaining tradition was taken seriously, very seriously. Once the pleasantries and photographs and formality matters were taken care of, another topic of significance but off-the-official-record was implicitly tackled. James M. "Jim" Ray, former Texas Ranger but now Chief of the DPS's Criminal Division, which included the Rangers, called newly appointed Texas Ranger Jack O'Day Dean to one side for a little "one on one" conversation. Chief Jim Ray's soft-spoken intent was subtle, but the words registered real loud and real clear: "I want you to go down to that Lower Rio Grande Valley and get along and I don't give a damn if you ever make an arrest!"[6]

While it necessitates a backwards glance, changing times had overtaken the Texas Rangers: DPS's organizational upper-brass was confidently trying to keep up, though sometimes it seemed a challenge absent any hint of a sound and workable solution. And nowhere did institutional worry manifest itself more plainly than in South Texas and the Lower Rio Grande Valley. Although his boss's scheduled retirement date due to mandatory age restrictions had already been set in stone, Ranger Jack Dean's first thirty days would be under supervision of the interminably irascible and illustrious Captain Alfred Young "A.Y." Allee, Sr., then overseeing the command of Company D Texas Rangers from his headquarters at Carrizo Springs, due east of Piedras Negras/Eagle Pass and seventy-five-odd miles north of Laredo, Webb County. Working out of Carrizo Springs was handy for Captain Allee; his home and 1,200-acre ranch were just north of town, an easy commute.

Captain Allee had begun his career with the Texas Rangers a half-dozen years before Jack Dean was even born, reminiscently proclaiming of the Rio Grande's treacherous twist and tangles: "When I started to work in this Ranger Service in 1931 it was still pretty doggone rollicky up an down this border and a pretty bad situation. . . . It wasn't anything when we rode this river horseback for somebody across that river to shoot at you. . . ."[7] When Jack Dean was but a lad of ten years, A.Y. Allee was awarded the captaincy of Company D. Offering a colorful descriptive assessment, one prominent historian shone the spotlight on Texas Ranger Captain A.Y. Allee: "Short and blocky, turning paunchy as he neared sixty, bushy white eyebrows sprouting from 'a face like a sunburned potato,' an unlit cigar dangling from his mouth, he projected the image of the old-time frontier Ranger. . . . He got along well with South Texas sheriffs, some of whom bore Spanish surnames. To a man, Allee's Rangers respected and loved their captain."[8]

By most accounts men who worked for Captain Allee did revere him, knowing the crusty and gutsy Texas Ranger would lead from the front and back them to the hilt. Though it's somewhat out of chronological sync, the story of the attempted jailbreak at Carrizo Springs is somewhat useful. Prisoners had somehow acquired guns kept downstairs at Sheriff Tom G. Brady's office and were foolishly occupying the upstairs lockup with cerebral acuity gone haywire. How they thought they were going to escape or where they hoped to go, is answerable only in the abstract reasoning of impetuous dupes and dopes, especially now, taking into account the fact that upstairs the erupting canisters of teargas were misting the *mal hombres* with an irritation of stinging palpability. Captain Allee was downstairs backed up by several of his Company D Texas Rangers but now hopelessly short of any more gas or tolerance. Time was passing and Captain Allee was an impatient man. Fiddling around was foreign to what good lawmen did. Hollering loudly in an unnecessary warning, Captain Allee generously gave the prisoners the benefit of a ten count to throw down their guns and surrender. One! Two! Three! Four! Then, abruptly but characteristically announcing, "None of my Rangers are gonna get killed in front of me," Captain Allee carrying a borrowed submachine gun raced up the stairs, spitting lead as he went—bullets ricocheting hither and yon against concrete floors, iron bars and steel bunks but, fortunately, not killing or critically wounding anyone—fellow Texas Rangers or scared and shaking inmates now standing in little yellow puddles of their own making. Rounding up the wannabe bad men and recovering a misappropriated arsenal ended the bedlam. Later, when it was inquisitively but naively pointed out that he hadn't waited for the count of ten, Captain Allee gruffly retorted, "Them sonuvbitches can't count."[9]

Though sometimes being accused of being flippant with his remarks, Captain Allee was just short on words but long on meaning. One time when a overly confident trial lawyer asked him if it wasn't true that he had attempted, on a previous occasion, to arrest his client, Captain Allee's quick-witted answer cut the legs out from under the implication and somewhat amused the court: "I have never *attempted* to arrest anyone in my life."[10]

For another instance of Captain Allee's dry wit, one only has to review an account penned by another of his Company D men, Bob Favor, about his first day on the job as a Texas Ranger. Near Asherton, southeast of Carizzo Springs, two outlaws had stolen a car and wounded a deputy sheriff. During the manhunt rookie Ranger Favor was forced to return fire, ultimately shooting but not killing one of the suspects. Afterwards in town and in his new employee's presence, Captain Allee told the local telephone operator to get "Homer" on the line. Accordingly, when DPS Director Garrison was on the line—absent any other exchange—Captain Allee brusquely made his obligatory notification: "Homer, you sent me a damn good man. He's already shot a son-of-a-bitch." Then absent another word or a response, Captain Allee hung up the phone.[11] Though much has been said—good and bad—about Captain Allee, none could say he ever shied away from taking care of business:

> Several years ago, a certain South Texas group imported a Mexican pistolero to assassinate Capt. Allee, but the gravel-voiced Ranger learned of the plot and, a few days later, spotted the hired gun in a Laredo restaurant.[12]

Unhesitant, with the stub of an unlit cigar clenched in his teeth, Captain Allee strolled over to where the imported badass was sitting. Looking him over from several different angles, as if measuring him for a pine-box, the nervy captain said: "Yep, you'll make a nice-looking corpse." Then he turned his back on the Mexican gang-ster and walked out of the café. Rather quickly, penned a newspaper-man, "The paid pistol went back to Monterrey."[13]

None dared or had reason to question his raw courage in a tight spot and, rightly so, though Captain Allee's saltiness and quick-trigger temperament lent itself very well to some private censure and considerable public criticism—sometimes not unwarranted. But even he ruefully decried: "I guess some times I use a little poor judgment. I try not to. You show me an officer that hadn't made a mistake and I'll show you an officer that hadn't done a damn thing!"[14]

Instances of the captain's less than praiseworthy judgment are legion, if they are, indeed, true. Purportedly, during one dustup with a presumptuous *Newsweek* photographer, Captain Allee had warned the picture taker: "You put that camera away, boy, or I'll kill you dead on the sidewalk, you S.O.B., and I don't have to ask anyone's permission."[15] *¿Quién sabe?*

That Captain Allee operated *ad infinitum* at the full-cock notch is not hyperbolic, but he could go off half-cocked, such as the time when Allee and a THP Patrolman engaged in a roadside tête-à-tête regarding the family's operation of a motor vehicle. For Allee the problem resolution was uncomplicated. Allee simply jerked out his "pistol and swatted the trooper up the side of his head, knocking him senseless. The patrolman was transferred across Texas before the swelling went down."[16] Though it wouldn't be the last time a Ranger struck a THP Patrolman, such unruly behavior would be causing undue public relations heartburn at the DPS front office, even after the rough-edged Captain A.Y. Allee had settled into a comfy armchair pensively bemoaning just what in the hell had the world come to? Like all this damn crazy business with "the countercultural movement, with its hippies, rock festivals, protests, and drugs. . . ."[17] And what was all this nonsense about Mirandizing a defendant, telling him that he didn't have to talk and the government could and would pay for his greedy mouthpiece, some red-mouthed lawyer? Which panty-waist activist judges were coming up with all that drivel? Captain Allee waxed philosophically: "I've always said if a man really wants to lose his religion and lose all he's got, just get him to be a peace officer."[18] A vinegary veteran of showdowns and shootouts, Captain Allee was a survivor. He could withstand almost anything that those liberalized politicos and feisty agitators or mean thugs threw his way. In his mind he did not have to give ground to anyone, at anytime. He'd mapped his career to operate as an autonomous force to be reckoned with, very nearly 100 percent of the time.

The real kicker, however, had been the brouhaha pertaining to striking farm workers, a labor movement eliciting statewide notice—and far-reaching coverage by the national news media. The spectacle would prove to be no laughing matter on the ground and in real time. Afterwards, the partisan versions are actually comical in a weird sense, for they are ostensibly retold relying on agenda-driven and cherry-picking expediency.

Delving into the story with at least minimal treatment is necessary because in all truth the resultant upshot, as will be made clear, significantly affects Jack Dean's narrative, even though he wasn't involved and wasn't even a Ranger when the drama unfolded with hurtful headlines. Denying that there was racial and economic discrimination in the space and at the time is lunacy. Equally, making Texas Rangers the sole whipping boys for everything from a lack of Hispanics' entrepreneurial enterprises and/or holding public office and/or the imperfect ratio of Latino classroom teachers, to not correcting the calculus of Spanish speaking cheerleaders at football games is, likewise, inane.[19]

The 1966–67 uproar in the Rio Grande Valley put Rangers in an "impossible situation."[20] Adjacent to the Río Bravo lay Starr County and her seat of government Rio Grande City, home to the 1,600 acre La Casita Farms, big-time fruit and vegetable growers wholly dependent on stoop labor. Union organizer Eugene Nelson, affiliated with the National Farm Workers Association based in California, was incensed and demanded that South Texas farm workers be compensated at the Federal Minimum Wage of $1.25 per hour, rather than the typical pittance of pennies then being paid: anywhere from 40¢ to 80¢ per backbreaking hour. The labor strike and protest march to Austin, a 300-plus mile trek, unquestionably captured headlines, as well as notice by the state's powerbrokers and politicos. Befuddled planters and the Texas Farm Bureau were adamant—they wished they could pay more—but "the union demands were economically unrealistic and, if accepted, would drive the growers from the Rio Grande Valley."[21] There was, too, at the time that aforementioned unrest sweeping the country and not just a few allegations were being hurled that *La Marcha* was underpinned by Communists and there was a distinct possibility that acts of violence might very well accompany the "social revolution."[22]

Though telling this story in the round would mandate mention of such high-profile figures as Texas Governor John Connally, Attorney General Waggoner Carr, Texas Speaker of the House Ben Barnes, United States Senator Ralph Yarborough, United States Representative Henry B. Gonzales, and the United States Justice Department civil-rights' wheel-horses, publishing reality appreciably pares the word count. Cutting to the nub, the growers and the workers were at an impasse—resorting to colloquialism, a sure-enough Mexican Standoff.

With the "record-breaking" melon crop in the field and well-aware that there was but a short window of time to gather and transport the highly perishable crop, Vice-President of the Farm Worker's Union, Gilbert Padilla, issued his nonflexible taunt to La Casita Farms' management: "Negotiate or let them rot." Jim (Ray?) Rochester, Vice-President of La Casita Farms, would not bend, knowing full-well that Mexican nationals would willingly cross the river and take up the slack any strikers might wreak with regards to the time-sensitive harvest. Padilla's twofold strategy, then, was simple on its face: prevent Mexican "scabs" from crossing picket lines or stop growers from shipping by shutting down transportation—preventing trains carrying costly produce from leaving the Lower Rio Grande Valley. Such would be a stranglehold on South Texas commerce. The potential for violence seemed imminent. Starr County officialdom cried for help—Captain A.Y. Allee and his Company D Texas Rangers answered. Whether or not there's any truth to it may beg credulity, a campfire tale taking on a legendary life, but when notifying his Rangers to report to Rio Grande City and put the kibosh on agitators breaking the law, orders were explicit: "Kill all but six and save those for pallbearers."[23]

Whatever the truth, Captain A.Y. Allee's irrefutable mindset was unsophisticated. The great State of Texas had laws on the books and, therefore, as the law's sworn steward: He *was* the law! "I'm not on the side of management or the Unions, but when they're putting sugar in gasoline tanks, burning railroad bridges, trying to derail trains and damage irrigation pumps, I think it's time to stop them. As far as the union is concerned, I am not prejudiced. They can strike until doomsday as far as I am concerned so long as they obey the law."[24] All that poppycock regarding ingrained prejudice, social injustices, workers' rights, and labor union activists' anarchy, could just take a damn backseat to Captain A.Y. Allee's interpretation as to when and how to enforce the law—no fooling, no arguing!

From the old-school brand of law enforcement Captain Allee had little comprehension of just how hot was the political potato he had been handed. On the one side, certain church leaders, liberal politicians, union kingpins and laborers, and progressive newspapermen spouting their editorial causes, were sturdily lined up against the state's "power structure" and years and years of Lone Star tradition and independence—unhampered by enlightened twentieth-century thinking. Captain Allee was in the middle, damned if he did, damned if he didn't.

Nevertheless, whatever he was, Captain Allee was not a man of muddled thoughts or inaction: Declaring that he had always done his best "to enforce the law and the peace and dignity of the State of Texas. I took an oath years ago to enforce this law and to protect life and property to the best of my ability and that's what I intend to do."[25] And he did!

At the international bridge on the eleventh day of May 1967, Texas Rangers earned their title as "strikebreakers" in the minds of farm workers when they *protected* "green carders" crossing into Texas at the Roma U.S. Port of Entry. Not unexpectedly during the hullaba-loo and hollering, jeering and jostling, profanity and pushing, Texas Rangers made arrests for criminal infractions, most registering on the misdemeanor meter. The arrests angered and inflamed labor organizer Eugene Nelson, who *purportedly* had a hard message for Captain Allee, one to be verbally delivered through the voice of the utterly shocked Starr County Constable Manuel Benavides: "You tell that s.o.b. he had better lay off or there will be some dead Rangers." Following the filing of a formal Complaint, charging him with what today would be called Terroristic Threats, the red-faced Eugene Nelson, now claiming his words had been misinterpreted, spent a night in the cold and dark and dank jailhouse—a real dungeon of sorts—located in the basement of the Starr County Courthouse.[26]

As days went by, union activity escalated and the strikers "became more militant and hostile," which understandably jumped the Rangers' arrest count to the neighborhood of near sixty folks representing both genders. The public outcry was not unheard: "the Rangers received bitter, galling criticism as well as statewide demands for an investigation of their law enforcement methods and techniques. Soon there "would be a number of court suits, with accompanying affidavits, charging them with unnecessary brutality and unlawful confiscation or destruction of private property."[27]

The intense heat was ratcheted up several notches on 26 May 1967, following Captain Allee's arrests of the Reverend Edgar Kruger, an on-the-ground figurehead for a special "team ministry" sponsored by the Texas Council of Churches, along with his wife who had her Kodak seized. From Captain Allee's outlook the Krugers and their eighteen cohorts were clearly violating the law as they picketed a train at the railroad bridge near Mission, Texas, slightly west of McAllen. Inescapably the arrests netted DPS and the Rangers news coverage they'd rather not have had. Peace in the Valley—the Lower Rio Grande Valley—was elusive.

Not a week later, during the whirlwind of discontent, a hurricane blew in at La Casita Farms. On the night of 31 May 1967, at the loading dock sheds, according to Foreman Jim Rochester, the Mexican-born Magdaleno Dimas, accompanied by Benito (Benjamin) Rodríguez, drove up the ramp, impertinently brandishing a rifle and threatening to take Jim's life—something he had done several times before. Rochester jerked out a six-shooter or grabbed his own long-gun and tried, ineffectively, to shoot out one or more of the rubber tires on Dimas's vehicle. Magdaleno and his sidekick—by this time—were making haste. Not surprisingly such hot information was soon in the leathery hands of Captain Allee. He, along with Texas Ranger Tol Dawson, were on the hunt. Using surveillance techniques the lawmen, at last, located their men at the home of Kathy Baker. The nighttime identification had been mutual. At the same time Captain Allee had shone his spotlight on Magdaleno, standing on Baker's front porch, Dimas also recognized Allee, panicky threw his rifle down and ran into the house.[28]

At this juncture, though it might surprise some when considering Captain Allee's hardcore law enforcing tactics, he focused on the Rules of Criminal Procedure and legality. Not having any outstanding arrest warrants for Magdaleno and/or Benito, or a search warrant for Baker's residence, the Texas Rangers checked their hard-charging momentum and summoned a judge. Shortly a Justice of the Peace, a lower-level judicial officer, yet one with authority to issue warrants and set bail, was onsite in front of Kathy Baker's abode. For this touchy arrest scenario Captain A.Y. Allee wanted to play it by the book—the law book. And, with good reason!

Although a member in good standing of the United Farm Workers Organizing Committee, Magdaleno Dimas was also a fellow owning a lengthy rap sheet, with "arrests and convictions dating back to 1954."[29] One Ranger there at the time, Haynie Joaquin Jackson, unabashedly characterized Magdaleno Dimas as an "enforcer, a cross border thug." Allegedly Dimas was issuing death threats, specifically tasked with "keeping strikers in line" and "intimidating" Mexican Nationals from crossing the borderline and working the harvest.[30] Part of Magdaleno's criminal record included Murder Without Malice and a charge of Assault to Murder in or around Floresville, Wilson County, just south of San Antonio. Those felony convictions had netted him a three-year stretch with the Texas Department of Corrections, the state's penitentiary system. Added to that little retreat was the one year of jail time at Rio Grande City for Aggravated Assault. Whether they were inked prison etchings is indistinct, but the twenty-nine year old ex-convict was "heavily tattooed. There is a dragon on his right arm, and there is a rose on his left arm." Adding to his documentable criminal history were arrests in West Texas at Brownfield and Farwell for drunkenness. And though there is paperwork perplexity, it seems that Dimas also had had run-ins with federal lawmen at both Lubbock and Del Rio with regards to investigations of alien smuggling two years earlier, 1965. From a lawman's viewpoint, Magdaleno Dimas could be graded a tough and dangerous cookie: Given the right opportunity, at the right time, he just might hurt you.[31] And that's not even factoring in that sidebar tidbit: Benito Rodríguez, "a union friend was also dogged by a long police record."[32] Captain A.Y. Allee would do what he had to do, but assuredly would not sidestep commonsense and take needless chances.

Arming himself with a double barreled shotgun and sending Tol Dawson to the backdoor, Captain Allee made ready for a peaceful capitulation or war. The choice would be Magdaleno's and Benito's to make. Failing to comply with his order to open the front door, Allee's boot served as a key—in police lingo—it was a "dynamic entry." Inside, sitting at a Spartan kitchen table with their hands underneath and hidden from view were the placid Dimas and Rodríguez. With "street smarts" in their catalog of criminality Magdaleno and Benito were not dummies with regards to anxiety attendant to not knowing what's in adversaries' hands. They would, in an act of spiteful defiance and dissent, keep their hands out of sight, and cause worry to that pudgy round-faced cigar chomping old man that bossed everyone around, just because he could, just because he was one of those damned Rangers. Predictably and understandably the scattergun wielding Captain Allee asked—demanded—that Magdaleno and Benito slowly show him their hands, an indemnity that they weren't artfully palming pistols or penknives, six-shooters or switchblades. The men stood pat. Now the precautious choice was Captain Allee's to make. Should he hazard being shot or skewed?

There are two versions to what happened next. One belongs to Captain Allee, the other was owned by a pair of foolish Hispanic guys and a trio of doctors at an area hospital. For scenario number one: "I found Dimas and another man sitting behind a table with their hands under it. I told them to put their hands on the table, since I didn't know if they had guns under the table or not, and to stand up. They refused even after I told them several times. So I tilted the table back against them and hit Dimas on the head."[33] Though from a charitable secondary perspective, Captain Allee's assertion could be half-in-half paraphrased: When the intended arrestees failed to comply with lawful orders, Captain Allee tipped over the table and "tapped" Magdaleno on the head "lightly" with his twin shotgun barrels. Then, in an effort to escape, the two quarrelsome fellows, well, they just "stampeded," stumbling and bumbling into each other knocking over furniture and crashing against an open door, just before they abruptly collapsed at the toes of his hand-stitched cowboy boots in an uncoordinated "tangled heap." Scenario number two is more explicit: Attending physicians were more articulate and technically precise, medically reporting that during patient Dimas's five-day hospitalization they noted he had "bruises all over his arms and body," and that one laceration required several sutures to close. Too, an X-ray "revealed a blow to the back so severe as to curve the spine away from the point of impact." Two of the three attending doctors knowledgeably "diagnosed a brain concussion." Benito did not come through totally unscathed either, suffering "cuts and bruises all over his body and a broken finger."[34] Figuratively spitting in the face of authority had not been smart. Defying Captain Allee, allowing him to think—to even slightly suspect—that hands secreted under that kitchen table were holding weapons was very nearly suicidal. Texas Ranger A.Y. Allee's chips were always all in: He played for keeps! Captain Allee safely survived executing the warrants, arresting Dimas and Rodríquez, but it would not be without cost.

The weakening dam holding back negative publicity broke. Up to this point in their history Texas Rangers had weathered tough pecuniary and politicized attacks, but the close in period following the trying and tumultuous farm strike in the Lower Rio Grande Valley during 1967's harvesting season was "furious" and, for awhile, unrelenting. Following La Casita Farms' quieted but unsettling labor dispute, the U.S. Commission on Civil Rights during 1968 conducted its starched investigation, *Mexican Americans and the Administration of Justice in the Southwest*. Unfortunately, perhaps, was the fact that many witnesses

were drawn from a pool "sympathetic to the plight of the impover-
ished workers, and the witnesses were Anglo and Latino participants
with a loathing of the Rangers."[35] Not surprising then, was their findings which said in part: "Rangers conferred with and acted on behalf of
the growers and joined with local law enforcement officers in attempting to break the strike and denying the strikers and strike sympathizers their legal rights. More than a hundred arrests were made of farm
workers and union sympathizers on such charges as trespass, unlawful
assembly, secondary boycotting, illegal picketing, abusive language,
impersonating an officer, interfering with the arrest of another."[36]
Although Texas Ranger detractors were abhorred to acknowledge,
there was not credible evidence that Captain Allee and his Company
D Rangers were actually "trying to break the strike," in light of the fact
they were sent to Starr County only to keep the peace, protecting lives
and property, no matter who they were or who it belonged to. And,
with regards to unlawfully and/or wrongly resorting to the employment of "excessive force in making arrests," the theoretical jury hung:
"If so, they infringed legal rights; if not, they merely enforced the laws
then on the books."[37] What, in the end, transpired was not a mistrial.
Right or wrong, good or bad, in general DPS and, in particular, the
Texas Rangers felt the sting and discoloration of a PR punch black-eye.

There would be landmark court cases and even rulings by the
United States Supreme Court that were critical and condemning,
questioning the propriety of using Rangers as buffers between organized laborers and corporate executives or when low-wage workers
were conscientiously pondering or being pushed into unionizing.
Really, some folks were questioning, was it any business of Rangers
when and/or if contract negotiations fizzled into intractable stale-
mates? Certainly DPS management was looking for a resolution.
The upper echelon was growing sick and tired of tainted publicity.
For sure, one Texas Ranger had an answer and an attitude. During
discussions about the Lower Rio Grande Valley farm strike with a
political friend, Texas State Senator Don Kennard of Fort Worth, an
always opinionated and not shy Captain Allee said: "Son, this is the
goddamndest thing I've ever been in." [38]

And those strident but salient remarks more or less bring the story around full circle. Like it or not, times were changing: a new age of societal and workplace enlightenment. With regards to the soon to retire Company D Captain, Texas Ranger Rudolfo Rodriguez hammered the coffin's last nail of transitional times overtaking an iconic institution both blessed and blighted and sometimes blinded by deep-rooted tradition: "He [Allee] was an outstanding captain, a good captain back in his time. He worked with a rough element and I didn't think he was so rough with them. The whole country was changing, and bless his heart, Cap tried to change. But he was from the old school and he didn't know how to."[39]

Brand-new Texas Ranger Jack Dean was from a different school, a different age. As he drove south, motoring back towards McAllen, Chief Ray's words ricocheted like a BB in a boxcar. Jack Dean's head was spinning: "I don't give a damn if you ever make an arrest!" What did the Chief mean? Jack Dean was now a Texas Ranger and Texas Rangers were supposed to make arrests, weren't they? Time and distance kept rolling by as Ranger Jack Dean was traversing the fascinating and lonely and rattlesnake-infested Wild Horse Desert, that expansive chunk of Texas real-estate south of an imaginary line strung between parched Laredo and breezy Corpus Christi. From a scholarly notion Dean's familiarity with South Texas history was but that of layperson. On the other hand, he was and always had been somewhat gripped by the Lone Star State's saga. He was a voracious reader of Texas history, especially about the so-called blood and thunder era. So as he checked off miles his mind skipped back and forth.

Although he couldn't recite chapter and verse about all of the badness that had taken place, Jack Dean knew well that the region he was traveling was steeped in Wild West-type history, those exhilarating stories that kept readers turning pages. He knew, of course, about the time Mexican bandits attacked some store just west of Corpus Christi (in Nuecestown), burned it to the ground, and killed several folks during their raid from south of the Texas/Mexico border, some 150 horseback miles away.[40] As he journeyed farther south from Alice, west of Kingsville, he remembered hearing about

Mexican outlaws Andres Davila and Hipolito Tapai and their gang of cutthroats attacking a store on the Gulf Coast's Baffin Bay, where they callously murdered four fellows, stealing clothes, whiskey, and the store's cashbox, before they were tracked down by a mean-eyed posse and hanged following Nueces County courtroom convictions.[41] Texas Ranger Jack Dean rolled south at a clip—the highway cutting straight through part of the well-known King Ranch—an empire he would soon become more than familiar with, though he knew not at the time he was burning miles back toward McAllen. As he got deeper and deeper into the Lower Rio Grande Valley he recalled that during 1875 another Texas Ranger, some guy named McNelly, had shown not an iota of sympathy and resorted to extreme actions, piling up dead bodies during a firefight and having them hauled to Brownsville and dumped into a heap as a not subtle warning to banditos on the far side of the river at Matamoros, State of Tamaulipas.[42] Nearing his new post of duty, though the finer points were not committed to memory, Jack Dean recalled that during the early 1900s during the Mexican Revolution epoch, specific Rangers had cleaved unto themselves a pretty unsavory reputation; a ranking not erroneously awarded for acts of murder, mayhem, and madness; perhaps the darkest time-period in their institutional history. Too, he summoned up something, vaguely, about that same timeframe, regarding a foolhardy and ghastly story vis-à-vis *El Plan San Diego*, wherein Mexicans and *Tejanos* were conspiring to compulsorily detach Texas and other states from America, and then summarily execute all Anglo males over the age of sixteen years.[43] The Lower Rio Grande Valley's borderland twentieth-century history was dripping with bloody narratives of derailing trains, sabotaging trestles, dynamiting infrastructure, plundering stores, executions—torture and terrorism—raids and retaliation.[44] And had not at that very setting Jack and Janie and the kiddos would call home, Hidalgo County, a sheriff, at an earlier time while serving as a duly commissioned Ranger, shot and killed two Hispanic brothers during standalone episodes—one of whom was yet a teenager, purportedly wholly unsuspecting and totally unarmed?[45]

That was the past, this was now. And what in the heck was all this noise about mad Mexican American farm laborers and their disgruntlement with Texas Rangers—the hearings, lawsuits, and verbal spankings newspapermen, radio, and television commentators were freely distributing to anyone who would but read or listen or watch. Were Captain A.Y Allee and the three other Company D Texas Rangers really named defendants? It was well after dark when Jack Dean, bushed and baffled, finally pulled his newly assigned unmarked sedan, Unit PO-643, a 1970 Plymouth, into the driveway at 1204 Tamarack, cutting off the car's headlights.[46] It was then the light came on! The bulb in his psyche had switched from befuddlement to understanding, shining brightly on Chief Ray's instructions, those words about *getting along* taking priority over simply thumping heads and handcuffing ne'er-do-wells.

Ranger Jack Dean's first-line-supervisor for the short-go would be Texas Ranger Sergeant John Mansel Wood, then fifty-six years of age, with DPS for twenty-eight years and a Ranger for twenty-one. Ironically, Sergeant Wood owned the in-house distinction of being a Ranger sergeant twice—by competitive examinations! "He was first promoted to sergeant in 1955; however, the promotion meant a transfer from Midland. He accepted a demotion back to Ranger and stayed in Midland. In 1957, when the Rangers reorganized their districts and headquarters for Company 'E' was placed in Midland, he was again promoted to sergeant," where he stayed until 1967. Then, leaving West Texas in the rearview mirror, he transferred into Company D, accepting the posting at Corpus Christi. The scuttlebutt really wasn't idle gossip; when Captain Allee retired Sergeant John M. Wood would move up the career ladder and accept command of Company D. In the meantime he would remain at his assigned Gulf Coast station.[47] Adhering to proper protocol and not jumping the gun by not showing the proper deference, Sergeant Wood instructed Ranger Jack Dean to immediately make the trip to Carrizo Springs, respectfully, seeking the wise counsel and good practical advice from Company D Commander A.Y. Allee, even if the famous captain was a short-timer.

Though he'd been back at McAllen but two days, on the morning of 3 September 1970, at 5:30 a.m., Texas Ranger Jack Dean set off on his jaunt to confer with the legendary captain. Four hours later, after covering 235 miles, halfway point of the day's roundtrip, Jack Dean understood why Rangers were enamored with the cussing and cigar-chomping cedar-stump of a man.[48] With less than a week on the job, Captain Allee treated Jack Dean with the respect due a veteran Texas Ranger. He would have it no other way than to drive Jack out to the ranch for a visit and meet the love of his life, Miss Pearl, his now retired school-teaching wife. The trip to the ranch north of town was uneventful—much to Jack Dean's relief. Riding with the grizzled captain was, as Jack Dean found out, an experience. The farther he got out of town the heavier the captain's foot pressed the accelerator, unbridling the state's under-the-hood horsepower. To Ranger Dean it surely seemed the faster the car went, the less attention Captain Allee paid to the windshield, unconsciously chewing the stogie, expressively turning his head and deliberately conversing with his new-hire about everyday Ranger business and vicious desperadoes he might encounter in the Lower Rio Grande Valley. At the ranch, in the presence of Miss Pearl, Captain Allee's rawness and characteristic earthiness gave way to gentlemanly words and docile behavior—so Jack Dean noticed as he partook of genuine hospitality and Miss Pearl's delectable lunch. Subsequent to retuning to Carrizo Springs—with newfound knowledge about "weekly and case reports"—the awestruck Jack Dean set sail for McAllen. Arriving at seven o'clock in the evening, Jack Dean was tired but in his mind a better man.[49]

There is little doubt that rookie Texas Ranger Jack Dean had taken seriously the words of the Chief of the Criminal Division, Jim Ray. Though actually on duty in the Rio Grande Valley but a short time, the personnel appraisal for a greenhorn Texas Ranger was terrific:

> Dean is a new man and has established a good relationship and good image with good citizens in the Valley. He gets along well with other officers and is an asset to the Texas Rangers. With supervision and instruction he will become an outstanding Ranger and promote better relationships with the public.[50]

5

"Cocked and locked"

Texas Ranger Jack Dean, to scrounge the phrase, hit the ground running. But a cursory glance at his first few months' work is informative. He immediately conferred with McAllen's Police Chief Clint Mussey and Detective Boyd Guilford regarding a homicide investigation. Ranger Dean had inherited a genuine whodunit. The unwarranted offense had happened exactly one month prior to Jack Dean becoming a Texas Ranger. Twenty-five-year-old nighttime clerk George Edward Crawford had been murdered—execution style—inside the walk-in cooler at a McAllen 7-11 Convenience Store. The murder weapon was a .22 caliber and there were no eyewitnesses, save the killer or killers.[1] Thoughtfully, Texas Ranger Jack Dean composed a letter to Worth Seaman, Manager of the DPS's MO (*Modus Operandi*) Section, asking that investigative files of similar crimes be researched, mined for meaningful clues.[2] Then, at Edinburg, the county seat, Jack Dean formally introduced himself to the multi-term Hidalgo County Sheriff, Claudio Castaneda and his stalwart Chief Deputy, Ray Rogers. The committed lawmen "cut up business," discussing investigative problems and open cases. At Mission, due west of McAllen, he met with Police Chief Tony Peña about criminality in his city—and that afternoon had an insightful meeting with DPS Intelligence Agent Donald L. "Don" Lee regarding "information on militant persons and organizations" in the Lower Rio Grande Valley. By the end of the week he was involved in a jail-break manhunt at Edinburg and was by Saturday back near Austin: a

"Special Detail," upholding "Law and Order" at the Bastrop pop festival.[3] It was a whirlwind. That nonstop activity consumed week one, not even counting the tiring full-day trip to Carrizo Springs and the enjoyable and edifying lunch with Captain Allee.[4]

The following week he met with a District Judge and an Assistant District Attorney, hunted for the jailhouse escapees, and at Brownsville, Cameron County, had a huddle with Chief of Police Gus O. Krause, before he dropped everything to help out another Ranger on one of those aforementioned collateral investigations—wherein that work took precedence over his own. After locating folks and conducting the requisite interviews he forwarded written reports of same to Ranger Bob Favor at Brady, who was anxiously awaiting the outcome.[5]

On Sunday, 13 September 1970, Jack Dean was called at home, and asked by the Mayor, City Councilmen, and Police Chief Peña at Mission to help them with the investigation of an episode of "large scale vandalism." The bad behavior centered on a "series of brick throwing incidents." Someone was obviously holding and acting on a grudge, bricks being hurled through glass windows on four separate occasions at attorney Neal King's office. The town's local newspaper, the *Mission Times*, likewise had been targeted for four nighttime incidents. Somewhat lucky it seems, at Carl's Minimax and the Walsh Lumber Company the brick thrower chunked but once. Dean took two statements from witnesses and interrogated a suspect. The next day he discussed the case with the fifty-four-year-old District Attorney Oscar McInnis, a native Texan from the tiny hamlet of Fred, Tyler County, and a WWII era Navy veteran.[6]

While the DA was mulling over that evidence, Ranger Dean struck out for Corpus Christi with a suspect in tow. He had scheduled an appointment with DPS Polygraph Operator Ed DeSha regarding the armed robbery and murder at the McAllen 7-11 Convenience Store. Amid all this, Ranger Dean received information regarding an illicit gambling operation, and conferred with Sheriff Castaneda regarding that intelligence, cautiously blueprinting plans for a covert and close-to-the-vest investigation. Then Jack Dean's investigations were, again, pushed to the backburner while he took up the causes of two collateral investigations: One for Texas Ranger Stuart Dowell of Company B at Dallas, the other for Ranger Glenn B. Krueger, Company D, at Beeville, near the halfway point between Corpus Christi and San Antonio. Ranger Jack Dean also, somehow, found the time to confer about criminal matters with the police chief at Weslaco, Harold George. And by week's end he was headed back to Corpus Christi, this time with two possible witnesses to the 7-11 murder and armed robbery. Back at McAllen, Jack Dean pulled into town just in time to accompany Detective Bob Jefferies on a fresh felony theft investigation and the passing of a couple of $100 bills, which could possibly be part of the booty taken in the theft. That was Friday, this was Saturday. In response to a request from the local Justice of the Peace at San Juan, Roy Trevino, due east of McAllen, Texas Ranger Jack Dean was on the QT updated with regards to several gambling operations that were active in Alamo and Pharr-San Juan. These were places with casino-type gaming tables, allegedly. How could they be operating without at least some local officer or officers looking the other way, so pondered the judge. Texas Ranger Jack Dean promised he would—as soon as he had time—look into the matter.[7]

Ever gracious to his band of Rangers, Captain Allee invited the whole of Company D to his ranch north of Carrizo Springs for a celebratory wingding, a farewell party. Naturally the affair could be and would be billed as a company meeting. The feisty old captain, forced out of service due to a sixty-five-year age curb, revealed a touch of sentimentality: "I would like to get one more picture of all Rangers in Company 'D' and bid them adue [sic]. This is the only way and time I have to do it in and hope you, your family and/or wives can attend." A latter sentence neatly exposes that this ostensible Company D meeting was, well, "not compulsory, but a wish."[8] Even though he was a new kid on the block—the Lower Rio Grande Valley—and on the job less than a month, Ranger Jack Dean, deferentially and wisely replied: "My family and I will be proud to attend the company meeting at your home. . . ."[9]

At Edinburg and after consultation with District Attorney McInnis, Jack Dean kept diligently working on a major forgery investigation with multiple offenders. Then he conferred with Chief Deputy Rogers regarding a possible polygraph examination for a murder suspect. After that it was off to Corpus Christi where he obtained written confessions from the principal suspect in the forgery investigation; in one, the paper-hanger implicated his step-father as a coconspirator. While at Corpus Christi, Texas Ranger Dean too, attained bullet samples from 22 cal. handgun in a Corpus Christi murder for matching to the bullets recovered in George Crawford's homicide. The next day, at Edinburg, Texas Ranger Dean obtained an arrest warrant for one of the suspects in the forgery investigation, before he called on Acting Police Chief Raul Garza for a sit-down discussing criminality in his area. The next day, after interviewing witnesses with regards to the ongoing homicide investigation, he also checked on possible agitators passing out leaflets for a rally at McAllen. The following day, back at Corpus Christi, Ranger Jack Dean executed his arrest warrant—and locked up one of the forgery suspects. Then on Saturday, 26 September 1970, it was time make a courteous appearance at Captain Allee's last Company D "meeting" which he did, returning to McAllen at 12:00 Midnight.[10]

As the month of September 1970 was fading away, Texas Ranger Jack Dean, aside from following up on his forgery and murder investigations, met with Chief of Police Mussey; rumors of big trouble were brewing. There was the possibility of a "civil disturbance" set to take place and knock the local school board meeting out of whack. Hispanic-oriented organizations like the Mexican American Youth Organization (MAYO), United Farm Workers, and La Raza Unida were dead set on addressing and resolving—one way or the other—their communal grievances: be they solidly grounded and genuine or simply perceived to be extant. Ranger Jack Dean, a professional peace officer, had no dog in the hunt. That night, though the school board meeting was very, very, well attended, Ranger Dean absent an ounce of condescension or six-shooter arrogance, self-assuredly circulated through the throng, and with an easygoing demeanor visited and talked and, most importantly—listened. Who was this new Ranger in town—a levelheaded and soft-spoken and, apparently, no-nonsense fellow? He wasn't barking commands and scowling, gruffly ordering attendees to do this or do that. To be sure, his over-all deportment foreshadowed that he was friendly and fair-minded. Too, his composure also suggested that testing him with purposeful acts of misconduct and/or unlawfulness would be very imprudent. Thankfully, at about 10:00 p.m. the school board meeting ended and the gathering of concerned folks disbursed—maybe not happily, but peaceably.[11]

And herein it is germane to mention a sometimes misunder-stood dynamic of good policing: the interplay between lawmen and lawyers. America's practice of impartial criminal justice is built around an adversarial system. Theoretically two sides competing—defense lawyers and prosecuting attorneys—within the framework of a written Code of Criminal Procedure will, in the end, yield an objective and truthful verdict. Too, as the nonaligned and neutral arbitrator, a judge "stands above the fight as a disinterested party," an umpire of sorts calling fair or foul.[12] Anyway, that's the presump-tion. Unfortunately, there is room for and there are miscarriages of justice, but competent investigative and evidence-gathering work on the part of those sworn to serve and protect is the doorway to the defendants' destiny. The final verdict will register as *Guilty* or *Not Guilty*, but never is a verdict of *Innocent* returned. The state's attor-ney, who has the burden of proof Beyond a Reasonable Doubt, will either make the prosecutorial grade—or not! Good lawmen have nothing to fear from defense attorneys, though the barristers' antics at trial sometimes register as funny and futile. In reality there is more to be gained than lost by working with a defendant's lawyer than blindly going to courtroom war with an air of downright hos-tility. As will become evident, Texas Ranger Jack Dean owned a keen knack for getting along—with victims and witnesses, informants and perpetrators, district attorneys and judges—and yes, even defense lawyers. And, for the latter instance, sometimes that no-nonsense demonstration of fair-play netted noteworthy outcomes.

Unquestionably Jack Dean had a practical sense of the boots he was filling and the positive parts of Texas Ranger tradition he was tasked with maintaining. Too, and it did not escape his notice, especially since he was an armchair history buff, is the fact that academic analysis could be and would be an independent and open-minded judge as to whether during his career he had performed admirably or miserably. He felt the weight of the past and the promise of the future:

> To be a Ranger, a man's gotta not only be pretty smart, but he's got to be a self-starter, a self-reliant person with a lot of common sense and able to get along very well with a lot of different people. . . . it's amazing when that [Ranger] badge is pinned on him. . . . I guess it might be peer pressure and the strong traditions of excellence among Rangers, but when a man wears this badge, it always seems to improve his demeanor and his personality.[13]

Replacing their former commander on 1 October 1970, Captain John Wood astutely and practically moved the Company D Texas Ranger headquarters to San Antonio. Headquartering at Carrizo Springs had been a concession to Captain Allee, not necessarily a convenient location. Serving as the Company D Sergeant would be the recently promoted Company A Texas Ranger from Navasota (in Anderson County), Walter August "Bob" Werner, who would likewise oversee his supervisory duties from an office in the Alamo City.[14] Geographically the Company D territory was "bounded on the north by a line generally from just below Eagle Pass at the Border, across to San Antonio and over to Port La Vaca at the coast."[15] Texas terrain south of that line, all the way to the Rio Grande/Río Bravo for Texas Ranger law-enforcing purposes belonged to Company D. A quick peek at the then-current and updated staffing pattern for the everyday working Rangers of Company D, dividing up thirty-nine of the Lone Star State's 254 counties, is fitting: Litt Truitt "Carpe" Carpenter, San Antonio; Arturo Rodriguez, San Antonio; John M. Hoff, Corpus Christi; James R. Peters, Corpus Christi; H. Joaquin

Jackson, Uvalde; William C. Nelson, Victoria; Glenn B. Krueger, Beeville; Billy J. Green, Falfurrias; Jack Van Cleve, Cotulla; Jack O. Dean, McAllen; Pedro G. "Pete" Montemayor, Laredo; and Jerome H. "Geronimo" Preiss, San Benito.[16]

For the treatment in hand and from here on out, it would be relatively uncomplicated to follow Ranger Dean's footsteps as he perambulated throughout the Lower Rio Grande Valley conducting complex and/or clear-cut and easy to wrap up criminal investigations. Thankfully, DPS and Texas Ranger bureaucracy demanded paper documentation as to just what Rangers were doing—or said they were doing—on any given day: where they had been, who they had visited with, interviewed, interrogated and/or arrested, how many hours had they worked, how many miles had they driven, and how many dollars and cents of the state's funds had they spent? Long past were the days when curt but comical Texas Ranger summations would suffice: "This morning we were fired on by Chas Small a noted desperate character and he was Killed by me."[17]

With regards to tracking Texas Ranger Jack Dean's day-by-day movements, the task is made even easier by his forethought in contemporaneously maintaining *Daily Reminder* journals to supplement the written reports and accountings required by the front office folks at Texas Ranger headquarters. Jack Dean, too, realized the inherent value in preserving Texas Ranger history. Therefore, when an opportunity arose for him to acquire DPS's all-inclusive record of his service with THP and the Texas Rangers, before an official order of destruction for that paperwork was undertaken, he jumped at the chance to save those papers for posterity. With parallel prescience Jack Dean realized that the voluminous collection of primary source documents could not be properly safeguarded by cardboard box storage inside his garage; nor if that were the course, would those records make any contribution with regards to quenching history's timeless thirst. For those reasons Jack Dean donated that wealth of data to the Anne and Tobin Armstrong Texas Ranger Research Center at the Texas Ranger Hall of Fame & Museum, as designated by the Texas State Legislature, the Official Repository for the Texas

Rangers. There the material would be and has been professionally catalogued and archived in a climate controlled atmosphere in accordance with orthodox museum standards. All that said, there is a straightforward caveat to this biographical chronicle as it unfolds: Much of what Texas Ranger Jack Dean actually did, sometimes very interesting doings, will be—must be—skipped past in deference to other equally attention-grabbing episodes.

Almost immediately after changing of the guard for Company D, Ranger Jack Dean conferred and started making plans with McAllen's Chief Mussey with regards to a protest march and rally promoted by MAYO, the United Farm Workers, and La Raza Unida. Understandably the lawmen were concerned about the potential for trouble should any radical elements from within instigate and agitate for something more than just a peaceful protest.[18] As planned the marchers marched, the protesters protested, and if there were champions for violent commotion their voices were either drowned by others' sensibleness or somewhat intimidated by the rigid police presence. Later that week, Texas Ranger Dean conferred with the area THP Lieutenant and Chief Mussey, agreeing that a combined effort at the Friday night football game would in all likelihood staunch particular agitators rumored plans. Subsequent to the referee's last blast on the whistle and the saxophone's final note, Texas Ranger Dean acknowledged: That although many known agitators had been observed, the show of force had defused any demonstrations at the football game or afterwards at the school sponsored sock hop.[19]

Plainly, he was a Texas Ranger, and Jack Dean did see himself as a Lone Star State lawman, approaching his job through those eyes. On the other hand, he was ever cognizant that carefully measuring his words and methods, while endeavoring to gather information and knowledge of future acts of any Hispanic protestors, and how best to control protest marches of the future by radical groups, could best be managed through flexible negotiation rather than an inflexible nightstick.[20] The old policing saw, "If feasible, talk first—shoot last," was sensible. Jack Dean was a smart man.

So sharp it was presumed, Ranger Dean was summoned to a meeting. The District Attorney, County Sheriff, and the new Chief of Police at Mercedes, on the eastern edge of Hidalgo County, requested that he reopen their dormant case, unraveling truths regarding an unusually brutal homicide. On the night of 5 December 1969 ,Alfredo Cavazos, Jr., aka Pee Wee, had simply disappeared. Days later Cavazos's dead body had been found floating in the Rio Grande and it was not a pretty sight. The sometimes bartender and suspected dope trafficker had suffered stab wounds near the heart and the gut had been sliced open. The murdered victim was also tied hard and fast.[21] It was, indeed, a gruesome crime, but not necessarily a shocker for borderlanders with heads not buried in the sands of complacency. There were viable allegations worth follow-up inquiries.[22] Texas Ranger Jack Dean agreed to their request, and immediately started the review process of inspecting investigative files and generating plans for conducting interviews and exploring leads.[23] As he would relatively soon discover, one gal, a purported witness to the homicide, had fled to parts unknown indisputably thinking she might be killed for what she knew.[24] Indicative of the fact that right from the get-go Texas Ranger Dean exuded confidence and confidentiality is the verity that an area lawyer was in receipt of not public knowledge about the Alfredo Cavazos homicide, an investigative lead he passed along to the Lower Rio Grande Valley's new face from the DPS.[25]

On the morning of 13 October 1970, Ranger Dean and Sheriff Castaneda traveled west, their ultimate destination being Falcon Dam on the Rio Grande. There, at that juncture connecting Starr and Zapata Counties, was a field office for the United States Customs Agency Service. Collecting and digesting intelligence regarding the murder of Alfredo Cavazos was their mission. Special Agent Joe Rizzo gladly opened files and shared his knowledge, which was wide-ranging. The premeditated homicide, Dean and Castaneda learned, spun on the same axis so familiar to borderland lawmen: the smuggling and distribution of illicit narcotics. Absent a shred of doubt, according to Agent Rizzo, the killing was in regards to a shipment of narcotics. Pee Wee Cavazos had been in way over his head, swimming with sharks in the undertow of a significant dope-moving operation. As Ranger Dean had, and would continue, to discover, there is a distinct difference between homicide investigations resulting with regards to affections of jealous barmaids and strippers and jilted spouses, and those barroom arguments fueled by too much beer and belligerence. The premeditated Cavazos homicide was a different brand of nastiness it seemed, a killing for blood-money and/or burnt feelings about splitting the spoils of criminality or being caught behind-the-scenes deal making and snitching to the "Man."

Alas, Texas Ranger Jack Dean, too, would have to circulate in the unsavory world of paranoid dope dealers, know-nothing barmaids, confidential informants with agendas driven by a desire to stay out of jail or get someone else put into jail or money—and now and then all of the above. This particular case, too, was sullied with allegations that certain physical evidence pertaining to Pee Wee Cavazos's cold-blooded murder case was missing—maybe intentionally missing—from Mercedes Police Department's property room.[26]

In but the sudden click of the Texas Ranger's radio's mike button the murder investigation stopped—temporarily! Quite out of the ordinary Texas Ranger Jack Dean was called upon by Sheriff Castaneda to meet him at the aforementioned San Juan, a congenial Hidalgo County community sited just east of McAllen. The situation was not rooted in run-of-the-mill criminality. Someone, in a defiant and deliberate act, had flown a Piper Cherokee 180, a four-place single-engine airplane, into a large church, the Basilica of Our Lady of San Juan del Valle. Deliberateness of the horrendous occurrence was confirmed by radio-traffic between the pilot and the control-tower. The warning had been weird: All Lower Rio Grande Valley area churches along a flight path were to be evacuated at once—now. Something real bad was about to happen! Not surprisingly the alarming message had been vague, impossible to understandably interpret. Bewildered folks on the ground were scrambling, but the explosion and ascending fireball pinpointed their attention. Subsequent investigation revealed the pilot to have been fifty-two-year-old Francis B. "Frank" Alexander, a former school teacher and aviation instructor. Curiously, in light of Alexander's targeting a Catholic Church and school, was the fact that his educational core specialty was centered on teaching young children of migrant farm workers. Inexplicably, although property damage was extensive, $1,500,000, on-the-ground injuries were but minimal, with no fatalities save for the haywire pilot who perished in the dramatic and bizarre suicide. Some parishioners believed the sparing of God's 200 children inside the school's cafeteria was, indeed, miraculous, an absolute and veritable Miracle. Consequent to supportive consultation with sincerely stunned church officials, Sheriff Claudio Castaneda and Ranger Jack Dean were in wholehearted agreement. The FBI, by now on the scene, and they having particularized resources, were the best suited institution to continue as the lead agency until U.S. Department of Transportation investigative personnel arrived.[27]

The previously mentioned Justice of the Peace, Roy Trevino, was in a quandary with regards to classifying a questionable death: homicide or suicide? The deceased teacher had been shot while in bed beside his wife, the apparent instrument of death lying on his chest. The JP had turned to Texas Ranger Jack Dean for help. Assuredly DPS and its vast resources, including the local Texas Ranger, could be and would be of service. Dutifully, on Saturday the thirty-first of October, Texas Ranger Dean collected death scene photographs and what was purported to be the suicide note. The following Monday, he obtained known handwritings exemplars of the deceased, and submitted them to the laboratory for comparison by the Questioned Document Section.[28]

Also at the end of October, his second month on the job, Texas Ranger Jack Dean received disturbing news. An informant passing him information regarding the Alfredo Cavazos murder investigation had been cautioned to keep quiet. It seems, if the snitch's news was spot on, Alfredo Cavazos's involvement with marijuana and heroin distribution had far-reaching tentacles, straight into Chicago, where the thriving financier called the shots—figuratively and literally.[29] Pushing his story—candidly or crookedly—the confidential source passed Ranger Dean the account of another murder that had been disguised as an auto accident fatality, which occurred within the same gang. The informant believed he could shortly gather more definitive details.[30] Within the week the informer apprised Texas Ranger Dean that the fellow from Chicago would soon be making an appearance in the Lower Rio Grande Valley—which was for real—and Jack Dean again noted for Texas Ranger headquarters consumption: That the smuggling operation tied directly into the Cavazos murder.[31]

Friday the thirteenth that November of 1970 was decidedly unlucky for a man and wife, apparently street-level dope pushers. Working in conjunction with DPS Narcotics Agents Walter McFarland and James Kellner, Texas Ranger Jack Dean helped strategize an illicit narcotics raid for that night at Weslaco. When bewitching hour came—joined by DPS Intelligence Agent Don Lee—Dean, McFarland, and Kellner safely executed the search warrant at the private residence and directly arrested the flabbergasted couple, seizing a half-dozen packets of heroin.[32] Validity of the snitch's tip had been bulletproof.

Though it is somewhat easy to throw stones from an armchair, it's true that the Rangers were on the short-side with regards to inclusive "minority" hiring practices. It's also true that upper-tier management recognized the deficit and was trying to apply Band-Aids until recruiting and testing and training remedied the societal and cultural imbalance. Company D Rangers were assigned counties with predominantly Spanish-speaking populations. Therefore it was incumbent that, at a bare minimum, Company D Texas Rangers be somewhat conversant in speaking and understanding the Spanish language. The orders were specific: "If you have not already started Spanish classes, do so at your earliest convenience. The Senior Ranger Captain [Clint Peoples] has ordered Border Patrol Handbooks for each of the rangers and they will be sent to you as soon as they are available. In the very near future, it will be a requirement that you be able to converse in Spanish, as well as English. . . ."[33]

The uneasiness of being thrust into a land where everyone spoke in a tongue foreign to one's native language exhibited itself—somewhat ingeniously—at the Dean household. Until there was a settling-in period—an assimilation period—for Janie Dean those earliest days at McAllen were to a degree somewhat lonesome, not hearing grownups speak English as she went about her daily home-making business at the supermarket, cleaners, and the five and dime store. The kids were in school during the day, and Jack worked—seemingly—all the time, day and night, and not just a few weekends. The old adage that crime takes no holiday was damn sure right; at least such was true in the Lower Rio Grande Valley. During those initial days after relocating to McAllen, an adult conversation in English for Janie Dean beat a box of chocolates any day! Texas Rangers adapt. Janie Dean was a Ranger's wife. Snowbirds, pulling travel-trailers or navigating traffic driving RVs looking like shoe-boxes, flocked to the Lower Rio Grande Valley for their home away from home during the freezing-cold white winter months that Northerners knew—and didn't like. To a shuffling man and jabbering woman they were one and all English speakers and they regularly washed their dirty clothes at campgrounds' coin-operated laundries. Although at home Janie had a washer and drier, it was much more fun to bundle the duds and mosey over to the tourists' campgrounds and enjoyably pass time with those talkative Yankees from Minnesota or Michigan or Massachusetts.[34]

An out-of-state visitor to the Lower Rio Grand Valley would not be engaged in any casual conversation with Texas Ranger Dean. The mobster from Chicago connected with the Cavazos murder—by all accounts—was scheduling his trip to McAllen. Without tipping their hand DPS Narcotics Agents, U.S. Customs Agents, and Ranger Jack Dean were coordinating their plan, which was straightforward and simple, but logistically nightmarish. They would surreptitiously place the Illinois gangster under surveillance around the clock "during his stay in the valley." Furthering the major "dope trafficking" investigation, identifying illicit contacts and, in the end, hopefully making a prosecutable "narcotics case" on the Texas side of the river was their prime objective. Establishing just which country actually hosted the Cavazos murder-site was jurisdictionally problematical, but lawfully necessary for courtroom conviction.[35]

Such international and/or intrastate criminality was knocked off Jack Dean's drawing board. McAllen's Acetylene Oxygen Company had been burglarized and Detective Bob Jefferies needed help. There were suspects—two brothers—and surveillance was called for. Purportedly, they and an associate thug had a cache of stolen firearms in Harris County, and were dead-set on moving them across the river for money.[36] Wiley Coyote may have been comically chasing after the Roadrunner but, seemingly, every lawman in Hidalgo County was metaphorically hounding after the Lower Rio Grande Valley's newest Texas Ranger. Jack Dean was a team player.

Thanksgiving may have been a welcome holiday for most folks, but not for Renato Cardenas, twenty-three, of Weslaco. Certainly not an everyday scenario for investigative Texas Rangers, but it happens: a peace officer killing someone—while not actually on the job. Whether a simple misunderstanding or something much more serious is vague, but the regrettable outcome is not. In the parking lot at Burton's Auto Supply, Cardenas and a companion, standing outside the car window of Weslaco off-duty policeman Cipriano Rodriguez, twenty-three, made their move. Cardenas reached through the open window and started slapping Officer Rodriguez while Renato's companion grabbed the policeman's arm. Cipriano may have pulled away and fell back onto the seat. While telling both of them to move back, he pulled his service pistol from the console between the front seats. Cardenas's crony stepped back, but Cardenas continued the attack.[37] Rodriguez's revolver, a .357 Magnum, was loaded all the way around, but a half and half recipe, certainly not an infrequent practice at the time. Revolvers chambered for the .357 Mangum will also accept and fire .38 Special ammunition, but not vice-versa. Rodriguez's Smith & Wesson, as the old-time saying goes, "had six beans in the wheel [the cylinder]." The first up were three Super-Vel brand .38 Specials, to be rotationally followed as the trigger was pulled by three Remington-Peters brand .357 Magnums.[38] No doubt fearing for his life, Cipriano Rodriguez, with his first-up .38 Special Super-Vel, drilled a round into Renato's upper chest. Two hours later at Knapp Methodist Hospital, Cardenas died.[39] As would be expected Chief Harold George suspended Officer Rodriguez, pending outcome of the criminal homicide or justifiable homicide investigation—and allowed that Cipriano would be free to go, subsequent to the court setting his bond at $5000, and him posting it. District Attorney Oscar McInnis wanted Jack Dean to look into the matter, interview witnesses, and make known his findings.[40] There were witnesses aplenty, and Texas Ranger Jack Dean interviewed them all, taking statements and gathering evidence for submission to the DPS Crime Lab. Particularly, one witness, a cohort of Cardenas, readily revealed that Renato might have been looking for a fight and had stated that he wanted to fight someone. Other bystanders thought Officer Rodriguez had vocally instigated the hubbub.[41] Shortly the assiduous Hidalgo County Grand Jury opted to forego bringing an Indictment charging Cipriano Rodriguez with any criminality. In their minds he had committed no crime, self-defense the logical justification for his resorting to lethal force.[42] Texas Ranger Jack Dean, as he should have, had served as but an impartial gatherer of facts and evidence, not as a predisposed advocate for either party.

Certainly since the mid-twenteith-century mark and beyond, the Texas Ranger management staff had ever been attuned to professionalizing by third-party schooling and/or continuing education. Particularly noteworthy, just the year before Jack Dean pinned on his coveted Ranger badge, Captain E.G. "Butch" Albers, Jr., soon to be Commander of Company F, had attended the FBI National Academy, the first active duty Texas Ranger to do so.[43] Closer to home and of importance to Jack Dean was the mandatory duty to be at Austin and in the classroom at the DPS Academy, bright and early on Monday morning 30 November 1970. There he would remain until the forty hours of Ranger-in-Service training were completed. Quite liberal were the allotted travel days: Sunday to get there, Saturday to get back home.[44] Texas Ranger Jack Dean certainly complied with orders and successfully completed the academic course work and field exercises, i.e., photography practice, simulated crime scene investigation, diagramming and collection of evidence, and practical combat marksmanship maneuvers on the firing range.[45]

With regards to handguns, Rangers were not restricted to but carry the DPS issued holster weapon, which at the time was a Smith & Wesson Model 19 six-shot .357 Magnum revolver. Texas Rangers were allowed leeway to carry and qualify with the shooter that suited them best, and most went for the famed Colt Model 1911 .45 autoloader, or a customized clone built on that time-proven platform.[46] The pistol was a superb man-stopper.[47] During Ranger Jack Dean's era, the majority of Texas Rangers sported one or two 1911s—not only because it was a damn fine piece of fighting hardware, but conforming to tradition was also important—something not to be sneezed at! In an earlier day Ranger Doyle Holdridge (now retired) asked the late and somewhat legendary West Texas lawman, Clayton McKinney, why he preferred the .45 caliber and the Texas Ranger's comeback was short and snappy: "because they didn't make a .46!" Holdridge went on to remark that the Colt 1911 .45 "was the gun that all others were judged by. . . . The Colt had a lot of knock-down power. . . ." [48] Texas Ranger Jack Dean was, really, sold on the merits of the .45 autoloader but sometimes along the border or when crossing into Mexico on Texas Ranger business—which was regularly then the case—he opted for a .38 Super caliber, but always a Colt and always a 1911.[49]

These particular handguns—1911s—are carried in what is commonly referred to as the "cocked and locked" mode, which to an untrained eye appears patently unsafe but in truth is not. Safety features abound.[50] But admittedly, appearances can be and in this case are deceiving. Sooner or later, at one time or another, a truly concerned citizen will all-knowingly but kind-heartedly point out to a Texas Ranger that the hammer on his/her pistol is back—in the cocked position—warning him/her that such a visibly and unintended slipup is rather dangerous. There is a stock rejoinder. With tongue in cheek, nine times out of ten, a Ranger will courteously reply: "Thank you, but if it wasn't dangerous I wouldn't be carrying it!"[51]

Before the 1970 arrival of a man captaining the sleigh and reindeer, Texas Ranger Jack Dean was again reminded that interstate criminals were just as mobile as Santa Claus. Along with Hidalgo County Chief Deputy Rogers and others, Ranger Jack Dean executed a search warrant at the Echo Motor Hotel in Edinburg. They'd tapped a goldmine! Two couples were placed under arrest: David L. Casady and James R. "Scotty" Dameron, aka Jack Hammer, and their wives. The unsmiling quartet's widely spread hometowns were illustrative of floodwaters draining, in due course coming together, and pooling in a stagnating swamp. David was from Cheyenne, Roger Mills County, Oklahoma, the far western part of the state, at the southeastern edge of the Black Kettle National Grasslands; his wife called the San Francisco, California, area home. The other gal was from Richmond, Fort Bend County, Texas, site of the horrific Jaybird/Woodpecker Feud of 1889, and Scotty Dameron was an Oklahoman, from Calera, Bryan County, just north of the Red River and six miles southwest of Durant. Legally, due to prior felony convictions in Louisiana and Arkansas, outlaw Scotty Dameron could be classed and charged as an Habitual Criminal, exposed to a life sentence, suffering in cop talk what was commonly referred to as the "Big Bitch."[52]

The court approved look-see had netted big time results: $222,250 in stolen and forged money orders and seventy-nine blank money orders. The cache of negotiable instruments had been stolen from the Hub City Bank and Trust Company, Lafayette, Louisiana. Productively eliciting information from witnesses, perpetrators, and informants is a skill-set not all lawmen own; their expertise may revolve around other attributes: forensics and the collection of evidence, or an uncanny ability to assume undercover identities with perilous performances worthy of Academy Awards. Texas Ranger Jack Dean was developing into a master interrogator—an investigator who knew what questions to ask, when to ask them, and how to keep quiet when someone wanted to blab. One of the jammed-up folks had something to say and Ranger Jack Dean had something he wanted to hear. After their little confab, an additional discovery was found at the Echo Motel, certainly now not the No Tell Motel.

It seems that Scotty Dameron had stashed twenty-seven counterfeit $100 bills under the carpet in the room's closet, bogus currency Texas Ranger Jack Dean now dutifully marked as evidence.[53] And if it was to be believed, Ranger Jack Dean's newfound friend could and would finger a fellow at Dallas in possession of stolen Treasury Bills, $2,500,000 worth, part of a larger, almost unbelievable stash of $13,000,000. Such is the honor of crooks. Lazily resorting to the lexicon of underworld characters and police officers, Ranger Dean "duked the Secret Service in on that part of the deal."[54]

Working another Saturday, Texas Ranger Dean obtained known handwriting samples from David Casady and, as well, specimens from the suspected typewriter used to imprint the stolen money orders.[55] At 4:00 a.m. on Monday, four days before Christmas, Texas Ranger Jack Dean left home transporting said evidence to the DPS Crime Lab at Austin. Afterwards on the way back through San Antonio he stopped and conferred for awhile with Captain Wood at the Company D headquarters, then tired but satisfied with the investigative accomplishments, pulled into his driveway at McAllen an hour before midnight—a short nineteen-hour day.[56]

Cracking the stolen money order caper and making arrests had been a case of terrific police work, exactly what was expected of Texas Ranger Jack Dean. Top-tier DPS brass had not sent him into the Lower Rio Grande Valley for rest and relaxation. Captain Wood had reiterated the words of Chief Ray—Jack Dean was specifically tasked with *getting along* and establishing "liaison with everybody in the Valley."[57]

Creditably Jack Dean was, even though he'd been a Texas Ranger and in the Valley but four months, doing a bang-up job at getting along and enforcing the law. Hidalgo County's top lawman had no complaints, especially after the stolen money order episode. For Sheriff Claudio Castaneda, an elected official, it was a public relations coup: "The county probably would have been flooded with stolen documents and counterfeit money. . . . Several people would have been defrauded. The information was received just in time."[58]

6

---◆---

"Stern but friendly"

Texas Ranger Jack Dean was personable. In but a reasonably short time he had gained the confidence of the Lower Rio Grande Valley's law-enforcing personnel, prosecutorial officials, and judicial officers—and a cadre of confidential sources of information. The New Year of 1971 had been ushered in with the usual string of business burglaries and bomb threats and bogus checks. Of particular note, however, for Texas Ranger Jack Dean was realization that his proximity to the Rio Grande exposed him to another cheerless dynamic of borderland criminality. Certainly high profits accompanied illicit drugs successfully smuggled into Texas, but certain commodities finding their way into Mexico also fostered its own brand of lucrative illegality. There was no insignificant traffic regarding transshipment south of the Río Bravo for such items has hard-cash American dollars, stolen vehicles—cars, trucks, big and little tractors—and guns.[1]

And of the latter, Ranger Dean was rich with hot data—if his secret snitch was on the money. There were, according to his spy, at least 1500 M-1 Grand Rifles stashed in Houston that could be had at a bargain basement price, $25 per unit—no questions asked. Purportedly it was an element of traditional Organized Crime—the Mafia—on the East Coast that was funneling the firearms into an otherwise legitimate Gulf Coast business for distribution. Somewhat earlier, according to Texas Ranger Jack Dean's confidential informant, a large shipment of .45 autoloaders had been the nucleus of another clandestine deal. Appropriately, Ranger Dean shared his newfound data with DPS Intelligence Agent Don Lee. Quite interestingly, and valuable to Special Agent Lee, was the fact that Ranger Dean's information was paralleling intelligence he was receiving from a separate and, apparently unrelated, source.[2] Ranger Dean and Agent Lee agreed to continue developing and sharing information from their informants. Although Jack Dean's investigative intentions had been righteous as rain, they were quickly to be short-circuited.

And speaking of rain: It ruined the day for Ranger Jack Dean that eighth day of January 1971. "The roadway was wet and there was a slight drizzling rain." Behind the wheel of his state-issued 1970 Plymouth, Dean, accompanied by passengers Sheriff Castaneda, Chief Deputy Rogers, and DPS MVI Patrolman Ray Shafer, were on their way to lunch. Proving that Ranger Jack Dean was but human is effortless, as were the findings of THP Patrolman Dale Johnson investigating the minor traffic accident. Though there might have been room for disagreement between two motor vehicle operators, as to just how and just why the collision happened during one of those tricky left-turn situations, the prize and penalty went to the somewhat embarrassed Texas Ranger. Dutifully, Senior Ranger Captain Clint Peoples noted in his official Fleet Accident Report that liability would be charged to the driver.[3]

On 6 February 1971 the receiver sounded at the home of Jack and Janie Dean. Even after working all day, and though it was Saturday, Jack Dean answered the 7:55 p.m. telephone call. The message would kick off one of the most significant events in Jack Dean's law-enforcing life and, it may be reasonably argued, heralded a new day for the Texas Rangers in South Texas. There was a riot underway at Pharr, just east of McAllen. Five minutes later Ranger Jack Dean had let-the-hammer-down, pedal to the metal.[4]

What he found at Pharr was most troubling. The wheels had come off. The city police department building was under siege, a fire truck's windshield had been demolished, and a militant crowd was, aimlessly it seemed, roaming the town's streets and back alleys carrying rocks and bottles. One newspaper editor allowed that "the front of the station was the scene of broken glass, hurled rocks, tear gas and discharging riot guns. Inside the station police held several dozen youths in custody."[5] In but quick time Texas Ranger Jack Dean was brought up to speed. The once peaceful MAYO demonstration had artlessly morphed into a full-scale riot. The explicit premise of the protesters' grievances were allegations of systemic police brutality on the part of Pharr's law-enforcing officers. There were, however, other irritations plaguing not just a few South Texas schoolchildren, at least according to a smattering of thoroughly committed activist adults: "The Chicanos want courses in Mexican-American culture with all students required to learn contributions made by Mexicans in Valley history. . . . Anglos run rough-shod over Mexican groups and this is institutionalized in the schools. . . . Let small Anglo children 'experience the same horror' learning Spanish that their Mexican classmates must now undergo to learn English. . . ."[6] The seesaw of social unrest—seemed perpetual.

As would be expected, competing versions of what provoked the movement from marching to maliciousness are grounded in perspectives filtered by whether one were protesting or policing. A subset of the crowd of several hundred Hispanics, on cue began hurling rocks and bottles at policemen and pelting the police department headquarters, so said besieged Chief of Police, Alfredo Ramirez. During the bedlam, after the run-amok rioters failed to cease and desist, Chief Ramirez ordered Pharr firefighters to drench the agitated crowd with water from a high-pressure hose—firemen complied. Although many taunting protestors were saturated, their spirits were not near dampened. The riot raged![7] Such an insensitive tactic fanned the indignity demonstrators underwent, sustaining their main point and hardening their resolve—so claimed the fuming discordant voice of one demonstrator, a paid political organizer and ardent activist.[8] His version of events was somewhat different from that of Chief Ramirez. The wholesale hurling of hard stones and empty beer bottles was plainly a direct result of, not the precursor for an uncalled for, drenching by city employees. Outlooks often are at odds—markedly in clement South Texas for that period. There was at the time—and would be later—that ever finicky query: Which came first, the drenching or the brickbats?

Anyway, by and large, Pharr police personnel were hunkered prisoners in their own Bastille. Such was the case by the time Texas Ranger Jack Dean arrived at Pharr. Credibility or lack thereof of the angry protestors' allegations, at the time, meant little difference to Ranger Dean. Restoring order and ultimately prosecuting lawbreakers was his top priority. And disorder there was aplenty, as Texas Ranger Jack Dean right away discovered:

> I came in on North Cage going South into Pharr. I observed a large number of people up and down the street in the business section where all the bars are in Pharr. As I came behind the police station, I observed quite a few officers, a couple of fire trucks, a lot of shouting. I could hear some breaking glass. Of course, as I got out of the car and got closer, I could see every once in awhile there would be some type of missile thrown toward the police station, either rocks or some bottles.[9]

Quite expectedly, law enforcement personnel from nearby jurisdictions began pouring into Pharr. Peace officers from McAllen, Edinburg, and San Juan hurried to the volatile scene of havoc. Generally they were deputy sheriffs and municipal policemen. However, in this instance there was also a rather healthy showing by DPS patrolmen from surrounding stations, all under command of THP Sergeant S.M. Moxley, a salty and plain-spoken veteran, one well versed in putting the clamps on loud-mouthed and belligerent behavior.[10]

At the time, whether he realized it or not, Jack Dean was standing at the precipice separating customary Texas Ranger practice of bygone days and more progressive thinking for dealing with activists' orchestrated furors. Captain A.Y. Allee had retired; DPS had buried a frame of mind. Though he didn't have time to focus on anything but the job at hand, not worrying about political repercussions or in-house criticism, Ranger Dean's actions could prove to be a true watershed moment—not only for his personal career but for institutional viability of the Rangers as well. Psychologically Texas Ranger

Jack Dean was bent more toward being cool and collected, rather than excitable and scatterbrained. Dean would fight, but much preferred palavering to fisticuffs. At tumultuous Pharr that night of 6 February 1971, genuine levelheadedness would be the prescription for preservation, safeguarding lives and property.

More or less taking charge, but in consultation with Sergeant Moxley and other departmental commanders, Texas Ranger Jack Dean began organizing forces for the first order of business, which was "to try and clear the people from directly in front of the police station." From time to time someone would "periodically run out of the dark and throw rocks at any policemen or firemen who moved and at the building itself." Yes, that was the first order of business. Marshaling manpower, the responding lawmen were divided into two separate forces, both intent on clearing the streets leading to and from the police station. Texas Ranger Dean, himself, was struck by a flying "missile of some type, a rock," he believed. Besides being struck and having to duck the occasional bombardment, Texas Ranger Dean also noted: "During this sweep, the people from various bars along the street, there were quite a few, were milling around, quite a few people seemed to be intoxicated or partially so, a lot of verbal abuse, we just tried to tell them to go on and tried to clear them out." Yet not everybody on the street was in a compliant mood: "we would get rocked and every once in awhile somebody would throw a bottle. Several people that were partially intoxicated, I would say, gave us some verbal abuse and refused to move. At this time we had decided to close all the bars and as we went by a bar, we were going in and asking them to turn out the lights and told everybody to leave. Also, every time we saw anybody standing in the street, we ordered them to clear the area." Troubling too, was another unnerving reality: intermittently the sound of gunfire had punctuated the riotous uproar at Pharr.[11] "I did not see anyone fire any weapons. I did hear earlier in the night when we were at the P.D. some small arms fired. I would say smaller than anything policemen would be carrying. To me it sounded like a .22, short crack, there were three, four, five of these reports when we were at the police station and I am nearly sure before we made any sweep. . . ."[12]

But there was more troubling news to ingest. Alfonso Loredo Flores, twenty-two (or twenty in other reports), lay dying on the sidewalk, flat on his back, profusely leaking blood, hands in his pants' pockets, a ghastly and ragged injury into the top of his head below blood-matted hair. A sizeable rock was nearby—within two feet. With an ambulance already on disaster standby, Texas Ranger Jack Dean personally observed emergency personnel place the unconscious Flores onto the gurney and set sail for the trauma center at McAllen General Hospital. Though Ranger Dean was later apprised that Flores had been transferred to Valley Baptist Hospital, the surgeons tried—valiantly—but their coordinated optimal efforts, in the end, were sorrowfully ineffective: Alfonso Loredo Flores died. That compounded Texas Ranger Jack Dean's duty. Once the riot was brought under control, and surely it would be sooner or later, he had another death-investigation on his heaped-high investigative plate.[13]

In the meantime there were tempers to cool and stability to restore. The demonstrators had been effectively swept from in front of the police station, but pent-up restlessness prevented many Pharr residents—primarily the younger set—from simply going home, jumping into bed, catching a forty wink *siesta* before sunlight. Agitation was fermenting. According to at least one account, "The mob leaders were holed up in a building," and the enraged Chief Alfredo Ramirez "intended to arrest them all."[14] Already, if the newspaper account reflects accurate numbers, twenty-three adults and eight juveniles were ensconced inside the little police station at Pharr.[15] Other arrests seemed eminent if judiciousness didn't materialize. Assuredly there had not been a media blackout, for inside the police stationhouse at Pharr was none other than Don Mallory, the news director for KGBT-TV at Harlingen, from neighboring Cameron County. He was an eyewitness from the outset. And, he had been there reporting "when the demonstration turned to violence."[16]

And it's perhaps at this moment that the calculated optimism of DPS's Colonel Speir and Chief Ray were realized. Texas Ranger Jack Dean, in assessing the situation at hand, wisely counseled Chief Ramirez that restraint might prove more beneficial in the long run than bravado. The city was a powder-keg, the fuse was short, and the eruption of more violence was sure to be a byproduct of wading into an already militant crowd, swinging nightsticks and flinging tear-gas grenades. John Wayne and Rangers of a different era may have done it that way, but realistically times had changed—smart lawmen changed with them. Did they really need to increase the jail population? Already, so it was reported, other area departments were helping out, housing some of those noncompliant folks arrested at Pharr.[17] Overcrowding jailhouses guaranteed its own nightmares for police administrators and county sheriffs. And, besides that, hadn't one fellow already been killed, two firemen and one policemen injured, not counting the more-or-less minor bruises and scrapes and knots on the head suffered by other intrepid first-responders?[18] Would they have to resort to deadly force for the next go-round, pulling .45s and .357s and 12 gauges? Pragmatically a noble Hidalgo County Grand Jury's after indictment warrants could issue—sometime after the fervor and fever of discontent and sincere frustration had somewhat cooled. Astutely, after giving it a second thought, Chief Alfredo Ramirez acquiesced; averting violence was also a part of his sworn duty. What had to be done would get done—safely for everyone concerned—and in due time.[19]

Suggesting that overnight tempers cooled at Pharr would simply be fraudulent. The embers of smoldering social discontent were in and around town, susceptible to reigniting into another full-blown conflagration with but a spark of agitation. The situation, to put it mildly, was tense. The protestors—and in some case rioters—grievances real and/or imagined had not been resolved. There were purposeful activists championing causes, exonerating lawlessness in the name of overdue societal change. Purportedly city officialdom at Pharr was in purchase-order process of requisitioning "riot equipment."[20] Ranger Jack Dean owned enough savvy to recognize communal volatility against the backdrop of more than a handful of clear-cut unlawful offenses. Neither could be excusably ignored. Diplomacy would have to—hand-in-glove—accompany any prosecutorial proceedings. Wisely, Ranger Jack Dean sought counsel from District Attorney McInnis. There were many potential defendants and a multitude of criminal charges to choose from—and an actual homicide investigation to untangle. By this time—short as it was—DA McInnis had discerned that Texas Ranger Jack Dean did not solely depend on brute and brawn to accomplish his objectives. Yes, he had a cocked and locked Colt 1911 .45 at his hip, but Jack O. Dean's savoir-faire was inherent, exceptional, and evident. The Rangers' new face in the Lower Rio Grande Valley owned skill-sets worthy of trust and confidence. Therefore, the district attorney wanted—and requested—that Texas Ranger Dean and DPS be the lead agency with regards to investigating and preferring charges against those exhibiting wholly illegal and riotous behavior, as well as deciphering just how and just who was responsible for the death of Alfonso Loredo Flores.[21] Though the tasks really seemed somewhat insurmountable, Ranger Dean began his multipronged criminal investigation—at the same time smoothly salving festering passions—or trying to—an approach that did not go unnoticed by Hidalgo County folks that were paying attention, which equated to everybody.

According to at least one newspaper report, picking up details from an Associated Press dispatch from Pharr, reason was beginning to take hold and, in large part due to a DPS lawman: "Texas Ranger Jack Dean told two priests who visited the police station that remnants of the mob could go home in small groups without fear of molestation by cruising police."[22]

Remembering that these were the days before such conventions as federal laws limiting time spent at the workplace is germane. Good investigators followed leads into the night if necessary and Jack Dean was a good Texas Ranger. Such restrictive foolishness as a forty-hour workweek was unheard of—not when there was evidence to be gathered and folks to be interviewed while recollections were yet fresh and, in some instances, before prospective criminal defendants had time to cunningly align their stories. As but a relevant example, subsequent to the Pharr disorder, during the first week, Ranger Jack Dean's *Daily Reminder* registered 100 hours of investigative time—there were no eight-hour days and no days off. Admissible evidence, written statements and/or Miranda compliant voluntary confessions—all within the Code of Criminal Procedure framework—are obligatory for placing alleged defendants on the criminal justice conveyor-belt. Simply saying he/she "did it" is insufficient.[23] And though at the very first, the brouhaha at Pharr might have qualified as a case of One Riot, One Ranger, such hyperbole was short-lived. By Monday night, 8 February 1971, Texas Ranger Sergeant Bob Werner and Texas Ranger Glenn B. Krueger, were at Pharr lending a helping hand—for a few days. There was plenty of work before them, namely locking down eyewitness testimony and coordinating contingency plans for any further eruption of property destruction and physical injury—or deaths.[24]

Examining subsequent primary-source documents reveals that Texas Ranger Jack Dean was swept into a whirlwind of activity, even seeing to it that a DPS pilot and observer made overhead photos of Pharr. The city's mayor had coordinated with the THP Lieutenant with regards to calling out the Texas State National Guard. Not surprisingly, this caught Texas Ranger headquarters somewhat off guard. Texas Ranger Jack Dean—amid all the other duties—was ordered to check into the matter and make his personal assessment known. Sidelining criminal investigative matters—Ranger Dean gauged the necessity for a hefty manpower buildup solely dedicated for keeping the peace. In Jack Dean's finite estimation there was, at least at that time, no need to call on military forces, and he so advised Senior Ranger Captain Clint Peoples.[25] Sometimes there is truly a fine-line between a show of force and a show of too much force. Occasionally, if one was not prudent, unintended consequences could spill forth. Ranger Dean was levelheaded. The community's underlying mood was volcanic.

With regards to the general public's and news-media's interest, likely flashpoints were near: The funeral of Alfonso Loredo Flores and a subsequently scheduled protest march. Texas Ranger Jack Dean was in receipt of covert information from a reliable and confidential source that the "Hidalgo County Courthouse would be bombed to draw law officers away from the Pharr demonstration. . . ."[26] And furthermore, according to Texas Ranger Jack Dean's spy, he and

Sheriff Claudio Castaneda had been "marked" though he couldn't definitively affirm or "elaborate on what 'marked' meant."[27] Sheriff Castaneda cancelled his deputies' days off.[28] Pharr Police Chief Alfredo Ramirez tactically issued "'military flack jackets' to his men, called in reinforcements from neighboring cities and asked [owners of] bars and grocery stores not to sell beer after sundown. . . ."[29] Staying within character, Texas Ranger Jack Dean brokered a meeting with MAYO spokesman Efrain Fernandez, attorney David Hall representing the United Farm Workers, John Hart, and Father Mike Allen, Catholic Chaplain, Pan American University. Understandably, the frank but cordial discussions focused on activists and demonstrators remaining peaceful and lawful during the upcoming protest march and mass meeting, as well as lawmen's professional duty to act with decorum and respect—and restraint.[30] Defusing impending catastrophe with words—or trying to—was much easier and more desirable than cleaning up public relation messes and mopping up blood in Pharr's streets after-the-fact. Constructively Texas Ranger Dean coordinated with all factions, and they effectively blueprinted a strategy wherein protestors would enlist their own voluntary "cordon of parade marshals" to make sure that "everybody cools it."[31] Certainly the Catholic Chaplain took note of Texas Ranger Jack Dean's efforts: "During the days preceding the march in Pharr, Texas, he willingly communicated with groups from both sides of the political sphere and for this reason I believe that he opened doors which were never before opened to some of our Mexican-American youths."[32] By any stretch of the imagination Texas Ranger Jack Dean was not perfect—but he was sensible and inclined to temper his actions by wrangling with words before going to war in the streets.

Texas Ranger Dean, too, was in receipt of intelligence that not just a few, 200-plus, folks from outside the Lone Star State were already at Pharr, sympathizers and possibly mischievous militants "from such scattered points as California, Arizona, and New Mexico, with more still coming in."[33] Just within boundaries of Texas, according to Efrain Fernandez, MAYO chapter members in Waco, San Antonio, Corpus Christi, and Mathis, had been invited to make their presence known—and felt—at Pharr, as well as an extended invitation to NAACP membership throughout the state.[34] The tightrope between peace and pandemonium could snap with the first toss of a protestor's rock, or the first swing of a policeman's baton.

The old adage about hoping for the best but preparing for the worst was not a message lost on Lower Rio Grande Valley lawmen. For hungry newspapermen hounding after scraps for the morning and evening editions' deadlines, Sheriff Castaneda confided:

> police at Mercedes, Weslaco, Alamo, Edinburg and Pharr and sheriff's deputies have all been placed on stand-by alert. . . . a McAllen Police Department fogger, which sprays tear gas, will be [would be] available. The fogger, the only one in the Valley, is equivalent to 50 men. . . . a helicopter will be available for observation purposes, if needed. . . . Two Texas Rangers will be on hand [Jack Dean and Captain John Wood], plus 32 Department of Public Safety officers, including a squad from Corpus Christi.[35]

While subsurface possibilities for bloodshed and property destruction were indeed real, the planned protest march came off without a serious hitch or overt—unlawful—acts of hostility. Texas Ranger Jack Dean's spirit of understanding and cooperation with activists and their desire to be heard absent an unwanted and expensive ticket to the county's calaboose, was a refreshing change in traditional theatrics from both camps, peacekeepers and protestors. From the splintery wooden floor of a "flat-bed field truck," a Roman Catholic priest associated with the Texas Conference of Churches fanned collective discontent: "We're here to protest the way we've been treated here and to defend ourselves." With regards to the fact that rumors were circulating that various merchants had armed themselves with "high-powered rifles" to protect their business houses during the protest march, a rep from the United Farm Workers Organizing Committee chided: "Look what they've spent on guns and ammunition—they should have taken that money and given it to the poor people." One of the protest's outspoken organizers was campaigning for an economic boycott: "This is the only weapon we have. Shop someplace else, but don't shop with them," he harangued to the "predominantly Spanish speaking crowd."[36] Understandably strident voices—rightly or wrongly—capture the attention of media correspondents.

Doubtless Jack Dean was building a good name for himself in the Lower Rio Grande Valley. The mayor of Pharr—the city torn by riot, protests, and death—recognized the calming but firm touch that the Ranger was having on municipal affairs. It was a reassuring Texas Ranger approach, one heretofore somewhat unknown by a sizeable segment of the Hispanic population. Mayor R.S. Bowe particularly noted: "the mere presence of Ranger Dean has prevented in several case the possibility of instances similar to the riot here in February of this year. Several times he has asked that order be called in City Commission meetings that he attends at the request of the City Commissioners. As representative of the people of Pharr I want to express appreciation for Ranger Dean, and the smooth and intelligent manner in which he handles situations such as mentioned above. He also has been able to keep a certain amount of communication open between our local police department and the militant group, which has been most helpful." Admiringly city officials gifted Dean with an engraved Colt Python revolver.[37]

Solidifying his positive standing in the jittery community is buttressed by two dynamics. Jack Dean, from an investigative perspective, would—as should be—simply let the chips fall where they may. In his own words Ranger Dean—even with a few fog of war discrepancies—said:

> This incident began several weeks ago with the arrest of several pickets, picketing the Pharr Police Department. There seems to have been no reason for the arrest other than that the Mayor ordered it because they were against him. The charges were later dismissed, but the pickets have filed suit in Federal Court.
>
> Last week MAYO and United Farm Workers again raised a loud cry for two drunks who were arrested by Pharr Police. They accused the officers of brutality of these two.
>
> On Saturday, February 6, the pickets were again at the City Hall and Police Department. This began at 10:00 AM and was

peaceful all day. As dark approached the crowd grew and became loud and began using obscene language. The Chief of Police asked the leader of the pickets. . . . to quiet his people. He said that he couldn't and gave the raised fist sign. At this time rocks began to fly and several firemen and at least one police officer were struck. Fire hoses were used and only added to the fury.

The Chief then called for help from the State, County and several nearby Cities. After we arrived I observed several hundred persons milling around on the main street. Rocks were being thrown from alleys and dark corners at any officer that they could see. Cars coming down the street would throw rocks and bottles.

A group of officers moved the people from the side of the main street near the Police Department and from alleys and yards nearby. The rioters then moved across the main drag and continued to throw rocks. Again a sweep was made on both sides of the street. This broke up the main body and only a few individuals caused any more trouble.

It appears that the rock throwing was not spontaneous. Rocks used had to be brought to the scene, they could not have been found there. There were 31 arrest made, all for disorderly conduct. There were reports of snipers, but I did not see nor hear any myself. Police officers did fire several shots, but no one was believed shot. The only serious injury was a young man standing in front of a bar. He was first believed to have been struck in the head by a rock. This young man died Sunday, February 7. . . .

Attorney David Hall and three priests arrived about 11:00 PM and asked for a conference and Chief Ramirez of Pharr, Chief Gonzales of Edinburg talked to them and they stated that the riot leaders wanted to call the riot off. They were advised that their people would not be molested and asked that they just send them home. By 1:00 PM the streets were quiet and most officers were released.[38]

Complementing the fact evenhandedness was paramount, the state's prosecutor had confidence with regards to Ranger Jack Dean's facility for keeping those things secret that were supposed to be kept secret—i.e. just who was saying just what when testifying before the Hidalgo County Grand Jury. Quickly addressing a legal point is appropriate and might prove helpful. In accord with the Texas Code of Criminal Procedure any number of folks may be present when sworn testimony is presented to the impaneled Grand Jury, though they must keep secret what they saw and/or heard. However, during the process of actual deliberations—deciding to indict or not—only sitting members of the Grand Jury may witness and take part in those deliberations—no outside spectators and/or witnesses.[39]

However, before any Grand Jury can act they need something to mull over and, in this instance, Texas Ranger Jack Dean—if he could—was tasked with bringing legal closure with regards to the as yet unexplained death of Alfonso Loredo Flores. Committing suicide with a rock, while both hands are inside front pockets of one's trousers is improbable, if not impossible. There was an answer. Texas Ranger Jack Dean was an investigator.

Following consultation with the pathologist, Ranger Dean was aware of scientific conclusions. Texas Ranger Jack Dean initiated his probe, a forensic investigation. Alfonso's cause of death was a bullet wound to the top of his head—not from a whole and intact bullet but fragments thereof. Carefully adhering to a documentable chain-of-custody, Texas Ranger Dean had the pathologist retrieve and hand over to him bullet fragments from the deceased Alfonso Flores. The partial projectiles' trajectory was problematic, as was just who pulled the trigger launching the death dealing shards. Competently as it turned out, Dean photographed and diagrammed to scale the crime scene. Still, it was rather puzzling trying to trace the metal fragments' flight path. Ranger Dean meticulously searched for some clue that would unravel the mystery. His stellar work netted its dividend. Overhead where Alfonso Loredo Flores had been standing in front of a barber shop was the building's metal gutter. Closer inspection revealed two momentous findings. First, the gutter's channel was thoroughly clogged, solid with debris and dirt, packed tightly, theoretically hard as concrete. Secondly, on the outside of the gutter was an indention, one that correlated handily as if made by a recently fired bullet. The discovery was dramatic and decisive. Unable to penetrate the gutter's tin outer wall due to now rock-hard rubble inside, the bullet had splintered and ricocheting pieces had struck the quite unsuspecting victim in the top of his head. The factual cause of death was now well established. The means of inflicting that cause was now not inexplicable. Sometimes police work is exciting, but sometimes doing it right is drudgery. Texas Ranger Jack Dean physically removed the critical section of gutter for preservation, and its likely evidentiary value. There was, however, that all important unknown: Whose gun could be—would be—a ballistic match tying shooter to shards?[40]

Not only was Texas Ranger Dean investigating the killing of Mr. Flores, DA McInnis had also tasked him with procuring evidence of other criminality taking place during the Pharr riot. Consequently Ranger Jack Dean was conducting interviews of firemen and policemen, deputies and the sheriff. A picture was emerging, one made much clearer in light of analysis by the DPS Crime Lab specialists regarding bullet fragment submissions from the field. Particularly one tidbit of data was more than relevant: According to the ballistic experts, though they could not conclusively identify the exact caliber of a suspect firearm, their scientific finding was somewhat specific. The portions of lead are or were at one time possibly pieces of a copper-coated bullet but were not the core of a jacketed projectile. The combined weight of the fragments was too hefty to be less than a .32 caliber.[41] The latter was telling, at least from a purely circumstantial standpoint. Law enforcement personnel on scene the night of the dustup and demonstrations, one and all, were armed with a sidearm of more than .32 caliber, chiefly .38 Specials and/or .357 Magnum revolvers. Cutting to the nub, Texas Ranger Jack Dean through investigative finesse and with the defendant's remorseful cooperation and confession, deductively determined that a Hidalgo County Deputy Sheriff, Robert C. "Bob" Johnson, thirty years of age and a former Edinburg policeman, had fired a round from his service weapon into the air—and a bullet from that discharge had struck the gutter, splintered, and those slivers ricocheted, causing the sad, but unintentional death of Alfonso Loredo Flores. Although result of the act had assuredly been inadvertent, it registered in the law books as a prosecutable case of Negligent Homicide, and so Bob Johnson was legally and formally charged.[42] Texas Ranger Jack Dean, despite the uncomfortable fact that Deputy Bob Johnson was a fellow lawman, had stood tall with regards to application of evenhanded justice. DPS's chain-of-command structure, prosecutors, defense lawyers and, for the most part, the whole of the Lower Rio Grande Valley's majority populace took an especial and brand new note: Texas Ranger Jack O. Dean was a thoroughly relentless criminal investigator—but always fair-mined, never allowing fear or favor to knock him off the principled course.

And that principled course was also decidedly uncomfortable—at least to some degree—for the Valley Community Center's hierarchy at Pharr, a facility operated by the Methodist Board of Missions. While tremendously swamped with more pressing investigatory matters, Texas Ranger Jack Dean had also managed to unwind a morsel of financial reality. By interviewing a local bank's vice-president and subsequent to the formal issuance of and service of a subpoena it was unequivocally shown that one of the leading—and most vocal—activists for Pharr's riot was receiving funds from the Methodist Church.[43] Such awkward and embarrassing news was not received lightly by Methodist Church officialdom when the Hidalgo County Grand Jury made public one of its findings:

> The present course of philosophy and leadership in the center, we feel, has contributed to the unrest that now exists in Pharr. It is a matter of record that organizations of a militant nature have been encouraged to use the Valley Community Center as a meeting place. Demonstrations have been advocated and planned within this church sponsored facility. Actions of this kind that lead to death, property damage and general disruption of the peace cannot be looked upon by this grand jury as acts of Christianity. It is our recommendation to the responsible leaders of this center that the directorship be changed and that a new course of public servitude be undertaken. . . .[44]

Due to the undisputed fact that the Director had allowed the facility to be used as an open meeting place for not just a few MAYO sponsored protestors, and that he had actually marched with said confrontational demonstrators, the Methodist Board of Missions bluntly and right fast dismissed the Director "on grounds of inability to cooperate with the board, churches, city officials and others."[45]

Amid the cyclone of interconnected investigative duties dealing with the Pharr disturbance, Texas Ranger Jack Dean had to bring his field work—interviews and statement taking—to a halt. In a judicial sense, if such work cannot stand scrutiny it's meaningless. Reflecting well on his knowledge of the horrible affair and of his high-level of competence is this fact: "District Attorney Oscar McInnis and Texas Ranger Jack Dean were inside the grand jury room as the suspects were called in one at a time."[46] The DA had Dean's integrity pegged—right and tight. Yes, when it came time for actually pinning down testimony and staking hard proofs, Texas Ranger Jack Dean would do to tie to.

Unlike some Rangers of an earlier epoch, Jack Dean was fully cognizant that his part was an integral role in the administration of justice—but as an adjunct player—not a law unto himself. Elsewhere throughout the Lone Star a new age was dawning for the Texas Rangers, but for that snapshot in time, it was manifesting itself in the Lower Rio Grande Valley. Notably due to his exercising "maturity of judgment. . . . [and] professionalism that every law-enforcement officer should have," Jack Dean, even-tempered and sensible, was amending attitudes about Rangers in the Texas/Mexico borderlands.[47] Assuredly such benevolence measures above a biographer's unintended hyperbole. The thoroughly seasoned and well-respected Ranger Captain John Wood openly noted: "We have received many good reports from officers and citizens regarding this Ranger [Jack Dean]. He is doing a good job and has a good working relationship with the public and other officers in south Texas."[48]

After hearing the testimony of about sixty witnesses during nine sessions, the Hidalgo County Grand Jury, consisting of nine men and three ladies, returned a dozen sealed Indictments resulting from the riot, naming ten fellows; prospective defendants ranging in age from eighteen to forty-seven years, including the now relieved of duty deputy, Bob Johnson.[49] Understandably Sheriff Claudio Castaneda lamented that arresting Johnson was, indeed, "an unpleasant duty."[50] Texas Ranger Jack Dean assumed duty at the Hidalgo County jailhouse as lawmen fanned out through the Lower Rio Grande Valley effecting post-Indictment arrests.[51]

Though it would be an innocent misnomer, was one to suppose that all of Jack Dean's investigative time was singularly centered on social unrest and resultant criminality at Pharr, such thinking would be wrong. For that posting to McAllen and the Lower Rio Grande Valley, Texas Ranger Jack Dean may not have psychologically qualified as a wretched workaholic, but you couldn't prove it through the testimony of Janie Dean. Admittedly a selective device, but highlighting a sampling of other cases somewhat rounds out the picture.

One episode that consumed a great deal of Ranger Dean's time was an armed robbery of note. At McAllen on the second day of March 1971 the doorbell at Gilbert Weisberg's residence sounded. The only person home was the Weisberg's maid, a conscientious and amiable lady of Hispanic lineage. She was not terribly suspicious. The two fellows standing on the front porch were attired in business suits, ties, and armed with broad smiles and smooth talk. When apprised that the homeowners were not there—pleasantness blanched. The two men forced their way inside, one placing the barrel of pistol against the housekeeper's temple. The other outlaw removed a roll of silver duct tape from his pocket and brusquely taped the startled woman's hands behind her back, rendering her helpless and afraid. Without fanfare or small talk they marched the scared-to-death lady upstairs to the master bedroom and then, placing her on a sofa, taped her ankles together. Though not blindfolded it was obvious to the victim that the men were not willy-nilly hunting for loot, but were on a dedicated mission—they knew exactly what they wanted and came to take it! Within ten minutes the wicked fellows had gathered their plunder: 34 pieces of jewelry valued at $27,000, a significant yet undetermined number of U.S. and Israeli Savings Bonds, and $100,000 in cash taken from the now standing open safe, attacked by slipping the vault door's hinges rather than a sledgehammer frontal assault. Threatening to return and kill the lady if she alerted the police, the guttersnipes quietly left—not attracting neighborhood attention. At last, the frightened woman worked loose from the restraints and called Mr. Weisberg, who in turn did notify the police, and they asked for assistance from Texas Ranger Dean.[52]

Even a rookie lawman would at once know the Weisberg robbery was not a run-of-the-mill spur-of-the moment act carried out by amateur nitwits. Somebody, somewhere, had fingered the target and professionals had conspired and executed the plot to enrich themselves with the Weisbergs' loss. Texas Ranger Jack Dean set to work. Professional highjackers were then living in or had come to the Lower Rio Grande Valley. Either way they were big-time crooks and this was a big-time case. Texas Ranger Jack Dean was up to the challenge. Though it's relatively easy to summarize, the on-the-ground investigative time and travel was extensive. In the end, however, it was productive. Coordinating his exhaustive detective work with DPS Intelligence Agents Joe Murphy and John McNelly in Harris County, as well as Houston PD Burglary & Theft Detective Jerry W. Carpenter, Texas Ranger Jack Dean had cleverly identified at least one of the prime and mean suspects: thirty-two year old Prentice Noel Ellard, now a transplanted Texan, originally from El Dorado, Union County, Arkansas.[53] Unarguably, Prentice Noel Ellard was no angel. Prentice, an ex-convict, owned not only a shameful criminal record but, at one time, status as an Outlaw Biker, a member of the Bandidos.[54]

He also owned a gun—specifically a Smith & Wesson Model 39, 9mm. At Houston during the evening hours of 16 January and/or the morning hours of 17 January 1970 the retail gun shop of H.C. Alexander was burglarized. Forty-two firearms were stolen. Later, a presumed legitimate gun dealer, subsequent to telephonic negotiations regarding the sale of a quantity of handguns from an unknown character, handed the telephone number over to a Houston city detective. It traced to a Houston house occupied by Ellard. The above cited handgun was—unfortunately for him—in Prentice Noel Ellard's possession when he was arrested near Little Rock, Arkansas.[55]

Prentice Noel Ellard might have been able to fork the leather seat of a Harley-Davidson with "Ape Hanger" chrome-plated handlebars, but he could not fly an airplane. Through far-reaching analytical theorizing "working the bricks" Texas Ranger Jack Dean located a charter aircraft pilot who had innocently flown Prentice Noel Ellard and another guy—unknown—from McAllen to Houston, "about an hour after the robbery."[56] According to Detective Carpenter, within circles of the Houston underworld it was no secret that Prentice Noel Ellard had made a big score, a real big score, at McAllen. In fact soon after he had flown back into Harris County, Prentice Noel Ellard paid cash for a Lincoln Mark III, bought a new Mercury Cougar for his girlfriend, paid six months' advance rent for quarters in the Ambassador Apartments at 5030 Ambassador Way, which at that time rented for $225 per month, a not insignificant sum for the early 1970s. Prentice Noel Ellard no longer wore Bandido colors indentifying himself as member of the 1 percent gang of misfits that your mother warned you about. No, his dirty Bandido rags had changed into new rich wealth. Now, with an air that he always had, he turned out in "fine new clothes, good clothes, and alligator shoes. . . . Ellard spent a lot of money after the robbery."[57]

Texas Ranger Jack Dean presented all of his findings to the Hidalgo County Grand Jury, and they, among other criminal indictments, returned an Indictment for Robbery by Firearms against Prentice Noel Ellard—an arrest warrant issued.[58] Texas Ranger Jack Dean had a teletype with the warrant number sent to Houston— followed up later that day with a paper copy via the United States Postal Service.[59]

Prentice Noel Ellard was an outlaw—one not wanting to sleep on a steel bunk at Huntsville. Foolishly, when DPS Intelligence Agents Murphy and McNelly and other officers went to arrest him at Houston on the outstanding Hidalgo County warrant, Prentice Noel Ellard fired three shots at the officers before he was ultimately taken into custody and handcuffed. Thankfully, no lawmen were injured. Around the corner from Prentice Noel Ellard's and girlfriend Bonnie's hangout, the Greek Cat Club, was parked his Mark III Lincoln. A protective inventory pursuant to a tow was legal—and revealing. Inside the trunk was a "dismantled machine gun, 22 silver dollars, assorted old coins, two Israeli coin mint sets, cameras and a German Luger."[60]

Ranger Jack Dean made the trip to Houston, picked up the prisoner, and returned him to Hidalgo County.[61] At the Edinburg bond hearing, crucial testimony was elicited from Harris County Deputy Sheriff Paul Champion and Harris County Assistant District Attorney John Holmes. The latter, in reply to a most logical and most pertinent probe, "testified that Ellard was [currently] under $440,000 in bonds at Houston."[62] And what fate befell Prentice Noel Ellard? Prosecutorial authorities opted to go with Assault to Murder a Police Officer in Harris County, first, betting that the defendant would catch hard time—and somewhat relieved not to have had to wholly depend on the testimony of the Weisbergs' frightened Spanish-speaking housekeeper. The gamble was not ill-advised. Prentice Noel Ellard was convicted and imprisoned—but his luck would, later, eventually play out inside his personal residence at 406 Oxford, Houston. Furiously inflicted stab wounds to his chest, a homicide, had ended the criminal misdoings of Prentice Noel Ellard.[63] Texas Ranger Jack Dean's industriousness and sound reasoning did not go unnoticed at the San Antonio headquarters of Company D.

And certainly during that same March of 1971, a blue 1970 Chevrolet with an after-market camper did not go unnoticed either. Especially after it perfected a slick one-eighty two miles south of Falfurrias, obviously dead-set against an inspection at the northbound BP Checkpoint. The resultant chase and eventual traffic stop netted dead bodies under the topper: a pair of Aoudad sheep, an Axis buck, a Muflon sheep, and a Whitetail buck. The truck's occupants—road hunters—had been busy as bees with their stinging .243 caliber Winchester and the snipping of high-fence wires. Since the initial stop had taken place in Brooks County, Texas Ranger B.J. Green and Sheriff Rep F. Moore and TP&W Game Warden L.H. Griffin, were first called. After it was determined that the actual destructions had taken place in Hidalgo County, but a half-dozen miles north of Edinburg off of US 281, Texas Ranger Jack Dean caught the case.

Upon receipt of the lawfully drawn Complaint by the Justice of the Peace and subsequent to the issuance of warrants, physical detention and setting bond was the next step. Working the distasteful investigation in conjunction with TP&W Game Warden Jeff Cordell, Ranger Dean arrested the two downtrodden poachers—who were ultimately convicted.[64] Hardly had Ranger Jack Dean had a break before the sound of gunfire reverberated again in Hidalgo County.

During the wee morning hours of 3 April 1971 at the parking lot in front of Martin's Café at Pharr, the earlier trouble at the Longhorn Bar came to a head. Jamie Zuniga was shot in the back by Santos Almanza Zuniga (no relation). And here, it's relevant to mention, this certainly was not a whodunit offense, but nevertheless the legal i's had to be dotted, and the legal t's crossed. Even more or less easy crimes to solve, however, are voracious consumers of valuable time. District Court and Appellate Court Judges could be and can be persnickety—and rightly so! Texas Ranger Jack Dean made his investigation, took written statements from the victim and witnesses and, subsequent to skillful interrogation, obtained the voluntary and written confession of Santos Zuniga, which eventually resulted in courtroom conviction.[65]

The following month on the twenty-ninth at 2:45 a.m. at the Kayo Service Station in Pharr, night attendant Eulogio Cisneros was highjacked by a gang of Spanish-speaking hoodlums, taking not only cash from the till but cartons of cigarettes as well. The most meaningful clue, as it turned out, was their getaway vehicle, a gold and white 1965 Chevrolet, one with "several black spots that looked like primer spots. . . ." Texas Ranger Jack Dean, ever on call it seemed, began his investigation. The fresh trail led to Edinburg. Through sharp detective work he ultimately began making arrests, the prospective defendants' rolling over on each other like falling dominos. Adult courtroom conviction resulted, and the lone juvenile offender was placed in an authorized "Correctional School."[66]

Playing "chicken" with Texas Ranger Jack Dean was not intelligent. Well, more precisely fighting chickens. On Sunday afternoon, the thirteenth day of June 1971, east of McAllen at Donna, an even dozen "Cock Fighters" were segregated from a throng of more than a hundred—including women and children—and hauled to Donna where the local Justice of the Peace accepted their bonds and/or fines. The joint operation with Sheriff Castaneda was a misdemeanor winner but not necessarily a long-lasting victory.[67]

The following Thursday, 17 June 1971, the whole of the Lower Rio Grand Valley's attention turned to the Hidalgo County courthouse. Courtroom doings were on tap. A resident of Elsa east of Edinburg, a twenty-five-year-old McAllen school teacher, was standing trial for his alleged February participation in the riotous uproar at Pharr and, more specifically, legally accountable for "interfering with police during a civil disturbance."[68] Ranger Jack Dean, besides providing courtroom security, was a witness in the criminal proceedings. Prosecuting the case was the aforementioned Oscar McInnis, and the defendant was represented by attorneys Rafael Flores and Robert Yzaguirre, who shortly made a very public statement about Texas Ranger Jack Dean. The long and the short of the battling barristers came down quick and decisively. District Court Judge Joe R. Alamia, after the trial jury deliberated three hours, received their verdict of *Guilty*. Not unexpectedly, assessing exactly how certain factions within the Hispanic community and their ardent supporters would act in response was problematic, especially for a compassionate but concerned Texas Ranger. Via a teletype through the Hidalgo County Sheriff's Office to the DPS Office at Harlingen in neighboring Cameron County, to be at once forwarded to Captain Wood and Sergeant Werner at Company D headquarters in San Antonio, Ranger Dean apprised:

"JURY IN 92ND DIST COURT HIDALGO CO FOUND [the defendant] GULITY IN FIRST OF PHARR RIOT CASES JURY OUT AT THIS TIME TO SET PUNISHMENT CONDITIONS UNCERTAIN AT THIS TIME SEVERAL THREATS HAVE BEEN MADE TO PHARR POLICEMEN LEADERS OF THIS GROUP SAY THAT THEY MAY NOT BE ABLE TO CONTROL THEIR PEOPLE TEMPERS RUNNING HIGH WILL KEEP YOU INFORMED OF ANY NEW INFO"[69]

Rather quickly the felony penalty assessed by the jury in the bifurcated punishment phase of the proceedings was rendered; according
to one newspaper reporter's understanding it was set at five years—
suspended sentence, which Jack Dean noted was actually five years
probated.[70] There was, no doubt a degree of community hostility—
not actual violence—regarding the trial's outcome, but not directed
at DPS or the Texas Rangers. In fact, one of the defendant's lawyers was plainly outspoken and audaciously emphatic: "Yzaguirre
described Ranger Jack Dean and Highway Patrol Sgt. S.M. Moxley
as 'the finest officers I know.' He said they testified there was a riot
and 'I believe every word they said,' and they helped settle the trouble, 'because Ramirez (Pharr Police Chief Alfredo Ramirez) could not
handle the situation.'"[71]

Not just a few other Hidalgo County folks—illicit controlled substances purveyors—had abruptly learned that they really couldn't
handle the situation either. A crafty and courageous undercover
DPS Narcotics Agent had been circulating amongst the Lower Rio
Grande Valley's underground subculture, guardedly buying commercial amounts of marijuana, heroin, LSD, and other illegal products
designed to euphorically alter mindsets and radically dull mental
alertness. These evidence purchasing outings were not what lawmen
tagged a "Buy-Bust" operation, when an actual custodial arrest immediately followed the unlawful transaction. No, this business, in policing lingo, was termed the "Buy-Walk" approach, wherein the bad guys
kept the money and the good guys walked away, keeping custody of
and inventorying the contraband for prosecutors' presentation in the
courtroom—a little later. This latter technique allowed for the overall investigation's viability and guaranteed its ongoing integrity; until
continuing with the undercover performance was at the pinnacle—not
too much more to be gained evidentiary wise by continuing with the
charade. It was super secret stuff to be sure. Texas Ranger Jack Dean,
working with Narcotics Agents Kellner and McFarland was a part of
the scheme from the get-go. The dope dealers' world came tumbling
down after the Hidalgo County Grand Jury handed down a string of
felony Indictments, and the subsequent arrest warrants issued.[72]

Again resorting to the lexicon of lawmen, it was time for the "Roundup," a preplanned and highly coordinated enforcement action—simultaneously timed raids and arrests. The casual entry from Texas Ranger Jack Dean's *Daily Reminder* journal is explicit in one sense, but a seeming laid-back citation to the very real danger possibly attached to such fundamental operations. "Leave McAllen 8:00 a.m. to Edinburg for Grand Jury. Also contacted Narcotics Agents Kellner and McFarland reference Narcotics Raids planned for this date. Help set up location for organizing raids and processing people. Also worked on arrest team which arrested 5 people and served 2 search warrants." For this particular law enforcement engagement Ranger Jack Dean's workday—before his head finally hit the pillow—measured at twenty-three hours.[73]

A perfunctory review of official reports relating to these raids and arrests reflects that Texas Ranger Jack Dean's defendants eventually banked hard time—prison sentences—from eight to eighteen years. These particular fellows, both Anglo and Hispanic, weren't nonchalantly and innocently playing hopscotch or shooting hoops, they were big-time dope traffickers.[74]

On the twenty-fourth day of August 1971, one minute before noon, a solitary white male, at the point of a pistol held-up the McAllen State Bank, making off with $10,600 and leaving a terrified bank teller behind. Texas Ranger Jack Dean—via the radio broadcast—was the first lawman onsite, and he quickly gathered information from witnesses who had seen the suspect flee in a green Dodge pickup truck. Without delay Texas Ranger Dean, through the DPS Dispatcher in Harlingen, relayed the key data to units in the field. Fortuitously and fast, DPS Motor Vehicle Inspection Patrolman Calvin F. Cox (a future Ranger) spotted the suspect vehicle, turned around, activated his red lights, and at the point of a wicked looking pump shotgun, apprehended forty-year-old Maurice Melvin "Pete" Green. On the pick-up truck's bench-seat was a .45 caliber autoloader, cocked and locked, and a manila folder containing greenbacks, $10,600 to be exact. Patrolman Cox physically turned the suspect over to Ranger Jack Dean for further investigation. After warning the alleged perpetrator of his specified Constitutional Rights pursuant to Miranda requirements, and after consulting with Pete Green's attorney, Ranger Jack Dean discerned:

> In talking with Green it was found that he was a Engineer and had been connected with the Space Program but was not working now due to a cut back (This was found to be true). He was living at Harlingen at this time and was attempting to open a cattle feed lot. He had made a application for a SBA loan and it had been approved. The only thing he would say about the robbery was that he was in a tight and needed money.[75]

Who was not emphatically uptight was the 92nd Texas Judicial District Judge. At Edinburg, in the Hidalgo County courtroom, defendant Pete Green caught a nickel, five years to do with the Texas Department of Criminal Justice at one of their high-fenced facilities.[76] And Texas Ranger Jack Dean pocketed a laudatory letter from G.E. Roney Executive Vice-President of the McAllen State Bank: "It is certainly gratifying to all or our people to know that we have such capable law enforcement people in the Valley to take charge in such situations as this."[77]

Comprehending Texas Ranger Jack Dean's everyday working history is wholly dependent on understanding that—unlike TV murder mysteries—where an investigation starts and finishes before the next episode, real life criminality does not confine itself to convenience. Offenders worry not about overworked lawmen's schedules and whether or not they've concluded one investigation before moving to the next, as if their wild and foolish actions had some semblance of suitable order. Though Texas Ranger Jack Dean was disposed to concern himself with an upcoming trial regarding the social untidiness at Pharr, several mean fellows figuratively knocked him off track.

Miguel Angel "Mike" Longoria, a middle-aged McAllen clothing salesman, had seemingly vanished, his whereabouts unknown to family and friends. Farmer Edward L. Good, catching his mail west of McAllen at Mission, discovered the decomposing body of Mike Longoria in his fruit orchard. For Texas Ranger Jack Dean and fellow officers it was another of those situations, a bona fide mystery? Soon the autopsy revealed that the unfortunate victim had been bludgeoned about the head and face, the instrument causing death unknown. Whodunit homicides, speaking with generality, are customarily worked backwards—tracing the deceased victim's last known footsteps—rather than helter-skelter rushing, trying to establish a motive. Though it wasn't easy, investigators finally determined from taxicab drivers and other witnesses—some reluctant—that the last time Mr. Mike Longoria had been seen alive and well was at the Astro Club in McAllen, partying and having a good time visiting with the gals and guys, dancing and drinking beer. Texas Ranger Jack Dean and his committed area law enforcing partners, Hidalgo County Sheriff Deputy Pat Ramsey, and Detectives Paul Conde and V. Rosser from the McAllen Police Department were steadily chipping away at chinks and inconsistencies in the Astro Club's barmaids' and patrons' stories. Every one of the tenacious investigating officers was pitching in with their pieces of the puzzle. A not so pretty picture was taking shape. In fact, due to his outstanding reputation for investigative integrity and a knack for not having to grandstand, an area attorney arranged for one of his clients to meet with and verbally update Texas Ranger Jack Dean with consequential information the person possessed. The secretive confab was more than constructive, the confidential source passing along criminal intelligence that, coupled with written statements, was more than a little insightful at pinpointing certain ancillary players' knowledge about disposition of the dead man's personal property.[78]

The old-time saying that "too many cooks spoil the broth" may very well be apt in this case; there being too many scared accomplices and/or witnesses for actually getting away with murder. In the parking lot behind the Astro Club—though non-participating folks weren't blind—the unwary and arguably naive Mike Longoria had been beaten to unconsciousness and stuffed into the trunk of a car. What started as a foul strong-arm robbery had jumped to Aggravated Robbery and Kidnapping. Not knowing what to do with their victim, the distraught perpetrators, finally found themselves in Edward Good's orchard—a real dark and real secluded spot.[79]

After regaining consciousness, from inside the automobile's trunk, Mike Longoria began banging and beating—screaming: "Open it! Open it!" The *mal hombres* opened the trunk and the victim began pleading for his life—swearing he would give them everything he had, would they but spare his life. He was knocked to the ground, senseless. Logically fearing that Longoria could and/or would finger them, the heartless decision was made to terminate the problem.[80] While the others held Longoria's arms, in the absence of a tire-tool, one of the gangsters grabbed a caulking gun and bloodied and battered their prisoner's head with the impromptu murder weapon—until Mike moved no more. Then, after artlessly covering the dead body with a little grass, the coldhearted killers went on their merry way—that is until they met Ranger Jack Dean and his law enforcing comrades. Four perpetrators were ultimately arrested subsequent to the Hidalgo County Grand Jury's return of sealed indictments.[81]

Though it took awhile, and a little wheeling and dealing plea bargaining and the calculated granting of immunity, the book finally closed—almost. There would be another exciting chapter: Geronimo Ochoa Quintanilla caught four-bits—fifty years—for Murder With Malice and Roberto Ruiz Gonzales entered his guilty plea to a lesser charge of Aggravated Assault, catching a deuce—two years in the Hidalgo County Jail. Interestingly, and somewhat ironically in light of later events, on the day he was formally sentenced to the lengthy prison term, Quintanilla made a break for freedom but was shut off from liberty by a securely bolted door.[82] For this case, the detective work had been terrific. After all was said and done, Texas Ranger Jack Dean, and assorted officers of the McAllen Police Department and the Hidalgo County Sheriff's Office had interviewed more than thirty individuals and taken as many as fifteen sworn written statements from witnesses and/or defendants during their—from start to finish—three-month Longoria murder investigation.[83]

At the end of 1971 Texas Ranger Jack Dean was yet involved in another appalling whodunit murder. At Alamo, east of McAllen and west of Donna, the body of Sarah O'Neil, a sixty-one-year-old fourth-grade schoolteacher, was found by her nephew who was making a welfare check due to the victim not answering repeated, but routine telephone calls. Mrs. O'Neil, a widow, lived alone on her tree shaded and secluded property, her nearest neighbor being about half-a-mile away. The victim had obviously received head trauma and suffered numerous stab wounds. Texas Ranger Jack Dean's presence at the crime scene was asked for and he responded, as did newspaper reporters baying after the hot story. Unluckily, the only witness, Mrs. O'Neil's small terrier, was a mute witness, prompting Ranger Jack Dean to apprise an on-scene journalist, "I wish that dog could talk. . . . he appeared to be in shock when [I] arrived. He backed against a washhouse and didn't say a word." Furthermore, according to Dean, "Time of death has not been determined yet. . . . There doesn't appear to be anything missing. . . . Guns and portable television sets were left there. However, we're not ruling out the possibility of an attempted burglary and that they got surprised. They may have killed her and gotten spooked. . . ." Texas Ranger Dean, after the crime-scene was processed for latent fingerprints and other forensic evidence mentally cataloged another unsolved mystery.[84]

And herein, at this point, it's salient to underscore hardcore reality: Not all crimes close with a defendant serving time or placing an order for their last meal. Following numerous interviews, laboratory analyses of blood, hair, and fiber, administering polygraph examinations, and after poking around in legally subpoenaed telephone toll records, Sarah O'Neil's gruesome murder remained a whodunit.[85] That is from a legal standpoint. Ranger Jack Dean, in his own mind, pretty well knew who was responsible for the dedicated teacher's heartless demise, but in the jargon of lawmen, the suspect "lawyered up." From that point forward it was rough sledding with regards to building a sustainable criminal case with admissible evidence; one with sufficient Probable Cause for an arrest and/or the likelihood of an Indictment and courtroom conviction.[86] The good guys don't win every time. Understandably, this was one of the most personally frustrating criminal cases Texas Ranger Dean ever worked; especially knowing the culprit slyly pulled the wool over the Blind Mistress of Justice's eyes.[87]

Shortly, another mystery facing Ranger Dean would be the outcome of one of the protestors' trial for breaking out the fire-truck's windshield during the night of the Pharr riot. The multi-day courtroom drama was well attended, "drawing large crowds," but as reporter Gary Garrison penned, a cogent observer "can quickly determine that most of the spectators" were championing for the defendant. The audience's feelings were exhibited repeatedly during the questioning of witnesses. An answer sympathetic to the defendant "brings an almost audible hum to the courtroom, while a reply favoring the prosecution frequently causes some audible grumbling."[88] Interestingly, but not surprisingly, courthouse security was of paramount concern for Hidalgo County officialdom, including the retired judge from Corpus Christi, Tillman Smith, who had been asked to referee the heated contest between DA Oscar McInnis and the defendant's legal lineup, lawyers Warren Burnett from Odessa and David Hall of McAllen. There were, in point of fact, two fellows singled out to ensure that sanity didn't give way to stupidity. When any noise level began to rise, Judge Tillman glanced at the audience and then to his quieter:

> Bailiff John Brewster jumps to his feet and shouts, "Let's have some order." Brewster then walks through the courtroom and sometimes points an accusing finger at some of the more noisy spectators.

And:

> Texas Ranger Jack Dean, a tall, muscular lawman who packs a .45 caliber automatic on his hip, keeps order in the hall and at the courtroom door. He remains stern, but friendly.[89]

Attesting to the fact that Texas Ranger Jack Dean was seen as being scrupulously honest is easily digested by a strategic decision reached by both the prosecution and the defense teams during the Pharr protestor's trial. Jack Dean was the last witness called by the district attorney. And, he was the first and only witness called by the defense.[90] Texas Ranger Jack Dean's under oath candor was never debatable; his answers cut straight to the fact, the proverbial chips falling where they may. Whether or not the defendant on trial actu-ally threw a rock at the fire-truck was in dispute; could it have been someone else's rock that shattered the windshield? In the jury's col-lective minds the State of Texas had not proved its case by that stan-dard of Beyond Reasonable Doubt. Their verdict was *Not Guilty*.[91]

Texas Ranger Jack Dean had been sent to the Lower Rio Grande Valley to shore up the public relation's image of the Rangers. In a relatively short time the headway he was making was showing posi-tive results. Civilians and supervisors were favorably impressed and said so in writings and personnel evaluations. Mayor Bowe, Pharr's Chief Executive, noted, among other things that Texas Ranger Jack Dean's working demeanor was "smooth and intelligent" allowing him to successfully handle and defuse those disagreeable political and sociological situations.[92] The aforementioned Priest, Michael Allen, made sure the DPS Colonel, Wilson Speir, knew that Texas Ranger Jack Dean was made of the right stuff: "His own political and social convictions may be different from mine, but I have found him easy to communicate with, mature in judgment and capable in his profes-sion. I had heard many stories about the Texas Rangers but he was the first that I had come into personal contact with."[93] Naturally such praise is fine and good, but from the purely practical sense, in-house recognition is much more meaningful and appreciated. Company D Captain John Wood, for obligatory personnel assessments was not blind to reality: "We have received many good reports from offi-cers and citizens regarding this Ranger [Jack Dean]. He is doing a good job and has a good working relationship with the public and other officers in south Texas."[94] Six-months later, the performance appraisal was consistent:

> This man shows a very keen interest in his work objectives, is dis-playing an active interest in community participation as shown by his work with the youth in Hidalgo County. Ranger Dean is a good investigator, a diligent employee and has advanced the image of the Texas Ranger in south Texas by his relationships, both with the general public and other law enforcement officers.[95]

Photo Gallery
2

Jack Dean is officially commissioned a Texas Ranger, handed his star-in-wheel badge by the DPS Director, Colonel Wilson E. "Pat" Speir, while Lieutenant Colonel Leo Gossett looks on. *Courtesy Jack Dean.*

Recognizing the necessity for Texas Rangers sculpting a new image in South Texas, Jim Ray, Chief DPS Criminal Law Enforcement Division, specifically drove that message home to rookie Texas Ranger Jack Dean with regards to his being assigned to duty at McAllen, Hidalgo County. *Courtesy Texas Ranger Hall of Fame & Museum, Waco, TX.*

One of the first to welcome Jack Dean into his newfound DPS investigative career was Lewis Rigler, an old-hand Texas Ranger—with service dating back to the days when North Texas was yet wild and woolly, populated with not just a few big-time gamblers and low-down gangsters. Texas Ranger Rigler had investigated the premeditated murder of Herbert "The Cat" Noble, blown to smithereens north of the Dallas/Fort Worth Metroplex. *COURTESY TEXAS RANGER HALL OF FAME & MUSEUM, WACO, TX.*

The ever salty and gutsy and universally adored—by his men—Alfred Y. Allee, Sr. would be Jack Dean's Company D Captain, at least for the first thirty days of his Texas Ranger service. *COURTESY TEXAS RANGER HALL OF FAME & MUSEUM, WACO, TX.*

Outfitted in what was then considered traditional Western wear, Texas Ranger Jack Dean embarks on his first day's rounds of getting acquainted in Hidalgo County. COURTESY JACK DEAN.

Early in the deployment to the Lower Rio Grande Valley, Ranger Jack Dean developed a close working relationship with Claudio Castaneda, Sheriff of Hidalgo County. COURTESY JACK DEAN.

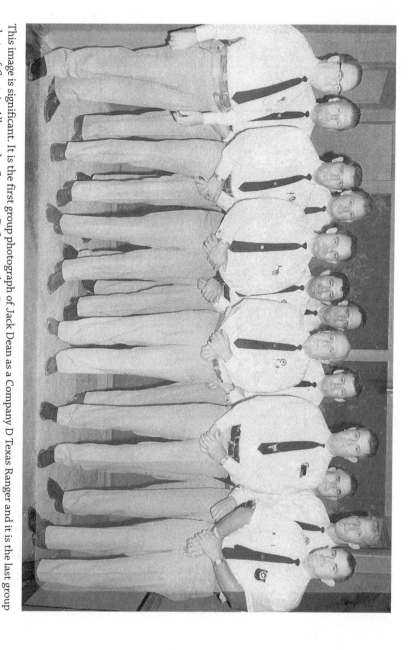

This image is significant. It is the first group photograph of Jack Dean as a Company D Texas Ranger and it is the last group photo of Captain Allee as the Company D Commander. *First row, L to R:* Dudley White, B.J. Green, Walter "Bob" Werner, Captain A.Y. Allee, Sergeant John Wood, and Litt Carpenter. *Second row, L to R:* Bill Nelson, Glenn Krueger, Art Rodriquez, Jerome Preiss, Jack Dean, Jack Van Cleve, and Jim Peters. COURTESY TEXAS RANGER HALL OF FAME & MUSEUM, WACO, TX.

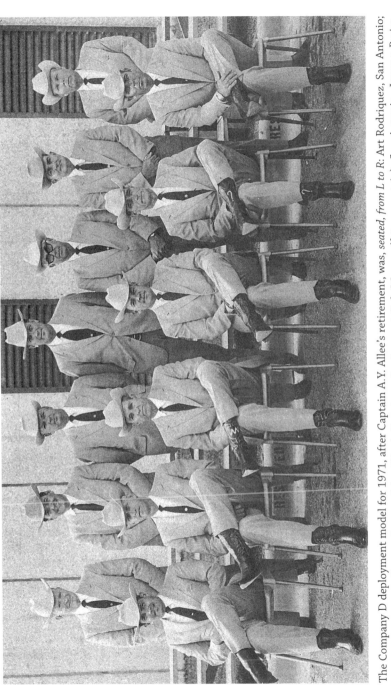

The Company D deployment model for 1971, after Captain A.Y. Allee's retirement, was, *seated, from L to R*: Art Rodriquez, San Antonio; Jim Peters, Corpus Christi; Captain John Wood, San Antonio: Sergeant Bob Werner (future captain), San Antonio; Jerome Preiss, Harlingen; and B.J. Green, Falfurrias. *Standing, from L to R*: John Hogg, Corpus Christi; Jack Dean, McAllen; Glenn Krueger, Beeville; Joaquin Jackson, Uvalde; Jack Van Cleve, Cotulla; Litt Carpenter, San Antonio; and Bill Nelson, Victoria. *Courtesy Texas Ranger Hall of Fame & Museum, Waco, TX.*

Subsequent to the civil unrest and riot at Pharr, and in recognition of Texas Ranger Jack Dean's levelheaded and diplomatic and nonpartisan handling of the matter, the mayor and city fathers gifted him with this beautifully engraved Colt Python .357 Magnum revolver; now on display at the Texas Ranger Hall of Fame & Museum. *Courtesy Jack Dean and the Texas Ranger Hall of Fame & Museum, Waco, TX.*

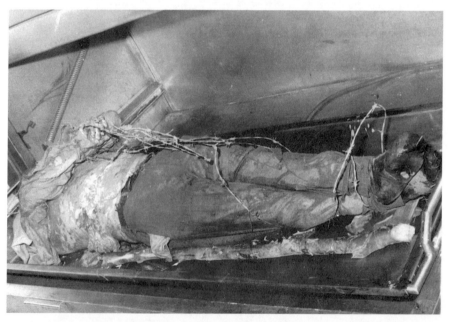

As mentioned in the text, Texas Ranger Jack Dean was called upon to investigate not just a few murders—some with known perpetrators—while others registered as time-consuming whodunits. *Courtesy Jack Dean.*

Another category of criminality for the Lower Rio Grande Valley was the transshipment of tractor-trailer rigs and bulldozers into Mexico. This outfit was stolen in Chicago but recovered through the efforts of Texas Ranger Dean and his DPS counterparts. In fact, Ranger Jack Dean would receive laudatory commendation from the FBI for his efforts at spearheading an investigation which broke the back of a sophisticated international motor-vehicle theft ring. *COURTESY JACK DEAN.*

During this timeframe, before the common usage of computers and online banking, there was an underworld subculture of professional safecrackers. Texas Ranger Jack Dean was frequently called on for lending a helping hand to local authorities, as this brand of nefarious outlaws was quick and mobile. The Texas Rangers statewide reach was effectual. *COURTESY JACK DEAN.*

Regardless the crime, cockfighting or counterfeiting or con-gaming, normalcy—regrettably—for the Lower Rio Grande Valley called for the discovery of dead bodies. Texas Ranger Jack Dean was busy—near twenty-four and seven. *COURTESY JACK DEAN.*

An ever vibrant and personable couple, Jack and Janie Dean, were exceptionally well-known and extraordinarily well thought of by a colorful cast of Lone Star celebrities; herein photographed with the Texas State Artist, Jack White. *COURTESY JACK DEAN.*

During 1974 Texas Ranger Jack Dean was promoted to be the Sergeant of Company F, stationed at Waco in McLennan County. Director Speir and Assistant Director Gossett make it official. *COURTESY JACK DEAN.*

Though Jack Dean had known Robert K. "Bob' Mitchell while stationed at Tyler as a THP Patrolman, the bond of an unbreakable friendship was welded tight when Ranger Sergeant Dean worked as Captain Mitchell's first-line Company F supervisor at Waco. *COURTESY TEXAS RANGER HALL OF FAME & MUSEUM, WACO, TX.*

William D. "Bill" Wilson, subsequent to Captain Clint Peoples's departure from the Rangers, became the Senior Captain stationed at the Austin headquarters. For whatever the reasons Bill Wilson, Bob Mitchell, and Jack Dean naturally gravitated toward each other, becoming exceptionally close personal friends—both on and off the job. *COURTESY TEXAS RANGER HALL OF FAME & MUSEUM, WACO, TX.*

Company F Texas Rangers about the time Jack Dean was promoted as Sergeant of the company. *Standing, L to R:* Ranger Sergeant Jack Dean, Jim Ray, James A. Wright (future captain), Bobby Prince (future captain), Wallace Spiller, Ed Gooding, Bill Gunn, Henry Ligon, and Captain Bob Mitchell. *Kneeling, L to R:* Bill DeLoach, Dale Brice, Bob Connell, Bob Favor, Joe B. Davis, and Troy Porterfield. COURTESY TEXAS RANGER HALL OF FAME & MUSEUM, WACO, TX.

During the abortive 1974 prison break at Huntsville, the convicts asked that an armored car be placed in the prison yard for their escape and bulletproof iron helmets be constructed in the unit's welding shop. Armed with smuggled revolvers and ammunition the outlaws supposed they were good to go. Wrong! The ensuing shoot-out—unfortunately—took lives. It also demonstrated the need for and hastened the formation of a Texas Ranger SWAT Team, a task handed to Texas Ranger Sergeant Jack Dean. *Courtesy Texas Ranger Hall of Fame & Museum, Waco, TX.*

Company A Captain Pete Rogers, a WWII fighter-pilot Ace and Texas Ranger commander having geographical jurisdictional authority over Huntsville in Walker County and its numerous TDC Units. A simple look into Ranger Pete Rogers' eyes reveals he was and could be a sure enough no-nonsense foe. During the horrific shoot-out during the afore-mentioned prison break, Captain Rogers, other Texas Rangers and DPS personnel, an FBI Agent, and TDC Correctional Officers stood tall. COURTESY TEXAS RANGER HALL OF FAME & MUSEUM, WACO, TX.

Although, perhaps, not universally endeared to all Texas Rangers, Captain G.W. Burks was by everyone's standard fearless. During the 1974 siege inside the TDC Walls Unit at Huntsville, the Company B Captain stood tough during the horrifying shoot-out with convicts. Here Burks poses as an old hand two-gun man with single-action revolvers and a tooled-leather Buscadero rig. COURTESY TEXAS RANGER HALL OF FAME & MUSEUM, WACO, TX.

Constable Ivor Montgomery, from Essex County, England, and Sergeant Jack Dean became close personal friends while both were students at FBI training. Here, Constable Montgomery pays a visit to Waco and is given a cowboy hat by Sergeant Dean at the Historic Fort Fisher, the Texas Ranger Hall of Fame & Museum. Note Sergeant Dean is wearing a revolver, and not a cocked and locked .45 autoloader. Such was common practice in and around the office and/or at the shooting range for mandatory qualification during certain courses of fire. COURTESY JACK DEAN AND THE WACO TRIBUNE-HERALD.

From his beginning tenure as a Texas Ranger supervisor Jack Dean recognized the tactical, strategic, and political advantages of training and learning from the U.S. Military. Herein is a joint exercise at San Antonio. Texas Rangers and a civilian supporter are kneeling, *from L to R: Jack Dean, Bruce Casteel, Dr. Vincent Walker, Rudy Rodriquez, Ray Martinez, and Lefty Block. COURTESY JACK DEAN.*

Thomas Rufus Hickman, like Jack Dean, but for an earlier timeframe, would study overseas policing procedures and departmental organization. Arguably, Captain Hickman was one of several ardent voices calling for structuring a statewide policing agency, ultimately leading to formation of the Texas Department of Public Safety (DPS). *Courtesy Texas Ranger Hall of Fame & Museum, Waco, TX.*

Upon receipt of particular grant monies, DPS sent representatives to study state and national policing organizations throughout the United States and overseas. Luckily, Jack and Janie Dean managed a trip to England. Here Constable Ivor Montgomery and Ranger Jack Dean stand still for the photographer. *COURTESY JACK DEAN.*

At the Company F headquarters at Waco, Sergeant Jack Dean stands proud with Texas celebrities Tom Lea, noted writer, historian and artist, and his lovely wife Sarah. Throughout his law-enforcing career Jack Dean would be favorably known—far and wide. *COURTESY JACK DEAN.*

On more than once occasion Texas Ranger Sergeant Jack Dean would be tasked with coordinating and providing security for the Lone Star State's Chief Executives such as the above pictured Governor Dolph Briscoe. High-profile exposure to high-profile dignitaries could have its career enhancing rewards—or a career killing penalty. *Courtesy Jack Dean*.

While the Company F Sergeant, Jack Dean also had the privilege of visiting with past acquaintances and meeting other Texas Rangers—some with near legendary standings, such as this 1975 reunion at Waco, wherein attendees received commemorative Winchester lever-action carbines. The attendee roster was—within Texas Ranger circles—illustrious. *From L to R, kneeling:* La Fetra E. Trimble, Jerome Preiss, Walter A. Russell, Norman K. Dixon, Dudley White, A.Y. Allee, Byron Currin, Arthur Hill, Homer T. Milton, Trenton Horton, Ernest Daniels, and Dan Westbrook. *Standing, L to R:* George M. Roach, Eddie Oliver, Selwyn Denson, E.J. "Jay" Banks, M.D. "Kelly" Rogers, Frank Probst, E.G. "Butch" Albers, Bennie C. Krueger, A.L. Barr, and Clint Peoples. *Courtesy Texas Ranger Hall of Fame & Museum, Waco, TX.*

7

◆

"Lead will get your attention"

massing more praise, Texas Ranger Jack Dean and Sheriff Claudio Castaneda were proud recipients of the "Lawmen Of The Year Award," an enviable tribute formally awarded by the Hidalgo County Civitan Club.[1] Such highly favorable recognition would extend will past the geographical borders of Hidalgo County, as evinced by the favorable "thank you" letter to Texas Ranger Dean from Lorenzo Ramirez, Southwest Regional Director, U.S. Department of Justice, Community Relations Service. Director Ramirez noted: "Dialogue among responsible officials, such as yourself, is imperative as we seek to find better solutions to the multitude of problems facing our communities."[2] Later, subsequent to a personal invitation from Gene Ann Herrin, Texas Youth Council, Ranger Jack Dean was invited to attend and participate in "Dialogue '71." Texas Ranger Dean was, understandably sought for the session, "Law Enforcement: The Search for Understanding."[3] Yes, Jack Dean seemed to be a different breed of Texas Ranger than what many citizens of the Lower Rio Grande Valley had been accustomed to or afraid of. And here, it's but important to mention that throughout the whole of DPS—Rangers included—a more enlightened mindset was nudging previous law enforcing attitudes aside, statewide. More and more emphasis was being placed on education and training, forensics, courtroom demeanor, and professional approaches to public relations.

Captain John Wood wasn't fooling. In a written directive to his South Texas Company D Texas Rangers the message was not vague: "It has been brought to my attention by some responsible citizens that some of the Rangers in Company 'D' have used loud and indecent language in public and in front of ladies and young children. . . . Please refrain from cussing and using foul language in public and where there are women and children. We are attempting to build up the image of the Rangers in South Texas and each one of us must do our part in every way possible to correct this situation. . . . Of course, this will not effect many of you because you are gentlemen at all times."[4] Captain Wood, however, was not blinded to reality, reminding his Company D Rangers in a face to face meeting: "If any man gets in a fight, write a report of the incident to the Ranger Captain giving details."[5] A few myopic Ranger critics, sometimes hiding behind the mantel of armchair scholarship—never making dicey life or death decisions—or slow roasting bizarre guesswork over the fires of political correctness, just for the sake of expediency, now and then are loathe to acknowledge hard truths: Sociological changes really come slowly. American society was in transition and the Rangers were in transition, too!

Although as a veteran THP Patrolman and now a Texas Ranger, dealing with death, whether accidental or premeditated or runaway emotions stampeding over the cliff of sensibleness was, sad to say, part of the job. Most lawmen hardened to that reality. On the other hand a child's death would upset the majority's state of minds. Jack Dean wasn't exempt. Three teenage girls went missing—last seen during lunch at San Benito High-School 11 April 1972. Late that same afternoon, a Cameron County farmer driving his truck along an irrigation canal's embankment shockingly discovered a lifeless form floating at the water's edge. From the pay telephone at a nearby service station he summoned authorities. The body of one of the missing fifteen year old girls had been located. First responders, from the beginning, knew they had a homicide on their hands. Although San Benito police personnel had handled the preliminary Missing Persons report, the body had been discovered outside the city limits and, now, the Cameron County Sheriff's Office was in charge. Deputies at once notified Texas Ranger Jack Dean. His initial crime-scene findings were explicit:

> She was fully clothed with the exception of her shoes. There was a small rope wrapped several times around her right arm and she had been strangled. A search of the area turned up her shoes, which were found a short distance from the body and appeared to have been thrown from a vehicle into the bar ditch. . . .[6]

Miss Patricia Segura's seven sisters and seven brothers were dumbfounded and numbed at the discovery, not to mention the heartache of her tearful and distraught parents, Felix and Amelia. From the law-enforcement perspective, at that time, it was another whodunit. The urgency to find the other girls was more than intense, but nightfall embargoed continuing the quest till morning's light peeked over the eastern horizon. Sunlight ended the search. Maria Norma Delgado's five sisters cried as did her loving parents Mr. and Mrs. Julian C. Delgado. Maria Norma had been murdered, too. Her lifeless remains had been discovered by a "volunteer civilian" in another nearby canal, a green bath towel wrapped around her neck: "The condition of her body indicated she had put up a struggle and had been criminally assaulted. Both girls appear to have been killed, then thrown into the water."[7]

Understandably the murder of two teenage girls was a legit newsmaker, headline material for area papers and, for this true-crime story, a lurid feature piece for *Inside Detective Magazine*—a nationally distributed tabloid, enhanced with contemporary photos, one of which for this article was of Texas Ranger Jack Dean. Though it couldn't come quick enough, two wedges of good news broke. The third missing female student hadn't been with the two unfortunate victims; she had, despite her parents' wishes, run away to neighboring Matamoros and married her seventeen-year-old boyfriend. Correlating to the murders, her untimely disappearance—elopement—had been but a coincidence. Texas Ranger Jack Dean was relieved. He, too, was energized.

Working very closely with Cameron County authorities, Deputies Edward Moody Jr. and James W. Parker, and San Benito City Detective Edelmiro Lucio, Texas Ranger Dean and they, had a viable suspect in mind for the double homicide. Subsequent to circumspect interviews with folks owning scattered tidbits of information and the specific description of a vehicle, a green Ford Mustang, turned out to be a meaningful clue. Investigators zeroed in on that particular detail. Following tedious investigative work with all hands on deck, motor vehicle registration data merged with what High-School students were divulging. Texas Ranger Dean and Deputy Sheriff Moody arrived at the residence of Antonio Rios "Tony" Zepeda, Jr., nineteen. Ranger Jack Dean expounds:

> . . . Deputy Moody and I went to his residence and found him in the carport with his green Mustang. I introduced myself and I asked him if he would come to the Police Department and talk with us. He stated that he would and said, "I guess it is about the missing girls and that he did know them but had not seen them in several days." While we were talking I was standing beside his vehicle and by looking in I could see a piece of rope laying between the front seats. Moody and I returned to the Police Department with Zepeda. When we arrived at the Police Department, Zepeda was interviewed by Deputy Parker and myself. I gave Zepeda the Miranda warning before we interviewed him. This was done in the presence of Deputy Parker. I also told him that he was not under arrest, that he came to the Police Department under his own free will, but that we believed he was involved and that I wanted him to know his rights. He acknowledged all of this. . . . After further talking with Zepeda by Parker and I he admitted that he had taken the girls to the waterfall at the canal because they wanted to go swimming, and that he had left them there, and when he returned he could not find them.[8]

Matching wits with Texas Ranger Jack Dean and Deputy Parker, both experienced investigators, was a lopsided contest for Tony Zepeda, Jr. Facing mounting psychological pressure due to what he was keeping inside and shaken by clues—physical evidence that could be traced to him—such as a pair of the victim's shoes, the section of rope, and the green towel, Tony Zepeda, Jr. ever so quickly "let his milk down," a policing euphemism equating to an admission of guilt, a confession:

> He then began to cry and stated he was not sure what he had done and to please help him. He said Pat was tied up and fell and was in the water and she would not quit screaming, then she went under the water and he was scared. He then told Norma Delgado that he was going to leave her there and wanted to untie her, but she tried to get away and he caught her. He stated that he pulled on the towel, which she had around her neck until she didn't make anymore noise, that they were both in the water and he was scared because he could not swim. . . .[9]

Now with sufficient Probable Cause the voluntary journey to the stationhouse had changed. Tony Zepeda Jr. was no longer free to go; he was under arrest. Not surprisingly, the hurricane of hot news blew through the San Benito area with hustle and hostility. Outside the magistrate's office a crowd—100 folks—were screaming for payback, a blood atonement from Tony Zepeda. When being transferred to the judge's courtroom, the spiteful crowd "threw rocks and spat on" the alleged murderer. At the Arraignment (Initial Appearance) Justice of the Peace Romeo Garza ordered that the prisoner be held without bond, articulating a veiled but clearly understood logic: That denying bond was done for "several good reasons, and I think you know what they are." Translation is effortless: Zepeda wouldn't be safe on the streets. Texas Ranger Jack Dean, when broached by a snooping reporter didn't shy away from answering questions, acknowledging that authorities had "obtained a statement from Zepeda and that the search for other suspects is closed. He indicated he would continue to assist in obtaining evidence for trial."[10] Texas Ranger Dean harbored no vindictiveness—good lawmen couldn't afford that luxury—he just did his job. Too, and it demands mention, this did not go unnoticed by numerous spectators and/or lawmen: "Texas Ranger

Jack Dean of McAllen, who headed most of the investigation, agreed to allow Zepeda a chance to talk with his father before he was taken to the county jail."[11] Dean's sense of fair-play was a deep-seated core value. And that fidelity to duty demanded that now he would dedicate himself to protecting Tony Zepeda, Jr. from lynch-mob mentality, regardless how he personally felt about someone capable of strangling the life out of two innocent girl children. Texas Ranger Jack Dean had a precious eleven-year-old daughter at home.

Working diligently to corroborate what he already knew, Texas Ranger Dean began the meticulous process of identifying and gathering admissible physical evidence for submission to the DPS Crime Lab: All of the murdered victims' clothing—including undergarments—hair, soil and grass samples, the green towel and the section of suspect rope. Knowing what happened is but part of the game—the Burden of Proof resting with the State of Texas—admissibility is key. Were statements legally obtained? Did the defendant understand guaranteed Civil Rights were applicable to him/her? Had there been undue coercion? Had the crime-scene been contaminated? Was the evidentiary chain-of-custody documentable and properly maintained? Would lawmen faithfully honor their oaths? Darlings that they are, wily defense lawyers hunt hard for holes in the case and/or contraventions of the Code of Criminal Procedure. A criminal proceeding that will not stand up in the courtroom is pointless.

With regards to Tony Zepeda's case, though it necessitates that vexing chronologic forward skip, defense attorneys harangued that "the trial should have been called the 3-C Case, standing for credibility, contradiction and confusion. . . ." Specifically of the Texas Ranger, the defense scolded that ". . . Dean and Cameron County Sheriff's Deputies Jim Parker and Ed Moody grabbed the first person handy and pinned the rap on him without bothering to investigate other leads." Such did not withstand a sharp-witted comeback: "Prosecutors countered with a different 3-C definition, crafty, cunning and cold-blooded. . . ." And in fact Zepeda "had been crafty enough to tell only parts of the story of his cold-blooded strangulation murder of the two girls." Once the case actually went to the trial jury for deliberation the defense team danced to a different tune. Somewhat unexpectedly Zepeda's word-wolves whimpered that, now, the Murder defendant wished to change his plea from *Not Guilty*. Antonio Rios Zepeda, Jr. would voluntarily settle for taking some hard-time in the state penitentiary.[12] Texas Ranger Jack Dean duly noted that defendant Zepeda had changed his plea while the jury was out, pleading *Guilty* to both counts of Murder With Malice.[13]

Since this is Jack O. Dean's biography and this was a news-maker of a criminal investigation, perhaps, hearing in part from the Cameron County Sheriff's Office is just:

> We had the assistance from various members of the Department of Public Safety including one of your Helicopters. We were able to clear this case in a matter of less than twenty-four (24) hours with the assistance from Ranger Jack Dean and a confession obtained from the killer. In my opinion Ranger Dean is one of the most efficient investigators that I have met in more [than] twenty-six (26) years that I have been working with your Department. He is a fine gentleman in addition to being an outstanding officer.[14]

Rest assured, upon receipt of the above-cited letter of commendation from Cameron County Sheriff Boynton H. Fleming's headquarters, DPS Colonel Pat Speir was pleased and gratified, more than pleased that a Texas Ranger had done a bang-up job with regards to clearing the books of a double murder. On the other hand, he was personally gratified about the decision to post Jack Dean in the Lower Rio Grande Valley. From reports filtering into the DPS front office, Texas Ranger Jack Dean was accomplishing what he had been sent to McAllen to do: Re-sculpture the Texas Ranger institutional image in South Texas. Having supervisory decisions validated is rewarding for anyone—and Colonel Speir was happy.

Texas Ranger Jack Dean was making a favorable name for himself not only with regards to investigative work in the field, but on the baseball diamond as well, not as a player but as President of the McAllen Pony League. The McAllen State Bank's sponsored youth baseball team, for the second straight year, took the league

championship. Where he found the time for such off-duty public service is yet a mystery, but Texas Ranger Jack Dean was, and always
had been, systematically committed to supporting good citizenship
through kiddos sports programs. For a *McAllen Monitor's* Sunday edition, decked out in a business suit and wearing a necktie, and no visibly exposed six-shooter, Jack Dean is captured in a photograph with
bank officials but, more importantly with youthful team members
and their hard fought-for trophy.[15]

The month following the Zepeda murders, on the third day of
May, Texas Ranger Jack Dean was in possession of some very hot
news—something requiring immediate attention. One of his confidential informants (Cis) revealed that two fellows, one an armed-robbery defendant in the Hidalgo County calaboose thanks to Jack Dean's
investigative talents, was dangerously close to making an escape,
freeing himself and other enterprising detainees. The fleeing jailbirds would fly the coop and wing themselves across the Rio Grande.
If playing odds was an indicator it would probably prove successful:
the crafty inmates, if the snitch's information was rock-solid, had
two lethal undersized smuggled pistols and magazines full of copper-coated ammunition. Immediately Ranger Jack Dean orchestrated
a systematic search of the particular prisoner's cell. The snooping
expedition proved victorious. A .25 caliber autoloader and cartridges
were seized and an outlaw's wistful daydreams of ill-obtained freedom shattered.[16] During that jailhouse search Ranger Dean also seized
an additional small .25 caliber autoloader, from another inmate, but
more of that episode later as it is weaved into the Ranger's dramatic
story. Provably, it seems, Jack Dean's spider-web network of spies was
multiplying, and rightly so. Ranger Dean grasped when to press, when
to retreat, and how to keep a secret—key ingredients for a CI toying
with the notion of squealing and/or just who he/she should squeal
to—whatever the underlying motive for snitching. Texas Ranger Jack
Dean could be trusted—the underground and underworld scuttlebutt
was, in that regard, not Top Secret.

Certainly thirteen-year-old Kyle Dean wasn't concerned—at
least for now—with jailbirds, but two feathered and flying things

had plucked his interest: Whitewing dove and Bobwhite quail. Even by his own admission, when first arriving in the Lower Rio Grande Valley, as a youngster Kyle suffered somewhat of a cultural and geographical shock. At McAllen there were towering and swaying palm trees, instead of the rolling tumbleweeds at Pecos or the tall pines at Tyler. Nearby the meandering Rio Grande was an international landmark boundary—but even then not a truly safe playground for little children or budding adolescents trying to shake loose from supervision. The predominant portion of Kyle's classmates spoke Spanish fluently. Too, they were for the most part genealogically tied to the historically rich Valley, having kinfolks on both sides of the twisting and tangling Río Bravo. The relocation from East Texas to South Texas, at first, had been overwhelming and Kyle introverted, isolating himself in his bedroom and escaping being ill at ease by reading and reading and reading some more. He was, like his daddy, enthralled with the rich history of Texas. The self-imposed exile from real world reality—in the bigger picture—was short-lived and Kyle soon morphed back into his more recognizable and extroverted self. Jack Dean during those same early years had earned trust enough to have a shotgun—now, Kyle did too.[17]

Texas Ranger Jack Dean, a sportsman in off-duty time, enjoyed the challenges of shooting dove on the fly, a tricky feat to master. Jack was a fantastic wing-shooter and a good teacher. Kyle followed in his footsteps, capably husbanding shells and filling his game-bag with the limit. North of Hidalgo County was the aforementioned Brooks County, and it was there between Falfurrias and Encino that the elder Dean acquired a lease—a quail hunting paradise. Fond memories of those outing were—and are—forged into the psyches of father and son.[18]

On the home front the Dean girls were busy too. Kelly Lenea was at that identifiable and emotional and awkward physiological stage; sometimes a cherished and sweet little girl and sometimes a princess with dreams of Prince Charming in her and her friends' dreamy futures. She, like Kyle, was growing up—despite parental druthers. Janie Dean had gone back to work, supplementing the household income and satisfying an internal drive to make her meaningful contribution in the workplace. She had been recruited for and had accepted administrative—not policing—employment at the McAllen PD. Chief Clint Mussey wishing to capitalize on Janie's intelligence and experience had plenty to keep her busy and, perhaps most importantly, knew she could be explicitly relied on with regards to those sensitive topics that are intrinsic to criminal investigations and in-house personnel matters.[19] Valley lawmen knew Janie could be trusted. They, too, knew Texas Ranger Jack Dean's word was good.

Someone else's word was not good! Charles Voyde Harrelson, a native Texan, was a career criminal. Though its necessitates that break in remaining on chronological track for passing on Jack Dean's story, the two fellows on opposite sides of society's norms each owned lives that would intersect and entangle, time and time again. The telling of Texas Ranger Jack Dean's story in the round and skipping past at least a minimal biographical sketch of Charles V. Harrelson would, in short, be journalistic malfeasance. Respectfully, indulgence is sought.

Harrelson, born east of the Trinity River at Lovelady in Houston County, was but a year younger than Jack Dean. Certainly one of Houston County's most noteworthy employers was the Texas Department of Corrections at their Eastham Unit located in the southern portion of the county—and just north of Huntsville in Walker County and its storied multiplex of high-walled and high-fenced prisons such as The Walls, Byrd, Ellis, Estelle, Holliday, Wynne, and Goree. Historically speaking the Eastham Unit was rich—in a sad sort of way. For it had been there during the sixteenth of January 1934 that Major (name not rank) Joseph "Joe" Crowson was murdered during a classic prison break: the gunplay liberation of gangster Raymond Hamilton and four other inmates, orchestrated and conducted by Clyde Barrow and James Mullen, laying down a symphony of covering fire with .30-06 Browning Automatic Rifles (BARs) while hoodlum Bonnie Parker harmonized with screams of support and the honking of the getaway car's horn.[20] Within the big picture Raymond Hamilton and Joe Palmer would meet the state's executioner for their murderous deeds that day, but for the short go they uncaringly and mortally wounded Correctional Officer Joe Crowson with .45 autoloaders previously stashed under a bridge near a field crop's turn-row.[21] Any way were one to cut it, by any or all standards Eastham was no Sunday School.[22] Inmates inside Eastham didn't want to end their last days there. According to at least one adroit penman, Lovelady, with its store, café, feed mill, and solitary stoplight wasn't too homey either: "It was a fundamentalist town, not so much conservative as reactionary, a town that dared and begged young people to escape."[23]

Charles Voyde Harrelson escaped by dropping out of high-school and joining the United States Navy but heartfelt patriotism and honesty were not part of his syllabus for living life. Sanctioning a traditional and enduring family life was not for Charles Harrelson, though by one early on marriage he did father three sons before being lured from stability into the world of gamblers and gangsters and greed. He was a traveling man. The swathe he cut would be newsy and wide. Harrelson didn't toil away his days working for a living; criminality winked and he was seduced. And as history will bear witness, putting any misplaced romanticism or fascination regarding convicts and contract-killers aside, and subsequent to evenhandedly and judiciously tallying his measurable accomplishments and ultimate failures, there is, really, a hard and fast bottom-line: Charles Harrelson proved to be an inept outlaw.

Apparently, though he had adopted the persona of a genuine bad-man from Bitter Creek, Charles V. Harrelson wasn't an accomplished and/or dexterous *pistolero*, having one time let a haphazardly fired round from his atypical weapon of choice, a diminutive .25 caliber autoloader (commonly called a "pocket pistol") furrow a painful channel into his very own leg. Ostensibly a Texas MD at the ER removed the spent bullet and offhandedly gave Charles V. Harrelson the souvenir of his handiwork with a handgun, then dressing the throbbing wound sent him on his way. Wounded pride? Well, that may have registered a bigger caliber hurt.[24] So, Harrelson, like the Wild West era's Wyatt Barry Stapp Earp, had the slipshod mishandling of a gun as a part of his personal history.[25] Charles V. Harrelson and Wyatt B.S. Earp each owned another common denominator: both had an affinity for profiting from—at least for awhile—the loose labors of loose ladies.[26]

Like most desperadoes—though they more often than not deny it with lame excuses—the lad from Lovelady could and would wear a wire and snitch—self-interest always at top of his list.[27] Subsequent to spending prison time in California, Harrelson returned to Texas consorting with characters and cardsharps. On the third day of June 1968, Charles Harrelson came up short at Kansas City, Missouri. Capably working their underworld connections, Kansas City PD detectives did what detectives are supposed to do: follow through on informants' ratting. Lawmen learned through a telephone call on the above-cited date that

> a 1967 or '68 red Cadillac was parked near Twelfth and Broadway, near a shoeshine parlor; it had Texas license No. NJP-[xxx]; the driver was a white male, approximately thirty years of age, wearing a yellow shirt and brown trousers; underneath the front seat on the driver's side was a quantity of heroin wrapped in a rubber prophylactic; and that in the trunk of the automobile was a loaded sawed-off shotgun. The information was relayed to another Kansas City detective who, in company with a third detective, proceeded to the area near Twelfth and Broadway, in an unmarked police car, where the two detectives observed a red Cadillac convertible, 1967 or 1968 model, with Texas license No. NJP-[xxx], parked on Twelfth Street near Broadway, near a shoeshine parlor; At approximately 2:25 p.m., the detectives observed a white male, wearing a yellow shirt and brown trousers, approach the automobile, open and close the trunk, and then enter the automobile, and drive away. The officers followed the defendant to a parking lot, where they identified themselves, searched the defendant and his automobile, and then formally placed the defendant under arrest. The officers held the defendant at gunpoint while searching him and the automobile. A Search of the automobile located the loaded sawed-off shotgun in question in the trunk of the car. No narcotics were found in the car.[28]

Charles V. Harrelson, as he would do quite often, had stepped in it again. The shotgun had been altered with a hacksaw from its legally manufactured nomenclature to an illegal weapon with a barrel length of but "thirteen and a quarter inches, and an over-all length of twenty-two inches." The shotgun's deficit in inches, unreservedly qualified Mr. Charles V. Harrelson to appear before a United States District Judge and explain his justification for having something he wasn't supposed to have—a clear-cut violation of federal firearms statutes.[29] And what of the condom stuffed with heroin? As detectives cautiously approached, "Chuck" Harrelson had slyly slipped the prophylactic out of his pants pocket, dropped it to the pavement, and with a shuffling kick scooted it beneath the car parked next to the rag-top Cadillac, so said Sandra Sue Attaway.[30] Somewhat later the discarded dope was discovered and delivered to officers, but by then it could not be directly tied evidentiary-wise to slick Charles Harrelson. There was though, a back story revolving around that tightly stretched condom and it would burst forth in due time.

The strikingly good looking—by all accounts—"shapely" brunette had plenty to say it seems. The out-of-state installment in Missouri with regards to cunningly disposing of the heroin would register as hearsay, which doesn't necessarily make it fallacious, but deflates its courtroom value. On another matter Sandra Sue Attaway wasn't dealing in second-hand allegations.[31] She was not only a principal witness but an onsite player—along with Harrelson—when Alan Harry Berg had been kidnapped and stuffed into the car at Houston in the Brown Jug Club's parking lot. Later, after winding their way through Fort Bend County (county seat Richmond) Sandra Sue Attaway said Harrelson, with a small .25 autoloader, shot and then strangled Alan Berg before they dumped his body in the isolated sand dunes between Brazoria County's waterfront Surfside Island and the Texas Gulf Coast's tourist's Mecca, Galveston.[32] Crossing the causeway back onto the mainland, Sandra Sue Attaway noted that predator Harrelson didn't want to chance getting caught with the .25 caliber murder weapon: "As we drove over the bridge to the Gulf Freeway Chuck took the clip out of the gun and pitched the gun out and over the car to the right and into the water."[33] This half-assed planned but coldblooded and ruthless killing had taken place prior to Jack Dean pinning on the iconic star-and-wheel badge, but that should not suggest the Texas Rangers were not involved in this and another merciless and premeditated homicide credited to desperado Charles V. Harrelson's criminal account for whoring his personal services as a lowly paid professional assassin.

In fact, Texas Ranger James Lambright "Skippy" Rundell, later Captain of Company C, along with Jimmy Jones, Chief Criminal Investigator for Brazoria County and Joe Thorpe of the Harris County SO at Houston, had traveled to Atlanta, Georgia, and arrested Charles Harrelson where he had been hiding under an assumed name after jumping bail on the criminal charges lodged against him at Kansas City. At that time, Charles V. Harrelson, with two dead bodies on his back trail, naively presumed Texas officers were clueless. He was wrong. They were holding good paper (warrants) in their hands. Alan Berg's homicide was a whodunit no longer, not for Texas lawmen traveling to Georgia. The befuddled prisoner was flown back to Texas in chains courtesy a DPS pilot and airplane.[34] And though it's but anecdotal, the loquacious prisoner's incessant rattling got under Skippy's skin. So much so, that with a stern countenance the irritated Ranger threatened to throw Harrelson out of the airplane if he didn't put the whoa on his blabbering.[35]

As but a quick sidebar there should be no implication that Ranger Skippy Rundell didn't own a good sense of humor. While a THP Patrolman during the WWII years, when "fuel shortages made a 30 mile an hour speed limit necessary," Rundell, in his marked state squad car, was leisurely cruising the two-lane highway in Harris County, just outside Houston. All of a sudden an excessively speeding ice cream truck overhauled and passed the THP unit, the driver not realizing until the very last second that he had just blown by a police car. Then, when the mental light came on, the truck driver "hit his brakes and waved frantically" for Patrolman Rundell to stop, even before he could activate red-lights or siren. Inquisitively but cautiously Skippy approached the driver who bailed out of the truck and began excitedly jabbering, making sure he got in the first figurative lick, the words: "Man, you're the hardest fellow to catch. . . . I've been trying to stop you and give you some ice cream." Skippy smiled and warned the truck driver to slow it down, and as his tongue swirled through the tasty and creamy vanilla, mused that someone that quick-witted really didn't deserve a traffic citation.[36]

Now, returning back to the real story at hand. The aforementioned Texas Ranger Tol Dawson did append to one of his mandatory DPS-PRs the lengthy type written and voluntary statement of Sandra Sue Attaway, one she made while ensconced in Korean War veteran and veteran lawman Sheriff Robert R. "Bob" Gladney's lockup, the Brazoria County Jail at Angleton.[37]

Though actually keeping the unfolding drama perfectly in sync is a short-space challenge, for the present task a synopsis will suffice. Subsequent to Charles V. Harrelson running off to the Peach State, Lone Star State policing authorities—Jack Dean was still with THP at Tyler—in the Lower Rio Grande Valley, after an exhaustive search had finally located the lifeless remains of an until-then much sought Missing Person, Sam Carmelo Degelia, Jr., a grain dealer from Herne, Robertson County, not far northwest of Bryan/College Station and Texas A&M University.[38] Sam Degelia had been slain, execution-style, inside an irrigation pump-house southwest of McAllen. And, like the ill-fated and no doubt horrified Alan Berg, Sam Degelia, Jr. had been popped in the head at close range with spinning .25 caliber projectiles.[39] This too, especially after prosecutors' wheeling and dealing with Sandra Sue Attaway, was no mysterious whodunit. Harrelson would face the music and district attorneys in Brazoria and Hidalgo Counties would play the fiddles.

Dancing into the courtroom, representing Charles V. Harrelson for killing Messers Berg and Degelia on two different dates at two different places, was the ever idiosyncratic and colorful and flamboyant defense attorney Percy Foreman.[40] He was what everyday working and underpaid paycheck to paycheck lawmen refer to as a "tall building lawyer" or a "plush carpet attorney." Which plainly translates: He was pricy. Foreman's most high-profile case of late had been the spectacular legal representation of James Earl Ray, the fellow that cold-bloodedly assassinated Dr. Martin Luther King, Jr. at Memphis, Tennessee. Percy Foreman, somewhat surprisingly and incredibly chiseled the plea bargain that put Ray in the Big House, but saved him from waiting to meet his Maker and a Mortician in the Death House. Lawyer Percy Foreman was, or could be, a defendant's dream, a prosecutor's nightmare, and/or a trial-court judge's needling provocateur. On the positive side even his knowing critics would have to credit Percy Foreman for bringing into play ingenious courtroom tactics and brilliant theatrics. There was, however, that troubling downside—some thought Percy was downright unscrupulous and blatantly dishonest, not at all above resorting to out-and-out illegalities to win a client's acquittal, even Subornation of Perjury if that's what it took.[41]

With regards to the calculated and bounty-money murder of Alan Berg, the trial took place at Angleton about two years after the victim's decomposing remains had been found at Surfside. The State of Texas was represented by first-term District Attorney Ogden Bass, while the aging and experienced Percy Foreman, raring to go, sat alongside Charles V. Harrelson at the defense table. The big trial, a typical Texas headlining newsmaker, would consume more than a month. When it started, technically speaking, Jack Dean was a THP Patrolman at Tyler and when it ended he was a Texas Ranger at McAllen. In the interim an adversarial contest between Bass and Foreman raged—well, kinda raged. Thinking the state's murder case was a slam-dunk due to the granting of immunity to Sandra Sue Attaway had been imprudent. Percy Foreman acted true to form. Fair play was fine for tennis matches and tiddlywinks. In the courtroom Percy performed with the tenaciousness and viciousness of a proverbial junkyard dog, attacking witnesses and chewing on their character flaws and then spitting out gristles of doubt for the all-male jury to digest. District Judge G.P. "Jeep" Hardy's efforts to keep barking and blustering Percy Foreman chained within the general norms—whatever they were—of traditional courtroom decorum were ineffectual. Brazoria County and the watching world were in want of a good show and Percy was the superstar. There's little room for doubt that tenderfoot law students escaping the classroom would have been aghast, had they been spectators in the courtroom.[42]

Insurance is helpful for car wrecks and house burglaries, and just to be on the real safe side Percy Foreman threw his policy on the table, two *alibi* witnesses, which surprised courtroom onlookers but not shrewd Houston lawyers; all familiar with his shenanigans and sleights of hand. Although their remembrances seemed to have holes big enough to ride a Thoroughbred through, the *alibi* witnesses, at the very last minute, swearing that Charles Harrelson was elsewhere when Alan Berg was shot in the head and choked and left to rot in Texas Gulf Coast remoteness, did what the ever foxy Percy Foreman knew their testimony would do—create that smidgen or scoopful of the jury's Reasonable Doubt. Subsequent to the verdict of *Not Guilty*, Harrelson figuratively and legally "walked."[43] His criminal exposure though was far from being history. Charles Voyde Harrelson literally walked straight into the arms of waiting lawmen with handcuffs, belly-chains and leg-irons, one of whom was the dutiful Texas Ranger Jack Dean.[44] There was that littlie niggling difficulty in Hidalgo County—the law demanded that somebody answer for the Degelia homicide.[45]

District Attorney McInnis during an earlier trial had been successful—to a tiny degree—with the prosecution of Pete Thomas Scamardo, a former childhood friend and business associate of Mr. Degelia. Not surprisingly Percy Foreman, the wily fox, had been hired as defense counsel and not surprisingly was his long-established pattern of trial tactics for Scamardo's criminal case. Though Charles Harrelson was the triggerman, Pete Scamardo was a conspirator who would see financial gain through the killing of Degelia, so said DA Oscar McInnis and the State of Texas. Tying Harrelson and Scamardo together really was no prosecutorial stretch, not with irrefutable facts and the testimony of Sandra Sue Attaway and Jerry O'Brien Watkins, an ex-convict who had plenty to say about the day he and Charles Voyde Harrelson spent at McAllen, Texas. Nonetheless, Foreman could ill-afford to gamble and lose, so he played his hole-card Ace, a bombshell *alibi* witness—a nightclub entertainer for the El Toro Club at McAllen's Holiday Inn. The jury may not have bought into Percy's full-bore defense arguments, but the purported killer wasn't on trial so they found Pete Thomas Scamardo *Guilty*, but assessed his punishment at but seven years—and that was to be served by a conditional Probation. Award the coup to Percy. When it was all said and done, the Scamardo trial had been the longest, sixty-eight days, and the most costly in Hidalgo County history.[46]

Perhaps the casual reminder is really unnecessary, but at the time of Pete Scamardo's murder trial Jack Dean was not yet stationed in the Lower Rio Grande Valley and he was unacquainted with the key players. That changed quickly and decisively—Charles Voyde Harrelson was to have his day in court.

Texas Ranger Jack Dean's first introduction to the fact-gathering part of the case (not just transporting the prisoner to Edinburg) was at the bidding of Oscar McInnis. There were trial details to prepare for and witnesses to be served with subpoenas, routine preliminary steps for any upcoming courtroom campaign. Of particular note was the fact that McInnis trusted the Texas Rangers. The DA had confidence that Jack Dean could and would safeguard sensitive information: The secret whereabouts of Jerry O. Watkins, the fellow who "flipped" and who now owned immunity from prosecution if he told the whole truth, and nothing but the truth—so help his or somebody's God. Early one morning, before daylight, Texas Ranger Dean left McAllen and after arriving at San Antonio formally served the required subpoena on Jerry O. Watkins, particularly noting the need for cloak-and-dagger intrigue, theorizing that the witness was taking somewhat of a life or death chance by testifying.[47]

Too, and it's more than germane for the true-life drama herein unfolding, Texas Ranger Dean, at DA McInnis's request, was particularly tasked with ensuring that Sandra Sue Attaway was where she was supposed to be—when she was supposed to be there. Her testimony was essential. Therefore Ranger Jack Dean in his witness protection and chauffeuring role came to know Sandra Sue Attaway reasonably well, transporting her to and from court—for this and that hearing about first one thing then another. In due course, quite naturally they

partook of meals and banter, an amicable but strictly business relationship. Though after acknowledging that Sandra Sue Attaway was
attractive, in Jack Dean's estimation she was a "little ditsy" which
wasn't said in a demeaning tone, just that she had allowed herself to
become involved with the wrong crowd, doing the wrong things—
and Chuck Harrelson was the bandmaster playing the wrong tune—a
dirge. Sandra Sue Attaway's choices had been bad.[48]

Paring to the nub may shortchange the reader of a damn good
true-crime story but, for this, Texas Ranger Jack Dean's biography,
a snapshot must suffice. Pete Thomas Scamardo wanted Mr. Degelia
doornail dead and turned to Charles V. Harrelson to accomplish what
he didn't have the stomach for—an execution. Harrelson wasn't
bothered by conscience, and the pittance paid for the hit would be
nice—he was always strapped for cash. And, in addition to that,
according to pretty Sandra Sue Attaway, Harrelson "owed a favor" to
Scamardo because it had been Pete's prophylactic stuffed with heroin that Charles had surreptitiously kicked under the convenient car
at Kansas City, Missouri.[49] In the world of dope dealing a $10,000
shortfall with somebody else's product is not good—balancing the
books with a "favor" is one path to setting things right. Such might
even be a sound indemnity against a premature departure from
the land of the living. So, according to Sandra Sue Attaway, Charles
Voyde Harrelson left Houston for a daytrip flight to McAllen, her
full-well knowing that the Devil's dirty work was afoot.[50]

Implausibly it would seem, and speaking to his aforementioned
ineptness when it came to covering his tracks of outlawry, Harrelson
didn't make the trip to McAllen alone. Jerry Watkins was a traveling
man, too. What had ostensibly been arranged as a legitimate business meeting with some drinks and recreation across the Rio Grande
at Reynosa, figuratively went south when Sam Degelia was literally
at gunpoint made a prisoner and his hands bound behind his back.[51]
Chalk another kidnapping to Harrelson's scorecard? Shortly, after
Charles Harrelson marched Degelia into an isolated irrigation pump-
house south of McAllen, Jerry Watkins waiting at the car heard two
"pops." Charles Voyde Harrelson, .25 caliber autoloader in hand,

straightforwardly returned to the parked car, cool and unworried—
and in a characteristically talkative mood said: "This is not the first
son of a bitch I had to ring the bell on and won't be the last. . . ."[52]
According to Jerry Watkins's sworn courtroom testimony, while he
drove back to McAllen, Charles V. Harrelson busily disassembled the
murder weapon and, as they motored down the getaway roadway, haphazardly pitched pistol parts out the car window. Such was, really, a
boneheaded stunt of ineptitude. Later, apparently yet wanting recognition for his pistol work after returning to Houston, Charles V.
Harrelson advised Sandra Sue Attaway that he had shot Degelia twice,
because the first round hadn't capped the life out of Sam:

> Chuck [Harrelson] said he tied the man's hands behind him and
> walked him out to the shack and that he shot him once in the head
> with a .25 pistol. The man Degelia said "Oh, My God, Why?" Chuck
> said he fell, but that he shot him again because he was a big man.[53]

Though at the time of the Degelia killing Jack Dean was not yet a
Ranger, Tol Dawson was. Since policing and prosecuting authorities
had already turned Jerry Watkins into a helpmate of sorts, one who
had to tell the truth or lose his free pass avoiding prison, the search
for pistol parts was not easy, but not futile—they knew about where
to look for the pot of evidentiary gold at the end of Hidalgo County's
rainbow—the weedy bar-ditch between the pump-house and McAllen.
The gist of the story is simple and short. Ranger Tol Dawson's tireless search was concluded. The .25 autoloader's frame—the part with
the unique serial number—was located and traced: The tiny pistol's
history was now known.[54] Earlier in their western state travels to Las
Vegas, Charles V. Harrelson and Sandra Sue Attaway had stopped for a
spur-of-the-moment look-see inside Bob's Sportsman's and Appliance
Center at Vernal, Utah, not too far west of western Colorado's state-
line.[55] There is where the gun had been purchased. The fellow selling
the .25 autoloader would later testify that he never would forget the
specific transaction—due to a signal fact, stating for the record: "If
you had seen that girl [Sandra Sue Attaway] in that purple dress, you
would probably remember her too."[56]

One would think DA McInnis was ecstatic. Though he had been by circumstances and reality forced into making deals with persons owning varying degrees of culpability, the facts and testimony of other disinterested witnesses were lining up rather nicely with the murder-mystery story Sandra Sue Attaway and Jerry O. Watkins were telling. Pete Thomas Scamardo had been legally scorched. Charles V. Harrelson's fat was in the fire, his goose cooked! Percy Foreman thought otherwise—and as usual—had a trick or two on the grill. The show was not over till the fat lady sings, and the pompous and flaunting legal beagle had a songbird in mind, that piano bar vocalist at El Torro Club, Louise Scott Gannon. Charles Voyde Harrelson was in dire need of an *alibi*, one that could put him elsewhere when Sam Degelia died. That *alibi* witness business was, by certain detractor's sustainable assertions, Percy's specialty.[57]

Therefore, once again, in the Charles Voyde Harrelson murder trials, an *alibi* witness, a last minute witness, this time Louise Scott Gannon, testified she had been having dinner with the defendant when the homicide was alleged to have happened. Oscar McInnis had proved his case to eleven men on the jury—they were convinced beyond a Reasonable Doubt—ready to convict Charles V. Harrelson for a premeditated and pitiless act of enormity—offing a father of four.[58] However, unanimous jury verdicts are obligatory, a tilt of the scales in the defendants' behalf. The only female member of the trial jury wasn't waffling and flailing; she was swimming in a reservoir of doubt and she was unsinkable, no matter how other jurors docked their logical votes or threw the life-rings of reason. The judge—after an appropriate time—had but little choice to declare a mistrial. Lawyer Percy Foreman, with a little help from Louise Scott Gannon, had awarded Charles V. Harrelson a do-over. And, for the next installment Texas Ranger Jack Dean would be primed and ready—to make his investigatory contribution.

In the meantime there was other criminal and peace keeping work. Charles V. Harrelson was not convicted but, he was not free— he couldn't post bond and his father couldn't post it either, the family farm near Lovelady having been conveyed to a tall building lawyer from Houston.[59] The case styled *State of Texas vs. Charles V. Harrelson* was docketed for a new day, a new trial. The wheels of justice turn slow, but they turn—grind—nevertheless.

While Percy Foreman's eleventh-hour *alibi* witnesses may have taken prosecutors and a public enthralled with a scandalous soap-opera type murder-mystery by surprise, Texas Ranger Jack Dean had other work demanding his attention. So, while Charles V. Harrelson languished in the jailhouse, Ranger Dean forged ahead into the swamp of ceaseless criminality. Though the list is long, for illustrative purposes a short peek is appropriate. Texas Ranger Dean was called to the scene of a homicide wherein a fellow was "shot three times in the chest and once below the belt buckle" before his wallet was taken and he was left "face up in a ditch."[60] Then there was the case of a Mexican national cabdriver from Matamoros, who north of the Rio Grande had been lethally stabbed twenty-five times by an unknown assailant or assailants. The unfortunate fellow's taxi, a 1966 Chevrolet, was ultimately located "6 miles from the body." A hardened crime reporter writing for the *Brownville Herald*, penning the all too routine narrative, jotted: "Texas Ranger Jack Dean has been called in to the investigation and various specimens of evidence will be submitted to the Texas Department of Public Safety laboratory for analysis and reports."[61] Shortly, an extortion minded nitwit thought he could enrich himself by threatening severe bodily harm to a thoroughly frightened female dentist south of the Río Bravo at Reynosa. Surreptitiously Texas Ranger Dean, aided by two DPS Narcotics Agents, "set up surveillance." The stakeout was short. A snapshot newspaperman pulled the trigger on the story, duly noting the stunned suspect "was arrested by Texas Ranger Jack Dean and local officers as he was allegedly picking up a bundle of newspapers, which had been substituted for the extortion money at a supermarket in Hidalgo County."[62] Score one for the good guys. Time really is unstoppable. There never is a shortage of crooks, conmen, crazed impulse killers, or police characters pirating for profit and/or payback. Jack Dean was busy.

And though the personal dilemma would not be exclusively owned by Ranger Jack Dean by any stretch of the imagination, due to his workload and the docketing of his criminal cases, finding vacation time was problematic, notifying Captain Wood: "I respectfully request that one week of my vacation, scheduled 6-19-72 thru 6-25-72 be postponed to a later date. This is due to a murder trial scheduled in Hidalgo County on June 19, 1972 and a Grand Jury in Cameron County on June 21, 1972. I am to appear in both of these."[63] Expectedly, Captain Wood notified Ranger Dean that his then-scheduled vacation time was officially canceled and his request to reschedule sometime later in the summer was approved.[64] The old saw about working from can to can't seems to mesh handily with Jack Dean's workaday actions.

Properly laying the foundation for the policing fraternity, it's germane to quickly clarify and not mislead. Simply said, though law enforcing can be a deadly game—it's a team sport. With that in mind, even though this is Texas Ranger/U.S. Marshal Jack Dean's narrative, he readily acknowledges that DPS colleagues and/or other local, state, and federal lawmen were and would be co-equal partners throughout his long-lasting law enforcing career. The old saw, One Riot-One Ranger certainly has a ring of blood and thunder excitement, although its practical application is best left to script-writers and movie moguls and greenhorn idealists. The lasting framework of trust is tricky to build, easy to topple. For hammering out a legit sense of trustworthiness and nailing down solid friendships Jack Dean was a damn good carpenter.

As previously noted during selective highlights of Texas Ranger Jack Dean's deployment to the Lower Rio Grande Valley, proficiently and safely maintaining custody of inmates in a county jail can prove nightmarish. At Edinburg the overworked and underpaid jail staff was operating in a 1920s constructed structure, one Sheriff Claudio Castaneda was championing to be replaced with the Hidalgo County Commissioners' set-aside of $825,000, supplemented with funds from some federal revenue-sharing grants.[65]

Geronimo Quintanilla was not up for bureaucratic dawdling and a promise of what might come; he wanted out of the steel-barred hotel—right now!

Awaiting an appellate court decision regarding his conviction and fifty-year sentence for killing Mike Longoria, Quintanilla was marking off days in Hidalgo County rather than at Huntsville. Geronimo and his fellow pal and prisoner, Guadalupe Gonzalez, made their break for liberty on the nineteenth day of October 1972. Undoubtedly the county lockup was porous; Geronimo and Guadalupe had a gun—and shanks. During the second-floor takeover of the facility, jailors Arturo Garza, sixty-three, and Ruben Flores, fifty-six, were wounded, not fatally, but nevertheless shot and/or stabbed.[66] Thankfully another jailor slipped his coworkers out of the unfolding mayhem and madness. Others spirited Garza and Flores to Edinburg General Hospital. Sheriff Castaneda immediately notified Texas Ranger Dean, who in response raced to the scene. Not surprisingly law enforcement personnel from area police departments and THP units reacted as dispatchers broadcast the alarm. At the county lockup, the beleaguered but cool and collected sheriff requested—because he thought well of Dean's judgment—that the Texas Ranger take command of policing operations outside of the jailhouse.[67] Such sagacity was well advised.

Troubles facing lawmen were twofold: run amok prisoners inside the jail, and impetuous spectators in the parking lot: "A huge crowd of several hundred surrounded the jail to watch the tense drama. Many of them stood unprotected, well within pistol range of the holed up prisoners."[68] Simultaneously corralling crooks and onlookers is complex. The inside outlaws were shooting outside indiscriminately; the outside rubberneckers were ducking and dodging at each sharp crack of Geronimo Quintanilla's second-rate six-shooter trying to catch a look inside. The exchange of gunfire was not one-sided, however. A plucky onsite newspaperman for the *McAllen Monitor* was trying his dead-level best—bobbing and weaving—to keep score, reporting that "he counted 22 shots from the jail and about a like number by lawmen." That same reporter turned his eyes to the sky: "A helicopter took three officers and a Texas Ranger over the jail, but they reported when they passed by the window, the shades were drawn. The officers carried M16 rifles."[69]

Confining the rogue prisoners to the second floor was tactically smart but fraught with peril. Nevertheless lawmen do what lawmen do: "Texas Ranger Jack Dean of McAllen and other officers finally raced to the lower floor of the jail in an exchange of gunfire."[70] The covering fire was effective—nobody, good guy or bad guy—caught a bullet. Somewhat later, Texas Ranger Jack Dean remarked to an interviewer: "I've been shot at a couple of times and that lead will get your attention.... Most of the time I'd say it's about 90 percent boredom and 10 percent terror, that's about what Rangering is."[71] Trapped as he was, a yet defiant Geronimo Quintanilla was making a demand that, before he surrendered, he wanted assurances he would not be prosecuted for his actions that day. He was playing a weak hand. He could fold or raise the bet—Sheriff Castaneda would stand pat, no deals whatsoever. But, being reasonable he would allow others to give it their best try. Sheriff Castaneda and Ranger Dean didn't want to kill anyone:

> Quintanilla's mother, Mrs. Arisilia Quintanilla, his sister and common-law wife were brought to the scene and appealed to him to give up about 9:35 a.m., but they were unsuccessful. His court-appointed attorney Servando Gonzalez arrived a little later and attempted to talk him into surrendering. Attorney David Hall talked to another prisoner, who had apparently been released by Quintanilla, and asked him to come out. The prisoners did not respond at the time.[72]

Ultimately, Geronimo Quintanilla reached the same conclusion as lawmen strategizing on the first floor; the tightly clinched jaws of a criminal justice bear-trap anchoring his ankle to the jailhouse floor was indestructible. Geronimo and Guadalupe surrendered. Is there a back story?

A Grand Jury had indicted Norma Quintanilla Morales, Geronimo's sister, for smuggling the revolver into the jail. Later, at trial, the prosecution had no shortage of credible witnesses, including Texas Ranger Jack Dean. Hidalgo County Assistant District Attorney Joe Friend "traced the .22 caliber 'Saturday Night Special'

Quintanilla used in the jail shootout to Mrs. Morales through a long chain of witnesses." As the one and only defense witness, Mrs. Morales testified in her own behalf, denying in oath "ever having the gun introduced in evidence. She said she had given a similar gun to her mother who is now critically ill and unable to testify." The calculated move by her defense lawyer, Roman Gutierrez, to put Mrs. Morales on the witness stand and create that smidgen of Reasonable Doubt proved risky but brilliant: After but two hours deliberation the jury returned their verdict of *Not Guilty*.[73]

Illustrative of inter-agency cooperativeness within the law enforcement community is Ranger Jack Dean's tiring investigative probe into stolen firearms—primarily pistols—being sold in the Lower Rio Grande Valley. During the wee morning hours of 24 November 1971 burglars had burrowed a hole through the metal backside of White-Jones Hardware in the Watson Village Shopping Center at Anderson, South Carolina. Before police were on the scene, the thieves had made off with thirty-seven brand-new firearms, four shotguns and thirty-three handguns. These were not cheap Saturday Night Specials, but a nice assortment of Colt, Ruger, Walther, and Smith & Wesson handguns.[74] Due to federal legislation, firearms dealers were required to be licensed and keep fastidious acquisition and disposition records of their inventory. Months later Texas Ranger Jack Dean had received intelligence that a particular fellow in the Lower Rio Grande Valley, an insurance salesman, was actively peddling pistols to friends and/or acquaintances out of a sizable cardboard box. No brain-teaser is necessary, these were guns stolen earlier at the White-Jones Hardware Store. Running down leads and recovering the stolen firearms is time consuming. Texas Ranger Jack Dean—slowly but surely was nailing down testimony, taking written statements and building a case, steadily working his way backwards toward identifying at least one of the thieves; a long-haul truck driver with a lengthy rap sheet. Muzzle blasts changed Texas Ranger Dean's course.

Laying aside his investigation into the South Carolina firearms burglary, Ranger Dean had to jump to, again: Another Saturday, another killing. This was a daytime crime, 1:30 P.M. on 16 December 1972. The crime-scene northwest of Mission was sickening and bloody. According to Ranger Jack Dean, the unfortunate victim, twenty-five-year-old Russell Dow Hinton, was DRT. He had "been shot several times at close range with a shotgun." According to the first officer on the scene, THP Patrolman Paul Starnes, it wasn't even necessary to "go near to see if Hinton was dead. He could see from the driveway various parts of Hinton's skull scattered about."[75] Somewhat incredibly it seems, Hinton's pregnant and gutsy wife "struggled with her husband's assailant after he was shot." This was no whodunit! William Bert Crosswhite was identified as the shotgun wielding culprit. The newly made widow, Mary Jane Hinton, had plenty to say:

> She told of knowing Crosswhite since she was 11. She said she was preparing lunch in the kitchen which was in the center of their nine room dwelling when her husband of a year and Crosswhite went behind her through a door into their carport. Almost immediately she heard a shot, ran to the door and saw Crosswhite standing over the prostrate form of her husband and pumping shot after shot from a pump gun into her husbands' head from six inch range. She called "stop" ran to Crosswhite and took the gun away. . . . he picked up a double barrel 20-gauge lying beside Hinton and emptied that into her husband also. . . . Cosswhite got into his car, told her "He's allright man" and drove away. . . . [She] admitted her husband and she had smoked marijuana from time to time and that Hinton had obtained his first marijuana cigarette from Crosswhite.[76]

Justice of the Peace Reynaldo Ruiz of nearby La Joya in the western stretch of Hidalgo County accepted a sworn Complaint and straightforwardly issued an arrest warrant. During the process of unraveling the sordid mess, in addition to the double-barreled 20-gauge, Ranger Jack Dean recovered several empty casings and a 12 gauge pump shotgun.[77] He, too, recovered at the murder scene what was a substantial weight of marijuana.[78] Later, the seizure of burlap bags containing green grassy substances in brick form and wrapped in brown paper was officially somewhat downsized. The actual weight of tightly pressed bricks is always a rather tricky guesstimate, while on the street and/or at the scene. Texas Ranger Dean turned the suspected marijuana over to DPS Narcotics Agent Don L. Stout for safekeeping and the necessary laboratory analysis. The certified weight of the product tipped the scales at 77.6 lbs and, indeed, the chemical analysis confirmed that the green bricks were marijuana.[79]

While hunting for the twenty-four-year old William Bert Crosswhite, at his home, lawmen learned that he was severely injured. An ambulance was called and he was at once rushed to McAllen General Hospital, purportedly in critical condition, lacerations to his left arm near the elbow. The not-so-alleged killer was immediately placed under guard. Texas Ranger Dean interviewed William Bert Crosswhite. Though suffering the self-inflicted injuries in a failed suicide, Crosswhite had his side of the story, and it wasn't quite the same as the widow Hinton. According to Texas Ranger Dean, although not giving a conclusive motive for the shooting, he did mention narcotics, stating that he and Hinton had smoked marijuana a short time before the shooting. Crosswhite claimed that Hinton was the one who had introduced him to drugs several years ago and he had often thought that if he would kill Russell Hinton, that all the trouble he had had with narcotics and other legal problems would disappear and he could start life anew.[80] Critically, Texas Ranger Jack Dean determined that Crosswhite had voluntarily and rationally answered questions in a normal manner subsequent to the shooting.[81] Such layman's analysis as to Crosswhite's deportment and frame of mind was very important.

Subsequently, at trial, William Bert Crosswhite's canny attorney, Joe Evins, opted trying for *Not Guilty by Reason of Insanity*. The inherent odds with such a plea were quite risky. For the murder defendant to succeed within such legal argument there had to be an admission that, indeed, he had killed Russell D. Hinton, but he was, in actual fact, mentally incompetent at the time of the shotgun shooting mêlée. Resultantly: "The defense did not contest the killing, but asked to have Crosswhite declared insane and to be committed to an institution." District Court Judge Fidencio Guerra overruled the defense motion to suppress introduction of crime-scene photos and other evidence. The defense lawyer, it seemed valiantly, tried to sell his premise and unfortunately for him and his client, the jury was not in a buying mood. They deliberated three hours and twenty minutes before reaching their verdict. Bold print newspaper headlines nailed the story: "Jury Finds Crosswhite Guilty in Murder Trial."[82] William Bert Crosswhite caught the quarter, twenty-five years.[83] Understandably, not even the attentive jury nor psychiatrists can predict the future. Despondently while waiting to "catch the chain" to TDC, William Bert Crosswhite, inside the Hidalgo County Jail, succeeded in taking his own life.[84]

And here, though it does not relate to Crosswhite and the murder investigation, it's but relevant to mention an underreported dynamic associated with lawmen engaged in hard-core criminal matters. During a Company D meeting, Captain Wood advised his Texas Rangers to be on guard: "Lock-type gas caps have been purchased due to the fact that in recent months some militants in the Gulf Coast area have placed incendiary devices in the gas tanks of police units. These devices explode when sufficient time elapses for the protective covering to melt in the fuel and cause destruction of the vehicle."[85] The message was shortly driven home to Texas Ranger Jack Dean in the Lower Rio Grande Valley: At approximately 1:00 A.M., on 26 April 1973, a blue 1972 Plymouth belonging to the Texas Department of Public Safety and assigned to the DPS Narcotics Service personnel stationed at McAllen was torched while parked on the west side of the McAllen Police Department.[86] Policing is dicey business.

Subsequent to the filing of a homicide case against Crosswhite but before the District Court's final disposition, Texas Ranger Jack Dean, working with DPS Intelligence Agent Don Lee, had pretty well corralled data about a yahoo blameworthy as the key link that would ultimately unravel the Anderson, South Carolina, gun-theft caper. He was, now, serving time in the United States Penitentiary at Marion, Illinois. The bad-boy was in the hoosegow due to concurrent convictions for thefts from Interstate Shipments in Missouri and Illinois. Texas Ranger Dean's and later Agent Lee's investigative talents had put them about as far as they could go with the case in the Lone Star State. Texas Ranger Dean authored a letter to Anderson County Deputy Wayne Coker naming the suspect and cutting to the nub: "I have no proof that this subject stole these pistols but as you will see by his rap sheet he has pulled time for burglary in the past. . . . I have been able to check these [pistols] back through several people to the subject. . . ."[87]

About this same time another bit of good news broke for Texas Ranger Jack Dean. For about a year he had been working a Home Invasion Robbery at the McAllen residence of Frank Norris, a genuinely hospitable and well-respected fellow within the American Numismatic Association: the official coin collectors' society. On the night of 12 December 1971 three ne'er-do-wells had invaded the Norris home, bound and gagged Mr. and Mrs. Norris—and then rifled the home ultimately making off with swag and a coin collection valued in the neighborhood of $15,000. Due to the hard work of Texas Ranger Jack Dean and McAllen Detective Bob Jeffries, the Hidalgo County Grand Jury was furnished sufficient Probable Cause to return Indictments. Warrants issued for three fellows: two from the city of Irving, Dallas County, and Teddy Keith Thrush, twenty-eight, of Lubbock. The surprised Dallas County desperadoes were arrested first, then U.S. Immigration officials arrested Thrush at an El Paso Port of Entry as he returned from Ciudad Juárez. Ranger Dean and Detective Jeffries traveled to San Antonio, where Thrush had been transferred to, then returned him to Edinburg, where his bond was set at nifty $100,000.[88] A newspaper reporter enlightened: "McAllen police said the three men are wanted at various other cities across the state in connection with similar robberies."[89] For a Sunday edition, the *McAllen Monitor* was effusive in its praise for a particular DPS employee:

> Law enforcement officers in general and Texas Ranger Jack Dean
> in particular were commended by members of the Hidalgo Coin
> Club at their January meeting. Club members took note of the fact

that Dean never retired to an inactive file his investigation of the burglary of the home of fellow coin club member Frank Norris, who lost a good many choice coins when the house was invaded. After more than a year, Dean did apprehend the alleged culprits. A report of his long hours on the case was forwarded to the American Numismatic Association.[90]

In a personal typewritten letter from Miriam Gilmore, Editor, the Texas Numismatic Association Newsletter, *TNA News*, Texas Ranger Dean was again singled out for adulation: "Without the fine efforts and protection of our law enforcement officers, coin collectors would not be able to pursue an enjoyable hobby such as numismatics. . . . may I offer our sincere appreciation for your continual investigation interest in the apprehension of the individuals allegedly responsible for the Frank Norris robbery. . . ."[91] And it didn't end there! At the annual Board Meeting of the American Numismatic Association in Colorado Springs, Colorado, a $500 reward payment was approved and a check was made out to Texas Ranger Jack Dean. In McAllen, on behalf of the Texas Numismatic Association, L.G. Davenport, TNA District 14 Governor, presented Ranger Jack Dean with the organization's very first "Golden Bullet Award," and the $500 check, declaring the Ranger had "done the most for the security of the hobby's collectors and dealers." Humbled, but not speechless, Texas Ranger Jack Dean accepted the honors "for all of several officers who worked on the case."[92] The beer and the barbeque were on Jack.

8

"I located Harrelson's pistol"

On a much more serious front there was not any notion or room for celebration—whatsoever. The nearly nude twenty-three-year-old body of Candice Fletcher Mora, mother of a three-year-old daughter, was shockingly discovered inside her Harlingen apartment. Another all too familiar headline heralded: "Ranger Joins Investigation." The young mother's death had been sadistically violent and nauseatingly gruesome as Texas Ranger Jack Dean presently learned: The autopsy revealing she had been strangled, stabbed about twenty-five times, slashed about the neck and stomach and suffered a broken neck. The plot thickened after it was learned that there had been no forced entry into the apartment and the toddler had been found sound asleep, unharmed, in her bed. Items of evidence were sent to the DPS Crime Lab at Corpus Christi. Although too frequently in a whodunit murder the spouse is an initial suspect, in this case that seemed not to ring true. The victim's husband, Daniel, at the time was in the United States Army and indisputably deployed to South Korea—he had a bulletproof *alibi*.[1]

Another case dealing with death had ground through the court's docket and was at hand. Although it was now a misdemeanor case and would be heard by a jury of but six, five women and a man, it was of general interest to the public and of particular interest to the defendant, the dismissed Hidalgo County deputy sheriff, Robert C. Johnson. The charge arising out of the civil disturbance at Pharr was being heard:

Hidalgo County Sheriff Claudio Castaneda and former Chief Deputy Ray Rogers, who is now chief at Mission, told the jury in Judge Walter Kelly's court that Johnson had told them he possibly shot a man while firing his pistol above the man's head.[2]

Texas Ranger Jack Dean, understandably, would be called on to testify as to his findings with regards to the apparent bullet indention, the hard-packed metal gutter, and the overall situation at Pharr on the night he was called into action. Part of that testimony clearly illustrated why area attorneys—prosecution and defense—had faith in and trusted Jack Dean. He would tell the truth. In this instance, among the hard evidentiary facts, Texas Ranger Dean open and above board related that during the riot he never "fired his weapon" and added: "I myself was not confronted with such a situation," even though he, too, had been struck with a rock. The Chief of Police from Edinburg, A.C. Gonzalez, followed suit, declaring "that he did not see any justification for officers to use weapons during the 1971 riot at Pharr."[3] Though it would have been effortless to shade their testimony—justifying brother officers popping caps—Dean and Gonzalez, to coin the phrase, cut the wheat from the chaff. Certainly there was no criminal intent on the part of Johnson to kill bystander Alfonso L. Flores. The death had been a tragedy to be sure, yet it had not happened on purpose. Legalese and leniency sometime intersect. The jury was sympathetic: Robert C. Johnson was acquitted.[4]

Someone else had to pay their debt—years. Though his appellate murder case was yet in process, there would have been nothing but hopelessness for Geronimo Quintanilla had he tried to legally skate past criminal charges resulting from the previous year's dismal jailbreak and the wounding of two jailors—and the shooting at near everyone else. Geronimo entered his *Guilty* plea to charges of Assault With Intent to Murder and waited, but not for long. Although it would make for a sixteen hour day and was a Saturday, Texas Ranger Dean and Deputy Pat Ramsey cuffed and chained Quintanilla inside the Hidalgo County Jail and set off on their jaunt to Huntsville. The prisoner was safely deposited with Texas Department of Corrections caretakers and the frazzled lawmen returned to the Lower Rio Grande Valley.[5]

One classification of criminality was a reoccurring nightmare for Texas Ranger Jack Dean and other Lower Rio Grande Valley lawmen. Mexico, it seemed, was a wide-open floodgate for fellows with stealing cars, trucks, farm machinery, bulldozers, and front-end loaders north of the river and illegally exporting to the Lone Star State's south of the border neighbor. Even a cursory review of Jack Dean's TRWRs reveals enormity of the illicit traffic. Fastidiously following Texas Ranger Dean's investigative trail in this regard is doable, but not necessary for perception of the overall picture. Frequently are the days Ranger Dean spent working with local lawmen, DPS-MVT Agents such as Ralph Byrd, who he had previously worked with while in THP at Tyler, NATB Agent Henry Lipe and TP&W Game Wardens.[6] Repeatedly roadblocks were manned north of McAllen and south of Falfurrias, and at Texas' end of the International Bridge crossing the in-between river. Not infrequently, too, were the days Ranger Jack Dean spent south of the Río Bravo working with Mexican authorities, identifying and recovering stolen vehicles of one category or another. With regards to these criminal investigations, during a Company D meeting, Captain Wood made particular note:

> Ranger Jack Dean has been very successful during this period in returning stolen vehicles from Mexico. . . .[7]

Though the arrests and recoveries were numerous, the problem was then, and is now, one of the reoccurring migraine headaches South Texas lawmen suffer—daily.[8]

Almost unbelievably but it is fact, ever intent on self-improvement Texas Ranger Jack Dean had enrolled at various times for educational classes at Texas' Southmost College at Brownsville and at Pan-American University, no little feat for a grown fellow on call twenty-four and seven. There was no shortage of homework and papers—and no shortage of felonies needing resolution. How he pulled it off may be unanswerable, but Captain John Wood had noted of Jack Dean's personal performance: "You are leading this company for the month of March [1973]. Keep up the good work!"[9]

Although it awkwardly skews the chronological narrative to an extent if examined too meticulously, an amalgamation of hard facts paints a mosaic of meanness. Texas Ranger Jack Dean and Charles Voyde Harrelson were destined to share space and time. With reasonably sound basis a prominent historian and writer posited that regarding Harrelson, Jack Dean knew "more about him than any lawman."[10]

This unfolding scenario, in part, was mentioned in the preceding chapter, but the notation here about the rest of the little story seems much more fitting for context. Guns inside Hidalgo County's lockup seemed a failing grade test for lawmen—not mentioning out-and-out embarrassment. Charles V. Harrelson somehow had a pistol in his cell. Another sly prisoner also had a tiny handgun, another .25 autoloader. Big plans were brewing for a big-time breakout. Harrelson had little to lose. Exhibiting his characteristic tendency to rattle rather than hold his tongue, Charles Harrelson's secret blue-steel treasure was no secret—one of Ranger Dean's spies knew the scoop. Action came quick. Working in unison with Sheriff Claudio Castaneda and Chief Investigator Ramsey, along with DA Oscar McInnis, Texas Ranger Jack Dean had paid an unannounced and unsmiling not so social visit to chatty Charles V. Harrelson's "house," the euphemism employed by prison convicts and/or long-term jailhouse inmates when referencing their involuntarily assigned cell. Texas Ranger Jack Dean elaborates—tellingly:

> Informant revealed to me that accused murderer Charles Harrelson had a Beretta .32 Auto hidden in his cell. Informant was not sure how it got in there but that it was there. The cell was searched by Sheriff, Deputy Ramsey and I, and the pistol was found as stated. It was found in a wall in a plastic bag. It was a .25 Cal Beretta [Jetfire model] instead of a .32. Also found was a new hacksaw blade. Charges will be filed at a later date at request of District Attorney.[11]

The ever loquacious Charles V. Harrelson was now outfoxed, flabbergasted, and weaponless. Turning to ATF to trace the Beretta Jetfire's wholesale and retail history Texas Ranger Dean assumed—temporarily—the standby mode with regards to the trace, but noted for headquarters: "I located Harrelson's pistol."[12]

Texas Ranger Jack Dean had located other things as well, holes in the story surprise *alibi* witness Louise Scott Gannon told regarding her's and Harrelson's whereabouts when a ruthless triggerman eternally anesthetized Sam Degelia by inserting two hard-cast pills into his cranium. Since that dark day Percy Foreman and Charles V. Harrelson cabbaged onto the declared mistrial at Edinburg, despite his other law enforcing duties, Texas Ranger Jack Dean had been ferreting fact from fiction, exactness from discrepancy. His day by day tireless work was geographically widespread and multipronged. Ranger Dean conducted family interviews, mining tidbits of value ever so slowing tipping the scales—but not in Louise Scott Gannon's benefit as a credible witness. He interviewed and/or corresponded with blood-relatives, casual acquaintances, previous employers, law enforcing and prosecutorial departments in California and Nevada, accessed oil company credit card invoices, scrutinized telephone toll records, and perused bank account details from Houston. Ranger Jack Dean's efforts were exhaustive—not confined to a day or two, but painstakingly measured in month after month doggedness.

Aside from the inconsistencies with hard facts and her Court of Record testimony, was the underlying theme that Louise Scott Gannon had been forewarned about Percy Foreman and his tactics, and she should be wary lest he push her into troubled waters—in way over her head. According to one of Ranger Dean's sources, Louise Scott Gannon had been told of an unnamed someone from California, a man, who originally was going to come to the Lone Star State and back up her story about Charles Harrelson but, in the end, he had refused—and had been killed. Was such prattle bona fide or bogus? ¿Quién sabe?

Ranger Jack Dean's obligation with regards to the investigation of Louise Scott Gannon's purported tainted testimony was to gather evidence. He was a cog in the criminal justice system. And that system slowly inched forward when Texas Ranger Jack Dean presented his finding to the Hidalgo County Grand Jury.[13] The Grand Jury at Edinburg, on the other hand, had its responsibility too, and in the case of the errant nightclub singer it acted. Louise Scott Gannon was, within the four corners of a sealed indictment, charged with Perjury, a felony violation of the Texas Penal Code. She was not, though, in the Lone Star State. And, that was reason for the Grand Jury's temporarily secret findings—so the law could nab her before she skipped into the smoky nightclub haze of whiskey sippin' anonymity. The purported perjurer was at Las Vegas singing her sultry songs, and trying her flat best to elude the legal limelight. Her efforts, like Harrelson's botched jailbreak, were a colossal flop. Texas Ranger Jack Dean was back in the picture and upon receipt of the bench warrant for her arrest, followed through by coordinating with law enforcement authorities at Las Vegas.[14] Louise Scott Gannon was arrested.[15] And although it should come as no real shocker, the taken aback and worried Percy Foreman was figuratively, not literally, Johnny-on-the-spot: "She is free on $3,000 bond posted for her by Percy Foreman of Houston, Harrelson's lawyer."[16] Louise Scott Gannon was in a pickle.

While Harrelson marked time in jail awaiting trial, and his star *alibi* witness stewed in the juices of indecision and apprehension, Texas Ranger Jack Dean and Janie had a weekend road trip on their agenda—a pleasure trip to be sure—but nevertheless an officially sanctioned trip. There was to be a formal groundbreaking ceremony for the Texas Ranger Hall of Fame at Waco overlapping with the Texas Ranger's Sesquicentennial celebrations. A worldwide audience would be watching, and scores of the Lone Star State's most distinguished dignitaries would be in attendance. Additionally, it was reasonably anticipated that several sovereign nations would also be courteously sending their high ranking law enforcement officers.[17] Not surprisingly it would be a perfect opportunity and setting for an endorsed Texas Ranger meeting. These were big doings and Texas Ranger officialdom—namely Senior Captain Clint Peoples—was leaving little to chance. For Rangers, there would be a strict dress code for both the afternoon ceremony and the nighttime banquet. No regular suit coats and black ties were required for the afternoon, as they would be for the keynote program and dinner—short sleeves and light colored straw hats would be okay for the daytime festivities—but there were common denominators for both ceremonial occasions. All Texas Rangers would wear black boots, and be outfitted with black pants' belts and black gunbelts. For this day there was to be absolute uniformity, and each Texas Ranger was unequivocally ordered to carry his state issued Smith & Wesson .357 Magnum revolver, no cocked and locked .45s.[18]

Senior Captain Peoples would not suffer embarrassment by having his Texas Rangers attend the get-together armed with what many—if not most—normally carried, Colt 1911s. A deal had been cut with Smith & Wesson to produce a Special Ranger Commemorative revolver, a .357 Magnum Model 19, similar to the handguns then being issued by DPS to Texas Rangers and THP Patrolmen. The cased commemorative revolver was one of several fundraising products especially timed to coincide with the Sesquicentennial Celebration at Waco. How would it look to spectators and spenders if they were being politely urged—for a good cause—to purchase a Smith & Wesson memorial revolver, while the Texas Rangers were walking about carrying their cocked and locked Colt .45s? Captain Peoples—good or bad—had a flair for burnishing an image: Sometimes a commendable and sometimes a censurable talent.

Texas Ranger Jack Dean without delay acknowledged that he and Janie would gladly participate in the gala, fully cognizant of the institutional and historic implications of having an officially authorized Texas Ranger Hall of Fame overlooking the grand Brazos River at Waco.[19] Traveling on Friday, 3 August 1973, the Deans were onsite and ready to involve themselves in Saturday's scheduled events.[20] It would be a wonderful day of socializing and inter-department camaraderie, as well as metaphorically carrying the Texas Ranger's public relations flag.

At the Saturday afternoon groundbreaking formalities more than 3,000 spectators braved the August heat and were on hand, including all eighty-two of the then-commissioned Texas Rangers. A not insignificant number of retired Texas Rangers were there too. Naturally, there was a robust contingent of the DPS hierarchy, including Director Wilson E. "Pat" Speir, Assistant Director Leo E. Gossett, and Chief of Criminal Law Enforcement James M. "Jim" Ray. Outdoor music was provided by the renowned Fifth Army Band from Fort Sam Houston at San Antonio, and the honor guard duties were executed by the vibrant Ross Volunteers, Texas A&M University's crackerjack drill squad. Also taking part in the superlative affair were several heavy-hitter Texas politicos, such as Governor Dolph Briscoe, Lieutenant Governor Ben Barnes, and Mark White, future governor of the Lone Star State. Entertainment celebrities were also a part of the majestic show: Clint Walker of the *Cheyenne* television series, character actor Chill Wills, along with Don "Red" Barry, and Country/Western singer Johnny Rodriquez enchanted the gathering. Several topnotch and talented Western artists such as Bob Moline and Donald M. Yena, and his vivacious wife Louise, were noteworthy attendees that scorching summer afternoon. Well-known businessmen and entrepreneurs and cattle ranchers and oil-men were part of the fanfare—it was, to put it plainly, a don't miss it Texas shindig.[21]

Two memorable and correct quotations bear repeating. In his remarks Governor Briscoe said: "It is more than a monument. It is a Hall of Fame for the heroes of the past, but it is also a hall of progress for the future. The 150th anniversary of the Rangers is a milestone, not a marker at the end of the road." That sentiment was forwarded with the engraved inscription on the gold-plated ceremonial ground-breaking shovel: "As long as there is a Texas, there will be a Texas Ranger." Such prophecy did not then, nor does it now, ring hollow. Nearing a half-century later, the illustrious Texas Ranger Hall of Fame & Museum—the officially sanctioned repository of the Texas Rangers—yet kindly welcomes visitors from around the world. Also housed thereat is the first-class Tobin and Anne Armstrong Texas

Ranger Research Center, an "especially important. . . . archive to which Rangers could [can] donate personal and official papers for historical research." And doing their part in maintaining tradition, the modern-era Rangers are intricately involved in a multitude of criminal investigations and peace keeping assignments.[22]

That evening at the banquet in the Waco Civic Center, the crowd had dwindled to but 1,500 fortunate ticket holders. Actor Clint Walker assumed his position as Master-of-Ceremonies and the audience was treated to something special besides the scrumptious steaks: a premiering of *The Texas Ranger: A Certain Kind of Man*, a thirty-minute documentary flick produced by the Jamieson Film Company of Dallas. Actor Slim Pickens acted in and had admirably narrated screenwriter Robert L. Lusby's script. Filming of the production had taken place at the legendary Southwestern movie-set, Alamo Village near Brackettville in Kinney County.[23]

All and all the whole day had been a splendid affair—a key ingredient in the recipe for preserving and promoting Texas Ranger history. Such consequence was not overlooked or lost. A unique hardcover volume commemorating the big day and the fêted institution was published, *Texas Rangers, Sesquicentennial Anniversary, 1823–1973: Pictorial Edition*. Of particular relevance of the biography in hand is the caption underneath Jack Dean's portrait photograph. Though many good Texas Rangers were pictured, clearly the fellow from Fort Worth was by the luck of the draw—temperament and timing and tenacity—sculpting a new image:

> Entered the Texas Ranger service on September 1, 1970, and holds an Associate of Arts Degree in Law Enforcement. He works diligently with the youth in the Rio Grande Valley area and has been instrumental in creating better relations between the Rangers and the citizens of South Texas.[24]

Assuredly Jack and Janie had stockpiled pleasant memories of the trip to scenic Waco and all the breathtaking hoopla associated with the outing, but good things last not forever. Jack had to get back to work, there was a momentous matter on the criminal enforcement horizon—and time stands still for no man—not even Texas Rangers. A murder trial was on tap.

Charles V. Harrelson by most accounts was a good conversationalist, a fellow with a broad repertoire of general knowledge and intellectual insight. The character dichotomy was weird. Harrelson was likable yet deceptively dangerous, congenial on the surface but conscienceless if self-interest promised profit or personal benefit. Harrelson's handshake could seem sociable and gracious at the very time his off hand was toying with the .25 autoloader in his pocket, as he planned an unwelcome surprise—or someone's demise. Ranger Jack Dean, through numerous routine and sporadic not so routine contacts with Charles V. Harrelson, erected a somewhat unique relationship with the incarcerated fellow from Lovelady. Jack Dean, though part of the personality assessment is short, thought that Charles V. Harrelson was "an easy man to talk to and [that] he always got along well with him."[25] Harrelson was personable and quite intelligent, so said Jack Dean.[26] The interplay between officer and outlaw is challenging to encapsulate, nonetheless, the dichotomy is real. By this time in his life Jack Dean was a veteran lawman. Due to his years in the THP at Pecos and Tyler making violator contacts and, now, in the Lower Rio Grande Valley working major felony cases, Ranger Jack Dean had internalized a critical point: No matter the mesmerizing melody the swaying and squatted player is piping, never solely focus on the charmer—ignoring the snake.

For the second bite at the legal apple the court was petitioned that to be justly impartial a Change of Venue should be granted for the upcoming murder trial. The scheduled courtroom action was moved to Brownsville, Cameron County.[27] A local attorney, Thomas G. Sharpe, Jr., would lend his expertise to Percy Foreman, a not unwise trial tactic, adding a prominent and familiar face to the defense team.[28] And therein, the relocation to Brownsville is genesis for a heretofore untold story.

Stringent adherence to vital security protocols would dictate that the prisoner be quietly transferred from Edinburg to Brownsville without fanfare and absent public or newspapermen's or television broadcasters' tipped-off notice. Mum was the word. In the middle of the night, unannounced, Texas Ranger Jack Dean and Chief Investigator Pat Ramsey utterly surprised Charles V. Harrelson inside his house at the Hidalgo County Jail. It was time to go! No personal effects; what little he had would be tagged and bagged and would follow later. The dumbfounded prisoner—maybe for once—was speechless. Though exhibiting the utmost friendliness the lawmen were somewhat tight-lipped with regards to the impending trip's precise route or destination. Charles V. Harrelson was utterly clueless, other than the fact he was going somewhere with a Ranger and a deputy into the middle of the night and he was completely at their mercy. Jack Dean took his position behind the steering wheel, the anxious Charles Harrelson beside him in the front seat. Deputy Pat Ramsey took his place in the state vehicle's backseat, directly behind the mystified inmate—a particularly convenient spot should Mr. Charles Voyde Harrelson opt to jump tacky and try any funny business. In a flash, a choke hold could—would—interdict stupidity.

Texas Ranger Jack Dean's duty was to get Harrelson to Brownsville absent undue delay. Therefore it was but natural to take a shortcut, traveling several isolated nighttime farm roads which in the daytime would be teaming with tractors and irrigation people and migrant workers. Though Pat Ramsey's gesture was easygoing and innocuous, he leaned forward and tapped Harrelson on the shoulder, asking Charles if wanted them to stop so he could step out of the car and relieve himself since they had left the jailhouse in such a hurry. There was nobody around to take notice, absolutely nobody. Charles Harrelson, according to Jack Dean, figuratively turned white—his complexion ashen, his deportment near comatose. What goes around comes around! Was this to be his last ride?

Texas Ranger Jack Dean would welcome a quick stop, his bladder was begging for clemency. He pulled to the side of the road and stopped, turning out the squad car's headlights, moonlight illuminating the turn-row soon to meet a deluge of diluted coffee and kidney-filtered Coca Cola. Charles Voyde Harrelson was for a moment paralyzed. Charles Harrelson's epiphany came quick: if he had to take it, he'd take it like a man, standing up. He stepped out of the car, unzipped and let nature take its course, knowing he'd never hear the gunshot. Though somewhat dehydrated—sweat drenching his orange jailhouse coveralls—Charles Harrelson, at the direction of his custodians, again took his place in Ranger Jack Dean's sedan, and the snaky back road trip to Brownsville was reactivated. And it was but then, once the trip had begun, that Texas Ranger Jack Dean had his epiphany, realizing the real reason Charles Harrelson had had such a forlorn and resolved expression subsequent to his braking to a stop in the lonesome wilds of nowhere. The irony was memorable—not to be soon forgotten by a good guy with an untarnished badge or a bad guy known by institutional numbers.[29]

Fatefully, Charles Voyde Harrelson's second trial for the killing of Sam Carmelo Degelia Jr., would be heard before the bench of District Judge Darrell Hester, aka "Hang 'Em High Hester." As the nickname brashly insinuates, the forty-eight-year old judge, raised due west of Corsicana, Navarro County, near the blackland farming village of Frost, was a sure enough no-nonsense but exceptionally well-read legal authority. Judge Hester was religious but not too churchy, tough or compassionate as challenging circumstances dictated. A WWII veteran of the Navy serving on destroyers in both the Atlantic and Pacific, in the 197th District Court's courtroom Judge Hester ran a tight ship—real tight.[30] Monkeyshines and misconduct in Judge Hester's court were not tolerated, not even at the hands of a melodramatic and sensationalist lawyer from Harris County. Percy Foreman had drawn the short straw.

At that time (1973) and maybe it still holds true, Charles Voyde Harrelson owned a somewhat distinctive and dubious standing, an honor highlighted in pages of the *Dallas Morning News*: "Harrelson has been jailed continuously since Nov. 20, 1968, when Texas Rangers arrested him in Atlanta, Ga.—longer than any Texan not convicted of a crime."[31] Judge Hester denied lawyer Foreman's motion to have Harrelson's bond reduced; he knew right where the defendant was and right where he would be when the court's bailiff commenced his call to order. Judge Hester's court and time would not be wasted while Lower Rio Grande Valley lawmen hunted for some wayward defendant on the lam, and Harrelson had previously proven he would flee.[32]

The trial—as with any where Percy Foreman drummed doubt— was a super big story for newspaper subscribers in the Lower Rio Grande Valley and throughout Texas. As opposed to his earlier trial for murdering Degelia for money, this time around Judge Hester, a different judge, allowed for the record that testimony of Sandra Sue Attaway regarding Harrelson's possession and then loss of the convicted Pete Thomas Scamardo's prophylactic tightly packed with heroin: "I will allow testimony regarding an extraneous offense admitted only to show a possible motive for the murder."[33] Percy Foreman wilted, the jury was learning way too much about dope and sawed-off shotguns and easily concealable .25 autoloaders. But, perhaps, what the attentive jury would not hear would prove even more detrimental to the effectiveness of Percy Foreman's arguments and the ultimate fate of Charles Voyde Harrelson.

Damned if she did and damned if she didn't, Louise Scott Gannon skipping the whole damn mess had jumped bond and had taken a holiday in Aruba—out of the country—not out of mind. The Perjury charge yet loomed un-adjudicated and Jack Dean held an arrest warrant in his hands. And, adding heat to Louise Scott Gannon's distress, who knew what Charles V. Harrelson might do should he slither through prosecutorial hands? Rhetorically it might be asked, did or did not Percy Foreman foot the bill for Louise Scott Gannon's Caribbean vacation? If he did such, and if such was slyly designed to cheat the Blind Mistress of Justice, it backfired. Harrelson's lawyers wanted to read for the record and for the jury Louise Scott Gannon's earlier *alibi* testimony. Louise, it was proffered, like no other witness, could unfetter any assertion that Harrelson was in the pump-shack when Degelia was killed. Naturally, not being in the courtroom she would not now be subject to cross-examination by DA McInnis. Much more was now known about her personal history and veracity. The Hidalgo County Grand Jury had not returned their indictment on a whim. Jack Dean had developed hard facts during an in-depth investigation. Judge Hester was not buying. If Gannon had testimony to offer, she could do it in person and in his court. Otherwise, move on![34]

With the defense team's legs cut out from under them, in a last ditch and predictable effort Charles Voyde Harrelson took the witness stand. He denied cold-bloodedly murdering Degalia and with his characteristic shiftiness tried to finger Jerry O. Watkins as the actual and merciless triggerman. Given that the murder weapon—purchased in Utah—could be directly traced to him, Charles V. Harrelson swore under oath that he had "loaned it to Watkins a few weeks before the Degelia slaying."[35] Normally a real slick talker, from the witness stand Harrelson's testimony seemed to register as a lame excuse, delivered with anemic verve.

Failing thus far to blunt the testimony of Sandra Sue Attaway and/or Jerry O. Watkins, the creative Percy Foreman turned to excoriating investigating lawmen—namely the Texas Rangers. During closing arguments to the jury Percy Foreman harangued and scolded that his client was wholly innocent of wrongdoing and it was the state-paid boys who were guilty of mischief and malfeasance, in that "the Texas Rangers had preconceived ideas about the case and framed Harrelson for the Degelia killing."[36] With nothing to lose and everything to gain, the slippery lawyer didn't shy away from shrilly naming names, not according to the *The Odessa American*: ". . . Harrelson is being framed by a group of Texas Rangers including Tol Dawson. . . . and 'Skippy' Rundell . . . I'm [Foreman] not a cop hater. I would be a poor man if it wasn't for peace officers. . . . [but] hell hath no fury like a Ranger who sees someone he arrested acquitted."[37]

What the eight men and four women of the jury thought as they listened to dribble and debate is, understandably, not retrievable absent polling them individually. What they did inside the jury room is known. Subsequent to but six hours of weighty deliberations, they rendered their verdict: *Guilty!*[38]

Perhaps, just perhaps, for the sentencing phase of Harrelson's case the jury had taken into account the probated sentence of Pete

Scamardo and the decision to grant immunity to shady Sandra Sue Attaway and ex-con Jerry O. Watkins. At any rate the jury wasn't bowled over by Percy Foreman's ranting theatrics; they assessed Charles Voyde Harrelson's sentence at fifteen years, to be served with the Texas Department of Corrections. Predictably, Harrelson wanted to breathe fresh air while his case wormed though the appellate courts, and he asked for liberty until a final decision would be handed down. That is, if someone—anyone—would make his bond. The takers were almost nonexistent, well, save for a couple. Texas Ranger Charlie Moore, Company B, contacted the Dallas County Sheriff's Office and conferred with the supervisor of the "bond desk" with regards to a particular Big D bonding agency. Ranger Moore was advised in no uncertain terms that due to criminality in the past "he would not approve bonds made by these subjects for the amount that is set on Charles Harrelson."[39] A West Texas bonding agency pledged that they would up $22,500 to guarantee Charles Voyde Harrelson's presence whenever and wherever he was ordered to be. Texas Ranger Jack Dean and DA Oscar McInnis failed to see the humor in the proposal after the necessary investigation and upon learning that the bondsman was "a former convict and had been a patient in a mental hospital" as result of "three separate charges of fondling minor female children."[40] Charles Voyde Harrelson was Texas penitentiary bound, albeit with a U.S. Marshal's detainer scotched in place for that 1968 federal sawed-off shotgun rap at Kansas City.[41]

For the part he contributed in this phase of Charles Voyde Harrelson's cheerless story Texas Ranger Jack Dean's stellar investigative acumen and hard work had not gone unnoticed—not in the Lower Rio Grande Valley and certainly not at DPS headquarters at Austin. Pleased as punch it would seem, Colonel Wilson E. Speir commented in regards to a formal letter of acclamation: "As you might know, we are always pleased to receive a commendation on our Rangers and the work they are doing. . . ."[42] Texas Ranger Jack Dean went back to work in the Lower Rio Grande Valley, but said: Charles Harrelson would be "like the [Energizer] battery bunny in my life."[43] He just kept showing up—but more of that story later.

Understandably the hard work Ranger Dean had put in attendant to the Harrelson murder investigation and trial was not news missed by his captain. For Jack Dean's regularly scheduled performance appraisal following days spent at the Cameron County courthouse, Captain Wood duly noted:

> Ranger Dean is doing a good job in public relations and is well liked
> by the prosecutors in his area as well as the officers. He is doing a
> good job with the young people and is an outstanding officer.[44]

Another Texas Ranger that would garner rating as an outstanding officer made his appearance in the Lower Rio Grande Valley. On the fifth day of September 1973 Texas Ranger Dean met with Ranger Bruce M. Casteel, recently posted at Harlingen, northwest of Brownsville in the western quadrant of Cameron County.[45] Ranger Casteel brought investigative experience with him. Prior to becoming a Company D Ranger on the first day of September 1973, Bruce Casteel had pulled time as a city police officer at bustling Killeen on the outskirts of the U.S. Army's Fort Hood. Later, under the administration of Sheriff Lester Gunn of Bell County, Bruce Casteel served a stint as Chief Deputy. Then, during 1967 it was off to the DPS Academy, and upon graduation THP Patrolman Casteel earned his state paycheck at Bryan, Brazos County, before a transfer back to Killeen. Thereafter Bruce Casteel underwent the rigorous training to acquire accreditation as a DPS Polygraph Operator and later as a qualified Hypnotist. Though still a topnotch lawmen, gritty and gutsy when need be, like Jack Dean, Bruce Casteel was among that new breed cadre putting their stamp on improving the overall Ranger image statewide and, most particularly, in South Texas through examples of professionalization and progressive thinking.[46]

Early on Texas Ranger Casteel's practical philosophy—paralleling Jack Dean's—was made emphatically clear: "sure I'll take on a riot alone. One riot, one Ranger. Sure with fifteen hundred state troopers behind me." More pointedly Ranger Casteel tossed the catch-rope loop around reality, allowing that self-respect and showing genuine respect for others paid measurable dividends: "You get more by being mindful of the personalities, the politics, than by bulling your way in and throwing your weight around."[47]

Janie Dean was put in the position of having to do some thinking and thanking. Were one to have asked McAllen Police Chief Clint Mussey who his favorite person was, it quite likely would have been the very personable and vivacious Janie Dean. At the time and place Janie Dean was the only female employee that Chief Clint Mussey would wholly trust with confidential material. She was, in his mind, special. Illustratively, Ranger Jack Dean through hook or crook—a legal bamboozling of course—was trying to talk Chief Mussey into parting with a clean-as-a-whistle Winchester, a Model 1907 carbine, a .351 caliber autoloader. As previously mentioned Jack liked guns— good guns—and this one was a sure enough dandy. Within Clint Mussey there lurked a streak of devilment, as Texas Ranger Jack Dean soon discovered. Rather than banter back in forth about a trade and the giving up of boot-money (added *dinero*) the wily chief put the quietus on Jack's incessant howling. He gave the Winchester to Janie— no strings attached. Should Jack really be dead-set on owning title to the polished blue-steel prize—he could pester Janie till the cows came home. Not a smart move, as Chief Mussey slyly mused.[48]

As if Texas Ranger Jack Dean didn't already have enough to worry with, during and after the Charles Harrelson trial, a newsmaker bombshell shattered peacefulness at the city of Weslaco. Ranger Dean duly noted for his TRWR: "To Weslaco at request of City Commission to assist in handling and setting up police protection for this city. At 5:00 P.M. the whole police department walked out leaving the city without any police force."[49] The city's fifteen officers had simply walked off the job in a fit of temper during a salary dispute, suddenly calling it quits: no warning, no contingency plan for the good citizens of Weslaco. For a suspended moment in time the Hidalgo County municipality was unprotected, teetering at the brink of chaos should crooks eye opportunity before there was a fix. Though not riding white stallions, other area lawmen rode to the rescue, one of whom was Jack Dean. Though he may have been the lone Ranger, Jack Dean wasn't alone. DPS Narcotics Agent Walter

McFarland stepped to the plate, ready to help ensure peace and quiet. Right fast they were enthusiastically backed up by four THP Patrolmen, five of Sheriff Claudio Castaneda's deputies, as well as at least one or more commissioned peace officers from the cities of Mission, Mercedes, Donna, Alamo, and Elsa.[50]

According to one witty blurb in an area paper, Weslaco's chief executive, Mayor Pablo Peña, extended the greeting to Jack Dean with humor, putting a lighter touch on the momentous mess: "What? Only one Texas Ranger!"[51] Though he would put in a tiring twenty-hour day, Ranger Jack Dean working with out of town policing administrators, finally managed to schedule and coordinate around-the-clock coverage with what was fast tagged a "Substitute Police Force."[52] The work was far from over. A lasting remedy would have to be placed on the drawing board. Texas Ranger Jack Dean, being called upon by "City Officials" was one of the instrumental consultants with establishing a new and permanent police department in Weslaco.[53] Once again taking note of the leadership role Texas Ranger Jack Dean was playing in yet another Lower Rio Grande Valley crisis, DPS Colonel Spier pledged his support in providing extra men if they were needed for an interim timeframe.[54] In the end all was well, and Texas Ranger Jack Dean could bank another formal letter of commendation and appreciation.[55]

Just because 1973 was winding down and preparations for the holiday season were underway does not mean everyone was in a cheerful giving mood. One area Hispanic was intent on taking something—satisfying sick lust and gifting his victim with fear and humiliation. During the night of 4 December the *mal hombre* crawled through a window in the apartment of a young single lady, an eighteen-year-old secretary for a Lower Rio Grande Valley PD. Whether his target was selected by happenstance or specifically targeted is hazy. Armed with a knife in his hand and meanness in his heart and psychosis in his head, the thirty-one-year-old bilingual violator overpoweringly violated the teenager. Though Ranger Jack Dean's DPS-COR is necessarily graphic there is no need here to offer verbatim testimony of what the crook did or demanded that the frightened young lady do, vigorously gratifying his twisted itch. Forcible rape is unspeakable. Thankfully the victim was—through it all—observant and provided Texas Ranger Dean with a meaningful clue—a peculiarity with regards to the rapist's hand. Working with Detective Peña of Pharr PD and Investigator Vernon Rosser of McAllen PD, Texas Ranger Dean was fortunate enough to develop hard evidence leading to an arrest and the subsequent filing of criminal charges—principally for a similar offense occurring at McAllen. The suspect was jailed.[56]

For Texas Ranger Jack Dean some January 1974 fireworks were not detonated in a grand nighttime extravaganza bursting overhead. No, the afternoon's belching muzzle blast took place at a used car lot west of Rio Grande City in neighboring Starr County. Such madness seemed but par business for the Lower Rio Grande Valley, another Saturday, another nonsensical killing. Though he had been rushed to Roma for medical help, Esiquio Gonzales, carrying a small caliber bullet wound, had died. The Starr County Sheriff, Reymundo "Rey" Alvarez, was in need of a helping hand for the murder investigation, and sought—not surprisingly—the investigative talents of Ranger Dean. After probingly talking with witnesses and taking written statements, Jack Dean had positively identified the perp, but the shooter had scooted south of the Río Bravo. And therein justifies the word count for even citing this, another moderately easy case to crack. The fact the violator fled to Mexico was not odd, but a midnight extradition was not necessary. Texas Ranger Dean had solid contacts throughout the Lower Rio Grande Valley, on both sides of the river and both sides of the law. Due to his trustworthiness Texas Ranger Jack Dean let it be known through the right underground crowd that he would personally protect the offender and guarantee the alleged suspect a fair trial. The killer's defense attorney, Ruben Cardenas, knowing Jack Dean's genuineness, made thoughtful arrangements to surrender his client to the Texas Ranger at the Hidalgo International Bridge.[57]

Shortly, solving another homicide was on Texas Ranger Jack Dean's agenda. This time called from home on a Sunday morning, Dean rushed to the crime-scene six miles east of Edinburg and north of Alamo. There, in an aromatic orange grove was Francisco Gonzales "Kiko" Tello, DRT. The thoroughly deceased Tello, forty-five, had been coldly executed, a bullet behind his left ear. From the best reasoning it appeared the murder had taken place elsewhere and the body dumped in the orchard. The local newspaper reporter duly noted: "Heading the investigation team for the department is Texas Ranger Jack Dean," who was most competently assisted by Hidalgo County Deputies, Max Mendiola, Albert Garcia, Elias Juarez, and Chief Investigator Pat Ramsey. It was a damned whodunit, and Deputy Ramsey told the impatient newshound the patently obvious: "we just hope one of his friends will come forward and tell us where he was last seen. All we can do now is just try to backtrack were Tello had been before his death." Quickly, Justice of the Peace A. Gutierrez ordered an autopsy.[58] Ranger Jack Dean revealed preliminary findings:

> Tello had been shot one time behind the left ear with a .45 automatic. The bullet struck his spine and severed it at the base of the brain. The exit wound was 2 inches below the right ear and the bullet came to rest on his right shoulder. It appears that Tello was shot inside a vehicle which was traveling north on Alamo Road. A vehicle had been stopped in the bar ditch and a small pool of blood was in this area. Drag marks lead from this spot to the body. It appears that only one person was dragging him and using Tello's arm to do so. . . .[59]

Although inquiry into the deliberate homicide of Kiko Tello would consume an inordinate amount of investigative time, i.e., submission of evidence to the DPS laboratory, interviewing witnesses, and the administration of not just a few polygraph examinations, there would be a hard bottom-line and it wasn't pretty. From the outset one of the leading persons of interests for the crime had been Matias Lopez Morin. Ranger Jack Dean was never betwixt and between for this case—even though Morin was at the time "a Deputy Sheriff (Jail Guard)." Also, during his visit with Ranger Jack Dean, Morin had opted for deceitfulness—telling "several known lies."[60]

Though sorting though the falsehoods and outlandish deceptions was no overnight success, ultimately, on the eighth day of May
1974, Deputy Pat Ramsey and Texas Ranger Jack Dean "arrested
Deputy Sheriff (Jail Guard) Matias Morin for this murder."[61] Not
surprisingly there would be fits and starts, continuances and bargaining, bluffing and blustering, but in the end and, that's what
counts, Matias Morin at the Hidalgo County Courthouse entered a
plea of *Guilty* and caught eight years with TDC and a $2,500 fine (the
court costs?).[62] Deputy Sheriff Matias Morin had, after a gut-check
and consultation with his lawyer, surrendered to reality.

Someone else had something to surrender. On his own accord
Senior Captain Clint Peoples was calling it quits with DPS—
maybe before the shoe fell and he was booted out of the Rangers.
Confidently, from an unbiased standpoint, Captain Peoples can
be credited with acts of good police work and an undying commitment to fostering a wholesome public relations image for the Texas
Rangers, including a championship role—or taking credit for a
championship role—in politically bringing the superlative facility at
Waco, the Texas Ranger Hall of Fame, from dreamscape to fruition.
Then there was that other side, the downside. Within Texas Ranger
ranks Clint Peoples's personal reputation ebbed and flowed and,
more often than not, ebbed.[63]

To the outside world Captain Clint Peoples could do no wrong.
However, to know Peoples was not to love him, and many a Texas
Ranger didn't—including one stationed at McAllen. Perhaps in the
shortest of succinct characterizations, Jack Dean crisply said: "Captain
Peoples dragged the Rangers behind him."[64] Translation? The Senior
Captain's self-interest came first. A case in point is illustrative from
Dean's perspective. Subsequent to the harvest of a particular strain—a
delectable strain—of Lower Rio Grande Valley onions, Texas Ranger
Jack Dean was ordered by a phone call from the Senior Captain, to
acquire several bushels, put them in his state car and report to headquarters—a round trip of several hundred miles. Captain Peoples had
tasty onions on his mind, not offenders and offenses. At the time a
rookie Ranger, Jack Dean complied but did not forget.[65] Texas Ranger

Dean was unaware of those looming clouds casting shadows of doubt on Clint People's character. The storm broke overhead.

Colonel Speir had caught wind that Peoples was negotiating a private pecuniary arrangement with some Hollywood types. In return for a $500 per-week finder's and consulting fee, the good captain would throw open Texas Ranger case files for an upcoming television production, similar to the popular series about the FBI. Though but a rumor of misconduct, Colonel Pat Speir was honest as a nun and persistent as a devil. Director Speir without delay dispatched Chief of Criminal Enforcement Jim Ray to Los Angeles to look into the matter and measure its veracity or lack thereof. A degree of vagueness stifled certainness: Would Clint Peoples pocket the money while he Rangered or subsequent to retirement?[66] "In any event, Peoples had obviously lied to the producers by representing himself as the only one who could provide the services needed. In any event, also, Peoples must have seen the coming crash."[67] In light of the possibility of a pending appointment as a politically appointed U.S. Marshal for the Northern District of Texas, Clint Peoples submitted his formal resignation ahead of any firestorm of financial impropriety.[68] Perhaps, if reading between the lines is at all applicable, the location of Senior Captain Clint Peoples's retirement party and farewell gathering is telling. "On Wednesday, February 20, 1974, there will be a retirement party for Senior Ranger Captain Peoples at the DPS Cafeteria in Austin. . . . Barbeque will be served and tickets will be sold at $3.00 each."[69] No sure-enough ostentatious goodbye wingding at the legendary King Ranch or picturesque YO Ranch or the downtown Waco Civic Center.

The mention of Clint Peoples's tribulations and *adios* to the Texas Rangers is not gratuitous. His replacement will play heavily into to Texas Ranger Jack Dean's biography. Moving up a notch and into the position of Senior Captain was William D. "Bill" Wilson, a veteran of DPS with twenty-two years' service. Through those years Bill Wilson had seen service as a THP Patrolman, Academy Instructor, Internal Security Section Agent and every ranking stage within the institutional framework of the Texas Rangers.[70] As a Lone Star lawman Bill Wilson was, unquestionably, the Real McCoy. Senior Captain

Bill Wilson feared not man or beast, though he had fully no use for straddling skittish horses or soaring the heavens in belly-churning airplanes; suddenly empty saddles and full barf-bags were an anathema to the otherwise audacious Ranger. According to one historian, backed up by folks on the ground and really in the know, Wilson was blunt and straightforward—saying what he meant—"tactless or indiscreet." And, in fact, a newspaper writer quizzed him about one arrest scenario wherein the bad guy had already shot a deputy sheriff in Guadalupe County. Subsequent to wrestling around inside a dark house for do or die possession of the rifle, Texas Ranger Wilson finally bested the crazed culprit, rendering the outlaw unconscious. Bill Wilson remarked: "When the fight was over I thought I had broken his neck, and I meant to." Luckily, the addled violator woke up, but alas the *mal hombre* was "just as healthy, and just as mean as ever."[71] Of this particular tetchy state of affairs a Ranger says more and it's spellbinding:

Bill Wilson. . . . I had known him as a Ranger when I was a Highway Patrolman and been in some incidences with him, shooting hostage situation over in Guadalupe County. . . . There was a guy who had mental problem and. . . . had gotten into a house there at Lake McQueeny and. . . . scared his parents to death, he had whipped his mother. And they had run out of the house and went to a neighbor's house and called the Guadalupe County Sheriff's office. And when the deputy drove up he shot him, didn't kill him, but he knocked down behind his car and continued to shoot the car. But he was able to get to his mike and call for help and a lot of us responded. And we got there and he was in a brick house set up on a hill, no cover, and he was steadily popping at everything that moved there. And somebody, I don't know who, called the Rangers and Jim Riddle and Bill Wilson responded. And they had an old tank in Austin at that time, each company had one, but they had the Highway Patrol driving that tank up there intending to just run through the house and get him, run through the wall, cause that was the only way we felt like we could get him out. But the tank broke down in San Marcus and it was way on up in the morning then, still dark and Bill and Jim said, "We're going to get that son of a gun out of there tonight." And old Bill [Wilson] worked his way around to the back door and we had shot gas in it for two or three hours. Every once in awhile he'd come and bam, bam, bam, so we knew he was still in there, no doubt about that, but we couldn't figure out how he was staying in there without. . . . with that gas. And what he had done, he had turned the shower on full force and on each side of it there was some windows and he was standing there with his face right in that water and every once in awhile he'd load that gun and pop it out those windows and shoot. Well old Bill worked his way up to that back door and he could hear the shower running and then he saw him run to the window and shoot and right back into the shower. And old Bill eased that door open and just eased down that hallway and just snatched him out of that shower and the hunt was over. . . . That's the first experience I ever had with Bill. . . . But we were involved in a lot of things together.[72]

For most Texas Rangers, Senior Captain Wilson was a refreshing change from his immediate predecessor.[73] And, cutting to the bone, Senior Captain Bill Wilson had no use then or later for Clint Peoples.[74]

Bureaucracy is capricious, and in this case interesting—especially for firearms enthusiasts. Since the State of Texas was issuing Texas Rangers handguns, they best not leave them at home—so said a direct order from headquarters: "you can in the future wear any type gun that you are most efficient with, but be sure to carry your 357 magnum in your car trunk or have it readily available when you are away from your station."[75] Assuredly Texas Ranger firepower was not solely limited to holstered handguns: "Remington Model 1100 12-ga. Semi auto-auto shotguns with short barrels and either a Ruger Mini-14 or Colt AR-15 in .223 cal. also are issued to each Ranger. Each company also possesses anti-sniper equipment. . . . Two especially trained Rangers in each company are issued Remington BDL bolt-action rifles in .308 or .223 cal. Special nightscopes are available."[76] Being armed and loaded for a bear or a badman was crucial preparedness for Texas Rangers—hell can rush forth in but a heartbeat!

Candidly and, factually, being prepared to met the challenge with a drawn weapon, more often than not negates the necessity of actually having to pull the trigger—a truism thoughtfully emphasized by Texas Ranger Tol Dawson: "I had a couple of friends, patrol officers, killed because they didn't get out their guns when they should have. They let things get past the control point before they realized it, and they were killed. But I'd as soon not have to shoot a man. I don't hold with gunplay unless it's absolutely necessary."[77]

Another criminal investigation with international implication earned Texas Ranger Jack Dean recognition from none other than Clarence M. Kelley, Director, FBI. Director Kelley particularly noted: "Your dedicated work in this investigative case contributed greatly to the rapid solution. My colleagues and I are indeed grateful for your cooperation and they join me in expressing deep appreciation."[78] In a second letter of exaltation written that same day, Director Kelley made sure Director Wilson E. Speir, was properly updated with regards to DPS's personnel being integral components—the tip of the spear— in the major investigation.[79] The case revolved around a considerable amount of traffic involving stolen truck-tractors and transshipment. Working closely with other Texas Rangers, MVT Agents, NATB Special Rangers, and an FBI Special Agent, Jack Dean was part of a highly qualified team that made numerous vehicle recoveries and ultimately, with arrests of five of the linchpin offenders, effectively broke the back of a sophisticated organized theft-ring.[80]

What was not being broken was Texas Ranger Jack Dean's spirit. Though Jack Dean had the utmost respect for law-enforcing entities within and outside DPS, and such diverse national outfits as Scotland Yard and the Northwest Mounted Police and, yes, even the FBI, he thought the Texas Rangers were the best; their mystique and tradition and capability had captured his body, mind, and soul. He was now a Ranger through and through. Unquestionably Jack Dean's work in the Lower Rio Grande Valley had been laudable and sometimes meritorious; there was, however, a move underfoot—a gentle nudge—not for him to move out, but up.

9

◆

"Just handle it"

Captain John Wood's endorsement would prove meaningful in the law-enforcing career of Texas Ranger Jack Dean: "Ranger Dean is doing an outstanding job in public relations as well as investigations. This man is ready for promotion at the first opportunity and would make an excellent supervisor."[1] With a heartfelt and critical endorsement in his back pocket, Ranger Dean formally made his desire to sit for the Sergeant's Examination known to Emory W. Muehlbrad, Manager, DPS Personnel and Training Section.[2] Rangers are real persistent and Captain John M. Wood wasn't about to quit and unsaddle the promotion pony: The Company D Captain was eyeing his subordinate's future law-enforcing career with DPS most promisingly and constructively—and he wasn't loosening the cinch:

> Ranger Dean's general appearance is very good and he is always neat and his physical appearance and condition are good. He has the ability to think out a question and to organize replies. He is a good investigator and his judgment is always good. His ability to communicate with others is good. His ability to get along with other officers and the general public, *as well as the militants* [emphasis added], is very good. His capacity for advancement and for assuming greater responsibility would be considered very good. It is my opinion that this man would make a good leader and would be dependable. We have had no letters of complaints at all on him.

I believe that his potential is great. This man is ready for promotion and would make a good supervisor.[3]

On the twenty-first of July 1974 Texas Ranger Jack Dean, with permission of Captain Wood, traveled to San Antonio taking his next step in climbing rungs on the career ladder. The following day he sat for the written examination for Texas Ranger Sergeant. Sweating test results, Jack Dean shortly returned to the Lower Rio Grande Valley and went back to work doing what Texas Rangers do, in this case trying to solve several Aggravated Robberies.[4] Then, Texas Ranger Dean had to perform a near immediate about-face, making a 31 July 1974 appearance at Austin, sitting for a grueling interview before the Oral Examination Board.[5] That the questioning was a take-no-prisoners ordeal might be overstatement—but it was tough and thorough. In the midst of the administrative personnel matters, a volcanic news story broke at Huntsville.

Prognosticating that temperature inside the Walls Unit of TDC was stifling and repressive would be an underrated misnomer—it was damn hot: Bodily sweltering and a situational crisis! Hard-time convicts Ignacio "Nacho" Cuevas, Rudolfo Sauceda "Rudy" Dominguez Jr., and the gangsters' boss henchman, Federico Gomez "Fred" Carrasco, a murderous Mexican Mafia drug smuggling kingpin, had taken a dozen correctional employees and several other inmates as hostages. Inside the facility's education center and library, but two days after Jack Dean sat for his written promotional exam, the untamed convicts holed-up. On the twenty-fourth of July the world had turned upside down inside the Walls. Amazingly, somehow, the trio of white-suited kidnappers had ably armed themselves with revolvers and a bountiful stockpile of ammunition. The crazed convicts were desperate and delusional: desperate in that they had made the play, delusional in presupposing prison executives would bend while facing the pointed gun of malevolent pressure. The allegorical alarm was sounded and Texas Rangers responded. Ranger John Wesley Styles (former sheriff of Baylor County) assigned to Huntsville was onsite inside of fifteen minutes, quickly notifying his company captain.[6]

Hurrying to Huntsville were Captain James Frank "Pete" Rogers, commander of Company A headquartered at Houston, and Sergeant Johnny Krumnow along with several other Rangers. Arriving from Dallas, were additional Texas Rangers and Company B Captain, G.W. Burks, a somewhat eccentric comrade but a man with plenty of grit and gumption for any emergency.[7] Captain Rogers, a thoroughly well-seasoned veteran Texas Ranger and a distinguished and decorated WW II fighter pilot, would stand in charge of the Rangers deployed to Huntsville; that jurisdictional sphere was within his territory. Moreover, the DPS was also officially represented by Agent Winston Padgett of the Intelligence Division, while the FBI's cooperative foothold was faithfully maintained by the RAC from reasonably close-by Bryan-College Station, Robert E. "Bob" Wiatt, a toughened investigator with twenty-three years' experience and gunplay in his chocked-full résumé. Thereafter, over the next few days, the fierce media frenzy swamped the small prison and college town. Folks from nationally affiliated news associations and magazines were calling in pay-phone reports ahead of inflexible deadlines. Aside from the lengthy string of Texas commentators and writers at Huntsville, scribes and photo journalists and broadcasters from as far away as Miami, New York, Atlanta, Chicago, and Montreal added to the noise.

For eleven dreadful days the hostages endured, never certain of their fate while TDC administrators and weary lawmen strategized—and newshounds piped out stories of varying degrees of veracity. Purchasing precious time the good guys acquiesced to the fanatical convicts' demand for shop-made iron helmets (bullet-proof) and delivery of an armored car into the prison yard. Stupid, indeed, had been the inmates' thinking. Penitentiary officials and Texas Rangers knew from the outset that the borrowed Purolator Security truck would never pass back through the gate carrying armed convicts and hostages into the cosmic world, no matter the costs. That was a given! Cutting to the nub, the convicts concocted a plan of moving to the getaway vehicle—with several hostages—concealed inside a gigantic cardboard box with peep holes, a Trojan Horse of sorts.

Lawmen, too, had blueprinted their plan. At the right time, employing water from high-pressure fire hoses, they would knock over the oversized *piñata*, rescuing the prison personnel and abruptly disarming the *mal hombres*. Donning bullet-proof vests, Captains Rogers and Burks, Intelligence Agent Padgett, and FBI RAC Bob Wiatt and several others made ready for war—or optimistically, surrender. Suddenly a ruptured fire hose depowered the high-pressure stream and the blaring shooting commenced from inside and outside the colossal carton now euphemistically referred to as the *Trojan Taco*. RAC Wiatt as well as the two Ranger Captains took hits to the chest, but were saved by their protective vests and continued to fight. Confronting gunfire TDC Lieutenant Willard N. Stewart managed to cut the net-rope fastening several hostages as human shields outside the now soaked cardboard contraption. While the gunsmoke dissipated and the screaming faded away, chilling reality set in. Cowardly and coldheartedly convict Carrasco had put a bullet into teacher Elizabeth Yvonne "Von" Beseda's heart, murdering her, before he ate the barrel, killing himself. Rudy Dominguez triggered three rounds into the back of librarian Julia C. "Judy" Standley, executing her before bullets fired by Winston Padgett and Bob Wiatt forevermore capped his worthless career as a hostage taker and horrible human. Inmate Nacho Cuevas survived unharmed until—seventeen years later—the Lone Star State's long overdue pharmaceutical injection dispensed justice and eternal good behavior. As but a quick sidebar, the Texas Ranger's intense post incident investigation revealed that trustee Lawrence James Hall, an inmate with outside duties, really wasn't too trustworthy. He had smuggled the three revolvers and near two hundred rounds of ammunition behind the ivy-covered tall red-brick walls concealed in carved-out hollows in fresh cuts of meat and cunningly altered and relabeled tin food containers. Before then, a six-time loser, for his part in the catastrophic and heartbreaking episode, Larry Hall caught another life sentence, ultimately dying in prison during his fifty-seventh year.[8]

In addition to the post-incident investigation as to just how the convicts acquired arms and ammunition, an after-action critique was revealing and somewhat troubling. Though the Rangers had acted admirably during the crisis—brave as grizzly bears—it had been a seat-of-your-pants operation. Refining tactical approaches to perilous situations with uniformity and forethought and specialization had been gaining favor within professionalizing police circles throughout the United States and the world. For the fêted Texas Rangers—and DPS—the ugly situation at Huntsville had driven home an uncomfortable law-enforcing message: They were working on the deficit side of the ledger book. And though Texas Ranger Jack Dean was elsewhere when the mad dogs and meanness chewed misery in the prison yard, the aftermath would soon impact his life and legacy—favorably.

Certainly the high-drama at Huntsville was a showstopper, but the administrative wheels at Austin ground onward, no single event ever putting an end for the Texas Rangers' momentum. As a result of his written test score and placing high during the rigorous Oral Examination Board's questioning, Ranger Jack Dean was put on the eligible list for promotion, his ranking was at the top of the list— slot *numero uno*.[9] Unless there were unforeseen circumstances Dean would figuratively pin on sergeant's stripes when the next vacancy presented—and in keeping with customary practice—in all probability would have to relocate.

With the appropriate foresight, knowing Jack Dean would most likely be transferred out of the Lower Rio Grande Valley, a replacement was named. Joseph Ronald "Ronny" Brownlow, thirty, with THP since 22 May 1967, was promoted to Texas Ranger and assigned to McAllen. Like the Deans, the Brownlows, recently of Jacksonville northwest of Rusk in the East Texas Piney Woods, would marvel at the geographical and cultural character of their newfound residence. At any rate, Ranger Jack Dean took Ranger Ronny Brownlow under his wing, showing him the ropes and introducing him to the Lower Rio Grande Valley lawmen he would be working with on a daily—near twenty-four and seven—basis. Conscientious Texas Rangers depended mightily on close interpersonal relationships and building trust. Ronny Brownlow quickly toed the mark. He was a good Ranger.[10]

Another Lower Rio Grande Valley resident, however, was not good. Texas Ranger Jack Dean was in receipt of some hot news, thanks to an informant. There was, on that third day of September 1974, a fellow with an objective on his agenda: Assassinating the President of the United States. In fact, that very day was his departure date for embarking on the trip to Washington, D.C. to kill President Gerald R. Ford. He had previously authored two threatening letters to the nation's Commander in Chief. Purportedly the assassin and coconspirators, who had already acquired firepower, by coordinated prearrangement, would flee the country after declaring mission accomplished. Sound farfetched? Particularly troubling for Ranger Jack Dean and, now, FBI Special Agent Howard McCook, was a bothersome detail. The suspect owned an extensive criminal history and documented prison time, for auto theft and for shooting a Utah State Patrolman, also for making threats against President Richard Nixon. Dean and McCook located and interviewed the fellow and he did acknowledge that he was about to leave for Washington just as they had arrived, and also admitted that he had written letters to President Ford. During the course of their probing interview the accommodating subject verbally stated he was dead set on getting President Ford. Texas Ranger Dean and Special Agent McCook certainly weren't trained and accredited psychiatrics, but the concurring diagnoses and treatment plan was spot on. Not surprisingly the man was without unnecessary delay taken into custody—authorized by an Assistant United States Attorney—and quickly turned over to Secret Service Agent Joe Cappasso for the proper disposition and/or criminal prosecution.[11]

In the meantime, however, knowing that Jack Dean would be a frontline supervisor, Captain Wood chose to enroll his McAllen-based Ranger in an upcoming Homicide Investigation School slated for the latter part of September 1974.[12] The classroom work and practical exercises would, in anyone's book, be rated as intensive as well as instructive. Scheduled course work included classes in Homicide Penal Code, Sex Deviates in Homicide, Infanticides, Bloodstain Evidence, Ballistic Telltale Patterns in Homicides, Psychological

Aspects and Approaches to Homicide, Postmortem Examinations, Hit and Run Murders, Identification of the Deceased, Prosecutors' Views and Problems in Prosecuting Homicides, Defense Views in Defending Homicide Suspects—last but not least and certainly critically important for a Texas Ranger, Appeals and Reversible Errors in Homicide Cases.[13] Texas Ranger Jack Dean attended and completed the course work at Austin before starting for his return trip to McAllen, rolling into his driveway at 10:00 P.M. on the night of 27 September 1974.[14]

A month later, ghastly news broke. It was not an enviable first for the DPS Narcotics Service. During an undercover buy and walk, things went awry. Narcotics Agent Patrick Allen Randel, the father of three and just four days after his fortieth birthday, was murdered during an attempt to purchase illicit amphetamines in Live Oak County near quaint George West, the county seat. Agent Pat Randel's gun-shot body was found slumped in the front seat of his unmarked state car. Needless to say it was but a whodunit for a short time.[15] Although it really merits a story within this story, such dastardly intrigue and dubious courtroom machinations must be short-circuited. In Cameron County, assisting Texas Ranger Bruce Casteel, Ranger Jack Dean participated in surveillance on a subject in San Benito, believed to be involved in drug traffic connected with the death of Pat Randel.[16] In due course arrests were made and DPS Narcotics Agent Hector Sanchez seized Agent Randel's pearl-handled .380 automatic pistol from one of the defendants' waistbands when arrested at San Benito.[17] Texas Ranger Casteel had the wheels and tires of the suspects' vehicle (a stolen car) removed for forensic comparison with tire tread marks preserved at the roadside park where Randel was shot.[18] Shortly, a .38 Special revolver was recovered from a bar-ditch near the crime scene. It proved to be Randel's shooter and, subsequent to ballistics testing, the murder weapon.[19] In this instance the figurative lawdogs were like literal bloodhounds—on the right track. The long and short of the grim tale ends at Huntsville. There outlaw Doyle Edward Skillern, already with a homicide conviction for murdering his brother, Milton, and penitentiary time on his back trail, awaited his fate. The killing of time was prolonged but deathly inescapable.[20] After wolfing down his last meal of sirloin steak, a baked potato, peas, hot buttered rolls and banana pudding, and after sardonically bidding his "compliments to the chef," Skillern was executed via lethal injection for DPS Narcotics Agent Pat Randel's gutless and tragic homicide. For his operative part in the senseless Capital Murder, Doyle Skillern's fall-partner arrested for the same crime, Charles Victor Sanne, forty-one, who was actually the culpable triggerman, caught a bona fide break, subsequent to appellate court review and commutation of his sentence from death to life in prison.[21]

Shortly after the killing of Agent Randel, another Lone Star State Peace Officer working the South Texas drug corridor was murdered. A former South Texas deputy sheriff and a past policeman at Garland PD (in Dallas County), Matthew Charles "Matt" Murphy, thirty-three, had returned to familiar stomping grounds at Alice, Live Oak County, and had taken a position with the city police department. While executing a chancy one-man vehicle stop at the intersection of West Main and U.S. Highway 281, Officer Matt Murphy was fatally gunned down during the wee morning hours of 1 December 1974, four .22 caliber bullets fired into Officer Murphy's arm and chest, eternally ending his hopes and dreams. Whether or not the killer was a revenge seeker for Matt's earlier South Texas law-enforcing efforts, "a two-month long, extremely hazardous undercover" assignment which netted thirty-five alleged dope-dealing defendants, was then rather vague, resting across the fulcrums of innuendo and guesswork.[22] Some years were good years for wine, but 1974 was an astonishingly bad year for commissioned Texas Peace Officers; nineteen fallen officers would mark memorial inscriptions.[23] But not all news was bad news—everlastingly.

Matt Murphy's murder was a whodunit—for more than four decades. Texas Ranger tenacity is one of the building-blocks of legend and the Matt Murphy murder investigation exemplified true grit and doggedness—and respect. As this narrative—Jack Dean's biography—is being put to paper, a press-conference at Corpus Christi in November 2017, revealed Texas Rangers may sleep but they do not forget. Though the act of criminality had happened even before he was born, Company D Texas Ranger Nathan R. Mutz finally put the cold case to bed with a warrant issued for the arrest of Matt Murphy's killer. Although the suspect was/is doing a life sentence in Alabama for Armed Robbery, and had been in the Big House since 1984, Texas Ranger Mutz and his diligent local law-enforcing team-mates—and a cooperative district attorney—skillfully hammered tight a prosecutable case of Capital Murder. Now the wheels of justice are grinding toward irrevocable resolution, pending indictment and trial—or a *Guilty* plea.[24]

Gunfire wouldn't be the sole means of issuing death to Lower Rio Grande Valley police personnel, folks that Texas Ranger Jack Dean knew. Familiar voices were forever silenced when the helicopter crashed to the ground in the clouds of swirling dust. Forfeiting their lives that tragic day were Harlingen PD Dispatcher Douglas Lee Dodson and Mission PD Dispatcher Humberto Javier Avila.[25] Sadness overwhelmed Cameron and Hidalgo Counties.

Seemingly never at rest, Texas Ranger Jack Dean's 1974 work-year was fading, but his change in career status was emerging. As of the first day of December, the same day policeman Matt Murphy had been murdered, Texas Ranger Jack Dean would become Sergeant Jack Dean, assigned to Company F at Waco.[26] Waco was no border country posting, but crime statistics clearly revealed that Central Texas owned her fair share of outlaws. The aforementioned Captain Butch Albers had been in command of Company F, but "burn out" and the titillating promise of a substantial salary increase with a private commercial enterprise had lured him into retiring before age forced him out.[27] Backfilling behind Captain Albers was Texas Ranger Bob Mitchell, who had been holding down the Company F Sergeant's position at Austin, dealing with high-profile personalities and politicos flocking to be a part of the capitol city scene. Too, there was, sad to say, no little shortage of genuinely unpleasant but sensitive investigations involving personnel of the Lone Star State's governmental agencies and in select cases, a smattering of corrupt elected city and/or county office holders. At that time Company F Texas Rangers stationed in the Hill Country at Kerrville and Llano, as well as the three Texas Rangers then posted at Austin, also counted Sergeant Bob Mitchell as their direct first-line supervisor. And in speaking of an official assignment to Travis County's shiretown, the Chief of Criminal Enforcement, Jim Ray, posited: "When I die I don't have to worry about going to hell, I already did ten years in Austin."[28]

The forty-year-old Bob Mitchell, a veteran THP Patrolman and Texas Ranger, originally from the rural community of Troupe, straddling the borderline separating southern Smith and northern Cherokee Counties, was extraordinarily well-thought-of and respected throughout East Texas. Already a Ranger Sergeant, William Troy "Bud" Newberry worked for the newly commissioned captain "for two or three months," before requesting to fill an opening and reassignment to his West Texas homelands. Bud Newberry's wish came true. That supervisory vacuum at Waco was newly promoted Sergeant Jack Dean's career ticket out of the Lower Rio Grande Valley, though he had mixed feelings about leaving. Bob Mitchell and Jack Dean had been acquaintances when both had been stationed at Tyler, the former as a Texas Ranger, the latter as a THP Patrolman; their relationship had been cordial but for the most part casual.[29] That changed!

Besides being Texas Rangers and new faces at Waco, Captain Mitchell and Sergeant Dean shared a mutual conundrum. Both had kiddos in school. Their fixes were, likewise, in harmony. Until the end of the school year Mitchell and Dean had independently decided to "batch" while their families remained behind at Austin and McAllen, respectively. Fortuitously for their individual needs, the Company F headquarters at Fort Fisher—on the same grounds as the Homer Garrison Museum and the under-construction Texas Ranger Hall of Fame—had, besides the investigative equipment storeroom, an overnight facility: an inside the office bunkhouse, a lavatory, privy, and shower stall.[30]

From those days working long hours and more or less living together at Fort Fisher, Captain Bob Mitchell and Sergeant Jack Dean forged an unbreakable friendship. Heretofore personal comments about a fellow Texas Ranger were best carefully spoken lest there be room for misinterpretation. Was an offhand remark measured as undue criticism, jealousy—or even a case of downright backbiting? On the other hand, supervisors were obligated to evaluate their personnel. So now, with a clear conscience Bob Mitchell and Jack Dean could rationally converse about the individual Rangers of Company F. Gauging strengths and weaknesses of the existing workforce is okay and their candid opinions could be mutually shared—confidentially! Just which Texas Ranger was best suited to successfully accomplish a specific job? Who were the most formidable interrogators? Who owned the best skill set for reconstructing a crime scene? Was there a crackerjack photographer in the company? Which Texas Ranger could best plan and coordinate an extended surveillance? Could someone scrutinize financial records and identify bookkeeping discrepancies with aplomb? Who looked right and talked right for capably carrying the newfound Texas Ranger public relations message? Which Company F Ranger could assume an undercover role with Academy Award composure? Was there a genuine dead-eyed Dick in Company F if some horrible hostage or fanatical kidnapping episode took a bad turn? Those earnest behind closed doors discussions—albeit sometimes at night over a drink—and the interpersonal trust that ensued welded tight mutual respect and admiration.

Though it bubbled to the surface rarely, nevertheless there was an uncomfortable drawback inherent to assuming a supervisory role in any outfit. Texas Rangers were not entirely exempt from humanity's frailties. Captain Mitchell and Sergeant Dean, though it troubled them, were also obligated to identify and unmask transgressions that might negatively impact Company F and, in turn, hamstring those very palpable efforts underway designed at professionalizing the whole workforce. Collectively the Texas Rangers were trudging into the latter quarter of the twentieth-century, shedding negative infringements of earlier epochs subdividing their vivid past. Who needed prodding with regards to submitting timely written reports? Was there a Company F Ranger lax in upholding their mandatory vehicle maintenance schedules? Were any, now that they had gained their place as coveted Texas Rangers, just flat lazy? Was all individually assigned and accountable property in good order? Should there be any worry with a skirt-chaser throwing caution and discretion to the wind? Were any of their Rangers tormented by the lurking mercilessness of demon rum? Which Rangers—if any—were slipshod spenders of government funds? Did any of their subordinates find comfort in coattail riding? Was there someone among them that just couldn't seem to get along with coworkers—or anyone else?

Captain Mitchell was not blindsided by taking command of Company F but was realistic regarding his responsibility: "having to discipline a co-worker or a subordinate is probably the most difficult thing that a Supervisor can do. Because the Rangers are a very, very close knit organization, almost like brothers and. . . . thank goodness you don't have to discipline many of them, but occasionally something will happen that you do have to, that was [is] difficult."[31] Pocketing the managerial paycheck is not cost free. Idealistically implying that the rank and file—no matter the outfit—always stand in awe of their bosses would be flawed thinking, and especially does such ring true for badge-wearing and pistol-toting peace officers— men and/or women: Anywhere, not just Texas Rangers. Simply said, it's a vocation where true approval and genuine respect are earned. Sergeant Dean had embarked on a new phase of his chosen career, and though the promotion was creditable, at ground level there was and is always room for whispered criticism and threads of green-eyed envy. Dean could measure up, or he wouldn't. Texas Rangers are people too!

Herein it's but fair to make a point. By and large Texas Rangers are autonomous creatures, a management philosophy filtering from the front office to personnel in the field performing the frontline tasks. Striking, indeed, is the noticeable dissimilarity between the Texas Rangers and certain federal agencies. In general, the blueprint for getting the job done is, if a Texas Ranger is working, step aside and let him/her do what they have been trained to do. Supervisors are in place to lend support and/or advice, not to interfere or to carpingly second-guess. On the other hand, in other law-enforcing bureaucracies the management model seems more heavily focused on reaping permissions to act from afar—Washington, D.C. or some arbitrarily drawn regional headquarters. Amid the seasonally blooming cherry blossoms and along banks of the Potomac, CYA is a well fertilized proclivity. An in-the-field Texas Ranger remembered his first day on the Company F job working for Bob Mitchell, and his remarks epitomize the Captain's management philosophy:

> You're a Texas Ranger now. By definition, that means you are the best of the best, and I expect you to act like it. Take care of your area and don't call me with ever little nick-picking thing that comes along. Just handle it. But if you do need me, I'll be right there.[32]

Another Texas Ranger, one who would advance through the ranks to the Captain of Company A, when it was mentioned that many of Bob Mitchell's subordinates thought he could walk on water, Jim Miller nodded in unqualified approval with simplicity and succinctness: "He can!"[33] An additional Texas Ranger who knew and respected and worked for Captain Bob Mitchell was Lieutenant George Turner who more or less seconded Ranger Miller's assessment, declaring that he had never heard anyone utter a foul word about Mitchell—on or off the job.[34]

Initially, so it seemed, Sergeant Jack Dean was transfixed in an awkward state of limbo, sometimes a supervisor and yet an everyday working Texas Ranger with numerous criminal case reports prepared and filed in Hidalgo County, but in want of final adjudication. Courts take their own time, and Sergeant Jack Dean was at their mercy, although the judicial processes offered him the avenue for returning to McAllen and seeing Janie, Kyle, and Kelly. For a time it seemed that Sergeant Jack Dean, at an alarming rate, was purposefully grinding Goodyears into scrap-heap baldies.

As the theme of this biographic treatment implies, Jack Dean was at all times cocked and locked, ready for any assignment. Although it tends to shoot down romantic imagery, one of Jack Dean's very first delegated tasks after becoming the Company F sergeant was pretty tough stuff. On the ninth day of January 1975 he jumped into his radio-equipped state police cruiser—one fully stocked with law enforcing paraphernalia, big and little guns and lots of ammo—and hit the high road for Hillsboro. Sergeant Jack Dean's date was not with destiny, but was with the local ladies' club, where he would be the lunchtime speaker. And, in truth, a packed full room of inquisitive women oftentimes can prove as challenging as capturing a sneaky safecracker. As far as the girls were concerned, Jack Dean was a hit—his noontime talk charming and informative. The importance of positive public relations—carrying the Texas Ranger flag—had not been lost on Sergeant Jack Dean: Good things come from good PR.[35]

Also, apart from hardcore criminal investigative dealings facing Rangers were the occasional demands on their time for security matters. As previously mentioned, prior to his first-line promotion Jack Dean had worked with the United States Secret Service—ultimately arresting a clueless fellow who had threatened the president.[36] That was, admittedly, somewhat out of the ordinary. Working other security details, however, was but routine. As but one example, not long after Ranger Bruce Casteel came to work, he and Jack Dean were assigned to provide security for Governor Dolph Briscoe as he made the hurried trip from Harlingen to Raymondville in Willacy County for a public appearance.[37] Subsequent to his promotion to Ranger Sergeant, Jack Dean, working in conjunction with Captain Mitchell and Senior Captain Bill Wilson, was deeply involved with helping coordinate security arrangements for the inauguration festivities for Governor Dolph Briscoe's second term.[38] Security protocols and details in and about Austin were—for Texas Rangers and other DPS personnel—nightmarish. There was, though often unspoken, that other correlating dynamic. Were one on the career path and not abjectly guilty of wetting on his/her own résumé, high-profile exposure to high-profile people could have its windfall bonus—justifiably or unjustly—in many instances workplace politics being somewhat of a metaphorical blood sport.

Though precisely weaving the family's relocation to Waco with an exacting chronology is doable, it's not crucial for advancing Ranger

Sergeant Jack Dean's story. Kyle was a teenager, a high-school student, now well-adjusted to life in the Lower Rio Grande Valley, and the reality of leaving his friends behind was upsetting but surmountable. Kyle was a good kid. Kelly, too, was paddling the same canoe but, in the end, soothing waters at Waco washed away adolescent misgivings. Janie twenty years earlier had made her commitment; another move, one closer to Fort Worth might break the piggy-bank but would not be a heartbreaker. In fact, there was a poignant part of her repositioning narrative. Before departing the Lower Rio Grande Valley on that very last day, McAllen Police Chief Clint Mussey handed Janie a small gift-wrapped package supplemented by a plainspoken admonition: "Whatever you do, don't open this until you're north of the Nueces." Janie complied with the instructions, though the thoughts of cheating had been tempting. Would a quick peek hurt anyone? When appropriate Janie opened the small present and her heart fluttered and her eyes misted. For her outstanding work and as but an undersized token of his utmost personal respect, Chief Mussey had gifted Janie with an exceptionally crafted McAllen PD badge, one bearing the engraved numeral—"1"—in all honesty a purposeful show of sincere admiration and genuine thanks.[39]

At Waco's John Connelly High-School student Kyle Dean dressed out for football and baseball, while Kelly did what little girls did—dance to the drumbeat of pop tunes on the radio and giggle with girlfriends first about this—then that. Certainly not content to sit at home twiddling her thumbs and/or watching *Days of Our Lives* or *As the World Turns*, Janie sought and gained meaningful employment in the office of a Waco based mobile-home manufacturer. At the time Texas Rangers were not drawing fantastic salaries, and Janie Dean was staunchly committed to doing her part—no matter where they made their home.[40]

When not in the Lower Rio Grande Valley testifying or on seemingly ceaseless standby waiting to testify regarding one case or another—which in truth would take several years—at Waco, Sergeant Jack Dean divided his time between administrative duties and staying abreast of Company F criminal investigations. For

Sergeant Jack Dean part of those administrative duties was breaking new ground for Texas Rangers. Due to his exceptional skill and interest in firearms proficiency—and demonstrated coolness under pressure—Company F's newly commissioned sergeant was handed the knotty task of organizationally formalizing, equipping, and overseeing the training of a Texas Ranger SWAT team. Potential for another horrifying episode within one of TDC's facilities was omnipresent and that was not factoring in some nitwit taking hostages during a bank robbery or a misguided yahoo barricading himself/herself behind closed doors during a domestic dispute ratcheted beyond good sense, or putting the kibosh on meth-cooks and fugitives safeguarded by unchained Pitbulls and bullet spittin' AKs. Times and enforcement tactics were changing and Ranger management—as they had been since nineteenth-century days of the Frontier Battalion—was fully cognizant that smart adaptability equated to survivability. Sergeant Jack Dean's assignment was not to assume leadership of a SWAT team, but to build the platform for future commanders to stand on.

Sounds simple! Such was not the case. Working within a bureaucracy, public or private, is never easy. By mid-February 1975 Sergeant Dean was frequently at Austin in conference with Senior Captain Wilson and his second in command, the aforementioned Skippy Rundell, who had by now worked his way through ranks, earning a captaincy and eventually the number two spot in the Texas Ranger command structure. The high-level discussions revolved around the anticipated SWAT Team schools and training.[41] For Sergeant Dean to effectively accomplish his mission, a better understanding of SWAT type operations—aside from dramatic television episodes—was deemed imperative by the Texas Ranger front office.

With less than six months' supervisory service at Waco, Texas Ranger Sergeant Jack Dean was enrolled in the Special Tactical Firearms School to be conducted at the FBI's Quantico, Virginia, instructional facility March 23–28, 1975. There would be a full schedule of classroom and field work—and no little time spent on the firing range. Aside from the knowledge Jack Dean assimilated for the future blueprinting of Ranger SWAT teams, one of the significant outcomes of the trip to Quantico was the fusing of another friendship—unlikely as it might have seemed as the intense training session began. Also in attendance was Sergeant Ivor Montgomery, representing the Essex County, England, constabulary. The fellow with the distinct Southwestern drawl and the guy with the "thick British accent" hit it off admirably—becoming *bueno amigos*. Though both shared equivalent law enforcement time, the Texan and the Brit had come from two divergent theories of policing. Sergeant Montgomery clarified the English philosophy of arming their peace keepers:

> We don't carry guns. . . . We do have a need for firearms on special occasions but the Bobbie on the beat never carries one. They leave it to the discretion of the local chief constable. In Essex County an elite group of 40 men out of 2,500 officers has been formed into a highly trained "task force" to handle serious crimes such as bank robberies and terrorist activities. Within the group is a smaller group of 26 men trained further in tactics and special weapons. The group is so highly trained that they can respond to any emergency in the county of 1 ¼ million persons within minutes. There's always two sections (10–12 men) on patrol at all times, ready to respond to any emergency. In an emergency, the special section goes into action just as soon as three or four men have equipped themselves with weapons and body armor, or whatever is needed. The rest come behind as a backup. . . . Showmanship plays another part in police confrontation. When a large group of police officers are called out, they roll up to the scene in large white vans with lights flashing and sirens sounding. . . . Many times the mere sight of police force is enough to control a situation.[42]

Jack Dean successfully completed the fifty-hour tactical firearms schooling course at Quantico, earning his Certificate of Training and returning to Waco with newfound knowledge and its practical application in the field, valuable lessons he could impart to other Rangers as the SWAT team concept steadily marched to fruition.[43]

Naturally, there were conferences regarding same with Senior Captain Bill Wilson.[44] Following up on 6 May 1975, Sergeant Jack Dean dutifully and formally "Presented SWAT Team Program to the Captains. [He] also conferred with Captain Rundell reference setting up training for this program."[45] Later in the week Captain Rundell and Sergeant Dean delved into specific matters of funding for the proposed SWAT team.[46] Such niggling details with regards to dollars and cents could not be sneezed at, especially with a big-time meeting on tap. On Wednesday, 28 May 1975, Sergeant Dean met with the executively appointed Austin based Criminal Justice Council and Captain Rundell.[47] Important? Crucial! A second anxious meeting with Captains Wilson and Rundell, along with the Criminal Justice Council regarding the Texas Ranger's proposal took place 11 July 1975.[48] Good news broke quick.

The ever-ravenous print media, always looking for a story, especially one involving Rangers, rolled the presses: "Gov. Dolph Briscoe's Criminal Justice Council has approved funds to create special SWAT teams of Texas Rangers. . . . Council Member Oscar Soliz of Corpus Christi pointed out that the Rangers are already the 'elite of the police in Texas, so I guess that a SWAT Ranger is the elite of the elite.'" With a touch of humor Soliz added that "he'd seen the television show SWAT, and most of them were young, agile men. I haven't seen too many young Rangers." Then the enthralled newspaperman turned to an actual on-the-ground player for comments: "Ranger Sergeant Jack Dean of Waco said, 'We don't plan to be jumping off buildings like they do on television. If that needs to be done it can be by the city police SWAT teams.' Dallas and Houston have full time SWAT teams." At this point in time Texas Ranger management was ever attuned to somewhat softening their sometimes merited hardcore image: "The Rangers have changed what the initials SWAT stand for. For the Rangers, it is Special Weapons and Training. On television it is the Special Weapons Assault Team."[49]

That the murderous hostage-taking incident behind prison walls the preceding year had served as a wakeup-call for Texas

Ranger hierarchy at Austin was confirmed during Sergeant Dean's impromptu press-conference: "Dean said that the Rangers would be trained to handle situations like the Carrasco affair at Huntsville and sniper situations. He said they already do that job, and this would just create special Ranger units to be assigned when the problems arise." Somewhat summing-up Sergeant Dean made it emphatically clear that the Rangers were not setting out to usurp local law enforcement authorities, telling the reporter that "the idea is to give smaller cities and counties around the State 'S.W.A.T.' capability. . . ."[50] The Texas Rangers would be there to help—not hamper or take over when a situational scenario turned hot.

Reviewing archived paperwork—in this regard—is more than revealing. The complexities associated with a from-the-ground-up fashioning of specialized personnel tasked with problem resolution—potentially—deadly problem resolution, is truly daunting. Outfitting SWAT teams with the necessary arms and accoutrements might prove mindboggling to the uninformed. Sergeant Dean was compelled to estimate costs and budget for procurement of

Firearms & Accessories:

Ruger AC556, .223 caliber folding stock carbines [11]

.223 Ruger 30 round magazines [22]

Remington 870, 12 gauge folding stock shotguns [3]

Remington BDL .308 caliber rifles, glass bedded with bull barrels [3]

H&R automatic rifles, .308 caliber with bipods and magazines [2]

Colt .45 1911 model pistols with spare magazines [11]

Bushnell 20x Spotting Scopes [3]

7x35 Leopold Binoculars [3]

Redfield accutrack scopes and mounts [3]

5,000 rounds .223

5,000 rounds .45

4,000 rounds .308

300 rounds 12 gauge

60 Assorted gas shells

24 Assorted gas grenades

Walkie Talkies [11]

Clothing:

American Body Armour—
soft [11]

Victor Ballistic Helmets [11]

Rain Gear [11]

Boots [11]

Caps—baseball [11]

Carryall Combat Vests [11]

Two Piece Uniforms [22]

Field Jackets [11]

Gloves—leather [11 pair

Rappelling Equipment:

150' Kermantle Rope [5]

Carabinis [5]

Jump Ascenders [5]

Rescue Harnesses [5]

Seat Harnesses [5]

Figure 8's [5]

Carry Bags [5]

Also necessary for a fully equipped SWAT team were other items of major importance, such as Fire Extinguishers, SEI Emergency Oxygen Kits, High Intensity Lights, Tripods, Portable Generators, Hand Held Search Lights, Stretchers, Ring Saw Rescue Kits, Grappling Hooks, Bolt Cutters, Quic-Bars [forcible entry tools], First Aid Kits, and hundreds of feet of 5/8 inch Nylon Rope, etc., and etc., and etc! All equipment was—according to plan—to be appropriately divided and transported in tandem axle trailers with designated and clearly marked storage compartments. When called out, rolling fast to the scene of action, there could be no timeouts for a trip to the hardware-store.[51]

Although it might tend to somewhat diminish drama—vicarious armchair drama—not a 100 percent of the Texas Rangers were chomping at the bit to become SWAT team members. As with any organization the individual interests are varied. For the most part, all Texas Rangers could be metaphorical man-eating tigers when need be. But within the law-enforcing discipline, including Texas Rangers, furthering and fine-tuning other skill-sets and techniques regarding criminal investigations and interrogations and forensic fascinations held sway over flash-bangs and door kickin' dynamic entries. Beneficially it was well-documented and well-known that the makeup of the Texas Ranger workforce was an amalgamation of multi-talented individuals.

Thoughtfully it was also recognized that those selected as SWAT team members would have to undergo specialized training. And at the very minimum their expenses and per diem would have to be budgeted for and approved. They couldn't be expected to travel on their own dime. Scratching heads and crunching numbers of estimated expenses were calculated with regards to sending select Rangers to varying training sessions, i.e., FBI Sniper Training at Quantico, highly focused courses work on Rappelling, Tracking, Team Problems, and Firearms Familiarity with the United States Air Force experts at Camp Bullis in San Antonio, as well as an updated SWAT session conducted by Houston PD. Additional tactical firearms training could be and would be attained by attending specialized schools at the U.S. Army's Fort Hood southwest of Waco. Unsaid, of course is the fact that all Texas Rangers—SWAT team or not—were by job description and performance appraisals compelled to maintain firearms proficiency and register acceptable scores at the regularly scheduled qualification sessions, range-time normally taking place in conjunction with company meetings.[52]

Holding a supervisory position with the Texas Rangers was no exemption from undergoing advanced training and continuing education. During September 1975 Sergeant Dean successfully completed In-Service Training for Texas Rangers, earning his certificate of recognition. Shortly, the following month, Sergeant Dean was at Fort Hood enrolled in the U.S. Army's Small Arms Firing School. During this classroom familiarization and firing-range time Sergeant Jack Dean was brought up to speed with the nomenclature, functionality, and safe operation of a number of weapons, including but not limited to some of the following examples: .357 Magnum Revolvers, Government Model 1911 .45 caliber autoloaders, .45 caliber Thompson submachine guns, Colt AR-15 rifles and their fully automatic cousins, the U.S. Army's officially issued M-16s, grenade launchers, and .30-06 caliber long-range sniper rifles.[53] Not only was the technical firearms training worthwhile, but it is at about this point that Ranger Sergeant Jack Dean recognized the importance of building and nourishing an amiable and cooperative working relationship with military personnel. All so soon, Jack Dean would be circulating in private and public settings with the U.S. Army's and other military services' topflight officers' corps. It would, in reality, and in the definitive breakdown, serve the Texas Rangers well—quite well.

Of course, some men/women seem to be natural supervisors (there are no *superiors* in the Ranger service), but even they need fine-tuning with regards to oversight responsibilities and effective leadership, a fact Texas Ranger management was now incorporating into their overall game-plan of transitioning into a new and more enlightened era. So-called on-the-job training, simply "learning the ropes" from seasoned Texas Ranger comrades was yet very important, but certainly no singular panacea for professionalization. Sergeant Dean was enrolled at Austin for a seriously thought through and methodically planned week of demanding classroom course work. Not surprisingly—failure was unacceptable—and also not surprisingly was the neat little fact that Sergeant Jack Dean graduated from the DPS sponsored Supervision School.[54]

With a year in harness as a first-line supervisor Sergeant Jack Dean banked a well-deserved and favorable personnel evaluation, one penned by Captain Mitchell: "Sergeant Dean is doing an outstanding job in all phases of work assignments. In addition to his regular workload during this reporting period he has devoted many hours to the SWAT Team formulation and training curriculum in the Texas Ranger Service." Then, Captain Mitchell handed noncom Jack Dean what may have been the highest of compliments: "Sergeant Dean is good Captain material and in my opinion should be given strong consideration when vacancies exist."[55]

Though as a matter of routine, Sergeant Jack Dean did not necessarily undertake firsthand criminal investigations, one Waco homicide drew him into the quest for justice. While details originated from Austin, not McLennan County, Sergeant Jack Dean was in receipt of important news—if it were, indeed, true. Desperadoes had killed Susan Highline, thirty-four, by breaking her neck. Thereafter they coldly put Highline in her own car, pushed the vehicle into Lake Waco west of downtown, hoping for a sunken and undisclosed waterlogged graveyard. This was, according to Sergeant Jack Dean's best knowledge, an attempted robbery, as the victim was thought to have—*alleged to have had*—several thousand dollars in her possession. At any rate, that was the information Sergeant Jack Dean now owned. Unfortunately for the outlaws, the hapless victim did not have the reported loot, $7000, but had been murdered anyway—which actually may have been the premeditated plan from the get-go. Fortunately for Ranger Sergeant Dean, he now had names of the suspected Waco killers.[56]

Ably coordinating on the Austin end with Detective Sergeant M. Wiley and on the Waco end with McLennan County Sheriff Jack Harwell, Chief Deputy Dan Weyenberg, and Chief of Police Al Rosnovsky, Texas Ranger Sergeant Jack Dean launched the full-scale investigation. Eighteen hours later Sergeant Jack Dean and his cohorts had three fellows in custody, none over the age of twenty-one years. Subsequent to their Initial Appearance before a Justice of the Peace, the trio were booked into the McLennan County Jail in lieu of failure to post bail, $100,000 each, all the way around.[57] Texas Ranger Dean's matter-of-fact DPS-COR sinks the offenders' ship, noting that all three suspects admitted their parts in the murder. Subsequent to letting their milk down, one of the defendants took impatient lawmen to the scene of the submersion and pointed out where Susan Highline rested, tightly secured by seatbelts in her impromptu casket, a 1972 Chevrolet station-wagon. The next morning, after good daylight, scuba-divers recovered Susan's body and the automobile from Lake Waco.[58] Later, in a plea bargain worked out with McLennan County prosecutors, after accounting for extenuating circumstances, one of the defendants accepted fifteen years, one five years, and for the third, *this* particular case was dismissed.[59] Like so many of Jack Dean's homicide investigations—this one, too—typified the tragedy of wasted lives, not only for the victim, but for the perpetrators as well. Legal salvation is, though, certainly possible. On the other hand, internal redemption is a private matter.

What was not a private matter was the grand celebration attendant to throwing open doors to the brand-new Texas Ranger Hall of Fame at Waco. As with the groundbreaking ceremony in early August of 1973, the February 6–7, 1976, affair was a Texas-size gala of importance, even though blustery winter winds were at the facility's doorstep. Fifteen-hundred rapt spectators enjoyed the reception and dinner at the Waco Civic Center, especially enthralled by having then television super-star Danny Thomas acting as Master of Ceremonies. Also present for the two-day festivities were both of the Lone Star State's U.S. Senators, John Tower and Lloyd Bentsen, as well as the then-U.S. Marshal for the Northern District of Texas, former Ranger Clint Peoples. Numerous were the political power-players of Texas inside and outside of DPS and/or other local/state/federal bureaucracies. Highly successful entrepreneurial movers and shakers— big money players—were there too. Once again, it was big Texas doings at its best—no fooling, no kidding! Of particular substance for Sergeant Jack Dean can be summed up by a quick glance at his required TRWR for Saturday, 7 February 1976: "In Waco attending ribbon cutting and opening of Ranger Hall of Fame and furnishing security for Governor Briscoe at this function."[60] Yes, Jack Dean was "stepping in high cotton!"

Sadly, some other despicable and shameless folks were just steppin' in it. Seemingly, for a time period, Bell County was a hotspot for meanness and murder. Just prior to Jack Dean's 1974 promotion to the Company D sergeant's spot heartbreak haunted Bell County. Veteran THP Trooper Hollie L. Tull, forty-eight, the married father of two daughters, was stationed at Temple. He was by and large one of the most liked and well-respected DPS employees in Central Texas. On the fourteenth day of September 1974 two bank robbers did what bank robbers do at Walburg in Williamson County. Shortly thereafter in Bell County, Larry Ross and Selwynn Gholson, with a .32 caliber pistol and a scattergun, ended Trooper Hollie Tull's life during a traffic stop gone wrong. The outlaws were convicted and given death sentences in Bell County, but later those irreversible sanctions were commuted to life imprisonments.[61]

Though there were more than a fair share of sickening homicides, of particular infamy was the one where an infant—the unwanted child of a haggard prostitute—was callously murdered. One of Sergeant Dean's Company F men was stationed in Bell County, Edgar Dalton "Ed" Gooding, a veteran Texas Ranger. Of the homicide, Ranger Ed Gooding describes how the innocent baby was killed by the two guttersnipes going down the highway in a van, one driving and the other—after opening the rear door—"held the infant by his heels, letting his head hit the pavement. It took only a few licks to kill him." Thereafter the murderers "wrapped the baby in a blanket and stuffed him in a brown paper bag" and then "tossed the body by the side of a driveway and kept going." Thankfully, in the big picture they didn't go too far, time wise, before local lawmen and Texas Rangers turned the prosecutorial key opening TDC's brightly polished steel-barred doors. That the disgusting defendants skated past the executioner troubled not just a few Texas lawmen, Ranger Ed Gooding at the top of the list, thinking that one in particular should have been "fried."[62]

Too, Bell County was home to a throng of folks not necessarily with murder in their hearts, but certainly with naughtiness in their schema for stuffing purses and pocketbooks with soldiers' ready and, apparently, disposable cash. Fort Hood was a humongous military base and the city of Killeen was earning an unsavory reputation of parity. Payday at Fort Hood was also payday in cheap motels, barroom's back alleys and parking lots, or behind bushes where a "quickie" might, but sometimes not, escape prudish public notice. For a certain caste of gals industriously working a circuit turning tricks, the city of Killeen was utopia unparalleled. Well traveled working girls from Dallas/Fort Worth, Houston, San Antonio, and pretty coeds slipping in from Austin, could convert weekend time to *mucho dinero* overnight. For conscientiously concerned city fathers and the churchy community it was, unequivocally, a genuine and damnable nuisance, and an acidic pill way too big to cheerfully swallow—Something had to be done! Ranger Sergeant Dean turns up the volume of 25 May 1976 reality: "Leave Waco 9:00 a.m. to Killeen area and met with Mayor, City Manager, Police Chief and other state and Federal officials reference organized prostitution in the City of Killeen."[63] In this instance he attentively listened but really could not offer any substantial commitment of manpower to what in actuality DPS policy makers were considering misdemeanor offenses that should be addressed by county sheriffs and municipal police chiefs. Somewhat specifically, Sergeant Jack Dean recalled— rather humorously—a written synopsis from an earlier Company D meeting with regards to the subject at hand:

> Also, don't do any undercover work in bawdy houses. It is all right to conduct raids, but *no buying* [emphasis added]. Try to get local officers to take care of closing them down and go with them on the raid if they need help.[64]

Wrangling whores into the hoosegow was noble work—it was the law—but Texas Rangers devoted their time and resources—for the most part—to investigating serious felony offenses and appre- hending those predators and perpetrators. Prioritizing enforcement actions is continually tricky. Thankfully, left with the challenge, inge- nious thinking and legislative tinkering by local authorities fixed— reduced—the Fort Hood payday untidiness.[65]

Although the actual criminal acts had taken place before Jack Dean had been promoted to sergeant and relocated to Waco, he would, as a first-line supervisor, become involved with assisting Ranger Gooding with an ongoing and horrendous homicide inves- tigation, a sickening double murder.[66] During March of 1974 the bodies of two fifteen-year-old boys had been found in a sidetracked railroad boxcar near Temple, the same town where Jack Dean had earlier tried a stint as a management-trainee for the S.H. Kress & Company. The luckless boys had been bound and strangled with parachute cord and brutally sodomized.[67] The sadism, even to the untrained lay psychologist, was more than evident. Quite naturally the disgusting true-crime story was an indisputable Lone Star State newsmaker with articles appearing in the *Dallas Morning News*, the *Amarillo Globe Times*, the *McKinney Daily Courier Gazette* and the *Port Arthur News*.[68] The atrocious criminality was and would be—at least for awhile—another whodunit?

Sergeant Jack Dean's TRWR of 14 March 1976 reveals the Texas Rangers and Bell County lawmen had not kicked the unsolved case to the ash-heap of forgetfulness. Sergeant Dean's words were concise but real meaningful: "Leave Waco [10 March] 9:30 a.m to Temple with informant and contacted Ranger Gooding and Temple Police Department reference this case. Returned to Waco 8:00 p.m."[69] Melding varied data points into a reasonably coherent story may leave a smidgen of room for variances but, in the end, that ever consistent bottom-line emerges. For these ghastly murders—as would be expected—a seriously troubled fellow undergoing psychiatric treatment was identified. Texas Ranger Ed Gooding supplements:

> He said that he had been to Michigan to visit his mother and was returning to the Veterans Hospital in Temple, where he had been living for several months. He had been riding a bus, but when he got to Bellmead [in McLennan County], he ran out of money. He jumped [into] the empty boxcar, only to find it already occupied. . . . He didn't mind sharing a boxcar with two nice young boys. Somewhere between Waco and Temple, which is about forty miles, he had assaulted one of the boys. The other boy, who had been asleep, woke up and tried to come to his friend's aid. For his efforts, he was choked to death with a cord and then his corpse sodomized.[70]

Purportedly, and there is not even a smidgen of doubt to question Texas Ranger Gooding's remembrance, during interrogation the mentally disturbed killer had a fleeting brush with reality: "I'm crazy, and there is nothing you can do to me." He was half right! Though the fellow could not be legally tried and convicted and imprisoned due to his mental incapacity there was another remedy to protect the public. After certification that he was indeed incompetent to stand trial, the former Veterans Hospital patient was transferred to the Rusk

State Hospital, an institution housing—among other patients—the state's criminally insane. And there he died.[71]

Another killer had not died, and Texas Ranger Sergeant Jack Dean made mental note as he unfolded pages of the widely circulated Lone Star State newspaper. The *Dallas Morning News* for its Sunday, August 29, 1976, edition reported that The State Board of Pardons and Paroles had directed TDC officials to release Charles Voyde Harrelson from prison.[72] Perhaps some TDC inmates rejoiced at the news. According to Jim Willett, a long-time correctional employee and former Warden at the Walls Unit (and now Director of the Prison Museum) not just a few convicts were "leery" of Charlie, never trusting him and daring not to turn their backs on him.[73] Though it had been but three years earlier that he had been sentenced to a fifteen-year stretch for coldly executing Sam Degelia Jr., the cards fell right for hit-man Harrelson. Early on, after his formal sentencing on 27 August 1973 at Brownsville, Houston defense lawyers Percy Foreman and Dick DeGuerin had filed an appeal in Charles Harrelson's behalf. Their legal argument—in this instance—was not that the convicted defendant was guiltless, far from it, but in light of the fact that prior to formal sentencing Harrelson had been snugly confined since his arrest at Atlanta during late 1968, that he should rightfully receive custodial credit for time served from that date. That would be but fair, they flatly argued. The Court of Criminal Appeals of Texas concurred.[74] Crediting his time in county jails and the penitentiary, and applying same against his fifteen-year sentence—computed to the August 1976 release date. There was though an irrevocable downside; condemned offender Charles Voyde Harrelson wouldn't be heedlessly strolling straight into the "free-world," that convict jargon for life outside tall walls with guard towers and/or steel mesh-fences crowned by razor-wire. Lucklessly, Charles V. Harrelson still owed the feds three years for that irksome sawed-off shotgun conviction at Kansas City, Missouri. More than delighted and thoroughly committed to giving him a toll-free ticket to the Sunflower State, U.S. Marshals were standing by in Texas and, ultimately, did deliver desperado Harrelson to the

Big House in northeastern Kansas, just west of the Missouri River at Leavenworth, a government-run penal palace reserved for tough cookies—or convicts wanting everyone else to think they had been kneaded from soured dough.[75]

Purportedly, for Charles Voyde Harrelson the stint spent inside the federal lockup was the "happiest time in his life. . . . He probably had more respect in Leavenworth than anywhere else he'd been. . . . The hired killer has a certain aura about him. I'm sure he was happy in an environment where he was the upper crust of the establishment."[76] Such quixotic hyperbole is rich and, most likely, from stem to stern far-fetched. Another journalist—of Charles Voyde's compulsory occupancy at the maximum security federal prison—remarked that the incorrigible Harrelson "sometimes made it sound as though he had spent half his life in Leavenworth. . . ."[77] Whether or not the majority of other hardened inmates thought Charles Voyde Harrelson was the big dog with the brass collar is—in all probability—subject to logically reasoned debate. Rhetorically it might not come up as unfair to ponder or ask, had Charles Voyde Harrelson—by this point in time—become "institutionalized?" The phenomenon is not uncommon.[78] Not just a few inmates ease into a life where decisions are made for them, not having to choose between competing options and where the free-world becomes a very real and very scary place. Thus far in his admittedly intriguing life's story, convict Charles Voyde Harrelson's decision-making capacity had proved to be rather dismal—positively, beyond a reasonable doubt.

10

❖

"A contract-assigned assassination"

Though he had certainly been interested in the hot news about Charles Voyde Harrelson's removal to Leavenworth, Texas Ranger Sergeant Jack Dean's plate was full with matters of more pressing near-term importance, administrative and investigative. And, at that time Sergeant Jack Dean would understandably be clueless about any further interaction with the loquacious lawbreaker from Lovelady.

Somewhat disturbing personally for Texas Ranger Sergeant Jack Dean was the change in top leadership at Edinburg in the Hidalgo County Sheriff's Office: Claudio Castenado, Jr. was out, Brigido "Brig" Marmolejo, Jr., was in. Brig Marmolejo could rightly claim work experience as a Lower Rio Grande Valley lawman, having been the Assistant Chief of Police at Edinburg PD, their youngest top-tier commander at age thirty-two, and later as an Agent with the Lone Star State's Texas Alcohol Beverage Commission. Such law enforcing service had been banked before the heated 1976 political primary and November's general election. Understandably it might seem to register as self-serving hindsight though in reality such is not the case. From his earlier tenure in the Lower Rio Grande Valley, Texas Ranger Jack Dean had, from the get-go, an "uneasy" feeling about Brig Marmolejo, which would, in due time, pan out as being well-founded.[1]

258

Most Rangers abhor being confined behind the desk, and the supervisory staff is not exempt. Captain Mitchell was markedly pleased with availing himself of competency when he was away from the Company F headquarters at Waco. Pointedly, Captain Bob Mitchell was mentoring: "Sergeant Dean continues to do a good job on all work assignments. He is given more and more responsibility in the administration and supervision of the Company."[2] Practically speaking, then, though it was not a formalized and rigidly imposed policy, Captain Mitchell and Sergeant Dean alternated the routine workweeks, one or the other holding down the fort at Fort Fisher, while the other supportively visited with Rangers in the field, staying abreast of ongoing criminal investigations and offering managerial backing when appropriate, whether it be supplementary manpower, munitions, money, or a morale boost. And, too, both Captain Bob Mitchell and Sergeant Jack Dean were ever attuned to developing and/or maintaining a cordial and sound working relationship with their law enforcing partners, whether they were city, county, state, or federal badge wearers.[3]

Reviewing but a few 1977 first-quarter TRWRs is illustrative. Sandwiched between Sergeant Dean's completion of the SWAT Anti-Sniper School at Austin during January and continuing education, an In-Service School also at Austin during February, were not just a few in-the-field stopovers. Sergeant Jack Dean met with local officers regarding crime in their jurisdictional spheres in Brazos and Robertson Counties. Shortly he conferred with local law enforcing authorities at Taylor in Williamson County, and Cameron in Milam County, and at Marlin in Falls County before shutting down his workweek. Then, shortly thereafter, it was off to Clifton in Bosque County for a social call on the Chief of Police, before moving up country to Hamilton. Later, was a sit-down visit at Stephenville. Subsequent to these carrying the Ranger flag trips, Sergeant Dean motored into Centerville for a face to face with Leon County Sheriff Royce G. Wilson and Texas Ranger Bobby G. "Bob" Connell. Then it was off to Navarro County for a conference with Sheriff Jerry N. Shelton at the county seat, Corsicana. That next morning he traveled to Cleburne in Johnson County and, thereafter passing through Glen Rose was back at Stephenville conferring with Texas Ranger Billy J. DeLoach regarding a murder investigation. Though set to finish paperwork in the office the following week, Sergeant Jack Dean had to rush to Thorndale in Milam County, lending a helping hand to Ranger James E. "Jimmy" Ray, Jr.; the bank had been robbed. Next on tap was an overnight trip to Palestine, where Sergeant Dean conferred with Ranger Bobby G. Prince (a future captain) and local officers from there, as well as lawmen in Athens and Jacksonville.[4]

And herein is noticeable a truism. One of the trips to Jacksonville coincided with the end of the week, an arrival on Friday and a departure on Sunday. Ostensibly the meeting was between Sergeant Jack Dean and Captain Bob Mitchell and Senior Captain Bill Wilson—and certainly hashing out some Texas Ranger business was on the agenda—and perhaps running a trotline and toasting a tribute the Neches River fishing gods was too! At any rate, as time will tell, the forging of an earnest personal and professional camaraderie between Ranger supervisors Bill Wilson, Bob Mitchell, and Jack Dean would tightly bind, an unadulterated eternal friendship stronger than dynamite—or death!

Following Sergeant Dean's trail is easy. After taking a day off, Saturday, 26 March 1977, on Sunday he traveled to the Lampasas/Lometa area in Lampasas County, southwest of Waco and rendezvoused with Company F Texas Ranger Troy E. Porterfield. Working with local officers Rangers Dean and Porterfield assisted with raiding chicken fights. After his eleven hours and roundtrip of 320 miles, Sergeant Jack Dean pulled the plug on his workday at 8:00 p.m.[5]

During the first part of April Sergeant Jack Dean helped set up and coordinate a springtime Company F meeting at Junction in Kimble County, in the delightfully bluebonnet-studded and captivating Texas Hill Country. Aside from the updating with regards to DPS and Texas Ranger policies and procedures, the practical focus of the gathering was to qualify with shotguns and rifles—necessary items in every Texas Rangers' toolkit. And, too, these company meetings, after official workday hours, provided the platform to cement existing and build new friendships, at the same time developing *esprit de corps*, a cohesive dynamic essential for those frontline state and local and federal champions when things turn hot: Those times when everyday citizens, civilians, deserve defense from nitwits and outlaws and hired killers—or wannabes.

Not all of Sergeant Jack Dean's time was spent hunting good-for-nothings, or trying to help the Rangers and/or local officers that were on the hunt. A feature story in the *Waco Tribune-Herald*, head-lining special guests visiting with Jack and Janie Dean was a charm-ing touch for that blossoming friendship between a Ranger and an across the Big Pond cop. The aforementioned Constable Sergeant Ivor Montgomery and his lovely wife, Marion, had managed the trip to America and at Waco spent a few days with the Deans. Naturally while the girls chatted and shopped the men ambled down to the Texas Ranger Hall of Fame & Museum—and Jack's Company F office at the south end of the neatly appointed Fort Fisher complex. While touring the gemstone facility Sergeant Dean presented Sergeant Montgomery with a genuine cowboy hat, unceremoniously but for-mally anointing him as now being a legit Texan. Of course, given that Sergeant Ivor Montgomery taught classes in firearms and tactics for Essex County's specialized tactical unit, and Sergeant Jack Dean was heavily involved with the Texas Ranger SWAT team implementation and training, the pair energetically and cogently traded theories and application of real world experiences.[6]

Particularly Sergeant Ivor Montgomery noticed the striking dif-ference between policing in the United States and England. He had dutifully observed that—seemingly—in America the police "seem to be remote from the public," while across the Atlantic in England it was poles apart: "We've got a good rapport with the people at home. Americans' attitude toward police 'comes about from their walking around with a big gunbelt on.' They don't give the impression of friendliness." Furthermore, according to Sergeant Montgomery:

> In England the local police handle all crimes, every officer uses the
> same set of laws. There are no city ordinances, state, or federal

laws. They may wear a different badge, but they all work under the same set of rules. American law officers seem to be all trying to do the same job, but pulling against each other.[7]

All too soon, Ivor and Marion Montgomery's trip to Texas was relegated to fond memories and photograph scrapbooks, but their invitation for Jack and Janie Dean to, someday, come their way was heartfelt and honest. In the meantime, both had work—policing work—to do.

Though in the annals of criminality it would rank as somewhat amateurish, nevertheless, at least for awhile the bank robbery at Whitney about a dozen miles southwest of Hillsboro was dreadfully serious business for local Hill County lawmen and Texas Rangers. On 21 June 1977, the First National Bank's wall clock hour and minute hands convened at numeral twelve: high noon. During lunch hour, the two outlaws who had been waiting outside walked in—brandishing wicked looking pistols, demanding loot not theirs be right fast stuffed into a "black zipper bag." Their partner, sitting behind the steering wheel and revving the engine of a blue Pontiac Firebird convertible, was "jiggering" (acting as a lookout) and poised to propel the getaway vehicle out of normally laidback Whitney town at high-speed. Shortly, with just under $19,000, the inside outlaws became outside outlaws jumping into the Firebird geared for flight, and over the far horizon they flew. The hour hand had barely moved to 1:00 p.m. when he was notified, but from his Company F headquarters at Waco, Texas Ranger Sergeant Jack Dean raced to the scene of action "to assist in manhunt for subjects who robbed First National Bank of Whitney."[8]

Unbeknownst to the robbers the bank president and employees had not been compliant with orders to stay perfectly still—that part about everyone was to lie on the floor and not dare peek. Pluckily—bank folks through a "partially open drapery" caught a glimpse of the getaway ride and its license number. The tag registered to a Hill County resident, a character known to local policing people. The party was near over, yet the inept bank bandits then had not such a hunch. On the outskirts of town they met up with wives and girl-friends, the whole six-person crew interrelated either by blood or marriage. The gals had been fretfully standing by with a second get-away vehicle, a dazzling green and snazzy Lincoln Continental, one rather well known to the Alabama born Hill County Sheriff, near seventy-year-old W.R. "Ray" Pettit, and his deputies W.J. Graves and C.R. Chambers. Sergeant Jack Dean soon joined area lawmen. For his TRWR the hastily typewritten notation is somewhat characteristic Texas Ranger verbiage—minimal: "Six subjects arrested for bank robbery."[9] And though Sergeant Dean doesn't say it, it should come as no shocker. His natural geniality and honed interrogative knack led to a fixed end-game result. By now, an adroit newspaper reporter dutifully updated readership with lawmen's stellar performance: "Pettit said all six suspects gave statements admitting complicity in the robbery [and] still live in the area. They were being held on $20,000 bond each."[10]

Although Sergeant Dean was either day and night working in the office or seemingly always on the road between jurisdictional centers within Company F's assigned territory an underlying theme regarding his everyday activities emerges. Most likely not everyone in the Ranger service liked Jack Dean—*Homo sapiens*' personalities being what they are—but unmistakably the DPS front office was grooming him for supposed bigger and better things if, indeed, pecking-order ascension is, in the end, really something bigger and better.

At any rate, there was during that twenty-sixth day of April 1977 a Secretaries Seminar at Austin, and per the authority of Senior Captain Bill Wilson, Ranger Sergeant Jack Dean had been one of the participants involved with planning and coordinating and attending the splendid and instructive affair, an overdue inclusion of meaningful workplace value.[11] In reality, that assignment paled in comparison to his next supervisory gig dictated straight out of Austin's Texas Ranger headquarters. Sergeant Jack Dean, rather than having another Company Captain come to the capitol city for temporary duty, was to sit in Bill Wilson's command chair, for several days during the absence of the Senior Captain.[12] Clearly the administrative challenge was being presented. Would Sergeant Jack Dean pass the test?

Though Sergeant Jack Dean was not personally a participant, psychologically a heartbreaking and inadvisable event shook all of DPS and particularly Texas Rangers to their very cores. North of the DFW Metroplex, near Argyle (Denton County) on 21 February 1978, forty-one year old Texas Ranger Bobby Paul Doherty, a husband and father of two, was lending a helping hand to DPS Narcotics Agents during an illicit substance trafficking investigation. Gregory Arthur Ott, twenty-seven, the alleged drug dealing suspect and student at what was then North Texas State University (now University of North Texas) "jumped tacky and fired a shot through the house's rear door," mortally wounding Texas Ranger Doherty who had been stationed outside to interdict the efforts of anyone inside, should they have opted to hit the high grass, scampering down the Owl Hoot Trail. Once fired, the irreversible bullet, like an unseen thunderbolt of annihilation had, sadly, plummeted Texas Ranger Bobby Paul Doherty into a different and eternal world. Policing is a hard game. For the rulebook—and there is one—disposition of the law is uniquely read and imposed, applicable to but one team—the good guys. "The law-enforcing brotherhood collectively cried: But for the grace of God or Lady Luck there go I."[13]

Fortuitously for Sergeant Jack Dean, some rather pleasant news erupted at Austin, in the DPS headquarters office. Colonel Pat Speir, through unanticipated receipt of grant funds specifically earmarked for parallel agency assessments, had the agreeable duty of selecting a limited number of personnel for traveling to and studying the law enforcement operations of outside agencies. Jack and Janie had been planning a vacation to England and a visit with Ivor and Marion. Now, it certainly wasn't a state-sponsored boondoggle. Sergeant Jack Dean and Janie Dean could unmistakably make the delightful overseas trip with one-half of their expenses justifiably—and openly—picked up through the windfall of administrative funds.[14] Entries in Sergeant Dean's *Daily Reminder Journals* with regards to his assignment are explicit: "Leave Waco 3:00 p.m. to Dallas then by Plane to

England to study English Police methods." And: "England, in Essex, Kent and London England [to] study British Police methods."[15]

Such an educational application was—in fact—not necessarily a new approach for analyzing ways to better law enforcement within the Lone Star State. And of particular note, though his travel expenses had not been supplemented with public funds, during an earlier timeframe Thomas Rufus "Tom" Hickman, had somewhat done the same thing. A well-known Ranger Captain and rodeo showman, Tom Hickman had studied and made inspection tours of national policing agencies in Belgium, Holland, France, and England while taking a leave of absence from the Texas Rangers, touring Europe with renowned rodeo producer Tex Austin. In fact, and indisputably in his mind, Captain Hickman thought and penned that Scotland Yard was the "most efficient law enforcing system in existence."[16] Stateside, Tom Hickman also visited and reviewed state policing operations in New York, New Jersey, Pennsylvania, and Oregon. Clearly there were other notable players, but Captain Tom Hickman, in his day, had been one of the driving forces behind creation of DPS in 1935.[17]

For Jack and Janie the May 1978 trip to England was—understandably—quite memorable. Assuredly, those fond memories were banked in separate accounts. Although Sergeant Dean met and visited with law enforcing personnel from several agencies, he, too, was somewhat overawed with Scotland Yard and its patently observable organizational competence. There were good lessons to be learned from those folks—even the ones that didn't carry six-shooters everyday. Likewise there was a particular tutorial that was genuinely problematic for Texas Ranger Sergeant Jack O'Day Dean: One he hadn't counted on being different in England. He was given the grand opportunity to try his hand at pursuit driving on the law enforcers' oval automobile training track. According to Jack Dean, at reasonably high-speed he masterfully maneuvered through the corners, but had one helluva time on the straightaway's—the steering wheel was on the wrong side of the car and he was consistently accelerating on the wrong side of the roadway. Those blokes had it backwards!

What those Englishmen didn't have backwards was showing Sergeant Jack Dean a good time, treating him—almost—as if he were a king. The brotherhood of the badge knew no boundaries. Texas Ranger Sergeant Jack Dean—a stranger in a foreign land— was privileged to go places and see things that were off-limits to everyday Londoners outside select dignitaries, politicos, law enforcing and top-secret security personnel.

Particularly impressive was the Black Museum (now the Crime Museum of Scotland Yard), the showcased historical center currently housed at New Scotland Yard. Since crossing the threshold was/is reserved for law enforcing personnel from around the world, Janie Dean was not barred from touring the Black Museum because she was a lady, but due to the fact she held no policing commission. She would have to pass time elsewhere. The remarkable Black Museum was/is not unlocked for the general public. With a decidedly rich and macabre history, in one form another operating since 1874 (the year Texas Rangers were institutionalized as lawmen) when the doors were first informally swung open, and the following year with an official dedication ceremony, the first-rate facility has on display a splendid panoply of spellbinding and somewhat—for the faint of heart—gruesome artifacts:

> The assemblage grew from collection of prisoners' property under the authority of the Prisoners Property Act of 1869. The act was intended to help the police in their study of crime and criminals. By 1875, it had become an official museum, although not open to the public, with a police inspector and a police constable assigned to official duty there. In 1877 the name "Black Museum" was coined, when on 08 April a reporter from *The Observer* newspaper [first] used the term after being refused a visit by an Inspector. . . .[18]

Commendably, historic accuracy is the byword, not bending to mawkish sentimentality and/or American modern age safe-space denial. There are sword-canes and nondescript umbrellas concealing shotguns, ghoulish memorabilia from bona fide and demonstrably deranged serial killers, hangman's nooses, and morbid death masks of executed criminals and, for those with an extraordinary fascination and macabre interest, "the Hell letter allegedly from Jack the Ripper and other letters." The special treatment shown Texas Ranger Jack Dean did not go unnoticed and was most sincerely appreciated. Aside from the more-or-less secretive subjects and spots, Sergeant Dean found it fascinating to be personally guided along London streets on the actual cold trail of England's most noteworthy serial killer, the aforementioned Jack the Ripper.[19] Realistically it was pretty heady stuff for fellow from Cowtown.

Similarly, petite Janie Dean had a good story or two about her sojourn across the Atlantic. Doing things up right for the spouse of a visiting Texas lawman, but unable to pass through the archway at the Black Museum, Janie was spirited away while Jack was examining the grisly but fascinating artifacts. In a secret spot that was even off-limits for most Londoners, Janie Dean was shown amazing treasures usually unseen: A stash of dazzling riches too pricy for public display. She may not have had Royal lineage in her family tree, but she was being treated as if a queen. Particularly and permanently sealed into her mind was a bejeweled gold chain once the property of King Henry VIII. Guesstimating the weight—in excess of 20 lbs.—and/or its value was beyond Janie's ability. What was not past her was surprise and appreciation when the weighty ornament was draped around her neck and fastened. Reflection in the ornate mirror was stunning. Wow! What Fort Worth girl could top that?

There were other memorable highlights too. One was particularly centered about her and Marion being "kicked out" of Westminster Abby. Jack and Ivor teasingly jested that through the years they had both been kicked out of some pretty good barrooms and pubs, but for this shenanigan the girls had them topped. Having a wonderful time the girls were oblivious to the propriety of their surroundings. Partaking of an ice-cream cone seemed like a grand idea, and so both gals tightfistedly armed themselves with a delicious dripping treat, napkins in hand. And inside Westminster Abby they did go— for awhile. Soon after entering they were broached by an official— unsmiling—and certainly a fellow with authority. They were politely but convincingly ushered out of the edifice—somewhat embarrassed about being ejected from Westminster Abby. Now, that would be a good story to tell her back home Texas friends—wouldn't it?[20]

Returning to Waco from their overseas travels was, at last, accomplished and dealing with the world of everyday trials and tribulations was on the front-burner for Sergeant Dean and his bride. All so soon Sergeant Dean learned—with disbelief—that District Attorney Oscar McInnis was already scorched, his fat in the proverbial fire raging in Hidalgo County. If the allegations were true, the DA had conspired to have the former husband of a client kidnapped and murdered on the opposite side of the Rio Grande by a Mexican policeman. Preposterous? FBI Agents thought not, especially after electronically wiring a jailhouse informant and recording conversations between him and the unsuspecting Oscar McInnis. Federal Grand Jurors, after hearing from the FBI and carefully evaluating tape recordings, were in accord with the FBI. Furthermore, after listening to sworn testimony from Oscar McInnis, they pitched a charge of Perjury into the felonious mix. A public official suffering criminal indictments is not good. Adding to the Hidalgo County DA's woes was another niggling matter of no little concern: Attorneys for the Texas Prosecutors Coordinating Council were, in their very first cause of action, legally maneuvering to formally have District Attorney McInnis's license to practice law revoked.[21] Not surprising, then, would be the legal sparring before appellate tribunals, state and federal, with regards to both civil and criminal sanctions.[22] For those initial courtroom doings spider-webbing around the Hidalgo County DA's neck, Sergeant Dean at Waco would not be in the investigative loop. His good luck would be short-lived.

Company F Ranger Sergeant Jack Dean's investigative focus—from a supervisor's oversight perspective—was redirected to that seemingly always troubled vicinity outside the guard-post gates at Fort Hood, in Bell County. A blood-spattered atrocity put local lawmen and Texas Rangers into high-gear. Thomas Andrew "Andy" Barefoot, aka Darren Callier, was temporarily living in the bustling military town of Killeen, residing with four other fellows in a mobile home. Whether or not his housemates knew of his history is unknown and, in context, is relatively inconsequential but Andy Barefoot had a good reason for adopting an alias. He had successfully engineered a jailbreak from a Valencia County lockup, that geographically surveyed and settled subsection of real-estate just south of Albuquerque in the Land of Enchantment, New Mexico. There, in Valencia County, an outstanding criminal charge of "sexual penetration of a minor," a three-year-old girl, and "kidnapping," loomed on Barefoot's back trail. Andy Barefoot was on the lam, and had been so for the past half-year, ever since his 9 January 1978 escape.[23] The former oilfield roughneck from New Iberia, Louisiana, was a habitué of the Big Houses, already having racked up hard time in the Pelican State's and the Sooner State's penitentiaries.[24] Seemingly, comparable to Charles Voyde Harrelson and scores of other inept police characters, Barefoot was a traveling man, and just like Harrelson and so many of those caught and convicted ne'er-do-well outlaw Texas gunmen, he, too, seemed to have an affinity for those tiny pocket pistols, .25 caliber autoloaders.[25]

Purportedly, uncontrollably riled by the way he had been previously treated by a policeman in Harker Heights, Killeen's sister city to the east, Andy Barefoot vowed to one of his roommates that he intended to exterminate one of that town's peace officers; not necessarily the one that had upset him but, by his standard, any one of those Harker Heights boys in blue would do. Barefoot would deviously create a diversion "by bombing or setting fire to a building," pull a highjacking at the Oasis Club (or somewhere else) and, when the golden opportunity presented, mercilessly off a hoodwinked officer responding to the glowing orange scene of devastation. Andy Barefoot was serious—dead serious! Subsequent to catching his ride to Harker Heights and pausing at a quiet and isolated nighttime Stop and Rob (a convenience store/service station), Barefoot "filled an empty plastic milk jug with gasoline." After slyly disentangling from his impromptu chauffeur, he surreptitiously ducked behind the Silver Spur Lounge, a couple of hours prior to the 7 August 1978 sun peeking down on busy Highway 190 at about 5:00 a.m. Unfeigned sinister business was near. Schemer Andy Barefoot's toss was rather pathetic. The Molotov Cocktail rashly thrown atop the Silver Spur's roof temporarily illuminated darkness, but while it attracted attention, in fact, it did very little monetary damage nor caused very much physical destruction. Of course, that had not been part of the evil plan.[26]

Answering the call to investigate was Harker Heights' patrolman Carl Irvin Levin, thirty-one, a persevering policeman with previous law-enforcing service at Killeen PD, following his tour in Vietnam and honorable discharge from the U.S. Army. Court records reveal what happened next, testimony from an early-rising witness who lived on Amy Lane: "He was walking to work at 5:35 a.m. when he saw a patrol car parked at the intersection of Amy Lane and Valley Road with its emergency lights on and its spotlight trained on some bushes. Officer Levin was standing beside the patrol car. A man wearing a white T-shirt and blue jeans stepped out of the bushes and walked toward the officer. The man then shot Levin in the head at point-blank range and fled down Valley Road." Understandably, Harker Heights Patrolman Carl Levin expired, due to that penetrating gunshot wound to the left temple.[27] At close range a copper-coated .25 caliber projectile fired into someone's brain was, needless to say, nearly always lethal.

At the time of the gunshot, for saddened lawmen it was a whodunit, although that changed during the late morning, after scouring the brush and brambles, alleyways and neighborhood streets, hunting for a worthwhile clue and/or a worthless suspect. One of Barefoot's roommates had received a panicky telephone call from the shooter. After acknowledging that he had been listening to the local news broadcasts, the roommate pointedly inquired of Andy Barefoot, "did you do that?" Barefoot was not even slightly hesitant; the answer shocked sensibilities, "Yea, I shot him. I killed the mother fucker. I shot him in the head." During a separate phone call to another acquaintance, Andy Barefoot blurted reality, coldly declaring "he had to get out of town because he [had] wasted a cop, that he killed a cop."[28] Through those cooperative helpmates, who now had learned more than they wanted to know, and meticulous processing of the murder site for admissible evidence, the Texas Rangers and area lawmen were challenged with a nasty whodunit no more. The manhunt was, relatively speaking, short.

Lawmen learned that Barefoot had fled the area, catching a bus bound for Houston at Belton in Bell County, hoping to hastily lose himself in the throng of Harris County's scurrying masses. Barefoot's miscalculation was colossal, a slick truth confirmed in—as but one example—pages of the *Dallas Morning News*: "The 33-year-old Louisiana native, Thomas Andrew Barefoot, charged under the name Darren Callier in Monday's slaying of police officer Carl Levin, 31, was arrested [and disarmed] at a Houston bus station early Wednesday as he stepped from a bus. Barefoot was moved from Houston to Bell County within hours of his arrest by Houston police and Texas Rangers."[29] Sergeant Jack Dean was, indeed, pleased with the stellar work of his Company F Rangers, the whole Texas Ranger outfit and their employees—but equally cognizant that such investigative and apprehension doings were, often as not, gold-plated examples of inter-agency cooperation and commitment. The days of the Lone Ranger or the overblown nonsense of One Riot, One Ranger, were no more. The tragic and senseless murder, execution, of Carl Irving Levin had been another of those situations calling for an all-hands-on-deck approach: None shied from the storm of duty.

And that devotion to duty extended well past the lineup of lawmen with adhesive black tape symbolically garnishing their badges. As previously highlighted, the American system of criminal justice is based on an adversarial model: two sides battling for their interpretation of hard truth, with an impartial judge calling fair or foul, and a nonaligned jury keeping tally and rendering the final score. Although its shortcomings are sometimes questioned, it's the extant system in play. In Thomas Andrew Barefoot's case, the Bell County District Attorney, Arthur C. "Cappy" Eads, a multi-term elected career prosecutor, was calling for swift imposition of the death penalty for a criminal offense that registered in the Texas Penal Code as a clear-cut case of Capital Murder.[30] That then trimmed Andy

Barefoot's options. If he really wanted to live, entering a plea of *Guilty* to a charge of Capital Murder, without an indisputable and court approved pre-sentence deal in place, was tantamount to a suicide. Andy Barefoot and his defense attorney metaphorically chose to attack and fight like furious Comanche. Cappy Eads was not deterred by war-whooping bluff or bravado. He had a razor sharpened arrow in his quiver.

At trial the thoroughly well-respected First Assistant DA, Jim Leitner in opening remarks let fly the prosecution's pointed shaft, noting for the jury that "Barefoot was carrying a .25 caliber weapon when he was arrested by Texas Rangers."[31] Of course for an impartial jury that in itself was interestingly relevant but certainly not—by any stretch—close to conclusive. Testimony from a forensic ballistician, however, pierced through the defense breastworks and right into Andy Barefoot's odds of riding off into the free-world sunset. The bullet retrieved from Officer Carl Levin's cranium had been—according to a court-qualified expert—fired from the very same .25 caliber pistol taken by Texas Rangers from Barefoot's pocket at the Houston bus station. Additionally, testimony from fourteen witnesses about what they saw and/or heard Barefoot admit to, staked him on indefensible ground. The trial jury deliberated but ninety minutes before returning their verdict of *Guilty* to Capital Murder. That same jury—by law in a bifurcated criminal justice system—and after their welcomed weekend recess, took but fifty-five minutes before "recommending that Thomas A. Barefoot, convicted of shooting a policeman through the head, die by drug injection."[32] Though it naturally took several years through a mandated appellate review, the jury's judgment was levied, but not before Andy Barefoot uttered his last words from Huntsville at The Walls, inside the execution chamber. In part the sentiment seems somewhat incredible coming from a convicted cop killer: "I hope that one day we can look back on the evil that we're doing right now like the witches we burned at the stake."[33]

Plausibly, at the time Sergeant Jack Dean's recollection as to what really registered as barely a trivial blip on lawmen's radar, is imprecise. His policing colleagues if they noticed at all, paid but little attention to Charles Voyde Harrelson's release from Leavenworth and his return to the Lone Star State.[34] Although Charles Harrelson fancied himself a professional gambler—a whiz with a deck of cards—he also acknowledged that any fair play in his games was outlandish: Rationalizing, "But the people I play are like me. We cheat each other. I just cheat better."[35] Chaste history is not a kind mistress and Charles Voyde Harrelson's high-stakes gambling for greenbacks and/or trying to beat the state and/or federal criminal justice systems—despite any maudlin romanticism—had a bottom-line and his standing was on the deficit side of the ledger. Anointing oneself a king on the gambling circuit but racking up hard time behind tall walls and barbed-wire in California, Texas, and Kansas seems a rather elastic and hyperbolic dichotomy. Tilting with windmills is futile. Some outlaws learn—some don't.

Though abandoning a fussy chronology is herein appropriate, the overall message remains clear. Amalgamating his requisite DPS-PDSs (evaluations) into a singular storyline suffices. Sergeant Jack Dean for the preceding four years had been handed an escalating leadership role. Reviewing for the historic record succinctly is sufficient. Captain Bob Mitchell was adamant: "Sergeant Dean is doing an outstanding job in all phases of work assignments. In addition to his regular workload he has devoted many hours to the S.W.A.T. formulation and training. He has been given more and more responsibility in the administration and supervision of the Company. His performance in each assignment has been commendable. Sergeant Dean is good Captain material." Furthermore Captain Mitchell capitalized on his recommendation for Sergeant Dean's promotion, "During this reporting period Sergeant Dean has traveled in the field extensively on inspection tours and [at the same time] performed routine supervisory duties."[36] There was not a smidgen of doubt—and never was—with what Bob Mitchell said.

For Jack and Janie Dean's household the news broke big—a formal letter from the DPS Director barely ahead of an explanatory piece in the *Waco Tribune-Herald*. In the first instance Colonel Wilson

E. Speir made it an endorsed matter of public record: "It gives me great pleasure to congratulate you on your appointment to the position of Captain, Texas Ranger Service. Effective November 1, 1978, you will assume this position and be assigned to command Company 'D' in San Antonio. . . . May I take this opportunity to wish you success in this new position as I am confident you will perform in this capacity as you have so ably done in the position you are leaving."[37] On the same day as his letter to Sergeant Dean, 25 October, Colonel Speir followed up with a DPS station-wide teletype announcing the promotion. Ensuring that the word was not missed inadvertently, Colonel Speir directed DPS teletype operators throughout the state to acknowledge receipt of his message.[38] At the time within the ranks of Texas Rangers earning the captaincy of a company was, really, a big deal—though now, in the twenty-first century, individual Ranger company commanders carry the rank and pay-grade of a DPS major. The newspaper reporter covering Waco affairs posted their readership on the why and where: "Jack Dean, presently a Waco Texas Ranger Sergeant, was promoted Wednesday to Ranger Captain and named commander of Texas Ranger Company D in San Antonio. The veteran law officer replaces Captain John Wood who is retiring at the end of October after serving in the department since November of 1942."[39]

Thankfully there was an experienced Texas Ranger who would be acting as Jack Dean's right-hand man: Sergeant Hyman R. "Lefty" Block, at the time forty-three. Lefty Block had signed on with DPS in late 1957 and had promoted into the Texas Rangers ten years later.[40] He was a forward thinker as has been penned: Lefty Block sometimes "yearned for the old days while recognizing the new." He, too, pointedly theorized about a change in philosophy, commenting about times long gone: "I felt the manner in which some cases in South Texas, such as the farmworker strikes, were handled in the '60s and 70s' cost us a lot of respect. In recent history, we've handled similar situations and managed to keep the peace without losing face. . . . These days, we portray a professional image."[41] For an altogether separate assessment it was written that Lefty Block was popular with the rank and file, in large part due to his outstanding "reputation as a hardworking Ranger with a lot of successful investigations to his credit."[42] Sergeant Lefty Block working under the command of Captain John Wood and himself gaining valuable investigative and leadership skills through the years, ensured that the changing of the guard at the top of Company D would be seamless. As Jack Dean had learned, Texas Ranger Company Captains leaned on their Company Sergeants—heavily.

Not daring to let the opportunity of extending a hand of cordiality and fellowship slip by, the FBI SAC at San Antonio, Michael A. "Tony" Morrow, added: "It is with great pleasure that I congratulate you not only on your promotion to Captain, but enthusiastically welcome you to San Antonio. I was delighted to learn that you will be replacing Captain Wood here. Needless to say, I am looking forward to working with you and getting better acquainted."[43]

Subsequent to Jack Dean fast and figuratively touching base at San Antonio, and though he was officially a Captain as of 1 November 1978, there was the nice custom of actually being one of the guests of honor for an official "swearing in ceremony" at Austin. Proudly accompanied by Janie, on 3 November 1978 the ritualistic formalities of tradition were adhered to. Colonel Pat Speir commissioned Jack Dean and the DPS photographer forevermore captured the moment. Attentively and appreciatively looking on was Senior Texas Ranger Captain Bill Wilson, pleased as punch that one of his protégés had made the grade.[44] Then, it was back to San Antonio and back to work—there was always plenty of work.

The Alamo City was historic and charming. Picturesque were the city's old-world Missions and arched entryways into prettily landscaped courtyards. With its downtown River Walk and winding conglomeration of quaint shops and restaurants and gondola-copied boat rides it was, beyond doubt, a vacationer's delight: So boldly hawked the Chamber of Commerce mouthpieces. And they were right! Truthfully there was that other little side, the bad scene less talked about; the extraordinary city's underbelly. The very same month that Texas Ranger Captain Jack Dean was house hunting and tending to the family's relocation an incident grabbed headlines proving that San Antonio was yet staking claim to her Wild West heritage.

On the twenty-first day of November 1978, on his way to work, Assistant United States Attorney James Kerr, driving his polished high-dollar Lincoln Continental, was attacked—not fatally, but ambushed nevertheless. Would-be assassins tried to hem lawyer Kerr between a mint-green van and annihilation. The purposeful outlaws jumped out of the van's cargo doors and opened fire with a shotgun and M1 .30 caliber carbine, punching nineteen holes into prosecutor Kerr's automobile. A startled witness to the dastardly deed remarked, to her, "it sounded like cannons going off." The heavy car's engine block and dashboard saved the crouching and thoroughly frightened prosecutor, though he was bloodied by shattered and flying glass and bullet fragments, enough so that overnight hospitalization was on his bad day's program. Deputy U.S. Marshals were quickly onsite to provide James Kerr with twenty-four and seven protection. The United States Attorney for the Western District of Texas, Jamie Boyd, told ravenous reporters that the electrifying happening "has the overtones of a contract-signed assassination. It's scary." Afterward, subsequent to James Kerr's best description of the van, it was recovered in a nearby neighborhood—having been stolen in Austin but hours before. And even later, after looking through mug books at San Antonio PD headquarters, James Kerr tentatively identified outlaw bikers—Bandidos—as, in his mind, prime suspects. Bandidos were from time to time purported to be first-hand engaged offering personal protection—or worse—for big-time dope traffickers. Narcotic smugglers and distributors, and their attorneys, didn't like Kerr. He was, at the time, embroiled in some high-profile prosecutions of defendants with wheelbarrow loads of dollars and not an ounce of remorse or conscience.[45] Welcome to San Antonio, Captain Jack Dean!

11

"You're lucky to be alive"

Even prior to ringing in the New Year, Captain Jack Dean found himself in familiar territory, in the Lower Rio Grande Valley performing a critical background investigation on a Ranger applicant, Stanley K. "Stan" Guffey.[1] Too there was that other matter, a touchy not so little matter. Now, that he was the Texas Ranger Captain commanding Company D, what happened in the Lower Rio Grande Valley didn't necessarily stay in the Valley out of sight and out of mind. Crookedness throughout the hallways in the Hidalgo County courthouse was Captain Dean's business. Captain Jack Dean's words were cutting and precise regarding a 27 November 1978 discussion: "Conferred with District Attorney Pro-Tem of Hidalgo County reference McInnis investigation."[2] Shortly, before December was history, Captain Jack Dean would personally find himself at McAllen meeting with Judge Evins and other members of officialdom, including criminal investigators, sorting through evidence relating to what was generically being referred to as the "McInnis Investigation."[3]

In the midst of that supervisory inquiry, Captain Dean side-tracked those duties to assist Rangers Bruce Casteel and Rudy Rodriguez with transporting a high-profile prisoner. Ensuring that Archer Parr would be safely delivered—absent press interference—and, at least temporarily ensconced in the Cameron County Jail at Brownsville, Captain Dean lent a helping hand.[4]

For the most part—and it's relevant to note—the recent Texas Ranger's criminal investigation into the criminal and crooked activities of Archer Parr and the shenanigans in Duval County were taking place—generally speaking—while Jack Dean had been stationed at Waco as the Company F Sergeant, prior to his promotion and taking command of Company D.

A wolf may find disguise in a sheep's clothing, but an alligator cannot pass as a pig no matter the costume. Duval County politics were and historically had been just as perceptibly corrupt as that—transparently obvious. The notorious George Berham Parr, the "Duke of Duval," had a long and storied run at greasing wheels and palms of the Democratic machine in South Texas. And he did it with discerning and intuitive aplomb, becoming fluent in border Spanish and, too, the political master "tirelessly learned the names of his constituents and their children, and provided help in time of need for one concession—absolute loyalty. Under his leadership, both corruption and paternalism flourished in Duval County. . . . Parr stood as the undisputed political boss of Duval County. He amassed a fortune with income from banking, mercantile, ranching, and oil interest—and from the public treasury. His political influence extended into other South Texas counties as well."[5] Lyndon Baines Johnson, perhaps, owed the surefire outcome of his supercharged 1948 campaign for U.S. Senator to George Parr. Providently it seems, 202 behind schedule votes mysteriously came his way. The missing written treasures from Jim Wells County put LBJ ahead by 87 votes statewide, just before a list of registered voters vanished. "Even more sordid [Parr] controversies followed." Three of those spun around rivals' murders.[6] And doing it up just fine for Lone Star State political mischief, at one time he could be politely and formally addressed as Sheriff George B. Parr of Duval County.[7] Unfortunately for the general and generally poor public's unsullied interests there was a glimmer of hope—for an ephemeral moment—but while the sequence of 1950s investigations led to "over 650 indictments against ring members. . . . Parr survived the indictments and his own conviction for federal mail fraud through a complicated series of dismissals and reversals on appeal."[8] Not forevermore. His good luck melted.

For the story at hand the terse flashback is essential. Rather than do a stretch in federal prison for income tax violations, on the first day of April 1975, at his celebrated *Los Harcones* ranch south of Benavides, George B. Parr eluded further imposition of any court's calculated sanctions. Ranger George E. "Gene" Powell and other lawmen—federal, state, and local—had been hard hunting for Mr. George B. Parr, even with a DPS helicopter. He had knowingly failed to appear and show cause to U.S. District Judge Owen D. Cox at Corpus Christi why "he should not be declared a danger to others and his $75,000 bond on an income tax evasion conviction forfeited." Earlier he had allegedly—and perhaps did—threaten to kill Judge O.P. Carrillo, "his one-time political ally who had broken with him." Near what was known as the Julian Windmill tank and pond, at a remote section of the ranch, in a shady grove of trees was parked Parr's "late model Chrysler Imperial." Ranger Gene Powell, along with DPS Major Kent Ogden, a Regional Commander, and Duval County Chief Deputy Israel Saenz—and others were onsite. George Parr was inside the vehicle and: "According to Texas Ranger Gene Powell [Parr] was wearing light brown trousers and a light colored shirt. His glasses were covered with blood. His Stetson hat was on the seat beside him." Powell noticed other things as well. George Parr was sledgehammer dead, slumped over the Chrysler's front seat, a bullet wound to the head. His "favorite Colt .45 automatic pistol" and a Ruger Mini-14 semi-automatic rifle had also been inside the car within easy reach. "Parr, 74, whose political house was falling in on him on all sides, apparently took his life rather than go to jail. . . ."[9]

Subsequently a Task Force was constructed, its mission to delve into the unfinished public corruption yet rampant in Duval County. Texas Rangers Gene Powell, Rudy Rodriguez, and Ramiro "Ray" Martinez, along with a host of legal minds from the Texas Attorney General's Office, were prepositioned in the starting-blocks ready to do what needed doing—something. The aforementioned Archer Parr, a former Duval County Judge and the nephew of George B.

Parr, among not just a few others, was an in-the-sights target of the Task Force investigators. The whole uncorking drama makes for fascinating perusal but for this, Jack Dean's law enforcing and supervisory story, the quick cut must suffice. Archer Parr suffered both federal and state convictions for a myriad of violations.[10] From his temporary home at Marion, Illinois, in the federal lockup, a downtrodden Archer Parr was shuttled back to Texas and was in and out of court—in chains. One of these transfers from jailhouse to jailhouse was the trip referenced when Captain Dean assisted Texas Rangers Casteel and Rodriquez.[11] That Captain Dean wasn't just idly killing time but was truly interested in—and from the front office perspective—responsible for overseeing theses affairs is manifestly and shortly evinced in one of his soon after TRWRs: "To San Diego, conferred with Rangers Rodriguez, Martinez and [Morgan L.] Miller and local officials reference criminal activities in Duval County."[12]

Someone else was in need of assistance. A troubled Lower Rio Grande Valley lawyer turned to Captain Dean for advice. He had faith in Jack's sure creditability and counted on his candor. It seems the legal beagle had gotten himself in way over his head with "some people" and they had hungrily turned to a no-nonsense collection agent, Charles Voyde Harrelson. One way or the other, Charles V. Harrelson was to collect the now long in arrears debt. Obviously bewildered and somewhat frightened, rightly so, the puzzled lawyer asked Captain Dean what he should do. Jack parried: "do you owe him [them] the money?" The answer was truthful, cold and direct: "Well, yeah, it's their money." On the purely personal level—between adversaries—Jack Dean knew Charles Voyde Harrelson to actually be quite "smart and had a personality." Honestly, on the surface Charles V. Harrelson was really a likable guy, somewhat enjoyable to talk to. Captain Jack Dean's counsel to his friend was logical and straightforward regarding the deficit: "Then you're lucky to be alive."[13] The lawyer's choice, then, was plain: Financially settle his account right fast—or live the rest of his days in fear—if he was lucky.

After that, it was that unpleasant time wherein lawmen did what lawmen do—what's necessary. Friendship is fine, but fidelity to sworn duty is firmly fixed and indissoluble. Respectfully, but point-edly, on the seventh day of December 1978, Captain Jack Dean inter-viewed Oscar McInnis in reference to allegations about assaulting a witness.[14] Unquestionably Captain Jack Dean valued the friendship of Oscar McInnis and, professionally, graded the legally encumbered attorney a damn good prosecutor. Captain Jack Dean's visit was offi-cial but short. Wisely and, not too surprisingly, McInnis had little to say of substance—nothing incriminating: And, in point of fact had deboned the investigative viability of Captain Dean's trip to McAllen. Jack Dean's *adios* to McInnis was plainspoken: "Oscar, if you didn't do anything wrong you'll be okay—and if you did—it was really stupid."[15]

With the coming of a brand-new year, 1979 heralded new lead-ership at the tiptop of Texas state government. A wealthy oilman from Dallas, William P. Clements, "who had close ties to Ronald Reagan," would become Texas's Chief Executive, the state's first Republican elected to that position in more than a century.[16] With the pomp and ceremony of an inauguration, security precau-tions had best be in place lest the principal dignitary be physically harmed—or, perhaps worse, politically embarrassed. Naturally such work was within the realm of DPS, and more precisely for the up-close elbow-to-elbow work with the protectee, that task went to the Rangers. By virtue of his upper echelon standing within the outfit Captain Jack Dean was engaged with carefully coordinat-ing security arrangements during the Governor's Inauguration for the 16 January observances. On the big day, Captain Jack Dean, himself, working under particular authority of Senior Captain Bill Wilson, oversaw security during the Inauguration.[17] Although Captain Jack Dean politically identified himself as a Republican, he was at least moderately concerned with part of the platform that propelled Bill Clements into office—that part about reducing taxes and cutting the size of state government. Would the Texas Ranger budget be on the chopping block of austerity? As the Part I Index Crime Rate was rising would DPS be forced to downsize? Would the SWAT team be axed? Who knew?[18] Meanwhile Captain Jack Dean did what he had taken an oath to do: protect and serve the good people of the Lone Star State.

Lamentably for him perhaps, but germane for squinty-eyed statisticians who always haunt the hallways of bureaucracies, Jack Dean not only had to fight *mal hombres* but piles of paperwork. DPS topdogs at Austin wanted to keep score—it was vital for budgetary and manpower matters when testifying and/or justifying and/or petitioning for something more during fussy legislative hearings and/or committee meetings. Not fun, but necessary. A quick review of the Company D TRPR, only in part and just for one month—January 1979—is insightful. Not resorting to a crime by crime breakdown, which there is, and shutting misdemeanors out of the equation, these Texas Rangers served twenty-three felony warrants and made twenty-seven felony arrests; their courtroom tally was eighteen felony convictions for previous arrests and sentences of 175 years—as well as assessment of $11,692.00 in fines. The amount of personal property recovered during this cycle for Company D tipped the monetary scales at $140,013.00 and they assisted with the recovery of an additional $1,200. Texas Rangers of Company D for this reporting period logged 43,375 miles traveled by state automobile, and ten hours flying somewhere to do something. All in all, for this January the Company D Rangers submitted a total of 383 reports and worked 344 days in the aggregate.[19] Captain Jack Dean could hardly see daylight at the end of the month before the whole damn paperwork process started anew—until the end of time—he figured.

There was something else Captain Jack Dean had to take into account: state politicians were always on the make—running for office. And providing them security was just part of pinning the iconic star-in-wheel badge over one's heart. When ex-Governor John Bowden Connally, Jr. pitched his name in the hat—protective duty came Captain Jack Dean's way. At the Alamo City on Saturday 25 February 1979, Captain Jack Dean provided security for Presidential Candidate John Connally during a visit to San Antonio. The next day of course was Sunday, but that made no difference to the politico and little difference to a loyal Texas Ranger. His TRWR is clear-cut:

"To Floresville, provided security for Presidential Candidate John Connally during visit to area."[20] Although personable and professional—and probably knew it—Captain Jack Dean was smart enough to personally capitalize on association with high-level folks. Practically speaking it would serve him well—and certainly more importantly—it would serve the institutional interests of the Texas Rangers well, too!

Although hardly settled in at San Antonio, Captain Jack Dean was kept in touch with hardcore reality. It wasn't just high-profile prosecutors that walked the line of potential jeopardy. Trouble stalked the borderlands adjacent to the Río Bravo too. During the wee morning hours of 17 February 1979 in the very Lower Rio Grande Valley country where he had first earned credibility as a skilled and stand-up Texas Ranger, big news broke and it broke bad. In the middle of an intersection lay the motionless form of a Hidalgo County Constable, twenty-two-year-old Ricky Stephen Lewis. He had been shot DRT—and the nastily disposed shooter was nowhere about. Signs of a frantic fight were clear. Oddly, Constable Ricky Lewis was prostrate atop a .357 Magnum revolver, but not his duty weapon— his revolver of like caliber was missing. There was, surely, an oddity about this unnerving murder—one Captain Dean and his Company D Rangers in Hidalgo and Cameron Counties would muddle over in their minds time and time again. Saddened local lawmen, too, were at a loss for words or suspects—it was another of those mysteries, a shocking whodunit?[21]

What was beyond reproach and above-board was Captain Jack Dean's recognition of the positives to be gained from fashioning and maintaining amicable relationships, both inside and outside of his immediate organizational command structure: A case in point is herein mentioned. During April 1979 both Dean's Company D and Bob Mitchell's Company F organized a joint firearms training session at the legendary YO Ranch—in and of itself not an unwise political and/or public relations maneuver. FBI SAC Morrow was invited to attend and participate. Afterward he made sure DPS Colonel Pat Speir was apprised of the painstaking commitment to excellence, writing: "My purpose in writing to you is to express my respect for the men I have met who serve this State as Texas Rangers. This training session afforded me the opportunity to become better acquainted with the Rangers and, in my opinion they are one of the finest groups of law enforcement officers that I have ever met." That was the generalization; during the next laudatory paragraph the San Antonio SAC turned to personnel particulars: "I wanted you to know my thoughts in this matter and also I would be remiss if I did not mention the outstanding job Sgt. H.R. 'Lefty' Block of Company D did in coordinating the training program. Sgt. Block is a tireless worker and indeed a credit to the Ranger service. Finally, Captains Dean and Mitchell are two of the most professional and dedicated law enforcement officials I have ever had the privilege of knowing. Their cooperation to me and this office is indeed appreciated."[22] Colonel Speir responded, and with what later proved to be a telling closing comment, assured SAC Morrow: "Thank you for your commendation and we look forward to working with you at all times."[23] Little did Colonel Speir know, at the very time he was writing those words a sinister plot was being hatched.

A happening that was not evilly incubated was Captain Jack Dean's two-day participation in the Labor Relations Seminar conducted at Austin.[24] Clearly the Texas Ranger administrative philosophy had undergone a correcting modification as contemporary times and attitudes swirled about them. Of course it rings of romanticism and, perhaps, it was true, but a few memorable characterizations of Texas Ranger captains were passé in 1979: Captain Jim Riddles may have had "balls as big as two brass bathtubs," and Captain Alfred Allee might have in a certain sense been "mean as a snake," but that was then—not now.[25] The sociological upheavals of days not long removed had altered Texas Rangers' courses and hastened professionalism. Institutionally the Texas Ranger workforce could adapt and survive, or stagnate and die. There was a new breed of Texas Ranger in town. Though Jack Dean was not alone, he had—for whatever reason—been juxtaposed perfectly on that precipice separating the old from the new. Of that, the historical record is concrete.

By nearing end of the month, another springtime episode centered on possession of firearms, not a typical training exercise,
and it would not play pretty in the streets of festive San Antonio.
On the twenty-seventh day of April 1979 Captain Jack Dean, in his
office catching up on routine but never-ending paperwork and host-
ing supervisory conferences, was rattled by the hot news breaking
forth.[26] A hidden sniper was on a shooting spree and casualties were
mounting at the passing of each minute. As a relatively new arrival
in the Alamo City, Captain Jack Dean was not yet wholly aware of the
significance associated with the colorful Battle of Flowers Parade.
On the other hand, a WWII veteran, sixty-four-year-old Ira Attebury
was. Attebury had known the marching bands and cheering crowd,
and the number of unwary city policemen blocking and/or directing traffic would be substantial: a target-rich environment. Near the
parade route he had parked his Winnebago.[27] The motor-home was,
literally, an arsenal on wheels, fully stocked with a "double-barreled
shotgun, an AR-15 semi-automatic carbine, nine other rifles and
four .38 caliber pistols."[28] Parked in the parking lot of a tire store
drew not an ounce of suspicion—not even from the store's manager who had chatted with him briefly, noting that Ira seemed like a
"quiet, intelligent sounding man."[29] Sadly, the dreadful noise inside
Ira's head was not tranquil. He was mentally tormented. Subsequent
to a horrific automobile accident in which two women perished eight
years earlier, fretful Ira Attebury had unhappily waded into the troubled waters of paranoia, at least so theorized family members.[30]

What happened next is not just well-reasoned hypothesis. At
about 1:00 p.m. from inside the Winnebago gunfire emitted and
pandemonium spilled forth. Policemen and bystanders fell to the
ground wounded—others, in a panic, fled racing and stumbling for
cover, screaming and scared. Ira Attebury had slipped over the edge.
Though individual stories of derring-do could be carved out during
the ninety-minute standoff and exchange of shots between Ira
Attebury and police and San Antonio's SWAT team's tear-gas canister
response, word-count curbs are essential and real. When the ghastly
and foggy mêlée was over, three adults lay dead in the street and half

a dozen police officers suffered gunshot wounds—thankfully, none were mortal. Additionally, nursing injuries of one sort or another— acute or superficial—were as many as fifty-five unfortunate and dazed citizens. For the aggregate numbers of those wholly innocent folks shot and/or trampled, thirteen terrified children—not counting grownups—cataloged bullet wounds.[31] What of Ira Attebury? Through the haze of eye-blistering mist SWAT team fellows executed a dynamic entry, firing shotguns as they advanced. However, the Bexar County Medical Examiner, Dr. Ruben Santos, officially ruled that Attebury had died as result of a self-inflicted wound with a .38 caliber pistol "just above the right ear."[32]

The Battle of Flowers carnage again painfully drove home a hard message for Texas Ranger management. Although San Antonio was a big city—a population hub—and their PD had a gutsy and efficient SWAT team, many smaller jurisdictions—especially rural Texas— did not. And what of another hostage-taking incident at TDC? Their custodial facilities weren't situated in highly populated metropolitan areas—those with a SWAT team at the ready. And it was there, those sorts of places that Texas Rangers were frequently called upon by local lawmen to lend that helping hand when a prickly situation went Western. In fact, the very same month that Ira Attebury snapped, Texas Ranger SWAT team members at Junction underwent equipment familiarization and firearms training with shotguns, rifles, and gas.[33] Yes, Captain Dean's recurrent SWAT team training and more training, as well as the ongoing procurement of key material assets was, by now, an elemental component for building a multifaceted Texas Ranger capability, one proficiently and professionally administered, capable of reacting to any crisis.[34] Hot situations are unscheduled—and quick. And, seemingly unending emergencies on Captain Jack Dean's calendar there would be.

During the following month, on May 16, 1979, Captain Dean found himself at Austin attending a Homicide Seminar. Supervisors were not exempt from bettering themselves. During the course of this visit Captain Dean visited with DPS Narcotics Agent Walter McFarland regarding the illicit drug traffic in South Texas and the

Lower Rio Grande Valley. Disturbing news about questionable doings by Hidalgo County public officials—not just DA Oscar McInnis—were beginning to bubble forth. Was Sheriff Brig Marmolejo doing all that he could do?[35]

That was far South Texas. What was happening in North Texas? Although the acquisition didn't take place within Captain Jack Dean's swathe of officially assigned Company D territory, the seemingly, at the time, innocuous purchase would have a significant and long term effect on his law-enforcing life. At the well-established Hunter Bradlee Sporting Goods Store in Dallas, on the seventeenth day of May 1979, Faye L. King, subsequent to answering the required questions on a government document, ATF Form 4473, signed the questionnaire, and took possession of a .240 caliber Weatherby Magnum bolt-action rifle, a Mark V model.[36] From the happy salesclerk's perspective it was a good day—a standard everyday purchase—somewhat of an uncommon caliber to be sure, but it was a premier brand rifle and a pricey one, too!

Some of the rumblings Captain Dean had been hearing from the Lower Rio Grande Valley were to him, not now surprising, but troubling for someone owning integrity and professionalism. On 21 May 1979 Captain Dean made the trip Huntsville. Thereat he conferred with Warden Williamson. An inmate at one of the nearby TDC facilities had something to tell him, something about the crookedness of certain public officials in Hidalgo County. The convict put enough on the plate to keep Captain Jack Dean overnight—the cautious debriefing concerning official misconduct continued into the next day.[37]

From Huntsville it was but a reasonable drive to Waco, and that's where Captain Dean would spend the night. He would, according to his TRWR, be an attendee at Captain Bob Mitchell's meeting of Company F Rangers on 23 May 1979. Ostensibly his presence at the Company F meeting was in "reference to SWAT Team training." While there at Fort Fisher he, too, conferred with Texas Ranger Senior Captain Bill Wilson and DPS CID Chief Floyd Hacker, also regarding "SWAT Team training and the operations of Company

D."[38] Though it must have registered as but sheer coincidence—to be sure—a rather auspicious wingding was underway at Waco's Texas Ranger Hall of Fame & Museum that very week: the annual reunion of retired Texas Rangers. On hand for the gathering and barbeque were such notable former Rangers as LeFetra "Lee" Trimble, eighty-six, "who patrolled the Big Bend on a horse until the state bought him a Model-T." Captain Jack Dean's past captain, John Wood, was there too, unabashedly, in response to a newsman's probing question about capital punishment, spouting that a few folks were simply bad to the bone and theoretically "don't deserve to live." Certainly the presence of former Captain Frank Probst, "who could charm a bird from a tree," and manipulate the print media to "the advantage of law enforcers," was duly noted. Captain Jay Banks was there too: one of the lawmen who ended the murderous career of outlaw Gene Paul Norris and a North Texas area Ranger likely triggering dreams in a waffling young man on the mundane line at Convair. The gathering was rich with real tall tales and real true stories—mostly. And, not left out of the picture, of course, was the crusty Captain Alfred Allee, Sr., "the bushy-browed man, chomping his favorite cigar," still going strong at seventy-four. An onsite newspaper person, when noting ages of the oldest of the retired Rangers, harpooned and lampooned reality: "many of the more than 30 [retired] Rangers are mere striplings in their 60s."[39]

After returning to San Antonio and enjoying a three-day week-end, Monday being the Memorial Day Holiday, Captain Dean was back at his desk on Tuesday morning, 29 May 1979, probably clue-less about the fact that very same day the *Dallas Morning News* featured a human interest story about the Texas Rangers and the previous week's reunion at Waco. That would, in an odd sort of chilling way, turn out to be ironic. Although he may have taken a holiday, the incoming paperwork had not. Jack Dean's head was down. An urgent telephone call knocked any thoughts of complet-ing another routine day sideways. A lone gunshot had hammered calamity! United States District Judge John Howland "Maximum John" Wood, Jr. had been premeditatedly murdered in the driveway of his luxurious San Antonio condominium, the Chateau Dijhon.[40] Examples of cold-bloodedness were nothing new to Texas Rangers, though as Captain Dean well knew from the outset, the wanton killing of a sitting federal judge would spark big headlines and quickly generate an extraordinarily intense criminal investigation. Shortly and sharply Jack Dean acted, putting together a DPS Task Force-type immediate response, provisionally skippered by Company D Ranger Sergeant Lefty Block: "three Rangers, a narcotic agent, and an intelligence agent."[41] Captain Jack Dean figuratively burned up the land line, notifying the Texas Ranger and DPS command structure personnel about the Alamo City trouble, prior to his rushing to the scene and conferring with San Antonio PD detectives and, his friend, FBI SAC Tony Morrow.[42] Clearly the killing of Judge Wood was a whodunit—an epic whodunit.

From the outset two observations were well-grounded. This was not a typical street crime, not a harebrained armed robbery gone awry or a chance confrontation with some nitwit roaming the Chateau Dijhon's beautifully landscaped and manicured grounds. No, this killing was an execution—maybe pure, but not so simple. Someone—a sniper—had lain in wait. One shot to the back had done the trick! Who and why? That was the question.

Aside from the initial criminal investigation, another matter was even more pressing. Had all of the federal judges and prosecutors been targeted? Their personal security was paramount. Aside to Captain Jack Dean pledging his unadulterated support to FBI SAC Tony Morrow regarding investigative matters, he also synchronized DPS manpower deployment with the United States Marshals Service about around-the-clock protection to select federal officials at San Antonio.[43] Doubling down, not knowing the unfathomable depth of any malicious plots and/or grand conspiracies, United States Attorney General Griffin Bell called the assassination "a dastardly act" and perfectly "intolerable," then straightaway addressed security anxieties: "The four federal judges remaining on the bench in the Western District of Texas have been placed under guard, including one in El Paso, one in Austin and two in San Antonio."[44] It surely didn't stop there. The federal judiciary was under attack: "U.S. marshals placed all U.S. district judges under protection, and added extra measures of protection to the detail of AUSA Kerr."[45] The wheels had come off at San Antonio—again.

Working in tandem with the other local and federal investigators Captain Dean sifted through theories and suspicions and even cockamamie conjectures as to who had capped Judge Wood. The jurist's nickname, "Maximum John," was well-earned. He was tough on crime in general, and damn tougher on drug traffickers pirating and peddling poison for profit. Before Judge Wood's bench, sympathy for wrongdoers was in short supply: there was none. There was, if a leading newspaper's calculator was spot on, a statistical correlation between Judge Wood's antipathy for drug dealers and the sentences awarded thereto in his courtroom. For the caseload regarding ninety heroin traffickers, Judge Wood figured that 72 percent owed the government the maximum sentence and none—not one—would be worthy of probation.[46] Understandably some defense attorneys loathed Judge Wood personally and professionally, thinking his black robe demeanor tyrannical at best and, perhaps worse, with cast iron consistency he exhibited an "abysmal ignorance of the law and courtroom procedure."[47] Others, normally on the other side of the legal wrangling, were not quite so strident and harsh. But, even they would likely not bet their paycheck on slim odds, were they exposed to suffering a courthouse payback at Judge Wood's discretion.[48]

Captain Jack Dean's job, though, was not to like Judge Wood; the Texas Rangers and DPS CID Agents were assisting with a homicide investigation. Not even a cantankerous judge, if that's what he was, warrants being murdered. There was, though, that burning hot-topic. Who hated Judge John Wood enough to see him driveway dead? Were Bandidos now guzzling beer inside grimy clubhouses, smiling and joking about their brand of a maximum sentence? Was the East Coast or West Coast or Arizona Mafia implicated? Could a Mexican cartel kingpin have opted to settle an old score—balancing the books—finding solace for the past seizures of big loads and forfeitures of twin-engine airplanes? Was a Hollywood wannabe worth looking at? And what about flamboyant Jamiel Alexander "Jimmy" Chagra, that high-rolling Lebanese gambler and purported gangster from El Paso; was he involved? He was the guy then suffering "a 5-count indictment issued by a federal grand jury in Midland. . . . [that] he conspired to possess, import and distribute cocaine and marijuana."[49] Would the government add a supplemental indictment, throwing in another count, a charge akin to the Lone Star State's habitual criminal statute, that federal business about masterminding a "continuing criminal enterprise"? Now that was heavy. Without a doubt there was room for some commonsense curiosity about Jimmy Chagra. He was free-world walking on a $400,000 bond—his criminal cases re-docketed and moved to Austin, originally scheduled for 29 May 1979, the day Judge Wood went under.[50] Should he have been convicted in Wood's court, would the judge have slapped his wrists and spanked his bottom, telling him to go forth and be a good little boy in the future? Or, was it more likely—a surefire guarantee—that Judge Wood would have sent his ass to Leavenworth, doing hard time till the cows came home and the man jumped over the moon?

Captain Jack Dean dutifully manned the seesaw arcing between coordinating security details with the U.S. Marshals Service and processing analytical theories with the FBI. Texas Rangers, from top to bottom were more than aware of the significance of this investigation. Likewise and, perhaps rightly so, nationally known politicos were adding their two-cents' worth regarding the absolutely gutless but undeniably triumphant killing. President Jimmy Carter and both U.S. Senators from Texas, John Tower and Lloyd Bensten, were offering public comment. Likening the "assassination to terrorism," ex-governor and presidential hopeful John Connally jumped into the arena of communal condemnation.[51] The federal bureaucracy, at high levels, stays tuned to public and political sentiment—though the anemic denial is sometimes veiled and lackluster, it's commonplace. In this instance the FBI Director, William Webster, was of the mind to put Washington supervisory fingerprints directly on the murder investigation. FBI Deputy Director James O. Ingram, "with a formidable contingent of agents," arrived at San Antonio, ready to assume command and solve America's foremost whodunit, the "Crime of the Century."[52]

Although Captain Jack Dean and fellow Texas Rangers had seemingly been working nonstop and closely with San Antonio PD and local FBI Special Agents, with a heavy-hitter now in town the game changed. Although the FBI would welcome any and all information, it would come down a one-way street. The Texas Rangers and the San Antonio PD right then should make note, they were no longer an official part of the newsy murder investigation—and explicitly told so![53] Captain Jack Dean cordially smiled and mused: There would be no argument or objection or obvious disgruntlement. He was thoroughly committed to and now had a long and recognizable history of playing well with others. On the other hand, expecting a Texas Ranger to bow and scrape like a docile steer was past ludicrous! Captain Jack Dean and his trusty Task Force boys would and did, quietly and agreeably, continue "to gather evidence, question informants, and comb DPS files for leads."[54]

Captain Dean, in addition to continued interest and quiet effort dedicated to the Judge Wood murder investigation, had other matters to look after. The murmurs of wrongdoing at McAllen, inside the Hidalgo County courthouse, had become a crescendo of accusations and innuendo and tarnishing of badges. Incriminations were not an indiscriminate scattershot. Quite specifically a Hidalgo County Grand Jury had sought Texas Ranger help. The normally secretive investigative body wanted a not so secret "special investigation of the Hidalgo County Sheriff's Office."[55] Humorless allegations of out-and-out impropriety and favoritism and unseemly payoffs were becoming widespread. Sheriff Brig Marmolejo may have been captain of the boat, but he wasn't running a tight ship, not if the accusations were even half true.

Astutely, Jack Dean had recognized pitfalls all too common in the Lower Rio Grande Valley. Perhaps an accomplished journalist struck the nail on the head, it being a harsh land where "borders are easily crossed, of temptation ferried and ethics bartered."[56] Proximity to the Río Bravo/Rio Grande now and then accelerates acceptance of a well-greased borderland convention, *la mordida*—the bite—the bribe. That said, such doesn't make it close to ethical or anywhere near legal! During the first week of June 1979, Captain Jack Dean spent three days coordinating with his Company D Rangers stationed in the Lower Rio Grande Valley, checking on the "misconduct involving members of the Hidalgo County Sheriff's Office."[57] Aforementioned in this text, it might be remembered that Captain Dean owned a wide-ranging queasiness about the sheriff from the outset of his administration. His findings were intriguing, enough so that during June's second week starting on a Sunday Captain Jack Dean spent four more days at McAllen looking into alleged misconduct and illegalities at the hands of Hidalgo County Sheriff's Office employees and relatives of same.[58]

According to Jack Dean, he and Sheriff Brig Marmolejo had a verbal head-buttin' inside Edinburg's best hotel/restaurant/lounge— the Echo. From the Captain's perspective the Sheriff was riding the high-horse of asininity. Brig Marmolejo, as the high-sheriff of Hidalgo County, undertook lecturing Captain Dean as to "where he could go and what he could and could not do." Brig was a big man— bigger than Jack. Giving in to fisticuffs might prove tetchy and a wipeout. On the other hand, Captain Jack Dean was a Texas Ranger with statewide authority—and could not be and would not be hurrahed. He could and would go damn well where he pleased and/or where any criminal investigation took him. Luckily the wordy tête-à-tête at the Echo didn't escalate past the point of no return, where blows or shots were exchanged. In this instance, though Captain Jack Dean carried a cocked and locked .45 at one side—he creditably carried right on the opposite hip.[59] Of that, in due time, it would become crystal-clear.

Predictably, since this is Jack Dean's story and not that of Sheriff Marmolejo, squashing a few years and events into a singular brick of reality is somewhat obligatory. That Captain Dean spearheaded the early part of an investigation into the Hidalgo County irregularities is obliquely confirmed by Sheriff Brig Marmolejo himself: "Hell, nothing surprises me. . . . It never did. Over the years I've been investigated by everyone, from private investigators to the Texas Rangers to the FBI."[60] And over the course of those years an avaricious cancer of corruption began eating its way through the sheriff's honor and honesty and—by now abandoned humility.

Admittedly, what turned the legal tables on Sheriff Marmolejo's tax-paid and cartel sponsored gravy train were not solely the Texas Rangers. Though he may have thought to some extent railroaded, it was the feds hammering the last spike into the last crosstie and setting the criminal engine chugging down the tracks toward prison. Though coming subsequent to Captain Dean's earlier investigations into wrongdoing within the Hidalgo Sheriff's Office, there certainly would be big-time legal repercussions about what seemed systemic misconduct. The federal Indictment was one of eight counts, including bribery, money laundering, and racketeering:[61]

> The Organized Crime Drug Enforcement Task Force in Laredo conducted the investigation, with agents from the FBI, U.S. Customs Service, Drug Enforcement Administration, Internal Revenue Service's criminal enforcement division, Immigration and Naturalization's anti-smuggling unit and Texas Department of Public Safety. Federal investigations have been concentrating on South Texas law enforcement officials. Hidalgo County Sheriff Brigido Marmolejo Jr. was indicted last month on charges of accepting money and gifts in exchange for granting favors to inmates at the county jail.[62]

According to the lawfully brought Indictment, it was suspected that Sheriff Marmolejo had accepted upwards of $151,000 "in cash from inmates over a two year period. He allegedly received $5,000 [sic ?] in monthly bribes from a jailed drug trafficker, Homero Beltran Aguirre in exchange of special favors."[63] According to an AUSA in closing arguments to the jury, Beltran literally ran the Hidalgo County Jail from inside the facility—it being a "hotel and brothel for him. . . . For a fee of $6000 a month and $1000 a visit, the sheriff allowed Mr. Beltran to have conjugal visits in Mr. Marmolejo's private office with his wife and his girlfriend. . . . and to conduct drug-related business from his cell." [64] Subsequent to the trial at Laredo, the jury deliberated but five hours—then they rendered their verdict. Brig Marmolejo was stone-cold *Guilty* of everything the United States Attorney had alleged.[65] Though the legal wrangling would be rich, ultimately the appellate courts upheld the sheriff's conviction and seven-year sentence to the federal penitentiary.[66]

While the ultimate verdict and sentence had not been particularly surprising to Jack Dean, nevertheless, such bad borderland news was always disconcerting. Returning to the appropriate chronological timeline, June 1979, Captain Dean found time to check on the Judge Wood death investigation and made a scheduled courtroom appearance in the 224th District Court regarding closure of a Forgery investigation.[67]

There were, too, other serious and sensitive matters calling for Captain Jack Dean's attention. One, in particular, was certainly not a whodunit but it would prove to be a brainteaser of colossal proportion for a befuddled Company D commander. In fact, the brouhaha would soon be christened the "Christian Alamo,"[68] even if the high-drama took place in Nueces County not far from alluring Corpus Christi with its glistening beaches and bikini-clad coeds on spring break. Some other area girls were not skimpily clothed and gaily wading in the Gulf's warm waters. Unwed mothers-to-be, drug abusers, runaways from home, and other dejected girls had a place. They were domiciled behind a tall fence at the Rebekah Home with their wayward sisters of sin, sorely in need of the good Lord's corrective therapy—at least so thought dogmatic evangelistic theologian Lester Leo Roloff.

Were one so inclined, an in-depth exploration of Lester Roloff and his ministry makes for a good—though troubling—read. A native Texan from Navarro County, Lester Roloff could lay legit claim to graduations at Baylor University and Southwestern Baptist Theological Seminary. Subsequent to ably launching his power-amped radio program *Family Alter* and successfully founding a Christian Day School, Preacher Lester, independent as Burmese tiger, brought to fruition Roloff Evangelistic Enterprises. Whether one was uncomfortably sitting in the pew or looking in from the outside might influence a layperson's opinion: Was he, in fact, zealously doing God's work, or was he just a zealot? Powerbrokers at the Southern Baptist Convention, in large part due to Lester Roloff's controversial stances, broke ties with the reliably stubborn and unyielding fellow. Undaunted, as one might suspect, believer Lester Roloff persisted. Although in Nueces County there were Roloff Evangelistic Enterprises' facilities for boys and men, it was the Rebekah Home for Girls near Corpus Christi that spawned seaside headlines and netted Captain Jack Dean, reeling him to where he didn't want to be.[69]

At the Rebekah Home for Girls core discipline was blended with interpretative scripture and inquisitional secular reasoning, such as, "Withhold not correction from the child: for if thou beatest him with the rod, he shall not die." And, philosophically, for the modern age update, Lester Roloff would not shyly and publically harangue: "Better a pink bottom than a black soul." Not surprisingly other methods of punishment for girls' infractions at the Rebekah Home began to drip forth, until the leakage became a flood of accusations ranging from being "whipped with leather straps" and "beaten with paddles," to being handcuffed to drainage pipes and/or harshly imprisoned in solitary confinement, "sometimes for such minor infractions as failing to memorize a Bible passage or forgetting to make a bed."[70] Predictably the words waxed hot. An at the time Texas Attorney General, John Hill, parried Lester Roloff's corporal-punishment's vividly discolored derriere comment, brusquely pronouncing "that it wasn't pink bottoms he objected to but ones that were blue, black, and bloody."[71]

For emphasizing Captain Dean's role in the rich drama cutting to the nub is necessary, though that truly demands skipping through a few years and bypassing litigation in Texas courts.[72] Assuredly—just a month after Judge Wood was murdered—Nueces County pandemonium, not a circus—was exciting a statewide readership and eager listening audience. William Barret Travis metaphorically and/or literally had drawn his line in the sand 143 years earlier.

The intractable Lester Leo Roloff drew his. Through legislative passage of the 1975 Child Care Licensing Act, facilities such as the Rebekah Home for Girls were subject to on-the-ground inspections and licensing by the state; administered by an agency that would now be known as Texas Department of Family and Protective Services. Gabriel had blown his horn and resultant reverberations had not been pleasing to the ear of Lester Leo Roloff; the protracted legal battles and maneuvering had begun. Lester Roloff's position was plain and obstinate: There was, as everyone was supposed to know, U. S. Constitutionally guaranteed separation between Church and State. The state-paid folks could pound sand, and there was plenty nearby. He and his coterie would assuredly stand for no earthly inspection of the sacred Rebekah Home—and his license to operate came directly from above—the Almighty issued his permit.

Fast forwarding to Captain Dean's June 1979 conundrum is effortless. The law on the books was not tangled and unclear. The Rebekah Home for Girls would stand and pass inspection and be issued the proper license—or it would be closed and the teenaged residents would be shuttled elsewhere on buses fueled with state-paid diesel and considerately escorted by DPS Troopers. The showdown was near. Not unwisely it seems, Captain Jack Dean traveled to Austin and huddled with Senior Captain Bill Wilson about what was clearly shaping up to be a delicate and distasteful—but dutiful law-enforcing assignment.[73]

Two days later Captain Jack Dean was at Corpus Christi, where he "assisted Uniformed [DPS] Personnel and Department of Human Resources with situation at Roloff's school for Girls as per orders of Captain Wilson."[74] The State of Texas Supreme Court had rendered its opinion. A follow-up District Court's order had been unambiguous: Law was to be enforced and obeyed. One way or the other! Plunging seagulls overhead seemed to be taunting and dropping their collective white messages: "Okay you big-time Texas Ranger go get that big-time preacher and roundup all those mistreated girls. Captain you've got a big gun—a cocked and locked .45—and tall orders straight from Austin headquarters. What are you dithering for? Hoping for a miracle?" In truth, such silliness meant as much to Roloff as those allegorical white droppings on the sand. "They'll hang black crepe on Heaven's gate if they close these homes."[75]

Captain Jack Dean's challenge was real. Several hundred of Roloff's supporters rallied to the cause, essentially forming a devoted human and hymn singing chain around the Rebekah Home. With tightly locked arms and firmly planted feet, and God's righteousness in their figurative holsters, they would defy any mere mortals' orders—regardless the judgeship. Social workers, Texas Rangers and DPS boys, too, should pay heed.[76]

Of course Captain Jack Dean had been in tight spots before, but these disciples were not wildly rioting in the streets and throwing bricks and bottles at hunkered-down policemen. These committed folks were not laborers on strike, deriding and/or assaulting scab workers willy-nilly recruited from somewhere to brazenly cross union picket lines. This was a different kettle of fish. These believers were firmly fixed and not influenced by legislative and/or judicial decrees. Strategically they were strong—and passive—no six-shooters, knives, or Molotov Cocktails. Truthfully, the person in the fix was Captain Jack Dean—his options were few.

Inaction is not a part of Texas Ranger psyche. To be blunt, Senior Captain Bill Wilson, from behind a desk at faraway Austin, was wondering what the heck had happened at Corpus Christi? Wasn't Jack Dean, the Texas Ranger captain with executive jurisdiction over that region onsite? What the hell was going down?

The answer is short. While Captain Jack Dean had been toeing the line of commonsense and judiciousness, holding his foot on the fuse of potential overreaction, Texas Attorney General Mark White had been palavering with Lester Roloff. The law was to be enforced. On the other hand, should there be a legitimate way for Lester Leo Roloff to save face—well—that might be to everyone's benefit. There would be no head thumping and headlines above photographs of handcuffed pacifists being hauled off to the Nueces County jail by DPS Troopers and Rangers. Although it measured as a compromise, Lone Star State laws would be complied with for the short-go.

For the big rodeo, Lester Roloff would be allowed to remove Rebekah Home residents to religious facilities outside Texas—Georgia and Mississippi—where different statutory and/or regulatory strictures were applicable. True, it was a sure enough stopgap measure, but bloodied noses and knocked heads—or much worse would not be. Captain Jack Dean—at last after several days—breathed a sigh of relief. Company D Texas Rangers were crime fighters—not pastoral flock tending shepherds.[77]

Before 1979 June was history, Texas Ranger Captain Jack Dean had received a big-time clue about the big-time case. At the Texas Ranger office Virginia Goss, his devoted secretary, took the initial telephone call, someone asking to "speak with Jack." Virginia cupped her hand over the receiver and whispered: "Captain, there's a man on the phone but he won't give me his name, he wants to talk to you." The lifeblood of a good criminal investigator circulates on information. Sometimes reliable, sometimes not, but the law enforcing guy/gal incapable of instilling confidence and trust in a network of obliging spies is—and will remain—clueless forevermore: "So, I took the call and I'll never forget the old boy said, 'Jack,' didn't call me Captain or Ranger, he said 'Jack,' Charlie Harrelson was in San Antonio the day Judge Wood was killed. . . . Just wanted you to know Charlie was in San Antonio the day Judge Wood was killed." Quite naturally Captain Jack Dean asked the key bottom-line question: "Did he kill the Judge?" The CI—who was really taking a big-time chance—answered curtly and with inimitable finality: "He was in town." A dial tone amplified the fact he had no more to say—period![78]

Captain Jack Dean was not in a quandary. There were but two issues to digest. Neither was indefinite. There would be no hesitation. He would willingly and quickly share what he learned. On the other hand, there were but two people in the telephone conversation, Jack Dean and the "old boy" passing along the hot news. Captain Dean's record of remembrance with regards to the CI's real identity is now and was then charily couched: "I was really not sure who it was. . . . Never did know for sure." The "know for sure" aspect absolved Captain Jack Dean of breaking faith with anonymity—the

CI's anonymity. Since he wasn't *absolutely* sure—even if he had a good idea—he could ill afford a mistake. The good guesswork, he'd keep that to himself. Otherwise a guy might be dumped face-up in a sand dune or face-down in a pump-house.[79]

Texas Ranger Captain Jack Dean substantiated that, indeed, Charles Voyde Harrelson had been in the Alamo City when Judge Wood was ticketed to eternity.[80] That the FBI was floundering in the sea of no information and misinformation is not said gratuitously—it was fact. Judge Wood was dead. One accomplished journalist rightly penned: "The list of felons who had a motive to kill 'Maximum John' Wood was a mile long."[81] The suspect list—if one counted those he'd sentenced to the care and custody of federal prison wardens—really was extensive. Murder contracts can issue even from behind electronically accessed custodial cages—if the loot is right! Bandidos inside and outside federal and state prisons had a reach. Mafia wheel-horses and drug smuggling kingpins knew no boundaries—steel or surveyed. Measures of their morality had been mislaid. And, of course, that did not count the scores of hapless defendants docketed for pleas and/or courtroom trials before Judge Wood's bench.[82] The pool was deep!

Dutifully, subsequent to his passing along information regarding his shadowy telephone conversation, Captain Dean was summoned to meet with the FBI Deputy Assistant Director at San Antonio, the "one sent down to run the case." He had asked for a face to face with the Company D Captain. Jack Dean was to and would and did share every tidbit he knew about Charles Voyde Harrelson. The Bureau Boys had no knowledge—not an inkling—about the Texas outlaw from Lovelady. "We sit down and go over everything I've ever known about Charlie Harrelson for four or five years, just whatever it had been."[83] Pointedly, Captain Dean was asked if he would—since he knew Charles Voyde—assist them with interviewing Harrelson if and when the Bureau ever did choose to follow up, make personal contact, and pick him up. Captain Jack Dean willingly agreed.[84] Besides sharing his knowledge, Captain Jack Dean even provided the FBI Deputy Assistant Director with a mug shot of the talkative and debonair Charles Harrelson, "whose profession was robbery and murder for hire."[85] Texas Ranger Captain Jack Dean's receipt of a concluding comment is quite revealing and a bit unsettling: "Then [the FBI Deputy Assistant Director] said 'Thank you, we don't need your help anymore.' Kid you not. . . ."[86]

The assassination of a federal judge and the attempted murder of an AUSA were but part of mysteries confronting the San Antonio based lawman. Uncomfortable can best describe Captain Dean's anxiety, being thrust into an investigation revolving around a questionable death and the subsequent civil actions. Unfortunately for a pregnant lady—near full term—she was ostensibly denied medial treatment at one facility and advised to seek treatment elsewhere—a hospital with on duty doctors, twenty-four and seven. Sadly she died. Not surprisingly the Texas Ranger stationed at Corpus Christi, James Richard "Jim" Peters, had looked into the 8 March 1979 death, but unquestionably it was not homicidal. Fast-forwarding to 21 July 1979, a weekend, Captain Dean hustled to Corpus Christi and huddled with Ranger Jim Peters. The Company D Captain was to have a command appearance at Austin on Monday. An appointment he anxiously kept: Testifying before the Board of Nurses Examiners regarding the suspension of a particular RN's license to practice.[87] To be sure it was a far cry from chasing crooks and/or SWAT team training. Nevertheless, it was all in a day's work for a Ranger.

That Captain Jack Dean was stepping into the institutional limelight of the Texas Rangers is exhibited by the fact he was chosen to represent them at the prestigious International Association of Chiefs of Police gathering at Dallas. The Texas Ranger hierarchy at Austin knew well that Captain Jack Dean would mix and mingle effectively—maintaining meaningful contacts and building new ones—at the multi-day conference.[88]

The next month—October 1979—found Captain Dean back in the Lower Rio Grande Valley. There, working with Company D Rangers Bruce Casteel and Joaquin Jackson, aside from looking into allegations of jury tampering, they were tasked with providing special security for courtroom proceedings with regards to the legally entangled Oscar McInnis.[89]

As mentioned, chronological jumping back and forth is a disconcerting device, but sometimes necessary to keep this narrative moving. With regards to the trials and tribulations of Oscar McInnis such is required. There is a hard bottom-line, however. Noting what amounted to several legal technicalities, a federal judge had summarily dismissed criminal charges against the embattled former Hidalgo County DA. In due time, the government would appeal—but in vain. The arguments before and the reasoning of the court highlight intriguing jurisprudence regarding whether or not an alleged victim can actually "kidnap himself," and/or how American jurisdictional venue is applicable to a crime designed to take place on the opposite side of the Rio Grande.[90] Whether or not the defendants had been tricked by prosecutors with regards to being summoned before and testifying before the Grand Jury was also an issue that did not bode well for prosecutors.[91]

During the latter part of the month Captain Dean was at George West in Live Oak County conducting a background investigation of Texas Ranger applicant Kasey King. At the time, THP Patrolman Kasey King was opting to trade his starched and tailored uniform for the traditional Stetson and hand-tooled gun-belt. He was somewhat reflective of the new-age Ranger applicant. Kasey King was a Texas A&M University graduate and had earned U.S. Army officer's status during the Vietnam War. Thereafter, the legit cowboy had served DPS both at San Antonio and Beeville (in Bee County) and finally at his hometown at George West. Aside from Kasey King's well-established law enforcing knack, he was an expert marksman. Kasey King had nothing to worry about, his promotion to Ranger assured.[92]

Now, Captain Dean's focus was not narrowly confined to Texas Ranger personnel matters; he would sit in as an Oral Review Board member for DPS applicants wishing to move up the chain into the officers' corps: As reflected in this TRWR, "In Austin serving on Highway Patrol Lieutenant's Interview Board."[93] And, quite naturally by this time Captain Dean also served on the official Texas Ranger Interview

Boards. His opinion of applicants, positive or negative, was valued; and, too, they might very well be assigned to Company D.[94]

Little could he have forecast one of the year's closing San Antonio events, but Captain Jack Dean, due to geographical positioning as well as competency, drew one of those out-of-his-control assignments, another especially high-profile mission. American hostages were being held in Iran and the now deposed and exiled Shah of Iran, Mohammed Riza Pahlevi, was desperately hunting for a new home country, but the takers were scarce. During his travels and backroom diplomacy, the Shah, due to cancer and a gallbladder flare up, became deathly ill and in an act of civilized compassion was allowed provisional asylum in the United States for hospital admission at New York's prestigious Cornell Medical Center. Once stabilized, since the Empire State hospital was not a bed and breakfast or hotel, the sallow-faced Shah was much in need of other quarters for a period of doctor-ordered real rest and genuine recuperation. At the White House the command decision was reached to tolerate the Shah's period of downtime rejuvenation to take place at Lackland Air Force Base in San Antonio.[95] While there, safely but temporarily, the dethroned and sick Shah could rest "pending further onward travel plans."[96] Needless to say, at the time, during the broiling international intrigues with agitators, activists, and shrill protesters screaming for the overthrown Shah's head on a platter—literally—security concerns were paramount.

Not surprisingly, then, would be the participation of Captain Jack Dean working in conjunction "with local and Federal authorities on security and protection of life and property during visit of Shah of Iran and possible demonstrations." For two weeks during December 1979, Captain Jack Dean did little else than personally participate in and supervise the Texas Ranger manpower commitment, guaranteeing that the convalescing Shah would leave American soil with life and limbs intact, as would his entire entourage and their personal property.[97] Subsequent to the Shah's departure, standing as representative for his Company D subordinates, Captain Jack Dean accepted formalized acknowledgment and appreciation from the

Air Training Command of the United States Air Force at Lackland, which appreciatively read in part: "This is to certify that The Texas Rangers Department of Public Safety San Antonio, Texas is awarded this Certificate in Recognition for Assistance In The Protection of The Shah Of Iran, December 1979."[98]

Photo Gallery

3

Shortly before Sergeant Jack Dean's promotion to Captain of Company D, the Company F Texas Rangers at Waco stand for a group photograph. *From L to R:* Captain Bob Mitchell, Joe Davis, Bill Gunn, Ron Brownlow, James Wright, Henry Ligon, Bobby Prince, Bob Favor, Ed Gooding, Wallace Spiller, Troy Porterfield, Howard "Slick" Alfred, Bob Connell, James Ray, Bill DeLoach, and Sergeant Jack Dean. *COURTESY TEXAS RANGER HALL OF FAME & MUSEUM, WACO, TX.*

Here DPS Director Pat Speir presents Jack Dean with a coveted Captain's badge, handing him command of Company D, headquartered at San Antonio. *COURTESY JACK DEAN.*

Subsequent to Jack Dean's promotion to Captain of Company D, these were the Texas Rangers working the South Texas corridor: *Standing from L to R*: Bruce Casteel (future captain), H.R. "Lefty" Block (future captain), Jim Peters, Joaquin Jackson, Glenn Krueger, Gene Powell (future captain), Captain Jack Dean, and Morgan Miller. *Kneeling, from L to R*: Rudy Rodriquez, Al Cuellar, Stan Guffey (killed in the line of duty), Bill Nelson, Henry Manning, Ray Martinez, Frank Horger, Bobby Poyntor, and the Company D honorary physician, Dr. Vincent Walker. *COURTESY JACK DEAN.*

Camaraderie within the ranks of the Texas Rangers—despite supervisory status—was enviable, demonstrated here at the King Ranch by Captain Jack Dean and Texas Ranger Joaquin Jackson. *COURTESY JACK DEAN.*

L to R: Ranger H. Joaquin Jackson, Captain Jack Dean, Ranger Kasey King, Ranger Al Cuellar, and Senior Captain Bill Wilson. Throughout DPS Kasey King was known as a crack shot. *COURTESY JACK DEAN.*

Though the enumerated list is long, these law-enforcing stalwarts were working or had worked together, illustrating the necessity for joint cooperation. *From L to R*: FBI SAC Tony Morrow; Johnny Klevenhagen, Jr., Sheriff of Harris County; Jerome Preiss, Texas Ranger, Ret; Bobby Poyntor, Texas Ranger; Lee Trimble, Texas Ranger, Ret; unidentified; unidentified; H.R. "Lefty" Block; unidentified; unidentified; Emil Peters, Chief of Police, San Antonio; Captain Jack Dean, Texas Rangers; Pat Speir, Director of DPS; Captain Bob Mitchell, Texas Rangers; Emanuel Avant "Dogie" Wright, former Texas Ranger, Border Patrolman, and Sheriff of Hudspeth County; A.Y. Allee, Sr., Texas Ranger, Ret; James Wright, Texas Ranger; Dudley White, Texas Ranger, Ret; Rudy Garza, Sheriff, Bexar County; and Eddie Oliver, Captain, Texas Rangers, Ret. *Courtesy Texas Ranger Hall of Fame & Museum, Waco, TX.*

Texas Ranger Captain J.L. "Skippy" Rundell, Sr., along with local law-enforcing colleagues, had traveled to Atlanta and arrested Charles Voyde Harrelson in connection with two murder investigations, returning him to Texas. Purportedly—though it's but anecdotal—the prisoner was rattling so much that Ranger Rundell threatened to throw him out of the DPS airplane if he didn't put the quietus on his incessant blabbering. *¿Quién sabe?* Provably, Captain Skippy Rundell did have a sense of humor. *COURTESY TEXAS RANGER HALL OF FAME & MUSEUM, WACO, TX.*

A copy of the Charles Voyde Harrelson's mug-shot furnished to the FBI regarding the killing of Judge Wood subsequent to Captain Dean receiving the crucial tip from a gutsy and chance taking CI. Charles Harrelson "beat" the Angleton murder case, but not two others. *COURTESY JACK DEAN.*

Unbelievably it seems, the DPS Headquarters at San Antonio was burglarized, and along with IBM Electric Typewriters, Captain Jack Dean's personal collection of antique Winchesters was stolen. Fortunately, they were later recovered. Herein pictured is FBI SAC Jack Lawn returning one of the prized Winchesters to Captain Dean for a photo op. *COURTESY JACK DEAN.*

Texas Ranger Lieutenant Jim Denman is now on the Lone Star State's retirement roll. While a DPS Trooper at San Antonio, when muzzle blasts echoed throughout the DPSs headquarters, killing two folks, it was Highway Patrolman Denman that courageously rushed to—not away—from the roaring sound of gunfire. *COURTESY TEXAS RANGER HALL FAME & MUSEUM, WACO, TX.*

As mentioned many—if not most—Texas Rangers of Jack Dean's era preferred a Colt .45 autoloader built on the 1911 platform, and carried in the cocked and locked mode. Herein is a representative sample, a limited edition Colt Royal Combat Commander with genuine ivory grips—cocked and locked. Variations and clones on the 1911 platform are many. Note the grip safety under the cocked hammer. The thumb safety is positioned on the weapon's opposite side. Author's personal handgun, photo COURTESY TEXAS RANGER HALL OF FAME & MUSEUM, WACO, TX.

Pictured here subsequent to an intensive and multi-pronged investigation into South Texas public corruption are, *L to R*: Texas Ranger Rudy Rodriquez, defendant Archer Pharr, and Texas Ranger Ray Martinez. COURTESY TEXAS RANGER HALL OF FAME & MUSEUM, WACO, TX.

There always has seemed to be a strong bond between sports personalities and Texas Rangers. This image captures such a moment. *L to R*: Company D Ranger Captain Jack Dean, well-known commentator Curt Gowdy, and Company F Ranger Captain Bob Mitchell. *COURTESY JACK DEAN*.

Although this is not an authentic "hot" scenario, the training exercise demonstrated that tactical approaches to unfolding events must be multifaceted. Here, Captain Jack Dean proves supervisors were expected to be prepared, as well as the Texas Rangers of the specific Companies they commanded. *COURTESY JACK DEAN*.

From L to R: DPS Director, Colonel Jim Adams, and DPS Commissioners Bill Blakemore, Bill Perryman, and Charles Nash. Captain Jack Dean had a good personal relationship with all three DPS Commissioners—much to the chagrin in a light-hearted way, of Senior Ranger Captain Bill Wilson. *COURTESY JACK DEAN.*

And as particularly noted, Jack and Janie Dean were especially close professionally and personally with Captain Bob Mitchell. *COURTESY JACK DEAN.*

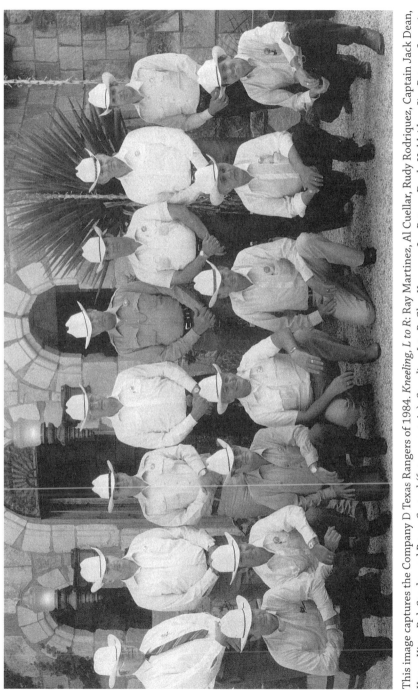

This image captures the Company D Texas Rangers of 1984. *Kneeling, L to R:* Ray Martinez, Al Cuellar, Rudy Rodriquez, Captain Jack Dean, Kasey King, Bob Steele, and Bruce Casteel (future captain). *Standing, L to R:* Glen Krueger, Joe Peters, Doyle Holdridge, Jim Peters, Joaquin Jackson, Steve Black, Morgan Miller, and Richard Sweaney (future captain). *COURTESY TEXAS RANGER HALL OF FAME & MUSEUM, WACO, TX.*

Following in his dad's career footsteps, Kyle Lynn Dean completes the rigorous DPS Training Academy and is posted at Crockett in Houston County as a THP Trooper. Jack and Janie and sister Kelly Lenea are button-poppin' proud. *COURTESY JACK DEAN.*

Though Captain A.Y. Allee, Sr. could project an image of genuine toughness if the going got rough, those that knew him would also come to know he was a sentimental push-over for kiddos. *COURTESY JACK DEAN.*

At the Texas Ranger Hall of Fame & Museum at Waco, Governor Ann Richards is flanked by Company Captains and the Senior Captain. *From L to R:* Captain Bobby Prince, Company A (Houston); Captain Jack Dean, Company D (San Antonio); Captain Bob Mitchell, Company F (Waco); Senior Captain Lefty Block, Headquarters (Austin); Captain James Wright, Company B (Garland); and Captain Bruce Casteel Company C (Lubbock). *COURTESY TEXAS RANGER HALL OF FAME & MUSEUM, WACO, TX.*

Captain Jack Dean, wearing his traditional cocked and locked Colt .45 autoloader, makes a necessary trip to the firing-range. Note the walkie-talkie in the foreground. He could never be far removed from the DPS communications network. *COURTESY JACK DEAN.*

This three-tiered photograph demonstrates firearms proficiency with a variety of weapons was not limited to the rank and file Texas Rangers. Captains lead from the front. COURTESY JACK DEAN.

Captain Dean capably demonstrates that even if one arm was disabled, the Ruger Mini-14 could be brought into play during a crisis. *COURTESY JACK DEAN.*

Karnes County Sheriff Robert W. "Bobby" Mutz. A jailbreak became the "longest day in the life of Sheriff Mutz." Thankfully—and courageously—the Sheriff and the Texas Rangers gained the upper hand sans shooting anyone. *COURTESY BOBBY MUTZ.*

Ranger Jim Peters [L] and Ranger Steve Black [R] exiting the jailhouse at Karnes City following the failed escape of a TDC inmate temporarily housed thereat. *COURTESY BOBBY MUTZ.*

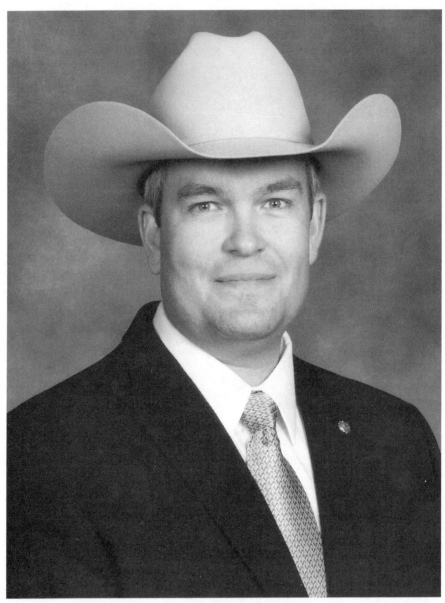

In November of 2017, Texas Ranger Nathan R. Mutz, the son of former Karnes County Sheriff Bobby Mutz, along with law enforcing colleagues, successfully developed Probable Cause and obtained an arrest warrant for the individual responsible for murdering Alice PD Patrolman Matt Murphy on 1 December 1974, the day Jack Dean had been promoted to Sergeant. It had been classed as a "cold case" for the previous forty-three years. COURTESY TEXAS RANGER HALL OF FAME & MUSEUM, WACO, TX.

12

"Baby rattles and beef"

Big doings were astir for DPS. The thirty-first day of December 1979 would be Colonel Speir's last day on the job—he welcomed retirement. Assuming command of DPS was an outsider of sorts, though he was a native Texan: James B. "Jim" Adams, fifty-four, a man who had earned his law-enforcing spurs with the FBI during a gratifying twenty-plus years and, at his federal career's pinnacle, distinguished service as its Assistant Director. He had picked up the DPS job at the urging of Republican Governor Clements. Admittedly, some Rangers looked at the appointment askance, bringing a so-called Washington bureaucrat into the inner workings of DPS. Taking the outfit's helm on 1 January 1980, Colonel Jim Adams proved himself up to the challenge. Perhaps hastening Colonel Adams's DPS success and, in turn, earned respect from the Texas Ranger camp, was an out-and-out appreciation and candid admission of blunt actuality: "A Ranger captain made more decisions in a month than an FBI SAC in a year." From the get-go Texas Rangers were instilled with the notion that they were expected to make individual and independent decisions, sometimes on the spur-of-a-moment and sometimes with the weight of life or death hanging in the balance. Frequently the sweet luxury of time was not on standby. Texas Rangers best be cocked and locked for any eventuality. Captain Jack Dean, contrasting Jim Adams's smallness of physical stature, had taken his earnest measure of the man, admiringly declaring that Colonel Adams's "brain was about ten feet tall."[1]

By this time Captain Dean had developed his own supervisory philosophy, albeit synthesizing the management styles of several previous commanders he truly admired. Captain John Wood had instilled a simple concept: When a man is doing a good job, leave him alone, step aside and let him do it. Captain Jack Dean's dear friend and mentor, Captain Bob Mitchell, as well as THP Sergeant Randal Howie were masters at "taking care of their people." That message was not lost. Senior Captain Bill Wilson, by now another close personal friend, had very simple but sound advice: Take care of the little things, and the big ones would usually take care of themselves.[2] Captain Jack Dean was smart enough to profit from the good, discarding the bad. That said, the Company D Texas Rangers never had to guess who was in charge; Captain Dean could, would, and did make hard decisions—no dithering and doubting.[3]

Referencing remarks by one of Captain Jack Dean's subordinates regarding the Company D commander's management style is earnest and insightful. Texas Ranger Adolfo "Al" Cuellar's appraisal was not vague: "When he tells you something, you know it's the truth. . . . when Captain Dean tells you something when talking, he doesn't make up anything. He's always straight forward and it's always the truth. Now what I liked about Captain Dean is that you know he wasn't like other supervisors. . . . If you do something wrong, he brought you in. He talks to you, closes the door and we talk about the problem. We resolve it and you open the door and you go on about your business and it's not to be brought up anymore because the problem was resolved. . . . He knows you're man enough to take care of business and that's the way I want to be treated and that's the way he treats his people. . . . And the men respected him a lot for that. . . . he always would talk in such a manner that you knew where he was coming from. You knew he was right. . . . nothing was made up, and it's just you're treated like an adult and like you want to be treated. And his men always tried to do right. Jack Dean has a very, very good way of supervising people. He kind of lets them compete against each other. He doesn't say you've gotta work harder. You just know that if the other Rangers are doing a real good job and keep doing good. . . . his attitude was the harder you work the luckier you get. And so every once in a while. . . . it all started when I said Bruce Casteel sure is lucky. He is always solving all his crimes. He [Captain Dean] said yeah, Bruce works very, very hard. . . . When you hear something like that. . . . that the harder you work the luckier you get, it rings a bell. And so it stays with you. Sometimes the investigation drags on and it's just that. . . . man, just knock on one more door and that may be the little thread you get that unravels the whole thing."[4]

Although already an experienced Lone Star State lawman, one fellow newly commissioned as a Texas Ranger transferring from the DPS Narcotics Service remembered—vividly—one of Captain Jack Dean's plainspoken commands. Doing undercover work buying dope DPS had paid the narcotics agent to "be in bars." Now, as a new Company D Ranger, Captain Dean cautioned: "I pay you to stay out of bars."[5]

And, he had an easy message for rookie Texas Rangers assigned to Company D. When and if possible—of course there would be untoward exceptions—their first priority was to develop and maintain an affable and professional relationship with the various Sheriffs, Chiefs of Police, and District Attorneys in the counties they looked after. From the start Captain Dean had taken to heart those earlier instructions from former CID Chief Jim Ray about the importance of actually getting along with counterparts and building a cooperative Texas Ranger image. The old adage was applicable: "if mama ain't happy, ain't nobody happy." Rolling it to reality, a Ranger that couldn't get along with the area officials had best get along down the lonesome highway—his effectiveness was nil. Proficient PR netted good results in the field, in the courtroom, in the media—and at the front office.[6]

Good fortune was also taking hold at Xerox. Ever conscious of keeping the home fires burning and making her financial contribution to the Deans' coffers, the ever industrious Janie went to work at San Antonio. Dexterously balancing on a teetering tightrope above the arenas of a professional career and personally running a household is never easy—working mothers would understand and agree. In this case Janie Dean pulled it off. Though, when she went to work at Xerox she had no idea how long her term of voluntary enlistment would be; ultimately those numbers added up to a guaranteed retirement income. She could adapt as circumstances and surroundings changed and there was a truism—Janie Dean was no quitter!

For Captain Jack Dean and the Company D Texas Rangers, 1979 ended calmly. As the New Year dawned for a new decade, no doubt they were, one and all, hoping for continued peace and good will. Perhaps another fellow was too, but he was a devotee of the green cloth, a good gambler so he said, but such tranquility was not to be in his deck—marked cards or not.

Though exactness is uncertain, between 1 July and 11 July 1979 a theft had happened. At a big-box discount store in Dallas County, at least one of their inventoried firearms came up missing, wholly unaccounted for following its receipt and recording in the store's compulsory FFL Acquisition and Disposition Book. Employees knew when they had received the revolver, a Colt Diamondback, caliber .38 Special, but not where it now was. At Houston, several months later, 1 February 1980 to be exact, Charles V. Harrelson knew where the hot six-shooter was—under his legs, on the floorboard, of the 1979 black Lincoln Continental he was driving. Over and over again the incautious outlaw from Lovelady seems to have had real bad days with the policing fraternity. This was one of them! Pursuant to a carefully drawn ATF affidavit and lawful issuance of a search warrant for the aforementioned automobile, lawmen acted. Charles Voyde Harrelson was sitting behind the steering-wheel when the Lincoln had been legally stopped and searched. Investigating officers knew that due to past felony convictions Harrelson was statutorily prohibited from possessing a firearm, any firearm, but in this case he had thoughtlessly fertilized the federal felony by adding four more counts: a Remington Model 870 slide-action shotgun with a real nifty folding stock, a Colt Cobra .38 Special revolver, a Colt Python .357 Magnum revolver, as well as a skillfully crafted and, for then costly, scope-sighted long-gun, a .300 Weatherby Magnum rifle.[7] Harrelson's out-and-out injudiciousness on this day, too, was many-sided. Also within the car was cocaine and illicit gambling paraphernalia.[8] Although it might have had significant and legit incriminating usefulness, but no evidentiary contraband consequence, found inside the luxury Lincoln was a fascinating audio tape recording between Jo Ann Harrelson "and another man in which the caller asked about 'Chuck's' availability to rob high-stakes poker games." And, according to an adept prosecutor, who was purportedly in the know; "the caller was shot and wounded shortly after the conversation."[9] Regardless, outlaw Charles Voyde Harrelson had stepped in it again! Dubiously, Harrelson claimed, hoping the slick chicanery would somehow let him off the hook, that he certainly "lacked knowledge that the weapons were in his automobile and that they were placed there by either the law enforcement agents or someone else without his knowledge."[10]

When hauled before State District Court Judge Thomas Routt for an initial appearance and bond setting on cocaine and gambling paraphernalia charges, Lady Luck winked at Harrelson. Judge Routt set the aggregate state bail at $60,000. Charles Voyde Harrelson walked out of the Harris County Jailhouse at thirty minutes before midnight 1 February 1980 after posting the small percentage of necessary surety. Harrelson would appear in court later—so he pledged. With regards to the firearms violations, that persnickety matter would be heard shortly by a Federal Grand Jury. When and if indictments returned, an arrest warrant would forthwith issue for Charles V. Harrelson. Whenever and wherever he was stumbled onto—intentionally or inadvertently—he would find a new home in the calaboose.[11] ATF Special Agents were not too concerned about running Mr. Charley Harrelson to ground. They knew Harrelson was never far removed from inserting his own foot in the bear-trap. Career criminality is predictably perilous. Company D Captain Jack Dean knew as much too—it was not hush-hush claptrap or delusional thinking about Charles Voyde Harrelson. By Harrelson's own volition he would trip into trouble given time and, generally, not too much time at that!

Little could Captain Jack Dean concern himself with Charles Voyde Harrelson's nightmarish reoccurring tight spots; DPS had some of their own in the Lower Rio Grande Valley, yet again! Negotiations were underway between TDC and the aforementioned La Casita Farms—the penal institution was in process of acquiring the vast agricultural enterprise's lands with state funds. The public outcry and possibility for civil and/or criminal disobedience from a dissident subset was real. Small sparks start big fires. With regards to social unrest, the few can wash community sanity aside—if not squelched promptly and properly. Captain Dean, not unexpectedly, was dispatched to the area, specifically tasked with protecting "life and property" during the public hearings. Levelheaded diplomacy was now Texas Ranger institutional policy, at least giving it a try before resorting to what had once been a more traditional hardcore and head-thumping methodology. Captain Dean would do his job— come hell or high water—if actually forced to. On the other hand, he too was a good ambassador. With his onsite presence, the potential for upheaval had been upended.[12]

What had not been upended was some burglars' skullduggery. Texas Rangers have a flair for the Western and Jack Dean was no exception. Within his office—on two wall racks—was an exceptionally nice collection of desirable lever-action Winchesters—primarily old Model 1894s and Model 1895s. The shooting hardware belonged to Jack, not the Lone Star State. Other items of interest at the DPS facility did have serial numbers recorded in the department's inventoried property ledger: IBM electric typewriters. Though in today's computer age it may ring hollow, at the time IBM typewriters were cutting-edge technology and costly—a hot ticket item on thieves' want list. Implausibly it would seem, one night burglars broke into the DPS headquarters at San Antonio. Apparently the brazen outlaws had plenty of time and not an iota of worry about getting nabbed: Carting off—undetected— upwards of twenty-odd typewriters and all of Captain Jack Dean's Winchesters. It was, for DPS, an embarrassing whodunit![13]

For the burglars, acquisition of Captain Dean's prized Winchesters had been but a whopping bonus—they had no way of knowing they were racked and displayed on the wall. Good luck the bad boys owned for a little while. Applying the right pressure to known fences (purveyors of stolen property) throughout Bexar County environs would be a common strategy for this type of criminality. Texas Rangers and DPS CID Agents diligently worked their sizable stable of CIs but, in the end, it would be the FBI boys bringing home the bacon. All of Captain Jack Dean's prized Winchesters were recovered—but none of the IBM typewriters: Gone for keeps. Therein lay the rub, in a snarky sort of way; Ranger Captains could get their personal property returned, even if the State of Texas couldn't. Captain Jack Dean never heard the end of such banter.[14]

Though a touch of literary license is necessary—regarding an exacting chronology—mention of a retirement and promotion is but herein appropriate. One of Charles Voyde Harrelson's old burs under the saddle was bailing out after an illustrious forty-year career with DPS. Captain Skippy Rundell, Senior Captain Bill Wilson's right-hand man, had opted to call it quits.[15] Though it now seems somewhat unbelievable, nevertheless it's true: none of the Texas Ranger Captains in the field wanted to relocate to Austin and fill the vacancy. One and all they were happy with their present assignments. And though it's certainly atypical, but it speaks well for Captain Dean's leadership abilities, his Company D Sergeant, Lefty Block, moved into the Assistant to the Senior Captain's spot without having served a single day commanding a company of Texas Rangers as a captain. Backfilling behind Lefty Block as the Company D Sergeant was Gene Powell, a sure enough first-rate Ranger.[16] Not unexpectedly the in-house chatter and scuttlebutt ran rampant—and was prolonged.

Something else never ended. Especially after the tragic Fred Carrasco affair at Huntsville, the Texas Rangers worked hand-in-glove with TDC officialdom. The close personal relationship between Director W.J. "Jim" Estelle, Jr. and the Texas Ranger front office was nurtured selflessly—lives swung in the balance between incarceration and independence. During those sweltering mid-year months of 1980, Captain Jack Dean as well several other Texas Ranger Captains, three unit Prison Wardens and Director Estelle reviewed well thought-out contingency plans with regards to "possible large scale problems at penitentiary during [the] summer."[17] Colonel Jim Adams had—and would continue—to demand that sufficient DPS investigative and uniformed personnel could be transitioned into a riotous situation, with the shortest possible response time. Accordingly, all of the Lone Star State's prison units were catalogued and dependent on geographical location a determination was on the drawing board as to just how many DPS personnel could make their presence felt at any given facility—hour by hour. Due to his previous endeavors with relation to SWAT Team birthing, Captain Jack Dean was an integral player in blueprinting the DPS answer to an inside-the-wire riot or to an outright prison-break.[18] Be that as it may, it seemed to Captain Jack Dean—in a peculiar sort of way—that a nemesis from days past was dead-set on breaking into rather than out of the Big House.

Culberson County as the crow flies or I-10 runs is a long way from San Antonio. Its western border is where one gains or loses an hour dependent on direction of travel. The county seat, located in the far southern reach of real-estate, is Van Horn, founded during 1912.[19] For an authentic Wild West setting Culberson County is legit: high mountains and dry deserts, rattlesnake and rocks, and a population of tough and independent-minded folks. No doubt with tongue-in-cheek, a hand-painted sign hanging in an antiquated Van Horn building says it all: "This town is so healthy we had to shoot a man to start a cemetery."[20]

The stage then is set, and who but Charles Voyde Harrelson would take the leading role, though now he was a fugitive from justice for not honoring his deal to make the scheduled Houston courtroom appearance. On the last day of August 1980, alone and driving a borrowed white Corvette, Charles Voyde Harrelson was armed and agitated—and high-riding a cocaine-induced euphoria or paranoia. At any rate, stopping along the Interstate east of Van Horn due to car trouble, the hysterical outlaw from Lovelady opted to fix his mechanical predicament. With a .44 Magnum revolver he took aim at the muffler, intending to just shoot it loose from the Corvette. He missed! The rear tire could hardly withstand the bullet's impact—and didn't. With a flat tire and flat out of his mind, wearing but shorts, sandals, and gold chains around his neck, it should be no big surprise that passing motorists were somewhat taken aback—enough so that authorities were notified about the wacky guy on the Interstate with a wicked-looking handgun pointed at his head. Soon on the scene were area law enforcing folks and the weird standoff was marked by the hour-hand, not the minute-hand. Benevolently not shooting him loose from his six-shooter, and following negotiations allowing his latest lady friend from El Paso to come to his rescue, Charles Voyde Harrelson had after six hours of craziness at long last laid down the .44 Magnum and nervously surrendered. The madcap ordeal was history. Aside from his revolver, an onsite THP Patrolman took possession of Harrelson's shoulder-bag, and during the requisite inventory was more than surprised at his find: over 200 grams of cocaine. But there was more. Though the writings were rambling, in a diary Harrelson had penned, "I'm sorry—not for me but for the pain I've caused others, both those who've loved me and who've loved the people I've killed—but I've never killed a person who was undeserving of it. . . . Please excuse my handwriting but I am high on cocaine (as usual). I, Charles V. Harrelson, killed John H. Wood, Jr. acting solely on my own. . . ."[21] Obviously, Harrelson had stepped in it, again! Seemingly, after a hard and cogent and not hyped analytical look, Charles Voyde Harrelson's free-world stints were just vacations.

Vacation days were temporarily rescinded for employees of the H-E-B Grocery Stores, at the outset in Waco, but the cancellations became widespread. Extortionists via an anonymous telephone call bragged that they had placed lethal doses of strychnine in consumable items in three of the chain's McLennan County retail groceries. For $60,000 the nitwit(s) would reveal which stores and which products were contaminated. Covertly, on two separate occasions the purported "drop sites" for the delivery of payments was placed under surveillance. Twice the extortionists failed to show—generating a predicament of epic proportion. Perplexed corporate executives could ill afford—morally, ethically, or financially—to hazard a chance. The order for the destruction of 680 tons of merchandise was issued. And that, in and of itself, was a massive undertaking. Working with the city of Waco, utilizing their garbage trucks, grocery store workers indefatigably destocked the shelves, hauling away load after load of the possibly tainted products. An H-E-B representative, Vice-President Bill Ault, reassured the public with supplemental details:

> We felt it was a hoax from the start but at that point we didn't have any assurance and had to take the action. . . . we absolutely were not going to take any risk that would endanger any of our customers. . . . About 50 percent of all the merchandise in the stores was taken out. . . . Things you don't eat or things in tin cans were left in the store. Non-food items, like soap or Clorox or things you wouldn't ever eat were left in. But all the animal food products or anything that you could put in your mouth—baby rattles, beef, produce, aspirin, everything like that—was taken out under very close guard. It was trucked to a special dump that was provided for us and buried and it remains under very close guard.[22]

For this act of Central Texas lunacy, random tests on selected items failed to produce even the slightest trace of any poisons. Though it may have been a ruse with regards to foodstuffs being laced with toxins, it was no joke for the three fellows "found guilty in the Waco extortion plots and their jail sentences range[d] from 15 to 20 years on the federal charges."[23]

Captain Jack Dean and his Company D Texas Rangers had not been involved in the Waco affair—but shortly he and they would get their taste—via a copycat. The scheme was tried again at San Antonio. In this instance, within hours the alleged violator was apprehended and the negative and scary publicity was avoided. Dan E. Butt, Vice-President and Treasurer of the gigantic food store enterprise made sure DPS Director Adams was updated, particularly singling out the tireless Company D Commander: "I wanted to let you know that we really appreciated the personal attention

Capt. Dean gave to this incident. He organized the apprehension efforts extremely well and kept us informed which we appreciated very much."[24] Presupposing such criminal madness was kaput would be an exercise in naiveté. Cats have nine lives; copycats, well, there are many.

Another H-E-B grocery store was under threat, this one in South Texas at Carrizo Springs in Dimmit County. Basically the MO was similar, though the demands were made in writing rather than over the telephone. A cash payment of $125,000 would downgrade the extortionist's ultimatum; otherwise he would poison H-E-B foodstuffs—and store management would be free to guess just which items had been tampered with. The Texas Rangers and FBI conducted a joint investigation, eventually arresting an H-E-B store employee.[25] Though the appellate case twists and tangles are many and interesting, once again Captain Jack Dean and his Company D Texas Rangers were lauded—this time by FBI SAC John C. "Jack" Lawn, who had backfilled behind Tony Morrow.[26]

And though the chronological context, once again, is not exactly in-sync there is a sidebar dynamic worthy of mention for the Carrizo Springs H-E-B extortion investigation: Hypnosis. One hallmark of Texas Ranger viability is adaptability. Whether it was acquisition of the latest technological advances in weaponry or forever improving forensic capabilities or cutting-edge communications, the Texas Rangers were game for giving it a try. In relation to the criminal case at hand, this is exemplified straightforwardly. Texas Ranger H. Joaquin Jackson and DPS MVT Agent Joe W. Haralson (who would later become a Texas Ranger), both active participants in the on-the-ground investigation and surveillance, voluntarily submitted to hypnosis during efforts designed at enhancing their subconscious perception of events. The legalities were ultimately addressed by the U.S. Court of Appeals, Firth Circuit, though not necessarily in the Rangers' favor.[27]

Somewhat later, this time as a sterling example of meticulousness, Texas Ranger Company D Sergeant Gene Powell (later Captain) then a trained and certified hypnotist, coordinated his skills with police forensic artist William H. Beechinor of Austin PD during the interview of a Sexual Assault victim. Productively the teamwork netted a "composite drawing of an unknown rape suspect." At San Antonio the sketch was shown on television. Overnight a tip from a citizen netted positive results and "a suspect was arrested and subsequently confessed to the rape and another attempt in the City of Live Oak. The suspect is also a suspect in a homicide in the City of San Antonio." Once again, Captain Jack Dean, along with Sergeant Gene Powell was singled out for recognition in a nice letter of commendation: "They and the other Rangers of Company 'D' truly epitomize the professionalism and dedication of the Texas Rangers."[28]

Although it may—for uninformed non-Texans—seem somewhat of trivial dimension in the never ending fight against criminality, Company D Texas Rangers were caught up in a violation that was all too repetitive. And it was no laughing matter! Every year preceding deer season, unscrupulous fellows were selling leases—hunting rights—for acreage they had no rights to. Using newspaper classified advertising they bilked many a non-suspecting and hopeful hunter out of hard-earned dollars. Much to hunters' surprise, on opening morning of the hunting season, they found themselves crowded by fellows that had likewise been duped—all having purchased permission to hunt the same ground—but from a now phantom landowner. When broached by an inquiring newspaperman about the arrest of a San Antonio man for such evil skullduggery, Captain Jack Dean fast clear-cut to reality: "It's not uncommon, we are investigating four other situations involving the same type operation."[29] Though now retired, Texas Ranger Captain James A. Wright underscores the seriousness of such investigations, recalling: "And early one morning, it was right at the beginning of deer season and early one morning I got a call that a man had been shot on a deer lease. And so I went out there immediately and was the first officer on the scene. And it turned out to be two deer hunters had a shoot out going around and around a pickup with deer rifles. And one of 'em eventually [had] killed the other one. They had a dispute over who was supposed to be legally on the place hunting deer and one of them. . . . they got into a fight. . . . they went around and around this pickup and shot several holes in the pickup before one of them eventually killed the other one. I thought that was rather unusual having a duel with deer rifles around a pickup."[30]

Aside from being—more or less—forced into fraudulent deer lease investigations, it seems the San Antonio print media was also fascinated with cockfighting. There were allegations that some members of the Bexar County law enforcement community were turning a blind eye, "having accepted bribes from the operators of the cockfights in return for not raiding the fights and the gambling operations that go with them." According to a newspaper account the FBI was investigating these reports of misconduct. Captain Jack Dean was interviewed, too. He told the reporter that his Texas Rangers had not—as of then—conducted a raid on a San Antonio area cockfight, "but noted that on several occasions, Rangers have told fight coordinators to close down, or else." Realistically, he also apprised the inquisitive newshound that cockfighting in the big scheme of Texas Ranger law-enforcing priorities was not at the top of the list.[31] Captain Dean, however, quickly refocused his attention on more pressing matters to the south.

Port Isabel on the shores of Laguna Madre and the site of a historic lighthouse, is gateway to the bridge allowing access to the very popular tourists' destination, South Padre Island and its Gulf of Mexico coastline shops, seafood eateries, and skyscraper beachfront condominiums and four-star hotels. This slice of eastern Cameron County in the Lower Rio Grande Valley was/is a delightful place to visit—or live. Thirty-eight-year-old THP Patrolman David Irvine Rucker, husband and father of three, had been with DPS since 1969 and he, too, "just loved the ocean." Life was good for Patrolman Rucker and his wife Thelma, a Registered Nurse.[32]

At 11:00 p.m. during the night of 29 September 1981, on State Highway 100 about fifteen miles west of Port Isabel, Patrolman Rucker was murdered during an apparently routine traffic stop. Like Constable Ricky Lewis, he had been shot DRT—and the nastily disposed shooter was nowhere about. Signs of a frantic fight were clear.

Rucker had been shot in the head and left for dead. Shortly, within minutes, an unknowing Los Fresnos PD officer, Enrique L. Carrisalez, twenty-five, stopped the very same automobile on Highway 100 and he too was caught off guard and gunned down, though he was not DRT. Certainly the double shootings had the Cameron County law enforcing community agog![33]

One of Captain Jack Dean's Company D men, the aforementioned experienced investigator Texas Ranger Bruce Casteel, responded and what he found at the David Rucker death-site was disturbing: The deceased trooper was "lying on his back. . . . in the westbound traffic lane of 100. His arms were sort of outstretched from his body. . . . There was not an eye there at all. . . . There was a lot of blood. Blood covered his face, completely draining down both sides of his body. . . . Rucker's hat lay near his body and his flashlight was across the road, 27 feet from his body. . . . Rucker was wearing his gun belt but the pistol had been removed from the holster. The pistol was never found [at the crime scene]." Richard Dickinson, a passing motorist who had initially found the slain officer and used the DPS patrol car's radio to notify Port Isabel PD, confirmed Texas Ranger Casteel's description of the deceased lawman: "I checked to see if there were any signs of life. There weren't. . . . There wasn't a left eye. There was blood covering the face."[34] Observantly, Dickinson found something else, too. There was a Social Security Card "near the body." Shortly on the murder scene, Constable Lupe Rosales also corroborated the presence of that crucial piece of evidence, a bloodied Social Security Card.[35]

Expectedly, Captain Dean was immediately notified and by the next evening he was in the Lower Rio Grande Valley meeting with Ranger Bruce Casteel with regards to the murder investigation of DPS Trooper Rucker.[36] Not surprisingly DPS Colonel Adams was there too. The Colonel was somewhat taken aback. He was relatively new and unfamiliar with the degree of autonomy typically afforded Texas Rangers. There had been no panicky call for flying in a squadron of Special Agents, as would have predictably taken place with an FBI-type response. Captain Jack Dean's follow-up TRWR entry for the next day, 1 October 1981, is reflective of two noticeable dynamics. First and foremost the tragic death of a fellow DPS comrade was priority business, categorically! Secondly, Captain Dean's TRWR commentary is illustrative of his Texas Ranger management philosophy. "In Harlingen assisted Ranger Casteel with continued investigation of David Rucker Capital Murder Case."[37] Perceptibly, the operative word in the Captain's entry is, *assisted*! Ranger Bruce M. Casteel knew what he should be doing and what he was doing—a painstaking criminal investigation.[38] The wise protocol for Company Captains was simple: If in good hands, step aside. Captain Jack Dean returned to Company D headquarters.

Fortuitously and fortunately the investigative leads and eyewitness testimony began to merge. Of critical importance had been that Social Security card located near David Rucker's bloodied body—the name on the lucky discovery was readable. At the time Officer Carrisalez had been gunned down, he had been accompanied by a ride-along civilian, Enrique (Henry) Hernandez. Collating the name on the Social Security card and license number of the vehicle Carrisalez stopped, doubled-down by a positive photographic identification of the suspect, Texas Ranger Casteel and other lawmen had a target for an arrest: Leonel Torres Herrera, thirty-four.[39]

Cataloguing their very best intelligence, lawmen thought that Herrera would be found at a house northeast of Edinburg on Chapin Road. Mobilizing a task force team of DPS and local officers was easy work; not just a few stepped to the plate for the takedown.[40] At the house, when Herrera realized he was being hemmed in, he broke for the brush but was fleeing into an open field. Coolly, not wanting to kill the hotfooting suspect, DPS Trooper Mike Stark fired an attention-grabbing warning shot—"When I fired the defendant was running. The best I could tell, it hit somewhere near his feet."[41] Fearing that he might not hear the next shot before it tore into meat and/or bone and/or gristle, Leonel Torres Herrera put on the brakes, fell to the ground, and dejectedly waited to be handcuffed. Texas Ranger Bruce Casteel elaborated from an evidentiary perspective what they found: items like a pair of blue jeans and a wallet with blood on them; "they belonged to Herrera." DPS Investigator Allen Helton noted that inside the house "were three 'bricks' of marijuana and $6000." Texas Ranger Bruce Casteel guesstimated the weed to weigh not ounces, but "several" pounds.[42] In this instance there was no real energy expended trying to tie the illicit leafy green substance to Leonel Torres Herrera: He was facing a death penalty case. The circumstantial and forensic evidence was stacking up, and not favorably, for Herrera—especially after DPS Crime Lab personnel processed the blood and fiber samples retrieved from the auto Lionel Herrera had been driving the night of such senseless shootings. The forensic matches were potent!

Leonel Torres Herrera, due to the fact he was arrested near Edinburg, was transported to the nearest lockup, the Edinburg PD. There, inside the juvenile office, because there had been no eyewitnesses to the slaying of THP Patrolman David Irvine Rucker, a Hidalgo County Assistant District Attorney, Joe K. Hendley, wanted to interrogate Herrera about that particular homicide. He most positively got more than he bargained for: First rattle out of the box, his very first question was, "Why did you kill David?" Herrera answered fast with his fist, furiously knocking Joe Hendley to the floor—unconscious—out cold. Unquestionably nearby officers heard the commotion and rushed to Joe Hendley's aid, thumping Herrera's head to get him under control. Whether or not it was excessive treatment may stand speculative debate; nevertheless, one would expect—anywhere in Texas—repercussions from pounding on a prosecutor. It's just not smart! Leonel Torres Herrera was ultimately taken to Edinburg General Hospital while the Assistant DA was waking up and being told what had happened.[43]

DPS Troopers Santiago Robles and Victor Escalon were stationed at the hospital to guard Herrera—and they got an earful when a caring nurse came to draw blood from the prisoner. According to Robles and Escalon, Leonel Torres Herrera swore at them in English and Spanish: "You all think you're God but you're not. Just because one of your own gets killed you go and get angry. . . . I am going to show you I am a man. I am going to kill you all one by one. . . . You are the ones who make us criminals and I will kill every one of you when I get out." Lest one be looking for a more or less neutral witness to the outburst, the nurse, Maria Guadalupe Aguilar, backed up the DPS Troopers' version, saying: "He (Herrera) said that he would kill the police officers one by one or he would take them all together and kill them if he had to."[44]

Sadly, for this late September 1981 episode, the death tally jumped. After clinging to life at the Valley Baptist Medical Center for nine days—and after positively identifying Herrera during a verbal Dying Declaration as the man who triggered the hot spiraling round into his chest, Enrique Carrisalez passed to the other side. He had been a policeman eleven months.[45]

And even before all this volatile mess, a year earlier, according to KGBT photographer Gregory Bader, when the prisoner had been legally sparring with officialdom regarding a charge of Attempted Capital Murder of a Police Officer, "Leonel Herrera rushed me and knocked me and the camera over. I was standing off to one side. . . . He broke away from deputies escorting him." Although fairness demands mention that Leonel Torres Herrera had been acquitted of that Hidalgo County felony charge, the intimidating incident had been burned into cameraman Bader's longtime memory.[46]

Another sidebar merits mention. For this particular case, during the searches and seizures a particular .357 Magnum revolver was recovered—one long missing. Earlier it was mentioned that young Hidalgo County Constable Ricky Steven Lewis had been foully murdered, his lifeless body sprawled in an intersection atop a .357 Magnum revolver, but not his own duty weapon. Ricky's .357 Magnum revolver was recovered as an offshoot result of the Leonel Torres Herrera investigation being made by Ranger Casteel.[47] Was there a legitimate and/or illegitimate tie-in to these officers' murders? Was Ricky's offing yet a whodunit?

At trial Leonel Torres Herrera opted to exercise one of his Constitutional guarantees and did not take the witness stand in his own defense. Though Herrera's attorney put forward a spirited defense, the seven-man, five-woman jury were not convinced. For them that obligatory standard of proof—Beyond a Reasonable Doubt—had been met, in spades. After rendering their *Guilty* verdict, jurors unanimously concurred that Leonel Torres Herrera should forfeit his life for what he had done. Transferred to Death Row, the appellate process for the convicted murderer kicked into gear.[48] And, for this particular case, though mentions here are out of chronological sync, somewhat later the try at scampering free from imposition of the 197th District Court's sentence does make for—even if not compelling—fascinating reading.

During an eleventh-hour appeal, Leonel Torres Herrera's assertion was that he was totally innocent, but that he knew well the guilty party—his brother Raul. It was Raul who had capped Trooper David Rucker and Policeman Enrique Carrisalez. For the Blind Mistress of Justice to extract lawful retribution for the eliminated lawmen, though, her dilemma was insurmountable. Raul Herrera was surefire dead—murdered—and really had been for quite a number of years, altogether unable to confess or deny anything. Death Row desperation is not atypical, but is rhythmic for those charged and convicted of capital crimes. Any simplicity linked with this solemn drama was negated by intricate and intriguing legal issues in want of momentous and, perhaps, precedent-setting resolution. The United States Supreme Court would examine the defendant's arguments—and did.

For the appellate case styled *Leonel Torres Herrera v. James A. Collins, Director, Texas Department of Criminal Justice, Institutional Division*, it would not bode well for the Petitioner, Leonel Torres Herrera. Subsequent to a truly exhaustive consideration and a step-by-step examination of the narrative and the legal issues pertinent thereto, the High Court had reached a decision. Included in their logically deliberative processes had been a most inconvenient fact, inconvenient for defendant Herrera. Although Leonel Torres Herrera had been found culpable by a jury in an actual courtroom trial for murdering Los Fresnos PD's Enrique Carrisalez, somewhat later he had—voluntarily—entered a plea of *Guilty* with regards to the killing of DPS Trooper David Rucker. In the end, the Supreme Court came down on the side of the State of Texas and not inmate Leonel Torres Herrera. As part of the majority opinion Justice Sandra Day O'Connor summarized: "Not one judge—no state court judge, not the District Court Judge, none of the three Judges of the Court of Appeals, and none of the Justices of this Court—has expressed doubt about petitioner's guilt."[49]

Though it had taken 4,128 days, convicted killer Leonel Torres Herrera had finally hit the metaphorical brick wall—the one inside the Walls Unit at Huntsville. The prison clock stopped for Leonel Torres Herrera at 4:49 a.m.[50]

13

"No neophyte at prison life"

O n the fifteenth day of April 1982 a Federal Grand Jury returned its Indictments regarding the gutless execution of Judge H. Wood, according to *Time Magazine*:

three defendants face charges: Charles V. Harrelson, 44, a convicted contract killer accused of shooting Wood for a payment of $250,000 from Jimmy Chagra, Harrelson's wife Jo Ann, 42, who allegedly bought the murder rifle; and Jimmy's wife Elizabeth, 28, who is charged with covering up the crime. Jimmy will be tried separately later. The final defendant was to have been the youngest Chagra brother, Joseph, 35, an El Paso lawyer. But last month he agreed to plead guilty to the murder-conspiracy charge and testify against Harrelson in return for a ten-year maximum sentence and the right not to testify against his brother.[1]

Chipping to more specific legalese is easy. For Jimmy Chagra and Charles Voyde Harrelson, were they to be lawfully convicted of whacking the judge, assured life sentences would be in their near-term futures. Husband and wife Chagra were to answer for Conspiracy to Commit Murder and Obstruction of Justice, while the distraught Jo Ann Harrelson had to face the music on the latter charge—and another federal case, a slam-dunk. The at times baffling and always trying investigative work had burned near three years.[2]

Though it's heretofore been reported—as a matter of general knowledge—for many, if not most versions of the Judge Wood murder tale this truth typically goes unmentioned. Perhaps a smidgen of jealous discomfiture had accompanied the furtive obfuscation. Nonetheless, FBI SAC Jack Lawn had stepped to the plate. He was a solid player. And, he did the right thing.[3] The "thank you" was personable and sincere. SAC Lawn had particularly noted the investigative value of Captain Dean's putting them on the convoluted trail of Charles Voyde Harrelson.[4] Jack Lawn played in the real world in real time with real folks. An eminent historian would several years later write: "That was all the recognition Captain Dean received. But for this lead, the FBI might never have ended the case. Yet the media spotlight fixed solely on the FBI, which never let the public know that Dean or any other state or local officers had been involved."[5]

Assuredly the scheming and dreaming and deceptions make for a super rich true-crime drama. With regards to trial strategy—prosecution and defense—the underhanded and the aboveboard machinations are not only titillating—but generally informative, legally enlightening. The sordid storyline is opulently stuffed with double-crossing dope dealers, jailhouse snitches, free-world CIs, assertions of attorney/client privilege, perjury, questionable pardons, shredded documents, hearsay, payoffs and payouts, clandestine deal making, upfront plea-bargaining, and hour after hour of electronic eavesdropping and taping—that's the short list. Beyond doubt book material and, thankfully, one is on the shelf.[6]

Of the many Aces in the government's hands, one concerning the *alleged* murder weapon was an indisputable showstopper. Apparently, obliviously unmindful with his earlier stabs at trying to personally distance himself from any connection with a supposed bullet spittin' homicide tool, Charles Voyde Harrelson had, again, bungled the job. His *Modus Operandi* for disposing of guns was to disassemble them and chunk parts across bridge railings or into bar-ditches. East of Dallas and just west of the Kaufman and Rockwall County lines is Lake Ray Hubbard, a rather large manmade reservoir. And into the drink did go, separated from each other, a hand-crafted hardwood rifle stock and a brightly polished steel-barreled action. Generally speaking the unique serial numbers of firearms are engraved on the frame and/or barrel—the parts made of metal. Beneficially for Charles Voyde Harrelson steel sinks but, unfortunately not factored into his miscalculated equation of slipshod criminality—wood floats. An elementary deduction one might presume. The rifle's stock was, at length, recovered from mud at the shifting shorelines of Lake Ray Hubbard.[7] Unbeknownst to Charles Voyde Harrelson— and not just a few crime fighters—is a little known fact, and, for this big murder case, a tremendously significant fact.[8] In this particular situation, characteristically, it would not bode very well for an unthinking Charles V. Harrelson. For some Weatherby firearms the serial number is also placed on the rifle's stock, nondescriptly stamped inside the furrowed framework and outside of ordinary sight. In this instance the .240 caliber Weatherby Magnum, Mark V model, qualified for dual numbering.[9] Lo and behold! The rifle, just the stock in question, was productively traced to the first retail dealer, in this case the aforementioned Hunter Bradlee Sporting Goods Store at Dallas. And as good luck or bad luck would have it, this proved to be the very firearm purchased on 17 May 1979, by someone identifying herself as Faye L. King—just twelve days before Judge Wood was coldheartedly assassinated in his driveway at San Antonio.[10]

And who would be Faye L. King and how did she play into this high drama? Unluckily for the defendants on trial, Faye L. King proved to be a phony name—one given by Jo Ann Harrelson, Charles Voyde Harrelson's conspiring wife. The address given on the government acquisition form, likewise, was fictitious. Jo Ann Harrelson's fingerprints matched those on the ATF Form 4473, Firearms Transaction Record, and after comparison, handwriting experts matched the questioned signature of Faye L. King to the known sample of Jo Ann Harrelson's exemplars.[11] True, it has been written: "Despite the tapes, there were still holes in the government's case. The government didn't have a murder weapon, merely the stock of one of the ten thousand Weatherby Mark V rifles sold in this country in recent years."[12] Yes, the government may have had the stock of but one of the thousands of Weatherby Mark V's sold in recent years, but it was the very one deceitfully and criminally purchased by Jo Ann Harrelson, aka Faye L. King. It would seem in Charles V. Harrelson's global existence, a bad twist of fate was commonplace. With a view turned toward lucid practicality, such irony and coincidence wouldn't be lost on a trial jury disposed to reasonableness and commonsense. Jo Ann Harrelson was, colloquially speaking, in a world of hurt—prison time on her upcoming calendar.

Nineteen eighty-two would be a meaningful year for Kyle Lynn Dean. After a stint in the oil fields at Somerville and Snook in Burleson County (county seat Caldwell), Kyle had worked his way through college at Sam Houston State University at Huntsville. Majoring in Criminal Justice with an emphasis on Law Enforcement and Police Science, Kyle had earned his Bachelor's Degree. Industriously Kyle had also supplemented his classroom education and labs with real work at the Ellis Unit of TDC. There he circulated in a distinct subculture wholly foreign to most folks in the free-world. By definition convicts weren't choirboys. Their institutional ticket had been bought with convictions for one or more felonies, not scatterbrained misdemeanors. Not just a few, like Charles Voyde Harrelson, were recidivists. Collectively they spoke their own language—prison jargon—with a glossary of terms having unambiguous meanings—manifestly decipherable if one was incarcerated for any length of time. There were in-house rules not laid down by persnickety prison administrators. Infractions within this subsection of humanity could extract a heavy penalty from fellow inmates. "Blood in, Blood out," was an oft repeated mantra of tattooed prison gang affiliates. Makeshift shanks and cunning schemes were commonplace. Lying to each other and to the correctional staff was but par business—part of the game. A bona fide hard-edged convict Kyle Dean explicitly recalls interacting with was Robert Excell White. The stone-cold killer was awaiting his execution date as a result of the machine-gun murders of three men at the Hilltop Grocery, a rural North Texas country store between the Collin County towns of McKinney and Princeton. The murder weapon had been stolen the day before from a Waco gun collector who had been robbed and stabbed to death.[13] Robert Excell White was but one of the several case-hardened convicts long on ferocity, short on friendliness and devoid of decency.

Like his father before him, Correctional Officer Kyle Lynn Dean had something burning deep inside—something only brothers/sisters of the badge know and feel in their heads and hearts. Kyle Dean forewent the big paychecks for psychological payback—he became a THP Trooper, graduating from the DPS Training Academy. He was posted at Crockett in Houston County just west of the alluring Davy Crockett National Forest and not too far north of Lovelady and the Eastham Unit of TDC. And though it necessitates that always uncomfortable digression from an exacting in-sync chronology, an utterly unexpected encounter of Trooper Kyle Dean was/is eerie. One of his personal friends—though he would go on to much bigger and better things—was TDC Lieutenant Rodney Cooper. For a noontime chat and lunch Trooper Kyle Dean stopped by at Eastham for a visit with Cooper. Therein an inmate "caught the wall" courteously asking Lieutenant Cooper if the DPS uniformed fellow was Jack Dean's son? He sure looked like him! Both Kyle and Rodney nodded in the affirmative, though somewhat puzzled. Then the convict in prison-issued whites whispered—respectfully—to Kyle Dean: "When you see your father tell him Charles Harrelson said hello."[14] Though he was undeniably yet the target of a full-scale federal investigation regarding the Judge Wood assassination, Harrelson was doing hard time with TDC. The roosters of state charges regarding firearms and narcotics violations in Culberson and Harris Counties had come home to roost: forty and thirty years respectively. Looming overhead was the federal case for offing Maximum John. "The FBI finally had Harrelson where it wanted him—in a Texas prison chopping cotton."[15]

Captain Jack Dean, too, was happy in a devilish sort of way during 1982. By nature he was outgoing and savvy about political doings inside and outside DPS. During a South Texas Company D meeting and dove hunt, one of the invited guests was William C. "Bill" Perryman and his wife Mary Ann of Athens in Henderson County. Bill Perryman was one of the executively appointed DPS

Commissioners. Senior Captain Bill Wilson particularly made note of the cordiality between Perryman and Dean, later calling Jack aside and somewhat jealously it seems quietly admonished him about "getting too close to the Commissioners." Jack Dean swallowed hard—trying to keep a straight face, not smiling when he replied: "Well, if that's the case, I guess you better take it up with the Commissioners." Senior Captain Wilson wilted.[16]

And herein it's but germane to mention the long-term friendship between Jack Dean and Wayne Showers. Businesswise Wayne Showers had been associated with Griffin-Brand Produce Company, perhaps the biggest onion producer in the Lower Rio Grande Valley. He, too, was on the Board of Regents for Texas A&M University at College Station. Jack Dean and Wayne Showers were frequent Whitetail deer and Whitewing dove hunting companions. They were *bueno amigos*. In fact, Jack Dean would and has openly declared that Wayne Showers was "the best non-pistol packin' friend I ever had."[17]

Even though he was faraway at San Antonio, another shooting episode in Hidalgo County caught Captain Jack Dean's attention—a bizarre six-shootin' affray with as many unanswered questions as there were spent cartridge cases. For several months Lower Rio Grande Valley Texas Rangers, his Company D Rangers, as well as local and federal lawmen had all been hunting for Mario Romero Leal, a twenty-six-year-old Mexican national. Fugitive Leal was being "sought in connection with the slaying of a Mexican federal officer at Reynosa, Mexico," just over the bridge south of McAllen. He had been laying low on the Texas side, living with a girlfriend at Edinburg. On the thirtieth day of October 1982, when leaving his lover's home, Leal had the pockets of his designer jeans stuffed; one was bulging with $10,000 cash, the other concealed a blue-steel .38 Special revolver—the gun that had capped the Mexican federal officer's career. Interestingly but unfortunately, soon developed tough confrontations. When dutifully approached by Hidalgo County Deputy Sheriff Lee Perez, Mario Romero got there first, shooting him in the right leg. Not unexpectedly the frantic pirate set sail—afoot. Exactly what mental gear Leal was operating in is indeterminate, though by now, he was in the pickup truck of a distressed Jesus Rosalez, Sr., holding the owner hostage at gunpoint—threatening to kill him if he didn't disengage the clutch and step fast on the gas pedal—for a speedy and unscheduled trip to somewhere. By sheer chance the truck owner's son just happened to be the Chief of Police at the small but pleasant community of Elsa, not too very far east of Edinburg. And, too, just by chance, Chief Jesus Rosalez, Jr. had come to his dad's house. At that point—again resorting to policing lingo—it turned Western. Mario Romero Leal quickly leaped out of the truck shooting. Chief Rosalez returned the favor. With blazing speed both fellows raced to milk their revolvers dry. The super scorching contest was fast and furious, an authentic Wild West shootout in deep South Texas. Was there a legit winner? It was a draw! Chief Rosalez crumpled to the ground, "a gunshot wound through the chest and abdomen with perforation of the liver and heart." Outlaw Mario Romero Leal's injury was not particularly detailed other than it being "a gunshot wound." Unhappily writing for the *Del Rio News Herald*, the newspaperman penned the bad news: "Rosales [*sic*] and Romero [Leal] died during a gunbattle as each man emptied the ammunition in his gun into the other."[18]

Another battle raged hot. Captain Jack Dean was near speechless and dumbfounded when he received the telephone call from Joaquin Jackson, his man then stationed at picturesque Uvalde, not too far west of San Antonio and, ironically, the semi-permanent campsite of nineteenth-century Company D Texas Rangers. The news was not good. Texas Ranger Joaquin Jackson had decked a THP Trooper for calling him a liar. According to Joaquin—when he told Captain Dean what had happened "the phone went dead." Shortly, Captain Dean quizzed: "You did *what?!*" Disciplinary action to some degree was a foregone conclusion. Giving in to personal fisticuffs with another DPS employee was a definite no-no! No matter the provocation. Captain Jack Dean interceded and championed Joaquin's case with the fuming DPS front office, ultimately whittling prescribed punishment down to a three-day suspension—unpaid—rather than outright dismissal. Subsequent to issuance of the short paycheck,

Captain Dean summoned Jackson to Company D headquarters at San Antonio. There he forked over to Joaquin a check for $300—the amount withheld from his pay. Joaquin's Company D coworkers had taken up a needed collection for one of their own—don't mess with Texas or a Texas Ranger![19]

On another occasion, once more, Captain Jack Dean, according to Joaquin Jackson, saved his job by interceding when the Texas Ranger headquarters command wanted to step on his neck and demand his resignation.[20] Although identifying exactly which incident Joaquin Jackson was making reference to is fuzzy—there were several—his gratitude to Captain Jack Dean was demonstrable with his handwritten note:

> *Cap: Just a note to say thanks for all your support during my crisis—I really appreciate everything you did for me and Mostly thank you for being a _Damn Good Captain_ and _Friend_. Thanks Again, Joaquin.*[21]

Though Captain Dean having to actually discipline a subordinate Texas Rangers was, indeed, rare, there was one thing he couldn't and wouldn't and didn't abide: best not knowingly lie to Captain Jack Dean. Though he shall herein remain nameless, one Texas Ranger did. He wasn't cashiered from the service and maybe he would have rethought his position, but if so it would have been after his transfer into another company—Captain Jack Dean had no longer a place for him in Company D.[22]

Upfront loyalty is admirable. Captain Jack Dean—a student of human nature—knew hard truths. Although it's not mentioned at this point for a show of gratuitous sensationalism, there should be no effort designed to shortchange readers of the reality—when, in due time, it will surely play into Jack Dean's biographical narrative. Certain truths may be inconvenient, but they are truths nevertheless. Within the sleazy world of gamblers and gangsters, convicts and conmen, drug traffickers and dope doers, the name of Charles Voyde Harrelson was well-known and, sometimes, dreaded. On the other hand, in the entertainment world one of his natural sons, Woodrow Tracy "Woody" Harrelson, was making quite a name for himself as a popular television personality and performer. And as writer David Hutchins penned for an article in *People Magazine* it was, indeed, "A Strange Family Twist."[23] The lighthearted NBC comedy, *Cheers*, was a high-ratings hit production. The multi-talented Woody Harrelson's on-set role as Woody Boyd "the most befuddled bartender in the land," demonstrably endeared him to a nationwide viewing audience. Later, his name would be under marquee lights on movie theaters throughout the country—Woody Harrelson's unrelenting trek toward stardom was not just some pie-in-the-sky fancy by a Hollywood wannabe. Like them or not, Woody Harrelson's on-screen characters were believable—at times chillingly so! During his childhood, he was not enamored with his flighty father; Charles Voyde Harrelson had skipped for parts unknown when Woody was a mere lad of seven, leaving his mother Diane to support their kiddos—ironically—as a hard working and superlative legal secretary.[24]

Undoubtedly and understandably Woody Harrelson was somewhat conflicted, an assertion that he himself realized and commented on: "This might sound odd to say about a convicted felon. . . . but my father is one of the most articulate, well-read, charming people I've ever known. Still, I'm just now gauging whether he merits my loyalty or friendship. I look at him as someone who could be a friend more than someone who was a father."[25] Captain Jack Dean could and did speak to Charles Voyde Harrelson's intelligence and deportment—not idolizing his misplaced scruples, abject criminality, and an absence of conscience—but confirming his likability and generally pleasing personality. On these traits Jack Dean echoed Woody Harrelson's feelings.[26] And to a certain extent so too did Justices on the United States Court of Appeals, Fifth Circuit, although their left-handed compliment was somewhat tempered: "It is unnecessary to consult the case law to conclude that one who expects privacy under the circumstances of prison visiting is, if not actually foolish, exceptionally naïve; Harrelson, highly intelligent and no neophyte at prison life, was neither."[27] Yes, setting aside Charles V. Harrelson's ineptness as an outlaw, he was, generally speaking, a damn smart cookie and charming. Career lawman Jack Dean was running in tandem with Woody Harrelson on another matter of import. Abstaining from actually awarding his daddy an opinion of *guilt* or *innocence* with regards to pulling the trigger on Judge Wood, the accomplished actor told adroit journalist Josh Young for a piece in *George Magazine* only that "under our justice system" his father—and everyone else—was surely "entitled to a fair trial."[28] Jack Dean would not argue against that premise.

At trial in San Antonio a jailhouse informant incarcerated with Harrelson testified that he had overheard an uptight Charles Voyde remark after watching lurid TV news coverage: "If she talks they'll burn me for ringing Wood's bell." Quite interestingly the colloquial phraseology about "ringing someone's bell" was exactly what Jerry Watkins claimed Harrelson had said after offing Sam Degelia, Jr. inside the dingy Hidalgo County irrigation pump-house several years earlier. Was such an out-and-out remark coincidence? The alluded to "she" was Teresa Starr—his grown stepdaughter—who had traveled to Las Vegas and picked up the blood money—$250,000—from Liz Chagra, an uncomplicated assertion not standing much dispute. Too, the fact, alleged fact, that Harrelson had once glibly bragged to Joe Chagra about Judge Wood going under was not good: "I saw him quiver, then twist and drop in his tracks. I knew it had been a perfect shot."[29] Throw in the blockbuster admission of guilt letter that Liz Chagra sent Mrs. Kathryn Wood, the Judge's widow, because she was now a "newly born Christian," and was desirous of making "peace with God. . . . and peace with mankind. . . . and especially you" and the hazy picture of nefariousness becomes radiantly clear.[30] Not citing a crude redrawn map about the missing rifle. The noose was tightening.

During the lengthy courtroom drama Charles Voyde Harrelson, it may be argued, didn't help himself when he took the witness stand, at one point even shaking his fist and snarly asking the federal prosecutor during cross-examination, "Did your mother dress you funny when you were a child?" Charles Voyde Harrelson prickled, too, when it was evoked that he was a hired hit-man. Presupposing that the jurors were detached from commonsense was whistling-in-the-wind risky: "It is my [Harrelson's] belief that rogue elements the Drug Enforcement Administration or some other agency perpetrated the killing and were perpetuating the cover-up. I still believe that." Really? Self-assuredly it now seemed outlaw Charles Voyde Harrelson thought he was secure standing pat, holding a winning hand. "I don't have to kill anyone to make a living. I can do very well with these ten fingers and a deck of cards. I can play God!"

On the other hand, apparently the jurors didn't look to the Deity for guidance—they relied mostly on earthly evidence. The trial had been lengthy—ten weeks—but that came to an abrupt end on the thirteenth day of December. Charles Voyde Harrelson drew short—convicted of assassinating Judge John Howland Wood, Jr. His life sentence in prison would be forthcoming.

Numerically calculating the cost in real federal dollars and man-hours for the Judge Wood murder investigation is interesting—but begs the fair question: Should there really have been any arbitrary cap on money and time? According to one consummate journalist—perhaps the most knowledgeable chronicler of the story in the round—he straightforwardly proffers figures he personally deems as "incredible" but dutifully sets them to paper: "Seventy full-time FBI agents had logged 82,000 man-hours and interviewed 30,000 [3000 ?] people. . . . The investigation had cost at least $5 million, maybe as much as $10 million. . . ."[31] He does not mention Captain Jack Dean, and the clue of the century!

Sadly, there were more murders in the state than those at the hand of Lovelady's news maker. Vicious criminals were not then—nor ever had been—in short supply for diligent Texas lawmen.

Not too long before Thanksgiving Day 1983 tragedy unfolded south of San Antonio. Adjoining Bexar County to the southeast was historic Wilson County. There, a fifty-four-year-old father, Ollie F. "Sammy" Childress, Jr. was employed by Sheriff Marvin H. "Pete" Baumann as a Deputy Sheriff. The fourth day of November turned bad somewhere along the highway between the county seat, Floresville, and the hamlet of Stockdale. Exactly how it happened is nebulous, but Sammy Childress was abruptly disarmed, handcuffed, and locked in the trunk of his patrol car. Two lawbreakers had concocted a wicked plan to rob the state bank at La Vernia, just south of the Wilson/Guadalupe County line. The vile outlaws' mindset was twisted. One would wear Sammy's uniform shirt with the attached badge. They would use the squad car as their getaway vehicle—and then murder the kidnapped deputy. The bank was robbed—$51,000—and Deputy Childress was shot in the neck the first and second time, wounds which understandably caused the cessation of life.[32] Needless to say, at least for awhile it was a genuine whodunit? Though numerous local and federal lawmen were investigating, particularly the FBI since a bank had been targeted, Texas Ranger energy due to workload pressure had been somewhat stymied, a niggling fact that tended to torture Captain Dean—but not for too long. With a gentle nudge he advised Company D Ranger Al Cuellar: "well you need to get on it. That's all he had to say, right? You need to get on it." Though having just come off of an intense but successful homicide investigation, Texas Ranger Al Cuellar jumped to—Captain Jack Dean meant what he said![33]

Painstakingly reviewing and reconstructing what had happened, Ranger Cuellar had the presence of mind to snap on a heretofore overlooked—or underappreciated—clue. When entering the bank the outlaws had with them grocery bags, sacks they wanted tellers to stuff full of greenbacks—no coins. During their craziness and apparent anxiousness to get away and off Deputy Childress, the yahoos had left an empty bag behind. Of course that was no big news to on-the-scene investigators. Texas Ranger Cuellar enhances the story—factually—after noting that there were, indeed, fingerprints on the abandoned sack: "But fingerprints back then was not like they are now. Now you can run them though a computer and they'll tell you who they are. Back then, if you had a fingerprint you had to get the suspect then check his prints to the latent prints that were left at the scene."[34] Times, indeed, were different then. Through diligently working the streets in and around Bexar County, Ranger Al Cuellar had a suspect in mind. Could that fellow be conclusively tied to the bank heist and murder?

The answer was yes—incontrovertibly. The fingerprint matched, leading to an arrest—well, two arrests, although it took several months to find the fugitive fellows. With due diligence, finally, Pedro Solis Sosa, in his early thirties, and his nephew Leroy Vargas Sosa, a seventeen-year-old, were taken into custody. Texas Ranger Cuellar was present, along with other lawmen, when oral admissions were made and written statements taken.[35] At trial the younger defendant unlatched the gate:

> testified that his uncle deliberately shot Childress once in the neck with the intention of killing him to avoid capture by identification. Leroy also testified that his uncle returned to the car to clear fingerprints from the trunk and fired a second shot into Childress when he was found still alive and conscious.[36]

Not unexpectedly Pedro Solis Sosa was convicted and caught a death sentence, while Leroy Vargas Sosa took up temporary residence at the Big House, owing the state a quarter—a quarter of a century.[37] Following the appellate process is intriguing but not relevant for putting a lid on Texas Ranger Al Cuellar's participation in the Capital Murder case. Interestingly, though, is the fact that the criminal offense had taken place during November 1983 and during May 2017—thirty-three years later—the Court of Criminal Appeals of Texas "reformed" Pedro Solis Sosa's original death sentence to "a term of life imprisonment."[38]

Assuredly Captain Jack Dean was not on-the-ground, involved in the everyday casework of his Company D Texas Rangers. They were, for the most part, crackerjack lawmen, well trained and talented forensic investigators and highly competent interrogators. Naturally, he reviewed their paperwork and kept abreast of their criminal caseloads, but generally stepped out of the way so that they could do what DPS was paying them to do—their job! There were, though, those certain times when hardcore policing—for whatever reasons—boiled to the forefront of his ever percolating psyche. For Captain Jack Dean, a case in point would be a horrific homicide just a touch northwest of the Alamo City.

Bandera (in Bandera County) billing itself as "The Cowboy Capitol of the World" is also home turf for the Old West genre museum founded by the noteworthy storyteller, editor and publisher of *Frontier Times Magazine*, J. Marvin Hunter. During early 1984 the picturesque county was also home to Marie Denise Walker, thirty-six, an attractive first-grade schoolteacher at Bandera. The experienced educator didn't live inside Bandera's corporate limits, but on a Hill Country ranch seven miles south of town. During early mornings, before heading off to work on schooldays, Marie Denise Walker would take her dog to her father William Walker's nearby home for tender and thoughtful care. The routine was expected. Five days a week—without fail! On the first Wednesday in February there was no daughter and no tail wagging dog greeting William when he walked out onto the front porch shortly before 8:00 a.m. The mental alarm bell sounded and a very concerned father decided to investigate. Upon arrival at his kiddo's place he discovered that her car was parked in the driveway with keys locked inside, and the residence was locked, too—tighter than a drum. With his spare key he made entry, and to his horror found his beloved daughter.[39]

Marie Denise Walker was disrobed, dead, and defiled.[40] There was not question about that, though the criminal meter, once again, registered a whodunit? Chief Deputy Mel Lemons, when quizzed by a newspaperman, didn't shy from hard truths, acknowledging that, while checking several leads, actually solving the case may result in "a tedious process."[41] A retired Postmaster but then the multi-term Bandera County Sheriff, Guy Vernon Pickett, welcomed help.[42] Texas Ranger Captain Jack Dean obliged. And shortly, the untimely departure of an area fellow warranted an inquiry—a real serious inquiry. Sheriff Guy Pickett noted publically what he and Captain Jack Dean knew privately: Gerald Rodger Sorenson, forty, had "disappeared the day after the murder." There was, though it was to a degree speculative, a smidgen of Probable Cause developed upon receipt of rock-solid backchannel details: "Officials at the Texas Department of Corrections said Sorenson was convicted in 1973 on rape and sodomy charges. He received a 15-year sentence and was released from

Huntsville on July 6, 1983." An arrest warrant issued and JP Tom Grant set a bail of $50,000 for Gerald Rodger Sorenson when and wherever he was apprehended.[43] That turned out to be the state of New York later in the month.[44]

After his return to the Lone Star State and at the Bandera County Jailhouse, the alleged murderer was given his Miranda Warning and interviewed by the sheriff and a "Texas Ranger." After some fits and starts, Gerald Rodger Sorenson, exasperatingly blurted what he knew to be the truth—he had, indeed, killed Marie Denise Walker. Then, not even reluctantly he gave and signed a written statement to that effect. Thereafter it was time to take the defendant before the court and put him on the conveyor belt of slow moving criminal justice. For the *Bandera Bulletin* it was above-the-fold news and the accompanying photograph updated readers with the story. The caption read: "Flanked by Bandera Sheriff Guy Pickett (left) and Texas Ranger Captain Jack Dean, suspect Gerald Rodger Sorenson is moved from the Bandera County jail to the courthouse for his arraignment in the death of Marie Denise Walker."[45]

Later on a Change of Venue the case was moved to Gillespie County for settlement and it was there, that the conscientious trial jury returned a verdict of *Guilty* for murdering Marie Denise Walker. They then determined that he should spend the remainder of his natural life behind polished bars and tall walls at Huntsville—or wherever TDC chose to put him— and to be on the safe side, for the Aggravated Sexual Assault of Marie Denise Walker, another ninety-nine years would do just fine, too![46]

Slipshod would be the telling of Captain Dean's life-story without repeatedly mentioning his closeness to Senior Captain Wilson and Company F's Captain Mitchell. The bond of friendship had been welded tight. In fact, Captain Dean would always remember Captain Wilson's homage: "I guess one of the biggest compliments Bill ever paid me, that I thought, he said 'You know, you and Bob Mitchell are a hell of a lot alike' he said. The only thing different is you're a whole lot more of a son of a bitch than Mitchell is. I think it was really sort of a compliment. Mitchell, if he had a fault it was he was too nice and

I never had that problem."[47] In Texas the smile or scowl accompanying tagging somebody a son-of-a-bitch is real relevant.

Though heretofore it's never been put to paper, there is, indeed, a sidebar story worthy of retelling. Sadly, at an all too early age Senior Captain Bill Wilson was handed a diagnosis and prognosis. His cancer was incurable. The news hit especially hard in two households: Jack and Janie Dean's at San Antonio and Bob and Gerry Mitchell's in Waco. There was but one want for the trio to do. Take a stag holiday. Then they could—one last time—reminisce about old days and good times, tell ribald jokes, play cards betting and bluffing, badmouth enemies, fish—and drink whiskey. And so it came to be, a *tres amigos* Gulf Coast outing. One night, measuring the amber current surging through bloodstreams or how much remained in the bottle is really moot. Finally everyone went to bed. In the wee morning hours Captains Dean and Mitchell were rudely awakened by the bleary-eyed Senior Captain Wilson. Sometime during the night Bill Wilson had come to terms with the Grim Reaper's unalterable design. Wiping sleep from their eyes Dean and Mitchell groggily set up on their economical motel beds. Half-awake they listened to Bill Wilson's last request as he handed them a tightly capped Mason Jar, one containing liquid with a yellowish hue. As he relinquished the glass container to his bosom buddies Bill Wilson's words were sincere and plainspoken: "Boys, I'll not live long enough to piss on Clint Peoples' grave." That could be accomplished by proxy if Jack Dean and Bob Mitchell truly valued his friendship. *¿Quién sabe?*

14

"They was laws to me"

A s the first month of 1985 faded into history, so, too, did Senior Captain Bill Wilson's thirty-two-year tenure as a Texas lawman. His last day on the job was to be the thirty-first and then it would be off to the fairways and putting-greens and, of course, traveling with his adoring wife Juanita, enjoying what time Fate had allotted, be it a few more days or a few more years. Particularly Captain Wilson wanted to express his appreciation to Captain Jack Dean and the other Texas Rangers. Thoughtfully, after pooling scant resources, their going-away gift to the Senior Captain was for everyday working folks, a stunner: "I wish I had the ability to express my sincere feeling toward you and the other friends who through your generosity made this old boy the happiest man alive. Never will I be able to convey to you my feelings. The pride I have every time I see, sit in, or ride on the golf cart is just a wonderful thing."[1]

The Texas Ranger's command position of Senior Captain was to be backfilled by the aforementioned Lefty Block, a Lone Star State native from Orange County just west of the Texas/Louisiana line, northeast of Port Arthur.[2] A DPS veteran, the former THP Patrolman had seen service with the Texas Rangers since 1 December 1967. Unlike Bill Wilson, Lefty Block was an avid and able horseman, breeding and showing Paints, as well as gainfully raising a World Champion roping horse and a Reserve World Champion halter stallion. Of the new command position at Austin, Senior Captain Lefty

Block would opine that it took him away from investigative work, having to be a behind-the-desk administrator and prepare budgets and habitually testify before the State Legislature's committees and subcommittees—such being the real upshot of his 1985 promotion.[3]

Quite interestingly, the following month the U.S. Court of Appeals, Fifth Circuit, returned its findings with regards to defendants convicted for the murder of Judge John Wood, and their wide-ranging assortment of grounds they claimed were reversible errors. The list was long. Looking back, with a palpable degree of irony is one of Charles Voyde Harrelson's contentions. He asserted that hypnosis had been improperly used against his trial interest with regards to the pre-trial questioning of two witnesses. Harrelson's appellate attorneys cited the H-E-B extortion case emanating from the grocery business at Carrizo Springs, the one wherein Texas Rangers had voluntarily submitted to hypnosis. With regards to that binding decision the Firth Circuit had determined that Texas Ranger Joaquin Jackson's hypnotic state had been "unduly suggestive," and was one of their justifications for reversing and remanding the H-E-B case for a new trial. Charles V. Harrelson, regardless whatever else, was a remarkably well-read and sharp-as-a-tack convict. Though now it cannot rise past a level of clean speculation, it's not patently unfair to suggest the appellant, too, internalized the genuine irony of trying to use the shortcomings in a previously cited Ranger/FBI investigation. Hoping to convert that court's decision into his status as a freshly released free-world walk-about was an inordinate stretch. Indeed, the paradox is rich. Alas, for a doing-life prisoner the black-robed adjudicators noted dissimilarities with hypnotic techniques, and found all of Charles Voyde Harrelson's arguments deficient of merit; assuredly in their minds there were no reversible errors.[4] The cell-door remained locked.

Even for Rangers most days blend into interesting but meticulous investigative assignments, not necessarily endless workweeks scored by blood and thunder excitement. In South Texas at Karnes City (Karnes County), about an hour drive north of Corpus Christi, 25 June 1985 would not be one of those pleasantly routine days.

Outside the summertime mercury was steadily rising. Inside Sheriff Robert R. "Bobby" Mutz's jailhouse the temperature was damn hot and dangerous. A prisoner, fashioning an eight inch shank out of the metal louvers from an air-conditioning vent, had made hapless prisoners of male jailer Eddie Garcia, and a female secretary/dispatcher, Daisy Villanueva (now a Karnes County JP).[5] The trio was locked behind the sealed steel door of a holding cell, one with a pay telephone on the back wall. Prisoners were entitled to phone calls on a scheduled basis. Unluckily, now, the only keys to the jail were in possession of the outlaw. At Karnes City on a bench-warrant from one of the TDC units, Roland Garcia was making his play—boneheaded— but nevertheless he had opted to shed himself of being confined in anyone's lockup. The thirty-eight-year-old convict was strapping and strong. In the prison recreation yard Roland Garcia was a dedicated lifter of heavy weights, and as a result the 225 lbs on his hulky frame was hardened and rippling muscles, not an ounce of blubbery fat. Truthfully, Roland Garcia was one tough *mal hombre*.[6]

Roland Garcia had a hard message for Sheriff Mutz. He wanted handcuffs for his hostages and a Karnes County patrol car placed at his disposal—his getaway ride. As with the horrible standoff with inmates at Huntsville during 1974, the good sheriff could not bend to demands for prisoners' freedom. That was in truth and fact a no-brainer from the outset. On the other hand, buying precious time palavering—well that was another matter altogether. Learning of the unfolding Karnes City drama, from the Company D headquarters office at San Antonio, Captain Jack Dean traced down Texas Ranger Jim Peters at Corpus Christi. Captain Dean's orders were not imprecise or complex. Ranger Peters was to "hop-tail it to Karnes City" evaluate the ongoing crisis and take the appropriate enforcement action.[7] That's what Rangers did and that's what Ranger Jim Peters had been told to do—right now! Rounding up Ranger Steve Black to accompany him, Jim Peters via a DPS helicopter ride was shortly onsite at the Karnes County jailhouse. When Ranger Peters asked for keys to the holding cell, Sheriff Mutz had to reply that the only keys were now in Roland Garcia's hands—there were no others. As would be expected that presented a perplexing problem. When quizzed regarding who had installed the cellblock hardware Sheriff Mutz advised that part of the interior construction had been formally contracted by an Alamo City firm, San Antonio Steel. Furthermore, Sheriff Mutz advised the specific number key to ask for would be #5509—that would be a workable key.[8] Interacting with Captain Dean and the Company D headquarters personnel and officialdom at San Antonio Steel, arrangements were made for Ranger Black to take another helicopter ride and retrieve a #5509. Everyone was pulling in tandem, the Rangers, the Sheriff, and the game corporate executives. Back at the jailhouse, now with a good key, Sheriff Bobby Mutz, disregarding the danger, warily slipped up to the holding cell door and quietly unlocked it, but did not open the steel door.

Cautiously taking peeks, Sheriff Mutz caught Roland Garcia off-guard and, on signal, lawmen rushed into the holding cell. Roland Garcia made a move at sticking Jailor Garcia with the shank, but soon backed off with the onslaught of plucky and resolute rescuers flooding the steel vault. The rush allowed the hostages to make good their escape—albeit on hands and knees during the pandemonium—though Garcia still had a bad attitude, clutching the wicked shank and daring lawmen to take another step. Though he could have punched Garcia full of holes with the sixteen rounds in his 9mm Beretta, Texas Ranger Jim Peters wanted a peaceful resolution, and so too did Sheriff Bobby Mutz. They were professional lawmen, through and through. Allowing Roland Garcia a short visit and talk with his daddy before pledging a safe return to Huntsville was not unsuitable. And so it was! After the hours-long drama, a relieved Sheriff Mutz declared it had been "the longest day in my [his] life."[9] No doubt Eddie and Daisy thought so, too! Subsequent to his trial at nearby Jourdanton in Atascosa County in the 218th District Court for the Aggravated Kidnapping case, a deflated and daft Roland Garcia caught six-bits to do—seventy-five years.[10] Even at the Company D office, Captain Jack Dean could oversee and support Texas Rangers in the field—he was right there when they needed him—not micromanaging when they didn't. Before long, another serious criminal matter, however, demanded more of Captain Jack Dean's investigatory and/or supervisory time—and it proved to be a newsmaker—a humdinger!

Inside San Antonio municipal limits another situation had the reading public, the elected and appointed city politicos, and policing personnel agog. A policeman had killed another policeman. Telling the story in the round would make—and has made—a most fascinating and spell-binding true-life drama, but is far too byzantine to interlace into Ranger Captain Jack Dean's biography, except for abbreviated remarks. The sad tale's underbelly is marked by allegations of misconduct and suspensions and vigilantism—perhaps cruel beatings and murderous vigilantism. And, too, the Texas tragedy is liberally salted with accusations of mismanagement by certain city administrators. Were one given over to crassness, the unseemly story has a tinge of soap-opera appeal but, truly, real death in real time is never benign—or entertaining.[11]

The snarly situation had long been festering. During the evening of 18 August 1986 gunfire put a period on part of the story. Inside a yellow compact car, five shots from a .357 Magnum rang out, loudly echoing through a northeast San Antonio neighborhood, before the car's sinking driver lost control skidding across a concrete curb and sidewalk. When the small auto finally came to a screeching and a hot rubber-stinking stop, the man behind the steering-wheel, an Alamo City cop, was leaking blood and "his torso [was] hanging from his yellow Chevette. . . ." He was sledgehammer dead—DRT. The addled passenger, another San Antonio policemen, the shooter—still holding the revolver—didn't flee but waited at the curb for the appearance of an EMS and SAPD Homicide Detectives.[12] It was, understatedly, a rather unusual situation, the uncorking melodrama not unnoticed by an after-the-fact newspaperman:

> What is unfolding in the nation's 10th largest city is a tale of guns and secret tape recorders, assassination plots and firebomb attacks, vigilantes and cops run amok, all seemingly too strange to be believed but too real to be fiction.[13]

The triggerman would assert it was a straightforward case of Self-Defense, a homicide yes, but a justifiable homicide according to elements of such an offense as printed in the Texas Penal Code. The driver had jerked out an autoloader, pointing it at the passenger's head, demanding he fork over his pistol—which he did. Rather shrewdly he was carrying a backup—the .357—in his waistband. What was he supposed to do? Something and be criminally charged or nothing and be whacked because he knew too much? There may have been big secrets, but it was no secret that earlier in the day he had met clandestinely with the Bexar County District Attorney, the city's Police Chief, and a Deputy Chief about the deceased plotting to assassinate them—one and all.[14] Did he not, too, hold hearsay intelligence about retributive murders—the vigilantism? Had not he been furnished a voice-activated tape-recorder to capture words and corral a gone-astray cop?[15] The untrustworthy gendarme was the first to go for a gun—wasn't he? Second place in a gunplay is last place!

Sliced, diced, or cubed was a political hot-potato: one city policeman offing a fellow officer. It should come as no surprise that a Special Prosecutor was appointed and equally there should be no shock value after learning that he smartly turned to Captain Jack Dean and the Company D Texas Rangers to lend that helping—but impartial—hand.[16] The FBI was there too. The whole affair—city police politics and suspected criminality had truly ginned a public confidence mess. There was, would be, however, an ambiguous and unanticipated legal hitch. The Bexar County Medical Examiner was of one dogged opinion, and it did not comport with the shooter's version as what was said to have taken place. There was, now, but one eyewitness inside the Chevette when spittin' distance bullets flew. He had his narrative—justification—to be sure. And therein and thereafter the killer's fat was in the fire, the post-Indictment conflagration fast burning toward a high-stakes jury trial.[17]

By any measure, it was an admittedly sordid story but Captain Jack Dean's function was not to judge, but to gather evidence and assimilate facts for the Special Prosecutor's courtroom presentation. Now Company D's Sergeant, Bruce Casteel, and Ranger Rudy

Rodriquez would help develop and ensure on-the-ground investigative truths. Theoretically the Texas Rangers didn't have a dog in the hunt—theoretically.

The legal sparring in reality was between battling court-qualified experts. The prosecution had one, the Bexar County Medical Examiner. The defense had one, a blood-spatter specialist from the Minnesota Forensic Science Laboratory.[18] In the first instance the San Antonio expert asserted that the deceased "could not have been holding the .45-caliber" and that gunshot residue found on the dead man's right palm was clear indication he was trying to fend off an attack.[19] Contrasting that testimony was the expert from Minnesota, who—due to blood spatter patterns and bullet wound placement—declared under oath that it was his learned opinion that the deceased could have definitely been "covering" the passenger "when he was shot."[20] The jury was, then, betwixt and between. They were ever trapped or lost in that legalized jungle where and when experts—physicians or psychiatrists or psychologists or ballisticians or DNA chemists or fingerprint technicians—disagree about proper protocols, procedures, and decisive opinions. How were plumbers, or firemen, or first-grade teachers or farmers or mechanics or retired oilfield roughnecks, those jurors tasked with rendering verdicts—to know the actual truth? The question may be fair. Nevertheless, the courtroom play is by rules. Moreover is the muddle when court-qualified experts cannot even agree amongst themselves.

In this instance the bar had not been met: Folks sitting in the jury box for nine days may or may not have had misgivings, but their ultimate decision was unanimous—the State of Texas had not overcome that obligatory standard, Beyond a Reasonable Doubt. The burden of proof was/is on the state, not the accused. Therefore, subsequent to but five hours of deliberation, the verdict was returned. The defendant was *Not Guilty*.[21]

Throughout the investigative and prosecutorial ordeal—and that's what it was—Texas Ranger Captain Dean had characteristically jumped hurdles and maneuvered around roadblocks quite deftly, commendable behavior brought to the attention of DPS Colonel Jim Adams by the Special Prosecutor:

> I also want to compliment the steady hand and patience of Captain Jack Dean. The relationship with the various agencies involved in this investigation, especially the San Antonio Police Department, was always strained and bordered on explosion. I don't believe the investigation would have progressed at the pace it did, nor with the tenuous inter-agency cooperation that resulted, without the calming and guiding presence of Captain Dean. The Captain was respected by all of the agencies, and managed to soothe ruffled feathers and inspire cooperation when it seemed impossible.[22]

Absent second-guessing, Captain Jack Dean unequivocally learned a valuable lesson—wherein the State of Texas had not sufficiently proved its case. Since the deceased was hanging half in and half out of the Chevette when it careened out of control, contamination on his hand could have resulted in nitrate particles from asphalt—not just telling gunshot residue. Quite important, too, the adamant Bexar County Medial Examiner had his theory but his conclusions—according to a contemporary newspaper account—required someone to "make a couple of assumptions" and the thoroughly attentive jurors didn't choose to *assume* anything.[23] Troubling as it might sometimes be, close may count for something in games of horseshoes and hand-grenades, but not in the courtroom.

Nineteen-hundred and eighty-seven would not be a good year for Rangers. The New Year kicked off with a kidnapping—a child abduction with monetary ransom the gateway to solution. Taken from her Horseshoe Bay home in the somewhat ritzy lakefront community northwest of Austin and southwest of Marble Falls, two-year-old Kara-Leigh Whitehead was the captive being held in lieu of a cash payment. Though his identity was unknown at the time, Brent Albert Beeler's telephone message to the prominent and prosperous William Whitehead was chillingly clear. If Kara-Leigh's father didn't fork over $30,000 in unmarked $20s his toddling daughter would be turned into "hamburger meat." In his mind Beeler had little to lose.

He was avoiding service of a Blue Warrant (a parole or probation violation—no bail) and his trip to the Big House was as predictable as his terrifying a baby was despicable.

Horseshoe Bay was territory within the Company F sphere and Captain Bob Mitchell and his Rangers were onsite in a jiffy. Like days long past during the Indian warfare era, for Rangers rescuing children their highest priority. Though Captain Dean was not present, due to joint Company D and Company F meetings and training, as well as his earlier days as Captain Mitchell's top non-com, he individually knew the Texas Rangers that were. In fact he had personally done background work on Stanley E. Guffey before his promotion to Texas Ranger and had acted as his supervisor while Stan had been stationed at Laredo. Ranger Guffey was now posted at Brady in McCulloch County, the pretty swathe of surveyed ground laying claim to the geographical center of the Lone Star State. Sergeant Joe Wilie (a future captain) and Texas Rangers Joe B. Davis, Jr., Fred Cummings, Johnny Waldrip, John Aycock and Jim Miller (a future captain) were on hand ready to act at a moment's notice. They, too, were working in conjunction with FBI Special Agent Sykes Houston and recent FBI Academy graduate Nancy Fernari. Serious business was at hand, a hardcore fact not escaping anyone's notice.

Hustling to prepare for the next telephone call, the Texas Rangers blueprinted their plan. Removing the backseat from a 1987 Lincoln Town Car, Rangers Aycock and Guffey would secret themselves beneath a covering blanket, prepared for the takedown when outlaw Beeler came to swap the baby for the booty. The call came! Mr. Whitehead was to drive the Lincoln down the street to a specific address, park in the driveway, leave the engine running, have the ransom money on the front seat, leave the headlights turned on and the driver's door standing wide-open. Then he was to right fast skedaddle not looking back. Beeler would then, he promised, come to the neighborhood, leave Kara-Leigh on the house's front yard, and quickly depart in his newfound luxury automobile with the briefcase on the front seat.

Mr. Whitehead did as instructed. Then Beeler came out of the house carrying Kara-Leigh wrapped in a table cloth in one hand, and a Smith & Wesson Model 29 .44 Magnum in the other. "Placing the helpless child in the front seat, he then shoved her across to the passenger's side, before the evil ne'er-do-well began shifting himself behind the steering-wheel. Seemingly the crook's plan was snapping in to place." Grabbing the briefcase of greenbacks, the desperate desperado pitched it onto what he thought was the big car's back bench-seat, certainly not Texas Ranger John Aycock's torso. At that point it turned Western. Texas Ranger Stan Guffey commandingly shouting 'State Police,' in perfect harmony with Beeler's spontaneously shrieked, 'Oh, Goddamn' while he clumsily unlimbered himself from the Lincoln. He discharged his six-shot wheel-gun twice as he lurched for safety and flight. His first shot missed. Unfortunately his second didn't: Texas Ranger Stan Guffey suffered a bullet to the forehead. "In those horrifying split-seconds, Texas Ranger John Aycock, sustaining a presence of mind, using his body as Kara-Leigh's shield, unleashed hellfire with his handgun, firing until Brent Albert Beeler went down DRT. . . ." Thankfully Kara-Leigh had been saved, but it had been a trade—Texas Ranger Guffey's life for hers. Too, after the shootout, behind the residence in a boathouse, investigators found the lifeless and sexually assaulted and tortured body of Denise Johnson, hands and ankles tightly restrained by silver duct-tape. Her sudden disappearance was no longer an out-and-out mystery. Kara-Leigh's missing nanny had not willfully abandoned her caretaking role—but had been burnt with cigarettes and foully murdered by an utterly remorseless thug.[24]

Aside from the natural nauseousness always accompanying such misfortunate news, Captain Jack Dean was pulled into—willingly—part of the psychological aftermath of the tragedy. As would any good leader, Captain Bob Mitchell was extraordinarily distressed by Ranger Stan Guffey's untimely demise. Of course, the rank and file Texas Rangers and DPS personnel throughout the state were deeply saddened, too, but Bob Mitchell had held the decision-making reins when the stagecoach went over the cliff. During private conversations with his good friend Jack Dean, Bob Mitchell, continually troubled, went through the understandable process of second guessing and what ifs. Confiding his innermost thoughts about the calamity with Dean brought Mitchell an emotional safety-valve of sorts—but, truthfully, the gunfire claiming Stan's life echoed though Bob's psyche until he, too, years later found his eternal peace.

One would have thought Captain Jack Dean's workplace in southeastern San Antonio's DPS complex at 6502 South New Braunfels Avenue would have been safe space. Such was not to be. On Sunday, the third day of May 1987, Captain Dean and other Texas Rangers were enjoying a carefree afternoon socializing at the renowned Witte Museum. A retired Texas Rangers reunion was happening. In but a split-second heartbeat a heartbreak had been triggered at the DPS Office. Understandably Captain Dean and Ranger Rudy Rodriguez forewent fun and rushed to the scene. What they found upon arrival was truly bizarre. Captain Jack Dean off-the-cuff told an onsite newspaperman the truth: "We've never had. . . . bodies on the front door. . . . This is a little different kicker."[25] And it was!

A potential crucial witness in a Cameron County public corruption case, Carlos Barrios, and his wife Elizabeth, had been courteously granted entry at the DPS Office through a backdoor. Mr. Barrios appeared to be highly agitated—somewhat paranoid it seemed—and was desperately trying to locate Ranger Rudy Rodriguez, ostensibly to pass along information regarding illicit narcotics smuggling and distribution. Texas Ranger Rodriguez was the lead investigator into the suspected wrongdoings at Brownsville's city hall, wherein seven indictments had already been returned. And, an after the fact analysis by Captain Dean confirmed: "the couple appeared nervous and jumpy."[26] The jumpiness was short-lived as was the couple from Brownsville.

Carlos Barrios slipped a mental gear, grasped his wife in a headlock, then quickly grabbed a .357 Magnum revolver from a nearby desktop, where it and other belt-gear had been laid while the DPS Trooper was completing weekly paperwork. For a very short while the fanatical Carlos alternately pointed the six-shooter first at the

Trooper and then at his wife. Suddenly a loud gunshot reverberated throughout the building. Elizabeth unwillingly accepted a bullet wound to the upper abdomen, dropping her to the floor. The twist of Fate proved weird. Was it accidental or was it intentional? During the life and death struggle the same bullet that had punched into his wife had also channeled its way through the shooter's shoulder, irreparably severing an artery. Conducting police business visiting at the DPS Office was Bexar County Precinct 4 Reserve Deputy Constable Alexcie Auzenne III, who managed to get off a round into Barrios's leg before Carlos hit the linoleum and bled to death.[27] Trooper James "Jim" Denman, now a retired Texas Ranger Lieutenant, who had been in the DPS Communications Center, rushed to, not away from the sound of gunfire. He made it before Elizabeth gasped for—and exhaled her very last breath. A pair of thoroughly dead bodies inside a DPS Squad Room was, indeed, an anomaly![28]

Aside from the personal tragedy for loved ones—any deaths being heartrending—Carlos Barrios's untimely demise was thought to perhaps fatally hamstring the Lower Rio Grande Valley public corruption investigation then underway. Captain Jack Dean said as much: "You lose a key witness and you're in trouble."[29] The dedicated Special Prosecutor assigned to the corruption case, Sharon McRae, was, too, manifestly flabbergasted: "They [the Barrios couple] were very important. . . . This is one of the oddest things I've ever seen in my lifetime. . . . I'm still trying to figure out if there is a way of getting around not having these folks anymore."[30] Regrettably Texas Ranger Rudy Rodriguez was forced to envisage a hardcore truth about the criminal intelligence closely held by Carlos and Elizabeth Barrios: "That information was dead when they died."[31] In speaking of DPS detections in public corruption cases Ranger Rodriguez quipped: "We collect the dirty laundry, but the DA is the detergent."[32]

Someone in real need of soap-suds was Janie Dean. There were diapers on her laundry line. She was now a grandmother, Kelly Lenea having given birth to a precious son, Dennis Cody on 19 November 1988. As it happens with most families, troubles of one sort or another seem to sidetrack the best laid plans of mice, men—and many marriages. With regards to baby Dennis Cody there is good history. Doing what needed doing at the time, Jack and Janie Dean formally and legally adopted Dennis Cody—officially giving him the family surname. And from that auspicious day forward Jack and Janie Dean have a daughter, Kelly Lenea, and two sons, Kyle Lynn and Dennis Cody.

Asserting that Captain Jack Dean was circulating in prominent company—which was serving the Texas Rangers admirably—can again be evinced by his special invitation to participate in tours of the United States Air Force Academy at Colorado Springs, Colorado, and from there the Nellis Air Force Bombing & Gunnery Range northwest of Las Vegas, Nevada. At the latter facility Captain Dean was particularly and reciprocally pleased with meeting Joseph W. Ashy, Major General and Commander of the USAF Tactical Fighter Weapons Center. General Ashy was favorably impressed with Captain Dean, writing that perhaps they could get together again "sometime in the future."[33]

Compressing a decade's worth of complimentary letters and commendations into a solitary paragraph is much more efficient and readable than interspersing them, one by one, within this text as they present chronologically. There are many. There is, then, herein a short sampling: An honorary membership at Lackland Air Force Base's Officers' Mess, courtesy Major General Spence M. Armstrong; Noted Houston attorney Vic Pecorino pledged to represent Captain Dean "if you or your men ever need legal assistance." A laudatory letter from Charlie Strauss, Assistant District Attorney, Special Crimes Section, Bexar County District Attorney's Office, regarding an investigation that led to the "discovery of a body near Smithville [in Bastrop County]; Former DPS Commissioner Ruben R. Cardenas thought Captain Dean should know: "I sincerely feel that you have been a role model for what anyone can expect of a Texas Ranger." The United States Attorney for the Eastern District of Texas invited Captain Dean to participate in the Voter Fraud Task Force; Colonel Carl B. Denisio, USAF, personally invited Captain Dean to not only attend the Air Force's Chiefs of Security multi-day meeting and, also, as a guest at the closing banquet; USSS SAC J. Barney Boyett personally thanked

Captain Dean for inviting him to a Company D meeting at the YO Ranch, declaring that he had "never been with a better group of men in or out of law enforcement." United States Senator Phil Gramm thanked Captain Dean for investigating and making a recommendation of a candidate to be appointed as United States Attorney for the Southern District of Texas; A wonderful thank you note for a wonderful visit to Captain Dean from J.B. Davis, Major General, USAF, DCS, Operations and Intelligence Headquarters, Pacific Air Forces; as well as deferential messages from General Andrew P. Iosue, USAF, Commander Air Training Command; Lieutenant General Robert C. Oaks, USAF Commander, Randolph Air Force Base, and Brigadier General Edward N. Giddings, USAF, and that's not factoring into the mix numerous state politicians such as Bob Bullock, Comptroller of Public Accounts, high-profile state politico Rick Perry (future governor and presidential candidate), and the then sitting Governor of Texas, Mark White. The catalog is thick—the examples herein but representative. There were good times—but, too, there were bad times.

Although it certainly couldn't be registered a total surprise, the news still deeply saddened Captain Jack Dean. The Texas Rangers' previous Senior Captain's bout with cancer had ended. On New Years Day 1990, Bill Wilson slipped to the other side at Austin. Characterized as a firm disciplinarian and tougher than a barrel of nails when need be, Bill Wilson's work ethics were widely known throughout the Texas Rangers service: eight hours work for eight hours pay, no long hair on the collar and no beards and/or mustaches. There was an appearance—the Ranger look—to maintain and years of tradition to uphold. The lean and lanky Wilson was a caretaker of that tradition. Nurturing same, even in death Bill Wilson's family personally made known that in lieu of flowers at the funeral, it was his fondest desire that a "memorial contribution" be made to the Texas Ranger Foundation at Waco. Understandably Jack and Janie Dean attended the funeral services in the Cook-Walden Chapel at Austin that fifth day of January 1990.[34]

Several months later, with a twist of melancholic irony in light of Bill Wilson's fondness for golf, Captain Jack Dean's donation to the

Bentwater Celebrity Golf Classic resulted in the personal thank you letter from Coach Jack Pardee, Houston Oilers.[35] Captain Jack Dean, as history will bear witness, was more than practiced at circulating with popular entertainment and sports celebrities—as well as the glad-handing politicos and the country's cadre of high-ranking military leaders. Image wise, Rangers of Jack Dean's era had taken on a whole new persona.

Later that same year another heartrending happening draped over the Dean household. Although she was an adult, Captain Bob Mitchell's middle child, Karen, unexpectedly passed away as result of a brain hemorrhage during 1990. Jack and Janie and toddler Cody were quickly at Bob and Gerry Mitchells' side, brokenhearted and showing the utmost respect for their very close but grieving friends. Jack Dean particularly has a poignant moment indelibly etched into his mind. Though Bob Mitchell was tough enough to "whoop two big men," the untimely death of his beloved Karen knocked him to his knees—figuratively. Literally, however, he picked up young Cody, carrying him about in his arms, all the while lovingly and tenderly caressing him. Even after an inordinate passing of time Bob Mitchell refused to relinquish the mystified child as he aimlessly wandered about, deep in despair, transfixed with thoughts of Karen's childhood. Jack Dean was emotionally touched—forevermore.[36]

Another shocking heartbreak tapped Captain Jack Dean; a fellow Texas badge-wearer went under. Ben P. "Doc" Murray, sixty-eight, had served the citizens of Dimmit County as Sheriff since his first election bid in November of 1972. Near twenty years later Doc Murray was still in office—a highly respected and thoroughly competent borderland lawman—doing what he loved to do—serve the people of his agriculturally diverse and wildlife brimming county.[37] Tragedy knocked at Sheriff Murray's residential backdoor on 6 January 1991, early in the morning—around 6:00 a.m. A few minutes later, after the backdoor had slammed shut, Doc was dead on the floor, a sharpened butcher-knife sticking out of his chest and a .45 caliber bullet wound to his forehead.[38] A friend, Maria Alma Cavzos, discovered the sheriff's body and alerted authorities.[39]

Not at all unexpectedly the distress call for Texas Ranger assistance was immediate. Shortly two of Captain Jack Dean's Company D men were expeditiously onsite, Ranger Doyle Holdridge stationed at Laredo in Webb County and Ranger Coy Smith assigned to Uvalde in Uvalde County. The crime scene was gruesome and horribly bloody, but even preliminary evidentiary sign indicated that Sheriff Murray had put up one helluva of a fight before breathing his last.[40]

The pair of investigating Texas Rangers astutely and quickly reconstructed the crime scene. For a brief newspaper account Ranger Doyle Holdridge was quoted, reporting, "that Murray apparently answered a knock at his back door shortly after returning home from work early Sunday. An altercation immediately broke out . . . They fought from the back door of the house, through the back bedroom through the kitchen, the dining room, into the living room. . . . The sheriff's body was found by the front door."[41] What wasn't said to the inquiring newshound was that inside the house, on the floor, was a piece of Sheriff Murray's ear.[42] Adept investigators routinely pocketed a clue, keeping it from public knowledge. Its handiness might prove valuable later—corroborating a confession or shooting down a mentally disturbed person's false one. Texas Rangers Holdridge and Smith were topnotch. Naturally the onsite Texas Rangers kept Company D headquarters at San Antonio updated via periodic telephone reports, particularly Lieutenant C.J. Havrda (later Senior Captain), who in turn made sure Captain Dean was in the loop—as he, too, was fending the press inquiries.[43] Lieutenant Havrda as would be expected administratively leaned forward in the foxhole, making sure a DPS crime lab team was dispatched to Dimmit County.[44] Though Captain Dean knew and cherished his friendship with Doc Murray, he remained at the Alamo City and dutifully continued fielding probes from ravenous news media outlets, such as the *Del Rio News Herald*: "Captain Jack Dean of the Texas Rangers in San Antonio said there was evidence that shots had been fired in the house. . . . Two Texas Rangers [Holdridge and Smith] who were sent to investigate told Dean there had been a struggle in the house. Dean said no motive had [yet] been established for the slaying. . . . Apparently there was lots of blood and some holes knocked in the walls. Dean said the body was being taken to San Antonio for an autopsy."[45] There was—in a practical investigative sense—no need for Captain Jack Dean to drop every-thing and frantically race to Carrizo Springs. With Texas Rangers Doyle Holdridge and Coy Smith taking the lead, Captain Dean knew without doubt that the Capital Murder case was in more than capa-ble hands—and sooner or later an arrest was sure to come.[46]

Captain Dean's confidence had not been misguided. Pulling out all the stops, with the DPS crime lab team gathering physical evi-dence, and Ranger Smith putting into play the use of nosey track-ing Bloodhounds, Ranger Holdridge, now joined by Ranger Johnny Allen from Del Rio, conducted beneficial interviews pointing in the right direction. Subsequently an accomplished jailhouse heart-to-heart clinched-off the coffin nails—the Rangers justifiably hypoth-esized. Fearing the worst—which was smart—Alberto Gonzales, twenty-four, had let his milk down, admitting he was there at the time Murray was murdered. Then Alberto fingered the remorseless butcher-knife wielder and triggerman. The main mean actor was a notoriously well-known Dimmit County native: Jose Garcia Briseno, thirty-three, a parolee with several sojourns at Huntsville inserted into his packed prison portfolio; Burglary of a Building, Burglary of a Vehicle, Forgery, and a twenty-five-year sentence for Aggravated Assault. He had, this time around, been dishonestly residing in the free-world for about a year, doing dope and duping parole officers.[47] As far as an understandable MO for the murder, logically it seemed robbery and revenge seemed to be handmaidens.

With masterful attention to detail, Rangers Holdridge and Smith—with the help of DPS scientific experts and other border-land lawmen—had wrapped up an airtight criminal case against Briseno and Gonzales. "A sample of blood taken from the sheriff's carpet matched applicant's [Briseno] blood, and a sample of blood taken from applicant's clothing matched the sheriff's blood."[48] The Texas Rangers and the good citizens of Dimmit County and through-out South Texas had to but wait for docket call of the 293rd Judicial

District Court—justice would be done. There is, however, an exciting sidebar story.

Jose Garcia Briseno, Ricardo Basaldua, and Roy Garcia engineered a jailbreak, stabbed a correctional officer with a shank, stole the fellow's truck and fled, later abandoning the getaway vehicle "behind a Wal-Mart Store in a different town."[49] Afoot the wretched outlaws hid in the South Texas *brasada* for three miserable days and nights. Roy Garcia, though he didn't know it at the time, was one lucky fellow. While lying low in the brush he had two epileptic seizures. Jose Garcia Briseno, thinking such would be their undoing, was about to kill him and be done with it—until Ricardo Basaldua stepped in and saved his bacon. Shortly, relatively speaking, the escapees were surrounded and rounded up—inmates again![50] Briseno's good luck, if he ever had any—had gone south. During time on the lam he had retrieved Doc Murray's Colt 1911, .45, the one he had killed the sheriff with and later buried. Allowing himself such was boneheaded! The ballistic match was easy and irrefutable.

The trial jury was convinced of Jose Garcia Briseno's guilt Beyond a Reasonable Doubt and sentenced him to death.[51] There the matter did not end. Through the mandated appellate processes Jose Garcia Briseno's guilt or innocence was not the overriding issue—his conviction was not overturned—the evidence was rock solid and legally admissible. However, due to issues of mental competency—the legal definition of retardation—the punishment phase of his trial was remanded for a second look.[52] For legal scholars in ivory towers it was, truthfully, problematic. Although that troubling chronological jump is necessary, the original sentence of death was commuted to Life Without Parole during 2013—twenty-two years after murdering the sheriff. Jose Garcia Briseno's conniving fall-partner, Alberto Gonzales, had caught a life sentence, too. Although Captain Jack Dean was exceptionally proud of the outstanding work exhibited by his Company D Texas Rangers, namely in this case Doyle Holdridge and Coy Smith, the shocking death of Doc Murray haunts him to this day.[53]

Sadly the violent death of a THP Patrolman again drove home for Captain Jack Dean the perilous route he and Kyle had taken to earn and deposit their DPS paychecks. Forty-three-year-old Bill Davidson, a THP Patrolman was working south coastal Jackson County as a one-man unit that fourteenth day of April 1992. Davidson was no rookie with DPS, but a veteran with nineteen years' service and eight commendations to his credit. One, was even the prestigious Director's Award "for his work in a 1985 hostage situation. He negotiated the release of a young gunman's grandmother and grabbed the 16-year-old as he emerged from the house with a shotgun."[54] Now, five miles southwest of Edna, the county seat, on U.S. Hwy 59, THP Patrolman Bill Davidson initiated a traffic stop on a 1986 GMC Jimmy operating with a broken headlight. Alas, somewhat earlier the vehicle had been stolen at Port Lavaca. Behind the steering-wheel was Ronald Ray Howard, an eighteen-year-old black male, sweating, and thoroughly committed to avoiding apprehension for a felony. Though Ronald Ray Howard had dropped out of school after but seven years, and had cocaine and marijuana in his system, he didn't drop the 9mm pistol he was cradling as THP Patrolman Davidson walked toward the driver's side of the stolen GMC and queried: "How you doing?" There is, if truth be told, not an absolutely sound indemnity for approaching a violator's vehicle during a traffic stop—not a conventional traffic stop. Caution is the watchword to be sure, but the vast majority of violator contacts cannot—and should not—be achieved with an officer's pistol pointed at the offender: Not for rolling through a stop sign or pegging past the posted speed limit—or a busted headlight. In this particular instance on the lonesome highway at night Bill Davidson was nakedly exposed and, frankly, unlucky. Ronald Ray Howard's snap-shot put a round into the THP Patrolman's neck—knocking him to the pavement. There he lingered unable to move, leaking blood, but maintaining a semi-conscious state of mind. When found he was able to tell witnesses he had been wounded by a "lone black male."[55]

Highway 59 angled toward Victoria and soon after gunning down THP Patrolman Davidson, the car chase began. Winding through Victoria streets at breakneck speed, officers in pursuit, was more than Ronald Ray Howard could handle with precision: He lost control of the Jimmy and crashed into a house. Thereafter the apprehension—though dangerous—was accomplished. Unfortunately for Ronald Ray Howard—some might say idiotically—he was yet feverishly clutching the 9mm autoloader.[56]

Whether or not Bill Davidson learned of Howard's arrest before he expired three days after the incident at the Victoria hospital is somewhat nebulous. For the prosecutor the evidence was overwhelming, surefire subsequent to damning testimony of the ballistician tying the retrieved murder bullet and spent shell casing to Howard's 9mm handgun. Adding to his court-appointed attorney's headache, Howard didn't deny, but had confessed during taped interviews. He, too, coughed up other acknowledgments: "Howard talked about his life in Houston's gritty inner-city dodging bullets, stealing cars and selling drugs. He also talked about the six children he believes he fathered by age 18 and about his love for gangsta rap music." And he moreover talked about policemen: "They was laws to me. They weren't people. They was laws."[57]

At Austin on a Change of Venue, the eight-man, four-woman, jury took but forty minutes to select a foreman, vote, and return their verdict: *Guilty*.[58] During the punishment phase, rather unfathomably, Ronald Ray Howard, or perhaps even more precisely his assiduous lawyer at trial, "blamed rap music for inciting him to kill the trooper."[59] Defense attorney Allen Tanner posited "his client should not die for the crime because he had a violent childhood in Houston's inner-city that included hours of listening to hard-core anti-cop music known as 'gangsta rap.'"[60] Abruptly the ingenious tactic caught national press attention. There was no little controversy about a brash assertion that the music and entertainment industries could be contributors to the triggering of deathly violence. In this instance and, in Texas, it would be Jackson County District Attorney Bobby Bell winning the courtroom contests. Apparently the appellate court judges reviewing Howard's Capital Murder conviction and death sentence were stone-cold deaf to the defendant's lawyering singsong defense strategy. The Devil made me do it did not sell well. Ronald Ray Howard was lawfully executed after placidly declining his last meal and forlornly droning his own dirge: "To the victim's family, I hope it helps a little. I do not know how, but I hope it helps. . . ."[61]

Captain Jack Dean needed some help. An off-duty—if there ever was such a thing—hunting outing was underway. Captain Dean was accompanied by several law-enforcing comrades, including his son Kyle. Riding in a crew-cab pickup, the ensemble was south of San Antonio, traversing Atascosa County on Highway 16 below the county seat, Jourdanton. Taking a quick but necessary roadside break, one of the travelers noted that Captain Dean's sleeping-bag was not where it was supposed to be, tightly packed with the rest of the duffle in the truck's bed. Most certainly it really did not take a Ranger to perform a crime scene investigation—obviously somewhere along the way the sleeping-bag had blown out of the vehicle. A quick call to Ranger Joe Peters at Jourdanton was initiated—could he check the highway headed south? They would search heading north—hopefully one of them finding the missing item before they met. Luckily, Ranger Joe Peters found the prize—in the bar-ditch not too far south of town. No doubt pleased at finding Captain Jack Dean's property, Joe Peters readied his wit. A few minutes later, while handing over Jack Dean's sleeping-bag he teased: "Captain I got it; the only thing missing is the teddy bear." The hunters resumed their fun-filled and carefree journey. Ranger Rudy Rodriguez updated the story. During a subsequent South Texas hunting trip, Captain Dean stopped by Jourdanton for a quick hello to Ranger Peters—who had sharpened his cleverness. He presented Captain Dean with a stuffed bedtime teddy bear, just to make up for the one he had "lost."[62] Sweet dreams Jack Dean!

Even as a pending retirement was on Captain Dean's horizon he wasn't asleep on the job. The 1992 Spring Break at South Padre Island, normally wild and crazy fun for hordes of college students flocking to the sandy beaches and warm Gulf Coast waters, this particular year figuratively washed tragedy ashore. The crime was—at least for awhile—Attempted Murder but according to the city's Police Chief, Edward D. Sanders: "I believe the charge will be changed to murder very shortly, as the victim has steadily gotten worse and is now on life support." Be that as it may, Captain Jack Dean overseeing the criminal investigative activities of Texas Rangers Bob Steele and Rudy Rodriguez, aided by DPS MVT Agent Henry Brume, helped identify the prime suspect. The search at San Antonio was intensive but, thanks to the DPS investigators network of cooperative citizens and CIs, the above cited lawmen located their target, making a custodial arrest and earning written adulation from Chief Sanders.[63]

There was other good news for Jack and Janie Dean that June of 1992. Kyle Dean's expended effort studying and satisfactorily sitting before the Oral Review Board had paid its big dividend. He was now a Texas Ranger—not supervised by his dad—but assigned to Company B, posted at Denton in Denton County. The twist of irony is real. Denton County was Captain Jack Dean's birthplace. And just like his Texas Ranger daddy before him, early on in his investigative career Texas Ranger Kyle Dean, too, caught a double murder.

The 1993 homicides were shocking and brutal. Shari Catherine "Cari" Crews, seventeen, had been found nude, her hands tied behind her back with her bra—she had been killed by a horrendous shotgun blast to the back of her head. The exceptionally gifted high-school girl was a National Honor Society student and, among other things, a talented classical pianist. An autopsy revealed DNA evidence orally, anally, and vaginally. At the time her body was discovered in Clear Creek her companion and classmate teenage Jesus Gilberto Garza was missing—and unaccounted for. Shortly, though, his lifeless body was found submerged in the nearby creek. He, too, had suffered a ghastly shotgunning, the cold-steel muzzle placed under his chin before the trigger was pulled. For a time, the double killing registered as an awful whodunit.

Naturally working these homicides was a full-court press. Kyle Dean, like Jack, is dead-set on conveying a truth: Most big-time investigations are multi-agency affairs—cooperation is crucial. The Capital Murder and Aggravated Sexual Assault of Cari Crews is a gold-plated example of teamwork. Collaboratively, possible suspects were identified, one being hospitalized with a nasty foot wound—an injury inflicted by a shotgun. Texas Ranger Kyle Dean's previous experience dealing with convicts and conmen netted results. He

had developed an interrogative knack. Placing two previously convicted felons and convicts at the crime scene did not prove to be a
real challenge for Ranger Kyle Dean and his thoroughly committed
investigating colleagues. Dissecting what had actually taken place,
well, that was a little more problematic. Both yahoos were claiming the other was actually good for the actual sexual assaulting and
coldblooded killings, honor among outlaws being but make-be-
lieve. There is none at the Big House or in the real world. Notably,
James Lee Clark, twenty-five, claimed—with a straight face—that
his fall-partner, James Richard Brown, twenty-one, before the murders had forced him at the point of a shotgun to engage in sexual
acts with the crying and horror-struck female victim. Ranger Kyle
Dean parried: "Were you aroused?" Incredulously James Lee Clark
lied assuring Ranger Dean that he was not—certainly not with a
shotgun shoved in his face. Then, Kyle Dean dropped the bombshell:
If James Lee Clark wasn't sexually stimulated why and how did the
medical examiner manage to collect his unique and identifiable DNA
from bodily orifices of Cari Crews? Strange indeed. For Texas Ranger
Dean the reply of, "I don't know," didn't cut it. At the time, Ranger
Kyle Dean definitely had never before investigated or heard of an
offense involving an Immaculate Erection. Apparently, the trial jury
and appellate courts hadn't either! James Lee Clark was convicted
and in due time would be strapped on the Death House gurney for
his last goodbye.[64] After skipping his last meal the potent solution
was lawfully injected into James Lee Clark's bloodstream. Before losing consciousness, James Lee Clark turned his head and, evidently,
was somewhat surprised to see witnesses gathered behind the glass
observation window. Apparently at a loss for words, James Lee Clark
simply uttered "Howdy" and then he passed to the other side—the
state's death sentence had been affirmed.[65]

Although Captain Jack Dean's late September 1993 goodbye
to the Texas Rangers would not near register as dramatic as James
Lee Clark's departure at Huntsville from the land of the living, he
would be saying "Howdy" to a brand new job—a rather tasty political
plum—one doubling his DPS salary.[66]

15

"I'll buy you a beer"

J ust ahead of Jack Dean's announced retirement date, U.S. Congressman Frank Tejeda presented a glowing tribute to the Captain as reflected in the *Congressional Record*, 103rd Congress, First Session, House of Representatives, which in part said:

Mr. Speaker, the Texas Rangers enjoy a long and distinguished history as one of this Nation's most formidable law enforcement agencies. Their heroism and bravery in the face of seemingly insurmountable odds is legendary. . . . It is with great honor that I pay tribute today to a modern Texas Ranger. Capt. Jack Dean, who is retiring after serving more than 30 years as a Texas lawman. . . . Admired by his colleagues, he has earned the respect of people of diverse backgrounds and interests. Integrity and honor remain his watchwords. . . . He cut his teeth in the 1960s as a Texas State Trooper. . . . Jack Dean's tenure in law enforcement took him literally to the four corners of the State of Texas. . . . On September 24, 1993, the Texas Rangers will honor Capt. Jack Dean on his retirement, a bittersweet moment for him and the Texas law enforcement community. . . .

Throughout the years, his dedication and skill earned him more than 30 commendations for meritorious performance. In more straightforward terms, Jack Dean saved lives, fought corruption, and defended public safety. . . . Captain Dean pursued a path of professional growth that serves as an example to all. He has undertaken more than 2,000 hours of training at various institutions, including the Federal Bureau of Investigation Academy's courses on special weapons and terrorism. What he learned, he shared with others as an instructor at the Texas Department of Public Safety Academy and other law enforcement organizations. Dean left his mark on the Texas Department of Public Safety, serving on committees overseeing the department's swat [*sic:* S.W.A.T] teams and revising ranger recordkeeping and statistical reporting. He took an active role in the local community with service on the San Antonio Crime Commission and the San Antonio Police Academy Building Committee. . . . Jack Dean provided the demanding qualities expected of a Texas Ranger, and his dedication to law enforcement, and to the people he served so well, will not soon be forgotten.[1]

Assuredly Jack Dean would not be forgotten. Within political circles his name was well-known. Regarding law enforcing issues, from time to time, two political appointments—patronage positions—are up for grabs. At the sole discretion of the U.S. President—and his advisors in the various states and territories—the vacancies are filled. That is, after successfully enduring confirmation proceedings by the U.S. Senate. There are at present ninety-four Federal Judicial Districts. Each has a presidentially appointed United States Marshal and a United States Attorney. Technically both serve at the U.S. President's pleasure. On the other hand, the Deputy United States Marshals and the Assistant United States Attorneys are classified as career positions with certain guaranteed civil protections screening them from political shuffling and/or dismissals—at least without demonstrable cause and mandated hearings. Practically speaking, then, when the political party at the top of the national ticket changes, so too do the United States Attorneys and United States Marshals, though their federally paid subordinates hold onto their jobs, benefits, and retirement plans.[2]

Historically the United States Marshals Service traces it beginnings to the Federal Judiciary Act of September 24, 1789, a birthing even before there was a fledgling Republic of Texas or a Texas Ranger.[3] The sizable Lone Star State is subdivided into four federal

Judicial Districts, Northern, Southern, Eastern, and Western, the latter coming to fruition through federal legislation on 21 February 1857. That same history reveals that just because one had fruitfully landed the politically appointed position, the bona fide potential for trouble is never on a holiday. One of Jack Dean's predecessors, Western District U.S. Marshal Harrington Lee "Hal" Gosling, had gone under subsequent to a blistering gunplay while transporting prisoners to court aboard an International and Great Northern train as it neared the depot at the festive German community of New Braunfels in Comal County.[4] Yet later, Western District Deputy U.S. Marshal George Wise and Calixto Garcia, a Special Deputy, were murdered, stabbed, on the same day near the School House Plaza at Laredo by fugitive Pancho Flores aka Francisco Flores. The known smuggler wetted his back in the Río Bravo, emerging in Mexico but lost to history.[5] Simply trading badges was no warranty from harm. Jack Dean, though, was a career lawman. Subsequent to his retirement from DPS, Jack O. Dean was appointed and confirmed as the United States Marshal for the Western District of Texas, filling the spot on the roster vacated by William J. Jonas, Jr.[6]

The Western District of Texas is undeniably gigantic, a vast real-estate reality reiterated by Jack Dean's comment: "it was about 460–70 miles across. It went from Brenham [Washington County] to El Paso [El Paso County] to Del Rio [Val Verde County]. I think it was the fourth or fifth biggest in the Nation."[7] Though unsaid, the Western District of Texas was also home to such municipalities as Austin, Waco, Midland/Odessa, El Paso, and the whopping Big Bend region of far West Texas, as well as all of metropolitan San Antonio and its environs. The Western District of Texas was a land mass of sixty-eight counties, some heavily populated, some thinly populated: all deserving attention, none warranting neglect.[8]

Herein at this point it's but germane to submit a gentle reminder highlighted in the Preface of the text in hand. From the historical perspective, in that broad sweep of time touching three centuries there have been but five individuals coming from the Texas Ranger officers' corps going on to serve as a United States Marshal. Jack

O. Dean is one, the only one registering such law-enforcing service from the twentieth and into the twenty-first century and until this journalistic undertaking, the only one lacking a full-scale biography. With regards to Rangers being commissioned or cross-deputized as Deputy USMs, there were/are many.[9]

Jack Dean's timing had been auspicious with regards to Texas Rangers transitioning into a more enlightened age; his selection as U.S. Marshal for the Western District corresponded with an updated change in managerial philosophy at the Washington headquarters. The former Chief of Police at Tampa, Florida, had been appointed as the USMS Director. Like Jack Dean, the new headman had banked years of meaningful law-enforcing service before becoming a federal employee. Prior to policing service at Tampa—which was relatively short—Eduardo Gonzalez had earned college credentials at Florida International University and after twenty-one years with the Miami-Dade PD he had left his Deputy Director position to assume command at Tampa. However, he all so soon tendered his resignation to assume the federal directorship. Taking into account the sizable budget and personnel numbers ($333 million and 3,500), Director Gonzalez had stepped up a notch—but he was a forward thinker. In his opinion U.S. Marshals in the field should be nominated and appointed "based on professional experience rather than purely for political reasons. . . . The proposal to make Marshal appointments based on career law enforcement experience alarmed [some of] the sitting U.S. Marshals, who benefitted from the current confirmation process. This led to inevitable conflict."[10] With a Presidential appointment tucked in their pockets U.S. Marshals named to the various Judicial Districts were somewhat of a federal dichotomy: They were wholly dependent on Washington for budgetary and logistical and personnel levels—but other than that, did damn well what they pleased—within the framework of legality, or course. Jack Dean, having both professional firepower and political horsepower, once again, had been juxtaposed just right!

U.S. Marshal Dean's reputation was solid. Director Eduardo Gonzalez undertook to make sure Jack could feel comfortable and most free to contact and consult with him personally if he could ever "be of assistance."[11] U.S. Marshal Dean appreciated the courtesy, internally noting that the gentlemanly gesture was good management style, something he nurtured—or tried to—in professional and personal interplays with his own subordinate Deputy U.S. Marshals. This philosophy was typified by his answer to a background and security investigation questionnaire: "I believe that if you show employees that you have confidence in them they will return your confidence with accomplishments. I have used this management style throughout my career as a supervisor and have seen new Rangers develop into outstanding investigators."[12]

Though certainly not the first or last, Jack Dean's appointment was somewhat of an anomaly. Circumstance he was not blind to—but he was most pleased to accept the exalted post anyway: "Yes, I was a Clinton appointee even though they read in the paper that they had checked my voting record and I was a registered Republican." Not surprisingly Jack Dean's key sponsors Congressman Frank Tejeda and U.S. Senator Robert "Bob" Krueger caught some "flak" from Democrats, but nevertheless Jack's sterling reputation and their wheeling and dealing carried the day for Dean.[13] Though he could have moved the Western District command center to any one of several cities within its wide swathe of jurisdictional territory, U.S. Marshal Jack Dean, not surprisingly, headquartered at San Antonio.

What U.S. Marshal Jack Dean couldn't do was spend like a drunken sailor. For the USMS operating within budget was difficult but demanded. Many legislators—while touting a good war on crime and criminality, in truth—were parsimonious penny-pinchers. About the time U.S. Marshal Dean held up his right hand to take the oath of office, lawmakers slashed dollars, severely trimming the hiring of new Deputy USMs and funding for government-paid PCS relocations. At Washington the USMS Director duly noted and advised staff and field personnel about the necessary request for "additional funding from DOJ to meet the shortfall, which was occurring because of circumstances largely beyond Marshal Service control."[14] U.S. Marshal Jack Dean, though healthily experienced with the ins and outs of governmental bureaucracy, was somewhat surprised when he learned that OIG had privately contracted with the well-known world-wide accounting firm of Price Waterhouse to audit selected District Marshals' financial accounts.[15] Endless paperwork and strict accountability were exacted. Jack Dean had weathered sequestration squalls at DPS. He was an old hand at managing a budget and cutting costs—still accomplishing the overall mission. Good leaders did that.

When broached with a question concerning the actual duties of the United States Marshals, Jack Dean owned a nutshell answer: "The U.S. Marshals are basically a Federal Sheriff. They're responsible for jailing [and transporting] all the federal prisoners, serving most of the federal process, court warrants and what have you, and they have the best warrant squads in the country serving federal warrants. The other agencies try it first to get their warrants served; if they can't get them served pretty quick then they send them over to the Marshal's office."[16]

U.S. Marshal Jack Dean's comment regarding execution of federal warrants and scooping up folks on the run—as it applied to Western District Deputy Marshals—was square on the mark. Within his supervisory purview would be The Southwest Border Fugitive Task Force operating out of El Paso. They were legitimately lauded for racking up an impressive array of "arrest statistics as criminals wanted for everything from murder to drug trafficking are [were] being hunted down and captured. The Marshals Service's Western District of Texas is in charge of this violent offender and narcotics task force. . . . Participating agencies include the El Paso Police Department, El Paso County Sheriff's Department, U.S. Border Patrol and the Federal Bureau of Investigation. Members have netted 1,227 federal fugitives and 1,219 state fugitives. . . ." Particularly interesting for U.S. Marshal Jack Dean was the rather quick arrest of a highly sought fugitive and parole violator by his Western District Deputy Marshals Fernando Karl and Al Sena, and a Supervisory Deputy, Javier Guerra. They had been hunting for a particular owl-hoot responsible for Auto Theft, three Armed Robberies and an Attempted Kidnapping. Through investigative ingenuity, U.S. Marshal Dean's deputies ably tracked the fugitive to Silver City, New Mexico. There they safely apprehended him. The interstate manhunt had burned but ten days and netted a good catch.[17]

Another classification of lawbreakers was not fugitives yet their apprehensions resulted in nightmarish headaches for several Southwestern United States Marshals, Jack Dean included. During but one fiscal year after his assuming command, the actual number of Western District prisoners in custody jumped by 72 percent—and regardless criminal charges the continually escalating workload was staggering. Overall, nationwide, the U.S. Marshals Service was breaking previous records with regards to housing and transportation of federal prisoners. The increased budgetary and manpower drain and strain was particularly impacting JAPATS as personnel tried to keep up with the responsibilities of "coordinating prisoner movements around the country."[18] Another federal convict was making his move absent any help from the U.S. Marshals Service.

With the ongoing capacity of the iconic Energizer Bunny, and though an inmate inside the federal prison at Atlanta, he was nonetheless a newsmaker and never far removed from trouble. Unquestionably, in light of Charles Voyde Harrelson's repeated and proven ineptitude at being a successful and thriving outlaw, U. S. Marshal Jack Dean was not wholly blown over when he learned the escape attempt had fizzled. Perhaps prisoner Charles Voyde Harrelson wasn't "institutionalized" after all!

> A guard foiled an attempt by Woody Harrelson's father to escape from the prison where he's serving life for assassinating a federal judge, authorities said. Charles Harrelson, 56, and bank robbers Gary Settle, 29, and Michael Rivers, 56, used a makeshift rope to scale a wall at the Atlanta Federal Penitentiary. They surrendered Tuesday night after a warning shot was fired from the guard tower, a prison official said. The men were placed in a special unit at the maximum-security prison pending an investigation, said prison spokesman Mike Binion.[19]

Definitively, Harrelson's misguided try at Atlanta had little impact—other than amusement—on the actual workaday life of U.S. Marshal Jack Dean. Shortly though, Charles Voyde Harrelson's transfer to a different federal penitentiary would. West of Pueblo, Colorado, and not too far from Canyon City in Freemont County was the town of Florence. There the Bureau of Prisons operated an Administrative Maximum Facility (ADX) known to the outside world as Supermax, but within USMS and BOP conversational circles it was commonly just referred to as Florence. Security at Florence was supreme—not whiny idealism. Dangerous and high-profile prisoners were housed thereat. Fellows like mad bombers and terrorists and cartel-affiliated convicts too mean or too risky for circulating in a general prison population were kept tight at Florence. Whether or not he would take perverse pride in being domiciled with the baddest of the bad is unknown. There is, though, a hard truth. Harrelson had earned his new home due to the bungled business unwinding at Atlanta. For sure Supermax was no Sunday School or Country Club. Excepting for sixty minutes for exercise each day inside a strong wire-mesh enclosure, Charles Voyde Harrelson would finally be caged behind concrete and steel for the day's other twenty-three hours. There would be no shortage of time to read and meditate, and/or bone up on appellate tactics in an effort to worm out of Big House residency.[20] In the free-world fleeting time is precious; in prison it drags—and drags.

Hardly had a week gone by since the botched breakout at the Atlanta lockup, when the Director of the FBI, Louis J. Freeh, made a trip to San Antonio. On the thirteenth day of July 1995 the Western District Marshal and the FBI Director had a face-to-face meeting in the Alamo City. Whether or not Director Freeh was aware of Jack Dean's tip about Charles Harrelson and the Judge Wood murder investigation goes unrecorded. However, Director Freeh did, in writing, commend U.S. Marshal Jack Dean: "You can be proud of the many efforts you have undertaken to assist other law enforcement agencies in the fight against crime."[21] Reading between the lines is not normally history researchers' finest methodology but, in this instance, the few words said much.

Much too was being said in hallways at the Texas capitol and in county courthouse corridors. Militants were declaring that laws and regulations promulgated at Austin were thus far wholly illegal, all due to the plain fact—in their minds—that the Lone Star State had been annexed to the United States inappropriately and therefore her 171,901,440 acres yet belonged to and were the sovereign territory embraced by a Republic of Texas of the 1830s era. They weren't fooling. There was no need for them to acquire driver's licenses or register vehicles or have safety inspections stickers for their windshields, "or anything else they deemed as forcing them into the funnel of lawful compliance if they chose otherwise. Crackpot as it may seem they were, in truth, dead serious!"[22] Compounding those niggling illegal botherences, ROT revolutionists were filing bogus liens throughout the state. Untangling a morass of frivolous filings was wearing thin. On the whole such silliness was really generating a burdensome and potentially dangerous mess. The crescendo of calamity was ratcheting to a fever pitch. Radically inclined ROT proponents fecklessly established an "embassy" in faraway West Texas in the decidedly picturesque and historically rich Davis Mountains, not too very far removed from the county seat of Jeff Davis County, Fort Davis.

Although the stew of the belligerents' discontent had been heating for several years, it boiled out of the kettle during April of 1997. Sheriff Steve Bailey had lawfully arrested the ROT's purported Chief of Security for state weapons violations. Other ROT constituents retaliated, orchestrating a violent home invasion, wounding an innocent fellow with reckless gunfire while taking him and his frightened wife hostage. The bleeding and scared kidnapped victims were now "prisoners of war."[23] Some type of inane madness had been long anticipated; now the lid had finally blown off the pot.

The ROT's top honcho, their "Ambassador," was Richard Lance McLaren, who had previously been found "in civil contempt of court" and was definitely a federal fugitive from justice but was not hiding. In fact, McLaren had boldly and incautiously made his intentions known should lawmen actually try to serve the U.S. District Court's warrant: "If they enter the embassy, they'll be in violation of international law. We have the right to remove them with bodily force, if necessary." U.S. Marshal Jack Dean had heard such big-ass badmouthing before. An out and out assault on the ROT compound would be an overreaction in his mind. He wanted to be reasonable and levelheaded, even remarking that he was not crazily adhering to anyone's timetable about serving the warrant issued by Judge Lucius Bunton, III: "We'll take it easy and it will get served."

Thoughtfully, it is now known, U.S. Marshall Jack Dean had charged several of his Western District Deputy Marshals with initiating a delicate and discreet surveillance on the comings and goings of ROT activists in the Fort Davis area. Naturally if they could "nab" McLaren absent chancing a bloodbath they were to do so, but gathering critical intelligence in the meantime likely would, as U.S. Marshal Dean knew, in the end donate to that overall peaceful objective. Unobtrusively Jack Dean's deputies learned minuscule details, even the "shopping habits" of ROT extremists, gauging the quantity of available food warehoused at the professed embassy. Such intelligence could and would prove beneficial.[24]

U.S. Marshal Jack Dean was, at that time, also privy to some inside investigative information, details he shared with now Texas Ranger Senior Captain Bruce Casteel, his former Company D Sergeant, Narcotics Service Lieutenant Doug Vance, recently named commander of DPS SWAT teams, and Mike Cox, Public Information Officer for DPS, as Chief Pilot Bill Isbell flew them to Alpine in the state-owned aircraft. From Alpine, the nearest airport to the scene of hostility, the hurrying lawmen would collaborate with the onsite Incident Commander, Ranger Captain Barry K. Caver, Company E, Midland, who with THP Captain David G. Baker (now DPS Lieutenant Colonel) via a fast whirling helicopter ride were already at Fort Davis. Accordingly U.S. Marshal Jack Dean related that it was highly anticipated that a sitting Federal Grand Jury in the Northern District of Texas would soon return Indictments charging McLaren and his wife with their issuance of fraudulent ROT money orders.[25] As a matter of course and Texas Ranger protocol Captain Caver would be calling the shots, owning the accolades or the condemnations—whichever—the decisions were his.[26]

The news transcended Jeff Davis County. Not only did concerned lawmen worry with ROT folks up the canyon at the embassy, but the vehement rhetoric of outside followers rushing to the Davis Mountain stronghold to increase numbers of an armed resistance was omnipresent and not to be indifferently brushed aside. As a matter of fact, Texas Ranger Captain Carl Weathers and Rangers Marshall Brown, Steve Foster, Larry Gilbreath, and Gary Henderson did find and productively arrest seven armed fellows at the Flying J Truck Stop at Pecos, far short of the 5,000 tough guys daubed with war-paint McLaren claimed were bravely riding to the rescue.[27] Overestimating strength is not uncommon for fanatical associations. For seasoned and committed lawmen, hot talk is cheap—and handcuffs plentiful.

Factually in the Davis Mountains at the ROT's dilapidated headquarters there was a standoff. There was, too, another truism about the uncorking madness. The miscalculating militants were outnumbered and outgunned from the get-go, as local, state, and federal lawmen converged on the normally serene vacation spot nestled below McDonald Observatory. In the aggregate, at roadblocks and the command center, upwards of 300 policing types and support personnel were on duty around the clock. Indeed there was a logistical nightmare attendant to scheduling and supplying so many folks with the basics: food, water, and downtime. Thankfully—for this brouhaha— the United States Forest Service Incident Command System assumed responsibility for matters such as scheduling the manning of specific posts and aptly rotating manpower, tribulations they had fine-tuned through years and years of frontline fighting wildfires.

And although the decision-making tasks were intricate and the peace-treaty talks intense, Captain Caver, at last, negotiated the surrender, navigating around pitfalls of any unnecessary heavy-handedness or blustery egomania. The "prisoners of war" had been safely returned and the ROT soldiers—at least some of them—would catch-the-chain for Huntsville, now owing the Lone Star State hard-time behind tall walls.[28] One ROT misfit opted for a backdoor escape into the wilds—and subsequent to his shooting and killing a tracking K-9, was himself shot and killed after taking potshots at a helicopter circling overhead.[29]

Afterwards U.S. Marshal Jack Dean was quizzed about the volatile incident and the number of and wide cross-section of participating agencies: "Police work around the Republic of Texas compound in Fort Davis operated smoothly for lots of reasons. . . ." Then reeling off agencies Jack Dean appreciatively mentioned that Deputy U.S. Marshals, Texas Rangers, Border Patrol Agents, FBI Special Agents, TDCJ K-9 handlers, U.S. Forest Service personnel, DPS Troopers, and Sheriff's Deputies were all a part to the mélange of on-duty defenders. Politely U.S. Marshal Jack Dean amplified, postulating: "Team members' assignments were clearly identified. That kind of cooperation flows from a better coordinating plan for these joint operations."[30] During those earlier days as a Texas Ranger in the Lower Rio Grande Valley, Jack Dean had learned well the value of inter- and intra- agency cooperation. He, too, by virtue of his patient psyche and levelheaded commonsense, was capable of allowing—when appropriate—the passage of time to assuage any tendency for rushed judgments and/or overreactions.

Steadiness was/is the watchword for hunting bear or badmen. Western District U.S. Deputy Marshal Randy Kruid had been looking for a particularly cunning outlaw—a major marijuana smuggler—for several years, a yahoo suspected of illicitly funneling as much as 1,000,000 lbs. of Mexican weed into America's insatiable marketplace for all things prohibited—"building a multi-million dollar trafficking organization." As Deputy Marshal Kruid appreciated and stated: "We knew he'd been a smuggler all his life. . . . And we knew he was catchable." U.S. Marshal Jack Dean found out—rather quickly— Kruid was correct. With an OCDETF warrant in hand and accompanied by Western District Deputy Tom Shaddix, Randy Kruid zeroed in on their man at Dallas—after soldiering after him at "California, New York, Pennsylvania and all throughout the Lone Star State." The smuggler's world came tumbling down at Big-D, when the federal boys and the Dallas PD and the DPS Narcotics Service "confiscated 9,031 lbs. of marijuana and eventually counted $530,000 in cash"—plus the seizure and forfeiture of a grocery store, a ranch, several vehicles, seventy-three firearms and, more importantly, the arrests of eleven taken aback coconspirators. Yes, as U.S. Marshal Jack Dean learned, the Western District Deputies were one widely disbursed set of busy folks.[31] Another fellow, though, was idling time.

The luckless prisoner at Florence was awaiting judgment—and it was a slow and drawn-out process. As a somewhat routine matter of allowable course Charles Voyde Harrelson was—once again—appealing his murder conviction and life sentence. As consequence of those legal maneuverings U.S. Marshal Jack Dean was summoned to hearings in Colorado. Dean moves the story: "So, I get to talk and visit with Charlie some more. He wasn't a bad guy to talk to. He'd just kill you, you know, but he wouldn't kill you unless somebody paid him to. He wasn't coldblooded, you know, go stab, kill everybody. . . . that wasn't Charlie. [But] if you pay him a million dollars or $500k well he would take out anybody. . . . He always said, 'Jack, I'm a gambler, this is all a bunch of crap, you know.' We caught him for three [murders] and we convicted him for two of the three. I don't think we caught him for everything he ever did. I think he slipped one or two around on us somewhere."

U.S. Marshal Jack Dean, by virtue of his past history with Charles Voyde Harrelson and because of his then-current federal position, was in a somewhat unique place in time—able to gauge the convict's character traits, as well as extending a personal yet harmless but, much appreciated, special favor: ". . . Charlie was smart and had a personality. You meet Charlie, I mean you'd say 'Yea, he's a good old boy,' you know. [As] We parted company the last time he said 'When I get out of here I'll buy you a beer,' and I said 'Charlie, if you get out of here [Supermax] I'll buy you the beer.' But, I've got a nice little note he sent me. He never has [had] seen his grandkids and he had three or four grandkids. I set it up so he could meet his grandkids. And, he sent me a nice little note."[32] U.S. Marshal Jack Dean had pull.

Unquestionably U.S. Marshal Jack Dean was rather well known in Lone Star State political circles, but that favorable notoriety would soon transcend statewide exposure. During one bill-signing ceremony at Austin, U.S. Marshal Dean was present and photographed, along with the other three U.S. Marshals of Texas and an assemblage of keenly interested dignitaries. Governor George Bush was signing into Texas law legislation that would "include [United States] marshals and deputy marshals as special investigators in the state, giving them power under the Texas Code of Criminal Procedure to make arrests, searches and seizures in felony cases under state laws."[33]

Though he was very proud of the work his Deputy U.S. Marshals were routinely doing, one particular case arrested Jack Dean's attention—if for no other justification, nostalgia would do. In faraway West Texas at Pecos—his very first law-enforcing post as a THP Patrolman—four federal inmates had cunningly escaped the Reeves County Detention Center. Milton Alarcon, Luis Castillo-Rodriguez, Jose Jarmillo-Hernandez, and Mariano Flores-Benavides had, with a touch of good luck, successfully scaled the several fences and disappeared into the night. Near Balmorhea on the county's southern edge the outlaws had secreted themselves in the brush of an area rancher's property. Unbeknownst to the escapees the observant cattleman had contacted Deputy U.S. Marshals Billy Johnson and Steve Clark. They teamed up with BP Agents and Reeves County Sheriff's Deputies. Though they were more than thirty miles from Pecos in the wilds of mountain and canyon country the alert lawmen found fresh tracks. Trailing the fugitives was not easy, but it was not an undoable chore. Score one for the good guys. The *mal hombres* were apprehended "without incident."[34]

Seasoned lawmen—and women—are always on the lookout. Through channels Jack Dean would learn that two of his Western District Deputies at El Paso had lent a helping hand to Deputy U.S. Marshal Barbara Gonzales from New Mexico. She had driven into El Paso to partake of a meal with relatives. At the restaurant she alerted on a particular table—there with a half-dozen *amigos* was Luis Pastor-Luque, a fugitive she had been hard after for at least six months. Discretely summoning backup from Western District cohorts at El Paso, in but short order Luis Pastor-Luque was jeweled-up nicely—handcuffs and leg-irons.[35] Deputy Gonzalez politely re-holstered her sidearm and picked up the Margarita—and deservedly so!

Another case of tracking a fugitive created more of a challenge for Marshal Dean's Western District Deputies. For nine months U.S. Deputies at the border town of Del Rio had been hunting hard for Jose Garza-Leija. The fugitive was wanted for Conspiracy to Possess Marijuana With Intent to Distribute. It was, too, alleged that the desperado was "an enforcer for a drug organization which stretched all throughout Texas and into the neighboring states. . . ." Purportedly, Jose Garza-Leija had also threatened the lives of DEA Agents, U.S. Customs Agents, and DPS personnel due to their previous arrest of his brother—as well as witnesses set to testify in court as to his sibling's alleged guilt. After following numerous false leads, through several Federal Judicial Districts, the slippery outlaw was purported to be living with his girlfriend at Fort Worth, Northern District of Texas. A wholly fresh approach was on the drawing board: "Deputies then turned to the Service's secret weapon against hard-to-find fugitives—the ESU. Through several, high-tech investigative techniques, ESU representatives were able to track Garza's girlfriend to Mesa, Ariz." Surreptitiously a physician's office was placed under surveillance and the pregnant girlfriend—in her eighth month—soon made her scheduled visit. The clandestine shadowing after her departure from the doctor's office soon led Deputy U.S. Marshals to their target. Surrounded by lawmen Jose Garza-Leija had little choice but to fight or surrender. The pick would be his—and his alone. He chose the latter option, smartly and thankfully. Gunplay was avoided. Accordingly the cautious takedown was graded: "This was a picture-perfect arrest—just like you'd see on TV," so reported U.S. Marshal Supervisory Deputy Kim Dawsey. And it was thanks to U.S. Marshal Jack Dean's man stationed at Del Rio, Deputy U.S. Marshal Joseph Johnson, that the lengthy and laudatory article was carried in pages of the September-October 1999 edition of *The*

Marshals Monitor—the service's newsletter.[36] Yes, U.S. Marshal Jack Dean was proud of his workforce.

And not all of that dedicated workforce were full-time Deputy U.S. Marshals; there were provisional CSO's, typically retired federal lawmen from one branch or another, working as needed providing security in and around United States District Courts. One such fellow at the time was Carl Raymond Fisher, Jr., a U.S. Navy veteran and a former old hand with the USBP, after his thirty years chasing and catching border jumpers and dangerous dope smugglers.[37] Sometimes Carl Fisher performed security assignments in San Antonio at the John H. Wood Federal Courthouse, an edifice named to honor the coldly assassinated judge of two decades past. In Sheriff Tommy Williams's bailiwick of Atascosa County, the twelfth day of October 1999 would be forever memorable—but not for good reasons—not for the sitting sheriff or the semi-retired bilingual borderland lawman. Or for that matter, U.S. Marshal Jack Dean!

In his revengefully warped state-of-mind twenty-one-year-old Jeremiah Justin Engleton had a serious bone of contention to pick with Atascosa County deputies, they having arrested him for domestic violence—spousal abuse—subsequent to an overheated and physical altercation with his wife Violet. Behind steel bars, away from deputies' hearing, Jeremiah boasted about the lawmen's future to an all-ears cellmate; "these motherfuckers don't know what they got coming," also saying to the aghast listener that he would very soon be making the "front page." And, as with Andy Barefoot in Bell County several years before, Jeremiah had but one solution to generate headlines, and that was to kill a cop— but more precisely in Engleton's case, massacre several cops if the opportunity presented—and he would damn sure make it present. Jeremiah, after posting the requisite bail monies, traveled to an area gun-shop with his friend Kenneth C. Vodochodsky where he bought several types of rifle and pistol ammo, $200 worth. At this point in time it seemed the evil plot but needed a short-fuse and booster-charge to detonate the core explosive wallop, cowardly murdering unsuspecting Atascosa County lawmen. Jeremiah

Engleton dialed 911 and then hung-up, a bogus call to be sure, but one guaranteed to, once again, rush evening-shift deputies to his mobile-home in a rural part of the county, east of Pleasanton, roughly thirty miles south of San Antonio.

Screened by brush and brambles, Jeremiah lay in wait, armed with an SKS Norenco assault rifle, a Mossberg 12-gauge slide-action, and three autoloading handguns—a Ruger 9mm, a Glock .40 caliber, and a Lorcin .380 caliber. Two Atascosa County deputies were dispatched to investigate the unknown emergency, both knowing who lived where they were going, but neither knowing exactly why they were making the 10-33 trip. To good deputies it wouldn't have mattered anyway—they just went. Twenty-nine-year-old Deputy Thomas Orville Monse, Jr. was first on the scene, pulling his squad car into the driveway at 8:28 p.m. Deputy Monse most likely didn't know what hit him, but the coroner would—"eighteen gunshot wounds caused by rifle, shotgun, and handgun fire." Close on his heels, at 8:30 p.m. Deputy Mark Louis Stephenson, three days short of his thirty-first birthday, went down for keeps in Jeremiah's dirt driveway, suffering "eleven gunshot wounds caused by rifle and handgun fire." Both deputies had been shot in the face at point-blank range—while down—clear evidence of a perverse *coupe de grâce*. Hearing naught from the deputies, a DPS Trooper, Terry Wayne Miller, thirty-eight, had been dispatched and raced to the scene of who knew what. Rolling up at 8:51 p.m. he immediately saw with headlights the two prostrate and lifeless uniformed deputies. Straightway, by training, Trooper Terry Miller radioed the universally understood lawman's distress call: "Officer Down!" A spiraling round from the imported rifle tore into Trooper Miller's head while he was yet sitting in the state-owned unit—seatbelt fastened—killing him instantly. Expectedly at this point in time radio traffic was more than intense, the airways jumbled as spur-of-the-moment possemen scrambled to help their ambushed brothers. What had happened? Where were they at? From the Pleasanton PD Officer Louis Edward Tudyk, thirty, launched into action, but, unluckily, at the crime-scene caught a bullet to the right forearm at 8:56 p.m. Upon hearing the squawking and garbled radio transmissions referencing the unfolding and bloody incident, the off-duty CSO Carl Fisher, now sixty and driving his personal pickup, raced at high-speed to the battlefront. Fellow lawmen were in trouble—arriving only one minute behind Officer Tudyk. Carl Fisher, too, suffered gifts from madman Jeremiah, who may have slipped a gear in his head, but the mental malfunction hadn't knocked his sights out of zero—he was dead on![38]

Not surprisingly it seemed the heavens had opened and it was raining lawmen at and near Jeremiah's habitation—he was surrounded no doubt—somewhere, but it was nighttime and damn dark and dangerous. Overhead a FLIR equipped helicopter from San Antonio PD, at last, detected and then illuminated Jeremiah Engleton lurking in the mesquite thicket, heavily armed and overtly defiant. The nighttime muzzle flashes were in harmony, a lawman's bullet striking Jeremiah, but as he had planned from the outset it was Jeremiah's self-inflicted gunshot wound that technically ended the madness—he was now DRT.[39]

With regards to CSO Carl Fisher, Western U.S. Deputy Marshal Dennis Collins, who had also responded to the uncorking mayhem, welded tight the wounded man's positive attitude declaring that he did not let the incident interfere with his work at the courthouse or interdict his positive attitude about life: "Carl was a good guy. . . . Carl was the kind of a guy you'd want to have as a neighbor and as an employee."[40] U.S. Marshal Jack Dean certainly seconded that notion.

But just as certainly the Texas Rangers who brought the case, the DA that prosecuted, and the jury that convicted and handed him a death sentence for Capital Murder weren't of two minds about Kenneth C. Vodochodsky—there was not a scrap of ambivalence. Accompanying shooter Jeremiah to buy bullets the day of the massacre did not look good. Big talk before the killings, allegations that he was onsite when the phony 911 call was placed and questionable statements post the luring of officers to their deaths had not portended well for Vodochodsky. The back-story, though, is somewhat intriguing. The Texas Court of Criminal Appeals reversed his conviction and impending sentence of death due interpretation as to inadequacy of evidence warranting a Capital Murder conviction. But, surprisingly that's not the end of the story. Previous to his being retried, during a carefully crafted and eruditely negotiated plea agreement Kenneth Vodochodsky confirmed to the court that he was, indeed, culpable for part of the heartrending tragedy—enough so to accept punishment—for making Atascosa County home for now mourning widows and crying orphans. Or, more simply stated, to a proficient interviewing *San Antonio Express-News* inquisitor: "I sure don't want to spend the rest of my life in prison. . . . At least this way, I wouldn't." Was Vodochosaky remorseful or realistic? *¿Quién sabe?* Nevertheless, Kenneth Vodochodsky took the deal, thirty years to do—wherever TDCJ chose to give him a cost-fee bunk and complimentary cafeteria chow, and clean whites, and an occasional haircut on the house.[41] Some other Big House residents weren't any too happy with regards to the freebees and the accommodations.

The news that U.S. Marshal Jack Dean received 13 December 2000—at the time—was somewhat routine, newsworthy but something lawmen throughout the United States sporadically tackled: A prison break. Shortly, though, this particular escape would morph into a manhunt of colossal proportion—at least one of the most intensive searches for fugitives in America's law-enforcing history.[42]

As earlier mentioned, while a Texas Ranger Captain, Jack Dean had focused some effort on the hostage taking and attempted 1985 jailbreak at Karnes City. Now, fifteen years later, he redirected his attention to TDCJ's Connally Unit, a 2500-plus prisoner maximum-security facility on State Highway 181 south of the Karnes County town of Kenedy, and not too terribly far west of the lazily meandering San Antonio River. Unbeknownst to anyone—save seven soured inmates—a dreadfully sinister plan for escape had long been engineered. The late morning on 13 December 2000 was E-Day, Escape Day. Inside the Maintenance Shop seven free-world minded outlaws began—one by one—taking flabbergasted and scared hostages, including employees and other inmates, during the scheduled

lunch hour. Gagging and binding them tightly with plastic ties and/
or duct tape and placing pillow cases over their heads, after conk-
ing them on the cranium with ax-handles and believably threatening
them with sharpened shanks if the scheming convicts deemed it crucial to their designs. The well-planned deviousness took a couple of
hours to fully orchestrate, but over time the hopeful escapees managed to violently overcome and subdue thirteen state-paid employees, as well as three luckless and utterly stunned inmates. Cunningly
donning civilian attire, several of the escapees with pals dressed in
prison whites productively worked a repairman ruse, gaining access
to a picket—guard tower—and ultimately acquired a portion of the
Connally Unit's firepower: a pump-action 12 gauge shotgun, a .223
AR-15 Assault Rifle, and fourteen handguns—.357 Magnum revolvers. A sixteen-count armament netted a ratio of two shooters apiece,
with a couple of spares if a shootout with authorities was to go down
in the very near term. One of the witty or witless outlaws—maybe at
the behest of the other six—penned a note to be left behind foretell-
ing the future, a figurative "Fuck You" to any pursuing lawmen and
to the whole world: "You haven't heard the last of us yet!" That was
true. Stealing a white prison maintenance truck, the outlaws—now
dressed in the hog-tied civilian employees' street clothes—scooted
for Kenedy, where they abandoned that standout ride behind a
Wal-Mart Discount Store. There, a getaway SUV—a Chevrolet
Suburban—provided by one of the outlaw's conspiring blood-relatives, but unknown then to lawmen—awaited, and the seven treacherous convicts, for practical purposes, evaporated.[43]

Quite naturally, however, their names and criminal records had
not been resultantly dissolved. Purportedly the outlaws didn't know
each other until registered at the penitentiary near Kenedy, but they
all had a somewhat common denominator past—none, while at the
Connally Unit, had committed any known punishable acts of "violent or assaultive behavior," which was a helpful precursor for their
behind-the-wire nonchalance and seemingly demonstratively harmless mobility. On the other hand they shared, one and all, a disparate
brand of equivalence: None of them were really nice guys: George

Angel Rivas, Jr., thirty, TDCJ #702267 was doing seventeen life sentences for Aggravated Kidnapping With a Deadly Weapon, Aggravated Kidnapping, Aggravated Robbery With a Deadly Weapon, Aggravated Robbery and Burglary of a Habitation; Demoralized convict Michael Anthony Rodriguez, thirty-eight, TDJC #698074 had been sentenced to life due to his Bexar County conviction for Capital Murder, hiring a hit-man to murder his wife; Randy Ethan Halprin, thirty, TDCJ #786259 had caught a tough 30 years to pull from Tarrant County for Injury to a Child/Serious Bodily Injury With a Deadly Weapon; Subsequent to his Travis County conviction for Aggravated Robbery With a Deadly Weapon, Donald Keith Newbury, thirty-eight, TDCJ #824631 and a three-time loser, was whiling away his 99 years as an unwilling institutional guest of the State of Texas; Dallas County was represented by Patrick Henry Murphy, Jr., thirty-nine, TDCJ #386888 who was chiseling away at his 50 year punishment for Aggravated Sexual Assault With a Deadly Weapon and Burglary of a Building; Joseph Christopher Garcia, twenty-nine, TDCJ #774391 was three years into his half-century stint for Murder With a Deadly Weapon in the Alamo City; and Larry James Harper, thirty-seven, TDCJ #861910 from faraway West Texas at El Paso was most reluctantly doing his four-bits worth—fifty years—because of his numerous convictions—running concurrently—for Aggravated Sexual Assault and Aggravated Sexual Assault With a Deadly Weapon.[44] Understandably, in the annals of prison breaks—state or federal—this was an epochal electrifier. It was unmistakably, as would be very predictable, not only a newsy, but a newsworthy story: Interesting and horrifying, seven bona fide outlaws somewhere on the loose. They would become known—Nationwide—as the "Texas Seven."

For the free-world folks the Texas Seven were definitely outlaws to be feared. For TDCJ inmates the Texas Seven bequeathed their brand of friendship, a hard right twist of rules and tightening restrictions.[45] That sordid legacy, though, meant nothing to instigator George Rivas: "I wasn't going to be an old man dying in prison."[46]

Not unexpectedly South Texas lawmen were searching hither and yon for any sign of the fleeing felons or any substantive leads as to their actual whereabouts or at that time what they were driving. And herein it is worth mentioning, for this humdinger, according to the former Karnes County Sheriff, Bobby Mutz, the news media was thought to be much more helpful than harmful—they could and did broadcast and spread the word about dangerous dudes on the run. Western District U.S. Deputy Marshals, Jack Dean's team, Texas Rangers, and THP Troopers and a slew of the DPS CID crew, USBP Agents, FBI Special Agents, and other U.S. Treasury and DOJ lawmen, as well as county sheriffs and policemen throughout the state and country were on the lookout. Deceptively the cordon of roadblocks had been slipped past.[47] These guys were armed, dangerous and, now, had nothing to lose and naught to fear about any hereafter. They had cut their deal with Devil.

A TDCJ command post was established. Western District U.S. Marshal Jack Dean, as had his counterparts from the state's other three federal districts, dispatched deputies to the impromptu clearinghouse for clues. Other lawmen and law enforcing agencies were drawn in, too. But for this particularly focused account it should be mentioned that Jack Dean was competently represented at the command center by two of his Western District stalwarts, Deputy U.S. Marshals Fernie Karl and Jose Chavarria. During the initial stages it was unknown whether the Texas Seven had subdivided or was yet ganged-up. Seven perfidious fellows on the run could be hunting succor from seven unrelated and widely-disbursed subsets of family, friends, and/or past criminal associates.

DPS CID Intelligence Agent H.L. "Hank" Whitman Jr., (subsequently Chief of the Rangers) pulled forty long days and forty short nights at the Texas Seven investigative headquarters. As a shrewdly trained hostage negotiator Hank's contribution to the manhunt was not on the street, cocked and locked .45 in hand, but at the command center buried in the analytical fine points. Each of the Texas Seven were individuals—and each individually owned their own wasted history—regardless failed rehabilitative reasons and/or maudlin excuses. Lawmen knew it would be but a matter of time before the Texas Seven were run to ground somewhere—either together or segmented or as loners. And therein was the foundation for CID Agent Whitman's analytic participation. Meticulous attention to case histories and social ties could yield a boundless data bank—if interpreted properly. That said, finding them together or separately solved but half the equation. How would each react when cornered? Therefore, for purely tactical reasons Agent Whitman also had to rank the Texas Seven by strength of personality and pure cussedness—who was the most dominant outlaw? In other words, when the leader at the top of the pecking-order surrendered or was tagged and bagged, who would take his place and what would that particular fugitive bring to the table of meanness? The breadth of the intelligence gathering process, now looking backwards—is mindboggling.[48] At the time, circumspectly exploring genealogical family-trees and psychological predispositions and the convicts' personal predilections were super important from the analytic angle, but the closeness or farness of any state or national borderlines was meaningless.

For the Texas Seven, also meaningless was any inclination for niceness. Two days after the breakout—15 December—at Pearland in Brazoria County just south of Houston, the Texas Seven highjacked a Radio Shack electronics store at gunpoint, scaring employees and stealing money, walkie-talkies, and police radio scanners. The store's manager was particularly distressed by the iciness of the gang's apparent leader George Rivas: "I knew by the cold, hard look in his eye, that if anybody moved he wouldn't kill just one of us, he'd kill all of us."[49] The Texas Seven also robbed an AutoZone Store and yet later, acquired a couple of uniforms that could be handily accepted as those of security guards. The Texas Seven's big score was yet on the drawing board—miles removed from the Gulf Coast.

Most folks on Christmas Eve 2000 were hustling and bustling tending to last-minute chores before Santa Claus began distributing gifts throughout the Texas municipality of Irving, a thriving suburban neighbor of Dallas, just across their northwestern city limits. At an Oshman's Sporting Goods Store—not long before closing—employees were, too, in a jovial holiday sprit. The Texas Seven weren't inclined to wait for a red-nosed Reindeer—and their

Christmas plans called for taking, not giving. Leaving Patrick Henry Murphy, Jr. as their jigger in the parking lot outfitted with a slide-action shotgun, an AR-15 and 60 rounds, a pair of .357 Magnums, a walkie-talkie, and the preprogrammed police radio scanner. He was, by any standard of badness, well prepared. The other Texas Seven gangsters entered the store—two wearing security-guard uniforms—deceptively giving an appearance they were at the store on official business, just as they had done at the Connally Unit's watchtower. The deception worked perfectly—and shortly all employees were corralled into a wad—staring into the business end of .357 Magnums—now aware evilness was inside the store as they were not politely marched—single file—into the windowless breakroom. After stuffing a duffle-bag full of cash—$70,000—and scooping up scads of winter clothing, the robbers' not guarding the hostages turned their attention to the store's firearms vault and display cases. The cache of weaponry and ammo seemed boundless. While busily engaged with nefariousness inside the store, the escapees had no idea that outside two witnesses had detected something was, well, just not right—and dialed 911.[50]

Already a reasonably seasoned lawman with service at other departments, twenty-nine-year-old Aubrey Wright Hawkins, a husband and father, now with fourteen months' service as an Irving policeman, was dispatched to the store. It was, at the time, classed as a Suspicious Persons call. Naturally due to Murphy's monitoring police radio traffic, Officer Aubrey Hawkins' after-dark arriving at the sporting goods store would come as no surprise. It would be Aubrey Hawkins that suffered the surprise—eleven bullets from Texas Seven shooters—then George Rivas ran over him with the pilfered property-packed Ford Explorer, one stolen from the store's scared manager. The whole Texas law-enforcing fraternity mourned the loss of a comrade. The Texas Seven were, again, ghosts. They were now armed even better—flush with cash—and the theft of winter clothing was clear indication they weren't planning a Caribbean Island holiday.

Electronic eavesdropping was methodology pulled from the USMS's bag of tricks. And, though it sounds somewhat over-the-top, at one point in time ESU had as many as thirty-five federal court-ordered surveillances in place, generating near immeasurable inklings. There were in fact, according to Chief John Clark, Domestic Investigations Unit of ISD, "mini task forces set up, each focusing on different fugitives. This investigation was huge there were a lot of players." The staggering amount of data being reviewed triggered an unremitting William Sorukas, ISD's Senior Inspector and Deputy U.S. Marshal, to remark, "We followed leads all the way to New York and California." The sheer magnitude of leads coming into the TDCJ command post was staggering, exceeding 5000. U.S. Marshal Jack Dean's Supervisory Deputy Fernie Karl was undaunted but to some extent awed: "The magnitude of this was incredible. Leads were funneled to districts all over the country. There were a lot of interviews and a lot of man-hours." With regards to this aspect of the joint agency manhunt, speaking appreciatively was the USMS ISD's Assistant Director Robert Finan: "Scores of field deputies, headquarters inspectors, intelligence analysis and administrative personnel from around the country made significant contributions to this investigation."[51]

Doubtlessly who turned out to be the most significant contributor to unraveling the mess would not be a lawman—local, state, or federal—despite all their commendable and tiring effort. True-crime television personality John Walsh had featured the Texas Seven saga on his popular program *America's Most Wanted* four times. A couple from Woodland Park, Colorado, northwest of Colorado Springs, after viewing the last segment knew right were the Texas Seven were: the Coachlight RV Park, staying in a Pace-Arrow motor-home, generally leaving an outward impression that that were pretty nice guys. Of course, lawmen knew better—and after confirming reliability of the hot tip—readied themselves for the peaceable takedown or war if the Texas Seven was of a mind that blazing gunfire would fetch glory.

Since U.S. Marshal Jack Dean was elsewhere, seeing to Western District investigatory and administrative duties, the recap will be truthful but short. George A. Rivas, Jr., Joseph C. Garcia, and Michael A. Rodriguez were captured fueling a gray Jeep Cherokee at an area convenience store/gas station; at Woodland Park; Randy E. Halprin, completely surrounded, exited the RV and surrendered, while Larry J. Harper stayed inside, opting to pull his own trigger—a suicide. Somewhat later, at a Colorado Springs motel, officers telephoned the room with a message real easy to decipherer—after the lapse of five hours, Donald K. Newbury and Patrick H. Murphy dejectedly but peacefully capitulated. The surviving six of the Texas Seven were returned to the Lone Star State—at trial the half-dozen were found guilty and juries awarded death sentences. As this is written (December 2017) Newbury, Rivas, and Rodriguez have been executed, and seventeen years after Aubrey Hawkins's coldhearted murder, Garcia, Halprin, and Murphy are imprisoned at the Polunsky Unit near Livingston in Polk County, TDCJ's Death Row.[52]

U.S. Marshal Jack Dean, especially subsequent to the December 2000 prison break, began facing several realities. He wasn't getting younger by the day; he was aging, having now banked forty-plus years as a state/federal lawman. And just as certainly as Captain A.Y. Allee was forced to take in, the real world and his world was forever changing—whether for the good or the bad. Regrettably, it never stopped spinning. There had, as Jack Dean learned from the outset, never been a shortage of paperwork at DPS, inside or outside the Texas Ranger service, but the federals had 'em swamped—hands down and quicksand proud!

For instance: Straight out of Washington the U.S District Marshals were instructed that they must retain certain forms for a specified period of years, where they were to store them, and how the appointed custodian of such paperwork was to administratively guarantee compliance. Furthermore, U.S. Marshal Jack Dean and his cohorts were updated: "Districts and divisions must ensure that there are memos in their files from OGC approving reimbursements from non-federal sources for employees' official travel. Whenever an employee is on official travel for which a non-federal source—such as state or local law enforcement agency or a non-profit organization—will pay all or part of the expenses, the traveler must receive approval from the ethics officer prior to the trip. . . . This may be with an e-mail or other writings but it must contain an estimate of costs. . . . If the general counsel approves the reimbursement from the non-federal source before the travel begins, the district of division may be reimbursed for the expenses. . . . After the travel is completed, the traveler must include the actual cost of the trip in the memo provided to the ethics officer. It is the responsibility of the districts and divisions to ensure that the memo of reimbursement is approved before the travel begins and that the traveler provides to the ethics officer actual cost of expenses after the travel is over. . . ."[53] True, governmental accountability is absolutely crucial, but the onslaught of e-mails and constant readjustments regarding this mater or that, can prove tiresome and irksome, especially to veteran lawmen—who by nature are an independent-minded lot. The old giving way to the new is simply part of the game, not a novel phenomenon, Texas Ranger Jack Dean had been a part of such in the Lower Rio Grande Valley—but that was then, this was now.

For Jack Dean it was time to go. His number of years as the United States Marshal calculated at ten, enough vested time to qualify for a modest retirement income. Coupled with the DPS pension and annuities from prudent financial management over the years, and Janie's sound contribution to the Deans' coffers, would enable them to maintain a comfortable lifestyle—not wildly extravagant but stable and secure. Financial security was, though, but one factor.

Old warriors know—instinctively—when peace comes at night reliving what has happened, rather than anticipating what terror or administrative entanglements or personnel problems might take place on the morrow. At a particular point in life the idea of pleasant memories altogether overrides uncertainty, and Jack Dean was astute enough to recognize reality. During those waning years it would be much more desirable in his mind to cordially visit with family, friends, and old-time Texas Ranger colleagues reminiscing about adventures gone by, than the surefire alternative: To keel over in his federal building office amid the mounds of paperwork and the constellation of mostly new-fangled working desktop computers, when not on the fritz. Steadily the Government Printing Office kept heralding up-to-the-minute new documents in need of timely completion. Messages from headquarters' office cubicles were unremitting. Quite often, though it's never satisfactorily explained, the replies were piercingly ordered before the close of business on Friday, as if someone would really be working weekends at Washington analyzing and/or filing routine reports from the field. In truth bureaucracy is unforgiving and that's the way it must be—institution before individual—otherwise workplace ethics, time spent on the job, and tradition are meaningless.

Jack Dean's service to the law enforcing community had been, by any reasonable standard, exemplary. Like his short-list of counterparts, former officer's corps Texas Rangers who also served as a Presidentially appointed U. S. District Marshal, Jack O. Dean now, too, has his biography. Though but a small tribute—the overdue historical debt—has been put right.

Jack Dean's formal farewell from the U.S. Marshals Service and the retirement reception were scheduled to take place on 26 March 2004. The location was fascinating; the festivities would be in the John H. Wood, Jr. United States Courthouse at San Antonio. The irony is—in a macabre sort of way rich. Assuredly the quirk of fate was not lost on U.S. Marshal Dean. Jack Dean never did get to make good on his offer to Judge Wood's assassin ensconced at Florence: "Charlie if you ever get out of here I'll buy you the beer."[54]

Photo Gallery

4

During 1987 these Company D Texas Rangers met at the famed YO Ranch. *From L to R, front row:* Al Cuellar, Rudy Rodriquez, Captain Jack Dean, Sergeant Warren Yeager, Doyle Holdridge, and Kasey King. *Standing, L to R:* Robert Garza, Morgan Miller, Richard Bennie, Ray Martinez, Charles Brune, Bob Steele, Richard Sweaney, Coy Smith, Ray Cano, and Joe Peters. *COURTESY TEXAS RANGER HALL OF FAME & MUSEUM, WACO, TX.*

At another outing, due to his undying support of the Texas Rangers, South Texas commercial farmer Warren Wagner was presented with a nicely engraved Smith & Wesson revolver from the men of Company D. Here, Captain Jack Dean steps up, making the presentation in the name of his Company D Rangers to a thoroughly delighted recipient. COURTESY JACK DEAN.

Texas Ranger Captain Jack Dean stepped up again, this time representing the Texas Rangers with heartfelt remarks during a memorial service for Stan Guffey, killed in the line of duty during the Kara-Lee Whitehead kidnapping investigation. COURTESY JACK DEAN.

The Texas Ranger command staff, Captains all. *From L to R:* Lefty Block, Maurice Cook, Bobby Prince, Bob Mitchell, James Wright, Gene Powell, Bruce Casteel, and Jack Dean. These captains liked each other—mostly! COURTESY TEXAS RANGER HALL OF FAME & MUSEUM, WACO, TX.

Captain Jack Dean [foreground] with his Colt .45 autoloader, illustrates that time on the firing-range was an ongoing phenomenon. Note when re-holstering his weapon, Captain Dean's finger is outside the handgun's trigger-guard. *COURTESY JACK DEAN.*

Texas Ranger Joaquin Jackson—wearing the apron—and long-time Dimmitt County Sheriff Ben P. "Doc" Murray take a break from the barbequing to visit. Unfortunately during 1991 Doc Murray would be found murdered in his own home. Captain Dean's Company D Texas Rangers conducted an intensive investigation (covered within this text) and arrested the guilty parties. COURTESY JACK DEAN.

Here Captain Dean is photographed at his San Antonio office. The saddle was once the property of William Warren Sterling, well-known Texas Ranger Captain and Adjutant General of Texas, but subsequently passed on to Jack. The teddy bear was given to Captain Dean—tongue in cheek—to make up for the one he allegedly "lost" during a South Texas deer hunting trip, an anecdote mentioned in this tome's text. COURTESY JACK DEAN.

Letter of provenance regarding the aforementioned saddle: Truly a noteworthy historic treasure. *COURTESY JACK DEAN.*

Here *bueno amigos* Captain Jack Dean and Wayne Showers have a pretty nice South Texas buck. A big-time Lower Rio Grande Valley farming executive and Texas A&M University Regent, Mr. Showers and Captain Dean were loyal pals. In fact, Jack explicitly characterized Wayne as "the closest non-pistol packin' friend I've ever had." *COURTESY JACK DEAN.*

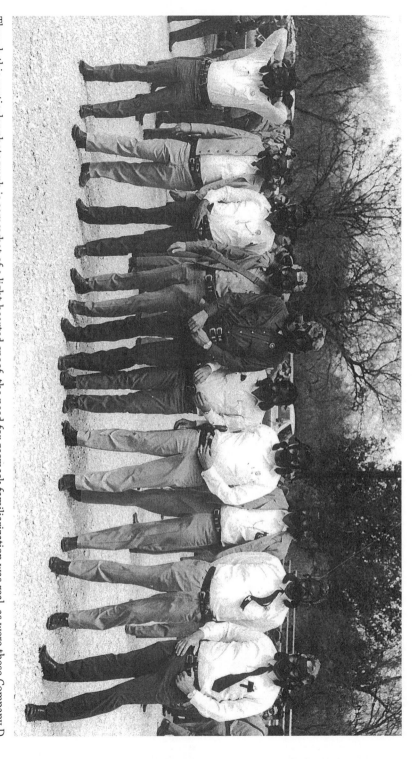

Though this particular photograph is somewhat of a light-hearted spoof, the need for gasmask familiarization was real, as were these Company D Texas Rangers. *From L to R:* Bill Green, Bill Nelson, Jerome Preiss, John Hogg, Jim Peters, Art Rodriquez, Jack Dean, Joaquin Jackson, John Wood, and Glenn Krueger. COURTESY TEXAS RANGER HALL OF FAME & MUSEUM, WACO, TX.

Subsequent to the intense testing and successful performance before the Oral Interview Board, Kyle Dean is promoted to Texas Ranger—first stationed at Denton. Though Captain Dean was yet—for a short time—a Texas Ranger he never formally supervised Kyle's Texas Ranger investigative activities. *COURTESY JACK DEAN.*

To Jack Dean —
A Good friend & great Texas Lawman —
Rick Perry Texas House 1989

Unquestionably the future Governor of Texas thought well of Texas Ranger Captain Jack Dean, characterizing him as: "A good friend & great Texas Lawman." *COURTESY JACK DEAN.*

Just as new faces come, old hands go. What was informally classed as a going away shindig for Joaquin Jackson was well-attended. Bruce Casteel [L] and Jack Dean [R] toast a tribute to Jackson wishing him the very best. *COURTESY JACK DEAN.*

Matt Cawthon left DPS's Criminal Intelligence Division to become a Texas Ranger, particularly so that he could work under the command of Captain Jack Dean, who he admired as a most capable leader and outstanding new era Ranger. Matt Cawthon, now a retired Texas Ranger, notes a quirk of fate: Not too long after he became one of Jack Dean's Company D Rangers in the Lower Rio Grande Valley, the Captain retired and became the Western District U.S. Marshal. Matt Cawthon went on to earn a noteworthy career with Company F at Waco and is now a sitting Board Member for the TRHF&M. *COURTESY MATT CAWTHON.*

Captain Jack Dean passes the torch of Company D Command to Charlie "C.J." Havrda, a college-educated and decorated combat veteran of the Vietnam War. Subsequent to his Highway Patrol service and assignments within Ranger ranks, he would in due time become the Chief, Senior Captain of the Texas Rangers, after Senior Captain Bruce Casteel's retirement. *COURTESY JACK DEAN.*

Though he would receive federal credentials, perhaps those that meant the most to Jack Dean was the official recognition that he had faithfully and honorably completed his Texas Ranger service—his retirement badge and official identification. *COURTESY JACK DEAN AND THE TEXAS RANGER HALL OF FAME & MUSEUM, WACO, TX.*

One of the most ardent political power players championing Jack Dean for the Western District U.S. Marshal's position was Congressman Frank Tejeda, herein shaking hands with his proposed candidate. *COURTESY JACK DEAN.*

Senate of the United States
IN EXECUTIVE SESSION

March 10, 1994

Resolved, That the Senate advise and consent to the following nomination:

Jack O. Dean, of Texas, to be United States Marshal for the Western District of Texas for the term of four years.

Attest: *Walter J. Stewart*

Secretary

Senate of the United States—U.S. Marshal Jack Dean's officially documented confirmation, as received at the White House. *COURTESY JACK DEAN.*

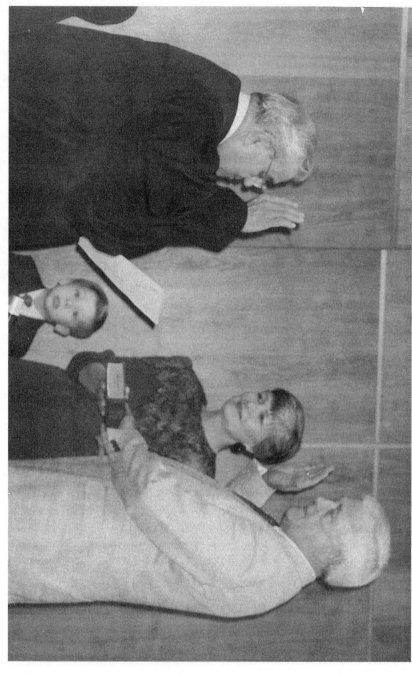

As Janie holds the Bible while young Cody stands as a witness, Jack Dean is sworn in as the United States Marshal for the Western District of Texas by Federal Judge Hipolito Frank Garcia in the John H. Wood, Jr. United States Courthouse at San Antonio. COURTESY JACK DEAN.

Suit and tie portrait of Jack Dean, United States Marshal for the Western District of Texas. *COURTESY JACK DEAN.*

As a special box-seat guest at the San Antonio Rodeo and Livestock Exposition, U.S. Marshal Jack Dean suffered a ricocheting lick from a hard rubber ball, one not checked by the arena's hard-packed ground. With ice in hand the thoughtful—though obviously saddened—rodeo clown administers first-aid. *COURTESY JACK DEAN.*

Upon surrendering, Republic of Texas leader Richard Lance McLaren, because of the coolness and respect he had been shown by Captain Barry Caver, requested to formally shake hands with the Texas Ranger. Although the handshake was somewhat awkward due to the prisoner being handcuffed, the gesture was accomplished by the Ranger Commander reaching inside McLaren's sports-jacket. Looking on was Texas Ranger Coy Smith, holing the prisoner's hat, and Texas Ranger John Allen. *COURTESY CAPTAIN BARRY CAVER, TEXAS RANGERS, RET.*

Arms and ammunition surrendered/seized by Rangers during the ROT drama in far West Texas. Thankfully no lawmen were killed. *Courtesy Captain Barry Caver, Texas Rangers, Ret.*

H.L. "Hank" Whitman. While a DPS Intelligence Agent, Hank Whitman would build mean-ingful psychological profiles and conduct critical behavioral analysis with regards to the Texas Seven outlaws. Later he would become Captain of Company D Texas Rangers, and at retirement from DPS be the Chief of Texas Rangers. Now (January 2018) Mr. Whitman is the Commissioner for the Texas Department of Family and Protective Services, as well as Chairman of the Board for the Texas Ranger Hall of Fame & Museum. *COURTESY TEXAS RANGER HALL OF FAME & MUSEUM, WACO, TX.*

Contrasting the days when Jack Dean first pinned on the iconic star-in-wheel Texas Ranger badge is clearly illustrated in this modern-age photograph. Company F Ranger Patrick Peña is outfitted to deal with near any emergency—investigative or hostile. Captain Jack Dean's era of Texas Ranger/DPS forward thinking and equipment procurement had—through the years—paid its dividend. *AUTHOR'S PHOTO COURTESY TEXAS RANGER CAPTAIN JAMIE DOWNS.*

Flanked by Jack and Janie, a graduate of Texas A&M University, Cody Dean, maintaining family tradition, too, pinned on the badge as a licensed Texas lawman. Working for the Seguin PD, he is thus far twice the recipient of formal recognition, earning explicit acclaim as the Seguin PD's Rookie of the Year and, later, bestowment of a Life Saving Award for his fast and valiant action during a violent confrontation wherein one fellow was critically stabbed in the neck. Jack Dean is exceptionally proud of Kyle and Cody, and they of he. *COURTESY JACK DEAN.*

Retirement Invitation for United States Marshal Jack Dean, Western District of Texas. Although the irony is legitimately poignant, it is also quite fascinating. The going-away gala was to be held in the John H. Wood, Jr. United States Courthouse at San Antonio—an edifice named after the murdered federal judge Charles Voyde Harrelson was convicted of assassinating—the possible killer Ranger Captain Jack Dean had fingered for the FBI. Fate, indeed, is a mysterious mistress. *COURTESY JACK DEAN.*

You are cordially
invited to a retirement reception
in honor
of
United States Marshal
Jack Dean

Friday, March 26, 2004
5:00 p.m. to 7:00 p.m.

John H. Wood, Jr. United States Courthouse
Rotunda
655 E. Durango
San Antonio, Texas

RSVP
(210) 472-6544

Notes

Preface & Acknowledgments

1. As examples a trio of venerating Texas Ranger histories would be C. L. Douglas, *The Gentlemen in the White Hats: Dramatic Episodes in the History of the Texas Rangers* (1934); Walter Prescott Webb, *The Texas Rangers: A Century of Frontier Defense* (1935); and Will Henry, *The Texas Rangers* (1957). Analytical caution is not unbefitting.

2. Three agenda-driven models aimed at disparaging the Texas Ranger story would be Américo Paredes, *With His Pistol in His Hand: A Border Ballad and Its Hero* (1958); Julian Samora, Joe Bernal, and Albert Peña, *Gunpowder Justice: A Reassessment of the Texas Rangers* (1979); and Gary Clayton Anderson, *The Conquest of Texas: Ethnic Cleansing in the Promised Land, 1820–1875* (2005). Here too, analytical caution is not unbefitting.

3. Interview with Christina Stopka, Deputy Director and Head, Ranger Research Center, Texas Ranger Hall of Fame & Museum (hereafter TRHF&M), 13 February 2017. Although the exact number of individuals who have actually served as Texas Rangers will probably always remain nebulous, Deputy Director Stopka judiciously guesstimates that the number likely was between twelve and fourteen-thousand over the course of time; some Rangers serving but a day or two, a week or two, several months, and some measured their tenure by decades. Understandably during the Indian fighting epoch Muster & Payrolls of provisional and part-time Texas Rangers range from the imperfect to nonexistent, somewhat thwarting calculation of precise numbers. This manpower approximation has been revised upward over the previous estimate provided to Melanie Chrismer for *Lone Star Legacy: The Texas Rangers Then and Now*, 124: "Over the almost two hundred years of Texas Ranger history, between ten and twelve thousand Rangers have served. The numbers are inexact because early records are incomplete." Chrismer was at the time basing her estimates on figures furnished by Rachel Barnett, Research Librarian, TRHF&M, 130, n.6.

4. Christina Stopka, *Partial List of Texas Ranger Company and Unit Commanders*, TRHF&M.

5. Texas Ranger Captain Frank Jones to Adjutant General Woodford Mabry, 30 December, 1892: "If you have no objection I would like to visit Austin

about the 6th of January on some business connected with my candidacy for the Marshal's office. I am very anxious to meet some parties who will be in Austin when the Legislature convenes." Texas State Library and Archives (hereafter TSA). For a biography of Jones see Bob Alexander's *Six-Shooters and Shifting Sands: The Wild West Life of Texas Ranger Captain Frank Jones*; The seminal work regarding outlaw Sam Bass is Rick Miller's *Sam Bass and Gang* which as well contains a biographical profile of Richard Clayton "Dick" Ware, 372–373, n. 13. Also for a brief biographical sketch of Dick Ware see Robert W. Stephens, *Texas Ranger Sketches*, 151–152; and Sammy Tise, *Texas County Sheriffs*, 378.

6. Eduardo Gonzalez, Director, United States Marshals Service, to Honorable Jack O. Dean, United States Marshal, Western District of Texas, 15 March 1994: "Congratulations on your appointment by President Bill Clinton to the position United States Marshal for the Western District of Texas," TRHF&M.

7. William Warren Sterling, *Trails and Trials of a Texas Ranger*, 363.

8. Harold J. Weiss, Jr., *Yours to Command: The Life And Legend Of Texas Ranger Captain Bill McDonald*, 6.

9. Paul N. Spellman, *Captain J.A. Brooks: Texas Ranger*, 56–63.

10. John D. Weaver, *The Brownsville Raid: The Story of America's "Black Dreyfus Affair"*, 80.

11. Bob Alexander, *Fearless Dave Allison: Border Lawman*, 104; Paul N. Spellman, *Captain John H. Rogers: Texas Ranger*, 128–129. Also see, Sterling, *Trails and Trials of a Texas Ranger*, quoting on page 379 Captain Rogers's report to the Adjutant General, ". . . I was completely in his power, and it looked as if he would kill me in spite of all I could do or say. This party [Hillary U. Loftis, aka Tom Ross] is an old time robber of a hard gang."

12. Weiss, *Yours to Command*, 9; Captain John R. Hughes to Adjutant General Thomas Scurry, 14 March 1901, TSA; Bob Alexander, *Winchester Warriors: Texas Rangers of Company D, 1874–1901*, 309; Captain Hughes to AG Scurry, 18 March 1901, TSA: "I will go to El Paso about tomorrow to see the Doctor and will probably stay about two days—My foot is doing well at present—I can walk on crutches but am very careful." Chuck Parsons, *Lone Star Ranger: Captain John R. Hughes*, 170–171.

13. Prior to embarking on this biographical project the author and Jack Dean, during face to face discussions, concurred that truth should override any tendency to favorably color the story. Jack Dean's candor is refreshing.

14. Jack Dean's personal participation with investigating and/or supervising the investigation of specific crimes will be enumerated as his biography unfolds in natural order—as it happened in context. That as a Texas Ranger he is

credited with putting the cap on a riot may be traced to numerous primary sources, two of which are herein cited ahead of chronological order: R.S. Bowe, Mayor, Pharr, Texas, to Colonel Wilson E. Speir, Texas Department of Public Safety [DPS], Austin, Texas, 29 July 1971 and Fr. Michael Allen, O.M.I, Catholic Chaplain at Pan American University to Wilson E. Speir, Director, DPS, Austin, Texas, 9 March 1971, TRHF&M.

Chapter 1: "That was kinda scary"

1. Luke Gournay, *Texas Boundaries: Evolution of the State's Counties*, 58–59. Any major study of Fort Worth's early days must include the adroit nonfiction treatment by Richard F. Selcer, *Hell's Half Acre: The Life and Legend of a Red-Light District.*

2. Clifford R. Caldwell and Ron DeLord, *Texas Lawmen, 1835–1899: The Good and the Bad*, 208–210. Quite probably correctly, author Richard F. Selcer hypothesizes that York's teenage killer was none other than the later infamous Joel Fowler, a Southwestern badman of no little repute. See, "Fowler Than the Kid," *Wild West*, October 2017. For closer study of Fort Worth lawmen killed during the early nineteenth and twentieth centuries the interested reader is advised to consult the laudable *Written In Blood: The History of Fort Worth's Fallen Lawmen, 1861–1909*, Vol. I and *Written In Blood: The History of Fort Worth's Fallen Lawmen, 1910–1928*, Vol. II, both by Richard F. Selcer and Kevin S. Foster. Also see, Richard Selcer and James W. Johnson, "Right Place, Wrong Man," *Wild West*, April, 2018. The definitive and insightful treatment of Courtright is Robert K. DeArment's *Jim Courtright of Fort Worth: His Life and Legend*. The latest research into the life of Luke Short would be the commendable work of Jack DeMattos and Chuck Parsons in the University of North Texas Press release of *The Notorious Luke Short: Sporting Man of the Wild West*. And, for the notorious White Elephant Saloon, see Richard Selcer, ed., *Legendary Watering Holes: The Saloons That Made Texas Famous*, 227–289. For a compilation of Wild West-era issuance of capital punishment in Fort Worth and Tarrant County the reader would be well-served by reviewing the creditable research and writings of West Gilbreath's, (lower case is correct) *death on the gallows: The Encyclopedia of Legal Hangings in Texas*, 313–322.

3. With regards to the Dallas Police Department and its nineteenth-century history, the interested reader is advised to consult researcher and writer Rick Miller's commendable work in *Tin Star Tales: Law and Disorder in Dallas County, Texas, 1846–1900*. A tabulation of slain peace officers is enumerated in Appendix 5, 355.

4. For examination of legal executions and lynch mob madness, an attracted reader should review Terry Baker's creditable enumerations in *Hangings and Lynchings In Dallas County, Texas—1853–1920*.

5. Gournay, *Texas Boundaries*, 49.

6. Texas Department of Health, Bureau of Vital Statistics, Certificate of Birth, "Jacky O'Day Dean" born 16 June 1937 to William H. and Juanita (Day) Dean. Unless otherwise noted, family details were provided by Jack Dean.

7. Ann Arnold, *Gamblers and Gangsters: Fort Worth's Jacksboro Highway in the 1940s and 1950s*. Citations of gangland murders throughout—check index for specific mention of perpetrators and/or victims.

8. Lieutenant George Butler, Dallas Police Department, to Captain R.A. "Bob" Crowder, Company B, Texas Rangers, Fair Park Station, Dallas, Texas, 26 October 1951. From Texas Ranger Captain James A. Wright Collection (Hereafter cited as JAW-C), TRHF&M.

9. *Dallas Morning News*, November 30, 1949; *Dallas Times Herald*, December 2, 1949. With regards to the accidental bombing of Mildred Noble, Lieutenant Butler's letter to Harold G. Robinson, Deputy Director, Criminal Law and Enforcement Division, Department of Justice, State Building, San Francisco, California, 10 March 1952, is both enlightening and speculative:

> [Delbert] Bowers told us that Lois Green had propositioned him to set a bomb on Herbert Noble's car, that Green showed him the bomb. Bowers described that particular bomb as being three sticks of high pressure 90% gelatin dynamite. Each stick had an electric cap inserted in the end. That particular brand of dynamite is considered very powerful and comes in 8" sticks. Bowers stated that Green offered him $10,000.00 for the job, and implied that he would be doing Benny Binion a big favor. Bowers, at that time, was an active Member of the Green mob. He stated that he told Green that "inasmuch as Herbert Noble was his brother-in-law that, he, Bowers, was not going to take a hand in the trouble on either side." We have had information for a number of years concerning Binion actually being the man behind the *attempts* [emphasis added] on Noble's life. . . . that the local underworld considers three sticks of 90% gelatin dynamite enough to kill anyone sitting in the front seat of an automobile. Informed sources say that three sticks will practically demolish any automobile." JAW-C, TRHF&M.

10. Arnold, *Gamblers and Gangsters*, citations to underworld murders throughout. For enumerating many of these gangland murders also see Elston Brooks, *don't dry-clean my blackjack*, [lower case is correct], 19–29; Also see,

Dallas Morning News, December 27 and 28, 1949, for the fatal ambush of Green. Though Hollis DeLois Green was understandably nicknamed "Lois" the proper pronunciation by his friends and enemies alike was "Loyce."

11. *Fort Worth Star-Telegram*, November 22, 1950.

12. *Life Magazine*, May 14, 1951; Texas Ranger Lewis C. Rigler, Company B, stationed at Gainesville, Texas, particularly updated his supervisor, Captain M.T. Gonzaullas, Company B, Fair Park Station, Dallas, Texas, about one attempt on Noble's life, in his official report 15 June 1950, JAW-C, TRHF&M.

13. Arnold, *Gamblers and Gangsters*, 128–129. With Regards to the bombing death of Herbert "The Cat" Noble, former Ranger Lewis Rigler, who was at the crime scene, descriptively noted: "The explosives which killed Herbert Noble tore a hole four feet deep in the roadway in front of his farm home. Noble's body was ripped apart; pieces of flesh and bone were found scattered over an area 200 feet in diameter. His black 1951 Ford sedan was demolished." See, Lewis C. Rigler and Judyth Wagner Rigler, *In The Line of Duty: Reflections of a Texas Ranger Private*, 127. Though the above cited sources about Fort Worth/Dallas gangsterdom are insightful, one of the most comprehensive and authoritative explorations of the Metroplex's underworld's battles for supremacy and cash during the time period is the estimable treatment by Gary W. Sleeper, *I'll Do My Own Damn Killin': Benny Binion, Herbert Noble, and the Texas Gambling War*. Again, specific name citations are indexed. For a summary of the Noble murder investigation a review of Butler to Crowder as cited is recommended. JAW-C, TRHF&M. For the death and underworld activities of Jim Thomas, see D.C. Robnett, Special Officer, to G.W. Dulaney, Sherman Texas, 13 September 1951, JAW-C, TRHF&M; and also see, Ranger Rigler and Lieutenant Butler, Memorandum: Herbert Noble Murder Investigation, 28 August 1951, JAW-C, TRHF&M.

14. T. Lindsay Baker, *Gangster Tour of Texas*, 276–277: "Back farther north on the hill stood a two-story wooden dwelling that housed a number of prostitutes, a further attraction for male customers on the hill." Accomplished journalist Doug J. Swanson, in the brilliant *Blood Aces: The Wild Ride of Benny Binion, The Texas Gangster Who Created Vegas Poker*, adds, "And behind the casino was the brothel. The whores were gorgeous, almost as lovely as the movie stars leaning on the roulette tables. Some wore black velvet capes from Neiman Marcus. Nothing but the best at Fred Browning's place." Quote on p. 41. Though critical caution is certainly appropriate, a book-length treatment of the Top O'Hill Terrace is Jim Gatewood's book, *J. Frank Norris—Top O'Hill Casino—Lew Jenkins and the Texas Oil Rich*.

15. Brownson Malsch, *Lone Wolf: Captain M.T. Gonzaullas*, 177–178.

16. Baker, *Gangster Tour of Texas*, 276.

17. Ibid. For a delightful pictorial peek at this swanky establishment the reader should peruse the photo gallery in *Top O'Hill Terrace* by Vickie Bryant and Camille Hess.

18. Enumeration of the so-called celebrities is a blend of persons identified by Bryant and Hess, *Top O'Hill Terrace*, 37–54; Mike Cox, *Time of the Rangers: Texas Rangers from 1900 to the Present*, 173; Sleeper, *I'll Do My Own Damn Killin'*, 103; and Swanson, *Blood Aces*, 40.

19. Certainly historic data is not lacking with regards to Top O'Hill Terrace, such as the excellent piece in Baker's *Gangster Tour of Texas* and Arnold's outstanding *Gamblers & Gangsters*. In fact, for the latter, the author includes the verbatim treatment of Gloria Van Zandt, a first-rate 1969 term paper prepared for a University of Texas history professor, 86–92. For Lester Ben "Benny" Binion's connection to the Top O'Hill Terrace, see, Sleeper, *I'll Do My Own Damn Killin'*, 102–104 and Swanson, *Blood Aces*, 41. Quite ironically, today the Top O'Hill Terrace compound is on manicured grounds comprising the Arlington Baptist College, and at the time of this writing Vickie Bryant serves as the old-time gambling enterprise's official historian. Aside from the above-cited secondary sources, with regards to Benny "Cowboy" Binion, perusing Ranger Captain Crowder to Colonel Homer Garrison, Jr., Director, DPS, 29 November 1951 is more than fascinating, JAW-C, TRHF&M. Also see, DPS Investigative Report, 17 March 1952: "Memorandum Regarding Benny Binion." Though the writer is not identified, more than likely the author was the Dallas Police Department's Lieutenant George Butler, who was working out of the Texas Rangers' Fair Park Station while working on the Herbert Noble murder investigation. The first sentence of the eight-page typewritten report teases the reader, enticing him/her to continue: "The following information was received from a very confidential source. . . ." JAW-C, TRHF&M.

20. Robert M. Utley, *Lone Star Lawmen: The Second Century Texas Rangers*, 173; Mike Cox, *Texas Ranger Tales II*, 189–190.

21. Malsch, *Lone Wolf*, 178–179; Robert W. Stephens, *Lone Wolf: The Story of Texas Ranger Captain M.T. Gonzaullas*, 74: ". . . Top of the Hill, an elaborate operation with guards at the gates to the grounds. The guards could not stop the Rangers from entering but often were successful in warning the gamblers of their presence. As a result, the raiders were sometimes frustrated by the ingenious ways devised to protect the operation. Once, after finding a virtually empty building an escape tunnel that led gamblers to safety was found, its entrance carefully hidden behind a rack of pool cues." Though there were escape tunnels, the hidden room behind the pool cue

rack was but a room where gambling paraphernalia could be quickly stashed in event of law enforcers' raids.

22. Texas Department of Public Safety (DPS): Application for Employment (Hereafter DPS-AE), for Jack Dean, 18 March 1958, TRHF&M.

23. Interview with Jack Dean by author, 8 March 2017.

24. Ibid.

25. Ibid.; and Oral History Interview (OHI): Jack Dean, 2013, TRHF&M: "there's nine years between my brother [and myself]. . . ."

26. J'Nell Pate, *North of the River: A Brief History of North Fort Worth*, 87.

27. Arnold, *Gamblers and Gangsters*, 12–16; OHI: Jack Dean, 2013, TRHF&M.

28. DPS: Interoffice Memorandum [Hereafter DPS-IM]: Edwin D. Pringle, Sergeant, Texas Highway Patrol [THP], to J.R. Arnold, Manger, DPS Personnel and Training, 14 November 1960, TRHF&M.

29. DPS: Applicant Investigation Report (Hereafter, DPS-AIR), 30 October 1960, by L.M. Hancock, Sergeant, THP, TRHF&M.

30. DPS-IM, 14 November 1960, TRHF&M

31. Interview with Jack and Janie Dean by author 14 March 2017.

32. Interview with Jack Dean by author 7 February 2017; DPS-AIR, 30 October 1960: "Expelled 3 Days in Senior year for skipping classes," in TRHF&M.

33. Arnold, *Gamblers and Gangsters*, 64–65.

34. *Dallas Morning News*, May 4, 1955; Sleeper, *I'll Do My Own Damn Killin'*, 220.

35. *Fort Worth Star-Telegram*, September 1, 1955; Arnold, *Gamblers and Gangsters*, 102–105; *The Brownsville Herald*, October 10, 1957. "[Gene Paul] Norris, was credited, among other things, with the deaths of gangsters Leroy (Tincy) Eggleston, Frank Cates. . . ." Quotation also appears in *The Lawton Constitution*, October 10, 1957.

36. Bill O'Neal, *The Reel Ranges: Texas Rangers in Movies, TV, Radio and Other Forms of Popular Culture*, 84–85; Mike Cox, *Texas Ranger Tales II*, 253.

37. Interview with Jack and Janie Dean by author 14 March 2017.

38. DPS-AE, Jack Dean, 18 March 1958, TRHF&M; Sleeper, *I'll Do My Own Damn Killin'*, 49; Pate, *North of the River*: "By the end of the 1940s, aircraft manufacturers employed more people than the livestock industry . . . ," 32.

39. Arnold, *Gamblers and Gangsters*, 119–120.

40. Ibid.; Brooks, *don't dry-clean my blackjack* [lower case is correct], 22–23.

41. Stan Redding, "Top Gun of the Texas Rangers," *True Detective* (double length feature article), February 1963:

> Only time will determine Norris' niche in the hierarchy of Southwest badmen, but not since the days of Raymond Hamilton and Clyde

Barrow had a desperado of his ilk plagued Texas and Oklahoma. In fact, if crammed police dossiers on his activities are only half-correct—and many have since been fairly well authenticated—Norris was on a par with Texas' most famed gunslinger, John Wesley Hardin, for Texas police generally agree that Norris was responsible for upwards of forty slayings. 71–72.

Garland Daily News, May 5, 1977: "Norris is said to have killed 40 persons. . . ."; *Family Weekly*, June 30, 1985, byline Dennis Holder, ". . . Gene Paul Norris had built a fearsome reputation as a hired killer. . . ."

42. Bob Alexander and Donaly E. Brice, *Texas Rangers: Lives, Legend, and Legacy*, 370.

43. Douglas V. Meed, *Texas Ranger Johnny Klevanhagen*, 173; *The Plainview Reporter-News*, July 22, 1966: "Norris had allegedly already killed more than 50 people during his outlaw career. . . ."

44. Ibid., 174. Also see, Gary Cartwright, "Talking to Killers," an exceptionally fascinating first-person article for the July 2002 edition of *Texas Monthly*, wherein the author highlights several face-to-face interviews with high-profile Texas murderers: "The first killer I ever interviewed was Gene Paul Norris, a notorious badass in Fort Worth in the mid-fifties. . . . Norris was a high-profile player in what was known as the Dixie Mafia, and every newshound in town would have given his trench coat for an interview."

45. Arnold, *Gamblers and Gangsters*, 155–161; Sleeper, *I'll Do My Own Damn Killin'*, 221; *Waxahachie Daily Light*, May 31, 1943.

46. Ibid., 160. The author opts for the nickname "Wimpy" for William Carl Humphrey, while other sources make reference to "Silent Bill" Humphrey.

47. Robert M. Utley, "Terminating Oklahoma's Smiling Killer," *Texas Ranger Dispatch*, No. 17, Summer 2005; *The Shreveport Times*, April 30, 1957. "[Gene Paul] Norris first gained notoriety when he blasted his brother, Pete, out of state prison. Pete went back to prison for a total of 256 years. The slaying victims at Houston were Johnny Brannan, 59-year-old gambler and his 58-year-old semi-invalid wife. They were found with their heads beaten in at their modest home in Houston last week."

48. Meed, *Texas Ranger Johnny Klevenhagen*, 220–222. Quite interestingly, the exact quote about Captain Klevenhagen, is also printed in what appears to be a newsclip from the *Houston Chronicle*, April 14, 1958, byline Stan Redding. For a "legend in his own time," see, Redding, "Top Gun of the Texas Rangers," 54.

49. *Fort Worth Press*, November 21, 1957: ". . . Norris planned to kidnap a woman employee of the bank, hold her and her child as hostages and then

kill them both."; S.E. Spinks, *Law On The Last Frontier: Texas Ranger Arthur Hill.* "Norris planned to enter the woman's home, kill her and her son, and obtain keys and credentials to enter the bank unnoticed." 132–133.

50. Utley, "Terminating Oklahoma's Smiling Killer."

51. *Lubbock Evening Journal*, May 1, 1957; Utley, *Lone Star Lawmen*, 210.

52. Alexander and Brice, *Texas Rangers: Lives, Legend, and Legacy*, 371–372.

53. Texas Department of Health, Bureau of Vital Statistics, *Death Certificate*: Gene Paul Norris, DOD April 29, 1957. Cause of Death: "Gun-shots by Texas Rangers."

54. *The Waco News-Tribune*, April 30, 1957; *Fort Worth Star-Telegram*, April 30, 1957; *Dallas Morning News*, April 30, 1957; Meed, *Texas Ranger Johnny Klevenhagen*, 173–186; Linda Jay Puckett, *Cast a Long Shadow*, 114–122; Susie Mills, *Legend in Bronze: The Biography of Jay Banks*, 4–16; *Dallas Morning News*, September 17, 1978, byline Kent Biffle.

55. Cox, *Texas Ranger Tales II*, 254.

56. Ibid.

57. DPS-AE, Jack Dean, 18 March 1958, TRHF&M.

58. James W. Robinson, *The DPS Story: History of the Development of the Department of Public Safety*, 30–31. Also see, Stephen William Schuster IV, "The Modernization of the Texas Rangers, 1930–1935," Master of Arts Thesis, Texas Christian University, Fort Worth, Texas, 1965.

59. Jack Dean to Personnel and Training Division, DPS, 17 April 1958, TRHF&M.

60. J.R. Arnold, Manager, Personnel and Training DPS, to Jack Dean, 22 April 1958, TRHF&M.

61. DPS Examination: Jack Dean, 22 May 1958, Fort Worth, Texas, TRHF&M.

62. Western Union Telegram to DPS Personnel and Training Division from Jack Dean, 22 July 1958, TRHF&M.

63. DPS Oath of Office, Jack Dean, 6 August 1958, TRHF&M; DPS Oath of Allegiance, Jack Dean, 6 August 1958, TRHF&M; DPS Loyalty Oath, Jack Dean, 6 August 1958, TRHF&M. Certainly at the time matters such as an "Oath of Allegiance" and "Loyalty Oath" were deemed critically important. For an insightful exploration of the Texas Ranger outfit during WWII and the subsequent Cold War era, the interested reader could hardly do better than *Chasing Thugs, Nazis, and Reds: Texas Ranger Norman K. Dixon*, by Kemp Dixon.

Chapter 2: "All these beautiful trees"

1. DPS Change in Status Report (Hereafter DPS-CISR) for Jack Dean, 7 August 1958, TRHF&M: "Resigned because of financial and personal reasons."
2. Jack Dean interview by author, 7 February 2017.
3. Ibid.
4. DPS-AE for Jack Dean, October 1960, TRHF&M; Jack Dean to Colonel Homer Garrison, Jr., Director, DPS, 4 October 1960, TRHF&M: "As for qualifications all I have to offer is a sound body and mind and a strong desire to become a Patrolman with Your Dept."
5. DPS-IM: Sergeant L.M. Hancock, THP, Belton, Texas to Captain Sam J. Gardner, THP, 31 October 1960, TRHF&M.
6. DPS-IM: Sergeant Edwin D. Pringle, THP, Fort Worth, Texas, to J.R. Arnold, Manager, Personnel and Training, Austin, Texas, 14 November 1960, TRHF&M.
7. DPS-CISR: Jack Dean, 7 December 1960, TRHF&M.
8. DPS: Recruit Training School—Part 1, Grade Record for Jack Dean, TRHF&M.
9. Jack Dean interview by author, 24 March 2017, Waco, Texas.
10. DPS-Field Observation Report [Hereafter DPS-FOR], for Jack Dean, by G.D. Winstead, THP, TRHF&M.
11. DPS-Student Evaluation Report—Jack Dean by DPS Sergeant J.A. Dumas, 5 April 1961, TRHF&M.
12. Fred Toler, Executive Director, Texas Commission on Law Enforcement Officer Standards and Education, to Wilson Speir, DPS, 24 March 1961, TRHF&M: "Dean, Jack Oday, is hereby certified by the Commission as being qualified to be a peace officer in your department."
13. Robinson, *The DPS Story*, 35.
14. *Fort Worth Star-Telegram*, March 25, 1961. Also see graduation photo, Texas Department of Public Safety *Golden Anniversary Pictorial and History Book, 1935–1985*, 113.
15. J.R. Arnold, Manager, Personnel and Training, to Jack O'Day Dean, 24 March 1961, TRHF&M
16. Jack Dean interview by author, 24 March 2017; Elizabeth Cruce Alvarez, ed., *Texas Almanac, 2014–2015*, 341.
17. Alvarez, *Texas Almanac*, 371.
18. Jack Dean interview by author, 30 March 2017.
19. Ibid.
20. Ibid. Also, Tise, *Texas County Sheriffs*, 436.

21. Ibid.

22. Ibid.

23. DPS Performance Development Summary (Hereafter DPS-PDS) for Jack Dean, 30 April 1961, TRHF&M.

24. Jack Dean interview by author 30 March 2017.

25. DPS-IM: THP Sergeant R.W. Howie, Pecos, Texas, to Joe S. Fletcher, Assistant Director, DPS, Austin, Texas, 29 September 1962, TRHF&M.

26. DPS-CISR: Jack Dean, 1 July 1961, TRHF&M.

27. DPS-PDS: Jack Dean, 31 August 1962, TRHF&M.

28. Kyle Dean interview by author, 18 April 2017.

29. Francis E. Crosby, Special Agent in Charge (SAC), FBI, El Paso, Texas, to Col. Homer Garrison, Jr., Austin, Texas, 23 October 1962, TRHF&M; Garrison to Crosby, 26 October 1962, TRHF&M.

30. Unidentified by date, newsclip from the *Pecos Enterprise*, TRHF&M.

31. Telegram: Texas Ranger Captain George Baylor to Texas Adjutant General Wilburn Hill King, 8 July 1883, TSA. For highlights of this Wild West shootout and the one listed in following citation, see Bob Alexander, *Whiskey River Ranger: The Old West Life of Baz Outlaw*, 34–40.

32. Telegram: Texas Ranger Captain James T. Gillespie to AG King, 19 August 1885, TSA; *El Paso Daily Times*, August 26, 1885; *Dallas Weekly Herald*, August 27, 1885.

33. Jack Dean interview by author, 30 March 2017.

34. Ibid.

35. Ibid.

36. This series of correspondence indicates that within DPS negative allegations—even be they near on the face ridiculous—are taken seriously. See, DPS-IM, Wilson E. Speir, Assistant Director, DPS, to Major Leo Gossett, Commander, Region 4, DPS, 6 May 1963; Ward County Judge Ed Keys to AD Speir, 17 May 1963; DPS-IM, Sergeant R.W. Howie, DPS, to Captain Ray B. Butler, DPS, 20 May 1963; DPS-IM, Commander Gossett to AD Speir, 22 May 1963; DPS-IM, Major Guy Smith, Commander, Region 1, DPS, to W.J. White, Captain, THP, Region 1, 31 May 1963; Captain White to Major Smith, 15 June 1963; Major Smith to AD Speir, 20 June 1963. All, TRHF&M.

37. Kyle Dean interview by author, 18 April 2017; Betty Dooley Awbrey and Claude Dooley, *Why Stop?: A Guide to Texas Historical Roadside Markers*, 402.

38. FBI SAC Herbert E. Hoxie, El Paso, Texas, to DPS Director Garrison, 18 February 1964, TRHF&M; DPS Director Garrison to Herbert Hoxie, 21 February 1964, TRHF&M.

39. Jack Dean interview by author 30 March 2017.

40. Ibid.

41. Ibid.

42. DPS-CISR: Jack Dean, 1 September 1963, TRHF&M.

43. Jack Dean interview by author 30 March 2017.

44. DPS-PDS: Jack Dean, 30 September 1964, TRHF&M.

45. DPS-IM: Sergeant Howie to Major Gossett, 19 September 1964, TRHF&M.

46. THP Patrolman Jack Dean to DPS Director Garrison: "I respectfully submit my resignation from the Department of Public Safety, Highway Patrol Service. This is done with much regret but due to a above average job and salary opportunity I feel it is in the best interest of myself and family. . . . I ask that my resignation become effective at 5PM, Wednesday, September 30, 1964." Received Personnel and Training, 24 September 1964, TRHF&M.

47. DPS-AE: Jack Dean, 24 December 1964, TRHF&M.

Chapter 3: "I have no right to ask"

1. Jack Dean interview by author 30 March 2017.

2. A.A. Archer, District Attorney, 143rd Judicial District of the State of Texas to Personnel Department, Montgomery Ward, Fort Worth, Texas, 19 April 1965, TRHF&M; D.T. Mead, Controller, Catalog House, Montgomery Ward, Fort Worth, Texas, to A.A. Archer, 4 May 1965, TRHF&M.

3. DPS-AE: Jack Dean, 24 December 1964, TRHF&M.

4. Jack Dean to Director Garrison, DPS, 24 December 1964, TRHF&M.

5. DPS Assistant Director Speir to Jack Dean, 01 March 1965, TRHF&M.

6. Alvarez, *Texas Almanac*: Population Reeves County, 13,798; Population Smith County, 214,821.

7. *Tyler Morning Telegraph*, March 18, 1965.

8. DPS-Probationary Progress Report (Hereafter DPS-PPR), 30 June 1965, TRHF&M.

9. DPS-PPR, 31 August 1965, TRHF&M.

10. Sergeant Fasel to Manager Arnold, Personnel and Training, DPS, 01 October 1965, TRHF&M.

11. DPS-PDS: Jack Dean, 28 February 1966.

12. Kyle Dean interview by author, 18 April 2017.

13. *Tyler Morning Telegraph*, July 31, 1970; unidentified newsclip (probably *Fort Worth Star-Telegram*); Jack Dean interview by author 4 April 2017.

14. Paul M. Bass, General Partner, Goodbody & Co., Dallas, Texas, to Major Guy Smith, THP, Dallas, Texas, 25 September 1969, TRHF&M.

15. Ibid.

16. Jack Dean to Colonel Garrison, Director DPS, 28 March 1966, TRHF&M.

17. DPS-IM: Sergeant Fasel to Major Smith, 15 April 1966, TRHF&M.

18. Jack Dean interview by author, 4 April 2017; unidentified newsclip: "We Are Proud to Announce the Association of Jack O. Dean, Registered Representative, Robert G. Day Investment Securities. . . . Private Wire to E.F. Hutton & Company." Clipping held at TRHF&M.

19. DPS-IM: Arnold, Manager, DPS Personnel and Training, to AD Speir, DPS, 28 September 1966, quoting applicant Jack Dean, TRHF&M.

20. DPS-IM: AD Speir, DPS, to Major Smith, DPS, 26 September 1966, TRHF&M.

21. DPS-IM: Major Smith, DPS, to AD Speir, DPS, 28 September 1966, TRHF&M.

22. DPS-IM: AD Speir, DPS, to Arnold, Manager, DPS Personnel and Training, 3 October 1966, TRHF&M.

23. DPS-IM: AD Speir, DPS, to Chief Glen McLaughlin, DPS Personnel and Staff Services, 23 December 1966 in TRHF&M: "The Commission also advised that due to the condition of his child that he would be stationed in Tyler." DPS-IM: Arnold, Manager, DPS Personal and Training to AD Speir, DPS, 28 September 1966, TRHF&M.

24. DPS-PPR: Jack Dean, 28 February 1967, TRHF&M.

25. DPS-PDS: Jack Dean, 29 February 1968, TRHF&M.

26. OHI: Jack Dean, 2013, TRHF&M.

27. Ibid.; For more about Texas Rangers Red Arnold and Glenn Elliott, see, Bob Arnold, *First in Texas: Three Texans and Their Contributions to Texas History, 1821–1978* and Glenn Elliott with Robert Nieman, *Glenn Elliott: A Ranger's Ranger* and Glenn Elliott and Robert Nieman, *Glenn Elliott: Still a Ranger's Ranger*.

28. Robert "Bobby" Nieman, "20th Century Shining Star: Captain Jack Dean, United States Marshall," *Texas Ranger Dispatch*, April 2008.

29. Jack Dean interview by author, 24 March 2017 and 4 April 2017.

30. Jack Dean interview by author, 6 April 2017.

31. Elliott, *A Ranger's Ranger*, 103. A first-hand recollection of the 1957 Lone Star Steel strike may be found in Rigler and Rigler, *In The Line of Duty*, 68–73. For another informative account of the 1957 Lone Star Steel strike, the reader might also wish to peruse Spinks, *Law on the Last Frontier*, 141–149.

32. Utley, *Lone Star Lawmen*, 223; Tise, *Texas County Sheriffs*, 384.

33. Ibid.

34. Ibid.

35. Elliott, *A Ranger's Ranger*, 103.

36. OHI; Robert K. "Bob" Mitchell, 1996, TRHF&M.

37. Bob Favor, *My Rangering Days*, 44.

38. Ibid.

39. Ibid.

40. OHI: Bob Mitchell, 1996, TRHF&M.

41. DPS-PDS: Jack Dean, 28 February 1969, TRHF&M.

42. Utley, *Lone Star Lawmen*, 224.

43. For a glimpse at this time of social unrest and illegality, specifically applicable to federal involvement, the interested reader may wish to review an excellent treatment, *Forging the Star: The Official Modern History of the United States Marshal Service*, researched and written by the organization's longtime historian, David S. Turk.

44. DPS Employee Biographical Sketch (Hereafter DPS-EBS): Jack Dean, 19 February 1982. With regards to "Riot Control," Jack Dean attended one school during 1965 and another during 1967. He would, also while serving with THP, undergo specialized training with regards to "Bomb Recognition." See papers in TRHF&M.

45. Gournay, *Texas Boundaries*, 39–40; Awbrey and Dooley, *Why Stop?* 308–309.

46. Roy R. Barkley and Mark F. Odintz, eds., *The Portable Handbook of Texas*, 970.

47. Ibid., 94, 970.

48. Ibid.

49. Jack Dean interview by author, 24 March 2017.

50. DPS-IM: Jack Dean to Colonel Speir, 21 April 1969, TRHF&M.

51. *Tyler Morning Telegraph*, November 5, 1969; DPS Criminal Case Report (Hereafter DPS-CCR), Jack Dean, 5 November 1969, TRHF&M.

52. Transcript, Tyler Junior College: Jack Dean, Fall Semester 1969, TRHF&M.

53. Unidentified newsclips (presumably from the *Tyler Morning Telegraph*), TRHF&M; Jack Dean interview by author 6 April 2017.

54. Ibid.

55. Kyle Dean interview by author, 18 April 2017.

56. J. Edgar Hoover, Director, FBI, Washington, D.C. to Colonel Speir, DPS, Austin, Texas, 3 December 1969, TRHF&M; Colonel Speir to Director Hoover, 9 December 1969, TRHF&M.

57. DPS-PDS: Jack Dean, 28 February 1970, TRHF&M.

58. DPS-IM: Texas Ranger Bob Mitchell, Company B, Tyler, Texas, to W.D. "Bill" Wilson, Captain Company B, Dallas, Texas, 1 May 1970, TRHF&M.

59. Director Speir to Jack Dean, 26 June 1970, TRHF&M.
60. Director Speir to Jack Dean, 13 July 1970, TRHF&M.
61. Director Speir to Jack Dean, 31 July 1970, TRHF&M; *The Texas Lawman: Official Publication of the Sheriff's Association of Texas, Inc.*, October 1970, 53.
62. Governor Preston Smith to Jack Dean, 12 August 1970, TRHF&M.

Chapter 4: "Good image with good citizens"

1. Texas Ranger Lewis Rigler, Company B, to Jack Dean, 3 August 1970, TRHF&M.
2. *San Antonio Times* (Tempo Section), November 19, 1992, byline Catherine Helland, "The Lone (Star) Ranger Rides Again." In this interesting piece, a biographical sketch of Jack Dean, the Texas Ranger comments on the philosophy of lending that helping hand to comrades: "Our group is close-knit even though we can fuss and fight like brothers. If a Ranger calls for help, unless you are in the middle of a shoot-out, you go." More recently this unwritten tenet was highlighted by H.L. "Hank" Whitman, Jr., Chief, Texas Rangers, Ret., during his 18 September 2016 presentation to the Heart of Texas Historians & Storytellers at Brady, McCulloch County, Texas; James L. Coffee, Russell M. Drake, and John T. Barnett, *Graham Barnett: A Dangerous Man*, 5: "across the entire state."
3. Alvarez, *Texas Almanac*, 312.
4. Jack Dean interview by author 6 April 2017; State of Texas Purchase Voucher, 21 August 1970, TRHF&M
5. DPS-Texas Rangers Weekly Activity Report [Hereafter DPS-TRWR], Jack Dean, 5 September 1970, TRHF&M; For a fascinating biography of James Abijah Brooks the interested reader should examine, Paul N. Spellman's *Captain J. A. Brooks: Texas Ranger*. For the federal lawsuit, see Utley, *Lone Star Lawmen*, 242–243.
6. DPS-TRWR: Jack Dean, 5 September 1970; Jack Dean interview by author, 7 February 2017 and 6 April 2017. Although he was sworn in by Director Speir on 31 August 1970, due to certain formalities and pay-period issues his official EOD (Entry on Duty) date in DPS records is listed as 1 September 1970.
7. Robert W. Stephens, *Tribute to a Ranger*, 2.
8. Utley, *Lone Star Lawmen*, 235.
9. Cox, *Time of the Rangers*, 277–278. With a slightly different take, H. Joaquin Jackson and David Marion Wilkinson, *One Ranger: A Memoir*, cover the jailbreak through Ranger Jackson's eyes, a first-hand participant, and it is from this account that the acreage of A.Y. Allee's Dimmit County ranch is drawn, although an unidentified newsclip in TRHF&M sizes Allee's ranch as 775

acres. And of particular interest is Ranger Jackson's rendering of the jail-break aftermath: "As we moved through the debris of the second floor, the effects of Captain's lone-man assault became obvious. Handguns lay abandoned, still cocked and loaded, on the floor. Two revolvers were stacked on the food trays like dirty dishes. We found a tossed rifle here, a shucked riot gun there. As the dust and gun smoke settled, an eerie quiet descended, like the stillness that follows a tornado. Everything had a bullet hole through it or in it. Inspecting the carnages, I was mighty glad the captain [Allee] was on our side." See pp. 77, 147–154.

10. H. Joaquin Jackson with James L. Haley, *One Ranger Returns*, 18.

11. Favor, *My Rangering Days*, 34.

12. Lengthy though unidentified newsclip in Vertical File (Hereafter VF), A.Y. Allee, TRHF&M.

13. Ibid.

14. Stephens, *Tribute to a Ranger*, 4.

15. *Detroit Free Press*, September 6, 1970.

16. Favor, *My Rangering Days*, 34; Robert W. Stephens, who actually interviewed A.Y. Allee, told this author that the captain struck the THP Patrolman in the back of the head with his pistol. On the other hand, when asked about this incident, Jack Dean related that Captain Allee never hit anyone from behind and further acknowledged that the story was, indeed, true—but that an argumentative Allee was standing toe to toe with the trooper and creased his skull with the barrel of his weapon. Also, Jackson and Wilkinson, *One Ranger: A Memoir*, 35: "Captain Allee was well known by my generation of highway troopers. During a disagreement, he had pistol-whipped one of my [THP] colleagues."

17. Utley, *Lone Star Lawmen*, 236.

18. Stephens, *Tribute to A Ranger*, 1.

19. In their sweeping indictment, authors Julian Samora, Joe Bernal, and Albert Peña, *Gunpowder Justice: A Reassessment of the Texas Rangers*, somehow try—ineffectively it may be argued—to correlate the lack of Hispanic cheerleaders at Crystal City, Zavala County, Texas, to their fixation on seemingly blaming Texas Rangers for all societal prejudice and discrimination in South Texas (125–126). Just as interesting—and fallacious—is the oft quoted characterization of Texas Rangers found in Adalberto Aguirre, Jr. and Jonathan H. Turner, *American Ethnicity: The Dynamics and Consequences of Discrimination*, 150: "In fact the general view of many Chicanos and Mexicans is that 'every Texas Ranger has some Mexican blood. He has it on his boots.'" The hyperbole is rich.

20. Ben H. Proctor, "The Modern Texas Rangers: A Law-Enforcement Dilemma in the Rio Grande Valley." This article first appeared as a contribution within

Reflections of Western Historians, edited by John Carroll, and was later reprinted in Glasrud and Weiss, *Tracking the Texas Rangers: The Twentieth Century*, 179–192.

21. Ibid. 181.

22. Ibid.

23. Favor, *My Rangering Days*, 34.

24. Maude T. Gilliland, *Horsebackers of the Brush Country: A Story of Texas Rangers and Mexican Liquor Smugglers*, quoting remarks of Captain A.Y. Allee. 141.

25. Stephens, *Tribute to a Ranger*, 4.

26. Proctor, "The Modern Texas Rangers," 185, "'Quite perturbed' over these episodes, union leader Eugene Nelson went 'looking' for Captain Allee the next morning to lodge a strong protest. When he arrived at the courthouse at Rio Grande City and Allee could not be found, he reportedly lost his temper. Constable Manuel Benavides claimed that he said: 'You tell that s.o.b. he had better lay off or there will be some dead Rangers.' By late afternoon County Attorney Randall Nye, who was also an attorney for the strike-bound Starr Produce Company, had charged him with threatening the lives of law enforcement officers. Nelson claimed that he had been misunderstood—that he had told the constable 'if the Texas Rangers don't stop, there are going to be some red-faced Rangers around here when the Senate investigators arrive.' Nevertheless he spent the night in 'a relic from the dark ages,' the cockroach infested Starr County jail"; Ed Blackburn, Jr., *Wanted: Historic County Jails of Texas*, 306.

27. Ibid.

28. Utley, *Lone Star Lawmen*, 241.

29. Cox, *Time of the Rangers*, 272.

30. Jackson and Haley, *One Ranger Returns*, 13.

31. Samora, Bernal, and Peña, *Gunpowder Justice*, quoting the *Texas Observer* of June 9, 1967, 151.

32. Utley, *Lone Star Lawmen*, 241.

33. Gilliland, *Horsebackers of the Brush Country*, quoting Captain Allee from a story carried in the July 7, 1967, edition of the *Dallas Morning News*. 140–141.

34. Utley, *Lone Star Lawmen*, 242. An alternative account of the arrests may be found in Jackson and Haley, *One Ranger*, 15–16.

35. Ibid. 240.

36. Ibid. Quoting partial findings of the U.S. Commission of Civil Rights, *Mexican Americans and the Administration of Justice in the Southwest*.

37. Ibid.

38. Proctor, "The Modern Texas Rangers," 184. For one interested in further probing this Lower Rio Grande Valley affair the reader may wish to access *Francisco Medrano, et al. v. A.Y. Allee, et al*, U.S. District Court, Southern District of Texas, Brownsville Division, 26 June 1972 and also, "Final Judgment as Modified Pursuant to Remand by The Supreme Court of the United States," 24 June 1976.

39. Utley, *Lone Star Lawmen*, 221; Jack Dean characterized Captain Allee, highlighting another dimension of his overall personality: "He was hard, and he was stern, but he helped a lot of kids out of his own pocket." See, Lee Paul, *Jim Peters: Texas Ranger*, 70.

40. Bob Alexander, *Riding Lucifer's Line: Ranger Deaths along the Texas-Mexico Border*, 38–51; For additional insight to this fascinating tale of Mexican banditry the interested reader might which to access Leopold Morris, "The Mexican Raid of 1875 on Corpus Christi," *Texas Historical Association Quarterly*, July 1900 and William M. Hager, "The Nuecestown Raid of 1875: A Border Incident," *Arizona and the West*, Autumn 1959.

41. Gilbreath, *death on the gallows* [lower case is correct], 277.

42. For McNelly's biography see the award-winning work of Chuck Parsons and Marianne E. Hall Little, *Captain L.H. McNelly: Texas Ranger, The Life and Times of a Fighting Man*.

43. The seminal treatment of this misguided manifesto is Charles H. Harris III and Louis R. Sadler, *The Plan De San Diego: Tejano Rebellion, Mexican Intrigue*.

44. For Ranger involvement during the exciting timeframe, see Spur Award winning writers Charles H. Harris III and Louis R. Sadler and their blockbuster treatment, *The Texas Rangers and the Mexican Revolution: The Bloodiest Decade, 1910–1920*.

45. Alexander, *Riding Lucifer's Line*, 199–209.

46. DPS-TRWR: Jack Dean, 5 September 1970, TRHF&M.

47. *Corpus Christi Caller-Times*, September 19, 1970. For biographical profiles of John Mansel Wood, see, "Commanders Lead Diversified Lives," *Borger News-Herald*, October 7, 1973 and *The San Antonio Light*, October 15, 1978; VF-John Wood, TRHF&M. Also of note, John Wood wrote a small book about some of his experiences in West Texas, *Texas Ranger in the Oil Patch*.

48. DPS-TRWR: Jack Dean, 5 September 1970, TRHF&M. The "cedar stump" analogy is from Jackson and Wilkinson, *One Ranger*, 150.

49. Ibid.; Jack Dean interview by author, 9 February 2017.

50. DPS-PDS: Jack Dean, 30 September 1970, TRHF&M

Chapter 5: "Cocked and locked"

1. DPS Criminal Offense Report (Hereafter DPS-COR): Murder-Armed Robbery, 01 August 1970, TRHF&M.
2. Jack Dean to Worth Seaman, Manager, MO Section, DPS, Austin, Texas, 24 September 1970, TRHF&M.
3. DPS-TV: Jack Dean, month of September 1970, TRHF&M.
4. DPS-TRWR: Jack Dean, 5 September 1970, TRHF&M; Tise, *Texas County Sheriffs*, 257.
5. DPS-TRWR: Jack Dean, 12 September 1970, TRHF&M.
6. DPS-TRWR: Jack Dean, 19 September 1970, TRHF&M; *McAllen Monitor*, September 15, 1970. This newspaper rightfully is *The Monitor*; however, adding the city name avoids confusion with the often-cited *Monitor*—the newsletter of the United States Marshals Service. *Valley Morning Star*, June 5, 1971. Biographical data regarding District Attorney McInnis is courtesy the award-winning nonfiction author Rick Miller, the now retired County Attorney for Bell County.
7. Ibid.
8. Captain A.Y. Allee to All Members of Company "D" Texas Rangers, 17 September 1970, TRHF&M.
9. Jack Dean to Captain Allee, 20 September 1970, TRHF&M.
10. DPS-TRWR: Jack Dean, 26 September 1970, TRHF&M.
11. DPS-TRWR: Jack Dean, 3 October 1970, TRHF&M.
12. David W. Neubauer, *America's Courts and the Criminal Justice System*, 32–33.
13. *The Current*, May 29–June 4, 1986.
14. *Texas Lawman*, Vol. 39, No. 8, 39; *Fredericksburg Standard Radio Post*, September 6, 1989, "Texas Ranger," byline Yvonne Hartman; VF-Walter Werner, TRHF&M.
15. *The Current*, May 29–June 4, 1986. "Dean of the Texas Rangers."
16. Texas Ranger Roster, Company D, 1 December 1971, TRHF&M. Also see, DPS-IM: Captain John M. Wood, Company D, to All Texas Rangers, 13 April 1972, TRHF&M. For a fascinating and informative piece regarding Texas Ranger Litt Carpenter, see, J. Lyn Carl, "Ranger, Daughter Keeps Tradition in the Family," *Nacogdoches Daily Sentinel*, December 16, 1979. Interestingly, for a time while serving as a Ranger, Litt Carpenter's daughter, Suzanne (Borden), was a THP Patrolman, marking a distinction as the only father-daughter team within DPS ranks; VF-Litt Truitt Carpenter, TRHF&M. A succinct biography of Texas Ranger Jack Van Cleve may be accessed in Gilliland's *Horsebackers of the Brush Country*, 144. Also, VF-Jack Van Cleve, TRHF&M. Watchfulness is noted. There are two Texas Rangers

named Jack Van Cleve: this one and his uncle who served much earlier and who perished in combat during WWI. For brief sketches of Texas Ranger Jerome Preiss, see Jacque Crouse, "The Last Cowboy," *San Antonio Express-News*, July 8, 1999, and Carmina Danini: "Preiss, 80, Traveled on Horseback as a Texas Ranger," *San Antonio Express-News*, July 15, 2000; VF-Jerome Preiss, TRHF&M.

17. Texas Ranger Sergeant Daniel Lynch Musgrave to Adjutant General Woodford H. Mabry, 22 July 1903, TSA. For a biographical profile of desperado Charles Small the reader may wish to review Chapter 6, "He Was Killed By Me," in Bob Alexander's *Lawmen, Outlaws, and S.O.Bs: Gunfighter of the Old Southwest,* Vol. 1, 103–118.

18. DPS-TRWR: Jack Dean, 3 October 1970, TRHF&M

19. DPS-TRWR: Jack Dean, 10 October 1970, TRHF&M.

20. Ibid.

21. DPS-COR: 12 October 1970, TRHF&M.

22. DPS-PR: Texas Ranger Sergeant Werner, 9 December 1970, TRHF&M.

23. DPS-TRWR: Jack Dean, 10 and 17 October 1970, TRHF&M.

24. DPS-PR: Jack Dean, 27 June 1971, TRHF&M.

25. DPS-PR: Jack Dean, 8 February 1971, TRHF&M.

26. Notarized Statement of Sergeant Felipe Pena, Police Officer, Mercedes Police Department, 19 October 1970, TRHF&M; DPS-TRWR: Jack Dean, 17 October 1970, TRHF&M.

27. DPS-TRWR: Jack Dean, 24 October 1970, TRHF&M; *McAllen Monitor*, March 8, 1971; William Martin, "Basilica of Our Lady of San Juan del Valle," *Texas Monthly*, January 2007; *Corpus Christi Caller-Times*, October 24, 1970.

28. DPS-TRWR: Jack Dean, 31 October 1970. TRHF&M; DPS-COR: Questionable Death, 31 October 1970. TRHF&M: Suicide Note and Physical Examination Report regarding deceased by Dr. H.W. Whigham, M.D., McAllen, Texas. TRHF&M; Ranger Jack Dean to DPS Crime Lab, Questioned Document Section, 2 November 1970, TRHF&M; Paul W. Hanson, Supervisor, DPS Questioned Document Section, to Ranger Jack Dean, 13 November 1970, TRHF&M.

29. Ibid.

30. DPS-TRWR: Jack Dean, 7 November 1970, TRHF&M.

31. DPS-TRWR: Jack Dean, 14 November 1970, TRHF&M.

32. Ibid.

33. Captain John W. Wood, Company D, Texas Rangers to All Texas Rangers, Company D, 4 November 1970, TRHF&M.

34. Jack Dean interview by author and Jan Devereaux, 24 March 2017.

35. DPS-TRWR: Jack Dean, 14 November 1970, TRHF&M.

36. DPS-TRWR: Jack Dean, 21 November 1970 and 28 November 1970, TRHF&M.

37. DPS-COR: 13 December 1970, TRHF&M.

38. Fred R. Rymer, Supervisor, DPS Crime Lab, Firearms Section to Jack Dean 1 February 1971, TRHF&M.

39. DPS-CCR: Murder, 27 November 1970, TRHF&M.

40. DPS-TRWR: Jack Dean, 12 December 1970, TRHF&M; *McAllen Monitor*, December 15, 1970.

41. DPS Investigation Progress Report [Hereafter DPS-PR]: Jack Dean, 13 December 1970, TRHF&M; Fred R. Rymer, Supervisor, Firearms Section, DPS Crime Lab, to Jack Dean, 1 February 1971, TRHF&M.

42. DPS Supplementary Criminal Case Report [Hereafter DPS-SCCR]: Jack Dean, 18 January 1971, TRHF&M.

43. E.G. Albers, Jr., *The Life and Reflections of a Texas Ranger*, 79–85.

44. James M. Ray, Chief, Criminal Law Enforcement to All Ranger Captains, 9 October 1970, TRHF&M

45. DPS-TRWR: Jack Dean, 5 December 1970, TRHF&M; TECLOSE F-6: Jack Dean, 4 December 1970, TRHF&M.

46. For this excellent piece by Pamela Colloff, "Law of the Land," [originally a *Texas Monthly* article] as carried by Glasrud and Weiss in *Tracking The Texas Rangers: The Twentieth Century,* now retired Texas Ranger Kyle Dean [Jack Dean's son] said: "Like a lot of other Rangers, I carry the Colt .45. It's a luxury we're afforded that the other services are not. We can carry the firearm that we think best fits our assignment. The way I see it, the Colt is a link to the past. That's what the Rangers who came before us carried, and we're continuing that tradition." See p. 254.

47. Ibid., quoting the remarks of retired Texas Ranger Matt Cawthon: "A lot of us carry the Colt Model 1911 semi-automatic, .45 caliber handgun. It has been around for nearly one hundred years [106 now], and it is tried-and-true. . . . Forty-five caliber does a good job, I'll tell you."

48. Doyle Holdridge, *Working the Border: A Texas Ranger's Story*, 45.

49. Jack Dean interview by author, 6 April 2017; OHI: Jack Dean, 2013. "I think it seems like the Rangers mostly favored .45 automatics of some breed, I always carried a Colt. When I was in the Valley I carried a Colt. 38 Super because I spent a lot to time across from Mexico and you can't get .45 ammunition in Mexico, you're not supposed to, it's illegal. But you can get 38 Super ammunition . . . ," TRHF&M.

50. For an insightful discussion of the "cocked and locked" mode for carrying handguns on the 1911 platform, see, Pete Dickey, "Handgun Safety and Design," *American Rifleman*, May 1988, 34–36.

51. Colloff, "Law of the Land" in Glasrud and Weiss, *Tracking the Texas Rangers*, quoting Texas Ranger, Ret. Lane Akin. While at the time a junior-high student, Lane Akin acknowledges that during a classroom visit by Texas Ranger Charlie Moore, he asked the lawman about the wisdom of carrying a "cocked and locked" pistol and Moore's stock reply. 240. The rejoinder is, by now, a well-used and standard response.

52. *McAllen Monitor*, December 16, 1970. Most newspaper accounts reference "David L. Cassidy" while Jack Dean's reports identify him as "David Casady," which is also the surname mentioned in a supplemental newspaper story and, more definitively, the spelling used to identify the man in the United States Department of Justice Criminal History, i.e. Federal Rap Sheet; *McAllen Monitor*, May 7, 1971.

53. DPS-TRWR: Jack Dean, 12 December 1970, TRHF&M; *McAllen Monitor*, December 13, 1970.

54. DPS-TRWR: Jack Dean, 19 December 1970, TRHF&M; *McAllen Monitor*, December 14 and 15, 1970; DPS-CCR: Possession of Stolen Property, 10 December 1970; numerous DPS-PRs: Jack Dean, December 1970, TRHF&M.

55. Ibid.; Hanson, DPS Questioned Document Section, to Jack Dean 8 January 1971, TRHF&M.

56. DPS-TRWR: Jack Dean, 26 December 1970, TRHF&M.

57. Utley, *Lone Star Lawmen*, 248.

58. Hidalgo County Sheriff Claudio Castaneda quoted in the December 23, 1970 edition of the *McAllen Monitor*.

Chapter 6: "Stern but friendly"

1. TRWR: Jack Dean, 9 January 1971, TRHF&M.

2. DPS-Intelligence Section, Intelligence Report [Hereafter DPS-IR]: Don Lee, 14 January 1971, TRHF&M.

3. DPS-IM: Ranger Jack Dean to Captain John Wood, 15 January 1971, TRHF&M: DPS-FAR: Senior Ranger Captain Clint Peoples, 18 February 1971, TRHF&M.

4. DPS-TRWR: Jack Dean, 6 February 1971, TRHF&M; Jack Dean's personal *Daily Reminder* journals (Hereafter JD-DRJ): 6 February 1971, TRHF&M.

5. *McAllen Monitor*, December 26, 1971.

6. Ibid., May 28, 1971.

7. Utley, *Lone Star Lawmen,* 248: "when Chief Alfredo Ramirez called in two fire engines manned by Anglo firefighters who turned high-pressure hose on the crowd. 'That made everybody go berserk. . . . it was a full-fledged riot.'"

8. *The Edinburg Daily Review*, March 9, 1971.

9. *State of Texas vs. Robert C. Johnson*, County Court at Law, Hidalgo County, No. CR-8032; Direct and Cross- Examination of Texas Ranger Jack Dean, 2, TRHF&M.

10. Ibid.; *Corpus Christi Caller-Times*, June 18, 1971.

11. Ibid., 4.

12. Ibid., 7.

13. Ibid., 8: ". . . I [Ranger Jack Dean] would say the time the ambulance got there and we got him [Alfonso Flores] in the ambulance and the ambulance left with him, it was not over five minutes. The ambulance was there nearly as soon as I was." Newspaper reports vary regarding Alfonso Loredo Flores's age, twenty in some, twenty-two in others and twenty-five in another.

14. Utley, *Lone Star Lawmen*, 248–249.

15. *San Antonio Express*, February 7, 1971.

16. *McAllen Monitor*, February 24, 1972.

17. *San Antonio Express*, February 7, 1971.

18. Ibid.

19. Utley, *Lone Star Lawmen*, 249: "Dean counseled delay. 'If we hit that place, it'll blow up again.' Ramirez accepted that wisdom, and the sun set on a tense, restless town."

20. JD-DRJ: 07 February 1971, TRHF&M.

21. DPS-TRWR: Jack Dean, 13 February 1917, TRHF&M; *Corpus Christi Caller-Times*, March 12, 1971. "The slaying of Flores as well as the entire riot was investigated by Texas Ranger Jack Dean of McAllen."

22. *Lubbock Avalanche Journal*, February 8, 1971. That Texas Ranger Jack Dean was at least one of the driving forces in restoring sanity and safety to the streets of Pharr came from David Hall, attorney for the United Farm Workers, and carried in the May 28, 1971, edition of the *McAllen Monitor*:

> Hall gave the militants' version of the Pharr riot—the police started it—and credited the Catholic priest, Ranger Jack Dean, Chief Deputy Sheriff Ray Rogers and Jesse Trevino of McAllen with getting the crowds to the Valley Community Center and negotiating with the police to get them back in to their homes.

23. DPS-TRWR: Jack Dean, February 13, 1971.

24. Ibid. Interestingly, Texas Ranger Glenn B. Krueger's father, Bennie C. Krueger was also a Texas Ranger, retiring from DPS during 1969. A book focusing on the elder Krueger's life story is Raymond West's *Bennie C. Krueger: Texas Ranger, Texas Gentleman.*

25. Ibid.

26. *The Edinburg Daily Review*, March 9, 1971.

27. *McAllen Monitor*, March 7, 1971; *Galveston Daily News*, March 7, 1971.

28. Ibid. February 11, 1971.

29. Ibid. February 12, 1971.

30. DPS-TRWR: Jack Dean, 6 March 1971, TRHF&M.

31. *McAllen Monitor*, February 12, 1971.

32. Father Michael Allen, Catholic Chaplin, Pan American University to Colonel Speir, 9 March 1971, TRHF&M.

33. *McAllen Monitor*, March 7, 1971.

34. Ibid.

35. Ibid. Interestingly during this or another protest, an eyewitness to Dean's demeanor and deportment apprised this writer with the following. On old business Highway 83 between Pharr and San Juan, militants had gathered and were burning tires and apparently making ready for action more impassioned. Though he was the only lawman onsite—One Riot, One Ranger—Jack Dean climbed into the bed of a pickup truck (not his or any lawman's) and addressed the milling crowd. His forcefulness registered as friendly—but decidedly clear-cut. The witness relates that Ranger Jack Dean simply said, in broken borderland Spanish, "This party is over." The protestors, apparently, believed him and took the message to heart. The tire burning ceased and there were no more problems. The eyewitness could hardly believe his eyes and ears that Jack Dean had acted "all by himself," and had not been "blown out of" the pickup's bed. Doug Mankin, Ranger, Texas, interview by author, 2 January 2018.

36. *The Edinburg Daily Review*, March 9, 1971.

37. R.S. Bowe, Mayor, Pharr, Texas to Wilson Speir, 29 July 1971; Wilson Speir to R.S. Bowe, 12 August 1971, TRHF&M; Peoples to R.S. Bowe, 3 September 1971, TRHF&M; Jack Dean interview by author 18 December 2017.

38. DPS-PR: Jack Dean, 8 February 1971, TRHF&M.

39. Attorney Rick Miller to author, 24 April 2017. "Article 20.011 of the Texas Code of Criminal Procedure defines who may be present during presentation of evidence to a grand jury. Statutorily, this includes witnesses presenting testimony and others who are necessary to assist the state's attorney in presenting evidence to a grand jury. However, no one but a grand juror

may be present while a grand jury is deliberating. In actuality, Texas law has long recognized a distinction between the presentation of evidence to a grand jury and grand jury deliberations. The general rule that has been accepted by Texas courts for many years is that others not associated with a case being presented to the grand jury may be present during the giving of testimony, but not during the grand jury deliberations."

40. *The State of Texas vs. Robert C. Johnson* as previously cited: Testimony of Texas Ranger Jack Dean, TRHF&M; *Brownsville Herald*, February 19, 1971.

41. Ibid., DPS Crime Lab Report, as stipulated by prosecution and defense. 25.

42. Ibid.; *Corpus Christi Caller-Times*, March 12, 1971; DPS-COR: 15 March 1971: "During the riot in Pharr of February 6, 1971, Alfonso Flores was killed. Autopsy report showed that Flores had been struck in the head by a bullet. Flores was standing on the corner of Bell and Cage and it is believed that he was not actively engaged in the riot." TRHF&M; DPS-CCR. 14 March 1971, TRHF&M.

43. DPS-TRWR: Jack Dean, 27 February 1971, TRHF&M.

44. *McAllen Monitor*, March 11, 1971. Clearly, it seems, Grand Jurors were somewhat troubled to report, but did report: "Another area that we, the grand jury, find a degree of responsibility for the unrest in Pharr, is in the realm of so-called social services by certain religious faiths. The Valley Community Center operated by the Methodist Board of Missions has served the Pharr community for some 50 years. Until approximately four years ago, it was a credit to its sponsors and a definite asset to Pharr."

45. *Corpus Christi Caller-Times*, March 12, 1971.

46. *McAllen Monitor*, February 24, 1971; DPS-TV: Jack Dean, months of February and March 1971, TRHF&M.

47. Father Michael Allen to Wilson Speir, 9 March 1971, TRHF&M. Certainly renowned author and historian Utley, *Lone Star Lawman*, wholeheartedly concurs: "After Pharr, Jack Dean's career had no direction to go but up. More important, he represented a transitional generation of Rangers, cherishing the old while looking forward to the new and adjusting accordingly." See p. 249.

48. DPS-PDS: Jack Dean, 28 February 1971, TRHF&M.

49. JD-DRJ: 11 March 1971, TRHF&M; *McAllen Monitor*, March 11, 1971.

50. *Corpus Christi Caller-Times*, March 12, 1971; *McAllen Monitor*, March 11, 1971.

51. JD-DRJ: Jack Dean, 11 March 1971, TRHF&M.

52. DPS-COR: 2 March 1971, TRHF&M; DPS-CCR, Armed-Robbery, 19 July 1971, TRHF&M. For another robbery of a coin collector and/or dealer

illustrating their vulnerability, see, January 5, 1972, edition of *Coin World*, "Bandit Holds Coin Dealer's Wife Hostage While Partner Robs Shop."

53. Background material concerning Prentice Noel Ellard is courtesy award-winning author and superlative researcher Rick Miller.

54. *Valley Morning News*, September 12, 1971: "Prentice Noel Ellard, a former member of the Bandidos motorcycle club. . . ."

55. *Prentice Noel Ellard vs. The State of Texas*. 509 S.W.2d 622 (Court of Criminal Appeals of Texas 1974).

56. JD-DRJ: Jack Dean, 21 July 1971, TRHF&M; Jack Dean interview by author, 26 May 2017.

57. Undated newsclip from *Houston Chronicle*, byline Zarkao Franks.

58. *McAllen Monitor*, July 29, 1971.

59. JD-DRJ: 14 July 1971, TRHF&M.

60. *Houston Chronicle* newsclip.

61. JD-DRJ: 16 and 17 July 1971, TRHF&M.

62. McAllen Monitor, August 16, 1971.

63. Rick Miller to author, 27 April 2017. Also, *Valley Morning Star*, September 12, 1971: "Conviction Returned In Shooting Case." Additionally, the defendant had in an appellate case attempted to impeach the testimony of Texas Ranger Jack Dean. See, *Prentice Noel Ellard vs. State of Texas*. 507 S.W.2d 198 (Court of Criminal Appeals of Texas, 1974).

64. DPS-COR: 15 March 1971, TRHF&M; Statement of Ranger B.J. Green, 29 March 1971. TRHF&M; Statement of Brooks County Sheriff Rep F. Moore, 23 March 1971, TRHF&M; DPS-CCR, Jack Dean, 22 March 1971, TRHF&M; DPS-SCR: Jack Dean, 10 August 1972. TRHF&M.

65. DPS-COR: 4 April 1971, TRHF&M; DPS-CCR: Assault to Murder, 4 April 1971, TRHF&M; JD-DRJ: Jack Dean, 4 April 1971, TRHF&M; DPS-SSCR, 30 May 1972, TRHF&M.

66. DPS-COR: Jack Dean, 01 June 1971, TRHF&M; DPS-CCR: Armed Robbery, 1 June 1971, TRHF&M; JD-DRJ: Jack Dean, 31 May and 1 June 1971, TRHF&M; DPS-SSCR, 3 July 1972, TRHF&M.

67. *McAllen Monitor*, June 14, 1971; JD-DRJ, 13 June 1971, TRHF&M.

68. *Valley Morning Star*, June 17, 1971.

69. Jack Dean's teletype to Company D headquarters, 17 June 1971, TRHF&M.

70. *Corpus Christi Caller-Times*, June 18, 1971; JD-DRJ, 17 June 1971, TRHF&M. Of the sentence handed out to the defendant, the *McAllen Monitor* of 24 February 1972, reports that he "was convicted of interfering with police and given a five-year probated sentence."

71. Ibid.

72. JD-DRJ, 30 March 1971, TRHF&M.

73. Ibid.

74. A series of DPS-CORs, DPS-CCRs, and DPS-SCCRs, TRHF&M.

75. DPS-COR, 31 August 1971, TRHF&M; DPS-CCR, 31 August 1971, TRHF&M; Statement of Calvin F. Cox, DPS, MVI Patrolman, 26 August 1971, TRHF&M.

76. DPS-SCCR, 3 July 1972, TRHF&M.

77. G.E. Roney, Executive Vice-President, McAllen State Bank, to Texas Ranger Dean, 25 August 1971, TRHF&M.

78. Texas Ranger Jack Dean's investigative case file regarding the Longoria murder investigation, TRHF&M.

79. Ibid.

80. Ibid.

81. *McAllen Monitor*, February 6, 1972.

82. Ibid., June 29, 1972. Also see, TRWR: Jack Dean, 1 July 1972, TRHF&M: "Defendant attempted to escape while being transported back to County Jail. Assisted in setting up security for this subject. . . . Worked with Deputy Ramsey in setting up security in courtroom for sentencing of Quintanilla. Also with Ramsey, transported defendant to and from the jail to courtroom. At Judge Smith's order all persons entering courtroom were searched. We also set up security for the District Attorney and the Judge due to threats made against them by defendant. Defendant's sentence set at 50 years."

83. DPS-SCCR: 10 August 1972 and 10 January 1973, TRHF&M; DPS-CCR, 7 February 1972, TRHF&M.

84. DPS-COR, 30 December 1971, TRHF&M; TRWR-Jack Dean, 1 January 1972, TRHF&M; Ranger Dean's cited quotations are a blend from the *Lubbock Avalanche Journal*, January 1, 1972, and the January 2, 1972, edition of the *McAllen Monitor*.

85. The thoroughness of Texas Ranger Dean's forensic investigation may be extrapolated from the following letters to Dean: C.H. Beardsley, Supervisor, Chemistry Section, DPS Crime Lab, 7 January 1972, and J.D. Chastain, Laboratory Manager, DPS Crime Lab, 7 January 1972, TRHF&M.

86. Jack Dean interview by author, 25 May 2017.

87. OHI: Jack Dean, 2013, TRHF&M.

88. *Corpus Christi Caller-Times*, February 20, 1972; *McAllen Monitor*, February 25, 1972.

89. Ibid.

90. *McAllen Monitor*, February 24, 1972.

91. DPS-TRWR: Jack Dean, 26 February 1972, TRHF&M; *McAllen Monitor*, December 31, 1972: Though the defendant "was specifically tried for

'malicious destruction' of Pharr city property, namely, a fire engine which was pummeled with rocks in the February, 1971, Pharr riots, the trial was conducted to connect him with instigation of disorders. A county jury acquitted him. He also gained dismissal of another charge, inciting a riot, since he cannot be placed in double jeopardy."

92. Mayor Bowe to Colonel Speir, 29 July 1971, TRHF&M. That Mayor Bowe was not popular with a segment of Pharr's residents is made clear in David M. Fishlow's piece in February 26, 1971, edition of *The Texas Observer*, "Poncho Flores Is Dead." "Police Chief Alfredo Ramirez is a tall, white-haired sharpie who likes to appear in court in a bright green suit and red cowboy boots. He, like every other city employee in Pharr, is utterly dependent for his job on R.S. Bowe, the balding, 60-year-old mayor and, as the front man for the little political machine that rules here, the undisputed czar of this community. . . . Mayor Bowe, the most elusive public official south of Austin, as usual, was nowhere to be seen. . . ."

93. Father Allen to Colonel Speir, 9 March 1971, TRHF&M.

94. DPS-PDS: Jack Dean, 28 February 1971, TRHF&M. Though it may some-what deflate agenda-driven Texas Ranger detractors, Jack Dean, though recognizing sociological inequities, was not greeted with hostility by the community at large. In point of fact, according to him: "I always hear of the Mexican dislike for Rangers, especially in South Texas. I found this to be wrong. I was welcomed by nearly all of the people in South Texas. There were and are many who backed the Rangers in the teens because they were attacked and abused by Mexican bandits." See, Utley, *Lone Star Lawmen*, 340; Jack Dean interview by author, 5 January 2018, confirmed his overall reception in the Lower Rio Grande Valley by the community. Of course out-laws of any stripe aren't fond of lawmen.

95. DPS-PDS: Jack Dean, 31 August 1971, TRHF&M.

Chapter 7: "Lead will get your attention"

1. *McAllen Monitor*, February 27, 1972, with photographs of recipients.

2. Lorenzo Ramirez, Southwest Regional Director, U.S. Department of Justice, Community Relations Service, Southwest Regional Office, Dallas, Texas, to Texas Ranger Jack Dean, 3 May 1971, TRHF&M.

3. Texas Ranger Jack Dean to Miss Gene Ann Herrin, Texas Youth Council, Austin, Texas, 13 July 1971, TRHF&M.

4. DPS-IM: Captain Wood to all Company D Texas Rangers, 13 July 1972, TRHF&M.

5. Summary Notes of Company D Meeting, 6 January 1972, TRHF&M.

6. DPS-COR: 17 April 1972, TRHF&M.

7. *San Benito News*, April 12, 1972. According to the report in *The Tyler Courier-Times*, April 13, 1972, the Justice of the Peace, Romeo Garza, conducting the Death Inquest, theorized that "a preliminary examination of the girl indicated she had been sexually assaulted."

8. DPS-PR: Jack Dean, 17 April 1972, TRHF&M. Later, at trial, defense lawyers argued that high-school dropout Zepeda did not knowledgably understand his Miranda Rights, see, *Dallas Morning News*, June 14, 1973. Interestingly for readers intrigued by courtroom machinations, was the attempt—feeble attempt—to support their contention that Antonio Rios Zepeda, Jr. was incapable of understanding certain Constitutional Rights. See, excerpt from the *Big Spring Herald*, May 23, 1973.

> A Pan American University professor and four high school teachers testified that Rios Zepeda *probably* [emphasis added] could not have understood many of the words in the constitutional rights warning on the statement form. Dr. George J. Garza of Pan American University testified that some of the words in the warning "are not commonly used words." Under cross examination by Cameron County Dist. Atty. Fred Galindo, Dr. Garza *admitted that he had never met or talked with* [emphasis added] Rios Zepeda. He said he could only base his opinion on *what he thought* [emphasis added] the average 19-year-old Mexican-American who dropped out of school in the ninth grade would understand.

Certainly the trial Judge, the Honorable J. R. Alamia, didn't buy into the defense theory, ruling that the accused defendant's statement would be allowed in the proceedings. See, *McAllen Monitor* May 18, 1973.

9. Ibid.

10. *McAllen Monitor*, April 13, 1972.

11. *The Tyler Courier-Times*, April 13, 1972.

12. *McAllen Monitor*, May 24 and 31, 1973; *Dallas Morning News*, June 14, 1973.

13. DPS-TRWR: Jack Dean, 2 June 1973, TRHF&M.

14. Cameron County Chief Deputy William J. Gatliff, for Cameron County Sheriff Boynton H. Fleming, to DPS Colonel Speir, 14 April 1972, TRHF&M.

15. *McAllen Monitor*, July 9, 1972.

16. DPS-PR: Jack Dean, 3 May 1972, TRHF&M; DPS-TV: Jack Dean, month of May 1972, TRHF&M.

17. Kyle Dean interview by author, 18 April 2017.

18. Ibid.; Jack Dean interview by author 25 May 2017.

19. Jack Dean interview by author, 9 February 2017.

20. Paul Schneider, *Bonnie and Clyde: The Lives Behind the Legend*, 1–12; Jeff Guinn, *Go Down Together: The True, Untold Story of Bonnie and Clyde*, 245–250.

21. Lon Bennett Glenn, *The Largest Hotel Chain in Texas: Texas Prisons*, 60–61; Clifford R. Caldwell and Ron DeLord, *Texas Lawmen, 1900–1940: More of the Good and the Bad*, 430; John Boessenecker, *Texas Ranger: The Epic Life Of Frank Hamer, The Man Who Killed Bonnie and Clyde*, 399–401.

22. Interview with Richard K. Alford, Texas Department of Criminal Justice, Correctional Institutions Division, Regional I Director, Ret., by author 7 May 2017. Of the Eastham Unit, Director Alford who once served there as a Major and later as the overall Director for Region 1, which included Eastham as well as numerous other institutional units, mentioned that the facility was basically an agricultural unit—and a "real tough place."

23. Gary Cartwright, *Dirty Dealing: Drug Smuggling on the Mexican Border and the Assassination of a Federal Judge*, 220; Lovelady, a pulpwood and ranching center, was founded in 1927. See, Awbrey and Dooley, *Why Stop?* 296.

24. *Amarillo Globe-Times*, March 3, 1970; DPS-PR: Texas Ranger Tol Dawson, 20 January 1969 and attachment. (Hereafter cited as Statement-Attaway), TRHF&M. Sandra Sue Attaway said:

> We were in a motel and I heard a gunshot in the other room and I ran from the bathroom and he [Harrelson] was sitting on the bed holding his .25 and turning ivory white. He said he had not known that there was a bullet in the chamber and the gun had fired striking him in the leg. We went to a hospital downtown and a doctor removed the bullet, gave him the bullet and the gun and filled out a report furnished by a policeman working the emergency room.

25. Nyle H. Miller and Joseph H. Snell, *Great Gunfighters of the Kansas Cowtowns*, quoting the January 12, 1876, edition of the *Wichita Beacon* on p. 83.

26. Roger Jay, "The Peoria Bummer'—Wyatt Earp's Lost Year," *Wild West*, August 2003, 46–52; William B. Shillingberg, *Dodge City: The Early Years, 1872–1876*, 170; Frederick Nolan, *The Wild West: History, Myth and the Making of America*, 139: "An almost forgotten relic of the old frontier. . . . Fueled first by books then movies, and later television, Wyatt Earp—a man who was never more than a deputy sheriff or an assistant marshal—was transformed into the most famous lawman of the frontier West. Controversy still swirls around his name and life. Was he a saint or sinner, a rugged frontiersman or a sly opportunist, a pimp and crooked

gambler or an incorruptible lawman, a small time peace officer or a mendacious fabulist?" Leon Claire Metz, *The Shooters*, 270: "In truth, historians are not certain if Earp was a bonafide frontier Paladin, or a scoundrel with a clever biographer. Right now the evidence leans toward the latter assessment." David Berg, *Run, Brother, Run: A Memoir*, 103; Statement-Attaway: "Also, when I met him [Harrelson] the previous summer he had been working some girls and when I protested vigorously he had stopped this activity as far as I know." Document in the TRHF&M.

27. *Jo Ann Harrelson, Charles Voyde Harrelson and Elizabeth Nichols Chagra vs. United States of America*. 754 F.2d 1153 (U.S. Court of Appeals, Fifth Circuit, 1985) Note 11: "Harrelson testified to personal knowledge of electronic eavesdropping in prison. While incarcerated in California, he had in fact cooperated with the authorities by recording the conversations of a fellow inmate and was thus not unfamiliar with the practice." *Dallas Morning News*, November 20, 1982: "Harrelson testified that he, too, once had been a government snitch. But he said it was for a good reason." Also see, Berg, *Run, Brother, Run*, 159–160; and Cartwright, *Dirty Dealing*, 221.

28. *Charles Voyde Harrelson, aka Charles S. Stoughtenborough vs. United States of America*. 442 F.2d 290 (U.S. Court of Appeals, Eighth Circuit, 1971); With regards to cheating folks out of money during card games, Harrelson himself would later testify: "But the people I play are like me. We cheat each other. I just cheat better," See, *Dallas Morning News*, November 25, 1982.

29. Ibid.

30. Statement-Attaway, TRHF&M.

31. *San Antonio Express News*, November 16, 1968.

32. For biographical data regarding the life and death of Alan [not Allen] Berg an interested reader should review the smartly penned *Run, Brother, Run*, written by Alan's brother, David Berg, an attorney and author; Also see, *Brownsville Herald*, November 15, 1968; And, *Dallas Morning News*, November 17, 1968; *The State of Texas Death Certificate* merely makes mention that Mr. Alan Harry Berg died as result of "a gunshot wound to the head, shot through and through."

33. Statement-Attaway, TRHF&M.

34. *Dallas Morning News*, November 21, 1968.

35. Nieman, "20th Century Shining Star: Captain Jack Dean, United States Marshal." Stopka, *Partial List of Texas Ranger Company and Unit Commanders*, 41.

36. *Austin American-Statesman*, September 6, 1981, byline Mike Cox.

37. Statement-Attaway, TRHF&M. For a succinct biographical profile of Sheriff Robert R. Gladney, see Tise, *Texas County Sheriffs*, 55–56.

38. *Dallas Morning News*, July 10, 1968, and July 12, 1968.

39. *Big Springs Daily Herald*, March 15, 1970.

40. *Dallas Morning News*, December 11, 1968.

41. Berg, *Run, Brother, Run*, 150–151.

42. Ibid. David Berg, an attorney with successful U.S. Supreme Court argument under his legal belt, offers a cogent analysis of the murder trial and the behavior and trial tactics of Percy Foreman and District Attorney Ogden Bass' ripostes. Certainly, even after taking into consideration the overstatements and inaccuracies attendant to newspaper stories, a brief sampling dealing with the execution of Alan Berg is insightful, such as: *Corpus Christi Caller-Times*, July 26, 1970 and August 22, 1970; *Victoria Advocate*, August 24, 1970; *Dallas Morning News*, July 27, 1970; *Amarillo Globe-Times*, August 13, 1970; *Big Spring Daily Herald*, August 14, 19, 21, 24, 25, 26, and 27, 1970; and the *Abilene Reporter News*, August 28, 1970.

43. *Dallas Morning News*, September 19, 1970.

44. OHI: Jack Dean, 2013, TRHF&M: "He [Harrelson] was in jail around Houston and the DA sent me and this deputy sheriff to get him. . . ."

45. *Brownsville Herald*, September 22, 1970.

46. *Corpus Christi Caller-Times*, November 14, 1971.

47. DPS-TRWR: Jack Dean, 30 October 1971, TRHF&M.

48. Jack Dean interview by author 5 July 2017.

49. *San Antonio Express*, August 1, 1973: "The shapely young woman [Sandra Sue Attaway] used to live with Harrelson and testified he had told her he shot Degelia to death as a favor he owed Degelia's business partner, Pete Scarmado [sic Scamado]. She said Harrelson had lost some heroin belonging to Scarmado and in repayment he killed Degelia at Scarmado's request." *Dallas Morning News*, August 1, 1973: "Miss Attaway, Harrelson's former girlfriend and a key state witness, testified the trip to Kansas City was to deliver heroin belonging to Pete Thomas Scamardo of Herne, who was a partner in a grain-cotton firm with Degelia. However, she said police in Kansas City stopped Harrelson and searched his automobile and that Harrelson kicked the heroin stashed in a prophylactic wrapped in a white sock hidden beneath the car. Officers later found the heroin, but could not prove it ever was in Harrelson's possession. . . ."

50. Statement-Attaway, TRHF&M; *San Antonio Express*, July 31, 1973: "Mrs. Attaway testified that Harrelson told her July 6, 1968 that he was going to fly to McAllen to kill Degelia. She said that he flew there with Jerry O. Watkins of Houston and that they returned late that evening to Le Bistro private club at Houston, where she worked. Chuck [Harrelson] told me [Attaway] he had done what he went to the Valley to do."

51. *Big Spring Daily Herald*, November 7, 1971.

52. Cartwright, *Dirty Dealing*, 222. A few years later, during another and wholly separate murder trial, testimony was offered which is a seeming parallel phraseology. "If she talks, they're gonna burn me [Harrelson] for ringing Wood's bell." See, *Dallas Morning News*, November 11, 1982.

53. *Dallas Morning News*, July 31, 1973; Statement-Attaway, TRHF&M.

54. Ibid. "After the slaying, the key sate witness said 'Chuck told me that he had done what he went to the valley to do and that he had dismantled the .25 and thrown it out of the window of the car'. . . . A pistol frame and barrel bearing the same serial number as the one bought in Utah was found along 2nd Street south of McAllen, not far from where Degelia's body was found sprawled face down in an abandoned pump shack."

55. Berg, *Run, Brother, Run*, 197; *The Odessa American*, December 8, 1971: "Sandra Sue Attaway, Harrelson's former girlfriend, said the gun was purchased in Utah."

56. *Dallas Morning News*, August 9, 1973.

57. Berg, *Run, Brother, Run*, 151.

58. *The Odessa American*, December 2, 1971.

59. Cartwright, *Dirty Dealing*, 222; Berg, *Run, Brother, Run*, 215.

60. *Corpus Christi Caller-Times,* March 21, 1972.

61. *Brownsville Herald*, May 10, 1972; DPS-COR: 15 May 1972, TRHF&M.

62. DPS-TRWR: Jack Dean, 22 July 1972, TRHF&M; *Abilene Reporter News*, July 21, 1972.

63. Ranger Jack Dean to Captain John Wood, 13 June 1972, TRHF&M.

64. Captain Wood to Ranger Dean, 20 June 1972, TRHF&M.

65. Blackburn, *Wanted: Historic County Jails of Texas*. 163–161; *McAllen Monitor*, December 31, 1972.

66. *Victoria Advocate*, October 20, 1972: "Two guards were injured when the two prisoners shot one in the back and stabbed the other several times."

67. DPS-TRWR: Jack Dean, 19 October 1972, TRHF&M.

68. *Victoria Advocate*, October 20, 1972.

69. *McAllen Monitor*, October 19, 1972.

70. *Victoria Advocate*, October 20, 1972.

71. OHI: Jack Dean, 2013, TRHF&M.

72. *McAllen Monitor*, October 19, 1972.

73. Ibid., June 7, 1973; DPS-CCR: [Aiding A Felon to Escape] Jack Dean, 20 November 1972, TRHF&M; Assistant District Attorney Joe W. Friend Jr., to Jack Dean, 7 June 1973; DPS-SCCR: Jack Dean, 8 June 1973, TRHF&M.

74. Anderson County [South Carolina] Sheriff's Office Criminal Offense Report, 71–456 and Inventory of thirty-seven firearms taken in the burglary, TRHF&M.

75. *McAllen Monitor*, April 13, 1973.

76. Ibid., April 12, 1973.

77. *Brownsville Herald*, December 17, 1972.

78. DPS-TRWR: Jack Dean, December 16, 1972, TRHF&M.

79. DPS-Narcotics Submission Report and Laboratory Report, 21 December 1972 and 3 January 1973, TRHF&M.

80. DPS-COR: 19 December 1972, TRHF&M.

81. *McAllen Monitor*, April 13, 1973.

82. Ibid. April 18, 1973.

83. DPS-TRWR: Jack Dean, 21 April 1973, TRHF&M.

84. DPS-SCCR: Jack Dean, 29 April 1973 (date of suicide), TRHF&M.

85. Notes, Company D Meeting, 6 January 1972, TRHF&M.

86. DPS-COR: 01 May 1973, TRHF&M.

87. Texas Ranger Jack Dean to Wayne Coker, Deputy, Anderson County Sheriff's Office, Anderson County, South Carolina, 16 February 1973, TRHF&M.

88. Undated newsclips, probably the *McAllen Monitor*, TRHF&M.

89. Ibid.; Thrush would eventually change his plea from *Not Guilty* to *Guilty* and take a dozen years to do. See, DPS-TRWR: Jack Dean, 01 December 1973, TRHF&M.

90. *McAllen Monitor*, January 14, 1971.

91. Miriam Gilmore, Editor, Texas Numismatic Association Newsletter, *TNA News,* to Texas Ranger Jack Dean, 8 January 1973, TRHF&M.

92. Copy of $500 Reward Check from American Numismatic Association, Colorado Springs, Colorado, to Texas Ranger Jack Dean, 29 March 1973, TRHF&M; *McAllen Monitor*, April 16, 1973.

Chapter 8: "I located Harrelson's pistol"

1. DPS-TRWR: Jack Dean, 27 February 1973, TRHF&M; DPS-COR: 12 February 1973, TRHF&M; *Lubbock Avalanche Journal*, February 10, 1973.

2. *Alice Echo-News*, February 7, 1973.

3. *Galveston Daily News*, February 8, 1973; TRWR: Jack Dean, 10 February 1973, TRHF&M.

4. *Wichita Falls Times*, February 9, 1973.

5. DPS-TRWR: Jack Dean, 10 February 1973, TRHF&M.

6. DPS-IM: Captain John Wood, Company D, to Senior Captain Clint Peoples, Austin, 2 March 1973, TRHF&M: "On January 28th and 29th, 1973, Rangers from this company worked with the Motor Vehicle theft Section, Texas Highway Patrol, Game Wardens and Sheriff's Officers on a twenty-four hour blockade of all major roads going into Mexico. This road check was conducted to stem the flow of stolen motor vehicles and property going into Mexico."

7. Ibid.

8. For but one example, see Captain John Wood, Company D, to Captain Pete Rogers, Company A, 4 April 1972, TRHF&M. The mentions of this category of criminality in Texas Ranger Jack Dean's DPS-TRWRs are too numerous to identify with specificity for this generalized statement. A particularized review of these documents does, indeed, reveal the magnitude of the cross-border traffic. It is a story within a story.

9. Jack Dean interview by author 9 February 2017; OHI: Jack Dean, 2013, TRHF&M; DPS-IM: Captain Wood to Ranger Dean, 6 April 1973, TRHF&M.

10. Utley, *Lone Star Lawmen*, 279.

11. DPS-PR: Jack Dean, 8 May 1972, TRHF&M.

12. DPS-TRWR: Jack Dean, 6 May 1972 and 13 May 1972. In the latter report Dean writes: "Leave McAllen 4:00 A.M. to Austin to submit two pistols taken from Hidalgo County Jail to lab. Pistols were taken from prisoners Charles Harrelson and Charles Morris." And the next day he types: "Also working with Deputy Ramsey in attempt to discover how firearms were being smuggled into the jail." Reports found in TRHF&M. Later, for his daily report of Saturday, 17 June 1972, Ranger Dean interviews a subject and then writes: "reference information he has on pistol found in jail cell of Charles Harrelson," TRHF&M. Also Ranger Dean to Chief of Police, Vienna, Virginia, 30 May 1972, TRHF&M: "The one in question [Beretta]. . . . was found in the cell of accused murder for hire suspect Charles V. Harrelson. This gun was smuggled to him and we are attempting to trace it." Bobby Nieman, ed., "20th Century Shining Star: Captain Jack Dean, United States Marshal": "a .25-caliber, automatic pistol that he [Texas Ranger Jack Dean] took from Harrelson's jail cell in a Hidalgo County jail," in the *Texas Ranger Dispatch*.

13. DPS-TRWR: Jack Dean, 15 April 1972, TRHF&M.

14. Ibid.

15. *Dallas Morning News*, April 22, 1972; *McAllen Monitor*, December 31, 1972, highlighting the year's significant events: "A key witness in the Harrelson trial in April was charged with perjury. Louise Scott Gannon, night club

singer gave Harrelson an alibi as a surprise witness. . . . Arrested in Las Vegas, Mrs. Gannon posted bond in the perjury case."

16. *San Antonio Express News*, July 22, 1973.

17. DPS-IM: Captain John Wood to All Company D Texas Rangers, 9 April 1973, TRHF&M.

18. Ibid., 9 March 1973, 5 July 1973, 6 July 1973, 26 July 1973, and 30 July 1973, TRHF&M.

19. DPS-IM; Jack Dean to Captain Wood, 23 April 1973, TRHF&M.

20. DPS-TRWR: Jack Dean, 4 August 1973, TRHF&M; DPS-TV: Jack Dean, month of August 1973, TRHF&M.

21. Aside from articles carried in the Sunday, August 5, 1973, edition of the *Waco Tribune Herald*, resource material for covering this event were—and may be—accessed by reviewing James M. Day's *One Man's Dream: Fort Fisher and the Texas Ranger Hall of Fame* and *Texas Rangers Sesquicentennial Anniversary, 1823–1973: Pictorial Edition*, Gene Hausenfluke, ed., written by Roger Conger.

22. First quotations from Day, *One Man's Dream*, 32; subsequent quotation from Utley, *Lone Star Lawmen*, 271.

23. Refer to the two preceding citations. Also, though it's somewhat outdated, *A Pictorial Tour of the Texas Ranger Hall of Fame Museum*, edited by Tom Burks, with its full-color plates is a fascinating volume to peruse, as is *Guns of Fort Fisher*, published by the Parks and Recreation Department, City of Waco, 1973.

24. Hausenfluke, *Texas Ranger Sesquicentennial Anniversary, 1823–1973: Pictorial Edition*, 78.

25. Nieman, "20th Century Shining Star: Captain Jack Dean, United States Marshal."

26. Jack Dean interview by author, 8 March 2017.

27. *The Odessa American*, March 30, 1973.

28. Ibid., July 15, 1973.

29. Jack Dean interview by author 5 July 2017.

30. *Dallas Morning News*, July 16, 1973; Genealogical profile of Judge Hester is courtesy Rick Miller, researcher and writer extraordinaire.

31. *Dallas Morning News*, June 30, 1973. For the newspaper's July 22, 1973 edition the distinction was again addressed: "Harrelson, now 34, has been in jail ever since [the arrest at Atlanta], but he has never been convicted of either slaying [Berg and/or Degelia]. His 56-month confinement is the longest for any person in the state not convicted of a crime."

32. *Brownsville Herald*, July 18, 1973.

33. *Dallas Morning News*, August 1, 1973.

34. Ibid., August 5, 1973.

35. *Victoria Advocate*, August 7, 1973; *Galveston Daily News*, August 7, 1973.

36. *Dallas Morning News*, August 11, 1973.

37. *The Odessa American*, August 10, 1973.

38. *Dallas Morning News*, August 11, 1973; *Brownsville Herald*, August 10, 1973; DPS-TRWR: Jack Dean, 11 August 1973, TRHF&M.

39. Texas Ranger Charles "Charlie" Moore, Company B, Dallas, Texas, to Jack Dean, 5 September 1972, TRHF&M. Though this bond agency inquiry for Harrelson was made at an earlier time, it is mentioned here for illustrative purposes.

40. *Dallas Morning News*, December 22, 1973.

41. DPS-TRWR: Jack Dean, 16 February 1974, TRHF&M: "Harrelson dropped appeal and asked to be sent to Huntsville to begin his sentence."

42. Oscar B. McInnis, District Attorney, Hidalgo County to Colonel Wilson Speir, Director, DPS, 12 November 1973, TRHF&M; Colonel Speir to DA McInnis, 15 November 1973, TRHF&M.

43. Nieman, "20th Century Shining Star: Captain Jack Dean, United States Marshal."

44. DPS-PDS: Captain Wood, 31 August 1973, TRHF&M.

45. DPS-TRWR: Jack Dean, 8 September 1973, TRHF&M.

46. Teletype: DPS Director Wilson E. Speir to All DPS Stations, 17 August 1973. "The following are promoted to the position of Texas Ranger effective September 1, 1973 and will be stationed as listed. . . . Bruce M. Casteel, CO D, Harlingen. . . ." TRHF&M; *Texas Lawman*, September-October 1973, 79; DPS-EBS: Bruce Casteel, TRHF&M; VF: Bruce Casteel, TRHF&M; *Floresville Chronicle-Journal*, August 23, 2001.

47. *Waco Tribune-Herald*, May 15, 1979, byline Dick Stanley.

48. Jack Dean interview by author, 15 August 2017. Also see, Robert D. Moser, *Texas Iron: Guns of the Texas Rangers*, 123.

49. DPS-TRWR: Jack Dean, 22 September 1973, TRHF&M.

50. *Del Rio News Herald*, September 23, 1973.

51. Unidentified and undated newsclip, probably the *McAllen Monitor*, in the TRHF&M.

52. Ibid.; and DPS-TRWR: Jack Dean, 22 September 1973, TRHF&M.

53. DPS-TRWR: Jack Dean, 29 September 1973, TRHF&M.

54. Unidentified newsclip as cited.

55. Pablo G. Pena, Mayor, Weslaco, Texas, to DPS Director Wilson E. Speir, 24 September 1973. In part: "I am sure a great disaster has been averted our

community due to your Jack Dean, W.C. McFarland and members of the DPS coming to the aid of Weslaco and for this I want to express the sincere appreciation of myself and the other members of our City Council." In the TRHF&M.

56. DPS-COR: 18 December 1973, TRHF&M; DPS-CCR: 26 December 1973, TRHF&M.

57. DPS-COR: 29 January 1974: "is believed to be in Reynosa, Mexico, at this time," in the TRHF&M; DPS-CCR: Jack Dean, 01 February 1974, TRHF&M: "surrendered to me on Tuesday, January 29, at the Hidalgo International Bridge." *The South Texas Reporter*, January 31, 1974; DPS-TRWR: Jack Dean, 26 January 1974, TRHF&M; Tise, *Texas County Sheriffs*, 474.

58. Unidentified and undated newsclip, probably the *McAllen Monitor*; DPS-TRWR: Jack Dean, 16 February 1974, TRHF&M.

59. DPS-COR: 18 February 1974, TRHF&M.

60. DPS-CCR: Jack Dean, 14 May 1974, TRHF&M.

61. DPS-TRWR: Jack Dean, 10 May 1974, TRHF&M.

62. DPS-TRWR: Jack Dean, 19 April 1975, TRHF&M.

63. Utley, *Lone Star Lawmen* 257: "Neither Colonel Speir nor criminal law enforcement chief Jim Ray had much liking for Senior Captain Clint Peoples. His exaggerated vanity, his posturing in the public spotlight, and his political ties into the legislature were irritating."

64. Jack Dean interview by author, 8 March 2017.

65. Ibid.

66. Cox, *Time of the Rangers*, 294: "Though Ray could not pin down whether Peoples had intended to collect money from the producers while still a state employee or had merely been planning to feather his eventual retirement, Peoples had no final authority over any Ranger records, which were government documents."

67. Utley, *Lone Star Lawmen*, 257–258.

68. Senior Captain Clint Peoples to Colonel Speir, 31 January 1974, TRHF&M.

69. DPS-IM: Captain Wood to All Texas Rangers, Company D, 6 February 1974, TRHF&M.

70. Hausenfluke, *Texas Rangers Sesquicentennial Anniversary, 1823–1973: Pictorial Edition*, 59.

71. *Austin American-Statesman*, January 3, 1985, byline Kay Powers.

72. OHI: Bob Mitchell, 1996, TRHF&M.

73. VF: William D. "Bill" Wilson, TRHF&M; Utley, *Lone Star Lawmen*, 258; Jack Dean interview by author, 8 March 2017; Proctor, *Just One Riot*, 16: Captain Bill Wilson said, "when ever there's a mean ass, they call on us."

74. Cox, *Time of the Rangers*, 294: "The two men [Wilson and Peoples] had never been close." Also confirmed by Jack Dean interviews by author as cited.

75. DPS-IM: Captain Wood to All Texas Rangers, Company D, 7 May 1974, TRHF&M.

76. Keith R. Schmidt, "Guns of the Texas Rangers." Quoting, Senior Captain H.R. "Lefty" Block, as carried in the May 1988 edition of the *American Rifleman*, 80.

77. *Houston Chronicle* [Texas Magazine], February 9, 1969.

78. Clarence M. Kelley, Director, FBI, to Jack Dean, 10 June 1974, TRHF&M.

79. Clarence M. Kelley, Director, FBI, to Colonel Wilson E. Speir, Director, DPS, 10 June 1974, TRHF&M; Director Speir to Director Kelley, 14 June 1974, TRHF&M.

80. DPS-TRWR: Jack Dean, 20 April 1974, TRHF&M.

Chapter 9: "Just handle it"

1. DPS-PDS: Captain Wood, 28 February 1974, TRHF&M.

2. Ranger Dean to Emory W. Muehlbrad, Manager, DPS Personnel and Training Section, 21 June 1974, TRHF&M.

3. DPS-IM: Captain Wood to Bill Wilson, Senior Ranger Captain, 11 July 1974, TRHF&M.

4. DPS-TRWR: Jack Dean, 27 July 1974. TRHF&M; DPS-TV: Jack Dean, month of July 1974, TRHF&M.

5. Teletype: To Ranger Jack Dean [and others], via McAllen PD, 25 July 1974, TRHF&M; DPS-TRWR: Jack Dean, 3 August 1974, TRHF&M.

6. Alexander and Brice, *Texas Rangers: Lives, Legend, and Legacy*, 377–378; book-length treatment of the purported brains behind the escape attempt is *Fred Carrasco: The Heroin Merchant* by Wilson McKinney.

7. OHI: Bob Mitchell, 1996, TRHF&M: "G.W. Burkes? G.W. Burkes and I never worked close, although our. . . . he was Captain of Company B for many years while I was Captain of Company F and we worked together. We never were close friends. . . . G.W. was a little bit different as I viewed Rangers. I never will forget the first time I met G.W. when I went into Company B, he came to a company meeting with a beard. . . . low quarter shoes, a turtleneck sweater, with a gold medallion around his neck. He was claiming to be working undercover." Utley, *Lone Star Lawmen*, 260: ". . . B Company's G.W. Burks, whose management style and sometimes bizarre behavior stirred resentment among his men, reprimands from his superiors, and company performance ratings embarrassingly lower than those of other companies." Jack Dean interview by author 8 March 2017,

likewise, held a somewhat jaundiced opinion of Captain Burks but did credit him as being fearless.

8. Alexander and Brice, *Texas Rangers: Lives, Legend, and Legacy*. Also see the skillfully written and adroitly researched *Eleven Days in Hell: The 1974 Carrasco Prison Siege at Huntsville, Texas* by William T. Harper. And see, the twenty-page written report of Warden Howell H. "Hal" Husbands, "The Escape Attempt of Inmates Fred Gomez Carrasco, #237163, Rudy Dominguez, #232414, and Ignacio Cuevas, #218121." In the TRHF&M. Also of significant value is the "Investigation of Attempted Escape at the Walls Unit of the Department of Corrections, Huntsville, Texas On July 24, 1974. This Investigation Ordered by the Honorable Governor Dolph Briscoe, Under the Direction of Texas Ranger Captain J.F. (Pete) Rogers." In the TRHF&M. Particularly useful, too, were the investigative reports of Ranger Wesley Styles and the voluntary written statement of inmate and coconspirator Lawrence Hall, in the TRHF&M. And for an insightful perspective focused on maintaining inmate security and operating the prison during the siege, which was, indeed, a real challenge, see former Warden Jim Willett's (now Director of the Prison Museum) and Ron Rozelle's exceptional *Warden: Prison Life and Death From the Inside Out*; Crawford, *Texas Death Row*, 39.

9. DPS-IM: Director Speir to Ranger Dean, 29 August 1974, TRHF&M: "This is your official notification that your standing among the group who competed with you is third. This places you in the number one position on the eligibility list for one year. The eligibility list will expire at midnight on August 2, 1975." DPS-PDS: Captain Wood, 31 August 1974, TRHF&M.

10. *McAllen Monitor*, November 17, 1974; VF: Texas Ranger Brownlow, TRHF&M; DPS-Texas Ranger Service Roster (Hereafter DPS-TRSR), TRHF&M.

11. DPS-COR: Jack Dean, 9 September 1974, TRHF&M; DPS-CCR: Jack Dean, 9 September 1974, TRHF&M.

12. DPS-IM: Captain Wood to W.D. Wilson, Senior Ranger Captain, 28 March 1974, TRHF&M.

13. B.R. McElroy, Training Officer, DPS Personnel and Training, to Captain Wood, 30 August 1974, with attached classroom schedule, TRHF&M.

14. DPS-TRWR: Jack Dean, 28 September 1974, TRHF&M; DPS-TR: Jack Dean, TRHF&M.

15. *Corpus Christi Times*, October 24, 1974; Ronald G. DeLord, ed., *The Ultimate Sacrifice: Trials and Triumphs of the Texas Peace Officer, 1823–2000*, 164.

16. DPS-TRWR: Jack Dean, 2 November 1974, TRHF&M; DPS-TV: Jack Dean, month of October 1974. Entry for 31 October 1974 in the TRHF&M: "To

Harlingen, assisted with surveillance of subjects believed involved in drug traffic connected with Randel Murder Case."

17. *Corpus Christi Times*, January 16, 1975.

18. Ibid., January 17, 1975.

19. Paul, *Jim Peters: Texas Ranger*, 77.

20. Ibid., 71–78. Author Paul cogently covers the murder of Walter Skillern.

21. Ibid.; also see, *Corpus Christi Caller-Times*, September 4, 1971, *Corpus Christi Times*, November 11, 1971, byline Lynn Pentony, *Corpus Christi Times*, November 12, 1971, byline Lynn Pentony, and *Corpus Christi Times*, December 20, 1971; Crawford, *Texas Death Row*, 5. Most interesting details of this murder of a DPS Narcotics Agent may be internalized by reviewing *Doyle Edward Skillern v. The State of Texas*, 559 S.W.2d 828 (Court of Criminal Appeals of Texas, 1977) and *Charles Victor Sanne and Doyle Edward Skillern v. The State of Texas*, 609 S.W.2d 762 (Court of Criminal Appeals of Texas, 1980).

22. *Alice Echo News*, December 2, 1974; *Corpus Christi Times*, December 2, 1974; DeLord, *The Ultimate Sacrifice*, 164; Program: *The Thirteenth Biennial Texas Peace Officers' Memorial Services, Texas State Capitol, May 1–2, 2011*.

23. DeLord, *The Ultimate Sacrifice*, 161–164.

24. Nathan R. Mutz, Texas Ranger, Company D, Laredo, Texas, interview by author 15 November 2017; *Alice Echo-News*, November 13, 2017; *San Antonio Express-News*, November 14, 2017, byline J.P. Lawrence.

25. DeLord, *The Ultimate Sacrifice*, 164.

26. DPS Director Speir to Ranger Dean, 11 November 1974, TRHF&M; DPS-EBS: Jack Dean, TRHF&M.

27. Albers, *The Life and Reflections of a Texas Ranger*, 127: "In 1974, I took early retirement and I thought I wanted to do something else that was not law enforcement. Part of my reason for taking early retirement was an offer of a job that paid considerably more than the state."

28. OHI: Bob Mitchell, 1996, TRHF&M.

29. Ibid.; Jack Dean interview by author 9 February 2017; VF: William Troy "Bud" Newberry, TRHF&M.

30. Ibid.; several interviews by author with Jack Dean, as cited.

31. Ibid.

32. Ed Gooding and Robert Nieman, *Ed Gooding: Soldier, Texas Ranger*, 253.

33. Ibid., 254.

34. Lieutenant George Turner, Texas Ranger, Ret., interview by author, 26 July 2017.

35. DPS-TRWR: Jack Dean, 11 January 1975, TRHF&M.

36. DPS-TRWR: Jack Dean, 7 September 1974, TRHF&M: "At request of U.S. Secret Service we interviewed and arrested subject . . . . for making verbal and written threats against the President of the United States."

37. DPS-TRWR: Jack Dean, 20 October 1973, TRHF&M.

38. DPS-TRWR: Jack Dean, 25 January 1975, TRHF&M.

39. Jack Dean interview by author, 5 July 2017.

40. Ibid.

41. DPS-TRWR: Jack Dean, 15 February 1975, TRHF&M.

42. *Waco Tribune-Herald*, April 18, 1977.

43. Certificate of Training: Jack O. Dean, Special Tactical Firearms School, FBI Academy, Quantico, VA, 23–28 March 1975, TRHF&M.

44. DPS-TRWR: Jack Dean, 5 April 1975, TRHF&M; DPS-TRWR: Jack Dean, 21 May 1975, TRHF&M.

45. DPS-TRWR: Jack Dean, 10 May 1975, TRHF&M.

46. Ibid.

47. DPS-TRWR: Jack Dean, 31 May 1975, TRHF&M.

48. DPS-TRWR: Jack Dean, 12 July 1975, TRHF&M.

49. *Corpus Christi Caller*, July 15, 1975.

50. *Victoria Advocate*, July 14, 1975.

51. Details with regards to forming and equipping Texas Ranger SWAT teams for this treatment are taken from Jack Dean's archived records catalogued at TRHF&M. Actions regarding his participation in this process were ongoing over the course of several years, until such was overhauled by a much more inclusive and overall DPS approach to specialized enforcement teams. For this chapter a synthesis of numerous reports and meetings was incorporated to convey the general story, though the facts and figures and places of training and names of participants are authentic.

52. Ibid., TRHF&M

53. Certificate of Training, In-Service Training for Texas Rangers, Austin, Texas, Jack Dean, September 1975, TRHF&M; Certificate of Training, Small Arms Firing School, Fort Hood, Texas, Jack Dean, October 1975, TRHF&M.

54. DPS-TRWR: Jack Dean, 7 November 1975, TRHF&M.

55. DPS-PDS: Captain Mitchell, 31 August 1975, TRHF&M.

56. DPS-COR: 5 August 1975, TRHF&M; DPS-TRWR: Jack Dean, 2 August 1975, TRHF&M.

57. *Waco Citizen*, August 7, 1975.

58. DPS-COR: 5 August 1975, TRHF&M; DPS-CCR: 5 August 1975, TRHF&M; *The State of Texas Death Certificate*: "Deceased was strapped inside motor vehicle and pushed into 40 feet of water in Lake Waco."

59. *Waco Citizen*, January 20, 1976, and February 13, 1976.

60. Day, *One Man's Dream*, 36–48; DPS-TRWR: Jack Dean, 7 February 1976, TRHF&M.

61. Kyle Dean interview by author, 31 October 1974; DeLord, *The Ultimate Sacrifice*, 164.

62. Gooding and Nieman, *Ed Gooding: Soldier, Texas Ranger*, 224–226.

63. DPS-TRWR: Jack Dean, 28 May 1976, TRHF&M.

64. Notes: Texas Rangers, Company "D" meeting 6 January 1972, TRHF&M.

65. In the early 1970s, Killeen, which is adjacent to Fort Hood in Central Texas, was plagued twice a month on military paydays by an onslaught of scores of prostitutes from around the state. The offense of prostitution at that time was a Class C Misdemeanor, for which the maximum $200 fine was not a deterrent. In 1977, at the urging of State Representative Stan Schleuter and new Killeen Police Chief Rick Miller, the Texas legislature increased the penalty to a Class B misdemeanor, which provided for county jail time. An increased enforcement effort then had teeth and the problem was greatly diminished in a short period of time.

66. DPS-TRWR: Jack Dean, 14 March 1976, TRHF&M. Newspaper profiles of Texas Ranger Gooding written by the prolific Stan Redding may be accessed by reviewing the *Houston Chronicle* of February 10, 1963 and the article penned by John W. Flores for *The Cleburne Times-Review*, Vol. 90, no. 159. Also see, *Palestine Herald-Press*, August 21, 2002, byline Cheril Vernon: "For 33 years, from 1949 to 1982, Gooding served as a Highway Patrolman and a Texas Ranger."

67. Gooding and Nieman, *Ed Gooding: Soldier, Texas Ranger*, 241.

68. *Dallas Morning News*, March 25, 1974; *Amarillo Globe Times*, March 28, 1974; *McKinney Daily Courier Gazette*, March 25, 1974; and the *Port Arthur News*, March 24, 1974.

69. DPS-TRWR: Jack Dean, 14 March 1976.

70. Gooding and Nieman, *Ed Gooding: Soldier, Texas Ranger*, 243.

71. Ibid.

72. *Dallas Morning News*, August 29, 1976.

73. Jim Willett interview by author, 17 November 2017.

74. *Charles Harrelson vs. The State of Texas*. 511 S.W.2f 957 (Court of Criminal Appeals of Texas, 1974).

75. *Dallas Morning News*, August 29, 1973; Cartwright, "Talking to Killers." ". . . Leavenworth, one of the toughest prisons in the country. . . ."

76. Berg, *Run Brother, Run*, quoting lawyer Percy Foreman, on 214–215.

77. Cartwright, *Dirty Dealing*, 223. Also see Cartwright's *Texas Monthly* article, "Talking to Killers."

78. Interview with Richard K. Alford by author 25 August 2017. Mr. Alford, a former and now retired Regional Director, Texas Department of Criminal Justice, Correctional Institutions Division, and an executive then responsible for the oversight and operation of fourteen Texas prison units, confirms that "institutionalization" is a rather common and well-recognized psychological phenomenon within prison administration circles. In short, according to Director Alford, not just a few inmates become accustomed to not having to make decisions regarding an array of day by day matters, i.e., when to get up, when to eat breakfast, lunch, and supper, how to dress, when and where to work, when to rest, where to stand, when and what they may purchase from the commissary store, when they are allowed visitation, who they can write or receive letters from, when they can get a haircut, when and how long they are allowed recreation, how to receive cost-free medical and/or dental procedures, or how to cleave unto themselves bona fide Bachelor's or Master's degrees, and when to go to bed—all while incarcerated. The list is, truly, *ad infinitum*. Over time, for certain individuals, the worry-free life of being ensconced behind bars is more comfortable than facing the hard music of everyday life in the free-world. Once settled into an unbendable and predictable routine—and if assiduously watching one's Ps and Qs, it's a somewhat trouble-free and non-stressful existence for letting the years tick by. Mr. Alford further elaborates that there are—and have been—those occasions when an inmate nearing the end of his/her court mandated sentence will purposefully assault a correctional staff employee or commit some other statutory offense, just so he/she can "catch another case," enter a *Guilty* plea, and thwart being released from custody on their original sentence. Additionally, as Mr. Alford pointed out, if a Death Row inmate after exhausting all hope of appellate relief and nearing his/her last date with a pharmaceutical injecting state-paid person, were to kill a correctional employee—a Capital Murder—and receive a sentence of death, the mandated appellate process would be started anew, a legal review forestalling the originally slated execution by a number of years. Simply stated it would be buying time with blood—someone else's.

Chapter 10: "A contract-assigned assassination"

1. Tise, Texas County Sheriffs, 257; Robert Draper, "The Sheriff Who Went to Pot," *Texas Monthly*, December 1994, 133, 162; Jack Dean interview by author, 5 July 2017.
2. DPS-PDS: Jack Dean, 28 February 1977, TRHF&M.
3. Jack Dean interview by author, 15 August 2017.

4. Partial compilation of Jack Dean's 1977 first-quarter TRWRs, TRHF&M.

5. DPS-TRWR: Jack Dean, 28 March 1977, TRHF&M.

6. *Waco Tribune-Herald*, April 18, 1977.

7. Ibid.

8. *Dallas Morning News*, June 23, 1977; DPS-TRWR: Jack Dean, 21 June 1977, TRHF&M.

9. Ibid.; Tise, *Texas County Sheriffs*, 259; DPS-TRWR: Jack Dean, 21 June 1977, TRHF&M.

10. Ibid.

11. DPS-TRWR: Jack Dean, 28 April 1977, TRHF&M.

12. DPS-TRWR: Jack Dean, 31 July and 07 August 1977, TRHF&M.

13. Alexander and Brice, *Texas Rangers: Lives, Legend, and Legacy*, 380; *Dallas Morning News*, February 23 and 24, 1978, March 4 and 8, 1978, May 31, 1978, June 14 and 17, 1978. Also, DeLord, *The Ultimate Sacrifice*, 172; VF Bobby Paul Doherty, TRHF&M.

14. Jack Dean interview by author, 15 August 2017.

15. JD-DRJ: 6 and 8 May 1978, TRHF&M.

16. Stephen William Schuster IV, "The Modernization of the Texas Rangers, 1930–1935," Thesis, Texas Christian University, Fort Worth, Texas, 1965. 38–39; Alexander and Brice, *Texas Rangers: Lives, Legend, and Legacy*, 365; Asserting that Texas Ranger Captain Tom Hickman was not drawing on state funds for his overseas travel is more than confirmed by Walter Prescott Webb's article, "Texas Rangers Quell Troubles," for the August 1924 edition of *The State Trooper*, 14.

17. Ibid.; And Steve P. Wharram interview by author 16 August 2017. Mr. Wharram, a TRHF&M Board Member, has in progress a comprehensive biography of Tom Hickman.

18. David Johnson, prominent researcher and writer, to author, 5 September 2017.

19. Ibid.; Jack Dean interview by author 15 August 2017.

20. Jack and Janie Dean interview by author 28 September 2017.

21. *Dallas Morning News*, June 21, 1978.

22. The interested reader may wish to peruse the following citations: *State of Texas v. Oscar McInnis*, 586 S.W.2d 890 (TX.Civ.App.—Corpus Christi 1979); *U.S. v. McInnis et el*, 601 F.2d 1319 (U.S Court of Appeals, Fifth Circuit, 1979); *McInnis v. State of Texas*, 603 S.W.2d 179 (TX 1980); *McInnis v. State of Texas*, 618 S.W.2d 389 (TX. Civ.App.—Beaumont 1981); and *Villanueva v. McInnis*, 723 F.2d 414 (U.S Court of Appeals, Fifth Circuit, 1984); Berg, *Run, Brother, Run*, 214.

23. *Thomas A. Barefoot aka Darren Callier v. State of Texas*, 596 S.W.2d 875 (Court of Criminal Appeals of Texas, 1980). Also see, *Dallas Morning News*, August 9, 1978: "Barefoot escaped along with at least one other man from a Valencia County, N.M jail in early April [*sic:* January] after he was accused in the rape of a 3-year-old Grants, N.M. girl. . . ." And see, Crawford, *Texas Death Row*, 4: ". . . Barefoot had been arrested for the rape of the three-year-old daughter of his estranged girlfriend. He escaped from jail by digging himself out with a spoon."

24. *Dallas Morning News*, October 30, 1984. Andy Barefoot had been living in New Iberia, Louisiana, but his actual POB was Centerville, Mississippi, on 23 February 1945.

25. *Barefoot v. State* (1980) as cited. Somewhat surprising, at least for this writer, was the number of times convicted murderers had opted to use the diminutive .25 caliber pistol. Particularly this proclivity was noted by reviewing Crawford's *Texas Death Row*, wherein when known, the murder weapon of those sentenced to pay the ultimate price for their criminality employed the .25 or .22 caliber weapons; citations throughout.

26. Ibid.

27. Ibid.; DeLord, *The Ultimate Sacrifice*, 173; *Texas Death Certificate*, Bell County, Carl Irvin Levin, 7 August 1978.

28. Ibid.

29. *Dallas Morning News*, August 10, 1978.

30. Ibid., August 26, 1978.

31. Ibid., November 15, 1978.

32. *Barefoot v. State* (1980) as cited; *Dallas Morning News*, November 18 and 22, 1978.

33. Crawford, *Texas Death Row*, 4.

34. *Dallas Morning News*, February 12 and November 21, 1980. Also, Cartwright, *Dirty Dealing*, 223.

35. Ibid. November 25, 1982.

36. DPS-PDS: Jack Dean, 31 August 1976, TRHF&M; DPS-PDS: Jack Dean, 28 February 1977, TRHF&M.

37. DPS Director Speir to Sergeant Dean, 25 October 1978, TRHF&M.

38. Teletype: All DPS stations, 25 October 1978, authority Colonel Speir, TRHF&M.

39. *Waco Tribune-Herald*, October 26, 1978.

40. VF: H.R. "Lefty" Block, TRHF&M; also see, Proctor, *Just One Riot*, 20–21.

41. Utley, *Lone Star Lawmen*, 302.

42. Cox, *Time of the Rangers*, 323.

43. FBI SAC Michael A. "Tony" Morrow, San Antonio, Texas, to Captain Jack O. Dean, Texas Rangers, Company D, San Antonio, Texas, 27 October 1978, TRHF&M.

44. DPS-TRWR: Jack Dean, 7 November 1978, TRHF&M; JD-DRJ: 3 November 1978, TRHF&M.

45. *Dallas Morning News*, November 22, 1978. Also see the U.S. Marshals Service Historian, David S. Turk's *Forging the Star: The Official Modern History of the United States Marshals Service*, 166–167; Headlines in the *Brownsville Herald* of October 18, 1979 were explicit: "FBI Says Kerr Identified Assailants." Furthermore, in the same newspaper article: "Assistant U.S. Attorney James Kerr, who escaped an assassination attempt last Nov. 21, identified his assailants in a police lineup as members of the Bandidos motorcycle club, an FBI agent says in a document released in court. FBI Special Agent Gregg Van de Loo also said in the document that a confidential informant claimed he was asked by Bandidos to participate in the assassination attempt." And see, Cartwright, *Dirty Dealing*, 132–133.

Chapter 11: "You're lucky to be alive"

1. DPS-TRWR: Jack Dean, 11 and 12 November 1978, and 7 December 1978, TRHF&M.

2. DPS-TRWR: Jack Dean, 28 November 1978, TRHF&M.

3. DPS-TRWR: Jack Dean, 6 December 1978, TRHF&M.

4. DPS-TRWR: Jack Dean, 7 December 1978, TRHF&M.

5. Barkley and Odintz, *The Portable Handbook of Texas*, 656, Evan Anders, contributor.

6. Ibid.; OHI: Ramiro "Ray" Martinez, 1999. "Right, from Jim Wells county, but it's really in San Diego which is Duval county because of the county lines come through San Diego, that's why they say Duvall county." TRHR&M.

7. Tise, *Texas County Sheriffs*, 163.

8. Barkley and Odintz, *The Portable Handbook of Texas*, 656.

9. *Corpus Christi Times*, April 1, 1975, bylines, Joe Coudert and Spencer Pearson.

10. *Alice Echo News*, May 10, 1974; *Washington Post*, November 3, 2000: Archer Parr "was one of the area's most influential men before convictions for perjury and stealing county equipment and services ended his political career."

11. Quite interestingly and informatively, Retired Texas Ranger Ramino "Ray" Martinez, a working member of the 1970s Duval County Task Force, cogently enlightens readers about this phase of investigate work in the

2008 autobiography, *They Call Me Ranger Ray: From the UT Tower Sniper to Corruption in South Texas*, 133–164.

12. DPS-TRWR: Jack Dean, 14 January 1979, TRHF&M. Two months later Captain Dean was at Alice, where he "conferred with local officials reference Archer Parr and situation in Duval County." See, DPS-TRWR: Jack Dean, 21 March 1979, TRHF&M.

13. OHI: Jack Dean, 2013, TRHF&M.

14. DPS-TRWR: Jack Dean, 7 December 1978, TRHF&M.

15. Jack Dean interview by author, 28 September 2017.

16. Barkley and Odintz, *The Portable Handbook of Texas*, Robert A. Calvert, contributor, 98.

17. DPS-TRWR: Jack Dean, 21 January 1979, TRHF&M.

18. Barkley and Odintz, *The Portable Handbook of Texas*, Carl H. Moneyhon, contributor, 720.

19. DPS-TRPR: Company D, January 1979, TRHF&M.

20. DPS-TRWR: Jack Dean, 28 February 1979, TRHF&M.

21. *Paris News*, February 17, 1979; DeLord, *The Ultimate Sacrifice*, 175.

22. FBI SAC Morrow to DPS Colonel Speir, 16 April 1979, TRHF&M.

23. DPS Colonel Speir to FBI SAC Morrow, 18 April 1979, TRHF&M.

24. DPS-TRWR: Jack Dean, 28 April 1979, TRHF&M.

25. Robert Draper, "The Twilight of the Texas Rangers," *Texas Monthly*, February, 1994, 110.

26. DPS-TRWR: Jack Dean, 28 April 1979, TRHF&M.

27. *Dallas Morning News*, April 28, 1979.

28. *Paris News*, April 29, 1979.

29. *Santa Ana Orange County Register*, April 29, 1979.

30. Ibid. Picked up from the *Chicago Tribune*, byline Timothy McNulty: "What I figure, with the parade and all, is that he must've thought everybody was ganging up on him,' said the 59-year-old brother. 'I know. . . . he thought people were breaking into his house and poisoning his water." Also, *Dallas Morning News*, April 30, 1979: Unfortunately it seems, Ira Attebury "was never the same after his semi-trailer tuck rammed a car that ran a red light in front of him eight years ago in Ohio. Both women occupants of the car were killed. . . . two brothers said he was not at fault in the crash. But they said the accident left him with a disabling injury and emotionally scarred. 'He thought the police were after him all the time after that. . . .'"

31. Ibid.: "More than 1,000 parade-goers and high school band members hugged the ground and screamed as Attebury traded bursts of fire with police." *The*

Dallas Morning News edition of April 28, 1979 carries a map of where the incident took place and a listing by name of the casualties, including the San Antonio police officers wounded during the mass shooting.

32. *Paris News*, April 29, 1979.

33. DPS-TRWR: Jack Dean, 14 April 1979, TRHF&M.

34. Jack Dean interview by author, 15 August 2017; and see, Martinez, *They Call Me Ranger Ray*, 207–208.

35. DPS-TRWR: Jack Dean, 21 May 1979, TRHF&M.

36. *Jo Ann Harrelson v. United States of America*, 705 F.2d 733 (U.S. Court of Appeals, Fifth Circuit 1983).

37. DPS-TRWR: Jack Dean, 21 May 1979, TRHF&M.

38. DPS-TRWR: Jack Dean, 28 May 1979, TRHF&M; DPS-TV: Jack Dean, March 1979, TRHF&M.

39. *Dallas Morning News*, May 29, 1979, byline Kent Biffle, "EX-RANGERS BRANDISH STARS, SCARS."

40. DPS-TRWR: Jack Dean, 31 May 1979, TRHF&M; *Dallas Morning News*, May 30, 1979.

41. Utley, *Lone Star Lawmen*, 279; Jack Dean interview by author, 15 August 2017.

42. OHI-Jack Dean, 2013, TRHF&M; JD-DRJ: Jack Dean, 29 May 1979, TRHF&M.

43. DPS-TRWR: Jack Dean, 31 May 1979, TRHF&M: "Assisted officers with security for Federal Judges at request of U.S. Marshal's Office."

44. *Dallas Morning News*, May 30, 1979.

45. Turk, *Forging The Star*, 167.

46. *Dallas Morning News*, May 30, 1979.

47. Utley, *Lone Star Lawmen*, 278.

48. Certainly one practicing attorney who had negative courtroom experiences with Judge Wood was El Paso's Raymond C. "Ray" Caballero. At least some of these less than positive dealings were enumerated in Cartwright's *Dirty Dealing*, Chapter 13, 95–105. Of course a contrasting look at Judge Wood is reckoned with in historian Turk's, *Forging the Star*, 166: "According to Deputy U.S. Marshal Ray Muzquiz, Judge Wood was strict but fair. Muzquiz was the court security coordinator for Western District of Texas, and would be among the closest deputies to the judges." In life—good or bad—personal perspectives are not infrequently at odds.

49. *Dallas Morning News*, April 5, 1979.

50. Ibid. Of his Las Vegas junkets, Jimmy Chagra bragged: "I'd win $60,000, $70,000 or more than $100,000 some nights. I just couldn't lose." And,

Dallas Morning News, April 3, 1979: "Jimmy Chagra drug trial moved to Austin, set May 29."

51. Ibid., May 30, 1979. As an editorial note: the *Dallas Morning News* articles regarding the prelude to and assassination of Judge Wood, as well as the aftermath criminal investigation and, in the end, successful federal prosecutions are for the most part methodical, comprehensive, and exceptionally captivating.

52. Utley, *Lone Star Lawmen*, 279; Cartwright, *Dirty Dealing*. Cartwright's skillfully penned tome is divided into three parts—part two is titled: "The Crime of the Century."

53. OHI-Jack Dean, 2013, TRHF&M; Cox, *Time of the Rangers*: "But as federal agents rushed to the Alamo City from Washington and elsewhere, the FBI soon said that while it would welcome any information the Rangers might develop, neither the state officers nor San Antonio detective[s] would be involved in the investigation." 306.

54. Jack Dean interview by author, 15 August 2017; For quotation, see, Utley, *Lone Star Lawmen*, 279.

55. DPS-TRWR: Jack Dean, 04 June 1979, TRHF&M; JD-DRJ: 04 June 1979. "Leave SA 5.00 a.m. to Edinburg McAllen area reference Special Investigation of Sheriffs Office requested by Hidalgo County Grand Jury." TRHF&M.

56. Draper, "The Sheriff Who Went to Pot," 132.

57. DPS-TRWR: Jack Dean, 04 June 1979, TRHF&M.

58. DPS-TRWR: Jack Dean, 14 June 1979, TRHF&M; Jack Dean interview by author, 15 August 2017.

59. Jack Dean interview by author, 28 September 2017.

60. Draper, "The Sheriff Who Went to Pot," 133. Herein for this text, but a capsule account regarding Sheriff Brig Marmolejo's tribulations and trials is forthcoming. For an incisive and full-bore examination, the interested reader should avail themselves of Draper's product in full, a first-class contribution.

61. *Brownsville Herald*, January 19, 1994; *Orange Leader*, February 13, 1994.

62. *Orange Leader*, February 19, 1994.

63. *Kerrville Daily Times*, July 17, 1994.

64. *New York Times*, March 24, 1997.

65. Draper, "The Sheriff Who Went to Pot," 133; *Brownsville Herald*, July 28 1994: "After nearly six hours of deliberations, a federal jury found Marmolejo guilty on all charges: two counts of racketeering; two of bribery; three of money laundering, and one of interstate travel in aid of racketeering."

66. *United States v. Marmolejo et al.*, 89 F.3d 1185 (U.S. Court of Appeals, Fifth Circuit, 1996). For reference to a related U.S. Supreme Court ruling in this matter, a capsule version may be accessed by reviewing the *Del Rio News Herald*, December 3, 1997.

67. DPS-TRWR: Jack Dean, 21 June 1979, TRHF&M.

68. *Dallas Morning News*, November 3, 1982, byline Helen Parmley: "He [Roloff] stood his ground with Texas officials once calling his standoff with state authorities 'the Christian Alamo.'"

69. Barkley & Odintz, *Portable Handbook of Texas*, 734, H. Allen Anderson, contributor.

70. Pamela Colloff, "Remember *the* Christian Alamo," *Texas Monthly*, December 2001, 96. Author Colloff, with her characteristic verve and cogent analysis and probing interviews, presents an insightful piece portraying life inside the Rebekah Home at the time.

71. Ibid.

72. Intriguingly in light of later rulings, was one that went the evangelist's way. The interested reader may wish to peruse a Texas Supreme Court finding: Ex-parte Roloff, 510 SW.2d 813 (TX 1974).

73. DPS-TRWR: Jack Dean, 21 and 28 June 1979, TRHF&M.

74. Ibid.

75. Colloff, "Remember *the* Christian Alamo," 97.

76. Jack Dean interview by author, 15 August 2017; *The New York Times*, November 4, 1982, byline Wolfgang Saxon: "in June 1979, state officials, armed with court orders and backed by troopers, moved in to shut the Rebekah Home."

77. Barkley and Odintz, *The Portable Handbook of Texas*, 734; Colloff, "Remember *the* Christian Alamo," 163. Although the *Roloff v. Texas* story is far from over, for Captain Jack Dean's involvement the Corpus Christi affair was history. The interested and thoughtful reader may want to access the rest of author Colloff's authoritative piece dealing with later happenings and entanglements and tacit support from the state's governors. The barefaced political tinkering—while disturbing—makes for an interesting insight into Lone Star State's political principles—or lack thereof.

78. OHI: Jack Dean, 2013, TRHF&M.

79. Ibid.

80. DPS-IM: Senior Captain W.D. Wilson, Texas Rangers, to Colonel James B. Adams, Director of DPS, 13 April 1982. A summary of Captain Jack Dean's (signed by Dean) participation in the Wood murder investigation

as it related to receipt of information concerning suspect Charles Voyde Harrelson is in TSA.

81. Elaine Shannon, *Desperados: Latin Drug Lords, U.S. Lawmen, and the War America Can't Win*, 241.

82. *Dallas Morning News*, May 31, 1979, byline Howard Swindle and George Kuempel: "Their potential suspects, investigators say, could come from eight years' worth of cases heard by a man whose stiff penalties—especially in narcotics cases—earned him his feared nickname."

83. OHI: Jack Dean, 2013, TRHF&M. Jack Dean does not identify the FBI Assistant Director from Washington, D.C. by name during this interview. However, in the above-cited Wilson to Adams DPS-IM, Captain Jack Dean is name specific. In the TSA.

84. Wilson to Adams as cited, TSA.

85. Utley, *Lone Star Lawmen*, 279. The author identifies the FBI Deputy Assistant Director as James O. Ingram.

86. OHI: Jack Dean, 2013, TRHF&M.

87. DPS-TRWR: Jack Dean 21 and 28 July 1979, TRHF&M. A review of and rulings in this civil case may be accessed by reviewing *Mary Lorene O'Dell Murphy, R.N., Appeliant, v. Margaret L. Rowland, R.N., et al., Appellees*, 609 S.W.2d 292 (TX.Civ.App.—Corpus Christi, 1980) and *Santiago and Guadalupe Valdez, et al., Appellants, b. Lyman-Roberts Hospital, Inc., et al., Appellees*, 638 S.W.2d 111 (TX.APP—Corpus Christi 1982).

88. DPS-TRWR: Jack Dean, 21 September 1979, TRHF&M.

89. DPS-TRWR: Jack Dean, 7 October 1979 and 21 October 1979, TRHF&M.

90. For the interested reader, the truly fascinating saga of Oscar McInnis and his legal sparring, may be accessed by reviewing several appellate court cases: *State of Texas v. Oscar B. McInnis*, 586 S.W.2d 890 (TX.CiV.App.— Corpus Christi 1979); *United States of America v. Oscar McInnis and Patricia Parada*, 601 F.2d 1319 (U.S. Court of Appeals, Fifth Circuit, 1979); *Oscar B. McInnis v. State of Texas*, 603 S.W.2d 179 (TX. 1980); and *Oscar B. McInnis, v. State of Texas*, 618 S.W.d 389 (TX.Civ.App.—Beaumont 1981).

91. Ibid.

92. DPS-TRWR: Jack Dean, 28 October 1979, TRHF&M; *Bee County Enterprise*, October 1, 1986; Jack Dean interview by author 28 September 2017; VF-Kasey King, TRHF&M; Holdridge, *Working the Border*, 157.

93. DPS-TRWR: Jack Dean, 07 November 1979, TRHF&M.

94. DPS-TRWR: Jack Dean, 14 November 1979, TRHF&M.

95. *Chicago Tribune*, December 3, 1979.

96. *New York Times*, December 3, 1979.

97. DPS-TRWR: Jack Dean, 7 and 14 December 1979.
98. Certificate of Recognition, Assistance in the Protection of the Shah of Iran, December 1979, TRHF&M.

Chapter 12: "Baby rattles and beef"

1. Utley, *Lone Star Lawmen*, 261–262; Cox, *Time of the Rangers*, 314.
2. Nieman, "20th Century Shining Star: Captain Jack Dean, United States Marshal."
3. Holdridge, *Working the Border*, 105.
4. OHI: Adolfo "Al" Cuellar, Texas Ranger, Ret., 2009, TRHF&M.
5. Holdridge, *Working The Border*, 105.
6. Jack Dean interview by author 28 September 1979.
7. *Charles Voyde Harrelson v. State of Texas*, 654 S.W.2d 712 (Court of Criminal Appeals of Texas, Houston, 1983).
8. Cartwright, *Dirty Dealing*, 212–213.
9. *Dallas Morning News*, February 3 and 7, 1980.
10. [Charles] *Harrelson v. State of Texas* (1983) as cited.
11. *Dallas Morning News*, February 7, 1980.
12. DPS-TRWR: Jack Dean, 21 May 1980, TRHF&M.
13. DPS-TRWR: Jack Dean, 14 June and 21 June, 1980, TRHF&M; Jack Dean interview by author, 7 October 2017.
14. Ibid.; Irrefutably not all of Captain Jack Dean's interaction with the FBI was positive. On one occasion there was rather heated fallout due to Dean refusing to reveal the identity of a CI—a brouhaha making it all the way to DPS Colonel Jim Adams's office. Captain Dean's fidelity to his informant was sustained, though Jack truly thought—for awhile—that his job was in jeopardy. Jack Dean interview by author, 5 January 2018. During another scenario revolving around a string of burglaries, the FBI took credit—calling a press conference, but purposely shuttling Captain Dean and San Antonio PD officials to one side during the self-serving performance. Such conduct came as no surprise. See, Utley, *Lone Star Lawmen*, 262–263, 375 n. 20. Also see Utley, 338, "But as an institution the FBI had few friends among Texas Lawmen. The FBI intruded where not needed or wanted, demanded a flow of relevant information from the Rangers but shared almost none of their own, insisted on taking the lead in any case involving other agencies, and grabbed the publicity when favorable while shifting it to others when not. Especially blatant instances of FBI arrogance occurred when the FBI withheld public recognition of the key role

of Ranger captain Jack Dean in identifying the hired killer of federal judge John Wood. . . ."

15. *Austin American-Statesman*, September 6, 1981.

16. Jack Dean interview by author 24 October 2017.

17. DPS-TRWR: Jack Dean, 14 June 1980, TRHF&M.

18. Jack Dean interview by author, 7 October 2017.

19. Gournay, *Texas Boundaries*, 117.

20. Bob Alexander, *Fearless Dave Allison: Border Lawman*, 193.

21. *Charles V. Harrelson v. State of Texas*, 668 S.W.2d 455 (Court of Criminal Appeals of Texas, El Paso, 1984); Utley, *Lone Star Lawmen*, 279; Cartwright, *Dirty Dealing*, 216, 320 and 321. During the Culberson County scenario Harrelson also alleged that he had assassinated President John F. Kennedy at Dallas.

22. *Brownsville Herald*, December 10, 1980.

23. Ibid., April 24, 1981. Also OHI: James Alvis Wright, Captain Texas Rangers, Ret., 1996: "through this vehicle it was. . . . turned out to belong to some small time thieves and hot check writers that I had dealt with before and eventually was able to run it down and arrest. . . . arrest. . . . made an arrest on 'em and got statement s from 'em and solved it [Waco H-E-B extortion]. . . . Well of course I think the H.E.B. food. . . . ah . . . extortion case was one of them that I thought was very satisfying or was very satisfying to me to solve that one."

24. Dan E. Butt to Colonel James Adams, 17 December 1980, TRHF&M.

25. *Del Rio News Herald*, April 23, 1981; *Eagle Pass News Guide*, April 23, 1981.

26. FBI SAC John C. "Jack" Lawn to DPS Director Adams, 17 November 1981, TRHF&M. Also see, Dan E. Butt to Captain Dean, 3 September and 11 June, 1982, TRHF&M; Jack Dean interview by author 24 October 2017. Jack Dean advised that his relationship with SAC Tony Morrow was a professional and personal friendship—on and off duty—while his relationship with SAC Jack Lawn, though most amicable, was confined to their workplace responsibilities. Furthermore, Jack Dean stated that he sincerely appreciated SAC Lawn—even if the adulation was not made public at the time—thanking him for furnishing the investigative lead regarding Charles Voyde Harrelson and the assassination of Judge Wood. From the analytical perspective, the clue was momentous.

27. *United States v. Joe Corona Valdez*, 722 F.2d 1196 (U.S. Court of Appeals, Fifth Circuit, 1984); Texas Ranger Joe Haralson interview by author 19 October 2017. Interestingly, Ranger Haralson—as of this writing (2018)—is at the top of the seniority list for Texas Rangers, having pinned on the iconic badge during June 1981. Ranger Haralson further advises that subsequent to a

new trial defendant Joe Corona Valdez was found *Not Guilty*, the state not having proved its case Beyond A Reasonable Doubt. Also, *Odessa American*, September 2, 1982; and, *Brownsville Herald*, March 30, 1984: "The jury took less than two days to acquit Joe Corona Valdez, 40, of the extortion charges. Valdez was accused of threatening to poison meat in H.E.B. stores unless $125,000 were left at a remote drop site." Historian and former Bell County Attorney Rick Miller to author, 19 October 2017.

28. Albert J. Lilly, Chief of Police, Universal City Police Department, Universal City [Bexar County], Texas, to Colonel Adams, 7 May 1984, TRHF&M.

29. *San Antonio Express*, September 24, 1981, byline Bruce Davidson.

30. OHI: James Wright, 1996, TRHF&M.

31. *San Antonio Light*, October 16, 1981, byline Robert Cahill.

32. *Dallas Morning News*, October 1, 1981.

33. DeLord, *The Ultimate Sacrifice*, 183. Seemingly the slain Los Fresnos PD policemen's name is interchangeably written as "Carrisalez" and/or "Carrizales" and/or "Carrizalez." A veritable smorgasbord of surname choices; sometimes more than one are employed in the same document. For this account, "Carrisalez" will be utilized, as it was for the 1993 United States Supreme Court opinion.

34. *Brownsville Herald*, January 15, 1982.

35. Ibid. "Constable Lupe Rosales said the Social Security card was seven feet from Rucker's body."

36. DPS-TRWR: Jack Dean, 30 September 1981, TRHF&M.

37. DPS-TRWR: Jack Dean, 7 October 1981, TRHF&M.

38. Jack Dean interview by author, 24 October 2017. During this interview Jack Dean graded Texas Ranger Bruce Casteel's investigative talents as "the best he had ever seen," particularly noting that Ranger Casteel was an exceptional and outstanding interrogator; The investigative presence of Company D Texas Ranger Bruce Casteel in this matter—aside from official reports and newspaper citations, is also found in *Leonel Torres Herrera, Petitioner-Appellant, v. James A. Collins, Director, Texas Department of Criminal Justice, Institutional Division, Respondent-Appellee*, 904 F.2d 944 (U.S Court of Appeals, Fifth Circuit, 1990).

39. *Leonel Torres Herrera v. State of Texas*, 682 S.W.2d 313 (Court of Criminal Appeals of Texas, 1984).

40. *Dallas Morning News*, October 5, 1981: "About 25 officers from the DPS, Edinburgh [*sic* Edinburg] Police Department, Hidalgo County Sheriff's Department and Texas Rangers took part in the arrest [of Herrera]."

41. *Brownsville Herald*, January 18, 1982.

42. Ibid.

43. Ibid., January 22, 1982; and see excerpt: *Herrera v. State* (1984) as cited. "Subsequent to appellant's invocation of his right to counsel, assistant district attorney Hendley attempted to interrogate appellant. Hendley, upon entering the interrogation room where appellant was situated, asked appellant why he had shot Officer Rucker. In response to Hendley appellant immediately decked him and continued to beat him until restrained by several police officers. The following morning while hospitalized, appellant in the presence of two officers, made several threats to the effect that he would kill all the police when released. These statements were admitted against appellant during the sentencing hearing on the issue of future dangerousness. Appellant alleges that since Hendley's interrogation of appellant was in violation of his rights under Miranda, supra, and Edwards, supra, that he would not, but for this illicit interrogation, have been hospitalized, and therefore have made these admittedly damaging statements. Appellant's argument fails for several reasons. First, we cannot agree that, but for Hendley's interrogation, appellant would not have been hospitalized. Rather we believe that, but for appellant's violent reaction to Hendley's interrogation he would not have been hospitalized. An illicit interrogation does not authorize the appellant to assault the interrogator. . . ."

44. Ibid.

45. DeLord, *The Ultimate Sacrifice*, 183; *Brownsville Herald*, January 19, 1982: "after witnesses testified of Carrizales' [Carrisalez] deathbed identification of Herrera as the man who shot him in the chest."

46. *Brownsville Herald*, January 18, 1982.

47. Officer Down Memorial Page, "Patrolman Enrique L. Carrizales, End of Watch, Wednesday, October 7, 1981:" "During a search of the suspect's home, the duty weapon of Constable Ricky Lewis was located. Constable Lewis had been murdered two years earlier. The suspect was never charged in Constable Lewis' death and the case remains officially unsolved. The suspect was sentenced to death for the murders of Trooper Rucker and Patrolman Carrizales. . . ."

48. *Herrera v. Texas*, (1984) as cited.

49. *Herrera v. Collins*, 506 U.S. 390, 113 S.Ct. 853, 122 L.ED.2d 203 (1993).

50. Crawford, *Texas Death Row*, 58. Leonel Torres Herrera was lawfully executed on 12 May 1993. It's but fair to mention that Leonel Torres Herrera's sister, Norma Herrera, has published an exculpatory and sanitized account of her brother's criminal involvements, tribulations, and his ultimate execution for murdering a duly commissioned Texas peace officer: *Last Words from Death Row: The Walls Unit*. Understandably and devotedly author Herrera was/is

sympathetic to her brother's plight. The thoughtfully interested reader, on the other hand, should have little trouble evaluating and discarding competing versions if logically or legally inappropriate—especially after even a cursory and layman's review of the United States Supreme Court's findings.

Chapter 13: "No neophyte at prison life"

1. Ray Cave, "Texas Sniper," *Time Magazine*, October 25, 1982, 38.
2. Cartwright, *Dirty Dealing*, 303.
3. Utley, *Lone Star Lawmen*, 280; Jack Dean interview by author, 24 October 2017.
4. Wilson to Adams, 13 April 1982, as cited, TSA.
5. Utley, *Lone Star Lawmen*, 280.
6. Cartwright, *Dirty Dealing*.
7. *Jo Ann Harrelson v. United States* (1983) as cited; It seems, as mentioned in this text, that author Cartwright, *Dirty Dealing*, was also somewhat innocently in the dark regarding the rifle's gunstock: "Despite the tapes, there were still holes in the government's case. The government didn't have a murder weapon, merely the stock of one of the ten thousand Weatherby Mark V rifles sold in this country in recent years." 308. And, also as mentioned in this text: "Yes, they may have had the stock of but one of ten thousand Weatherby Mark V rifles sold in this country in recent years, but it was the one purchased by Jo Ann Harrelson, aka Faye L. King. Such coincidence would not be lost on a jury disposed to reasonableness and commonsense." The inference is not at all vague, quoting straight from the above cited appellate case: "two local residents, alerted by publicity surrounding the search, produced a rifle stock they had found. [FBI Agent] Iden testified that through this physical evidence the authorities were able to trace the murder weapon to the defendant [Jo Ann Harrelson]."
8. Jack Dean interview by author 28 April 2017.
9. Interview by author with antique and modern era firearms researcher and writer, well-known authority Lieutenant Doug Dukes, Austin PD, Ret., 20 July 2017.
10. *Jo Ann Harrelson v. United States* (1983) as cited.
11. Ibid.
12. Cartwright, *Dirty Dealing*, 308.
13. Kyle Dean interview by author, 31 October 2017; Crawford, *Texas Death Row*, 173. Robert Excell White would meet his prearranged date with the state-paid executioner on 30 March 1999.

14. Ibid.

15. Gary Cartwright, "The Man Who Killed Judge Wood." *Texas Monthly*, September 1982, 262.

16. Jack Dean interview by author, 7 October 2017; W. C. Perryman to Jack Dean, 7 September 1982, TRHF&M.

17. Jack Dean interview by author, 9 September 2017.

18. *Del Rio News Herald*, November 1, 1982; *Galveston Daily News*, November 3, 1982; Certificates of Death, Hidalgo County, 30 October 1982: Jesus Partida Rosalez, Jr. and Mario Romero Leal; DeLord, *The Ultimate Sacrifice,* 186; *Program: The Thirteenth Biennial Texas Peace Officers' Memorial Services*, May 1–2, 2011, Austin, Texas.

19. Jackson and Wilkinson, *One Ranger: A Memoir*, 262–263; Jack Dean interview by author, 24 October 2017.

20. Ibid., 261.

21. Handwritten note from Texas Ranger Joaquin Jackson to Captain Jack Dean, no date, TRHF&M.

22. Jack Dean interview by author, 24 October 2017.

23. David Hutchings, "Woody Harrelson, *Cheers'* Cheery Bartender, Feels a Bit Mixed About Fame and a Strange Family Twist," *People Magazine*, November 14, 1988, 143.

24. Ibid., 144: Both Woodrow Tracy Harrelson and Charles Voyde Harrelson share the same birthday.

25. Ibid.

26. OHI: Jack Dean, 2013. "He wasn't a bad guy to talk to. . . . Yea, well Charlie [Harrelson] was smart and had a personality. You meet Charlie, I mean you'd say 'Yeah, he's a good old boy,' you know." Interview in TRHF&M.

27. *Jo Ann Harrelson, Charles Voyde Harrelson and Elizabeth Nichols Chagra v. United States*. 7544 F.2d 1153 (U.S. Court of Appeals, Fifth Circuit, 1985).

28. Josh Young, "ZEN AND THE ART OF HEMP CULTIVATION." *George Magazine*, December 1996, 121.

29. Cartwright, *Dirty Dealing*, 333 and 232.

30. Ibid., 313.

31. Cartwright, "The Man Who Killed Judge Wood," 262; Curiously, for this article and for the author's full-scale treatment *Dirty Dealing*, Captain Jack Dean's revelations regarding a possible Charles Harrelson connection to the murder of Judge Wood are not captured. Primary sources, however, are extant.

32. DeLord, *The Ultimate Sacrifice*, 189; Tise, *Texas County Sheriffs*, 547.

33. OHI: Al Cuellar, 2009, TRHF&M.

34. Ibid.; For contemporary newspaper accounts relating to this murder, the reader may wish to access, the *Brownsville Herald*, November 6 and December 20, 1983; *Galveston Daily News*, November 6, 1983 and February 8, 1984; *New Braunfels Herald*, January 31, 1984, and the *Del Rio News Herald*, February 6, 1984.

35. *Pedro Sosa v. State of Texas*. 769 S.W.2d 909 (Court of Criminal Appeals of Texas, 1989)

36. *Seguin Gazette Enterprise*, December 2, 1984, byline Gary Martin.

37. DeLord, *The Ultimate Sacrifice*, 189.

38. Ex Parte Sosa, No. AP-76, 674. (Court of Criminal Appeals of Texas, 2017. Unpublished)

39. *Kerrville Mountain Sun*, February 4, 1984. As will be later detected, court documents place the murder as taking place on 2 February 1984.

40. *Galveston Daily News*, February 17, 1984: Marie Denise Walker "was found clad only in a bra by her father, William Walker, police said."

41. *Kerrville Mountain Sun*, February 4, 1984.

42. Tise, *Texas County Sheriffs*, 28–29.

43. *Galveston Daily News*, February 17, 1984.

44. *Kerrville Mountain Sun*, June 16, 1984.

45. *Bandera Bulletin*, March 29, 1984.

46. Ibid.; Also, *Gerald Roger Sorenson v. The State of Texas*, 709 S.W.2d 319 (Court of Criminal Appeals of Texas, Texarkana, 1986) and *Gerald Roger Sorenson v. The State of Texas*, 709 S.W.2d 321 (Court of Criminal Appeals of Texas, Texarkana, 1986).

47. OHI: Jack Dean, 2013, TRHF&M.

Chapter 14: "They was laws to me"

1. W.D. Wilson to Jack Dean, 11 June 1984 and 31 January 1985, TRHF&M.

2. *Austin American-Statesman*, January 3, 1985, byline Kay Powers.

3. OHI: H.R. "Lefty" Block, 2009, TRHF&M. Decidedly interesting, is the photograph and caption appearing in the *Carswell* [Air Force Base] *Sentinel* of May 1, 1992. On a raised platform Senior Captain Lefty Block is photographed examining the painted depiction of an old-time Texas Ranger—pistol in hand—astraddle a falling bomb, painted on the nose of a B-52H bomber. "The nose art was dedicated in honor of the hard work and dedication of the Texas Rangers and the men and women of the 7th Wing."

4. *United States v. Jo Ann Harrelson, Charles Voyde Harrelson and Elizabeth Nichols Chagra*, 754 F.2d 1153 (U.S. Court of Appeals, Firth Circuit, 1985);

and *United States v. Joe Corona Valdez*, 722 F.2d 1196 (U.S. Court of Appeals, Fifth Circuit, 1984). The latter reasoning is cited in part:

> We consider the admissibility of an identification of the defendant made by a law enforcement officer after undergoing hypnosis. The officer had seen the defendant a number of times during the investigation and knew him to be a suspect but had previously been unable to identify him. Under hypnosis the officer identified the defendant as the person he had earlier seen at the scene of the crime. He later identified the defendant in court. We hold that it was improper to admit his post-hypnotic testimony. . . . Moreover, the procedures employed during the hypnotic session were unduly suggestive. In every particular, they were at variance with the safeguards required in New Jersey and Oregon. Several Texas Rangers, FBI agents, and an Assistant U.S. Attorney were present in addition to the hypnotist. Questions were directed to Jackson not only by the 'mental health professional' who hypnotized him, but also by an FBI agent. Both had evidently received information about the events being investigated before the session began. During the hypnotic session, additional questions were purposed orally by yet another FBI agent in the room. Only some of the agents present were videotaped; whether others may have unintentionally suggested 'recollections' cannot be determined. Because those present did not record their knowledge and beliefs relative to the investigation, we cannot examine what recollections could be attributable to their subtle cues. . . .

5. Interview with Robert R. "Bobby" Mutz, Karnes County Sheriff, Ret., by author 15 November 2017. Interestingly Mutz advised that Daisy Villanueva's brother, Wayne, is currently the Karnes County Sheriff, and is making an outstanding name for himself as a dedicated career lawman; Tise, *Texas County Sheriffs*, 296.

6. Paul, *Jim Peters: Texas Ranger*, 204–208.

7. Ibid., 205; OHI: Jim Peters, 2009, TRHF&M: "Well I had. . . . the Captain [Jack Dean] called one day and said you need to get up to Karnes City. We've got a hostage situation up there." Conformation is cited by Jack Dean's interview with author, 24 October 2017.

8. Interview with Bobby Mutz, as cited. Sheriff Mutz advised—at this date—there are absolutely no security concerns with identifying the jailhouse key by its number.

9. Ibid.

10. OHI: Jim Peters, 2009, TRHF&M.

11. *Seguin Gazette Enterprise*, August 19, 1986. For what the *San Antonio Light* dubbed as a "Chronology" of this truly bizarre story—with succinct biographical profiles—the interested reader may wish to peruse the edition of October 23, 1986.

12. *Odessa American*, October 27, 1986.

13. Ibid.

14. *Los Angles Times*, June 14, 1987.

15. *Del Rio News Herald*, August 21, 1986; *Galveston Daily News*, August 24, 1986.

16. *San Antonio Express-News*, August 27, 1986. "He said he had met with Texas Ranger Capt. Dean and received a briefing on what Rangers anticipate examining. The Rangers entered the probe at request of special prosecutor. . . ."

17. *New York Times*, October 23, 1986; *Kerrville Daily Times*, October 30, 1986.

18. *Kerrville Daily Times*, June 16, 1987.

19. *Galveston Daily News*, June 19, 1987.

20. *Kerrville Daily Times*, June 16, 1987.

21. *Galveston Daily News*, June 20, 1987; *Kerrville Daily Times*, June 21, 1987; *New York Times*, June 21, 1987.

22. Sid L. Harle to Colonel Adams, 30 October 1986, TRHF&M. This missive was written subsequent to the Grand Jury probe but before trial.

23. Jack Dean interview by author, 6 October 2017; *Odessa American*, October 23, 1986.

24. Alexander and Brice, *Texas Rangers: Lives, Legend, and Legacy*, 384–386. As mentioned in the endnotes, pages 595–596, the recreation of this kidnapping tale is a synthesis of resource materials. Particularly interesting was the oral history interview with Captain Mitchell by Robert Nieman, 29 October 1996, TRHF&M; Also see, *Dallas Morning News*, January 24, 1987; and "Eulogy Delivered by Colonel Adams at Guffey's Funeral," as carried in the March 1987 edition of the *Texas DPSOA Monthly,* the official publication of the DPS Officers Association, 39–41. A most interesting recap of the affair is mentioned in Jackson and Wilkinson, *One Ranger: A Memoir*, 177–185; also see, Utley, *Lone Star Lawmen*, 292–295.

25. Jack Dean interview by author, 6 October 2017; unidentified newsclip, TRHF&M.

26. *San Antonio Express News*, May 5, 1987.

27. *San Antonio Light*, May 10, 1987, byline Anne Pearson.

28. Jim Denman, Texas Ranger Lieutenant, Ret., interview by author 9 October 2017.

29. *San Antonio Express News*, May 5, 1987.

30. *San Antonio Light*, undated newsclip, byline Jim Michaels.

31. Ibid., May 10, 1987.

32. Walter Borges, "S. Texas Inquiry Expands," *The Texas Lawyer*, February 16, 1987. This article provides a succinct overview of the allegations and investigation. Also see, *Brownsville Herald*, January 29, 1987, bylines Basilio Hernandez and Armando Villafranca for additional data regarding alleged corruption at city hall. For a very brief biographical sketch of Texas Ranger Rodolfo "Rudy" Rodriguez, see Maude T. Gilliland, *Wilson County Texas Rangers, 1837–1977*, 134; Draper, "The Twilight of the Texas Rangers" underscores the Rangers' lack of success with this public corruption investigation, though he does not mention the untimely deaths of the state's purported star witnesses. See p. 118.

33. Major General Joseph W. Ashy, USAF, to Captain Jack Dean, 22 August 1988, TRHF&M: DPS-TV: Jack Dean, June 1988, TRHF&M.

34. DPS-Teletype, 2 January 1990, Authority, Senior Texas Ranger Captain H.R. Block, TRHF&M: *Austin American-Statesman*, January 3, 1985, for remarks about Texas Ranger's appearance; *Texas Lawman*, August 1981, for upholding Texas Ranger tradition, 14; Bill Wilson's funeral program, Colonial Chapel, Cook-Walden Funeral Home, Austin, Texas; Jack Dean interview by author 7 October 2017.

35. Coach Jack Pardee to Captain Jack Dean, 13 July 1990, TRHF&M.

36. OHI: Bob Mitchell, 1996, TRHF&M; Jack Dean interview by author, 7 October 2017.

37. Tise, *Texas County Sheriffs*, 160.

38. DeLord, *The Ultimate Sacrifice*, 209; Holdridge, *Working the Border*, 194–195.

39. Office of Texas Attorney General John Cornyn, Media Advisory, 9 July 2002.

40. Holdridge, *Working the Border*, 192. Retired Ranger Doyle Holdridge's account of the Doc Murray murder and resultant criminal investigation is heartrending, but interesting and insightful.

41. *Galveston Daily News*, January 8, 1991.

42. Attorney General's Media Advisory, as cited: "The investigation revealed that the sheriff suffered numerous stab wounds, including defense wounds on his hand, had piece of his ear missing, and had been shot in the head." Holdridge, *Working the Border*, 192.

43. *Galveston Daily News*, January 8, 1991: "Texas Rangers Capt. Jack Dean said investigators reported 'lots of blood.'"

44. Holdridge, *Working the Border*, 194.

45. *Del Rio News Herald*, January 7, 1991.

46. Jack Dean interview by author, 28 April 2017.

47. Attorney General's Media Advisory, as cited.

48. *Ex parte Jose Garcia Briseno*, 135 S.W.3d 1 (Court of Criminal Appeals of Texas, 2004).

49. Ibid.

50. Ibid.; Holdridge, *Working the Border*, 201.

51. *Jose Garcia Briseno, Petitioner-Appellant v. Janie Cockrell, Director, Texas Department of Criminal Justice, Institutional Division, Respondent-Appellee*, 274 F.3d 204 (U.S. Court of Appeals, Fifth Circuit, 2001).

52. *Ex Parte Jose Garcia Briseno v. State of Texas*, Non-published opinion. (Court of Criminal Appeals of Texas, 2010); Holdridge, *Working the Border*, 202.

53. Jack Dean interview by author, 28 April 2017. The late Joaquin Jackson particularly singled out Texas Ranger Holdridge for mention regarding this murder. See, Jackson and Wilkinson, *One Ranger: A Memoir*, 265: "Doyle Holdridge, from Laredo, who tracked down Sheriff Ben Murray's killers in fewer than twenty-four hours."

54. *Galveston Daily News*, April 15, 1992, quoting interview and press availability with DPS Public Information Spokesman Mike Cox.

55. Crawford, *Texas Death Row*, 350; DeLord, *The Ultimate Sacrifice*, 212.

56. Ibid.

57. *Orange Leader*, July 1, 1993, byline Pamela Ward.

58. *Galveston Daily News*, June 24, 1993; *Orange Leader*, July 9 and July 10, 1993.

59. *Los Angles Times*, September 17, 1992, byline Chuck Phillips.

60. *Orange Leader*, July 11, 1993.

61. Crawford, *Texas Death Row*, 350; DeLord, *The Ultimate Sacrifice*, 212. First quotation from DeLord, second quotation from Crawford. Also, *Ronald Ray Howard v. State of Texas*, 941 S.W.2d 102 (Texas Court of Criminal Appeals 1996).

62. *San Antonio Express-News*, September 7, 1993, byline Chris Bird; *Dallas Morning News*, September 11, 1993; Jack Dean interview by author, 24 October 2017; Kyle Dean interview by author, 31 October 2017.

63. Edward D. Sanders, Chief of Police, South Padre Island, Texas, to James R. Wilson, Director, DPS, 6 April 1992, TRHF&M.

64. Kyle Dean interview by author, 31 October 2017; Crawford, *Texas Death Row*, 391.

65. *James Lee Clark v. State of Texas*, No. 71, 991 (Court of Criminal Appeals of Texas, 1996); *James Lee Clark v. Gary Johnson, Director, Texas Department of Criminal Justice, Institutional Division*, 227 F.3d 273 (U.S. Court of Appeals,

Fifth Circuit, 2000); also, *James Lee Clark v. Nathaniel Quarterman, Director, Texas Department of Criminal Justice, Institutional Division*, 457 F.3d 441 (U.S. Court of Appeals, Fifth Circuit, 2006). Were one interested in following this murderous affair through newspaper journalists' eyes, the reader may wish to access, the *Fort Worth Star-Telegram*, June 8, 9, 10, July 14, 1993, May 4, 1994, and April 30, 1994; the *Dallas Morning News*, June 9 and 11, 1993 and April 21, 30, 1994; *Austin American-Statesman*, June 10, 1993; and the *Denton Record Chronicle*, April 11, 2007, byline Donna Fielder: "Investigator Danny Brown was lead investigator for the sheriff's office, but Texas Ranger Kyle Dean soon became case manager. Danny Brown said he and Dean didn't sleep for days as the case quickly unfolded and they hustled to get arrest and search warrants swiftly but with such accuracy they would stand up under scrutiny in court." *Houston Chronicle*, April 11, 2007, byline Michael Graczyk; and the *Huntsville Item*, April 11, 2007. Author's note, the phrase "Immaculate Erection," was not coined by case investigators to offer callous humor, but to illustrate the absurdity and impotence of defendant Clark's claim.

66. OHI: Jack Dean, 2013, TRHF&M; Utley, *Lone Star Lawmen*, p. 281, credibly acknowledges the new era transition of Texas Ranger leadership: "The exemplary record of Senior Captain Bill Wilson and such captains as John Wood, Jack Dean, Bob Mitchell, and Pete Rogers gave new faces and new prestige to the Texas Rangers."

Chapter 15: "I'll buy you a beer"

1. *Congressional Record*, 103rd Congress, First Session, House of Representatives, September 22, 1993.

2. Turk, *Forging the Star*, 5. For the reader interested in the modern-era of the U.S. Marshals Service, this excellent model is the seminal study.

3. Ibid., 1.

4. Ernst, *Deadly Affrays: The Violent Deaths of U.S. Marshals*, 120–123.

5. Ibid., 101–102; Caldwell and DeLord, *Texas Lawmen: The Good and the Bad, 1835–1899*, 385–386.

6. *Congressional Record*, 103rd Congress, Second Session, Senate, March 10, 1994; *The Marshals Monitor* [USMS Newsletter], April 1994, 4; *San Antonio Express-News*, March 12, 1994, byline Gary Martin; Roster of Western District U.S. Marshals, courteously furnished by U.S. Marshals Service Historian David S. Turk.

7. OHI: Jack Dean, 2013, TRHF&M.

8. *San Antonio Express-News*, undated newsclip, byline Cindy Ramos; *San Antonio Express-News*, March 11, 1994, byline Gary Martin.

9. As mentioned in the Preface, Richard Clayton "Dick" Ware also served as a Western District U.S. Marshal, but his prior nineteenth century service with the Texas Rangers was as a noncom, not from the officer's corps.

10. Turk, *Forging the Star*, 297–302.

11. Eduardo Gonzalez, Director, United States Marshals Service to U.S. Marshal Jack Dean, Western District of Texas, 15 March 1994, TRHF&M.

12. United States Marshal: Personal Data Questionnaire: Jack Dean, TRHF&M.

13. *San Antonio Express-News*, May 21, 1993, byline Bruce Davidson: "Bexar County records show Dean voted in the 1992 Republican presidential primary, and Dean confirmed it." From the personal perspective about retiring from DPS and the reality of an upcoming appointment as the Western District U.S. Marshal, Jack Dean soberly reflected: "[Bob] Mitchell had left, [Bill] Wilson was gone, [and] my contemporaries started to fade away. I was the young one of that bunch. All that bunch was gone, either passed away or they retired. And so, it was a good time for me to go out [of DPS] on top, I guess." See, OHI: Jack Dean, 2013, TRHF&M. Respected writer and historian Utley, *Lone Star Lawmen*, proffers an additional reason, implying that Texas Ranger management at the Senior Captain level hastened Jack Dean's decision. "The two ranking captains, Bob Mitchell and Jack Dean, chose to retire as Cook ascended, Mitchell in June 1992 and Dean in September 1993." See p. 304. Interestingly, Jack Dean interview by author 5 January 2018, offered no dispute for Utley's reckoning.

14. *The Marshals Monitor*, April 1994, 4.

15. *The Marshals Monitor*, January-February 1997, 10.

16. OHI: Jack Dean, 2013, TRHF&M.

17. *The Marshals Monitor*, November-December 1996, 6.

18. *The Marshals Monitor*, January-February 1997, 3.

19. *Desert News*, July 6, 1995; Berg, *Run, Brother, Run*, 218.

20. David S. Turk, USMS Historian, interview by author, 8 November 2017.

21. Louis J. Freeh, Director, FBI, to U.S. Marshal Jack Dean, 14 July 1995, TRHF&M.

22. Alexander and Brice, *Texas Rangers: Lives, Legend, and Legacy*, 388.

23. Certainly to date the most inclusive account of the buildup of the years in the making clash between lawmen and ROT militants is the rendition by former DPS Public Information Officer Mike Cox in *Stand-Off in Texas: "Just Call Me a spokesman for DPS . . ."* Author Cox traces ROT history and actions admirably, 83–110.

24. Ibid., 107, 128.

25. Ibid.; Alexander and Brice, *Texas Rangers: Lives, Legend, and Legacy*, 389; Jack Dean interview by author 24 October 2017.

26. Barry K. Caver, Captain, Texas Rangers, Ret., interview by author 17 October 2016. In this instance the home invasion and taking of hostages—state violations—superseded, in a practical sense, dealing with the federal cases.

27. Barry Caver and Robert Nieman, "Captain Barry Caver on the Republic of Texas Standoff," in *Tracking the Texas Rangers: The Twentieth Century*, edited by Bruce A. Glasrud and Harold J. Weiss, Jr., 221.

28. Alexander and Brice, *The Texas Rangers: Lives, Legend, and Legacy*, 389–390; Utley, *Lone Star Lawmen*, rightly and particularly makes note: "Although the Ranger Role in the ROT negotiations received almost no publicity as they unfolded, and not much afterward, in fact it represented a decisive success. A company of Rangers, headed by an exemplary captain, had achieved a difficult mission fraught with lethal consequences." 327.

29. This incident is particularly highlighted in Holdridge's *Working the Border*, 239–245.

30. *The Marshals Monitor*, May-June, 1997.

31. *The Marshals Monitor*, September-October, 1997, 6.

32. OHI: Jack Dean, 2013, TRHF&M. Purportedly, due to his celebrity status and financial wherewithal, actor Woody Harrelson sponsored an appeal for his father's federal conviction and imprisonment. That the effort was sincere was established by obtaining the legal talents and services of the prominent Alan Dershowitz of Harvard University as head of the defendant's appellate team. A sidebar story is not only interesting but informative with regards to Jack Dean's sense of propriety. During these legal challenges, at one point, Jack Dean was asked if he would like to participate in shooting hoops with the well-known actor at an area basketball court; other federal court personnel would be taking part in the off-duty fun. U.S. Marshal Jack Dean appropriately declined the invitation. Any final scores on the basketball court are not now known by Jack Dean, though ultimate outcomes are: A Federal Judge had to accept recusal from the hearings for the patent impropriety and the appellant reasoning, in the end, would prove unproductive for Charles Voyde Harrelson. See, Cartwright, *Dirty Dealing*, 383; Berg, *Run, Brother, Run*, 217–218; *Charles Voyde Harrelson v. United States* 967 F. Supp. 909 (United States Western District Court, San Antonio Division 1997); and Jack Dean interview by author, 8 March 2017.

33. *The Marshals Monitor*, January-February 1998.

34. *The Marshals Monitor*, January-February 1999, 5.

35. *The Marshals Monitor*, May–June, 1998, 11.

36. *The Marshals Monitor*, September-October 1999, 14–15.

37. DeLord, *The Ultimate Sacrifice*, 227: "A Pleasanton officer [Tudyk] and deputy U.S. Marshal [Fisher] were wounded. . . ."; *Amarillo Globe-News*, October 16, 1999, byline Kelley Shannon: "A deputy U.S. marshal [Fisher] and a Pleasanton police officer [Tudyk] were wounded."

38. *Kenneth C. Vodochodsky v. State of Texas*. 158 S.W. 3d. 502 (Court of Criminal Appeals of Texas, 2005).

39. *Paris News*, October 13, 1999; *Orange Leader*, October 21, 1999; *Texas City Sun*, November 4, 1999.

40. Undated newsclip, *San Antonio Express-News*.

41. *Houston Chronicle*, March 20, 2006, picking up a story in the *San Antonio Express-News*.

42. Glenn, *The Largest Hotel Chain in Texas: Texas Prisons*, 338.

43. A book-length treatment for part of this yet ongoing (appellate reviews yet working) drama is *The Texas 7* by Gary C. King. Also of particular value was the TDCJ Institutional Division, Serious Incident Review, December 19, 2000; *Orange Leader*, August 23, 2001.

44. *Houston Chronicle*, January 23, 2001, byline Jim Henderson and John Williams.

45. Jorge Antonio Renaud, *Behind the Walls: A Guide for Families and Friends of Texas Prison Inmates*, 164. The nonaligned Texas citizen—one far removed from felonious associations—may or may not find any merit in Renaud's conclusions and/or justifications. Proffering a convict philosophy akin to "fix us or we'll fix you when we get out," seems a rather arcane approach to attaining just goals—it might be deduced!

46. *Kerrville Daily Times*, August 29, 2001.

47. Bobby Mutz interview by author, 5 December 2017.

48. H.L. "Hank" Whitman Jr., Chief, Texas Rangers, Ret., interview by author 18 November 2017. Quite interestingly and speaking to his investigative acumen and personnel management skills, Hank Whitman was tapped by the Governor of Texas to assume responsibility as Commissioner, Texas Department of Family and Protective Services, the administrative chair he sits in today (January 2018). Interestingly with regards to the prison-break analytical component are two dynamics, both frustrating to a former and a future Texas Ranger Captain of Company D, Jack Dean and Hank Whitman. Though it's been written U.S. Marshal Dean was of the opinion that the Texas Seven had split up after the escape, during several interviews he clarified that while he didn't know at the time, he thought that it would have been the smart thing for them to do—to avoid identification and capture.

In the second instance convict George Rivas—the suspected ringleader—already had an Aggravated Robbery of an Oshman's Sporting Goods Store in his MO File—one wherein walkie-talkies were used, deceptive clothing was worn, and 58 firearms were stolen, as well as more than $5000 cash. Certainly these readily apparent facts were not lost on Hank Whitman. Sometimes in the crazy world of criminality the future is predictable; making someone listen—well—that's sometimes difficult too! See, King, *Texas 7*, 63–64, 82 for citations but not for conclusions proffered herein.

49. *Orange Leader*, August 23, 2001.
50. *Patrick Henry Murphy, Jr. v. The State of Texas*, No. AP-74, 851 (Court of Criminal Appeals of Texas, 2006).
51. *The Marshals Monitor*, January-February 2001, 1, 8–11.
52. Jim Willett interview by author, 17 November 2017.
53. *The Marshals Monitor*, July-August 2001, 9.
54. Jack Dean's Retirement and Reception Invitation, 26 March 2004, TRHF&M; Charles Voyde Harrelson died of natural causes in prison 15 March 2007.

Bibliography

Non-published sources—manuscripts, typescripts, theses, dissertations, tape recordings, official documents, courthouse records, appellate court decisions, tax rolls, petitions, correspondence, prison records, census records, licensing records, interviews, etc.—are cited with specificity in chapter endnotes.

Abbreviations and/or Acronyms:

APB	All Points Bulletin or All Points Broadcast
ATF	U.S. Bureau of Alcohol, Tobacco, and Firearms
AUSA	Assistant United States Attorney
BAR	Browning Automatic Rifle
BNDD	Bureau of Narcotics and Dangerous Drugs
BOP	Bureau of Prisons
CCE	Continuing Criminal Enterprise
CI	Confidential Informant
CPS	Child Protective Services
CPO	Customs Patrol Officer
CSO	Court Security Officer [USMS]
DOJ	Department of Justice
DPS	Texas Department of Public Safety
DPS-AE	Application for Employment
DPS-AIR	Applicant Investigation Report
DPS-CCR	Criminal Case Report
DPS-CID	Criminal Investigation Division
DPS-CISR	Change In Status Report
DPS-COR	Criminal Offense Report
DPS-DLS	Drivers License Service
DPS-EBS	Employee Biographical Sketch
DPS-FAR	Fleet Accident Report
DPS-FOR	Field Observation Report
DPS-IM	Interoffice Memorandum
DPS-MVI	Motor Vehicle Inspection Service
DPS-MVT	Motor Vehicle Theft Division

DPS-PDS	Performance Development Summary
DPS-PPR	Probationary Progress Report
DPS-PR	Progress Report
DPS-SCCR	Supplemental Criminal Case Report
DPS-SER	Student Evaluation Report
DPS-TR	Training Record
DPS-TRPR	Texas Ranger Periodical Report
DPS-TRWR	Texas Ranger Weekly Report
DPS-TV	Travel Voucher
DRT	Dead Right There
EMS	Emergency Services (Ambulance, Paramedics, etc.)
EPIC	El Paso Intelligence Center
ER	Hospital Emergency Room
ESU	Electronic Surveillance Unit (USMS)
FACE	Freedom of Access to Clinic Entrances (Act of 1994)
FEMA	Federal Emergency Management Agency
FFL	Federal Firearms License
FFL-A & D	Firearms Acquisition and Disposition Book
FFL-4473	Firearms Transaction Record
FLIR	Forward Looking Infrared Radar
FTO	Field Training Officer
HB	Harness Bull (Uniformed Officer Not Wanting Promotion)
IACP	International Association of Chiefs of Police
INS	Immigration and Naturalization Service
ISD	Investigative Services Division [USMS]
JAPATS	Justice Prisoner and Alien Transportation System (USMS)
JAW-C	Captain James A. Wright Collection
JD-DRJ	Jack Dean's Daily Reminder Journals
JP	Justice of the Peace
LEAP	Law Enforcement Availability Pay
MO	*Modus Operandi* (criminal method of operation)
NATB	National Automobile Theft Bureau
NCIS	Naval Criminal Intelligence Service
ODALE	Office of Drug Abuse Law Enforcement
OHI	Oral History Interview
OIG	Office of Inspector General
OGC	Office of General Counsel (USMS)
PD	Police Department

PCS	Permanent Change of Station
RAC	Resident Agent in Charge
ROT	Republic of Texas
SAC	Special Agent in Charge
SO	Sheriffs Office
SOG	Special Operations Group (USMS)
TDC	Texas Department of Corrections
TDCJ	Texas Department of Criminal Justice
TECLOSE	Texas Commission of Law Enforcement Standards and Education
THP	Texas Highway Patrol
TRHF&M	Texas Ranger Hall of Fame & Museum
TABC	Texas Alcohol Beverage Commission
TP&W	Texas Parks & Wildlife (Game Wardens)
TSA	Texas State Library and Archives
TSCRA	Texas and Southwestern Cattle Raisers Association
USA	United States Attorney
USBP	United States Border Patrol
USM	United States Marshal
USMS	United States Marshals Service
USSS	United States Secret Service
VF	Vertical File
WANT	Warrant Apprehension Narcotics Teams (USMS)

Books:

Aguirre, Jr., Adalberto, and Jonathan H. Turner. *American Ethnicity: The Dynamics and Consequences of Discrimination*. New York: McGraw Hill, 1998.

Albers, Jr., E.G. *The Life and Reflections of a Texas Ranger*. Waco, TX: Texian Press, 1998.

Alexander, Bob. *Whiskey River Ranger: The Old West Life of Baz Outlaw*. Denton: University of North Texas Press, 2016.

———. *Six-Shooters and Shifting Sands: The Wild West Life of Texas Ranger Captain Frank Jones*. Denton: University of North Texas Press, 2015.

———. *Winchester Warriors: Texas Rangers of Company D, 1874–1901*. Denton: University of North Texas Press, 2009.

———. *Lawmen, Outlaws, and S.O.Bs.: Gunfighters of the Old Southwest*. Vol. I. Silver City, NM: High-Lonesome Books, 2004.

———. *Fearless Dave Allison: Border Lawman*. Silver City, NM: High-Lonesome Books, 2003.

————, and Donaly E. Brice. *Texas Rangers: Lives, Legend, and Legacy*. Denton: University of North Texas Press, 2017.

Alvarez, Elizabeth, ed. *The Texas Almanac, 2014–2015*. Denton: Texas State Historical Association, 2014.

Anderson Gary C. *The Conquest of Texas: Ethnic Cleansing in the Promised Land, 1820–1875*. Norman: University of Oklahoma Press, 2005.

Arnold, Ann. *Gamblers and Gangsters: Fort Worth's Jacksboro Highway in the 1940s and 1950s*. Fort Worth, TX: Eakin Press, Imprint of Wild Horse Media Group, 1998.

Arnold, Bob. *First in Texas: Three Texans and Their Contributions to Texas History, 1821–1978*. Friendswood, TX: Self-published, 2011.

Awbrey, Betty D., and Claude Dooley. *Why Stop? A Guide to Texas Historical Roadside Markers*. Houston, TX: Lone Star Books, 1999.

Baker, Terry. *Hanging and Lynchings in Dallas County, Texas, 1853 to 1920*. Fort Worth, TX: Eakin Press, Wild Horse Media Group, 2016.

Baker, T. Lindsay. *Gangster Tour of Texas*. College Station: Texas A&M University Press, 2011.

Berg, David. *Run, Brother, Run: A Memoir*. New York: Scribner, 2013.

Blackburn, Ed Jr. *Wanted: Historic County Jails of Texas*. College Station: Texas A&M University Press, 2006.

Boessenecker, John. *Texas Ranger: The Epic Life of Frank Hamer, The Man Who Killed Bonnie and Clyde*. New York: St. Martin's Press, 2016.

Brooks, Elston. *don't dry-clean my blackjack* [lower case is correct]. Fort Worth, TX: Branch-Smith, Inc., 1979.

Bryant, Vickie, and Camille Hess. *Top O' Hill Terrace*. Charleston, SC: Arcadia Publishing, 2012.

Burks, Tom, ed. *A Pictorial Tour of the Texas Ranger Hall of Fame and Museum, Waco, Texas*. Waco, TX: Central Printing Company, n.d.

Caldwell, Clifford R., and Ron DeLord. *Texas Lawmen: The Good and the Bad, 1835–1899*. Charleston, SC: The History Press, 2011.

————, and Ron DeLord. *Texas Lawmen: More of the Good and the Bad, 1900–1940*. Charleston, SC: The History Press, 2012.

Cartwright, Gary. *Dirty Dealing: Drug Smuggling on the Mexican Border and the Assassination of a Federal Judge*. El Paso, TX: Cinco Puntos Press, 1998.

Chrismer, Melanie. *Lone Star Legacy: Texas Rangers Then and Now*. Gretna, LA: Pelican Publishing Company, 2016.

City of Waco. *Guns of Fort Fisher*. Waco, TX: Parks and Recreations Department, 1973.

Coffee, James L., and Russell M. Drake and John T. Barnett. *Graham Barnett: A Dangerous Man*. Denton: University of North Texas Press, 2017.

Cox, Mike. *The Texas Rangers: Wearing the Cinco Peso, 1821–1900*. New York: Forge Books, 2008.

———. *Time of the Rangers: Texas Rangers from 1900 to the Present*. New York: Forge Books, 2009.

———. *Texas Ranger Tales II*. Plano, TX: Republic of Texas Press, 1999.

———. *Stand-Off in Texas: "Just Call Me a Spokesman for DPS…"* Austin, TX: Eakin Press, 1998,

Crawford, Bill, ed. *Texas Death Row: Executions in the Modern Era*. New York: Plume Publishing, Penguin Group, 2008.

Cutrer, Thomas W. *Ben McCulloch and the Frontier Military Tradition*. Chapel Hill: University of North Carolina Press, 1993.

Dawson, Carol, with Roger Allen Polson. *Miles and Miles of Texas: 100 Years of the Texas Highway Department*. College Station: Texas A&M University Press, 2016.

Day, James M. *Captain Clint Peoples, Texas Ranger: Fifty Year a Lawman*. Waco, TX: Texian Press, 1980.

———. *One Man's Dream: Fort Fisher and The Texas Ranger Hall of Fame*. Waco, TX: Texian Press, 1976.

DeArment, Robert K. *Jim Courtright of Fort Worth: His Life and Legend*. Fort Worth: Texas Christian University Press, 2004.

DeLord, Ronald, ed. *The Ultimate Sacrifice: Trials and Triumphs of the Texas Peace Officer, 1823–2000*. Austin, TX: Peace Officers Memorial Foundation, Inc., 2000.

DeMattos, Jack, and Chuck Parsons. *The Notorious Luke Short: Sporting Man of the Wild West*. Denton: University of North Texas Press, 2016.

Dixon, Kemp. *Chasing Thugs, Nazis, and Reds: Texas Ranger Norman K. Dixon*. College Station: Texas A&M University Press, 2015.

Douglas, C.L. *The Gentlemen in the White Hats: Dramatic Episodes in the History of the Texas Rangers*. Dallas, TX: South-West Press, 1934.

Elliott, Glenn, with Robert Nieman. *Glenn Elliott: A Ranger's Ranger*. Longview, TX: Self-published, 1999.

———, and Robert Nieman. *Glenn Elliott: Still A Ranger's Ranger*. Longview, TX: Ranger Publications, 2002.

Ernst, Robert, and George R. Stumph. *Deadly Affrays: The Violent Deaths of the US Marshals*. n.p: Scarlet Mask Publishing, 2006.

Favor, Bob. *My Rangering Days*. Abilene, TX: H.V. Chapman & Sons, n.d.

Gatewood, Jim. *Benny Binion: The Legend of Benny Binion, Dallas Gambler and Mob Boss*. Garland, TX: Mullaney Corporation, 2002.

———. *J. Frank Norris, Top O'Hill Casino, Lew Jenkins and the Texas Oil Rich*. Garland, TX: Mullaney Corporation, 2006.

Gilbreath, West. *death on the gallows* [lower case is correct]: *The Encyclopedia of Legal Hangings in Texas*. Fort Worth, TX: Wild Horse Press, 2017.

Gilliland, Maude T. *Horsebackers of the Brush Country: A Story of the Texas Rangers and Mexican Liquor Smugglers*. Brownsville, TX: Springman-King Co., 1968.

———. *Wilson County Rangers, 1837–1977*. Pleasanton, TX: Self-published, 1977.

Glasrud, Bruce A., and Harold J. Weiss, Jr., eds. *Tracking the Texas Rangers: The Twentieth Century.* Denton: University of North Texas Press, 2013.

Glenn, Lon Bennett. *The Largest Hotel Chain in Texas: Texas Prisons.* n.p. Eakin Press, n.d.

Gooding, Ed, and Robert Nieman. *Ed Gooding: Soldier, Texas Ranger.* Longview, TX: Ranger Publications, 2001.

Gournay, Luke. *Texas Boundaries: Evolution of the State's Counties.* College Station: Texas A&M University Press, 1995.

Greer, James K. *Colonel Jack Hays: Texas Frontier Leader and California Builder.* College Station: Texas A&M University Press, 1987.

Guinn, Jeff. *Go Down Together: The True, Untold Story of Bonnie and Clyde.* New York: Simon & Schuster, 2009.

Harper, William T. *Eleven Days in Hell: The 1974 Carrasco Prison Siege at Huntsville, Texas.* Denton: University of North Texas Press, 2004.

Harris, Charles H. III, and Louis R. Sadler. *The Texas Rangers and the Mexican Revolution: The Bloodiest Decade, 1910–1920.* Albuquerque: University of New Mexico Press, 2004.

———. *The Plan De San Diego: Tejano Rebellion, Mexican Intrigue.* Lincoln: The University of Nebraska Press, 2013.

Hausenfluke, Gene. [text by Roger Conger] *Texas Ranger Sesquicentennial Anniversary, 1823–1973.* Fort Worth, TX: Heritage Publications Inc., 1973.

Henry, Will. *The Texas Rangers.* New York: Random House, 1957.

Herrera, Norma. *Last Words from Death Row: The Walls Unit.* LaVergne, TN: Nightengale Press [Lightning Source Inc.], 2007.

Holdridge, Doyle. *Working the Border: A Texas Ranger's Story.* Dallas, TX: Atriad Press, LLC, 2009.

Hughes, Alton. *Pecos: A History of the Pioneer West.* Seagraves, TX: Pioneer Books Publishers, 1978.

Ivey, Darren L. *The Texas Rangers: A Registry and History.* Jefferson, NC: McFarland & Company, Inc., 2010.

———. *The Ranger Ideal Volume I: Texas Rangers in the Hall of Fame, 1823–1861.* Denton: University of North Texas Press, 2017.

Jackson, H. Joaquin, and David Marion Wilkinson. *One Ranger: A Memoir.* Austin: The University of Texas Press, 2005.

———, with James L. Haley. *One Ranger Returns.* Austin: University of Texas Press, 2008.

King, Gary C. *The Texas 7.* New York: St. Martin's Press, 2001.

McCaslin, Richard B. *Fighting Stock: John S. "Rip" Ford of Texas.* Fort Worth: Texas Christian University Press, 2011.

McKinney, Wilson. *Fred Carrasco: The Heroin Merchant.* Austin, TX: Heidelberg Publishers, Inc., 1975.

Malsch, Brownson. *Lone Wolf: Captain M.T. Gonzaullas*. Austin, TX: Shoal Creek
Publishers, Inc., 1980

Meed, Douglas V. *Texas Ranger Johnny Klevenhagen*. Plano, TX: Republic of Texas
Press, 2000.

Metz, Leon C. *The Shooters*. El Paso, TX: Mangan Books, 1976.

Miller, Nyle H., and Joseph W. Snell. *Great Gunfighters of the Kansas Cowtowns,
1867–1886*. Lincoln: University of Nebraska, 1970.

Miller, Rick. *Tin Star Tales: Law and Disorder in Dallas County, Texas, 1846–1900*.
Bloomington, IN: Archway Publishing, 2017.

———. *Texas Ranger John B. Jones and the Frontier Battalion, 1874–1881*. Denton:
University of North Texas Press, 2012.

———. *Sam, Bass and Gang*. Austin, TX: State House Press, 1999.

———. *Rube Barrow, Desperado*. Bloomington, IN: iUniverse LLC, 2014.

Mills, Susie. *Legend in Bronze: The Biography of Jay Banks*. Dallas, TX: Ussery
Printing Company, 1982.

Moore, Stephen L. *Savage Frontier: Rangers, Riflemen, and Indian Wars in Texas,
1835–1837*. Volume I. Denton: University of North Texas Press, 2002.

———. *Savage Frontier: Rangers, Riflemen, and Indian Wars in Texas, 1838–1839*.
Volume II. Denton: University of North Texas Press, 2006.

———. *Savage Frontier: Rangers, Riflemen, and Indian Wars in Texas, 1840–1841*.
Volume III. Denton: University of North Texas Press, 2007.

———. *Savage Frontier: Rangers, Riflemen, and Indian Wars in Texas, 1842–1845*.
Volume IV. Denton: University of North Texas Press, 2010.

Moser, Robert D. *Texas Iron: Guns of the Texas Rangers*. Killeen, TX: Self-published,
2015.

Neubauer, David W. *America's Courts and the Criminal Justice System*. Belmont,
CA: Wadsworth Group/Thompson Learning, 2002.

Nolan, Frederick. *The Wild West: History, Myth and the Making of America*. Edison,
NJ: Chartwell Books, 2000.

O'Neal, Bill. *Reel Rangers: Texas Rangers in Movies, TV, Radio and Other Forms of
Popular Culture*. Waco, TX: Eakin Press, 2008.

Paredes, Américo. *With His Pistol in His Hand: A Border Ballad and Its Hero*. Austin:
University of Texas Press, 1958.

Pate, J'Nell *North of the River: A Brief History of North Fort Worth*. Fort Worth:
Texas Christian University Press, 1994.

Parsons, Chuck. *Captain John R. Hughes: Lone Star Ranger*. Denton: University of
North Texas Press, 2011.

———. *John B. Armstrong, Texas Ranger and Pioneer Ranchman*. College Station:
Texas A&M University Press, 2007.

———, and Marianne E. Hall Little. *Captain L.H. McNelly, Texas Ranger: The Life
and Times of a Fighting Man*. Austin, TX: State House Press, 2001.

Paul, Lee. *Jim Peters: Texas Ranger*. Bedford, IN: JONA Books, 1979.

Proctor, Ben. *Just One Riot: Episodes of Texas Rangers in the 20th Century*. Austin, TX: Eakin Press, 1991.

Puckett, Linda Jay. *Cast a Long Shadow: A Casebook of the Law Enforcement Career of Texas Ranger Captain E.J. (Jay) Banks*. Dallas, TX: Ussery Printing Company, 1984.

Raymond, Dora N. *Captain Lee Hall of Texas*. Norman: University of Oklahoma Press, 1940.

Renaud, Jorge A. *Behind The Walls: A Guide for Families and Friends of Texas Prison Inmates*. Denton: University of North Texas Press, 2002.

Rigler, Lewis C., and Judyth Wagner Rigler. *In the Line of Duty: Reflections of a Texas Ranger Private*. Houston, TX: Larksdale, 1984.

Robinson, III, Chas. *The Men Who Wear the Star: The Story of the Texas Rangers*. New York: Random House, 2000.

Robinson, James W. *The DPS Story: History of the Development of the Department of Public Safety in Texas*. Austin, TX: Texas Department of Public Safety, 1975.

Rubenser, Lorie, and Gloria Priddy. *Constables, Marshals, and More: Forgotten Officers in Texas Law Enforcement*. Denton: University of North Texas Press, 2011.

Samora, Julian, Joe Bernal, and Albert Peña. *Gunpowder Justice: A Reassessment of the Texas Rangers*. Notre Dame, IN: University of Notre Dame Press, 1979.

Schneider, Paul. *Bonnie and Clyde: The Lives Behind the Legend*. New York: Henry Holt and Company, LLC, 2009.

Schuster, Steve. *My Favorite and Finest Firearm*. n.p.: The Press of Waifs and Strays, 1993.

Selcer, Richard F. *Hell's Half Acre: The Life and Legend of a Red-Light District*. Fort Worth: Texas Christian University Press, 1991.

———, ed. *Legendary Watering Holes: The Saloons That Made Texas Famous*. College Station: Texas A&M University Press, 2004.

Selcer, Richard F., and Kevin S. Foster. *Written in Blood: The History of Fort Worth's Fallen Lawmen, 1861–1909*. Vol. I. Denton: University of North Texas Press, 2010.

———. *Written in Blood: The History of Fort Worth's Fallen Lawmen, 1910–1928*. Vol. II. Denton: University of North Texas Press, 2011.

Shannon, Elaine. *Desperados: Latin Drug Lords, U.S. Lawmen, and the War America Can't Win*. New York: Viking Penguin Inc., 1988.

Shillingberg, William. *Dodge City: The Early Years, 1872–1886*. Norman, OK: Arthur H. Clark and Company, 2009.

Sleeper, Gary W. *I'll Do My Own Damn Killin': Benny Binion, Herbert Noble, and the Texas Gambling War*. Fort Lee, NJ; Barricade Books, Inc., 2006.

Spellman, Paul N. *Captain John H. Rogers, Texas Ranger*. Denton: University of North Texas Press, 2003.

———. *Captain J.A. Brooks, Texas Ranger*. Denton: University of North Texas Press, 2007.

Spinks, S.E. *Law on the Last Frontier: Texas Ranger Arthur Hill*. Lubbock: Texas Tech University Press, 2007.

Stephens, Robert W. *Tribute to a Ranger: Captain A.Y. Allee*. Dallas, TX: Self-published, 1968.

———. *Texas Ranger Sketches*. Dallas, TX: Self-published, 1972.

———. *Lone Wolf: The Story of Texas Ranger Captain M.T. Gonzaullas*. Dallas, TX: Taylor Publishing, n.d.

Sterling, William W. *Trails and Trials of a Texas Ranger*. Norman: University of Oklahoma Press, 1959.

Swanson, Doug J. *Blood Aces: The Wild Ride of Benny Binion, The Texas Gangster Who Created Vegas Poker*. Viking Press [Penguin Group], New York, 2014.

Tise, Sammy. *Texas County Sheriffs*. Hallettsville, TX: Tise Genealogical Research, 1989.

Turk, David S. *Forging The Star: The Official Modern History of the United States Marshals Service*. Denton: University of North Texas Press, 2016.

Utley, Robert M. *Lone Star Justice: The First Century of the Texas Rangers*. New York: Oxford University Press, 2002.

———. *Lone Star Lawmen: The Second Century of the Texas Rangers*. New York: Oxford University Press, 2007.

Weaver, John D. *The Brownsville Raid*. New York: W. W. Norton & Co., 1970.

Webb, Walter P. *The Texas Rangers: A Century of Frontier Defense*. Austin: University of Texas Press, 1935.

Weiss, Jr., Harold J. *Yours to Command: The Life and Legend of Texas Ranger Captain Bill McDonald*. Denton: University of North Texas Press, 2009.

West, Raymond. *Bennie C. Krueger: Texas Ranger. . . . Texas Gentlemen*. Jacksonville, TX: J.A Staton, 1984.

Wilkins, Frederick W. *The Legend Begins: The Texas Rangers, 1823–1845*. Austin, TX: State House Press, 1996.

———. *The Highly Irregular Irregulars: Texas Rangers in the Mexican War*. Austin, TX: Eakin Press, 1990.

———. *Defending the Borders: The Texas Rangers, 1848–1861*. Austin, TX: State House Press, 2001.

———. *The Law Comes to Texas: The Texas Rangers, 1870–1901*. Austin, TX: State House Press, 1999.

Willett, Jim, and Ron Rozelle. *Warden: Prison Life and Death From the Inside Out*. Houston, TX: Bright Sky Press, 2004.

Wood, John M. *Texas Ranger in the Oil Patch*. Austin, TX: Woodburner Press, 1994.

Periodicals:

Borges, Walter. "S. Texas Inquiry Expands." *The Texas Lawyer*, February 16, 1987.

Cartwright, Gary. "Talking to Killers." *Texas Monthly*, July 2002.

———. "The Man Who Killed Judge Wood." *Texas Monthly*, September 1982.

Colloff, Pamela. "Remember *the* Christian Alamo." *Texas Monthly*, December 2001.

———. "Law of the Land." *Texas Monthly*, April, 2007.

Cox, Mike. "She Went to Join Her Husband—Found Death." *Startling Detective*, September 1972.

Dickey, Pete. "Handgun Safety & Design." *American Rifleman*, May 1988.

Dillow, Gordon. "The Lone Ranger." *Philip Morris Magazine*, July/August 1989.

Draper, Robert. "The Twilight of the Texas Rangers." *Texas Monthly*, February 1994.

———. "The Sheriff Who Went to Pot." *Texas Monthly*, December 1994.

Editors. "Texas Sniper." *Time*, October 25, 1982.

Hager, William M. "The Nuecestown Raid of 1875: A Border Incident." *Arizona and the West*, Autumn 1959.

Hutchins, David. "Woody Harrelson, *Cheers'* Cherry Bartender, Feels a Bit Mixed About Fame and a Strange Family Twist." *People*, November 14, 1988.

Jay, Roger. "The Peoria Bummer—Wyatt Earp's Lost Year." *Wild West*, August 2003.

Krell, Eddie. "The Girls Who Were Picked Up by Death." *Inside Detective*, August 1972.

Martin, William. "Basilica of Our Lady of San Juan del Valle." *Texas Monthly*, January 2007.

Morris, Lepold. "The Mexican Raid of 1875 on Corpus Christi." *Texas Historical Association Quarterly*. July 1900.

Nieman, Robert. "20th Century Shining Star: Captain Jack Dean, United States Marshal." *Texas Ranger Dispatch*, April 2008.

Schmidt, Keith R. "Guns of the Texas Rangers." *American Rifleman*, May 1988.

Selcer, Richard F. "Fowler Than the Kid." *Wild West*, October 2017.

———, and James W. Johnson. "Right Place, Wrong Man." *Wild West*, April 2018.

Redding, Stan. "Top Gun of the Texas Rangers." *True Detective*, February 1963.

Utley, Robert M. "Terminating Oklahoma's Smiling Killer." *Texas Ranger Dispatch*, Summer 2005.

Webb, Walter P. "Texas Rangers Quell Troubles." *The State Trooper*, August 1924.

Young, Josh. "Zen and the Art of Hemp Cultivation." *George*, December 1996.

Newspapers:

Abilene Reporter News
Alice Echo-News
Amarillo Globe-Times
Austin American-Statesman
Bandera Bulletin
Bee County Enterprise
Big Spring Herald
Borger News-Herald
Brownsville Herald
Carswell Sentinel
Chicago Tribune
Cleburne Times-Review
Corpus Christi Caller-Times
Dallas Morning News
Dallas Times Herald
Dallas Weekly Herald
Del Rio News Herald
Detroit Free Press
Eagle Pass News Guide
Edinburg Daily Review
El Paso Daily Times
Family Weekly
Floresville Chronicle-Journal
Fort Worth Star-Telegram
Forth Worth Press
Fredericksburg Standard Radio Post
Galveston Daily News
Garland Daily News
Houston Chronicle
Houston Post
Kerrville Times
Lawton Constitution
Liberty County Vindicator
Lubbock Avalanche Journal

Lubbock Evening Journal
McAllen Monitor
McKinney Daily Courier Gazette
Nacogdoches Daily Sentinel
New Braunfels Herald
New York Times
Odessa American
Orange Leader
Paris News
Pecos Enterprise
Plainview Reporter-News
Palestine Herald-Press
Port Arthur News
San Antonio Express-News
San Antonio Light
San Antonio Times
Santa Ana Orange County Register
Seguin Gazette Enterprise
Shreveport Times
Syracuse Post Standard
Texas City Sun
The Current
The Texas Observer
Tyler Courier-Times
Tyler Morning Telegraph
Valley Morning Star
Victoria Advocate
Waco News-Tribune
Waco Tribune Herald
Washington Post
Waxahachie Daily Light
Wichita Beacon
Wichita Falls Times
Winnipeg Free Press

Index